George D. Heaton
Myers Park, Baptist Church,
Charlotte, N.C.

THE MINISTERS MANUAL FOR 1952

THE VOLUME FOR THIS YEAR, BEING A STUDY AND PULPIT GUIDE, AND HANDBOOK OF SUGGESTION AND INSPIRATION FOR PASTORS, EVANGELISTS, MISSIONARIES, BIBLE READERS AND ALL OTHERS REGULARLY CALLED UPON FOR CHRISTIAN ADDRESS FROM PULPIT OR PLATFORM

TWENTY-SEVENTH ANNUAL VOLUME

Books by Rev. M. K. W. Heicher, PH.D.

LIVING ON TIPTOE
MEDITATIONS FOR DAYS AND SEASONS

Also Co-editor of

THE MINISTERS MANUAL, 1943-1952

Books by Rev. G. B. F. HALLOCK, M.A., D.D.

---

210 MORE CHOICE SERMONS FOR CHILDREN
THE PRACTICAL USE CYCLOPEDIA OF SERMON SUGGESTION
NINETY-NINE NEW SERMONS FOR CHILDREN
2500 BEST MODERN ILLUSTRATIONS
THE MINISTER'S WEEKLY MANUAL
FRATERNAL SERMONS AND ADDRESSES
PRAYERS FOR SPECIAL DAYS AND OCCASIONS
BEHIND THE BIG HILL. A YEAR OF SIX-MINUTE SERMONS FOR CHILDREN
THREE HUNDRED FIVE-MINUTE SERMONS FOR CHILDREN
HOLY COMMUNION CYCLOPEDIA
CYCLOPEDIA OF PASTORAL METHODS
CYCLOPEDIA OF FUNERAL SERMONS AND SKETCHES
CYCLOPEDIA OF SERMON OUTLINES FOR SPECIAL DAYS AND OCCASIONS
CYCLOPEDIA OF COMMENCEMENT SERMONS AND BACCALAUREATE ADDRESSES
ONE HUNDRED CHOICE SERMONS FOR CHILDREN
ONE HUNDRED BEST SERMONS FOR SPECIAL DAYS AND OCCASIONS
THE EVANGELISTIC CYCLOPEDIA
NEW SERMONS FOR SPECIAL DAYS AND OCCASIONS
SERMON SEEDS
THE HOMILETIC YEAR
BEAUTY IN GOD'S WORD
THE TEACHING OF JESUS CONCERNING THE CHRISTIAN LIFE
THE MODEL PRAYER
JOURNEYING IN THE LAND WHERE JESUS LIVED
CHRIST IN THE HOME
GROWING TOWARD GOD
UPWARD STEPS
GOD'S WHISPERED SECRETS
THE WEDDING MANUAL

Also Editor of

THE MINISTERS MANUAL, 1926-1952

The MINISTERS MANUAL

(Formerly Doran's Ministers Manual)

A Study and Pulpit Guide for the Calendar Year 1952

TWENTY-SEVENTH ANNUAL ISSUE
OF THIS "MINISTERS WORKING TOOL"

Compiled and Edited by
REV. G. B. F. HALLOCK, M.A., D.D.
and
REV. M. K. W. HEICHER, PH.D.

HARPER & BROTHERS PUBLISHERS
NEW YORK

Foreword

This is our twenty-seventh annual volume. Long continuance, growth in circulation and in approved use all prove worth. So we think and so we thank you all, our untold number of friends.

In each volume we seek to supply the clergy and all in kindred employ with an expert research service and vocational handbook of the same character as that enjoyed by other professions. This is the aim not alone in the section of Clergy Helps, but is equally true in all the many departments.

All the former departments are here, with additions to some of them. There will be found Outlined Sermons for Sunday Morning and Evening of the Entire Church Year, including the Special Days, with homiletic and expository seed thoughts and a goodly number of apt illustrations chosen from the best of widely varied sources; a School Year of Junior Sermons for Children and Youths; Themes and Outlines for Lenten Services for Deepening the Spiritual Life, for Good Friday and for Evangelism; an ample schedule of Studies in Neglected Texts, being Sermon Starts, or Vital Themes for Vital Preaching; Midweek Fellowship Meeting Topics with treatment; Pleas from the Pews; Christian Endeavor Society Topics for the Year; Brief Comments on the Year's Sunday School Lessons; Suggestive Sermon Subjects; and Monthly Bulletin Board Slogans. The new department introduced in 1950, The Conduct of the Holy Communion, is continued and enlarged. So also is the department For Missions and Missionaries, introduced three years ago. Section I, Convenient Clergy Helps, contains Calendars for 1952 and for 1953, The Ecclesiastical Year Calendar, Prominent Church-Year Days for Four Years, Table of Easter Sundays 1940 to 2000, Table of Wedding Anniversaries with Distinctive Gifts, Table of Choice Films for Church Use, a Roster of Prominent Historical Persons Whose Anniversaries Occur in 1952. Choices from these may be considered desirable for sermons or church observances at times during the year. Other features in this section are Prayers with the Choir, Entrance Sentences, After-Petitions Following the Scripture Lessons, Prayers before the Sermon, etc.

It is due our readers, we think, to definitely state the fact that there is no complete sermon in the book. All are closely considered condensations, sermon digests, with added outline suggestions. The illustrations also, chosen for the themes, all are independent, the very best at hand or available, carefully selected for appropriateness alone. The whole work is intended to be intellectually quickening, spiritually inspiring, and homiletically suggestive, a stimulus to creative reflection.

Besides its other practical uses, we think that as a time-saver and help in getting started the book can prove of very special value. Every minister is aware of how time is lost through lack of good leads and in efforts to conjure up usable ideas out of thin air. Every hour salvaged from such time-consuming endeavors is so much to the good. A single suggestion or briefest sermon starter may prove a great help.

This is definitely a pastor's book. Of course it is equally useful for evangelists, missionaries, seminary students, Bible teachers, and all others regularly called upon for Christian address from pulpit or platform. And it is an ample book, for it contains well over two hundred and fifty thousand words, equal to the combination of several volumes of quite customary size. Each successive issue, bringing together ideas from many of the outstanding preachers of our day, is an entirely new work, with freshly chosen content intended for the current year, yet permanently valuable.

The idea throughout has been to create an interdenominational handbook of both immediate and enduring usefulness that each minister will want on his desk every day of the year.

The material is made instantly available by a Condensed Index, an Alphabetical Table of Contents According to Subjects and Special Days and Seasons, and a Plenary Scriptural Index, all found in the beginning of the book.

G. B. F. H.
M. K. W. H.
Brick Church, Rochester, N. Y.
Community Church, Altadena, Calif.

CONDENSED TABLE OF CONTENTS

(A Complete Alphabetical Subject Index Immediately Follows)

CONTENTS ACCORDING TO SUBJECT

General Alphabetical Index

Morning Sermons:

SCRIPTURAL INDEX

Complete with the exception of references to which there is practically no comment or material.

OLD TESTAMENT

NEW TESTAMENT

SECTION I. Calendars and Other Convenient Clergy Helps

1. Civil Year Calendars for 1952 and 1953

1952

JANUARY

S	M	T	W	T	F	S
—	—	1	2	3	4	5
6	7	8	9	10	11	12
13	14	15	16	17	18	19
20	21	22	23	24	25	26
27	28	29	30	31	—	—

FEBRUARY

S	M	T	W	T	F	S
—	—	—	—	—	1	2
3	4	5	6	7	8	9
10	11	12	13	14	15	16
17	18	19	20	21	22	23
24	25	26	27	28	29	—
—	—	—	—	—	—	—

MARCH

S	M	T	W	T	F	S
—	—	—	—	—	—	1
2	3	4	5	6	7	8
9	10	11	12	13	14	15
16	17	18	19	20	21	22
23	24	25	26	27	28	29
30	31	—	—	—	—	—

APRIL

S	M	T	W	T	F	S
—	—	1	2	3	4	5
6	7	8	9	10	11	12
13	14	15	16	17	18	19
20	21	22	23	24	25	26
27	28	29	30	—	—	—

MAY

S	M	T	W	T	F	S
—	—	—	—	1	2	3
4	5	6	7	8	9	10
11	12	13	14	15	16	17
18	19	20	21	22	23	24
25	26	27	28	29	30	31
—	—	—	—	—	—	—

JUNE

S	M	T	W	T	F	S
1	2	3	4	5	6	7
8	9	10	11	12	13	14
15	16	17	18	19	20	21
22	23	24	25	26	27	28
29	30	—	—	—	—	—
—	—	—	—	—	—	—

JULY

S	M	T	W	T	F	S
—	—	1	2	3	4	5
6	7	8	9	10	11	12
13	14	15	16	17	18	19
20	21	22	23	24	25	26
27	28	29	30	31	—	—

AUGUST

S	M	T	W	T	F	S
—	—	—	—	—	1	2
3	4	5	6	7	8	9
10	11	12	13	14	15	16
17	18	19	20	21	22	23
24	25	26	27	28	29	30
31	—	—	—	—	—	—

SEPTEMBER

S	M	T	W	T	F	S
—	1	2	3	4	5	6
7	8	9	10	11	12	13
14	15	16	17	18	19	20
21	22	23	24	25	26	27
28	29	30	—	—	—	—
—	—	—	—	—	—	—

OCTOBER

S	M	T	W	T	F	S
—	—	—	1	2	3	4
5	6	7	8	9	10	11
12	13	14	15	16	17	18
19	20	21	22	23	24	25
26	27	28	29	30	31	—

NOVEMBER

S	M	T	W	T	F	S
—	—	—	—	—	—	1
2	3	4	5	6	7	8
9	10	11	12	13	14	15
16	17	18	19	20	21	22
23	24	25	26	27	28	29
30	—	—	—	—	—	—

DECEMBER

S	M	T	W	T	F	S
—	1	2	3	4	5	6
7	8	9	10	11	12	13
14	15	16	17	18	19	20
21	22	23	24	25	26	27
28	29	30	31	—	—	—
—	—	—	—	—	—	—

1953

JANUARY

S	M	T	W	T	F	S
—	—	—	—	1	2	3
4	5	6	7	8	9	10
11	12	13	14	15	16	17
18	19	20	21	22	23	24
25	26	27	28	29	30	31

FEBRUARY

S	M	T	W	T	F	S
1	2	3	4	5	6	7
8	9	10	11	12	13	14
15	16	17	18	19	20	21
22	23	24	25	26	27	28
—	—	—	—	—	—	—
—	—	—	—	—	—	—

MARCH

S	M	T	W	T	F	S
1	2	3	4	5	6	7
8	9	10	11	12	13	14
15	16	17	18	19	20	21
22	23	24	25	26	27	28
29	30	31	—	—	—	—

APRIL

S	M	T	W	T	F	S
—	—	—	1	2	3	4
5	6	7	8	9	10	11
12	13	14	15	16	17	18
19	20	21	22	23	24	25
26	27	28	29	30	—	—

MAY

S	M	T	W	T	F	S
—	—	—	—	—	1	2
3	4	5	6	7	8	9
10	11	12	13	14	15	16
17	18	19	20	21	22	23
24	25	26	27	28	29	30
31	—	—	—	—	—	—

JUNE

S	M	T	W	T	F	S
—	1	2	3	4	5	6
7	8	9	10	11	12	13
14	15	16	17	18	19	20
21	22	23	24	25	26	27
28	29	30	—	—	—	—

JULY

S	M	T	W	T	F	S
—	—	—	1	2	3	4
5	6	7	8	9	10	11
12	13	14	15	16	17	18
19	20	21	22	23	24	25
26	27	28	29	30	31	—

AUGUST

S	M	T	W	T	F	S
—	—	—	—	—	—	1
2	3	4	5	6	7	8
9	10	11	12	13	14	15
16	17	18	19	20	21	22
23	24	25	26	27	28	29
30	31	—	—	—	—	—

SEPTEMBER

S	M	T	W	T	F	S
—	—	1	2	3	4	5
6	7	8	9	10	11	12
13	14	15	16	17	18	19
20	21	22	23	24	25	26
27	28	29	30	—	—	—

OCTOBER

S	M	T	W	T	F	S
—	—	—	—	1	2	3
4	5	6	7	8	9	10
11	12	13	14	15	16	17
18	19	20	21	22	23	24
25	26	27	28	29	30	31

NOVEMBER

S	M	T	W	T	F	S
1	2	3	4	5	6	7
8	9	10	11	12	13	14
15	16	17	18	19	20	21
22	23	24	25	26	27	28
29	30	—	—	—	—	—
—	—	—	—	—	—	—

DECEMBER

S	M	T	W	T	F	S
—	—	1	2	3	4	5
6	7	8	9	10	11	12
13	14	15	16	17	18	19
20	21	22	23	24	25	26
27	28	29	30	31	—	—

2. *Ecclesiastical Year Calendar for 1952 (Including the Movable and Immovable Feasts)*

JANUARY

1. Circumcision.
6. The Epiphany.
13. First Sunday after the Epiphany.
20. Second Sunday after the Epiphany.
25. Conversion of St. Paul.
27. Third Sunday after the Epiphany.

FEBRUARY

2. Purification of St. Mary the Virgin.
3. Fourth Sunday after the Epiphany.
10. Septuagesima Sunday.
17. Sexagesima Sunday.
24. Quinquagesima Sunday.
25. Saint Matthias.*
27. Ash Wednesday.

MARCH

2. First Sunday in Lent.
5. Ember Day.
7. Ember Day.
8. Ember Day.
9. Second Sunday in Lent.
16. Third Sunday in Lent.
23. Fourth Sunday in Lent.
25. Annunciation of the Blessed Virgin Mary.
30. Fifth Sunday in Lent (Passion Sunday).

* Transferred from Feb. 24.

APRIL

6. Palm Sunday.
7. Monday before Easter.
8. Tuesday before Easter.
9. Wednesday before Easter.
10. Maundy Thursday.
11. Good Friday.
12. Easter Even.
13. Easter Day.
14. Easter Monday.
15. Easter Tuesday.
20. First Sunday after Easter.
25. St. Mark.
27. Second Sunday after Easter.

MAY

1. St. Philip and St. James.
4. Third Sunday after Easter.
11. Fourth Sunday after Easter.
18. Fifth (Rogation) Sunday after Easter.
19. Rogation Monday.
20. Rogation Tuesday.
21. Rogation Wednesday.
22. Ascension Day.
25. Sunday after Ascension.

JUNE

1. Whitsunday (Pentecost).
2. Whitsun Monday.
3. Whitsun Tuesday.

4. Ember Day.
6. Ember Day.
7. Ember Day.
8. Trinity Sunday.
11. St. Barnabas.
15. First Sunday after Trinity.
22. Second Sunday after Trinity.
24. Nativity of St. John Baptist.
29. St. Peter (Third Sunday after Trinity).

JULY

4. Independence Day.
6. Fourth Sunday after Trinity.
13. Fifth Sunday after Trinity.
20. Sixth Sunday after Trinity.
25. St. James.
27. Seventh Sunday after Trinity.

AUGUST

3. Eighth Sunday after Trinity.
6. Transfiguration.
10. Ninth Sunday after Trinity.
17. Tenth Sunday after Trinity.
24. St. Bartholomew (Eleventh Sunday after Trinity).
31. Twelfth Sunday after Trinity.

SEPTEMBER

7. Thirteenth Sunday after Trinity.
14. Fourteenth Sunday after Trinity.
17. Ember Day.
19. Ember Day.
20. Ember Day.
21. St. Matthew (Fifteenth Sunday after Trinity)
28. Sixteenth Sunday after Trinity.
29. St. Michael and All Angels.

OCTOBER

5. Seventeenth Sunday after Trinity.
12. Eighteenth Sunday after Trinity.
18. St. Luke.
19. Nineteenth Sunday after Trinity.
26. Twentieth Sunday after Trinity.
28. St. Simon and St. Jude.

NOVEMBER

1. All Saints' Day.
2. Twenty-first Sunday after Trinity.
9. Twenty-second Sunday after Trinity.
16. Twenty-third Sunday after Trinity.
23. Sunday next Before Advent.
27. Thanksgiving Day.
30. First Sunday in Advent.

DECEMBER

1. St. Andrew*
7. Second Sunday in Advent.
14. Third Sunday in Advent.
17. Ember Day.
19. Ember Day
20. Ember Day
21. Fourth Sunday in Advent.
22. St. Thomas.**
25. Christmas Day.
26. St. Stephen.
27. St. John Evangelist.
28. Holy Innocents (First Sunday after Christmas).

---

* Transferred from Nov. 30.
** Transferred from Dec. 21.

3. *Prominent Church-Year Days for Four Years*

Ash Wednesday, 1952, Feb. 27. 1953, Feb. 18. 1954, Mar. 3. 1955, Feb. 23.

Palm Sunday, 1952, Apr. 6. 1953, Mar. 29. 1954, Apr. 11. 1955, Apr. 3.

Good Friday, 1952, Apr. 11. 1953, Apr. 3. 1954, Apr. 16. 1955, Apr. 8.

Easter, 1952, Apr. 13. 1953, Apr. 5. 1954, Apr. 18. 1955, Apr. 10.

Trinity Sunday, 1952, June 8. 1953, May 31. 1954, June 13. 1955, June 5.

Ascension Day, 1952, May 22. 1953, May 14. 1954, May 27. 1955, May 19.

Whitsunday, 1952, June 1. 1953, May 24. 1954, June 6. 1955, May 29.

First Sunday in Advent, 1952, Nov. 30. 1953, Nov. 29. 1954, Nov. 28. 1955, Nov. 27.

4. *A Table of Easter Sundays for the Years 1940-2000*

1940, March 24.
1941, April 13
1942, April 6.
1943, April 25.
1944, April 9.
1945, April 1.
1946, April 21.
1947, April 6.
1948, March 28.
1949, April 17.
1950, April 9.
1951, March 25.
1952, April 13.
1953, April 5.
1954, April 18.
1955, April 10.
1956, April 1.
1957, April 21.
1958. April 6.
1959, March 29.
1960, April 17.
1961, April 2.
1962, April 22.
1963, April 14.
1964, March 29.
1965, April 18.
1966, April 10.
1967, March 26.
1968, April 14.
1969, April 6.
1970, March 29.
1971, April 11.
1972, April 2.
1973, April 22.
1974, April 14.
1975, March 30.
1976, April 18.
1977, April 10.
1978, March 26.
1979, April 15.
1980, April 6.
1981, April 19.

1982, April 11.
1983, April 3.
1984, April 22.
1985, April 7.
1986, March 30.
1987, April 19.
1988, April 3.
1989, March 26.
1990, April 15.
1991, March 31.
1992, April 19.
1993, April 11.
1994, April 3.
1995, April 16.
1996, April 7.
1997, March 30.
1998, April 12.
1999, April 4.
2000, April 23.

5. *List of Wedding Anniversaries with Distinctive Gifts*

Pastors when asked find it convenient to have the full list, which follows. The most important are the "Silver" after 25 years, the "Golden," after 50 years, and the "Diamond," after 60, 70 or 75 years.

1st, Paper.
2nd, Cotton.
3rd, Leather.
4th, Fruit.
5th, Wooden.
6th, Candy.
7th, Wool.
8th, Pottery.
9th, Willow.
10th, Tin.
11th, Steel.
12th, Silk.
13th, Lace.
14th, Ivory.
15th, Crystal.
20th, China.
25th, Silver
30th, Pearl.
35th, Coral.
40th, Ruby.
45th, Sapphire.
50th, Golden.
75th, Diamond.

6. CHOICE FILMS FOR CHURCH USE

Films for church use are worthy of more than a mere "showing." They deserve to become a religious experience for all who see them. Magnify their announcement. Of any suitable in length for a church service, speak about it as a message of importance, not as a "feature." And give it a churchly setting with hymns and prayers and a well-planned introductory message. For less formal meetings, as for Sunday evening clubs, fellowship gatherings, or for week-day use at missionary meetings, devotional services, or for social gatherings, short films can be used and in a less formal manner. All of suitable application may be used in Sunday school classes for all ages. Through the eye and ear to the mind and heart films have a sure future of greatly enlarged use.

We note below a few well-chosen religious films.

"Second Chance." Sound, black and white, 80 minutes. Highly recommended. On stewardship and evangelism.

"Barabbas the Robber." Sound, black and white, 38 minutes. Highly recommended. Good for Lent. Events as would have appeared to Barabbas as leader of a gang of rebels.

"Out of the Dust." Sound, black and white, 40 minutes. Highly recommended. Excellent for missionary education and social problems in Latin America.

"The Two Kingdoms." Sound, black and white, 62 minutes.

"In the Footsteps of the Witch Doctor." Sound, black and white, 20 minutes. Excellent on medical missions in the Belgian Congo.

"The Ninety and Nine." Sound, color, 10 minutes. Use in church service, men's club, ladies' society, young people's groups.

"Creation According to Genesis." Sound, color, 10 minutes. Highly recommended. Designed primarily to be used in worship.

"South of the Clouds." Sound, black and white, 35 minutes. Near East missionary education. Highly recommended.

"Reaching from Heaven." Sound, black and white, 80 minutes. Recommended. Carries strong call for personal evangelism.

"The Sickle and the Cross." Motion picture, 75 minutes. Luther League production. Thrilling entertainment with a wholesome message.

"Like a Mighty Army." Sound, black and white, 48 minutes. Openly religious, instructive, good for pointing up stewardship.

"Dust or Destiny." Sound, color, 50 minutes. Evangelistic emphasis. Recommended.

"Beyond Our Own." Sound, black and white. Highly recommended. Worship, evangelism or missions. Story of a man who recovered his faith.

"Pilgrimage Play." Sound, color, 90 minutes. Useful during Lenten and Easter seasons or for a general church audience. Life of Christ.

"And Now I See." Sound, black and white, 40 minutes. Highly recommended. Fine story for Christian stewardship.

"Calling of Matthew." Sound, black and white, 28 minutes. Recommended. Instruction on the ministry of Jesus.

"Make Way for Youth." Sound, black and white, 20 minutes. Recommended. Interesting both parents and young people.

"Answer for Anne." Sound, black and white, 40 minutes. Highly recommended. Displaced persons; appeal to be our brother's keeper.

"Two Thousand Years Ago." Series of five. Sound, black and white. "The Home," 19 minutes. "The Day's Work," 21 minutes. "The School," 16 minutes. "The Travellers," 22 minutes. "The Synagogue," 22 minutes. Showing life in Palestine. Recommended.

"Journeying into Faith." Sound, black and white, 34 minutes. Recommended. For worship, or instruction on the life of Jesus.

"Peiping Family." Sound, black and white, 20 minutes. Recommended. Excellent presentation with natural acting.

"Letter from China." Sound, black and white, 30 minutes. Highly recommended. Excellent for missionary education.

7. ANNIVERSARIES SUGGESTED FOR SERMONS AND CHURCH OBSERVANCE IN 1952

List to choose from:

500 years: September 21, 1452. Birth of Girolamo Savonarola. Religious reformer; burned at the stake.

400 years: Edmund Spenser, born 1552. Author of *Faerie Queen.*

300 years: December 23, 1652. Death of John Cotton, Puritan preacher, born in England, December 4, 1584. Religious and intellectual leader of New England.

200 years: Betsy Ross, born June 1, 1752. Traditional maker of first American flag.

200 years: June 15, 1752, Benjamin Franklin demonstrated the identity of electricity and lightning by use of a kite.

200 years: September 14, 1752, Great Britain and its colonies adopted the Gregorian Calendar.

150 years: Mark Hopkins, born February 4, 1802. Distinguished American educator.

150 years: March 16, 1802, U. S. Military Academy at West Point opened July 4, 1802.

150 years: Dorothea Lynde Dix, born April 4, 1802. Internationally famous pioneer in the reform of prisons, almshouses and insane asylums.

150 years: Victor Hugo, born February 26, 1802. French poet and novelist Author of *Les Miserables.*

150 years: Sir Edwin Landseer, born March 7, 1802. English painter, sculptor of the great lions of Trafalgar Square, London.

100 years: Louis Braille, died January 6, 1852. Blind French teacher of the blind, originator of the Braille System of printing and writing.

100 years: Daniel Webster, died October 24, 1852. American statesman and defender of the Constitution.

100 years: Horace Bushnell, born April 14, 1852. New England Congregational preacher, theologian, poet and mystic, and public-spirited citizen.

100 years: Friedrich Froebel, died June 21, 1852. Founder of the kindergarten system.

100 years: Arthur Wellesley, Duke of Wellington. Defeated Napoleon at Waterloo.

100 years: June 29, 1852, death of Henry Clay, American statesman.

100 years: Timothy Cole, born April 6, 1852. American wood engraver.

100 years: Birth of Albert Abraham Michelson, December 19, 1852, one of America's greatest physicists. Noted for his investigations of the velocity of light. The first American scientist to be awarded the Nobel Prize, 1907.

50 years: Charles A. Lindbergh, born February 4, 1902. Hero of American aviation. 25 years. Anniversary May 21, 1927, of completing the first nonstop flight from New York to Paris.

We add some noted hymn writers whose anniversaries of birth or death may well be observed. Each is author of a number of familiar hymns. For examples, see any hymn book.

Philip Doddridge, born June 26, 1702, died October 26, 1751. 250th anniversary of birth. Very many hymns.

Thomas Moore, born May 28, 1779, died February 25, 1852. 100th anniversary of death.

Nahum Tate, born 1652, day unknown, died March 12, 1715. 300th anniversary of birth.

Leonard Bacon, born February 19, 1802, died December 24, 1881. 150th anniversary of birth.

Timothy Dwight, born May 14, 1752, died January 11, 1817. 200th anniversary of birth.

Henry van Dyke, born November 10, 1852, died April 10, 1933. 100th anniversary of birth. Clergyman, author, poet, hymn writer, educator.

8. PRAYERS WITH THE CHOIR

(Pre-processional)

It is the goodly custom with very many ministers to offer prayer with the choir in the chapel or choir room before entering the service in the church sanctuary. The offering of such a prayer is in every way commendable and its influence good.

a. Open thou our lips, O Lord, and our mouths will show forth thy praise. Inspire these thy servants who have consecrated to thy glory the gift of song with which thou hast endowed them. And so sustain them in the leading of the congregation now met for worship that thy holy name may be glorified and thy people made truly to rejoice in thy presence. We ask in the name of Christ. Amen.

b. Almighty God who art worshiped by the heavenly hosts with hymns that are never silent and with thanksgivings that never cease, fill our hearts and souls with thy praise, that we may truly magnify thy name. And grant us, with all who fear thee and keep thy commandments to be partakers of the inheritance of thy saints in light. We ask through Christ, our Lord. Amen.

c. Thou author of Christian praise, we thank thee for the gift of song. May we use it for thy glory alone. May we keep our hearts and minds and souls in tune with thy great heart and mind and soul. Help us to practice on earth for heaven's choir. Be pleased to give us the spirit of prayer and praise in every song we sing. In Christ's name we ask. Amen.

d. Grant us, O Lord, the help of thy Spirit in our hearts, that we may enter into thy holy presence with reverence and gladness and render a service acceptable unto thee; through Jesus Christ our Lord. Amen.

e. Our Father, we bless thee that thou hast given us voices to speak forth thy praise. Help us to worship thee with our lips and with our lives. Help us to show forth thy goodness in praiseful song. Amen.

f. As we enter thy sanctuary, our Father, wilt thou bestow the spirit of worship upon us. While we sing the songs of Zion may our words and worship be acceptable to thee, O God. We ask in Christ's name. Amen.

g. Grant us, O Lord, the help of thy Spirit in our hearts that we may enter thy holy presence with reverence and gladness of heart and render the service of leading thy people in praise in a way acceptable unto thee and to the edification of all. In the name of Christ we ask. Amen.

h. For Christmas. On this glad morning may our experience of the Christmas spirit be such, that all who hear us may rejoice. May our hearts be in tune with our voices and our lips show forth thy praise. We ask in the name of the Christmas Christ. Amen.

9. PREPARATION, OR ENTRANCE SENTENCES

Here are a few out of many examples for the Order of Worship, Church Bulletin, or Calendar.

a. Whosoever thou art that worshipest in this church, enter it not without the spirit of reverence; and leave it not without one prayer to God for thyself, those who minister, and for all who worship here.

b. Let each one, on being seated, engage in silent prayer for those who lead in worship and all who worship here today.

c. On silent feet come in,
Bow low in penitence.
Whoe'er thou art
Thou too hast sinned.
Uplift in prayer thy heart.

d. The organ prelude is a pathway from everyday life to the presence of the Master. Be reverent. Be silent. Be thoughtful. Within thy spirit lift a prayer for thyself, for those who worship and those who minister here and for the work of Christ in the world.

e. Leave not this church without a prayer for our nation in these days of sacrificial burdens and difficult decisions; for all hapless victims of life's tragedies, and for the coming of God's world-wide kingdom of justice and peace; for the fellowship of the Christian Church universal among all nations and races; and for men and women of every faith who sincerely desire one human family under the Fatherhood of one God.

f. To all who mourn and need comfort, to all who are tired and need rest, to all who are friendless and need friendship, to all who are lonely and want companionship, to all who sin and want a Saviour, and to "whomsoever will," this church opens wide its doors of welcome in the name of Jesus our Lord.

10. SOME AFTER-PETITIONS FOLLOWING THE SCRIPTURE LESSON

Use variety. It indicates alertness of reverent thought. Here are a few out of many possible examples:

May God write these words upon our hearts.

May God's Spirit give us understanding hearts.

May God bless to our spiritual profit this great chapter (message, word, parable, Psalm).

May the Lord quicken our hearts to hear and obey his Word.

Sanctify us by thy Truth; thy Word is Truth.

Blessed are they that hear thy Word and keep it.

Grant unto us, O God, the spirit of wisdom that we may understand thy Word.

Grant unto us faith, O God, that we may keep thy Word unto life eternal.

Graciously impart unto us, our Father, the spirit of meekness that we may receive thy Truth.

May God add his blessing to this reading of his Word.

Thy Word is a lamp to our feet and a light to our path.

This is a portion of God's Word: he that hath ears to hear, let him hear.

Lord have mercy upon us and incline our hearts to keep this law.

May God bless the reading of his Word.

May God give us understanding minds and hearts to profit by this lesson.

11. PRAYERS BEFORE THE SERMON

Some ministers in beginning their sermon bow and offer a brief prayer. It always consists of very short audible petitions for both the preacher and the hearers. We give a few examples of such prayers:

a. Almighty God, our heavenly Father, we invoke thy presence and blessing in our speaking and hearing thy Word this day. Be to us the Fountain of Light, and send thy truth into our hearts. We ask through Jesus Christ our Lord. Amen.

b. O Lord, from whom all good things come, grant us as thy servants that we may think and speak those things that are good and true. By thy grace may we be both hearers and doers of the Word. We ask in Christ's name. Amen.

c. Merciful Father, pour the light of thy Spirit in our minds as we preach and as we hear. May we learn what is thy holy will that we may walk in all humility in the paths of heavenly wisdom and peace to the glory of thy holy name. Amen.

d. Our Father, quicken our insight that we may this day gain a deeper understanding of the gospel of Christ. And especially we pray that when we come to know we may have grace to do thy will. We ask in Jesus' name. Amen.

e. O God, author of eternal light and truth, do thou shed forth thy blessing upon us all, that our lips may praise thee, our lives bless thee, and our meditations glorify thee. We ask through Jesus Christ our Lord. Amen.

f. As we preach and as we hear this day, let the words of our mouths and the meditations of our hearts be acceptable in thy sight, O Lord, our Strength and our Redeemer. Amen.

g. O God, forasmuch as without thee we are not able to please thee, mercifully grant us that thy Holy Spirit may in all things direct and rule our hearts as we study thy Word together this morning. We ask in the name of Christ our Lord and Saviour. Amen.

SECTION II. Pleas from the Pews. The Question-box, Panel, or Forum Method for Responding to the People's Interrogations and Desires

The past has proven this to be a valued department. Really, what are our people thinking about? As pastors our contact on Sunday evenings is largely with young people in club or fellowship gatherings. What are they thinking about, and what subjects interest them most? Pastors can find out by studying these pleas from the pews, for they are very largely from the young people themselves. They are brought together here as quiz-quests or question-box queries, thus affording by selection a glimpse into the minds of youth. They also give suggestion as to what the young people would like to have their ministers discuss with them. It is sure also that many of these questions can prove most suggestive for other occasions or for brief popular pulpit preludes. Older people are likely to be equally interested. Such inquiries cannot but prove valuable in revealing or awaking thought and in giving opportunity to say many needed and intimate things.

QUESTIONS

1. How can I find out the way to choose a vocation of Christian significance?

2. I am a young man of eighteen. Am I old enough to marry?

3. Seeking matrimony, where are the most marriageable young women to be found?

4. Seeking matrimony, where are the most marriageable young men to be found?

5. Have my parents a right to say anything about my proposed marriage?

6. Was I born able to do either right or wrong if I want to?

7. How can I learn to say No to social pressure for drinking with the crowd?

8. How can we lessen the tension between capital and labor? Is it improving?

9. Why do young people have inferiority complexes. What causes them? How overcome them?

10. Ministers preach about "justification by faith." What does that mean?

11. Ministers sometimes say something about "original sin." What does that mean?

12. Is there any harm in petting? If so, what?

13. What conception should I have of the Christian Church?

14. How can we who are in school

make our vacation season most useful? Most profitable?

15. How can I find out more about my own abilities and aptitudes?

16. I am considering making a change from one job to another. How can I get best advice in the matter?

17. Is there a God? What is he like?

18. Why do some churches practice close communion? Why do not others?

19. What is the meaning of a phrase ministers use, "Means of grace"?

20. At what period in life does adulthood arrive?

21. Should the unity of the Church be in spirit and program rather than in ecclesiastical organization?

22. Should the Church ignore the present disorder in the world and devote itself to saving souls for the life beyond?

23. Should the Church use its influence in support of the United Nations?

24. Should Christians get into politics?

25. In what sense have we made the Negro what he is?

26. Why should we respect the Negro's personality?

27. If I am saved by God's grace, may I live as I please?

28. Is the sense of sin in our day declining? If so, why?

29. What relation has our bodily condition to our spiritual state?

30. Is it always necessary to defend oneself?

31. Can the Gospel remove conditions of poverty?

32. Has the Gospel in any degree spent its force?

33. What is the value of special evangelistic services?

34. What are the advantages of attendance on summer conferences?

35. Is Foreign Missions meeting with the success it had in the past?

36. What methods of evangelism are proving the most effective today?

37. Are there any substitutes for "shoe leather" in pastoral work?

38. Is there a growing public interest in religion? In the Church?

39. What does it mean to be a Christian?

40. Does present-day Christianity meet up with Christ's original teachings?

41. What can be said for or against the movies of today?

42. Are science and religion incompatible?

43. Will the different countries of the world ever cease their strife and discord and become one happy family?

44. Would I be happier married?

45. As this world becomes more educated will there be room for God?

46. How long does it take to prepare a sermon?

47. What is the difference between psychology and psychiatry?

48. Can one Christian be a better Christian than another?

49. Is a consecrated Christian immune from sin?

50. In what way does the Holy Spirit manifest himself now?

51. Can a positive faith be reasonable?

52. Until an ideal social order appears what shall be done with the criminal class?

53. Should the organist and sexton be members of the church by which they are employed?

54. What right have we to urge the Christian faith upon people brought up in other faiths?

55. How important is my vote on election day?

56. Is it a good thing to keep a diary?

57. Can a minister stay too long in one church?

58. How about "mercy killings"?

59. What are the benefits of regularity in church attendance which the nonchurchgoer misses?

60. How may God become more real to me?

61. How far is communism a substitute for religion?

62. Is it right to bet on a horse race or a ball game?

63. When another person does not return our friendship what can we do?

64. What is the Christian view of sex and life?

65. What are the dangers and opportunities confronting the churches?

66. Is it proper for high school boys and girls to "go steady"?

67. When high school boys and girls "go steady" is an unofficial engagement implied?

68. How can we develop an adequate program of Christian education in our church?

69. Why has Christianity always been divided? Is it likely always to be so?

70. How can a Christian determine what proportion of his income he should give to the Lord?

71. How can I learn to pray satisfactorily?

72. How can I keep from always condemning myself?

73. Where are the dead?

74. Can a rich man be a Christian?

75. Can a boy win a girl by merely spending money?

76. Does war promote human progress?

77. In what sense are all men brothers?

78. How long should courtship last before there is an engagement?

79. Should Christians put stock in a good company as an investment?

80. How train one's thoughts into proper and worth-while channels?

81. What is meant by self-expression?

82. Is the engagement ring as sacred as the wedding ring?

83. Should a woman work at a full-time job after she is married?

84. Matrimony: Can two live as cheaply as one?

85. Is courtship by mail possible? Advantages? Disadvantages?

86. How early should I teach my child to pray?

87. Is it right to carry insurance?

88. Why pray if God knows our needs already?

89. What should a parent do if a child does not want to go to Sunday school?

90. What is involved in the idea that man was made in the image of God?

91. What do you think of strikes?

92. Is the Church far behind the world in progress?

93. Is it possible to banish the fear of want?

94. Is the expansion of democracy into industrial life possible?

95. I have not chosen a college to attend. How can I learn of the one best fitted to my needs and ability?

96. Are young married people in danger of graduating from courtship? What remedy?

97. Is an elopement likely to end in a successful marriage?

98. Are the young people of today properly educated for marriage?

99. Do young people considering marriage need any guidance to choose mates wisely?

100. "Man proposes." Should it always be so?

101. Is it hard for men to understand women? If so, why?

102. How should we wisely behave toward each other in our betrothal period?

103. After marriage, how can I prove to be the perfect son-in-law?

104. How can young married couples best deal with those almost inevitable early quarrels?

105. How can the newly married best conclude on managing their family finances?

106. How can the newly-wed wife learn to "manage" her husband?

107. How can the newly-wed husband learn to "manage" his wife?

108. What is the Christian way of thinking about moral evil?

109. What is the Christian way out of man's moral distress?

110. What is the Christian way of understanding Jesus?

111. Should we choose to be married in church? If so, why?

112. What preparation do young people need for the responsibilities of marriage? How get it?

113. Do many young people go to their minister for premarital counseling? Should they? If so, why?

114. What do we know about God?

115. Is the dropping of an atom bomb ever morally justified?

116. Is war ever justified?

SECTION III. Vital Themes for Vital Preaching, Being Church Year and Other Sermons in Germ

---

SOME GOOD SERMON STARTS

Each year we are giving increased and more careful attention to the quality and suggestiveness of this section of the Manual. The warm commendation it has received shows that it is accounted especially useful.

A flash of illumination on a text that may seem unusual or obscure often makes it brilliant with suggestion. Its various phases of truth become glowing and glorious. In utter frankness, the aim of this section is at being both provocative and picturesque in the way of sermon starts. Here are half a hundred starting-point studies of striking texts and themes.

The purpose is to present a body of practical-use suggestions, also bringing to attention scores of texts almost wholly passed over by the pulpit, yet vital, full of beauty and spiritual value. There is decided gain in the direction of freshness and force in the selection of texts and themes from the comparatively unknown and neglected portions of Scripture. The preacher does well who often treads the unfamiliar byways of the Bible, visiting regions somewhat new and strange. The use of unusual and striking texts promotes attention, good hearing, interest, as also resultful retention in the memory of hearers. The truths uttered are more likely to strike and stick. They need be none the less vital and essential, for ministers are well aware that there is a direct road to Christ from every portion of the Word.

1. Topic: The Over-burdened Nail.

TEXT: "In that day, saith the Lord of hosts, shall the nail that is fastened in a sure place be removed, and be cut down, and fall." Isa. 22:25.

Eliakim was the nail fastened in a sure place and became overburdened. He was a strong man, just the kind to hold the nation together in a crisis. In old-time buildings some nails were used to fasten the timbers together, others were used as wall pegs on which to hang things; but such might be broken by having too much weight put upon them

I. This is what happened to Eliakim. The office to which he was appointed was one of distinction, but as soon as he entered upon his duties as minister of state all his family relations came round and hung themselves on him and the nail became overburdened and broke down. This kind of thing has been the undoing of many a city and state administration. A man can show his strength by the people he keeps out of office as well as by those he puts in. Looking upon civilization today men are beginning to ask, "Will civilization commit suicide?" Winston Churchill says, "Another war will mean the extermination of the white race." It looks as though the nail is in danger of becoming overburdened.

II. One may have the same conviction in regard to the burdens some people have to bear. But in some instances we make our own burdens. We take on too much. A minister once told me that he was on twenty committees, mostly outside his own church.

III. Some of us need to take a quiet hour and overlook our lists of engagements and dates, take a look at the things that have come by stealth and hung themselves upon our life. It is concentrated steam that moves the engine. Eliakim broke down because he was carrying too much.

IV. We become overburdened not always because of the weight of the burden, but through the unsufficiency of our strength We are not properly connected with the living God. "I can do all things through Christ which strengtheneth me." "They that wait upon the Lord shall renew their strength." This is the one great need, to link these overtaxed lives of ours to the infinite mercy and infinite might and find His strength made perfect in our weakness.—J. B.

2. Topic: Underbidding Christ.

TEXT: "And when he was gone forth into the way, there came one running, and kneeled to him, and asked him, Good Master, what shall I do that I may inherit eternal life?" Mark 10:17.

Underbidding Christ! Yes.

I. "So you want eternal life, young man. You can have it. Go sell what you have and give to the poor, and thou shalt have treasure in heaven: and come, follow me." The young man did not follow. He went away sorrowful. Did he give up his desire for eternal life, or did he say, "I know how to get it at less cost"?

II. How often we underbid Christ. In the matter of happiness, for example. Supreme happiness can be had of the Christ. It is a gift for which a high price has been paid. We underbid. We pay our little prices and we receive a shoddy article. And yet often it isn't the real article but a very poor substitute.

III. Life. Jesus said, "I came that they might have life, and that they may have it abundantly." And we say, "I know where life can be had for a smile, a song, a coin. Life is cheap if you know where to go." Not life, dead leaves. A bauble, a trifle will never buy life. The supreme gift is at supreme cost.

IV. Beware of low bids. Scrutinize the characters of those who offer their goods too cheaply. Investigate the article they offer. Beware of substitutes, often they are counterfeits.—M. K. W. H.

3. Topic: Tension.

TEXT: "They are not of the world, even as I am not of the world." John 17:16.

In Jesus' farewell prayer he interceded for his disciples. He knew the tension that they would be under in trying to live a Christian life in a non-Christian world.

I. The Christian awakes each morning to experience that tension in greater or less degree every hour of the day. Our temporal lives and our spiritual lives are never identified. In the perfectly Christian society they might become so. Or in the perfectly pagan society a perfect pagan might live a life without tension.

II. But here we are doing the best we can to make our life in the world and our higher spiritual life as harmonious as possible.

III. It encourages one to remember that Christ knows our difficulties. It helps to remember that it is by tension that we grow.

IV. When, under severe tension, we are compelled to choose between the life of the world and the higher life of the spirit, the latter must be given the primacy.—M. K. W. H.

4. Topic: The Outspread Hands.

TEXT: "I have spread out my hands all the day unto a rebellious people." Isa. 65:2.

This is an intimation of God's gracious attitude of love toward his rebellious people.

I. The outspread hands. "I have spread out my hands." What does that mean? What is implied? The outspread hands are hands of mercy, hands of compassion, hands of pity. Outspread hands indicate a waiting and urgent desire to receive and to save. God's hands are gracious hands, waiting hands, ready hands, longing to welcome the returning sinner.

II. Further there is suggestion of the persistency of God's loving readiness to save. "All the day." A day is morning, noon and night. It represents the entire time. It represents God's ceaseless, unfailing readiness to welcome and to save.

III. To what kind of people is God showing such grace and love? "To a rebellious people." That is just what those Jews Isaiah was speaking of had been. Rebels. Rebels against God, against his laws, against his love, against his holiness. The same is true among men today. "God commendeth his love toward us in that while we were yet sinners Christ died for us." But too many spurn his mercies. They ignore his blessings, their privileges, and his grace. We rebel against his Son, our Saviour, disregard his invitations and the strivings of the Holy Spirit.

Why not yield to God's waiting love? —J. B.

5. Topic: Ecce Rex (Good Friday).

TEXT: "Behold your King!" John 19:14.

I. Is he King there in his shame? Then assuredly he is King now that he has risen from the dead and gone into glory.

II. Is he King amid shame and pain? Then he is able to help us if we are in like case.

III. Is he King while paying the price of our redemption? Then certainly he is King now that the price is paid and he has become the Author of salvation.

IV. Is he King at Pilate's bar? Then truly he will be so when Pilate stands at his bar. Come hither saints and pay your accustomed worship! Come hither sinners and adore for the first time!—C. H. S.

6. Topic: The Lonely Cross-bearer (Good Friday).

TEXT: "And he bearing his cross went forth." John 19:17.

I. Bearing his cross for himself. Isa. 53:3. 1. An aggravation of his misery. 2. An intensifying of their sin. 3. A heightening of his love. 4. An enlargement of their hope.

II. Bearing his cross for us. 1. In expiation of our guilt. Col. 1:2; Col. 2:14. 2. As a pattern for our life. I Pet. 2:21.—T. W.

7. Topic: The Cross of Christ (Good Friday).

TEXT: "Where they crucified him, and with him two others, on either side one, and Jesus in the midst. And Pilate wrote a title," etc. John 19:18, 19 (A. S. V.).

I. Under the cross. 1. The weary pilgrim, Jesus. Burdened by weight. Exhausted by agony. Suffering through scourging. Degraded by tablet. 2. The varied attendants—robbers, soldiers, etc.

II. Upon the cross. Jesus in the midst. On either side a robber, proclaiming him the worst of the three. The nails. The pain. A spectacle of woe. Priests and people mocking.

III. Above the cross. The title, vs. 19. 1. Its conspicuous position, seen by all. 2. Its threefold language, to be read by all. 3. Its providential use, to attest to all. The meaning: Christ's true humanity, "Jesus of Nazareth." His messianic dignity, "King of the Jews." Israel's sin. Had crucified their Sovereign. The world's hope. He was the Saviour of men.

IV. Beneath the cross. Gambling for his clothes. Heartless cruelty. Moral responsibility. Appalling criminality. Unconscious instrumentality.

V. Near the cross. The Galilean women. Posts of love. Their names: the Marys and Salome. Their position. By the cross. Near the cross. Courage—not afraid of the soldiers. Their fidelity—in contrast with the male Disciples who had forsaken him and fled. Their privilege—gracious opportunity of hearing his last words.—T. W.

8. Topic: Heaven's Ascension Day Message (Ascension).

TEXT: "Ye men of Galilee, why stand ye looking into heaven? this Jesus, who was received up from you into heaven, shall so come in like manner as ye beheld him going into heaven." Acts 1:11 (A. S. V.).

Ascension Day is an important festival in the Greek, Roman and English churches. The time is more or less informally observed in nearly all denominations. It offers opportunity for the consideration, especially on the nearest Sunday, of the transcendent fact of Christ's exaltation to glory and mediatorial reign in behalf of his people. The time in the church calendar is the fortieth day after Easter.

I. The Ascension Day message is a rebuke to inactive curiosity. "Not for you to know the times and the seasons."

II. It is a reminder of human limitations. "Many things to say . . . but ye cannot bear them now."

III. It is an intimation for faith to be exercised in service. "Ye shall be witnesses."

IV. It is an assurance of a similar return. "In like manner as ye beheld him going to heaven," etc.—C. R. S.

9. Topic: An Ascended Yet Ever-present Lord (Ascension).

TEXT: "Lo, I am with you alway, even unto the end of the world." Matt. 28:20.

These are the final words of a gospel but the inaugural words of a ministry. They seem to mark the close of a dispensation, yet they open a perspective of the end of the world. They mark the end of a temporal relationship but the beginning of an eternal one.

I. This seems not impossible when the unique Speaker is taken into account, Jesus, the Christ, Emmanuel glorified and risen.

II. The only condition of fulfillment devolves upon the human chosen ones who receive and obey.

III. The resultant comfort is especially adapted to human longings. 1. In temptations: "Temptations lose their power when thou art nigh." 2. In sorrow or adversity. "Though I walk through the valley of the shadow of death, I will fear no evil, for thou art with me."—C. R. S.

10. Topic: No Compartments.

TEXTS: "Set your mind on the things that are above. . . . Put on a heart of compassion. . . . Do all in the name of the Lord Jesus." Col. 3:3, 12, 17 (A. S. V.).

Set your mind upon the Christ level. Clothe your heart with the Christ spirit. Do everything in the name of Christ. These were the teachings of Paul to his friends at Colossae.

I. Paul brings the mind, the heart, the will into inseparable relationship. They belong together. The set of the mind must be on the Christ for action to be in the name of Christ.

II. A man just doesn't do one way and think another, not successfully and not for long. Nor can one do all in the name of Christ if the heart's emotions are not Christward.

III. Even as knowing, feeling and doing cannot be put into separate compartments, so in presenting an "all" in the name of Christ it is difficult, if not impossible, to break life up into time divisions. Can we do on Sunday in the name of the Lord Jesus and let the weekdays go? Is it enough to give my mature years to Christ and let my youth be passed? Even one's early years must be consecrated, or if it is too late for that, they must be redeemed by Christ.

IV. Who can successfully offer Christ his home life and dedicate his business life to Mammon?—M. K. W. H.

11. Topic: Sent Ones.

TEXT: "I heard the voice of the Lord, saying, whom shall I send?" Isa. 6:8.

May be treated thus: I. The person wanted. II. The person offering himself. III. The work the person is called to undertake. Or thus: I. The Divine call. II. The proper response. III. The Divine acceptance of the offer.

I. The waiting one. "I heard the voice," etc. 1. Ready. "Here am I, send me." 2. The word to the sent one. "Go."

II. The waiting one sent. Matt. 21:28. 1. The place appointed, "In my vineyard." 2. The time arranged. "Today."

III. The workers must be: 1. Competent, I Chron. 9:13; 12:33. 2. Wholehearted, Neh. 4:6; 6:3. 3. Men of valor, II Chron. 32:7, 8. 4. Diligent.

12. Topic: The Larger Trust.

TEXT: "Trust in the Lord with all thine heart; and lean not unto thine own understanding. In all thy ways acknowledge him, and he shall direct thy paths." Prov. 3:5, 6.

We all need to learn the lesson of the larger trust.

I. It is not so difficult to trust in the Lord a little, but to trust with all thy heart—that must be learned. When one trusts a little then one enjoys a little peace. When one trusts greatly one finds the great peace which passeth all understanding.

II. The secret of acknowledging him in all our ways is to do so in each of our ways. Few of us can do so great a thing as to submit all of life at once to him, but we can give him the parts which make the whole.

III. This morning the path of duty lies ahead, I will acknowledge him in that. This noon I shall walk the road of friendship and there we shall find him. It may be that this afternoon he shall have to direct my path over Hill Difficulty but he will do it. Each part of the road knows his direction. Then when I look back I shall see that he directed all my paths.—M. K. W. H.

13. Topic: The Common Lot.

TEXT: "They . . . were tempted." Heb. 11:37.

William Penn once said, "God is better served in resisting temptation to evil than in many formal prayers."

I. Temptation is the common lot. Not all these saints were "scourged, stoned, slain," but all were tempted. A universal experience.

II. The unlimited breadth of this statement does not specify how all were tempted; but states the fact. "They were tempted." Some temptations are peculiar to self, some common to all, some to unbelief, some to immorality, some to religious declension.

III. Why does God so permit? Christ tempted "like as we are." Temptations sift, reveal, when resisted add strength. God has many good reasons. "So it seemeth good in thy sight."—H.

14. Topic: Thorns and Walls.

TEXT: "Behold, I will hedge up thy way with thorns, and make a wall." Hos. 2:6.

Divine restraints.

I. God puts forth restraints on the sinner here. "Hedge up thy way."

II. A way may be found through a hedge of thorns, though with pain and suffering.

III. Nature of restraints. Restraint of public sentiment. Restraint of conscience. Restraint of affliction.

IV. Such restraints are necessary. For the evildoer himself. For the world at large. What if wickedness were never reined in, wicked men having their full fling?

V. Thank God for thorny hedges. Sometimes even the best of Christians have occasion to thank God for their thorns. So with Paul. So with us, our troubles proving our greatest blessings. Said one, "I thanked God a thousand times for my roses, but not once for my thorns."—H.

15. Topic: Time.

TEXT: "A time to keep." Eccles. 3:6.

I. The quantity of a moment is infinitesimal. The quality of a moment may be infinite. It is proverbial that a second may hold eternity, which means that a period of time may be timeless.

II. One who experienced a moment of excruciating pain discovered it to be most revealing, for it was given him through it to understand more fully the pain of Christ upon the cross.

III. Time value. Traveling through Japan a company of us caught just one glimpse of Mount Fuji as the clouds broke; it would have taken hours, even days, of our other sight-seeing to strike an equivalent.

IV. The flash of inner light is often with no less speed than the light of a sun or star. The truth is discovered, the beautiful created, goodness appropriated in a split second. It is marvelous that man has been made with such capacity. Is this the token that he shares the timelessness, the eternity of God?

V. Shining moments help us through dull days. When we stumble in the dark how helpful and encouraging the light which flashes from our hands; by a single flash we may take many steps on the road. One glimpse of Christ on the Damascus road was a brightness that blinded Paul for days, but all his after life was lived in obedience to that moment of vision.—M. K. W. H.

16. Topic: An Unpainted Picture.

TEXT: "In that hour Jesus rejoiced in spirit." Luke 10:21.

Recall the great paintings we have seen of Jesus. All of us note the spiritual earnestness in his face as he talked with the doctors in the temple in Hofmann's picture. A less familiar picture is that painted by Cornicelius of Christ being tempted by Satan. Look at it for a few moments and the intense struggle as seen in his eyes will haunt one's memory for days. In William Holman-Hunt's "Light of the World" there is deep tenderness in the face of the stranger who stands at the door and knocks. What courage and dignity in the haggard face of Munkácsy's "Christ before Pilate."

I. Why has not someone portrayed the Christ of this text? One can be reading along in Luke's Gospel and easily miss this picture of the rejoicing or exulting Christ. One is unaware of the significance of the word "rejoice." Nowhere else except in this verse is anything of the kind recorded of him. Luke alone uses the word. It is to be found in the Song of Mary, "My soul doth magnify the Lord; and my spirit hath rejoiced in God my Saviour." Also in the book of Acts it is used twice. How variously it is translated, "He exulted," "He thrilled with joy," "He was filled with rapturous joy," "He was inspired with joy."

II. What brought this experience to Jesus? With his face set steadfastly toward Jerusalem, his hands on the plow and never looking backward, what could have brought this rapture to his face, this ecstasy to his heart? Read the story from the beginning of the tenth chapter. He had appointed seventy to go forth and spread for a season the message of the Gospel and do good in his name. They had returned with joy. They had followed his instructions and discovered themselves to be channels of the divine grace and instruments of his power.

III. They were common men. No one knows the name of any one of them, though tradition carries memory of a few. But here we have the will of Christ being done and the kingdom advancing through the labors of such men as perhaps you and I.

IV. Their success brought him rapturous joy. Today we, too, shall go forth in his name and when we return at evening may we bring joy to the face of the Master whom we love. That rapture may never be captured by a painter's brush; it may be reflected in our own exultant hearts.—M. K. W. H.

17. Topic: The Abuse of Prosperity.

TEXT: "Israel is an empty vine, he bringeth forth fruit unto himself." Hos. 10:1.

Proper translation is luxuriant, not empty. Denotes the outward prosperity and abundance Israel had enjoyed.

I. Vineyard planted, choice vines, cultivated, rich fruitage used to wretched purpose. Prosperity abused.

II. Some men very prosperous, every branch of life clusters with fruit.

III. When is prosperity abused? When used to selfish ends, in selfish indulgence, to self-aggrandizement, without regard to the claims of God.

IV. The right which prosperity gives is the right to lay it out for the benefit of others, the cure of human woes, the dispersion of human ignorance, the elevation of the human soul, the salvation of the world.

V. How are we as individuals and as a nation using our enormous prosperity? —H.

18. Topic: The Rights of Children (Children's Day).

TEXT: "And Jesus increased in wisdom and stature, and in favor with God and man." Luke 2:52.

Which means that his growth was normal and healthy. He grew just as your child or my child should grow. Some of the apocryphal books contain certain stories of the childhood of Jesus in which the miraculous and the supernatural abound; but not so the Gospel records. They contain these words showing the boy's development. The words contain that fine summary of which it is well often to remind ourselves.

I. Jesus increased in wisdom, developing intellectually.

II. He increased in stature, developing physically.

III. He increased in favor with God, developing spiritually.

IV. He increased in favor with man, developing socially.

V. And the development was in perfect proportion.

We are beginning to realize that every child born into the world has a right to grow. Are we seeing to it that, at whatever may be the cost to us, the little ones God has given to us are so developing, that they are growing as Jesus grew, in wisdom, in stature, and in favor with God and man? It is their right.—J. A. M.

19. Topic: Spiritual Bankruptcy (Lent).

TEXT: "And he wist not that the Lord was departed from him." Judg. 16:20.

A man may lose his strength and yet continue to live in the experiences of the past. Samson "wist not that the Lord was departed from him."

I. Samson's strength came from the Lord. God the source. Evidently then there was a supernatural element in it. Both beauty and strength come from communion with God.

II. God's Spirit departs if abused. When a man departs the Lord departs, the Spirit being grieved.

III. The Spirit departs silently. "He knew not." Lost grace may be unrealized.

IV. The consciousness of loss of strength will be realized when the strength itself is most needed. How much Samson in crisis needed his!

V. The person from whom the Spirit has departed finds himself a spiritual bankrupt. Locks shorn. Strength gone. Helpless.

Such thoughts should bring sadness, but not despair. Return! Return!—H.

20. Topic: Stand Up Like a Man.

TEXT: "Son of man, stand upon thy feet, and I will speak unto thee." Ezek. 2:1.

It is a great mistake to say that religion paralyzes or impoverishes manhood. To the contrary, its purpose is to help us realize highest values. It says, as God spoke to Ezekiel, "Stand upon thy feet," etc.

I. "Stand" in order to hear and bear a Divine message.

II. "Stand" in the attitude of self-respect. Religion a call to dignity, conviction, courage, character, uprightness.

III. "Stand" in the attitude of expectancy. "Speak, Lord," etc. To the man upon his feet and expecting God will have something to say.

IV. "Stand" in the readiness to act. "Here I am, send me."—H.

21. Topic: The Iron Pen.

TEXT: "The sin of Judah is written with a pen of iron, and with the point of a diamond." Jer. 17:1.

Striking figure, suggests:

I. The fixedness of sin. Carved as in granite with iron pen with diamond point.

II. The record deep and ineradicable.

III. The items are filling up page after page in the record of God's remembrance.

IV. The iron pen with its diamond point does not wear out. The long list assuredly will be made. No violation of Divine law passes unnoticed.

V. Be lovingly warned against the black catalogue which the iron pen has been recording.

VI. Sin thus stamped into us, ingrained into our nature, how can it be gotten out? Christ the cure, gives a new heart.—H.

22. Topic: Need and Supply.

TEXT: "Now when Jacob saw that there was corn in Egypt," Gen. 42:1, 2.

I. In sore straits, famine. The need was: 1. Essential—a famine not of luxuries but bread. 2. Universal—over all the land. 3. Absolute—not a meager crop but total failure.

"I perish with hunger," etc. "Man shall not live by bread alone," etc. "Labor . . . for the meat that endureth," etc.

II. Welcome news. "I have heard there is corn." "I am the Bread of Life." Bread. 1. Satisfies desires. 2. Sustains life. 3. Supplies energy. Christ does all this.

III. Sound advice. "Get you down and buy." 1. You need the Bread of Life. 2. You have every encouragement to procure it. 3. Invitation. 4. Testimony of those who have tried it. 5. It is free. Buy and eat without money and without price.

23. Topic: The Crisis of Prayer.

TEXT: "O Lord! how long shall I cry, and thou wilt not hear?" Hab. 1:2.

The question to be answered is this: How long will God suffer his people to pray and still neglect to hear? There are answers:

I. Until they see the plague of their own hearts. Until each one becomes conscious of his own individual iniquities and repents.

II. Until his people are willing to do whatever duty he requires in addition to praying. Some of us stop at praying. We do nothing else. That is not enough.

III. Until we remove the stumbling blocks out of the way of God's work.

IV. Here we discover: 1. Why so many prayers seem to be offered in vain. 2. We see some of the causes of spiritual declension in the Church. 3. We see the duty of every Christian to search his own heart. Often the hindrances to God's cause are the sins of individuals. —N. P.

24. Topic: The Meaning of Memorials (Memorial Day).

TEXT: "And these stones shall be for a memorial unto the children of Israel for ever." Josh. 4:7.

I. We have memorials whose strength and beauty recall to us today majestic figures and past deliverances (monuments: Washington, Lincoln, Unknown Soldier, and many others).

II. Wisdom of keeping alive memories of men who gave so much, asked so little—road-builders for order, freedom, and their nation. Their spirit is our priceless heritage. What they built and saved is ours to conserve and continue.

III. If we remember gratefully such, how much more we need to attend upon the Lord of all, Jesus our Saviour! "Lord God of Hosts, be with us yet, lest we forget!"—H.

25. Topic: The Man for the Times.

TEXT: "But my servant Caleb, because he had another spirit with him," etc. Num. 14:24.

Caleb was a man for the time, his work and influence strategic.

I. Consider the dignity of his character. His name means "All heart." The word "courage" also means "heart." He was embodied courage, with also sympathy and common sense. God called him "My servant."

II. Consider also his excellent spirit. "Had another spirit with him." Believing, fearless, eminently devout and faithful.

III. The reward of his fidelity. "Him will I bring into the land." God-approved. God-rewarded. Recall his notable inheritance in the land.

IV. Such men are men for crises times, turbulent times, good times, all times. God give us men!—H.

26. Topic: Lustrous Christians (Lent).

Text: "Let your light so shine," etc. Matt. 5:16.

Are we lustrous Christians, or has our light grown dim? Our Lenten services are aimed to rekindle your light.

I. Every Christian has a light peculiar to himself. Consider the power of good example. Most successful way of removing objections to religion, also of winning the esteem of the world. "A good example is the tallest kind of preaching."

II. There is a right way of shedding light. Hold it up. Make it winsome.

III. Men see the works, not the worker. "See your good works." Don't magnify self. Do good works.

IV. Men greatly influenced by what they see. Good life a great means of glorifying God.—H.

27. Topic: Keep in Fitness.

Text: "Be ready to every good work." Titus 3:1.

Sounds like challenge of coach or trainer of athletes.

I. Implies the readiness of a good foundation. Preparation. Knowledge. Training. Faith. Hope.

II. Readiness for what kind of works? For the bodies of others. For the souls of others. In behalf of the church and kingdom of Christ.

III. To what extent suggested? "Every good work." To full extent of ability and opportunity.

IV. Some implied features of this readiness. Disposition to do. Willingness. Promptness. Cheerfulness. Persistence.

V. Motives moving Christians to such works. The supreme motive, love to Christ. Next, love to souls for his sake. Others, great present joy, rich future reward.—H.

28. Topic: Straight Ahead!

Text: "Turn not," etc. Josh. 1:7.

Courage, Joshua! Go straight!

I. Straight is obedience. There is sure to be a right hand. Sure to be a left hand. Both are probably wrong. Go straight!

II. Straight is strategy. Avoid temptations, sinful inducements from either side.

III. Straight is most economic of strength. Is shortest way, most direct. No roundabout or zigzag. Straight!

IV. Straight is safety. Gives no opportunity for enemies. No dangerous parleying. No loitering. Straight!

V. Straight is happiest way. No doubtful vacillation, nor argument with self or others. Escapes misery of making repeated decisions. Not right. Not left. Straight ahead!—H.

29. Topic: Short-lived Pleasures.

Text: "For as the crackling of thorns under a pot, so is the laughter of the fool." Eccles. 7:6.

In Eastern countries where fuel is very scarce every combustible shrub, bush, and bramble is seized for culinary fires. These blaze hot but soon extinct. This is the picture, "crackling of thorns under a pot." So of worldly mirth, "laughter of the fool," short-lived "vanity."

I. It is noisy. More so than if there were anything in it.

II. It is short-lived. Like crackling thorns, hot, quick, little lasting. Recurring, increasing demand. There are physical limits to all gay pleasures.

III. It is unintelligent. "Laughter of fool" not founded on judgment or good sense.

IV. It is unprofitable. Empty, disappointing.

V. Evidently the reverse of all sound, sensible social and spiritual enjoyments. —H.

30. Topic: Christian Staying Power.

TEXT: "Let us not be weary in well doing," etc. Gal. 6:9.

The great desideratum in the Christian life is staying power. Impulse, spasm common, far less so perseverance.

I. The Christian's duty. That of "well doing." Sin is wrong doing. Well doing is duty to God, to self, to neighbor. Such duties great in number, in extent, important in nature, and require staying power.

II. The Christian's danger in duty. Of "weariness in well doing," of fatigue, discouragement, letup. Such weariness invites failure, dishonors Christ, forfeits reward.

III. The Christian's encouragement to duty. "Reap if ye faint not." Harvest may be delayed, but sure. Reap in time, God's time, best time, "in due season."—H.

31. Topic: Secret Sins Exposed.

TEXT: "When I looked, behold a hole in the wall . . . and there stood . . . Jaazaniah!" Ezek. 8:7, 11.

Judah was falling into heathen idolatry. Depraved worship of creeping things, abominable beasts, idols. In a vision God shows all this to his prophet. Ezekiel's mission was to bring the people back to God. Jaazaniah was one of the leaders of Israel, respected, venerated. Through an enlarged hole in the wall of the temple court, the priests' quarters, Ezekiel beholds midnight incantations, swinging censers, clouds of incense, actual worship of the horrible heathen monstrosities. The ministrants seventy elders of the people. Then these words, "In the midst of them, there stood Jaazaniah!" "Be sure your sin will find you out."—H.

32. Topic: The Grace of Having Enough (Thanksgiving).

TEXT: "I have enough." Gen. 33:11.

Here is happy converse between two brothers. Esau declines a present saying, "I have enough." Jacob urges his acceptance saying, "I have enough."

I. It is a great pity that contentment is not true of Christians more generally. We read of a poor woman breakfasting on bread and water exclaiming, "What, all this and Christ too!" A Puritan preacher asking a blessing on herring and potatoes said, "Lord, we thank thee that thou hast ransacked sea and land to find food for thy children."

II. Contentment surpasses riches.

III. It is pleasant to have to spare for others.

IV. Best of all is it to recognize God as giver.

V. "Enough" can hardly be true of spiritual blessings.—H.

33. Topic: Concern for Companionships.

TEXT: "What men are these with thee?" Num. 22:9.

The story of Balaam is exceedingly interesting but tragic. In this question God was not seeking information, but to arouse Balaam's conscience and caution, both as to his company and the sin they were tempting him to commit. "What men are these with thee?"

I. In his concern for our welfare God often asks the same question of us men, women, today. Asks through providences, by his Word, frequently through conscience.

II. This inquiry plainly indicates the importance of our companionships, also our responsibility to God concerning them. "A man is known by the company he keeps." Associates do influence character.—H.

34. Topic: Making Crooked Things Straight.

TEXT: "That which is crooked cannot be made straight." Eccles. 1:15.

This is probably a common proverbial saying.

I. There are at this moment many crooked things in this world.

II. It does not require much insight to see that there is much in human nature that is marred and crooked, in human conditions that are gnarled and twisted. In the mental world erroneous beliefs and false conceptions; in the moral world violations of both human and Divine laws.

III. The man who quoted this proverb beheld the obstacles, but he did not see God. Man's power is limited, God's is not. Co-operate with God.—H.

35. Topic: The Abundant Life.

TEXT: "I am come that they might have life, and that they might have it more abundantly." John 10:10.

Life in its source, Christ. Life in its blessings, salvation. Life in its fruit, glory to God.

I. Life in Christ for all. All life is in him. His perfect life given for us on the cross, v. 11. His risen life imparted to us by the Holy Spirit, vv. 15, 18. His life set before us as our pattern, v. 27. His eternal life presented to us as a gift v. 28.

II. Life in the souls of all who believe. "He that hath the Son hath life," I John 5:12. Life in its privilege by knowing, v. 13. Life in its power by living, v. 18.

III. Life abounding. The manifestation of life. Four things prove the tree to be alive, growth, leaves, blossoms, fruit. Life in the head, light, John 17:3. Life in the heart, love, I John 3:14. Life in the hands, labor, Phil. 3:10. Life in the feet, liberty, Gal. 2:20. Life in the pocket, liberality, I John 3:17. Life in its glory, lasting joy, I John 3:2; Col. 3:4.—Rev. C. Edwards.

36. Topic: How Shall We Measure Life?

TEXT: "And all the days of Methuselah were nine hundred sixty and nine years: and he died." Gen. 5:27.

I. Shall we measure life by time?

II. Shall we measure life by accumulation or possessions? See Jesus' parable, Luke 12:16-21. Read Tolstoy's story. "How much land does a man need?"

III. Shall we measure life by happiness?

IV. Shall we measure life by worldly success? Read II Chron. 26.

V. Shall we measure life by self-expression?

VI. Shall we measure life by experience?

Life is to be measured by growth. Read John 15.—M. K. W. H.

37. Topic: Value of the Past (New Year).

TEXT: "But call to remembrance the former days." Heb. 10:32.

Leutze's great painting of "The Course of Empire" represents a company of emigrant families at the crest of the great mountain divide looking forward into that new western country toward which they have been toiling. But in the back of the column are some thoughtful men and women looking back into the old country they are leaving. Their backward look and sober reflections may not make them any worse settlers in the new country.

I. The past includes all that we have done. Much of it fit only to be forgotten, but much of it done with honest purpose of good. That good purpose is a pledge that we will do more, as honest consistency requires, and there are few stronger obligations upon us than that pledge.

II. The past includes what others have done to our advantage. "Other men labored, and ye are entered into their labors." This Epistle advances from the thought of what we have done, to the glorious record of the "Heroes of Faith."

III. The best of the past is what God has done for us. His purpose of love; the gift of his Son; the continual leading with which Providence has brought us up to our present strength and opportunity. God in our past has made it sacred. We "hear a voice behind us saying, This is the way, walk ye in it."

38. Topic: God Forbids Pessimism.

TEXT: "Finally, brethren, whatsoever things are true . . . think on these things." Phil. 4:8.

There are cheering facts in the world, as well as discouraging facts. We ought to "think on" the cheering things.

I. Because looking at what is good makes us good; while looking at what is bad weakens and discourages our goodness, if it does not actually make us bad.

II. Because looking at the courage, truth and love of men strengthens their goodness. The recognition of moral qualities helps them.

III. Because good thoughts will make us happy and grateful to God; and we need to rouse our thankfulness.

IV. Because among the good things are those activities in which we ought to find our place of work.

39. Topic: The Beginning and the End.

TEXT: "I am Alpha and Omega, the beginning and the end." Rev. 21:6.

The description reveals the speaker's character, his personal nature, the duration and immutability of his being, his agency.

I. He is the Alpha and Omega of time.

II. He is the Alpha and Omega of rank.

III. He is the Alpha and Omega of salvation.

IV. He is Alpha and Omega of providence.

V. He is Alpha and Omega of his Church.

40. Topic: The Alpha and Omega.

TEXT: "I am Alpha and Omega, the beginning and the ending, saith the Lord, which is, and which was, and which is to come, the Almighty." Rev. 1:8.

Alpha is the first letter of the Greek alphabet. Omega is the last. So that Christ in this text represents himself as the A and the Z. Jesus is the Alpha and the Omega because of his all-sufficiency. Like the literal Alpha and Omega he includes everything within himself. He is the beginning and the ending, which is, and was, and is to come, the Almighty —the All-sufficient. There is nothing which the Christian needs but he will find it in the Lord Jesus, a sufficient Saviour, a perfect Pattern, a wise Counselor and Guide, his Life, his Hope, his Way.

I. He is the Alpha and Omega of the entire creation.

II. He is the Alpha and Omega of the Divine manifestations.

III. He is the Alpha and Omega of the inspired Volume.

IV. He is the Alpha and Omega of the plan of redemption.

V. He is the Alpha and Omega of spiritual life in the believer.

VI. He is the Alpha and Omega of future happiness. Men believe in a hereafter. All immortal aspirations are met in him.

41. Topic: Love Essential.

TEXT: "If I have all faith, so as to remove mountains, but have not love, I am nothing." I Cor. 13:2 (A.S.V.).

Love is essential.

I. Without love I am nothing. Without love the essential thing is lacking. The reason for my existence is that I may love. Christ died for us that we might be saved for love. The gift of life eternal is for the exercise of the abiding and eternal virtue, love.

II. The uttermost failure in life is not to love. It is for loving and for being loved that we were created and redeemed.

III. Love is essential too in that no other virtue can be substituted for it. One cannot substitute eloquent speech for love. One cannot substitute knowledge, scholarship, cleverness, inventiveness, for love. Nor is benevolence apart from love, giving all your goods to feed the poor, a satisfactory exhibition of the self. Nor is standing up for a principle until martyrdom results of any profit in itself. There is no substitute for love.

IV. It is essential for any understanding of Christianity that one grasp its distinctive idea of love. To grip this idea in any adequate way is not by holding some general theory of good will; it is by the practice of love.—M. K. W. H.

42. Topic: The Resurrection Fact (Easter).

TEXT: "Now is Christ risen from the dead, and become the firstfruits of them that slept." I Cor. 15:20.

I. The resurrection of Jesus Christ from the dead is a historical fact. As such it is proved like any other historical fact—by the testimony of competent witnesses and by the witness of related facts and results.

II. The resurrection of Jesus Christ from the dead is more than a historical fact. It is a spiritual force in the lives of men. Through fellowship with the risen Christ, men rise from a death in sin to a life in holiness. "Now is Christ risen from the dead." "Ye are risen with Christ." In Christ the believer is a risen man.

III. The resurrection of Christ is more than a historical fact and more than a spiritual force. It is prophecy and hope and assurance of future life. "Because I live, ye shall live also." Men have ever nursed and nurtured the thought of life beyond the grave. It is a sort of instinct of humanity. The thought is as old as the heartbeat and as natural.—Rev. John F. Carson, D.D.

43. Topic: Profit and Loss.

TEXT: "For what is a man profited, if he shall gain the whole world, and lose his own soul?" Matt. 16:26.

Here is a case supposed: "If he gain the whole world." Here is an inquiry instituted: "What is a man profited?" And an exchange proposed: "What shall a man give?"

I. Think first of the world of the soul. 1. Its nature. The text assumes an inherent dignity in the soul itself. 2. Its capacities. 3. Its duration. 4. Its purchase price. Its value in its origin, in its operations, in its redemption, in the duration of its existence.

II. Think of the possibility of its loss. 1. The loss of the soul is certainly possible. 2. The loss of the soul is utterly deplorable. 3. The loss of the soul is irreparable. 4. It is the loss of holiness. 5. It is the loss of happiness. 6. It is the loss of hope. 7. It is the loss of heaven.

III. The question proposed. 1. The gain is uncertain; the loss is inevitable. 2. The gain is imaginary: the loss is positive. 3. The gain is temporary: the loss irretrievable.

This problem deserves our most careful study. Nothing can compensate for the loss of the soul. It does not need to be lost. "Heaven is had for the asking."

44. Topic: Making New Year Accomplishments (New Year).

TEXT: "And the prophet came to the king of Israel, and said unto him, Go, strengthen thyself . . . for at the return of the year the king of Syria will come up against thee." I Kings 20:22.

What will the new year bring?

I. A renewal of life's battle. The nobility of the life conflict.

II. The return of the same old antagonists. The same old Syrians, with new faces possibly, but certainly with reinforcements.

III. The need for adequate preparation. In strength; in alertness; in self-possession.

IV. The same victorious leadership. To whom hill or valley battlefield is alike, and with whom menacing numbers and parading chariots do not count.

V. The call for individual loyalty and fidelity (5:39).—Rev. S. B. Dunn, D.D.

45. Topic: A New Year Resolve (New Year).

TEXT: "Ye have not passed this way heretofore." Josh. 3:4.

I. We must go on. There is no going back. Whatever the path before us we must tread it. Keep going. Time is an old policeman: he says, "Keep moving on."

II. As we go let us look out for the signposts. The bypaths are plainly marked "Misery," "Ruin," "Death." The right path is clearly shown: "Happiness," "Peace," "Heaven." Keep going. Keep in the right path.

III. Let us proceed slowly. Make haste slowly. It is better not to slip than to get up after a fall. There are green lights of caution; red lights of danger; the White Light of safety—the Word of God. Through the year keep the lamp of the Word high as a light to the feet.

IV. Let us not go alone. Let us look out for friends on the road. Let us also look out for those needing help on the way. We can have Christ with us every day and all the way.

V. Take the staff of God's promise in your hand. He promises help and comfort. Isa. 42:16.

VI. Look forward with hope to the end of the way. It is a holy way, a happy way. It may be an untried way now. Keep going. Keep in the right path. Fall not out to the right hand or the left. Go straight on. The road to heaven? "Take the first turn to the right and then keep straight ahead." The end of such going is heaven itself. In the new year make a year's journey toward heaven.

46. Topic: Some Other Way.

TEXT: "Are not Abana and Pharpar . . . better?" II Kings 5:12.

Naaman wished to be healed. He heard through his maid of the great prophet Elisha and sought him out. Told to bathe seven times in the Jordan, he interposed his religious and national pride in the question of the text.

I. Naaman's question. Abstractly his question is a noble one. He defends his Syrian traditions. He speaks patriotically of his own country. Most of all he vindicates the right of free inquiry. We have the right to compare our present faiths with the new affirmations that are offered us. If Naaman at last chooses the Jordan, it will be none the worse because he compared it with Abana and Pharpar.

II. Naaman's obedience. Naaman, however, did not finally stand on his pride. He knew well enough that Abana and Pharpar could not heal him. It was at last the Jordan or a leper's death. God does not choke off our inquiries, but by the reminder that we are dying men he calls us at last to choose. The struggle to climb up some other way may by its failure bring us to the critical alternative: "God's way or the sinner's death." Critical hesitation has its limits. When a man comes to Naaman's desperate condition he will choose.

III. Naaman's cure. It was the justification of the requirement. It showed, not the natural superiority of the Jordan to Abana and Pharpar, but the value of faith and the power of God.

47. Topic: Doors of Opportunity (New Year).

TEXT: "Behold, I have set before thee an open door." Rev. 3:8.

God is ever opening doors of opportunity. There is no time like the present, because the present is all we are sure of.

I. One of the finest sentiments we can entertain is: "Lord, for tomorrow and its needs I do not pray: keep me, my God, just for today." If we are strong tomorrow, it is because we were strong today. If we are faithful to the immediate duty, we shall be faithful to the wider obligations.

II. An individual will never influence a wide circle until he has learned how to influence his own environment. The accomplishments of our workaday world are not done by stored but current power. So long as the current flows, the light shines. So long as the wheels turn, the machinery moves.

So long as things need to be done, they will be done by men and women who are already doing. On one side of the open door is written the word "Opportunity." On the other is written the word "Responsibility."

The New Year has ushered us into new responsibilities and has laid upon us new and untried duties.

Another year is but another call from God
To do some deed undone and duty we forgot:
To think some wider thought of man and good,
To see and love with kindlier eyes and warmer heart,
Until acquainted more with Him and keener eyed
To sense the need of man and serve
With larger sacrifice and readier hand our kind.

—R. B.

48. Topic: Concerning Zeal.

TEXT: "Concerning zeal." Phil. 3:6.

Zeal has often been compared to a high-bred horse. Let us follow out the analogy.

I. It is necessary for zeal to start from the right point. It needs right motive. "Let nothing be done through strife or vainglory."

II. It is necessary for zeal to keep in the right course. Learn to do God's work in God's way.

III. It is necessary for zeal to be restrained. Unbridled, uncontrolled zeal is fanaticism.

IV. It is necessary for zeal to have attendants. Discretion, knowledge, charity.

V. It is necessary for zeal to seek the right goal. Paul mourns in this verse that once his zeal had for its object persecution of the Church. Our zeal should seek the welfare of the Church and the good of souls.

49. Topic: The Meaning of the Incarnation (Christmas).

TEXT: "Now when Jesus was born in Bethlehem of Judaea." Matt. 2:1.

I. When Jesus was born there was the realization of the supernatural. The birth of Christ was no ordinary birth. It brings us face to face with the supernatural. It means the visitation of God. For Christ is God manifested in the flesh. The incarnation signifies not the coming of an absent God into the world, but the manifestation of an ever-present Father. Christ was not a revealer of God, he was the revelation of God, and he alone could say, "He that hath seen me hath seen the Father."

II. When Christ was born in Bethlehem there was also the working out of God's eternal plan of salvation. The Incarnation of Christ is the first great earthly event in connection with this divine purpose. The angels sang a heavenly truth when they said, "Unto you is born a Saviour." Christ did not come into the world merely as a teacher, a lawgiver, or a reformer, but primarily as a Saviour. Man's redemption is wrapped up in Christ's incarnation. Humanity must pin its hope of salvation to him and him alone.

III. When Jesus was born in Bethlehem there was also the culmination of an eternal process. As Christ was the Incarnation of God, the advent makes possible the Incarnation of Christ in men. It is now possible for us to be made partakers of his divine nature. If that is so, then there must be a likeness between our redeemed nature and his divine nature. When we are most like him we think less of self and more of others. As the world grows more and more Christlike, it grows less and less selfish. The nearer we come to him in the likeness of our lives, the more practicable become his teachings.—W. W. B.

50. Topic: The Logic of Providence.

TEXT: "Therefore I say unto you, Be not anxious for your life, what ye shall eat, or what ye shall drink; nor yet for your body, what ye shall put on," etc. Matt. 6:25, 26 (A.S.V.).

"How much more." That is the logic.

I. There is here a condemnation of worry concerning physical necessities, worldly matters. 1. It is foolish. 2. It is useless. 3. It is unnecessary. 4. It is wicked.

II. There is here an argument for trust. 1. Your heavenly Father knows your needs. 2. He cares for the least, therefore he will care for the greatest, of his creatures. We are of much more value than lilies and birds. 3. He gives the greater, therefore he will not withhold the less. Life and body are more than food and raiment.

III. There is here a regulation for the quests of life: "Seek ye first the kingdom of God," etc.

51. Topic: Come and Dine.

TEXT: "Come and dine." John 21:12.

The third appearance to the disciples (v. 14). He had appeared in the meantime to a number of individuals.

I. Christ interested in our physical needs. Feeding 5,000; feeding 4,000; at Jacob's well; the wheat field on the Sabbath Day. He miraculously filled their nets. The breakfast on the shore:

"Come and dine." At the present time, his interest in man's need has not waned; sample prayer: "Give us this day our daily bread." He said: "Your Father knoweth that ye have need of all these things."

II. Christ vitally interested in our spiritual needs. He ministered to the body as a preparation for spiritual teaching; discourse on the bread of life, following feeding 5,000; "Feed my sheep," the command to Peter after breakfast.

It is a mistake to overemphasize the physical. Many would follow a "bread and butter" Church for the loaves and fishes; the importance of the body as compared to the soul is in ratio as time is to eternity.

"Come and dine" is Christ's call to his Church today. "Go feed my sheep," is the command which logically follows. Feed the hungry. Care for those in spiritual want.—A. F. H.

52. Topic: Abram the Pilgrim.

TEXT: "Now the Lord had said unto Abram, Get thee out of thy country," etc. Gen. 12:1-4.

One of the first heroic scenes of Old Testament history. At God's command, this father of the faithful went out from his country and kindred, not knowing whither he went (Heb. 11:8-10). He left a certainty for an uncertainty, a fixed home for a nomadic life.

There are some valuable lessons to be learned from this narrative:

I. It is always safe and blessed to follow God's clear leading.

II. Nothing should hinder or delay us when he calls. Property, and even family, are to be sacrificed for the sake of obedience.

III. God calls for no sacrifice for which there is not, sooner or later, ample compensation. Abram had a great inheritance, and, if he left friends behind, he became "the friend of God."

IV. God's double promise to all who thus obey him is: "I will bless thee, and thou shalt be a blessing." First, blessing to oneself, and then, through oneself, to others.

53. Topic: Some Lessons the Ants Teach Us (Children's Day).

TEXT: "Go to the ant, thou sluggard; consider her ways, and be wise." Prov. 6:6.

The Bible evidently intends that we shall learn lessons from the ants. Now what are ants? I think we all know, and that we all have seen them. The dictionary says that they are small social insects. What does that word "social" mean? It means that they live in communities. They are social, they mingle together, and like us human people, they live in communities. Their nests are ordinarily excavated underground, or some species make them in mounds above ground and to considerable height. They are remarkably busy and intelligent insects. But without describing them further let us seek to know some of the lessons these little creatures may teach us.

I. They may teach the lesson of what little people can do. Don't think you cannot do anything or are excused from trying because you are little.

II. They may teach us the lesson of industry. Ants are never lazy.

III. They may teach us the lesson of perseverance. They keep on at their tasks. They never give up.

IV. They may teach us the lesson of law and order. They live together and work together and do their work systematically and according to the rules they have among them.

There are many other lessons. Think them up. Learn them.

SECTION IV. Outlines and Themes for Lenten Services. Ash Wednesday to Easter

FOR DEEPENING THE SPIRITUAL LIFE

Theme: Beaten Tracks.

(Suggestive as Introductory to the Lenten Season.)

TEXT: "Some fell by the way side." Luke 8:5.

Christ himself interpreted this parable, the "seed," the "good ground," etc. What is the "wayside"? It is the "path through the field," the "beaten track." It represents the disposition hardened and rendered unresponsive by a variety of habits of mind.

Let us think of some of the beaten tracks on which the good seed is thrown away.

I. There is the beaten track of familiarity. We are all acquainted with the term, "Gospel-hardened." That may not describe our state, but there is a condition resembling it to which all of us are subject, even us ministers. We need to be saved from the perfunctory discharge of duty and from the evil of familiarity with sacred things. The like danger is incurred by church people in general, from the beaten track of familiarity.

II. And there is the beaten track of convention. We don't like to appear different from other people. For example, we would hesitate to go into our church on a weekday to spend a little time in quiet meditation and prayer. We are a little afraid of what others might think and say if we happened to be seen. Yet the advantage of a quiet ten minutes is quite incalculable to the spiritual life. What a pity that a fear of the unusual should so obsess us!

III. There is the beaten track of routine. Take, for example, our prayers. We have not forsaken them entirely. We say them. But sometimes only say them, even for long periods. Or how is it with us about going to the Holy Communion? We may go on year after year, as we did when we first united with the church. Has it become routine? The Saviour's unqualified invitation, "Come unto me," so often falls on the beaten track of a good yet inflexible habit.

IV. And there is the beaten track of prejudice. This is perhaps the most serious hindrance of all. We are in constant need of pardon and release from the bondage and burden of sin. We know it, yet we go on in complete ignorance of our real state, and very likely struggling unaided with some besetting sin simply because we are prejudiced against confession.

Christ told us that the Holy Spirit is at work in the world, available on our behalf to pulverize the rocky ground, break up the beaten tracks and prepare our souls for the reception of the heavenly seed. In this, as in all else, what he requires is our willingness. May this Lenten season be used to the glory of God and the growth of the spiritual life within us.—Abbreviated from T. J. H.

1. Title: An Important Lenten Inquiry (Ash Wednesday).

TEXT: "How many are mine iniquities and sins? make me to know my transgression and my sin." Job 13:23.

This is for us a most appropriate and befitting Ash Wednesday inquiry. This language of Job may well be uttered by us all.

I. Consider first the question: "How many are mine iniquities?" 1. The question is personal. "My." 2. It concerns his moral state. 3. It relates to number—"How many?" Our sins how many of heart, lip and life!

II. What is the expressed object in presenting the question? That he "might know." 1. That he might have consciousness of them. With us, with all, time is likely to obliterate and efface realization of our sins. But sometimes increases the same. 2. That he might have a penitent sense of them—to know in order to confess. 3. And that he might have their removal, forsaken, forgiven.

III. How deplorable to be ignorant of our state! Still more to be unconcerned for our sins' consequences. "How many are mine iniquities and sins? Make me to know my transgression and my sin." "Me." "Mine." Our message is, Repent and accept anew the blessing of the Gospel, of salvation through Christ.—B.

2. Title: The Joy of Salvation.

TEXT: "Restore unto me the joy of thy salvation." Ps. 51:12.

I. Salvation has joy. It is a state of safety and acceptance.

II. Salvation's joy may be lost. 1. By lack of cultivation. 2. By indulgence in sin. 3. By want of faith.

III. Salvation's joy may be recovered. Desirable. Attainable. "Restore unto me." God only can restore it. He alone can rekindle the flame. The Christian's happiness and usefulness are complete when he is in the full enjoyment of salvation. The soul that has known this joy can never be deeply happy without it.

3. Title: The Land of Nod. Where is it?

TEXT: "And Cain went out from the presence of the Lord, and dwelt in the land of Nod, on the east of Eden." Gen. 4:16.

The geography of Genesis is spiritual geography. Genesis looks at places in their relationship to God, near him or far from him. Cain settled "in the land of Nod, on the east of Eden," outside of Eden. The name expresses the nature and character of the locality. It signifies flight, or exile, or wandering. Nod is therefore the land of the wanderer.

I. Cain went out from the presence of God and dwelt in Wanderland. For is not that the place where men always find themselves when they go out from the presence of the Lord into a place of aimless, purposeless uncertainty?

II. In Wanderland Cain became jealous of his brother Abel and slew him. He had been born in Eden, but in this sin he put his own will against the will of God, turned his back upon Eden and went out into Wanderland. He went out from the Meaningful to the Meaningless. And that is always what happens when we get away from God.

III. When men or nations forsake God they always get into the land of Nod. Life goes to pieces with them. They go up and down and to and fro in Wanderland. They are like sheep without a shepherd. They drift. They are homeless. Their only hope is in a return unto God.—J. M.

4. Title: Religious Inconstancy.

TEXT: "O Ephraim, what shall I do unto thee? O Judah, what shall I do unto thee? for your goodness is as a morning cloud, and as the early dew it goeth away." Hos. 6:4.

It is not alone necessary to commence a religious course, but to continue in well-doing to the end. Israel and Judah had revolted from God even repeatedly. After presenting promising aspects of piety they had turned aside. How like unto many who are professed Christians in our day. They may well be asked, as were the Galatian Christians, "Ye did run well; who did hinder you that ye should not obey the truth?" This Lenten season offers a great opportunity to hindered Christians to get a new start.

I. First we may well consider the characters to whom this text applies. The metaphors used are very striking. The "morning cloud," which overhangs the scenery but flees so quickly before the rising sun. The "early dew," that moistens the parched earth, beautifying the flowers and the blades of grass, but is so soon gone leaving not a trace behind. 1. Such words apply to the forgetful hearer of God's Word. 2. They apply to backsliders in general.

II. What are the consequences of such religious declension? 1. God is deprived of the fruits he reasonably expected. 2. The Church is filled with mourning for her forsaking children. 3. The world is hardened and unbelievers confirmed in their unbelief. So Christ is wounded in the house of his friends. 4. And the condition is peculiarly sad for those who are the subjects of this inconstancy.

III. How is such inconstancy to be prevented? 1. In order that our religion be not as the morning cloud and the early dew we should cultivate the spirit of Christian watchfulness. 2. We should cultivate the spirit of entire dependence upon God. 3. We should be active and regular in use of the appointed means of grace. 4. We should live in close communion with God. In this Lenten season return, return.—B.

5. Title: The Selfishness of Mere Morality.

TEXT: "Did ye at all fast unto me, even to me?" Zech. 7:5.

It is not our purpose to present the matter of fasting, but the sort of morality it is to fast without meaning it. There is selfishness in mere morality. What God asked of the Jews through his prophet Zechariah was when they fasted, "Did ye at all fast unto me, even to me?" If it was a form and not a fact it was not even acceptable.

I. Some men are moral from very inferior motives. 1. Some for their health's sake. 2. Some from financial reasons. 3. Some from policy, to retain the respect of their fellow men. 4. Some just to maintain their own self-respect. 5. Some to avoid an accusing conscience.

II. Men are not saved by mere morality. The rich young ruler asked Christ, "What lack I yet?" He was moral. His conduct was correct. But he did not love Christ enough to sacrifice for him, truly trust and love him. Fasting is not postponed feasting. It is not enough just to fast. There may be a way of doing it that robs it of all its virtue and of all its significance. God asks, "Did ye at all fast unto me, even to me?" Mere fasting is not enough. It may be the selfishness of mere morality. God asks our faith and love and spiritual devotion. True religion says, "Believe on the Lord Jesus Christ and thou shalt be saved."

6. Title: The Church's Conservation Policy.

TEXT: "Break up your fallow ground." Hos. 10:12.

These words were spoken to a people nominally righteous; today they would have called themselves "Christians." Yet there was "fallow ground." While America is just awakening to conservation responsibilities in the physical realm, she should also hear the ancient prophet's call.

I. The need, as revealed in recent disclosures of frauds. "What America needs . . . is a revival of piety," *Wall Street Journal*. There is a waste of agricultural and mineral resources; but that is nothing compared with the waste of vital forces of young men and women. Nor is our educational system sufficient apart from the "plowshare of God's truth."

II. The method—not that we need a novel system; but that we should cultivate more intensively along the same recognized lines: 1. Using best system; as exemplified in the present movement in adult Bible study. 2. Going deeper. Isaac "digged again the wells of his father," but he probably digged deeper (Gen. 26:12-19). 3. Adaptation necessary —Isaac "sowed" whereas Abraham "herded." 4. Economic methods—right use of time. One of our honored statesmen spoke to the students of his alma mater on "Margins"—showing the right use of "odd moments." A man's "off hours" God asks for spiritual cultivation —reflection and meditation.

III. Lasting resources are often disclosed thus. Eternal possibilities are never on the surface. Intensive application alone reveals.

7. Title: Toward Christian Attainment.

TEXT: "Not as though I had already attained," etc. Phil. 3:12-14.

We have here presented Paul's ideal of the Christian life. These verses suggest much concerning the true Christian's aspiration and experience.

I. The recognized imperfections of attainment. "Not as though I had already attained." Humility. Reality. Yet aspiring.

II. The grandeur of our calling. "Perfect." The goal at which the apostle aimed was moral perfection. He acknowledges that he has not reached such attainment.

III. The necessity of effort. "I follow after." "Reaching forth, I press toward the mark."

IV. The prospect of reward. "For the prize of the high calling of God in Christ Jesus." Mountaineering. "The higher climbers climb the higher they want to climb."

8. Title: The Blessedness of Waiting upon God.

TEXT: "They that wait upon the Lord," etc. Isa. 40:31.

There are three blessings suggested as consequent upon this waiting upon God:

I. First, renewed vigor. "They shall renew their strength." The intellect is strengthened by exercise upon Divine themes. The affections are strengthened by exercise upon right objects. The will is strengthened by exercise upon good purposes. The whole soul gets strength by such employ.

II. Secondly, soul elevation. "Mount up with wings as eagles." Gratitude will wing the soul upward to its Benefactor. Love to God is a wing that will exalt the whole being.

III. Thirdly, interesting progress. "Run and not be weary," etc. 1. Godliness is progress. It is not a stationary state. It is a running and a walking. 2. Godliness is progress without fatigue. There is no weariness in love.—D. T.

9. Title: The Enriching Treasures of Wisdom and Knowledge.

TEXT: "For I would that ye knew what great conflict I have for you," etc. Col. 2:1-3.

Paul is expressing his great interest in and concern for the Colossian church, as also for other churches. He desires their comfort, their unity in love and that they may have understanding of the treasures of Christian wisdom and understanding.

I. First, we see here a noble anxiety. 1. The nobleness of Paul as here made evident is his purely unselfish anxiety for others. 2. Also his anxiety for the absent; those he had not seen and who had not seen him. He is thinking of the whole group of churches that he had not planted or even visited. His was pure disinterested love, a noble concern and solicitude.

II. Secondly, we have here a blessed experience. 1. He expresses hopes for their personal comfort. 2. For their complete unity, "knit together in love." 3. And a hope that they may enjoy the blessing of "full assurance."

III. Then further is expressed his desire that they may know the "mystery," the "open secret" of Christianity. By "mystery" Paul did not mean an unknowable, mystical something beyond ken. He meant the self-revelation of

Christ, and the riches of his truth and love and saving grace.

1. Love is the key to this treasury of wisdom in Christ. 2. Nothing but love will open up this treasury; and love does open it. 3. This love must be love to Christ and in him love to one another.—U. R. T.

10. Title: The Lord's Supper (Maundy Thursday).

(NOTE: This evening marks the anniversary of Christ's founding of the sacrament of the Lord's Supper. We suggest the observance of a special Communion Service in recognition of this great and solemnly important event.)

TEXT: "This do in remembrance of me." Luke 22:19.

The sacrament of the Holy Communion was instituted by Christ on Thursday evening, the night before his crucifixion. The evening of Maundy Thursday is an appropriate one of our holding an anniversary observance of the Supper.

I. This ordinance goes upon the supposition that we are apt to forget Christ. "This do in remembrance of me." In the world in general Christ is undeniably forgotten. This is too much so also by his own disciples. Much too true when we consider the common current of our thoughts. Equally so in our general conversation. Still more so in our habitual conduct.

II. The causes of such forgetfulness are various. Christ and the things of Christ have to compete for a place with the world at a disadvantage. The one is near, the others remote. The one is seen, the others unseen. The one is generally valued, the others are despised. The one is gratifying strong tendencies, the others are looked upon as insipience to weak tastes.

III. But plainly this ordinance and commandment imply that Christ is worthy of being remembered. We know that he is infinitely so. Yet contrast: 1. A great person of the world is remembered by men. His name is known. His life is written. His monument erected. His descent traced. His works preserved. His family and nation boast of him. Yet who of the sons of the mighty can compare with Christ? 2. A great event is remembered by men. Recorded. Monuments built, etc. But what victory can equal that of Christ? Yet how likely are both Christ and his work to be forgotten!

IV. Once more, this ordinance of the Lord's Supper implies that to remember Christ is most profitable and necessary. 1. Christ must be remembered if his last wish is to be respected, obeyed. 2. If the Christian's conscience would be clear. 3. If our spiritual life would be preserved. 4. If grace and strength would be enjoyed. 5. If Christ's life and work and example would be known and set forth. This do. Do often. Keep on doing. "Till he come." —J. S.

SPECIAL GOOD FRIDAY SERVICE

Theme: Crucified with Christ.

SUGGESTED SCRIPTURE READING: Luke 23:27-40.

SELECTED HYMNS: "Beneath the cross of Jesus."—E. C. Clephane. "O sacred Head, now wounded."—Bernard of Clairvaux. "When I survey the wondrous cross."—I. Watts. "There is a green hill far away."—C. F. Alexander. "In the cross of Christ I glory."—J. Bowring.

CALL TO WORSHIP: "Ye were not redeemed with corruptible things, as silver and gold; but with the precious blood of Christ, as of a lamb without blemish and without spot."

INVOCATION PRAYER: O Lord of Truth, whom to know is everlasting life, we would seek thee here in thy house today. For our sakes, O Christ, thou hast lived and died and won victory over sin and death. For thy sake we shall consecrate our lives to the highest this day. We love thee because thou didst first love us. We bow in deep reverence before thee, O God, as we remember the wounds of Christ. Forgive us the hurt we have given unto the world. Forgive us the hours and days when we have opened up afresh the wounds of Christ. But also make us glad in our day as we hear him speak peace unto our souls. —M. K. W. H.

Theme: Crucified with Christ.

TEXT: "I am crucified with Christ: nevertheless I live." Gal. 2:20.

INTRODUCTORY: From twelve to three on Good Friday our blessed Saviour hung in agony on the cross—for me. How shall I spend those three most sacred hours? They are too sacred to spend at my usual occupation unless compelled to do so by circumstances beyond my control. They are too sacred for a Christian even to think of spending them at a place of amusement. They are too sacred to be used in shopping, even if I did not want to encourage the merchants of our city to close during those hours by refraining from making purchases at that time. There is only one way in which I can show adequately my appreciation of what Christ has done for me on the cross, and that is to spend those hours in worship, meditation and prayer, in God's house if possible; if not then in some other public or private devotion. Shall I not spend those three most sacred hours in this way?

But this present service is to take a wide view, the theme being, "I am crucified with Christ: nevertheless I live."

I. In what sense can we be dead with Christ while still alive? It was in the war trenches that a chaplain said in a heart-to-heart talk with one of his boys, "Would you like to go home to England?" "Only God knows how much I would like to go." "Would you go now if you had the chance?" "Not till we have finished this job." That man was dead to the old normal life. To all such death is followed by a resurrection. "I die daily," said Paul. But he also protested that he knew the power of a spiritual resurrection.

II. To what do we die when we are dead with Christ? Certainly to sin, to all that is ignoble, gross, unworthy, debasing. This is as far as some of us ever go. It is a heroic thing to die to sin, to put down the ape and tiger and swine in us.

III. But Christianity has a bigger program. 1. We must leave our "low-vaulted past." We must die to littleness. It was said of a man who recently died, "He never consciously did a little thing in his life." Let us hope he had lived up to his epitaph! 2. The hardest death of all to die is that to self. Many a good man never learns this lesson completely. Do we not know some very pure souls who are nevertheless selfish? Genius, success, keen intellect, youth, even sorrow, tend to make us selfish.

IV. If we are dead with Christ and risen with him the passion of life is turned to seeking. But we seek the things Christ sought; fellowship with the Father and with his children; the enlargement of life by the increase of points of contacts with the world. By how many points of contact do we touch the world? Eye, ear, tongue, fingertips, mind. Christ used all of these and others. He knew the world by sympathy, by service, by suffering. He deliberately sought these points of contact, and these we are to seek, not as ends, but as means to an end, as means to power. Is power a thing to be sought in itself? No, only as means to the life more abundant.—C. C. A.

OUTLINES AND THEMES FOR LENTEN EVANGELISM

1. Topic. Seeking the Lord an Immediate Duty.

TEXT: "It is time to seek the Lord." Hos. 10:12.

It is time to seek the Lord. Now is the time. It is high time to do it. The farmer sows in seed-time. If that time be far spent he applies to the work with the more diligence. Seeking the Lord is to be every day's work, but there are some special occasions when by his providence and grace it is in a peculiar manner time to seek him.

I. Whom are we to seek? "The Lord," our Creator, Father, Redeemer,

Lord. Think of how able and willing he is to promote our happiness.

II. How are we to seek him? Earnestly. Put heart into it. Humbly. Because of helplessness in sin. Therefore penitently. Therefore prayerfully. Therefore obediently.

III. Why are we to seek him? We cannot be happy without him and his salvation. Seek him for our own sake. Seek him for God's sake, because he asks it. Seek him for others' sakes. Seek him because it is the happiest and wisest preparation for our future. It is performance of his will. It is due preparation of heart to receive his blessings.

IV. When are we to seek the Lord? Now. "It is time." 1. The Scriptures often urge haste. 2. Delay itself is evil. 3. The way to God is open. 4. The time is short. 5. There is great and immediate good to be received from such a course. There is urgency to this duty. There is certainty of success in it.—H.

2. Topic: Coming to Jesus.

TEXT: "And he, casting away his garment, sprang up, and came to Jesus." Mark 10:50 (A.S.V.).

This is a beautiful picture and teaches a wonderful lesson.

I. One who comes to Jesus may find barriers. 1. Many rebuked blind Bartimaeus, and commanded him to hold his peace. 2. Professed Christians sometimes hinder by unwise conduct, by indifference, or unwise conversation or criticism. 3. Or one may erect imaginary barriers against himself. By making excuses. By procrastination.

II. All barriers may be removed. 1. Manner of removal. One must recognize his need (Bartimaeus knew he was blind). One must heed the Master's call. "He sprang up and came." One must be willing to follow him. "He followed him in the way." 2. Result of such removal of barriers. He will be received. "He that cometh to me I will in no wise cast out." He will be made whole—spiritually. "If a man be in Christ, he is a new creature." He will find peace and happiness.

He is calling for you today. "Whosoever will may come." "If any man will open the door I will come in." —A. F. Hanes, D.D.

3. Topic: The Healing Virtue of Christ.

TEXT: "And the whole multitude sought to touch him: for there went virtue out of him, and healed them all." Luke 6:19.

I. There is sickness in man.

II. There is health in Jesus.

III. Contact with Jesus heals.

IV. This health and this contact are free to us.

4. Topic: The Folly of Procrastination.

TEXT: "Behold, now is the accepted time; behold, now is the day of salvation." II Cor. 6:2.

I. Repentance ought not to be delayed when we consider the nature of repentance and the command of God concerning it. 1. Its nature, a change of heart, and a change of life. 2. God's command, distinct and peremptory.

II. Repentance ought not to be delayed because delay will increase its difficulties. 1. From the power of habit, of sinful habit. 2. From the cessation of the strivings of the Holy Spirit.

III. Repentance ought not to be delayed, because circumstances may occur to render it impracticable. 1. There may be change of residence. 2. There may be loss of health. 3. There may be loss of mind. 4. There may be loss of will.

5. Topic: The Effect of Finding Christ.

TEXT: "And he went on his way rejoicing." Acts 8:39.

There was once a famous comic actor whose appearance always created laughter. Once he went to consult a doctor who did not know him, and told him of his low spirits and poor health. The doctor advised him to go and see the famous clown, and his patient answered, "Alas! I am that unhappy man." No, the secret of a happy life is to be found only in God. David, St. Paul, Mary, and others found it so. The Ethiopian found it so.

I. The effect of finding Christ. 1. Joy in the acquisition of spiritual information. 2. Joy in the glorious privileges. 3. Joy in the anticipation of usefulness. 4. Joy in the hope of a blessed future.

II. The causes of this Ethiopian's joy. 1. He had heard the best of news. 2. He had seen the most glorious of all sights, that of the grace of God in salvation. 3. He had found the richest of all treasures, John 1:41. "I have found him of whom Moses and the prophets did write." 4. He had attained to the greatest of all honors, the becoming a son of God by faith in Jesus Christ, an heir of God, and a joint-heir with Christ. 5. He had gotten his title-deed to heaven.

III. Some inferences. 1. Learn that pure and undefiled religion is not a melancholy thing. It is, or should be, full of joy. 2. That the Lord knoweth them that are his. 3. That the word and ordinances of God are means of communicating joy to the souls of men. 4. That there are means of feeding this joy. 5. That Christians themselves, when in the raptures of spiritual pleasures, cannot fully describe the excellence of this joy. 6. Learn to rejoice ever in the hope of the glory of God.

6. Topic: The New Heart.

TEXT: "A new heart also will I give you." Ezek. 36:26.

I. A new heart here contrasted with a stone. "I will take away the stony heart."

II. A new heart realizing a new spirit. The old spirit conforms to the world. The new does not.

III. A new heart means a new pilot. "I will put my Spirit within you."

IV. A new heart means a new life. "And I will cause you to walk in my statutes." Not dragged to heaven. It is a walk, not a limp. It is a willing walk, a glad and happy walk.

V. A new heart means new rules. "Ye shall keep my judgments." The finger posts point the right way. Following God's commands will keep us in the paths of righteousness.

VI. A new heart means new employment. "And to them." How happy we are in being assured that God will give us power to do his will! "My grace is sufficient for thee."

VII. God's guarantee. "I will do it." "I will give you." He can, he promises, he will. You can afford to trust him. —W. B.

7. Topic: Reasons for Uniting with the Church.

I. If you are a Christian it is God's desire and will that you go into his church, Acts 2:4-7.

II. You do not get the full joys of the Christian life until you do unite yourself with God's people, Ps. 55:14.

III. You will not grow much in the religious life until you do, Ps. 92:13.

IV. Christ loved his Church so that he gave himself for it, and if you love him you will love his Church enough to unite with it, Eph. 5:25-27.

V. If you are going to heaven you will want to go with as many of God's people as possible, and you will find them in his Church, Num. 10:29.

VI. The Church belongs to God, and if you belong to him you will wish to belong to it, I Tim. 3:15.

VII. How are you going to watch over and associate with other Christians unless you go into the Church when they are? I Cor. 12:25.—D. S.

8. Topic: How Resist Temptations (To the Newly Enlisted).

TEXT: "They were tempted." Heb. 11:37.

Christians are exposed to temptations. How they may be resisted and overcome. The following are a few of many good rules:

I. Keep out of their way. Avoid as far as possible.

II. Check their first risings.

III. Strategy. Be active in doing good.

IV. Depend much on the assistance of God.

V. Grasp the sword of the Spirit.

VI. Abound in prayer.

9. Topic: Prayer and Bible Study (To the Newly Enlisted).

TEXTS: "Lord, teach us to pray." Luke 11:1. "Wherewithal shall a young man cleanse his way? by taking heed thereto according to thy word." Ps. 119:9.

To be a Christian without praying is like living without breathing.

I. God wishes us to talk with him, and this is prayer. In prayer we should thank God for his benefits, praise him for his excellence, confess our faults, ask him to forgive them and help us to be better.

II. We may ask for anything we desire if he sees it best to give it. If we pray in faith and sincerity, with a heart surrendered to God, results are sure to come. We should have regular times to pray, but should pray also whenever there is special need.

III. We should expect God to answer our prayers. Listen and watch for the answer. The Lord's Prayer is a good model for us.

IV. The Bible is God's message to us. We should study it daily, looking for things that apply to ourselves. We should remember it, meditate on it, believe it, and heed it. How does the Bible help us? It gives us the truth of God concerning the way of life and guides us in that way. "Thy word is a lamp unto my feet, and a light unto my path," Ps. 119:105. The Bible is a record of how men in ancient times were guided by God. It is the greatest of books for inspiring men to character, righteousness and service.

FOR THE PASTOR'S COMMUNICANT CLASS

On Joining the Church

I. What the Church Is.

It is the living body of Christ's followers, of which he is the Head. To it he has committed the responsibility of preaching his gospel and establishing his kingdom in the world. We are not to think of it therefore as we do of other organizations which are purely voluntary and human in their origin, and which as Christians we may be under no obligations to join. If we are truly disciples of Christ it is our duty to join the Church. It is also a great privilege to do so, for membership in the Church is one of the most essential aids to living the Christian life.

II. Who Should Join the Church.

Since the Church is the body of Christ's followers, no one should join it who is not at heart a follower of his, or, as we say, a Christian. Joining the Church does not make one a Christian. Doing the best we can does not make us Christians. A Christian is a person who believes that Jesus Christ, Son of God and Son of Man, lived and died for him to save him from sin and its consequences, and who therefore feels moved in gratitude and love to enter Christ's service, trusting him as Saviour and obeying him as Master.

But we must not think that we must be perfect before we are entitled to call ourselves followers of Christ. He is the sinner's friend. His Church, his sacraments, his love, law and service are for sinful men, women and children who with his help are trying to overcome sin and do his will. All such may and should join his Church.

III. What the Sacraments Are.

The two sacraments, Baptism and the Lord's Supper, are solemn and joyful ceremonies intended, like the rites observed at weddings, inaugurations into high public offices and other important occasions, to impress those taking part in them with certain great truths and responsibilities.

1. Baptism is the rite of initiation into the Christian Church. It represents the washing away of our sins.

2. The Lord's Supper is primarily a memorial of Christ. He said, "This do in remembrance of me." The bread represents his broken body; the wine his blood, shed for us. They remind us in a touching and powerful way of what he suffered for us, and so tend to renew our love and devotion to him. Our

eating and drinking of them is a very striking symbol of our taking him as our Sacrificial Saviour, of his entrance into our souls and of our living spiritual union with him and all believers. This sacrament as a whole has the character of a solemn compact or covenant between him and ourselves. Like the Passover, which it displaced, it is a memorial of a great deliverance, and therefore not a mournful fast but a joyous feast. It is intended for those for whom Christ died and who accept him as their Saviour and Lord.

IV. Duties of a Church Member.

In general it is the duty of a Church member to try to be and to do everywhere and always what Christ would have him be and do.

To the church which he joins he owes some specific duties, especially these three:

1. To attend the services unless providentially prevented.

2. To contribute regularly, according to his means, toward both the current expenses of the church and its missions and benevolences.

3. To take some active part as he may be able in the work of the church.

V. How to Join the Church.

The necessary steps are very simple. Before each Communion season, meetings duly announced are held to receive new members. The applicants for membership are given an opportunity to confess their personal faith in Christ and purpose to follow him. They are publicly received at the next Communion.

SECTION V. The Conduct of the Holy Communion

Fellowship is one of the most used words in the Christian vocabulary. Sometimes it is used lightly to describe the loose ties that bind people in a church group, but at other times it signifies the real tie that binds. Whenever the Lord's Supper is celebrated it is peculiarly a fellowship service. People find it almost impossible to be insincere and unfriendly and at the same time partake of the sacrament.

The Lord's Supper is primarily a memorial of Christ. He said, "This do in remembrance of me." The bread represents his broken body; and the wine his blood, shed for us. They remind us in a touching and powerful way of what he suffered for us, and so tend to renew our love and devotion to him. Our eating and drinking of them is a very striking symbol of our taking him for our sacrificial Saviour, of his entrance into our souls and our living spiritual union with him and all believers.

The sacrament as a whole has the character of a solemn compact, or covenant, between him and ourselves. Like the Passover, which it displaced, it is a memorial of a great deliverance, and therefore not a mournful fast but a joyous feast.

We mention these familiar facts as a method of again introducing this department, which has been accepted with such great favor. As we have said before, by whatever title the ordinance is called, The Sacrament, The Communion, The Holy Communion, The Lord's Supper, The Eucharist, The Sacred Feast, or any other, its conduct is each minister's high privilege and yet one of his most important, oft-recurring and exacting special services. The ceremony is observed in practically all denominations, in some churches every Sunday, in others once a month, once in two months, or once in three months. Its frequent recurrence, together with its great significance, places the minister in special need of a strong body of suggestive material for ready reference. It is true, moreover, that no service is worthy of more careful attention for its sermon-meditation and other features, or demands more study for its appropriate, fresh and edifying conduct.

Testimonies of users also show that having all the material in one combined department, where it can be quickly found and most easily evaluated, is especially appreciated.

A. SUGGESTIVE SERMON-MEDITATIONS AND OUTLINES

1. Theme: The Song of Redemption.

TEXT: "Then sang Moses and the children of Israel this song," etc. Exod. 15:1, 2.

Recall the creation of the Passover and the exodus from Egypt. The Passover was the symbol of redemption from bondage. That in turn was the chief event in Hebrew history. There is nothing that appealed to the imagination of the devout Jew, outside the creation and the coming of the Messiah, quite so much as deliverance from bondage. He rejoiced in the mercies of God who led his people forth from slavery.

Today the Christian Church looks upon the Passover Feast as the Old Testament counterpart of the Lord's Supper. As we join with Christians everywhere in the celebration of a memorial to our Lord at his table, enacted before our eyes is the great story of God's redemption offered to you and to me. It brings from us the song of redemption.

I. As we compare God's deliverance of Israel through the Passover to God's redemption that is offered through Calvary, we think of the Song of Redemption as a song of experience. In the Exodus story of the Passover celebration, which is continued in the Christian communion service, observers are told how it should be explained to those who ask, "What mean ye by this service?" Back into the past one must go, recalling that this is a memorial established by God himself. There must be an experience involved or else this service has no meaning to us. In the heart there must be a vivid remembrance of a deliverance that has been acomplished. There is no other ground for communion with God. To know God one must experience his salvation.

Likewise, as we come to the Lord's Table, it is an hour of memory, and we sing a song of experience.

II. But this Song of Redemption is also a song of expression. This is a memorial. We do this in memory of Christ. Yet it is more than that. If that memory does not call forth an expression on our part—an expression of gratitude and thanksgiving, an expression of fellowship and communion, and an expression of humiliation and self-surrender, then we are of all men most miserable. This service is one of sacrificial love, and I cannot partake of it worthily until I search my heart and know that no hate is there, no envy, no meanness of spirit. I come as a penitent—not as one perfect, not as one sufficient in oneself, but humbly at the Throne of Grace to express my call of need.

III. Again, this Song of Redemption is a song of expectation. In fellowship we can go back to come into communion with that long line of believers that began in the Upper Room to partake of the bread and wine. It looks back on a glorious heritage. But it also reaches out to include every race and color—to include the great Church Universal with a fellowship that reaches around the world to all who believe. But greater still, it reaches into the future. With a forward step, it lays aside every fear, even the anxiety of the moment, to catch step with the people of God, past, present and future, to march on to renewed courage and assurance.

To have experienced, to give expression to the Song of Redemption, is to have a great expectation in the Heavenly Father.

As we come to the Table of our Lord, may we come in the full assurance that he is our Lord, that we are going forward with him into a richer Christian experience because we are willing to lay aside those weights that "so easily beset us" and hinder our spiritual growth and testimony. May our trust be in him who gives to us a hope that this world cannot know or understand.—Rev. William H. Boyd.

2. Theme: The Sacramental Service.

TEXT: "This do in remembrance of me." Luke 22:19.

The emphasis is to be placed on the initial word: "This." It is antithetic to what they had been doing. They had been celebrating the Jewish Passover that commemorated deliverance from Egypt. That deliverance was the sign of blood. "When I see blood, I will pass over you." This deliverance was by a paschal lamb, whose blood had no intrinsic redemptive efficacy. This deliverance is by the Lamb of God, whose blood cleanseth from all sin!

I. Here we have a momentous transition from That to This: From Judaism to Christianity, from types and shadows to reality and fulfillment, from the priesthood of men to the priesthood of the Son of God, from the transitory to the permanent, from the earthly to the heavenly. It is the most momentous and significant transition from one dispensation to another ever made.

II. "This do." This supremacy which the Lord Jesus assumed in his transition teaches that our Lord would have every disciple of his regard him as supreme in all things. "All power is given to me," etc. In regard to all he said and did, to the Scriptures he endorsed, to the vicariousness of his death, to the reality and importance of his resurrection, to the necessity of his return to his Father in order that the Holy Spirit might come to his disciples. No truth is more important to faith than this.

III. The great significance of the symbols he chooses to set forth the foundation on which rests this New Dispensation. "This is my body." We are taught that this universe was brought into being in order that the Son of God might redeem a lost race and bring it back to God. "He was the Lamb slain before the foundation of the world." Redemption through the precious blood of the Son of God being the great purpose of God in all ages reveals the reason why its importance is so vital and its rejection by unbelief so fatal.

IV. The sweet, pathetic, and loving tenderness with which our gracious Lord would have us ever partake of these chosen elements. "This do in remembrance of me." These words reveal at least three things: 1. The intense reality of the Lord's love for his disciples. "Having loved them," says the Apostle John, "he loved them to the end." These disciples were very imperfect, even as we are; yet Jesus loved them. He loved them not for the perfections of their character, but for the reality and simplicity of their faith in him, though their knowledge and conception of him were limited and crude. 2. They reveal the reality of his humanity. His human heart yearned for the loving response of these disciples, imperfect as they were. 3. The breaking of bread and the pouring of wine so vividly reproduce the crucifixion of Christ, that in order to awaken suitable feelings of love and gratitude and devotedness to him he has ordained throughout perpetual generations that his disciples should "do this in remembrance" of their loving Redeemer.—D. C. H.

3. Theme: The Peace of Christ.

TEXT: "Peace I leave with you, my peace I give unto you." John 14:27.

There is within man no desire deeper than his desire for peace. If we could unlock the doors leading to the hearts of men and women and see their secret thoughts, we should find these hearts straining for peace. People work and strive and for a time glory in the sheer thrill of being alive, but to everyone there comes a moment when he dreams of peace and seeks it with all his heart.

I. We may not be able to put it clearly, but we do know that this peace is essential to our happiness. It is this peace that Christ promises to those who are welded unto him by the bonds of discipleship. Shortly before his death, Jesus gave to his friends this strangely beautiful benediction: "Peace I leave with you, my peace I give unto you: not as the world giveth, give I unto you."

These are strange words and they create within our thinking a difference between the peace the world knows and the peace that Christ grants. Are we to assume that this difference is a difference in fact? Are we to assume that Christ actually implied that there is a difference between peace as the world understands it and the peace which he gives to men and women through his indwelling presence? What else could he have meant?

II. There is an abysmal difference between the peace of the world and the peace of Christ. No philosophy on earth can bridge the distance between them. No escape from the realities of life, no furious striving can heal this breach. The peace of the world is always a negative peace, for it consists in the absence of irritating factors. It is not positive. It is not creative. The peace of the world never consists in anything we possess; it consists in things which now we lack. It is the absence of noise that brings peace to our minds. So a mother after sending her boisterous brood to play in the yard, says with a sigh, "At last some peace."

It is the absence of a disturbing, haunting problem that brings peace to our souls. It is the absence of a nagging temptation that brings peace to our battered emotions and appetites. It is the absence of sorrow and pain that brings the peace of calm and serenity. It is the absence of armed strife, of bitter conflict and bruising hatreds that brings peace to nations.

So you see with us peace always lies in something negative. It is always to be found in the absence of that which irritates, confuses and disturbs. It is the peace of a city asleep. The shrieking of brakes, the roar of traffic, the clanging of bells have died down and the strange silence of a city asleep comes upon us.

But this peace is not real. It is an illusion. Soon the city will awaken again. There will be the clumping of hoofs, the shrill voice of the whistles, the roar of traffic—and peace will have gone.

III. The peace of Jesus is something else. It is positive. It is creative. It comes to us not in the absence of irritating factors; it comes in spite of them. It is the peace within ourselves.

It is the peace a man finds on a mountaintop when he looks down upon the city alive, throbbing and pulsing. It is the peace that gives to a man an inner light though there is darkness without him, that gives him a sense of strength though he is surrounded by danger.

It is the peace that brings to man the sense of assurance and certainty though he stands in the midst of doubts and confusion. It is the peace of security which makes a man say, "Yea, though I walk through the valley of the shadow . . . I will fear no evil, for thou art with me."

This peace a man must possess if his life is to have meaning. Without it, there are no lasting joys and no deep, satisfying pleasures. This peace we seek, for indeed it passeth understanding.—Rev. Arnold H. Lowe.

4. Theme: The Madness of the Cross.

Text: "This do in remembrance of me." Luke 22:19.

In the will of Franz Liszt, written when he was old and a bit weary of the world, there were found these sentences: "I am writing on the date (Sept. 4, 1860) when the Church celebrates the elevation of the Holy Cross. The voice of this feast also expresses the ardent and mysterious emotion which like sacred stigmata has transpierced my entire life. Yes, Jesus Christ crucified, the madness and elevation of the Cross, this was my true vocation."

I. The madness of the Cross! The gibbet on Calvary is the most foolhardy adventure ever made by the soul of man. It was no accident. Jesus could have escaped it.

But though his flesh shrank from it, his indomitable spirit held his feet on the road that led inevitably to the place called Golgotha. His friends begged him not to go to Jerusalem. Terror and tragedy awaited him there. He was young with life before him. He had won the attention of multitudes of his own people. Galilee would shelter him. The people of Galilee would yet follow him. Some day through them he would win his way to the kingdom of his dreams.

II. But no! He set his face steadfastly toward Jerusalem. His heart had reached the strange conclusion that love could win only by suffering. Love wins its battles by surrender. It conquers by abdication. It saves by sacrifice. Hardly known by men, often scorned by them in their blindness, and yet the most influential and creative power in souls and societies.

"No one taketh life from me." I lay it down—with divine recklessness I lay it down. My soul shall be love's offering for the world's sin and woe. I stake my all on the power of love that suffers and dares to die.

III. Was there ever such madness? It was in this kind of a world that Jesus did that. In this world of compromise and cowardice, this world of force and fear, Jesus turned from an earthly kingdom and took a cross.

And then on an eve of a gray day in Nazareth men about the marketplace said one to another, "Well, have you heard? They killed the Carpenter in Jerusalem the other day." "I expected it," said another. "He was mad—no other way to explain him."

IV. Nor does the madness end here—here, with a sacrifice at the stony Place of the Skulls. It actually reaches up and includes God in its sublime folly. It claims there is something cosmic in the act on Calvary. It says God climbed to the cross; that the Carpenter was only being true to a principle eternal in the heart of God; that Everlasting Love was suffering in that mangled body and broken heart of the beauteous young Nazarene.

Jesus was not making a sacrifice for God or to God. Jesus was joining—as no one else ever did—in the sacrifice of God which began at the dawn of days and is continuing to the end of the ages. Jesus' sacrifice helped fill the saving cup of a suffering God.

That is the glorious gospel of the cross. It points to love, sacrificing, dying, and says, "God is like that." God is not far off. He is here in the world's crowded ways. Because his love is perfect and complete, his anguish has no end. He will save by love, or not at all. That's the music that comes, singing and sobbing, from the storm-swept hill; that's the melody that echoes and re-echoes over the hill called Calvary.

God does not send suffering, but he is at the heart of all redemptive suffering. And no poor soul climbs alone any scaffold in the world. "This do in remembrance of me."—Abridged from William H. Boddy, D.D.

5. Theme: The Importance of Observing the Lord's Supper.

TEXT: "I must by all means keep this feast." Acts 18:21.

It is practically sure that Paul referred to the feast of the Passover. There he would meet former friends and have favorable opportunity of making known and commending the doctrines of Christ. Most naturally we can apply the passage to the Christian feast of the Lord's Supper, where the friends of Jesus have opportunity to meet and hold communion with him and with one another.

I. It is well for us to notice, first, that the Lord's Supper is a feast. As such it was very beautifully and fully prefigured by the Jewish feast of the Passover. Christ is our Passover, sacrificed for us. The symbols of the Passover can be applied at desired length to the Lord's Supper. This is a feast. It is a love feast. It is a Christian family feast.

II. We should recognize the fact also that Christ's disciples should by all means keep this feast. We should do so because the Lord himself has commanded it. "This do." We should do so because his Church asks it. We should do so because our own spiritual welfare requires it. In its observance our love to Christ is rekindled, our faith strengthened, our hope brightened, and joy and peace caused to abound. Our souls are refreshed and we are set forward anew in the Christian life. Let us not miss it.

III. Consider, lastly, some thoughts as to how we should keep the feast. In view of our sins and shortcoming, we should keep it with deep humiliation of mind and spirit. Yet it is a feast and we should observe it with faith and gratitude and real joy. We should keep it also with strong feelings of regard and love toward our fellow Christians. We should also attach great importance to the observance of the Lord's Supper regularly. He intended that we should. If we love him we will wish and delight to do so. Besides, there is great spiritual loss in failing to do so. As the time for the celebration comes around let us regularly and joyfully say, "I must by all means keep this feast."—H.

6. Theme: What Is the Lord's Supper?

TEXT: "For I have received of the Lord that which also I delivered unto you, That the Lord Jesus the same night in which he was betrayed took bread," etc. I Cor. 11:23-26.

What is the Lord's Supper?

I. It is a command of the Lord, "Do this."

II. It is a memorial of love, "In remembrance of me."

III. It is a bond of fellowship, "As often as ye eat."

IV. It is a testimony for Christ, "Ye do show the Lord's death."

V. It is a confession of hope, "Till he come."—Rev. C. Edwards.

7. Theme: The Remembrance of Christ.

TEXT: "This do in remembrance of me." Luke 22:19.

Christians are in danger of forgetting Christ. The causes are many, though he never forgets us. The Lord's Supper is a memory service, a reminder, to the true Christian a very welcome reminder.

I. Consider first the precious Object of memory. It is our Saviour, Christ.

II. Consider further the gracious benefits to be derived from a living remembrance of Christ. Love. Hope. Patience. Strength. Victory.

III. Its sweet aids to memory. How many!

IV. To it we are given a sweet command. "This do." We are commanded to highest privilege. 1. It is a memorial. 2. It is a means of communion with Christ. 3. It is the highest act of worship.—C. H. S.

8. Theme: The Nature and Importance of the Lord's Supper.

TEXT: "And when he had given thanks, he brake it, and said, Take, eat," etc. I Cor. 11:24.

The nature and importance of the Lord's Supper are manifest by the different names descriptive of the ordinance.

I. It is called the "Breaking of Bread." 1. Bread is considered the chief support of life. 2. Among the Jews the breaking of bread together was a sign of mutual friendship. 3. Christ's body was broken for the sins of men.

II. It is called the "Communion." 1. This may signify either a participation or communion between the receivers themselves, or between the receivers and the thing received. In both senses it is applicable to the Lord's Supper. (See v. 16.)

III. It is called the "Eucharist." This signifies thankfulness or thanksgiving. "And when he had given thanks." The word "eucharist" frequently occurs in the New Testament as a general expression of gratitude. Taking this view of the ordinance, how should our hearts overflow with adoring gratitude, love and praise whenever we approach the Lord's Table!

IV. It is called a "Sacrament." The word originally signified the solemn oath of allegiance which the Roman soldiers took to their commanders. So does every Christian solemnly engage to maintain irreconcilable warfare against the world, the flesh, and the evil one.

V. There are two other terms often applied to this ordinance. They are "Oblation" and "Sacrifice." In this sacred ordinance men are invited to "Behold the Lamb of God, who taketh away the sins of the world." In celebrating the Lord's Supper in obedience to his last command, "This do in remembrance of me," we view Christ as the great atonement and the only sacrifice for sin.—N. M.

9. Theme: The Meaning of the Holy Communion.

TEXT: "The Lord Jesus the same night in which he was betrayed took bread." I Cor. 11:23.

I. It is a memorial of the sacrifice of the death of Christ. 1. The time. 2. The action. 3. The meaning.

II. It is a means of present communion with Christ. "Lo, I am with you alway."

III. It is the highest act of worship in the Church.—C. W. F.

B. PRAYERS BEFORE, AT AND AFTER THE SUPPER

1. Invocation Prayer.

Almighty God, our heavenly Father, we rejoice that it has pleased thee to spare us to this hour of public worship and to this place of communion at the Lord's Table. May we now be in the spirit on the Lord's Day, and receive the blessings promised to all who wait upon thee in sincerity and in truth. Now that we are here in thy house help us to worship thee in the beauty of holiness. May we place upon the altar the offering which is acceptable to thee. May we not give of our money and refuse ourselves. May we not, bringing the homage of our lips, withhold the devotion of our hearts. Make us truly alert of mind and will in our worship. Quicken every power of our souls. Awaken our dull discernments. Mercifully give us an appetite for the things of the Spirit. May we thirst for the water of life. May thy grace unite us all in the receiving of a great and common blessing. We ask in the name of Christ, our Saviour. Amen.

2. Invocation Prayer.

Eternal God, in our very search for thee we need the help of thy Spirit lest we go astray. Let thy constraining influence lead us into the secret place. Guide us through the outer courts of the temple into the sanctuary of the Spirit. May the means of grace be highways through which we pass to the court of the King. May no transient thing hold us in bondage and put our souls to sleep. May our worship bring us into the intimate fellowship where we shall find the things which thou hast prepared for them that love thee. We would sit at thy Sacred Table as thy invited guests. Interpret our needs by the insight of thy love for us. Give unto us the bread with thine own hands. Let no human ministry stand between our souls and thee. May our disappointments incite us to deeper spiritual communion. Let our joys be to us like wings, helping us to soar into heavenly places in Christ Jesus. We ask all through Christ our Lord. Amen.

3. A Communion Prayer.

O Lord, look in mercy upon us and give us the reality of thy presence. Search thou our hearts with us and give us the courage to be unafraid to face those attitudes, purposes and habits that have clouded our vision and cautioned our initiative in spiritual adventure. Make for us this bread and wine into a picture of the cross and out of its parable may we be eager to find such a cross in our own experiences or in that of others, so that our fellowship with thee may be unobstructed and we shall somewhat understand thy purposes for us in the daily lessons of life. In giving ourselves afresh to thee we give thee back thine own. Grant us to love all and most of all to love thee, through Jesus Christ our Lord. Amen.—Rev. Peter Ainslee, D.D.

4. Private Prayer before Communion.

O Infinite Love, that comest to me so willingly, no sin of mine shall keep from thee this heart thou hast come so far to seek. I trust thee and I fear thee. But my trust is greater than my fear. For my fear is built upon myself, but my trust upon thee. Be it unto me according to thy word.—E. Herman.

5. Private Prayer after Communion.

Thou hast slipped quietly into my heart. I give myself to the consuming fire of thy love. Spare not, O Lord. If only I could return thee love for love. This is the pain I lift perpetually to thee. Teach me to love. Let there be in me no consciously crooked dealings with thee, no corner curtained off from thy sight, no subject on which it is understood we do not trench.—E. Herman.

6. Prayer of Confession.

Almighty and most merciful Father, before thee and one another we confess our sins in thought and word and deed. We are ashamed and sorry for all wherein we have displeased thee. In spirit and in truth we do repent, and of any whom we may have wronged we seek forgiveness. Purify our affections in the love with which thou hast first loved us, and lead us in the way of thy will, which is our peace, through Jesus Christ our Lord. Amen.—Unidentified.

7. Invocation Prayer (Communion).

Almighty God, Father of our Lord Jesus Christ, who hast revealed through him thy nearness to humanity and art graciously inviting us to the worship of thy house and the fellowship of thy Table, make us partakers of thy fullness, and let us enter into thy courts with joy. Prepare us that as we receive the sacred symbols of thy love we may feed on thee in our hearts by faith. Work in us unfeigned sorrow for wrongdoing, and suffer us not to return to the sins which we have solemnly renounced, neither let us brood over the sins which thou hast freely forgiven. Confirm our faith in those great mysteries of redeeming grace which we are this day to show forth. Inspire us with ardent love for the Saviour, and give us sincere and humble purposes of new obedience, that we may with a true heart devote ourselves to his service. We thank thee, that thou hast taught thy children the way of life. We thank thee that it is full of rich experiences. We thank thee that we can travel it together with loved ones and friends. We thank thee for Pilgrim songs to sing. We thank thee that every part of the road reveals the greater glory of Him who is both the Way itself and our Fellow Traveler. Amen.—M. K. W. H.

C. SOME SUGGESTED LORD'S SUPPER TEXTS AND TOPICS

Minds stirred to Remembrance: "I stir up your pure minds by way of remembrance." II Pet. 3:1.

The Presence of Christ in the Supper: "And he took bread, and gave thanks, and brake it, and gave unto them, saying, This is my body which is given for you." Luke 22:19.

Partakers of Christ: "For we are made partakers of Christ, if we hold the beginning of our confidence stedfast unto the end." Heb. 3:14.

The Bread of Life: "For the bread of God is he which cometh down from heaven, and giveth life unto the world." John 6:33.

The Worthy Communicant: "But let a man examine himself, and so let him eat of that bread, and drink of that cup." I Cor. 11:28.

Christ Our Passover: "Christ our passover is sacrificed for us." I Cor. 5:7.

The Upper Room of Harmony: "And when the day of Pentecost was fully come, they were all with one accord in one place." Acts 2:1.

Preparation for the Feast: "There make ready." Luke 22:12.

The Subject of Meditation: "We have thought on thy lovingkindness, O God, in the midst of thy temple." Ps. 48:9.

The Mount of Privilege: The transfiguration. Mark 9:1-14.

After the Mountaintop, What? Work awaiting at its base. Mark 9:14-27.

Good to Draw Near to God: "It is good for me to draw near to God." Ps. 73:28.

Duty and Obligation of Christians to Keep the Communion Feast: "Therefore let us keep the feast." I Cor. 5:8.

The New Passover Feast: "And they made ready the passover." Luke 22:13.

The Surroundings of the Supper: "After the same manner also." I Cor. 11:25.

Christ's Love to the End: "Having loved his own which were in the world, he loved them unto the end." John 13:1.

Christ at the Feast: "I will come in to him, and will sup with him, and he with me." Rev. 3:20.

The Finished Work: "When Jesus therefore had received the vinegar, he said, It is finished!" John 19:30.

Neglect of the Lord's Supper: "And they would not come." Matt. 22:3.

Meaning of the Lord's Supper: "What mean ye by this service?" Exod. 12:26.

The Guestchamber of the Soul: "The Master saith, Where is the guestchamber, where I shall eat the passover with my disciples?" Mark 14:14.

Invited Closer: A Day of Communion: "Master, where dwellest thou? . . . Come and see." John 1:38, 39.

Love's Question: "Lovest thou me?" John 21:16.

Communion Continued: "But they constrained him, saying, Abide with us," etc. Luke 24:29.

Under His Shadow: "I sat down under his shadow with great delight." Cant. 2:3.

Love for the Unseen Saviour: "Whom having not seen, ye love." I Pet. 1:8.

A Message First: "I will not eat, until I have told mine errand." Gen. 24:33.

God's Invitation: "Come ye, buy, and eat," etc. Isa. 55:1.

How Make the Most of It?: "Lord, evermore give us this bread." John 6:34.

D. SOME SUGGESTED COMMUNION HYMNS

Break thou the bread of life.—M. A. Lathbury.

Breathe on me, Breath of God.—Edwin Hatch.

Fairest Lord Jesus.—Munster.

Majestic sweetness sits enthroned.—S. Sennett.

Oh, blest memorial of our dying Lord.—J. R. Woodford, Tr.

Sweet feast of love divine.—E. Denny.

This is my body, which is given for you.—C. L. Ford.

Together with these symbols, Lord.—J. Cennick.

A parting hymn we sing around thy table, Lord.—A. R. Wolfe.

According to thy gracious word.—J. Montgomery.

At thy command, our dearest Lord.—Isaac Watts.

Bread of heaven! on thee we feed.—Josiah Conder.

Bread of the world in mercy broken.—R. Heber.

Draw nigh and take the body of your Lord.—J. M. Neale, Tr.

From the table now retiring.—J. Rowe.

Here, O my Lord, I see thee face to face.—H. Bonar.

Jesus, at whose supreme command.—C. Wesley.

Jesus, thou joy of loving hearts.—Bernard of Clairvaux.

Jesus, to thy table led.—R. H. Baynes.

My God, and is thy table spread.—P. Doddridge.

O bread to pilgrims given.—R. Palmer, Tr.

E. CHOICE SACRAMENT OF THE LORD'S SUPPER ILLUSTRATIONS

1. The Lord's Supper.

The Lord's Supper is at once a Memorial, a Covenant, a Communion, and a Call to Separation.—William L. Pettingill.

2. Till He Come.

In the celebration of the Lord's Supper we are commanded to observe it in remembrance of Christ. It is, however, no commemoration of defeat, for our Lord gained his greatest victory and his most signal triumph in his death upon the cross for the sins of men. It was through his vicarious atoning death that he bore our sins and carried our sorrows. It was through the cross that he achieved for his people the great deliverance. In commanding his people throughout all ages to remember his death in this helpful sacrament, he is virtually saying: Commemorate my victory, my triumph over sin and death and hell. Do this that you may with faith and patience await my return. "For, as oft as you eat this bread and drink this cup, ye do show the Lord's death till he come."

3. Note of Triumph.

We must not forget that even in this sad night when the Lord's Supper was instituted there was the note of triumph. The feast ended with a hymn. What they sang probably was the concluding portion of the Hallel, the special group of Psalms assigned to the Passover. It would contain such verses as Ps. 116:13, "I will take the cup of salvation, and call upon the name of the Lord"; and Ps. 118:29, "O give thanks unto the Lord; for he is good: for his mercy endureth for ever." The remembrance of what Christ has done for us should always fill our hearts with love and our lips with song. "The joy of the Lord is your strength."

4. It Rekindles Love.

Each recurring observance of the Lord's Supper rekindles love. You have an absent friend. You have not thought of him for a long time. But something starts a train of thought, and you allow yourself time to meditate. As you sit and think, how all his kindly ways and loving words and deeds come back to you, and you find your love for him burning warm and full. Your meditation of him is sweet. Going through your papers, you open an old letter. It is from a former and almost forgotten schoolmate. But as you read and reflect that friend seems almost to be at your side again. Just as does the remembrance of Christ in the Lord's Supper bless us and quicken love for him.—H.

5. The Form without the Spirit.

In our Communion we are to be watchful that we worship not in form alone without the spirit. In an old church at Valsbol the men for centuries followed the practice, when returning from the sacrament, of standing on a particular spot and bowing in a certain direction. Why they did it no one knew. But later, in cleaning one of the walls, a picture of the Virgin Mary was discovered. It had been covered up by whitewash four centuries before, and the worshipers continued to bow toward it long after everyone had forgotten that it was there. Are we by mere habit bowing before the lost religious experience of youth, or the religion of a former age unexperienced by us?—H.

6. Broken Things.

"Take, eat: this is my body which is broken for you." How often we have heard these beautiful words at the communion of the Lord's Supper, where we have offered the sacrifices of a broken heart and a contrite spirit! Is there not a blessing in broken things? We would keep them whole for our selfish enjoyment; but love flows forth from hearts that are broken and our Lord's love finds entrance into the riven side, enriching the soul with its infinite treasure.

Unbroken alabaster boxes are valueless, as many uncrushed flowers are odorless.

Broken earthly hopes make room for heavenly riches. Breaking the marble makes the statuary beautiful; breaking the grain gives bread to the hungry; breaking the rocks opens the way to gold and precious stones; breaking the earth gives oil and coal for commerce and comfort. So the breaking of the body of Jesus on Calvary gives the Bread of Life to famishing millions. "He that eateth of me shall live by me."

To become like our Saviour, we break the alabaster boxes of loving sacrifice for others, scattering the fragrance of devotion everywhere. The gifts of a little child or of a poor widow are as precious to Christ as the offerings of the rich and the great.—Rev. E. W. Caswell, D.D.

7. Communion Continued.

Like those disciples on the way to Emmaus, when we have the Saviour's company for a little while we will not be contented until we have more of it. Some liquors men drink increase thirst. Never is the Christian tired of Christ's company. Love's logic is always ready with a plea, "Abide with us, for it is toward evening." "They constrained him." The suggestion comes that if we would keep Christ with us we must constrain him. Christ will not intrude where he is not wanted. How can we keep him with us? First, allowing no rivals in your heart. Christ will never tarry in a divided heart. Then, retain no darling sin. And make your heart a fit temple for Christ's indwelling. Out with the money-changers and all unholy traffic. And give him goodly entertainment, suitable for such a Guest.—H.

8. Closed-door Communion.

"When the doors were shut—Jesus came." When the disciples locked the doors to prevent interruption, Christ knew that he was sure of a welcome. He had been waiting for this opportunity to manifest himself unto them. He could not speak to his friends in the presence of his enemies. He could not get their ear on account of the din and confusion that came through the open doors. Have you ever tried to carry on a conversation over the telephone in a room full of uproar? Then you know why "Jesus came, when the doors were shut."

Closing the door to the world is opening the door to the Master. He is always passing by those doors that are wide-open to all the frivolity and vanity of men; but whenever he finds the door shut to these things, he seeks admittance. He knows that there is room for him on the other side of the closed door.

Do not be afraid of shutting the door; it is the best invitation for the Master to enter. "Enter into thy closet and shut the door," and he will see that his presence is desired. In the busy modern world, with its multiplicity of interests, we must find time to be alone with the Master. When the doors are shut, Jesus still comes! And this feast of the Lord's Supper is a time of closed-door communion. He comes and sups with us when we shut the world out in an attitude of attention.

9. The Lord's Supper a Prophecy.

The Lord's Supper is a prophecy of Christ's second coming, of the perfect triumph of his kingdom, for we are to celebrate it till he comes. It contains a hope and a promise of victory and heaven. Our last view of Christ in the Gospels is not of death, but of an ever-living Saviour who once was dead, but now lives forevermore. It is the morning star. It is like the music of the unseen Highland regiment coming to relieve the siege of Lucknow.

The Holy Grail in legend is the cup out of which Jesus drank wine at the last supper with his disciples.

If a man
Could touch or see it, he was healed at once,
By faith, of all his ills. But then the times
Grew to such evil that the holy cup
Was caught away to heaven, and disappeared.

So it will ever be if the Church forgets its meaning of fellowship.—Rev. F. N. Peloubet, D.D.

10. The Spreading Tree.

There is the story of the king many of whose subjects rebelled against him. He might have crushed them, but he was a magnanimous monarch, who preferred to win them. So he appointed an envoy to confer with them, offering amnesty to such as conformed to reasonable requirements, and appointed a day and a place for them to come to him, relate the story of their wrongs as they conceived them, promising that if their complaints were well founded their wrongs should be redressed. The meeting place was at a distance from the king's palace and under the spreading branches of an ancient oak. The rebels came and were received by the king himself. They stated their grievances, which the king himself guaranteed should be redressed; and each rebel, putting his hands between the king's hands, swore to be his faithful man thereafter.

The parallel is not exact. We have no complaints against God. He has not wronged us nor oppressed us. Yet we are rebels, and he invites us to return and be reconciled to him. Now what is the cross? The cross is the spreading tree under which the king of heaven meets his rebel subjects and receives them with open arms and pitying heart. —Rev. Charles C. Albertson, D.D.

11. Spiritual Meditation.

The lack of spiritual meditation is one of the religious lacks of our time. The Lord's Supper observed is a help toward overcoming this lack. There are reasons for this lack. One is the tremendous rush and hurry of our modern life. Much of the superficial piety and lack of joy we see is not because Christians do not know and feel, but because they do not think. We read our Bibles, catch up a religious paper now and then, listen to sermons, hear addresses; we may even be thrilled with emotion for a moment, but how few of us ever sit down and spend an hour in earnest thinking on what we hear.—H.

12. The Antioch Chalice.

A number of years ago there was unearthed in Antioch, Syria, a large silver cup enclosed in a carved silver container which is now in the safety vault of a New York bank. The owners secured the services of an authority in archaeological treasures, who is confident, after several years of careful study, that this "Chalice of Antioch" dates from the first century of our era. The inner cup closely resembles in shape the representations on the Arch of Titus, Rome, of cups among the spoils taken from the temple of Jerusalem in the year 70. Two central figures, on opposite sides of the Chalice, represent, it is believed, Christ in his youth and in his maturity. Above the latter figure is a dove, and underneath it an eagle resting on a basket containing loaves of bread. Vines with their clusters of grapes connect these figures with twelve others. It is natural to suppose the symbolism to be that of the Saviour offering the bread and the wine, denoting his broken body and shed blood. The beautifully carved outer cup is so honored as being the very cup that Jesus used when he instituted the Lord's Supper. It has always been believed that the "Upper Room" where the supper was held was in the house of Mary, the mother of Mark. The cup might have fallen into his possession, and he might have carried it with him to Antioch when he went there from Jerusalem with Paul and Barnabas, Acts 2:28, 30.

13. Communion Sunday.

Archimedes wanted a fulcrum on which to place his lever, and then he said he could move the world. Calvary is the fulcrum, and the cross of Christ is the lever; by that power all nations shall yet be lifted. The Preparatory Service, Communion Sunday and the celebration of the Lord's Supper are to bring freshly to mind the meaning of the cross and to awaken anew in all disciples a love for and consecration to Christ and to his work for the world.

14. Just Loving You.

A wife was sitting beside the bed of her husband, who was so ill that he could not turn his head to look at her. He asked, "What are you doing?" She replied, "Just loving you!" As we come to the Lord's Table and he asks us what we are doing, may we reply from our hearts, "Just loving You!" When we feel all is a failure or that we do not know what to do and Jesus asks what we are doing, may we be able to reply, "Just loving You!" The little one on the train looked around and said, "Mamma, I love you." Her mother smiled a glad smile. Jesus likes to be told of our love. Let the redeemed of the Lord, say so. —H. G. C. H.

15. Back to the Cross.

What a strange persistence lives in the cross! Mr. M. L. Fisher tells in a sonnet how once he caught a glimpse in a museum of art of a sculptured head of the Crucified. He could not forget it. He must find it again. In his search he passed by cloths of gold, jeweled robes that kings had worn, famous pictures, graven gems. He had no eyes for these, eager only for one Face. Wherein is the power of Calvary? He admits that power and states it, though he has no explanation.

16. Her Need.

A lady was lying dangerously ill in the hospital. A clergyman had been sent for, that she might receive the sacrament at his hands. He came, and administered the rite, but it failed to give the desired relief. After the minister had left the sufferer turned to the occupant of the bed nearest her own and said in tones of sadness, "I thought it would have done me more good." Her fellow sufferer, an earnest Christian lady, quietly replied, "Ah! you don't want it, you want Him."

Her need, our need is for Him. But the Holy Communion is a blessed reminder of Him.

17. Love for Our Unseen Saviour.

It is to be feared the majority of professing Christians fail to appreciate all the joy or blessedness of sweet communion with Jesus. I have heard of a young girl whose growth in Christian character was very marked. No one seemed to understand the secret of it. It was noticed by an intimate friend that she wore a golden locket which she seemed to prize very highly. One day this friend was sitting with her by the seaside. In the course of an affectionate conversation the friend asked if she might look into the locket. Being urged, the girl consented. The friend opened it, and found these words: "Whom having not seen I love."

Here was the secret of her beautiful life. She had come under the transforming power of the love of Christ. She had a true Friend. There was One who loved her. There was One she loved. The purity of that daily communion and fellowship impelled her to struggle against sin and cultivate all that was pure and good—all that was pleasing to her unseen Friend.

At this Communion service let us cherish and cultivate this love for our unseen Saviour.

18. Despised and Rejected of Men.

Few pictures on exhibition in the world's great galleries have caused greater sensation than the painting by Sigismundi Goetze called "Despised and Rejected of Men," which was hung in the Royal Academy of London. The canvas centers, of course, about the thorn-crowned and spear-riven Son of Man, but this time he is exposed in one of the world's busy thoroughfares, where the feverish and hurried hosts of modern life roll by. Business, toil, profession, pleasure and even the church—all are represented here, but all alike are indifferent to the Man of Sorrows, whose touch upon their lives might mean so much for them. But the workman with his pick, the sportsman with his riding whip, the devotee of society, the scientist, the soldier, the newsboy shouting the sensation of the hour, the mother with her babe, and even the priest are either unaware that he is near, or, knowing, do not care. Of all the throng, only the hospital nurse turns her eyes upon the strange, and yet familiar, figure, but here is a look of alarm and not of concern.—William E. Biederwolf.

19. Christ Our Ideal for Imitation.

In his journey through the regions of the dead, Aeneas sought with a reverent curiosity for his father, the great Anchises. He found him in a verdant valley, where he was contemplating the ranks of his posterity, their destinies and worthy deeds to be achieved in coming times. When he recognized Aeneas approaching, he stretched out both his hands to receive him. "Have you come at last?" said he, "long expected, and do I behold you after such perils past! O, my son, how I have trembled for you as I have watched your career!" To which Aeneas replied, "O Father! Your image was always before me to guide and guard me."

There is no influence in life like that of a great personality. And Christ is the Christian's ideal. He is the Personality we study and seek to imitate. And it is to assist in this transformation, in this increasing likeness to Christ that we come to meet him here at his Table. It is a Table of fellowship, of communion with him. It is Christ's appointed place where in a special sense "we all with unveiled face beholding as in a mirror the glory of the Lord are transformed into the same image from glory to glory, even as by the Spirit of the Lord."

20. The Rent Veil.

One of the portents which accompanied the crucifixion of Jesus was the rent veil of the temple. On that day of crucifixion, as the priests entered the holy place to offer the evening sacrifices, they found the sacred veil rent in two from the top to the bottom. The Jewish Christians, as is seen in the book of Hebrews, interpreted the rent veil as a symbol of "the new and living way" of reconciliation with God which Christ had opened for all believers. The rent veil is also symbolic of other veils rent by Christ. Some of these are separation between nation and nation, race and race, culture and ignorance, and science and faith. Christ by his teaching and life makes possible the unity and harmony of all such dividing veils.—Rev. I. J. Swanson.

SECTION VI. For Missions and Missionaries

What is ahead for world Christianity? Where is world Christianity heading —and why? Is there valid hope, after these nineteen centuries, for an all-embracing world brotherhood? In our time Christianity is a world reality. At long last there is hope—and promise—that the Christian faith shall embrace men and women of every race and culture and stage of civilization. This is a period of life's widening horizons. The geographic world known to people of Bible times was relatively small. For fifteen hundred years into the Christian era the horizon was not greatly enlarged. Then came Columbus and the thoughts of men grew broader. In times much nearer ours daring spirits have enlarged the boundary of our knowledge of the world, until it is scarcely possible that any considerable land on the face of the globe is hidden from our knowledge. Political horizons have been greatly slow to enlarge. There are spiritual horizons, and their recognition is the chief difference between small souls and great. Great souls recognize that they have a world mission. We are our brothers' keeper, in whatever part of the world they are found. That means missions.

We would call attention to how a great soul recognized this fact. A large corporation sought a manager for a divisional opening in China. Many men were considered, but each was found lacking in some capacity. Finally, the company's agent heard of a missionary in China who possessed all and more of the necessary qualifications and who was then earning less than one thousand dollars a year. The agent called the missionary offering him ten thousand, twelve thousand, fifteen thousand dollars salary. He refused the position. Finally the agent asked, "What will you take?" The missionary replied: "The trouble is not with the salary; it is with the job. The job is too little. You offer a big salary, but a small job. I get a small salary but I have a big job. I can't quit helping men just to sell oil!"

The greatest satisfaction a man can have is that of doing the biggest job he is able to do. The best job is to work for the Kingdom, in whatever way he can.

I. SOME STARTING-POINT STUDIES FOR MISSIONARY SERMONS AND ADDRESSES

1. Theme: Christ's Farewell Commission.

TEXT: "Go ye into all the world, and preach the gospel to every creature." Mark 16:15.

I. The work designated. "Preaching the Gospel." 1. Speaking. Much of real and useful work in life is wrought by words. In preaching the Gospel they are the chief agency. 2. The Gospel. The central truths of the Christian religion. 3. A new work this. Not preaching merely, but telling the "Good News." "Gospel." 4. A divine work, commended and commanded by Christ himself. The Church's "Marching Orders."

II. The workmen chosen. 1. Common men, therefore in sympathy with the common people. 2. Men from ordinary secular occupations. 3. Great varieties of natural character among them. No two alike, yet all useful. 4. Although not perfect men, they were men to whom special promises were made—the presence of Christ, the power of the Holy Spirit. 5. But they were representative men. We too are representative men and women and called to duty.

III. The sphere of work. The whole world. No limitations of country or climate. No distinctions of barbarism or civilization, bondage or freedom, preparedness or unpreparedness. What a glorious sphere for working—the world, man, men, all men, "every creature." And what a work—builders of a temple that shall fill the world, stewards of a wealth that shall enrich the world, ambassadors on an errand of supreme importance to the world.

IV. The Master of the workmen. He who said "Go," himself came into the World. He has the right to command. We owe him obedience. With such a Master the lack of willing workmen is truly astonishing.—S. M.

2. Theme: The Conversion of the World.

TEXT: "God be merciful unto us, and bless us; and cause his face to shine upon us. That thy way may be known upon earth, thy saving health among all nations." Ps. 67:1, 2.

One of the most striking characteristics of the religion of the Bible is its universality. It is designed to and does meet the wants of all. It is expansive both in its nature and effects. All this is plainly manifest in this beautiful prayer.

I. Think first of the principles that pervade the prayer. 1. Humility. "God be merciful unto us." No claim for justice. No word of merit. But a plea for mercy. 2. Patriotism. It is a prayer by Jews for Jews; and we may take the words for ourselves. 3. A regard for others.

II. The object of the prayer. It is the conversion of the world. "Thy saving health among all nations." The world for Christ. This is what we are expected to seek, and for which provision has been made. There must be room for the world in our hearts, our prayers, our benevolences.

III. God's way at present is not known upon earth. It is his will that his way shall be known in all the earth and his saving health among all nations. How meaningful those two words, "saving health." How aptly descriptive of the result of missions!

IV. The means by which this object is to be accomplished. It is to be by human instrumentality. The direct instruments to be employed in making God's way known in all the earth are his own people.

Our duty: An enlightened, zealous, wise and consistent interest and enlistment in the cause of world-wide missions.

3. Theme: The Kingdom of Heaven.

TEXT: "The kingdom of heaven is like unto leaven, which a woman took, and hid in three measures of meal, till the whole was leavened." Matt. 13:33.

It is a singular thing that Jesus never attempted to define the kingdom of heaven. But again and again, in parables, he describes it by illustration, telling us what it is like. Why did he not define it? Because it is too great to be defined. But he borrows all sorts of figures as symbols of the kingdom. There is no more striking symbol of the kingdom than leaven.

I. It is foreign to the substance which it affects. It is a secret, silent, unobtrusive force. It is pervasive and powerful—so powerful as to change the character of that into which a small quantity of it is introduced.

Christianity is a force entirely alien to the world into which it came. It is not of the earth earthy—not a human religion. God's thoughts are not our thoughts, nor his ways our ways. See the multitude of human gospels—how different these!

II. Moreover, Christianity is a secret force. It comes without observation. It came into the world with no advertised program, no prospectus. Jesus raised no army, effected no organization. He did not cry aloud in the streets to advertise his wares. It strikes certain minds as exceedingly strange that Christianity did not at the beginning openly attack despotism or slavery; that it made no direct effort to diminish cruelty, to deliver women from bondage and children from barbarous conditions; that it organized no temperance crusade or purity movement. Only immature minds, however, dwell long on these "omissions." The surest way to fail would have been to do exactly what half-baked theories would have demanded. The leaven must first be planted in the meal. That was what Jesus did from the beginning of his ministry to the day when in the attitude of blessing he ascended to the heavens from which he came, thenceforth to give gifts to men.

III. The leaven has been working for centuries and its power is only beginning to be universally felt. There are still unleavened masses, so there is still work for us to do who were appointed to continue and to complete that which Christ began. Every church at home and every mission abroad, every Christian school and hospital, every evangelist and colporteur is neither more nor less than a purveyor of the leaven of the kingdom. We can do nothing more, though we were the mightiest on earth, and we must do nothing less, whatever the cost may be. —C. C. A.

4. Theme: The Coming of the Kingdom.

TEXT: "Thy kingdom come." Matt. 6:10.

I. Greater than all the kingdoms of the world is the kingdom of God.

II. Amidst all the breaking up of human kingdoms men seek one that will abide.

III. This is a kingdom founded not in might but by moral goodness.

IV. The kingdom of God is God's primeval thought.

V. The way of its coming is an inner, a spiritual, a moral one.—L.

5. Theme: A Worshiping World.

TEXT: "From the rising of the sun even unto the going down of the same my name shall be great among the Gentiles; and in every place incense shall be offered unto my name, and a pure offering: for my name shall be great among the heathen, saith the Lord of hosts." Malachi 1:11.

It is usual for the prophets to describe the dispensation of the Gospel by terms and analogies taken from the Mosaic ritual. "Incense" and "offering" are examples.

I. Here is first a glorious prediction of a worshiping world. "From the rising of the sun even unto the going down of the same . . . in every place." World-wide. Here is a prediction from the very highest authority, even that of God himself. And the image is very significant. It is taken from the wide circuit and prevalency of solar light which visits every portion of the globe.

II. The second image employed indicates the glorious season when true religion shall possess the hearts of men in all its purity and hallowed devotions. The contrast is lovely between the two figures used. "Light," the most beautiful element in nature. "Incense," perfume, the sweetest of elements.

III. The sweet incense and pure offering which Jehovah now desires and loves are spiritual devotions, true prayers, praise, obedience, love.

IV. It is predicted that these will be found "in every place." The coming glory of Christ in the conversion of the world is the earnest prayer of faith now. It is the glorious object of hope.

V. Our imperative duty is to extend

the Gospel of Christ in all lands. 1. It is the Christian's obligation. 2. Efforts to this end bring down richest blessings upon our souls.—J. A.

6. Theme: The Christian Debt.

TEXT: "I am debtor both to the Greeks, and to the Barbarians." Rom. 1:14.

I. The nature of the debt and our power to pay it.

II. The parties who hold our obligations.

III. The true test of piety is a sense of debtorship to souls.

IV. The earnestness with which we should strive to pay our debts.—C. S. R.

7. Theme: Have You Obeyed the Command of the Captain?

TEXT: "Go ye therefore, and teach all nations." Matt. 28:19.

The word "therefore" explains why Jesus sent the disciples forth. It was because all power was given unto him in heaven and in earth.

I. He had all authority to send them and all power to give them, and his own mighty personality to attend them. Therefore Jesus commissioned his apostles and every other follower to "go" and tell the story of salvation.

II. It is a "Go" Gospel, a Christ Gospel, a glorious Gospel of the truth as it is in Jesus. Christ stood for the Godhead, the Holy Trinity, when he died for lost men and when he sent men on a world-wide mission. He is a mighty Saviour because he has all love to die, all power to endure, all authority to command, and the all-cleansing blood to wash sins away.

III. Christ is the center and circumference of the Gospel. He is the Christ crucified, raised, glorified, coming again to gather the results of his mighty mission.

IV. Have you obeyed the command of the Captain? Are you going every day, everywhere, witnessing for the Master? Are you ministering with your pen, your tongue, your example, your gifts? Are you using your endowment of divine power to bring back a lost world into his kingdom? It may be you are a deserter, a traitor, worthy of being court-martialed for disobedience to divine orders. Let us ever hereafter be true, obeying the Lord's call to go; keep sacred his commandments, that we may love his appearing and be caught up with him when he comes.—Rev. E. W. Caswell.

8. Theme: The Lordly Grace of Giving.

TEXT: "God loveth a cheerful giver." II Cor. 9:7.

God loveth a cheerful giver because cheerful giving is born of love, and therefore it is a Lover loving a lover and rejoicing in the communion. Giving is the language of loving; indeed, it has no other speech. "God so loved that he gave!"

I. Love finds its very life in giving itself away. Its only pride in possession is the joy of surrender. If love has all things it yet possesses nothing.

II. But we must not confine our thought to material things when we think of the grace of giving. We must get back to the fontal giving of which the gift of money is only a single issue. It is of this primary spring that James Hinton has a suggestive word: "We must make our thinking too, a giving, an escape from the death of trying to get." That word has surely a very vital significance. Our real giving is to begin in our thinking, and first of all in our supreme thinking, which is in our prayers. Self is to be lost when we commune with our God, and our empty place is to be filled by others. We must be cheerful givers in our intercessions, fellow laborers with God in distributing the holy powers of grace over a needy multitude.

When a man begins to be nobly generous in his prayers, when his highest thinking is a giving and not a getting, we need have no care about his minor forms of beneficence. It will "stream from the hills and descend to the plains."

III. When our divine communion is cheerfully sacrificial the whole of life will be an unconscious sacrifice. That is a great epitaph on General Gordon's monument in St. Paul's, and it powerfully illustrates this law of genial and holy sacrifice: "He gave his strength to the weak, his sympathy to the suffering, his substance to the poor, and his heart to God." His great surrender was the offering of love, and it was made in the secret place; and out of that central giving, as streams from a fountain, there flowed all manner of radiant beneficence.

IV. The people who have no money to give are yet not deprived of those joys of cheerful beneficence. "Silver and gold have I none, but such as I have give I thee!" And he imparted a capacity which money could never have bought. The apostle Paul, "having nothing," longed to visit Rome, "that I may impart unto you some spiritual gift." In those supreme realms we can all be benefactors, ministers of a treasure more to be desired than gold, yea, than much fine gold. And all this applies also to our giving for missions.—J.

9. Theme: Our Debt.

TEXT: "I am debtor both to the Greeks, and to the Barbarians; both to the wise, and to the unwise." Rom. 1:14.

Paul's sense of indebtedness arose from a consciousness of having come into possession of that of which the world stood in need. A graduate of the Medical Department of the University of Pennsylvania, having finished his hospital interneship, visited China. One day, as he walked through the narrow streets of a crowded city, he saw so many people who were in need of medical and surgical assistance that his heart went out to them, and he said, "Am I not needed here more than in America?" There is no doubt Canton needed him more than did Philadelphia.

When he returned he said to the men of his university, "If you will back me up, I will go to China." They backed him up and he went not only to practice the art of healing but to be one of the founders of a medical college from which hundreds of well-trained young Chinese doctors and nurses have been sent out to bless their land. "Joe" McCracken, idol of the football field, was proud and glad to be a servant of the Great Physician. He was paying his debt even as Paul paid his.

Dr. Andrew Hall did a similar work in the Philippines. The Mission to Lepers is in some respects the most striking example of the application of this rule of indebtedness to the world. The men and women who support it, the physicians and nurses who minister to the lepers, might all say, "We are debtors, both to the clean and the unclean." All such workers are opening wells in the desert.—C. C. A.

10. Theme: One of the Haystack Band. Short Missionary Talk to Children and Youths.

This morning I am to tell you young friends about a little dark-eyed baby who was born in the town of Malden, Massachusetts. It was on August 9, 1788. He was named Adoniram, after his father, who was a Congregational minister. The father, and mother too, thought this baby a wonderful child. That is a way our fathers and mothers have, and we ought to try very hard not to disappoint their expectations. Mr. and Mrs. Judson thought that if the boy was to do a great deal of good in the world the best way to get him ready was to begin early to teach him as much as he could learn. Long pieces were given him to commit to memory when he was hardly more than a baby. He learned to read when he was only three years old. When he was four he liked to gather all the children in the neighborhood and play church. He always preached the sermon himself.

At sixteen he went to Brown University. He was a fine student. A great longing came into his heart to be a minister, and he studied diligently with this end in view. He became the leader of the noble pioneer band of American missionaries. He was one of the Haystack Band at Williams College. They had formed the first foreign missionary society in America and met at night to pray under a haystack. At the theological seminary he continued his interest in missions and was one of the first company of missionaries that set sail from our shores. He arrived in Burma, where he labored until his death.

When once asked what were the prospects of the conversion of the heathen, he made his famous reply, "They are as bright as the promises of God." During the war in which England conquered Burma, he was imprisoned by the natives and suffered horrible tortures. With great effort he had made a precious manuscript translation of the Bible into the native language. This he sewed into a pillow, which was taken as a keepsake by a native Christian, and so the valuable document was preserved.

For thirty-seven years he toiled on, several times returning to this country, but hastening back to his field. It was six years before he won the first Burmese convert. But before his death he was permitted to see sixty-three churches in Burma under the care of one hundred and sixty-three missionaries and helpers, and more than seven thousand converts had been baptized.

Worn out with long labor, the hero missionary, stricken with fever, was sent home, only to die on shipboard, and his body was buried at sea. But he had been permitted to see the Gospel firmly planted in that country.—H.

II. SOME GREAT MISSIONARY SAYINGS

These may well be quoted in sermons or addresses, printed on calendars, or posted on wayside bulletin boards.

The world has many religions; it has but one Gospel.—George Owen.

All the world is my parish.—John Wesley.

I see no business in life but the work of Christ.—Henry Martyn.

Fear God and work hard.—David Livingstone.

We can do it if we will.—The Men of the Haystack.

The bigger the work the greater the joy in doing it.—Henry M. Stanley.

We can do it and we will.—Samuel B. Capen.

The lesson of the missionary is the enchanter's wand.—Charles Darwin.

The work of winning the world to Christ is the most honorable and blessed service in which any human being can be employed.—C. F. Schwartz.

I am in the best of services for the best of Masters and upon the best terms. —John Williams.

Nothing earthly will make me give up my work in despair.—David Livingstone.

The greatest hindrances to the evangelization of the world are those within the Church.—John R. Mott.

Prayer and pains, through faith in Jesus Christ, will do anything.—John Eliot (on last page of his Indian Grammar).

What are Christians put into the world for except to do the impossible in the strength of God?—General S. C. Armstrong.

Christianity is a religion which expects you to do things.—Japanese saying.

Let us advance upon our knees.—Joseph Hardy Neesima.

Tell the king that I purchase the road to Uganda with my life.—James Hannington.

I am not here on a furlough; I am here for orders.—Hiram Bingham.

The medical missionary is a missionary and a half.—Robert Moffat.

Every church should support two pastors—one for the thousands at home, the other for the millions abroad.—Jacob Chamberlain.

I will place no value on anything I have or may possess except in relation to the Kingdom of Christ.—Livingstone's resolution made in young manhood.

Win China to Christ and the most powerful stronghold of Satan upon earth will have fallen.—Mr. Wong.

The word discouragement is not to be found in the dictionary of the Kingdom of Heaven.—Melinda Rankin.

We are the children of the converts of foreign missionaries; and fairness means that I must do to others as men once did to me.—Maltbie D. Babcock.

We cannot serve God and mammon; but we can serve God with mammon.—Robert E. Speer.

The prospects are as bright as the promises of God.—Adoniram Judson.

Your love has a broken wing if it cannot fly across the sea.—Maltbie D. Babcock.

III. SOME PRAYERS FOR MISSIONS AND MISSIONARIES

1. Ministering to the Multitudes.

O God, thou King of glory, we rejoice that thou dost send forth ambassadors from age to age. And they come still with the same spiritual credentials, healing the sick and preaching the gospel. We thank thee this day for all who minister to the multitudes of diseased and crippled and lunatic folk. O Lord of life and death, manifest thy presence in each asylum and hospital, each school of medicine and home of healing. Bless abundantly all doctors and nurses at home and abroad. Baptize them with Christ's own wisdom, and tenderness, and patience, in their work for the least of his brethren. Remember, O Lord, thy servants in far lands, who sacrifice themselves for the bodies and souls of the heathen. Fill them with the peace of the gospel which they carry. Guard them amid peril and sorrow. And wherever they enter, let thy kingdom come with power. Lord, may thy kingdom come in its fullness speedily; and may we all be owned in our labor to bring it in, for thy name's sake. Amen.

2. Lord of the Harvest.

O great Lord of the harvest, send forth, we beseech thee, laborers into the harvest of the world that the grain which is even now ripe may not fall and perish through our neglect. Pour forth thy sanctifying spirit on our fellow Christians abroad and thy converting grace on those who are living in darkness. Raise up, we beseech thee, a devout ministry among the native believers that all thy people being knit together in one body in love, thy church may grow up into the measure of the stature of the fullness of Christ. Through him who died and rose again for us all, the same Jesus Christ our Lord.—Amen.

3. To Every Creature.

O God our heavenly Father who didst manifest thy love by sending thy only Son into the world that all might live through him, pour thy spirit upon thy Church that it may preach the gospel to every creature and that it may send forth laborers into all the fields of the world. Defend thou those who in distant lands preach thy gospel amid dangers and temptations, and hasten the time when the minds and hearts of the multitudes of the world shall be saved through Jesus Christ our Lord. Amen.

4. Thy Kingdom Come.

Thy kingdom, O Christ, is an everlasting kingdom. Strengthen us to pray and labor for its appearing. Forgive our little faith and the weakness of our endeavor for its realization. And though it now seems far from our world, may we seek it in our times and in our own lives. Give us also faith and consecration to promote it everywhere. May thy kingdom come and thy will be done on earth as it is in heaven. In thine own name we ask. Amen.

5. The Good News of the Gospel.

We thank thee, O God, for the good news of the Gospel of Christ. We thank thee for the revelation of his face and for his wonderful words of life. The riches of his grace in us, our Father, is but the measure of our obligation to thee and to those who do not know thee. We would have all men rejoice in the Gospel. We would have India and China and Africa and Japan know our Saviour as we do. How can the nations be glad and sing for joy until they know thee and thy wonderful love in Christ? O send out thy light and thy truth into all the earth. Bless all missionaries and native workers. Bless the Church in our own land, and out of her increasing wealth may she freely give and freely go that the world may be saved. May thy kingdom come and thy will be done on earth as it is done in heaven. To this end wilt thou consecrate us anew to thy service. We ask in the name of Christ. Amen.

6. Invocation Prayer.

O God, who hast made of one blood all nations of men for to dwell on the face of the whole earth, and didst send thy blessed Son to preach peace to them that are far off and to them that are nigh; grant that all men everywhere may see thee and find thee. Bring the nations into thy fold, and add the unevangelized to thine inheritance. O our Saviour, who didst come to seek and to save the lost and to whom all power is given in heaven and on earth, hear our prayers for those who, at thy command, go forth to preach the Gospel to every creature, for those who help to heal the world's sicknesses, for all who teach young and old the saving truths of thy Word. Preserve them in all dangers, from perils by land and on sea; from the deadly pestilence; from the violence of the persecutor; from doubt and impatience; from discouragement and discord; from all the devices of the powers of darkness. While they plant and water, O Lord, send thou the increase; gather the multitudes of the unevangelized; convert in Christian lands such as neglect thy great salvation; that thy name may be glorified, and thy kingdom come, O Saviour of the world; to whom, with the Father and the Holy Ghost, be honor and glory, world without end. Amen.

IV. SUGGESTED MISSION TEXTS AND THEMES

His Wonders: "Declare his glory among the heathen, his wonders among all people." Ps. 96:3.

The Prediction: "The earth shall be full of the knowledge of the Lord, as the waters cover the sea." Isa. 11:9.

Prepare the Way: "Prepare ye the way of the Lord, make straight in the desert a highway for our God." Isa. 40:3.

World Around: "From the rising of the sun even unto the going down of the same my name shall be great among the Gentiles." Mal. 1:11.

The World Kingdom: "Thy kingdom come." Matt. 6:7-15.

The Seeking Greeks: John 12:20-26. Those men were not driven merely by curiosity. They were heart-hungry. It was doubtless, therefore, that Jesus saw in them the first fruits of the Gentile world coming to him.

The King of the Kingdom: Matt. 13:31, 32. The vital force of the kingdom is the person of Jesus himself. He makes alive. Life radiates from him. Everyone who comes under the influence of Jesus becomes a force for life.

The Gospel Mandatory: "Go ye therefore, and teach all nations." Matt. 28:19.

Ends of the Earth: "All the ends of world shall remember and turn unto the Lord." Ps. 22:27.

Ethiopia Saved: "Ethiopia shall soon stretch out her hands unto God." Ps. 68:31.

The Degradation of Image Worship: Ps. 115:8.

The Effect of Spurious Christianity: Jude 4:11-13.

The Call of the Neglected Continent: Acts 16:9.

What the Law of Love Demands: I John 3:16.

What Remains to be Done in Mission Lands: Matt. 9:36-38.

The Speedy Evangelization of the World. What is Needed? Rom. 12:1, 2.

Among All Nations: "That thy way may be known upon earth, thy saving health among all nations." Ps. 67:2.

The Isles Wait: "The isles shall wait for his law." Isa. 42:4.

The Great Commission: "Go ye into all the world, and preach the gospel to every creature." Mark 16:15.

Scattered Children: "That also he should gather together in one the children of God that were scattered abroad." John 11:52.

Commissioned: "As my Father hath sent me, even so send I you." John 20:21.

To Those Far Hence: "I will send thee far hence unto the Gentiles." Acts 22:21.

The Wisest Work: "He that winneth souls is wise." Prov. 11:30.

Fishers of Men: "I will make you fishers of men." Matt. 4:19.

The White Harvest: "Pray ye therefore the Lord of the harvest, that he will send forth laborers into his harvest." Matt. 9:38.

Thine Inheritance: "I shall give thee the heathen for thine inheritance, and the uttermost parts of the earth for thy possession." Ps. 2:8.

The Good Samaritan. Deeds of Medical Missions: Luke 10:33, 35.

The Missionary Motive: II Cor. 5:14.

God King of the Earth: Ps. 103:18-22.

Salting the Earth: Matt. 5:13-16.

Your Nearest Neighbor: Acts 8:5-12.

Incentive to Missionary Work: I John 4:19.

Encouragements in Missionary Work: Ps. 22:27-28.

An Old-time Missionary: Jonah 3:3-10.

V. CHOICE ILLUSTRATIONS UPON MISSIONARY THEMES

1. Representing God's Government.

"Go . . . and, lo, I am with you alway." Matt. 28:20. When the government sends an ambassador to accomplish some difficult and delicate piece of work, then, so long as he keeps strictly to his instructions, he knows that he is backed up by all the resources and power of the nation he represents. If he went simply as a private individual he might well feel powerless to affect the current of international politics, but when his nation says to him, "Surely I will be with thee," the case is entirely different. So it is with every worker whom God calls into his service. We go to execute God's commission, and God himself will undertake for us.

2. The Undelivered Message.

"I sent my love to you every day," said a little girl, indignantly, to a sick friend, who was beginning to be convalescent, and felt hurt because no word of remembrance had come to her. "They just took it and kept it all theirselves!" The childish way of looking at it sets in strong light the meaning of an undelivered message. Was it chance that just at the moment of hearing it there fell into our hands an article in one of the magazines in which the writer—a missionary—made a passionate plea for men and women to come and tell the story of a Saviour's love for sinners? "O, the people! the people!" she wrote earnestly, as if overwhelmed by the thought of their numbers and their need. "They are so dark and ignorant and lonely. Come and tell them that Christ loves them." Christ sends his love to them with each returning day—sends it by us. Do we deliver it? Or do we take it and keep it all ourselves? What does he think of us as messengers?

3. Three Things.

Three things the Master has to do
And we who share Him here below
And long to see His Kingdom come
May pray, or give, or go.

He needs them all—the Open Hand—
The Willing Feet—the Praying Heart—
To work together and to weave
A threefold cord that shall not part.
—Unidentified.

4. Love Thy Neighbor As Thyself.

A foreign missionary recently told of a woman who, on a schoolteacher's salary of $2,000, lived on one-half, and with the other half supported a substitute in China. She then felt that she was really two persons, and carried out her lifelong, devoted desire to be a foreign missionary. She received frequent letters from her substitute, prayed for her by name every day and realized the truth of what a friend of hers had said, namely: "This teacher serves the Lord twenty-four hours a day, and thus practically lives the life of the angels in heaven who serve God day by night; for at the antipodes her substitute is working while she sleeps."—*American Messenger.*

5. He Did What He Could.

A young man accepted for the African missionary field reported at New York for "passage," but found on further examination that his wife could not stand the climate. He was heart-broken, but he prayerfully returned to his home and determined to make all the money he could, to be used in spreading the kingdom of God over the world. His father, a dentist, had started to make, on the side, an unfermented wine for the communion service. The young man took the business over and developed it until it assumed vast proportions—his name was Welch, and his family still manufactures grapejuice. He has given literally hundreds of thousands of dollars to the work of missions. Every job is missionary work when we interpret it by stewardship.—*Presbyterian Advance.*

6. No Near and No Far.

There is no near and no far, but just one round world of lost and perishing souls to be rescued and saved through the world's Christ.—Hwai Yuen.

7. Are There Men There?

When a volunteer missionary to Polynesia was told of dangers to be met, he asked whether there were men there. "Yes," he was answered, "horrible cannibals." "That settles it," said he; "wherever there are men, there missionaries are bound to go."

8. How Much Does Christ's Presence Count?

"Lo, I am with you alway." Matt. 28:20. Frederick the Great wrote to one of his generals, "I send you with 60,000 men against the enemy." On numbering the troops, however, it was found there were but 50,000. The officer expressed surprise at such a mistake on the part of his sovereign. Frederick's reply was, "I counted you for 10,000 men." For how many does the living Christ count in the battle we are fighting in his name?

9. Why So Slow?

On one of his missionary tours Peter Cameron Scott, missionary to Africa, relates a most touching description of what was accomplished after preaching to the natives. A very old pagan man, having most attentively listened, came tottering up to where the missionary stood, and after asking a few most searching questions, became somewhat satisfied that the blood of Jesus could even cleanse away his sins, and while opening his heart to the Saviour closed the conversation by asking with deep pathos, in trembling tones, while tears were glistening in his eyes: "Why didn't you tell us the story sooner; why didn't you let us know?"

10. How Win the Women of China.

Recently it was necessary for me to return to America for a few months. One thing I noticed while at home was that women in attendance at church are much more numerous than men. In China the men are in the majority. There are reasons for this. The women seldom leave their homes and so do not hear itinerating preachers. Too, they are not used to walking long distances. They have children to care for and someone must guard the home. It is most natural to the Chinese that the women stay at home. It is for these and many other reasons that we need Bible-women to visit these home-keepers and tell the Gospel message to them.

We continually urge the men to bring their wives to church and win them to Christ. The better way in China, as well as in America, is to have the whole family come to church. A beautiful scene of my childhood was the sight of father, mother and a line of little people filling the church pew every Sunday regularly, rain or shine. May those days return and continue!—Testimony of H. G. C. H., a missionary in China.

11. Come Clear Out.

A converted Chinese, visiting America, was greatly puzzled over the little difference he saw between professing Christians and men of the world. Speaking of the matter he said, "When the disciples of my country come out from the world, they come clear out." This is what God requires of us, an out-and-out life for him.

12. Clergymen to Spare.

A Chinese Christian asked Archdeacon Moule how many clergymen there were in England. The Archdeacon asked the Chinese how many he thought there might be. "It is a little island," the man replied; perhaps there are a thousand." He was told, "More than forty thousand." "Then," said the Chinaman, "you can easily spare a few thousand for China."

13. We Are Debtors.

An African missionary tells of a community of Congo Christians that became aroused concerning the pagan Africans on the other side of the river. "We are saved, and they know nothing about Jesus," they cried. "What shall we do?" At last fifty of them took provisions and crossed the river and stayed among the villages for many days preaching Christ.

14. Converted to Missions.

An old gentleman who had traveled widely but not much away from the beaten tracks, was one day with a party of Americans in Algiers. For the first time he saw a real foreign missionary enterprise in the home of Miss Trotter's Mission there. The next day on the steamer he said to some friends, "I am perfectly frank to say that I have not been interested in foreign missions, but now it is all different. I now believe in foreign missions because of what I have seen," and he did not hesitate to tell others from that time on what the day had meant to him. Was he more blind than the rest of us? If you believe in the blessings that have come to us here in this neighborhood through the Word of God, and through the lives of Christian men and women, then you simply would have to believe in foreign missions. If you know the need in your own life then you know just a little of the need in the lives of millions who have not yet known Christ, but whom he loves just as much as he does you.—*5,000 Best Modern Illustrations.*

15. An Illustration from China.

Away back in the sixth century there lived in China a great religious poet whose name was Fu Hsi. One day he appeared before his emperor. On his head he had a Taoist cap; about his throat a Buddhist scarf; and on his feet were Confucian boots. The emperor said, looking at his hat,"You are a Taoist." Fu Hsi merely pointed to his Buddhist scarf. Then the emperor said, "Ah, then you are a Buddhist," but Fu Hsi only pointed to his Confucian boots. "Excuse me, then you are a Confucianist?" But Fu Hsi shook his head, for he was all three, a Taoist, a Buddhist and a Confucianist. Many of the Chinese continue to follow Fu Hsi's example and are today consistently Taoist, Buddhist and Confucianist simultaneously.

16. The Field.

"The field is the world," our Lord declared. "The world is my parish," John Wesley replied. What changes would be wrought if the Church of Christ would wake up to the great fundamental truth that she is designed to be not the field, but the force; "the field is the world." —David McConaughy.

17. The Unevangelized World.

Paint a starless sky; hang your picture with night; drape the mountains with long, far-reaching vistas of darkness; hang the curtains deep along every shore and landscape; darken all the past; let the future be draped in deeper and yet deeper night; fill the awful gloom with hungry, sad-faced men and sorrow-driven women and children: It is the unevangelized world—the people seen in vision by the prophet, who sit in the region and shadow of death, to whom no light has come; sitting there still through the long, long night, waiting and watching for the morning.—Bishop Foster.

18. Our Proxies.

Missionaries are our proxies. Our Lord sent every one of his followers forth into the world to win the world to himself. The world will never be won except as all Christians feel this missionary obligation. Christ does not want all of us to go to the field, for many must stay at home and earn the money to support those that do go. Moreover, some are better fitted to earning the money than to preaching and evangelizing. But those that stay at home are equally responsible with those that go. Indeed, the missionary obligation rests all the heavier upon those whom Christ permits to remain at home, in easy and pleasant places. Missionaries, our proxies, have many needs, because theirs is so vast a work. They are called to convert millions from idolatry and great iniquity.

19. Industrial Missions.

A group of Africans watched the missionary make a table from rough timber. One of them said, "Master, I thought God made these things and gave them to you white men; now I see that you do it yourselves." "I told him," said the missionary, "that our ancestors were once savage and knew nothing of handicraft, but through our contact with God we'd been given wisdom to do these things." Then at once the African asked, "Master, if you have done this why cannot we?" Industrial missions have a work to do. There is no limit to the opportunities through which the power of the cross can reach darkened minds.—I. L. Moulton.

20. The Value of Missions.

Diamonds found in the mud of Africa now adorn the diadems of princes and merchants, but the workmen who found them are unknown. Stanley, Livingstone, and Bishop Tucker never found a diamond all the time they were in Africa, but the immortal souls they rescued from heathenism have transfigured them before the whole world. God honors his workmen.

21. Motives to Missions:

I. We face a humanity too precious to neglect.

II. We have a cure for the ills of the world too wonderful to withhold. (Good news too good to keep.)

III. We have a Christ too glorious to hide.

IV. We have an adventure too thrilling to miss.

SECTION VII. Outlined Sermons for Sunday Mornings and Evenings for the Entire Church Year. With Recognition Also of Special Days and Occasions and Thematic Aids to Public Worship

SUNDAY: JANUARY SIXTH

MORNING SERVICE

Theme: This Year Also (New Year).

SUGGESTED SCRIPTURE READING: Ps. 9:1-17; Luke 13:6-10. After-petition: May God bless to our need these lessons for the New Year.

SELECTED HYMNS: "Another year is dawning."—R. F. Havergal. "O God, our help in ages past."—I. Watts. "While with ceaseless course the sun."—J. Nerton. "Rock of Ages, cleft for me."—A. Toplady.

CALL TO WORSHIP: "One generation shall praise thy works to another, and shall declare thy mighty acts. They shall abundantly utter the memory of thy great goodness, and shall sing of thy righteousness."

INVOCATION PRAYER (New Year): Ever-living God, by whose mercy we have come to the gateway of another year, grant that we may enter it with humble and grateful hearts; and confirm our resolutions, we beseech thee, to walk more closely in thy way, and labor more faithfully in thy service, according to the teaching and example of thy Son our Lord. Let not the errors and offences of the past cling to us, but pardon us and set us free, that with a purer purpose and a better hope we may renew our vows in thy presence and set forth under the guidance of thy Spirit to travel in that path which shineth more and more unto the perfect day. In the name of Christ we ask. Amen.

Theme: This Year Also (New Year).

TEXT: "And he answering said unto him, Lord, let it alone this year also," etc. Luke 13:8, 9.

INTRODUCTORY: The brief parable of the fruitless tree contains an appropriate text and motto for the new year. "Lord, let it alone this year also."

This is the plea of the vinedresser for delay of penalty, suspension of penalty upon the barren tree. It sums up the lesson of fruitfulness and the penalty of fruitlessness under these four heads.

I. The Just demand. "There is," says French, "a wonderful significance in the simple image running through Scripture according to which men are compared to trees, and their work to fruit."

As a tree is expected to bear fruit, and is known by his fruit, so is it with the Christian. "Herein is our Father glorified, that we bear much fruit." This is the demand of life, that we "make good," or show results. The greater our opportunities and privileges, the greater the just demand that our lives bless men and glorify God.

II. The bitter disappointment. "And found none." He had a right to expect fruit. The care and culture the tree had received involved the obligation of fruitfulness. How deep the disappointment to find none! After three years of care and cultivation, sunshine and shower, how disappointing to find "nothing but leaves." Is this not a parable of many Christian lives? The rest and luxury of religion appeal to them; but they are like seed in the sand, fruitless trees, doing no one else any good.

III. The threatened doom. This was to be "cut down." The owner's patience was exhausted. The fruitless tree cumbered the ground. It took the place of a better. It absorbed soil and sunshine that might have gone to produce fruit. And it became therefore subject to the stern law: produce or perish! Refusal to bear fruit results in loss of power to bear fruit. The profit of fruitfulness is offset by the penalty of fruitlessness. As one says, "Just as the neglected rosebush sinks gradually into decline, leaving fewer and fewer, smaller and smaller roses, and at length becomes woody and sterile, so the human soul which neglects opportunities, neglects duties and ceases to cultivate its best and richest life, yields to the inexorable law of deterioration."

IV. Hence the plea for delay; for another chance. "Let it alone this year also." This is the utterance of Christian optimism and hope. Perhaps "this year" will show different conditions and results. But, if not, then the doom must fall; "After that thou shall cut it down." What a lesson of the joy of fruitfulness, the doom of sterility. Fruit suggests abundance, variety, richness. Herein is our Father glorified; not merely in bearing fruit, but that we bear "much" fruit. To that end let us reverse the prayer of the vinedresser. Instead of "Let us alone," rather let us plead, "Leave us not to ourselves; take not thy Holy Spirit from us." Welcome the spade and pruning hook, if we may be saved from fruitlessness and death, and made to bear abundant fruit to the glory of God and the good of our fellow men. —W. S. J.

Theme Prayer: Grant unto us, Lord, we beseech thee, the spirit to think and do always such things as are right; that we, who cannot do anything that is good without thee, may by thee be enabled in this year upon which we have entered to love according to thy will; through Jesus Christ, thy Son, our Lord, who liveth and reigneth with thee and the Holy Ghost, ever one God, world without end. Amen.

Offertory Sentence: "There is that scattereth, and yet increaseth; and there is that withholdeth more than is meet, but it tendeth to poverty." "Freely ye have received, freely give."

Offertory Prayer (New Year): "In this new year, our Father, we would make new investments in the cause and kingdom of Christ. As we bring our gifts and dedicate them to thee we would also consecrate ourselves anew to thy service. In the name and for the sake of Christ. Amen.—G. B. F. H.

Illustrative Material

SEED THOUGHTS, HOMILETIC AND EXPOSITORY. This Year Also: I. Then there had been former years of grace. 1. Years of mercy. 2. Years of opportunity. 3. Years of unfulfilled resolutions. II. This year also implies a limit. Is this my last?—S.

Fruit or no Fruit: Now suppose the predestined interval pass away and you are not a fruit-bearer.—V.

The use of prolonged discipline: Pleading for a respite.

This Year Also! I. Suggests retrospect. II. Mentions a mercy. III. Implies a limit.—S.

The Sentence Suspended: I. The intercession of mercy. II. Its special end,

Time. III. Limited as to term. This year.

These Three Years: I. Youth. II. Middle age. III. Old age.—A.

Choice New Year Illustrations

NEW YEAR A NEW START. Moses got his new start at the burning bush. He caught a new vision of God and went forth. That is what we need in starting out on this new year.

LEARNING FROM FAILURES. Even our last year's failures may be turned to good account if we will regard them rightly. Some famous engine builders in this country were once asked if they ever had an explosion of one of their engines. They replied, "No, we have not. We wish we could, if no one were hurt. For we should like to know where the weakest part is." In great chain factories power machines are especially designed to make chains fail, so that the makers may know how and why and where the chains' weakest portions are. It is sometimes in the Christian life a distinct advantage to have learned by a failure. At least we may learn new year's wisdom from old year failures; we may get new year help from old year mistakes.—H.

A GOOD PRESCRIPTION. Don't worry. Don't hurry. "Too swift arrives as tardily as too slow." Sleep and rest abundaintly. Spend less nervous energy each day than you make. Be cheerful. "A light heart lives long." Think only healthful thoughts. "As a man thinketh in his heart, so is he." "Seek peace and pursue it." "Work like a man, but don't be worked to death." Avoid passion and excitement: a moment's anger may be fatal. Associate with healthy people: health is just as contagious as disease. Don't carry the whole world on your shoulders, far less the universe; trust the good Lord. Never despair. "Lost hope is a fatal disease." Trust the Master and go forward.

PUT IN YOUR TIME IMPROVING. Two men at the Boston Public Library were waiting for the books they had ordered. One of them fidgeted impatiently, snapped his watchcase, and gnawed his mustache. The other turned to the reference books and used his time in gaining some useful information. You may not see your chance this new year to get just the kind of a new start you would like; but while you are waiting for it, put in your time improving yourself as best you can.

Quotable New Year Poetry

JUST A MINUTE

I have just a little minute,
Only sixty seconds in it,
Forced upon me, can't refuse it.
Didn't seek it, didn't choose it,
But it's up to me to use it.
I must suffer if I abuse it;
Just a tiny, little minute,
But eternity is in it.

—Herbert M. Course.

NEW YEAR SONG

One song for thee, New Year—
One universal prayer;
Teach us—all other teaching far above—
To hide dark Hate beneath the wings of Love;
To stay all hatred—strife,
And live the larger life!
To bind the wounds that bleed;
To lift the fallen, lead the blind
As only Love can lead—
To live for all mankind!

—Frank L. Stanton.

A NEW YEAR WISH

What rarer gift than this can be?
What kindlier wish than this for thee?
That through the far tip-toeing years
That steal upon one ere he hears,
You still may know the simple joys
That came to us as girls and boys;
The sunny skies, the golden days
That lit our childhood's happy ways;
That honest faith in God and men,
That makes the heart beat high again:
The eager look for each tomorrow;
The buoyant heart that bears its sorrow;
The steadfast, onward, upward going
That reaps the fruit of all its sowing:
And through it all the joys that lurk
In daily toil and honest work.

—Edwin Osgood Grover.

Alternate Theme: "I Will Go before You" (New Year).

TEXT: "I will go before you into Galilee." Matt. 26:32.

INTRODUCTORY: As the old year goes we are more conscious of the finality of the past and more attentive to the hope of the future. What has gone before is irrevocably past. What is to come is full of opportunity. There is always possibility of change for the better. No matter how black things may look, few are wont to dwell upon the blackness. Hope springs eternal in the human heart. Our eagerness for the new turns our eyes from the past.

I. What do we Christians look for in this coming year? Does Christ still reign? And will God bring to fruition his promises of truth and peace and freedom? Does he still stand with men of good will to strengthen their arms and establish his kingdom? We have just heralded Christ's coming to us this Christmas season. Shall he truly be found in the days ahead? Will God stand in the shadow "keeping watch above his own"?

II. We might well turn to that last evening which our Lord spent with his disciples in the upper room. To them it seemed the end of a brave hope, the last faint glimmer of a glorious vision. But as they sang a hymn and went out into the blackness of the Mount of Olives, Jesus said, "I will go before you into Galilee." Soon the upper room which had seemingly been the end took on a new meaning. It became a starting point. There they gathered to gird their loins to face a blackening future. There they chose Matthias to close the ranks of their shaken fellowship. Instead of the dissolution, it was the gathering of forces for action. It was from that room that Peter went forth to preach so fearlessly. It was there that they gathered on the day of Pentecost to receive the Holy Spirit. That dark moment became the prelude to fearless action and indomitable faith. Each time they gathered they remembered Christ—and "he went before them."

III. As we gather in our church each Sunday this year, we cannot hope that our world will be free from danger or tragedy or strife, but we can know that Christ will go before us into whatever situation we shall meet. Perhaps the future is black because too often we have tried to face the world alone, with nothing but our own knowledge. How far would the apostles have gone had they faced the world of their day without Christ?

IV. In his earthly life Jesus was always leading on and on. How often the Scripture says, "From hence he departed into . . . ," and we can picture his followers feeling confidence because he led them! After his crucifixion his followers still sensed that they did not travel alone, but that his footsteps broke the path before them. So even today he leads on and on for those who will follow. We shall not fear the days ahead for he still says, "I will go before you." —Rev. Richard R. Northrup.

SUGGESTIVE NEW YEAR TEXTS AND THEMES

January Birthdays: "A physical birth —a spiritual birth." John 3:6.

A Young Year: "That the field bringeth forth year by year." Deut. 14:22.

New Things in a New Year: "Behold I make all things new." Rev. 21:5.

Young People's New Year: "This is the way, walk ye in it." Isa. 30:21.

Two-faced Janus: "I will go on to visions and revelations." II Cor. 12:1.

Spiritual Mobilization: "So you must take God's armor . . . stand and hold your ground." Eph. 6:13.

EVENING SERVICE

Theme: All Things New (New Year).

TEXT: "Behold, I make all things new." Rev. 21:5.

I. Man. "If any man be in Christ, he is a new creature: old things are passed away; behold, all things are become new." II Cor. 5:17. He shall be renewed in the spirit of his mind, restored to the image and likeness of God. Eph. 4:24; Col. 3:9.

His vile body shall be changed that it may be fashioned like unto his glorious body. Phil. 3:21.

II. Heaven and earth. "And I saw a new heaven and a new earth." Rev. 21:1. According to his promise we look for new heavens and a new earth, wherein dwelleth righteousness. II Peter 3:13.

III. City. On this new earth shall be a new city—the holy city, the new Jerusalem. It shall come down from God out of heaven, prepared as a bride adorned for her husband. Rev. 21:2. "Having the glory of God: and her light was like unto a stone most precious. . . . And the building of the wall of it was of jasper: and the city was pure gold, like unto clear glass. . . . And the twelve gates were twelve pearls." Rev. 21:11, 18, 21.

IV. On this new earth and in this new city the new man shall have a new home. He that overcometh shall pass by the cherubim and the flaming sword which keep the way, and shall eat of the tree of life which is in the midst of the paradise of God. Rev. 2:7. In this new home man shall live a new life, under new conditions, with new associations, and new experiences. There shall be no night there; and they need no candle, neither light of the sun; for the Lord God giveth them light. There shall in no wise enter into it anything that defileth, neither whatsoever worketh abomination, or maketh a lie. There shall be no more death, neither sorrow, nor crying, neither shall there be any more pain: for the former things are passed away.—Rev. W. Arthur.

Additional Theme: Waymarks.

Text: "Set thee up waymarks." Jer. 31:21.

Introductory: Travelers usually have reason to be thankful for the pioneers on their route who have left signs and indications of the way. In these sophisticated days we are glad to have the guideposts, the finger posts, along the roads. The voyager up the St. Lawrence will find floating buoys with small fir trees attached to them marking out the fairway. From Quebec past Three Rivers along to Montreal the vessel follows the course marked out by the early fishermen of over a hundred years ago. From the east coast to the west coast of the United States beacon lights guide the night-flying aircraft across the great plains of Nebraska and Wyoming, over the highest points of the Rockies at thirty-mile stages. Waymarks!

To the tribe of Ephraim was given the task of pioneering in adventurous living. This tribe was to set up waymarks for the guidance of others. "Set thee up waymarks," said God.

I. This injunction to Ephraim has point for all the followers of the living God. It was Christ's injunction that at all times each of us should help in creating and setting up standards for the future. It is unfortunately true that some pioneers mark a way to destruction rather than to the gates of heaven. Jesus spoke sternly of those who misled. "It were better for him that a millstone be hanged about his neck, and that he were drowned in the depth of the sea." We face the fact that our Christian duty is to guide men into all truth. What should our essential contribution be?

II. Christians as waymarks: Personal living should mark the way to God. An essential contribution the individual Christian must make in our day is to a renewed belief in God, leading to a new devotion to him. Does your life, and mine, stand as a finger post pointing others to God? As our contemporaries take their cue from us where are they being led? God speaks to us as individual Christians, "Set thee up waymarks." "Be ye examples one to another."

III. Marking the way to unity. Each age has found the Church making some great contribution to Christian living. What shall be the waymark set by the twentieth century? Many believe that God is calling us to set the mark of Christian unity. We must show that we are of one mind in Christ Jesus. If the twentieth century can heal its unhappy divisions and show that at the heart of the Christian Church there is more that unites than divides, we shall have added our contribution to Christian progress that is beyond measuring. At the moment the world is torn by divisions just because it cannot find a unifying agent. Can we in the Church of Jesus Christ show that we have One who does draw men and women together? The Church of Christ is being invited to set up a "waymark" for a disunited world. Let us rise up as men of God and show that love for Christ in the heart brings love for our fellows, and creates fellowship.

To us at this moment there comes the challenging call of God, "Set thee up waymarks"—waymarks by virtue of which others may adventure yet further along the road that leads to God, waymarks into whose creation we may throw all the energies of mind and sinew, and find the touchstone to life everlasting.—D. A. S.

MIDWEEK FELLOWSHIP MEETING TOPIC

(Church Night or Suggested Sermon Subject)

Theme: In the Beginning (New Year).

TEXTS: "In the beginning God." Gen. 1:1; "In the beginning was the Word," etc. John 1:1, 2.

I. How often we are at the beginning of things! 1. We have been at the beginning of our lives. 2. We began our school days. 3. We began our Christian lives. 4. Some of us have stood at the beginning of married life, of parenthood, of business. 5. We stand at the beginning again in this new year.

II. It is sometimes hard to stand at the beginning of things. 1. Have you ever pitied a baby because he knew nothing of life and could not care for or protect himself? 2. The bridal days are happy days, but they are hard days of necessary adjustments too. 3. The man beginning business usually has a hard row to hoe. 4. At the beginning of the year, we may know that it will hold some hardships and difficulties for us.

III. But a beginning is always a wonderful opportunity. 1. That baby has a hundred avenues of success opening before him. 2. The bridal days usually open a successful and happy marriage. 3. The new business may win golden returns. 4. The new year is ours. Begin it by offering yourself and the new year of your life to the Lord Jesus.

CHRISTIAN ENDEAVOR SOCIETY TOPIC

Jan. 6. Indispensables for Life: What Do You *Need* to Live? Luke 4:1-4.

BULLETIN BOARD SLOGANS FOR THE MONTH

By Earl Riney

Resolve not to criticize people this year but to understand them.

In this new year is a good time to get your faith lifted.

We are always getting ready to live but never living.

Choose the best life for habit will make it pleasant.

Conscience is God's throne in man.

A living religion is a way of living.

God reveals himself to us when we listen for his guidance.

Good books give new views of life and teach us how to live.

The trouble with most of us is that we try to defend our mistakes rather than to correct them.

Most people are about as happy as they make up their minds to be.—A. Lincoln.

The soul, like the body, lives on what it feeds.

SUNDAY SCHOOL LESSON

Jan. 6. Finding the Christ. John 1:35-49.

MEMORY SELECTION: "We have found the Messiah (which means Christ)." John 1:41.

In this first quarter there are fifteen lessons concerning early followers of Jesus and rising to a climax in his resurrection. This is an introductory lesson on finding the Christ. It may be well to discuss the Messianic expectations of the time and the preparatory preaching of John the Baptist. John points out the Christ who as God's Son can meet all human needs. It is all-important that each one of us make a personal discovery of Christ and accept him as Lord and Saviour. Finding the Christ is the privilege and duty of all mankind.

SUNDAY: JANUARY THIRTEENTH

MORNING SERVICE

Theme: I Believe in Man (Evangelistic).

Suggested Scripture Reading: Luke 15:1-32. After-petition: May God reveal to our minds the truths of this great chapter.

Selected Hymns: "Lord, I hear of showers of blessings."—E. Codner. "Revive thy work, O Lord."—A. Midlane. "He that goeth forth with weeping."—T. Hastings. "Come, Holy Spirit, heavenly dove."—I. Watts.

Call to Worship: "Lord, I have loved the habitation of thy house, and the place where thine honor dwelleth." "I was glad when they said unto me, We will go into the house of the Lord."

Invocation Prayer: We rejoice, O God, in the invitation that thou hast given us, "Seek ye my face"; and our hearts make answer, "Thy face, Lord, will we seek." One thing have we desired of the Lord, and that will we seek after, that we may dwell in the house of the Lord all the days of our lives, to behold the beauty of the Lord, and to inquire in his temple. On this day of rest may we see thee in thy beauty in the sanctuary. Thou art the hearer and answerer of prayer, in our daily cares and troubles be thou our daily comfort. Give us grace that each of us may learn to say after Christ, "Not my will but thine be done." Cure us this day of our pride and willfulness. Check us, O our Father, from all anger and violence and passion. Teach us to watch and pray lest we enter into temptation. We ask thee to bless all in thy house this morning with the blessing which addeth no sorrow. Let thy sunshine fall on the children and the aged, and thy healing visit the sick. Preserve all our dear ones from all evil, and gather us into thy home at last. Through Jesus Christ our Saviour. Amen.

Theme: I Believe in Man (Evangelistic).

Text: "So God created man in his own image." Gen. 1:27.

Introductory: Never has there appeared anywhere a greater champion of man than the Christian faith which on the surface seems so vilely to traduce him. Never has a greater compliment been paid to man than when the Gospel frankly described him as a sinner. It is just because it believes in him so much that it is so harsh.

It proclaims man's true greatness to consist in this, that God has set his love upon him. Never in all the experience of man has there been found a greater champion of the souls of men than in the Gospel of Jesus Christ. Yet it can find no better word for him than to call him a sinner. Let us review some aspects of its teaching about man.

I. In the first place, it begins by reminding man that he is a created being. This means, of course, that he is a dependent and a limited being, the true source of whose strength is not in himself but in another who created him. This may sound a commonplace statement in a Christian church, but in the world outside it is a surprising statement which contradicts all men's practice. For the heady wine of modern progress has caused men to believe they are sufficient unto themselves. Against this the Gospel lifts man out of the rut by saying that he is more than a physical body. Strangely compounded with the grosser elements of his make-up is a "vital spark of heavenly flame." His soul is the warm, living breath of the Almighty. What a claim to make for a man! What a glory it casts around his life! In upholding his title deeds to a royal heritage the Gospel does right to proclaim "I believe in man."

II. Then, in the second place, it goes on sadly but insistently to brand him a sinner. Here again, what seems an obvious thing is hotly disputed outside the Church. There is no such thing as sin, say some. There are mistakes, there is a lack of judgment, there is folly, but there is no such thing as sin, for sin implies that man is responsible, that he could be better if he chose. But that is precisely what the Gospel asserts. The Gospel denies that sin ever was part of the creation of God. It is neither in his purpose nor his method. He did not create it, nor is he responsible for it. It sprang out of man's pride and selfish desire. Sin is not part of the stuff of life. Therefore a man is capable of being better than his sin. The one who denies this is much in the position of those who assume that the pitiful deformity of a cripple is the true standard of health. But the cripple knows, and the man knows, that such evil is not his real nature. It is because the Gospel proclaims this that it has the right to say in face of all the contradiction of the world, "I believe in man."

III. In the third place, the Gospel declares that no man can save himself. Only the One who made him can remake him. God only has the creative energy with which to overcome the sin of man. By Jesus Christ, in whom the creative love of God was blended with a human life, the secret of redemption is made clear. Truly can the Gospel which offers so great a salvation to mankind, calling in the resources of the eternal world to redress the balance of this mortal existence, truly can it cry, "I believe in man."

IV. Then the Gospel withdraws the veil and points to those stirrings of man's heart, those longings after he knows not what, and it whispers, "These thoughts arise in you because you were made in the image of God. It is he who is active within your soul; it is he who is causing you to reach out beyond the possibilities of this world, for he has set eternity within your heart. See, eternity is before you. Go in and possess the land."

Surely the "glorious gospel of the blessed God," which exalts man as the son of a King, although a selfish and a wayward son—truly can it stand forth as a champion and declare, "I believe in man."—W. L.

THEME PRAYER: Almighty God, whose only Son, our Lord, walked before us in the living Way, give us grace to follow where he leads. Help us to see the vision, and to leave the lesser things behind. Give us grace to accept his invitation to the acceptance of life eternal. We ask in his name. Amen.

OFFERTORY SENTENCE: "And the King shall answer and say unto them, Verily I say unto you, Inasmuch as thou hast done it unto one of the least of these my brethren, ye have done it unto me."

OFFERTORY PRAYER: We would make new investments today, our Father, in the cause of Christ. In his name we would consecrate our talents and pledge our lives anew to his service. May these investments bring profit to others and return unto us treasures laid up in heaven. In Jesus' name we ask. Amen.

Illustrative Material

SEED THOUGHTS, HOMILETIC AND EXPOSITORY. Man in God's Image: I. The dignity of man's nature. II. The greatness of man's fall. III. The glory of man's recovery by Christ.—J. S. E.

Man in God's Image: I. In respect to intelligence. II. In respect to his moral nature. III. In respect to his dominion. IV. In respect to his immortality.

Man in God's Image: I. With intellectual powers. II. With feeling of moral obligation. III. With power of free will. IV. With power of exercising affections. Capable of love to God and love to man.—D. N. S.

Choice Evangelistic Illustrations

PERSONAL WORK. Has our Christian experience been such that we feel we must share it with others? When Andrew found Christ, it is recorded that "He first findeth his own brother Simon . . . and brought him to Jesus." When Philip had become convinced that Jesus was the Christ, his first act was to seek out and win Nathanael. So also with the woman of Samaria, who left her waterpot and hurried to the village to tell her neighbors of the marvelous Stranger, exclaiming to them, "Is not this the Christ?" There are many forms of Christian activity for which special talents are needed in order that one may give effective service, but personal witnessing to what Christ means to one's own life is possible to all. One who loves the Lord with all his heart will greatly desire that others shall know also the joy of fellowship with him.—Christian Observer.

MAKING NEW MEN. Cecil Rhodes, the great empire builder, once said to General William Booth: "You have the best of me, after all. I am trying to make new countries; you are making new men."

LIMPING BETWEEN. "What," exclaimed a stranger talking to an old farm laborer, "you've walked four miles to and from the farm every day for over sixty years? Why didn't you move nearer your job?" "Well, ya see," responded the cautious laborer, "I wasn't really sure whether it was a permanent job or not." It is a similar attitude of mind found in people who go limping between God and the world.—*Christian Herald.*

PERSONAL TOUCH. George Bernard Shaw has reminded us of the ancient story of Pygmalion, who chiseled the form of a beautiful woman out of marble. Working upon his masterpiece with all the devotion of his soul, he found himself falling in love with it. Forsaking everything else he labored day and night with painstaking care. Then the miracle occurred, and Galatea was transformed from cold marble to a living, breathing creature of great charm.

Every day the miracle of the loving personal touch is wrought when people go to others in the spirit of the Master —a friendly handshake, a word of encouragement, a loving invitation, and "chords that were broken vibrate once more." Lonely and discouraged people in the prison house of secularism come out into the sunlight of triumphant Christian living and into fellowship with God's folk.—Sidney W. Powell.

EVENING SERVICE

Theme: The Unspeakable Gift.

TEXT: "Who gave himself for us, that he might redeem us from all iniquity, and purify unto himself a peculiar people, zealous of good works." Titus 2:14.

How great a theme! How glorious a work! How worthy a study and appreciation! The unspeakable gift!

I. The Giver. "The great God." "God so loved the world that he gave," etc. 1. The dignity of the Person bestowing. 2. The sacrifice at which it was made. 3. The motive which impelled the Donor to bestow it. 4. The benefits which accompany it.

II. The Gift. "Himself." Christ gave himself for us. 1. Voluntarily. "Gave." 2. Personally and precious. "Himself." 3. Vicariously, sacrificially. "For us."

III. The purpose or object. "To redeem." Note Christ's work of redemption is practical, perfect, complete.

IV. Our answering gift. It is or should be ourselves. Christ's gift of himself calls for our gift of ourselves. Hearts are bought by hearts. Love is kindled by love. "The love of Christ constraineth us." Through love to him we become especially enlisted in his cause, purified people, "a peculiar people," a people devoted to good. A consecrated Saviour suggests a consecrating people.

V. This suggests the enthusiasm for

good this wonderful, vicarious, redeeming Gift should enkindle. "Zealous of good works." Zeal implies an intense earnestness for the accomplishment of an object. God's people are "zealous of good works" because the spirit of work is in them. Great zeal can spring only out of a great motive. The ultimate spring is love, the purest, holiest, sweetest and most abiding of all motives. The unspeakable Gift presents an unmeasurable motive.—H.

Additional Theme: God Reigns.

TEXT: "How beautiful upon the mountains are the feet of him that bringeth good tidings, that publisheth peace . . . that saith unto Zion, Thy God reigneth!" Isa. 53:7.

INTRODUCTORY: When the prophet Isaiah uttered these most descriptive words, he would at once take his people's thoughts back to bygone experiences, and as they relived those exciting moments they would feel a passing thrill. They would recall the many occasions when, years before, they had seen the messenger in the distance, far away on the mountain path, and had waited with bated breath to hear the message brought by those hurrying feet. But now, with a sigh, they would realize that those days had gone forever; for now desolation and poverty stared them in the face, seemingly forgotten by man and by God. They felt that their sinfulness and indifference to the claims of God had brought misery and desolation in its train.

I. Then it dawned upon them that there was a deeper meaning in these beautiful, memory-stirring words, namely, that the prophet himself was a messenger who had come with hurrying feet to tell them that, in spite of appearances, God still reigned; and that if they could only grasp the full significance of that message they could throw off their lethargy and arise and rebuild and sow ready for next spring. So, in a new setting, the old words came to life: "How beautiful upon the mountains are the feet of him that bringeth good tidings . . . that saith unto Zion, Thy God reigneth." A new day had dawned for the people of God.

II. The claim, then, of this Scripture is that the most wonderful news that this world can hear is, "Thy God reigneth." Now, this was a truth about which Isaiah was absolutely convinced. His early experience in the Temple when he had felt the Presence and heard the Voice, had made a profound impression upon his life. He knew he could be of no greater service to his nation than to arouse them to this same confident belief. And I am convinced that this is the belief that men and women need most today.

III. But how we are to "get it across" to them, is our major problem. The people to whom Isaiah spoke, though weary and depressed about the future, at least had something within them which was quickened into response by his words. His clarion cry lit up their memories, and so his words were able to bring new hope and encouragement. But today the majority of people seem to possess nothing with which to respond! The wonderful words of the Gospel fall on dull ears. As I see it, we must begin with ourselves. Are we convinced, in spite of appearances, that God reigns, with all that that implies?

IV. Further, if God reigns, then his kingdom is here and now. This, of course, seems a paradox, for the world is anything but Christian. Yet, in truth, the kingdom is both here and now and it is also coming. For while the kingdom of God on earth has yet to be realized, the kingdom of God is within you. And that means, surely, that we can enjoy all the benefits of that kingdom now. Even in a world torn with strife we can enjoy peace and salvation.

V. Finally, if God reigns, then we possess the needed dynamic for true reconstruction. "Thy God reigneth." The words of the prophet brought reassurance and joy to his weary, defeated, despondent countrymen. When their doubts were removed they were suffused with new strength, they threw off their weariness and began to rebuild their shattered world. Where are men going to find the strength to rebuild this shattered civilization? I believe God is calling his people today to show the way, to proclaim the truth, and to live the life that will both challenge, convince and inspire the world of men.—R. K. R.

Suggested Texts and Themes

The Works of Faith: "For whatsoever is begotten of God overcometh the world: and this is the victory that hath overcome the world, even our faith." I John 5:4 (A.S.V.).

Faith without Works: "But wilt thou know, O vain man, that faith apart from works is barren." James 2:20 (A.S.V.)

The Wages of Sin: "For the wages of sin is death; but the free gift of God is eternal life in Christ Jesus our Lord." Rom. 6:23 (A.S.V.).

The Wages of God: "For bodily exercise is profitable for a little; but godliness is profitable for all things, having promise of the life which now is, and of that which is to come." I Tim. 4:8 (A.S.V.).

MIDWEEK FELLOWSHIP MEETING TOPIC

(Church Night or Suggested Sermon Subject)

Theme: The Christian Name.

TEXT: "And the disciples were called Christians first in Antioch." Acts 11:26.

The name was not given by Jews. It was not given by the disciples. It was not given by Divine direction. Other names in use were "believers," "brethren," "saints," "friends." The name "Christian" was given either as one of reproach or as a convenient designation to a rapidly enlarging society.

I. The name was given. 1. It was personal, testifying to the pre-eminence of Christ in the first preaching. The facts came before the doctrines as they always should. 2. It was a name of distinction, or at least distinguishing. It indicated the worship of Christ. It indicated that the followers of Christ were showing the spirit of Christ. "See how these Christians love one another!" It indicated separation from the world, contrast with the heathen world. 3. It was a prophetic name. Christ's disciples preached hope, the resurrection, the ascension, heaven in prospect.

II. The name honored. "Called Christians." 1. The life should be evident before it is named. 2. If the world looks upon the life it will name it. Let us see to it that ours is named after Christ. 3. It is a great privilege to wear the name. Are we ashamed of it? 4. It is not what we are called that will decide our final state but what we are. Let us who bear his name depart from iniquity.—R.

CHRISTIAN ENDEAVOR SOCIETY TOPIC

Jan. 13. Indispensables for Life: What Makes for *Personal* Worth? Matt. 10: 28-30.

SUNDAY SCHOOL LESSON

Jan. 13. The call of the Fishermen. Luke 5:1-11.

MEMORY SELECTION: "Come ye after me, and I will make you to become fishers of men." Mark 1:17.

The Scripture selections point out the profound impression Jesus had made on these fishermen and their consequent readiness to respond to his call. So doing, Jesus gave to them a new lifework. They were to become fishers of men. Jesus has a lifework for each of us. As we engage in it we find life's most enriching experiences. In this lesson we may well discuss together what it means to be called of Christ, what discipleship may cost, and some of its rich rewards.

SUNDAY: JANUARY TWENTIETH

MORNING SERVICE

Theme: Using or Losing (Evangelistic).

SUGGESTED SCRIPTURE READING: Heb. 2: 1-18. After-petition: May the Lord enable us in heart and mind to receive the light and truth from his Word.

SELECTED HYMS: "God calling yet."—G. Tarsteegen. "Behold a stranger at the door."—J. Grigg. "O Jesus, thou art standing."—W. W. How. "The Lord is rich and merciful."—S. F. Smith.

CALL TO WORSHIP: "The Lord is nigh unto all them that call upon him, to all that call upon him in truth. He will fulfill the desire of them that fear him: he also will hear their cry, and will save them."

INVOCATION PRAYER: Almighty God, our Heavenly Father, we have come to seek thee here in thy sanctuary this holy Sabbath morning. May the peace of the Sabbath take possession of our souls. Quiet our minds with the gracious influence of thy truth. Quiet our hearts with the strengthening ministries of thy love. Make us receptive of the things which thou hast prepared for them that love thee. Make us ready to hear thy will and ever eager in our obedience to it. Remove from us the indifference which has so often marred our services. Transform our reluctance into spiritual delight. Forgive our sins. Cleanse our hearts. Exalt our aims. Strengthen our purposes. And through thy grace, direct us, we pray thee, toward a life of spiritual victory. We ask in the name of Christ. Amen.

Theme: Using or Losing (Evangelistic).

TEXT: "We ought to give the more earnest heed to the things which we have heard, lest at any time we should let them slip." Heb. 2:1.

INTRODUCTORY: Few thoughts are more serious than the knowledge that if we do not give heed to the teaching of the Master, it will slip by without influencing us.

I. This is an inescapable law. We cannot escape the natural law. Neglect education and there is ignorance. Don't use a limb and it will become useless. What we do not use we lose.

Man is no exception to the law which runs through all life. If man does not cultivate the garden of his soul he will find weeds growing. Should he be foolish enough to plant thorns how can he expect to gather grapes? If he does not plant at all how can he escape rags, hunger and misery? By simple neglect a man can commit spiritual suicide.

II. Here is a warning to the modern world. The present world may boast of its wisdom, but neglect has the same effect in an educated, as in an illiterate, age. Every teacher needs to tell his pupils it is a delusion to imagine there is any escape from losing what you are not using. It cannot be the same with the man who observes the laws of health and someone who neglects them; or with one person who makes a decision, and another who never reaches a decision.

Someone living by a river lets it glide without benefiting in any way. Another harnesses the water, capturing its power. The result is electricity, which revolutionizes life. The miller harnesses the water by the water wheel. To capture the power in the water needs thought and energy; and the man who is going to get most out of his religion will have to put most into it. Around us is the power of God, but it has to be harnessed. It will flow by us unless there is personal action.

III. The result of neglecting the warning. "Earnest heed" must be given to Divine matters. A man will tend to lose his moral sense by failing to respond to it. One result of sin is the weakening of moral perception. Dullness of moral feeling and dimness of moral vision are matters of experience and observation. The explanation why a man's moral sense seems to lose its edge is because a stimulus disregarded grows less. Sensitive nerves grow accustomed to the inactivity, and do not respond as once they did. Conscience grows weaker in proportion as its urgency is disregarded. The perception of ideals becomes dim through failure to respond to the vision already perceived. If you let an ideal go it will let you go.

The grace of God may be compared with daily food. If food is constantly rejected the power to assimilate it perishes; if people persist in rejecting heavenly food, may not the power to receive it disappear? If not using we are losing.

The Church has to sound a warning note to those who continually shirk decisions. If a man will not make up his mind he may lose a mind to make up. If the faculty for decision is neglected it will "run out like leaking vessels." The situation is this—he who defers decision decides. Those who never reach a decision concerning Christ are unconsciously practicing a refined method of refusing to accept him. By doing nothing in regard to Jesus people are losing him. It is a terrible thought that we can lose the Saviour by simply not using him.—A. J. C.

THEME PRAYER: O Power divine, we confess our need of thee. We are without power; we have no strength, no wisdom. All these gifts come from thee. Wilt thou bind our weakness to thy strength and our ignorance to thy wisdom, that we may possess, and be possessed by, thy power and thy truth. In the Saviour's name. Amen.

OFFERTORY SENTENCE: "How shall they believe in him of whom they have not heard, and how shall they hear without a preacher, and how shall they preach except they be sent?"

OFFERTORY PRAYER: Upon the first day of the week according as thou hast prospered us we would bring our offerings to thee, our Father. We would count it all joy to be used as helpers of thy kingdom. Bless us and these gifts of our hands we pray in the name of Christ. Amen.

Illustrative Material

SEED THOUGHTS, HOMILETIC AND EXPOSITORY. The Things We Have Heard: I. A message from heaven. Therefore important. II. No temporary consequence. III. Advantages flowing from duty.

Redemptive Truths: I. They are communicated. "We have heard." II. They are things to be retained. "Should be held" as important forces. III. Their retainment requires most determined effort. The loss of them would be a great calamity. IV. This calamity is possible. Many things tend to relax the soul's grasp upon them.

Letting Truth Slip: I. Great things we have heard. II. The easy peril of their loss. Hours slip. Feet slip. Tide slips. III. The intense attention demanded. —C. M. J.

Choice Evangelistic Illustrations

DRIFTING. One of our papers told of a man who took his book one afternoon during his vacation and strolled down to the river. He climbed into a boat tied to the bank and sat down in the stern to read. The weight of the man as he stepped in had set the boat adrift, but so gentle was the motion and so quiet was the current that he was unconscious of any movement. All at once he heard a sound. He looked up and saw that he was rushing toward the falls. It was only by a desperate effort that he escaped destruction. Drift is one of the most insidious and formidable enemies of the soul. And a close kin to religious drift is indifference which worships neutrality as a virtue.—S. N. Hutchinson, D.D.

IMMEDIATE DUTY. At Fife on the east coast of Scotland, on the shores of the Firth of Forth, are valuable deposits which can be mined only when the tide is out. When the tide turns and comes in, the miners must withdraw. Those few hours alone can be utilized. They are the accepted time.—W. P. Westfall, D.D.

TOMORROW. Tomorrow, and tomorrow, and tomorrow, creeps in this petty pace, from day to day, to the last syllable of recorded time; and all our yesterdays have lighted fools the way to dusty death.—Shakespeare.

OVER THE DOORSTEP. The Arabs have a proverb, "Over the doorstep is half the journey." What do you think of that proverb as applied to the beginnings in discipleship of Christ? Does the proverb apply in the journey of the Christian life? What detail at the beginning of the Christian life would you call "over the doorstep"?

SHUN DELAYS

Shun delays, they breed remorse;
  Take thy time while time is lent thee;
Creeping snails have weakest force;
  Fly their fault, lest thou repent thee.
Good is best when earnest wrought,
  Lingering labors come to naught.
    —Author Unknown.

EVENING SERVICE

Theme: The Desire of Humanity for Christ.

TEXT: "And when they had found him, they said unto him, All men seek for thee." Mark 1:37.

INTRODUCTORY: Christ had sought a lonely place for prayer. The people missed him, felt deprived by his absence and inquired with anxiety, "Where is he?" When the disciples had found him they said, "All men seek for thee." This suggests the fact of the desire or need of all humanity for Christ. The text carries also an unconscious prophecy. What these disciples said in their wondering delight shall one day be literally true. All men will be in search of the Saviour of the world. In the first instance, his coming to earth, the Saviour sought all men. In the second, all men will seek the Saviour.

I. What is it in men that leads them to seek for Christ? There are many motives inducing this search today, just as there were when he was here among men. 1. Curiosity leads men to seek him. In his early ministry in Galilee crowds sought him, following him even into the mountains and deserts. Many were only curious, wanting to see the new Prophet of Nazareth. 2. Admiration leads men to seek him. Even wicked men confess to the beauty of his holiness, and the young and ardent and aspiring feel the marvelous attraction of his person and character. 3. Need and suffering often lead men to seek him. It was so when he was here. It is so still. 4. The sense of personal ill-desert and need of pardon leads men to seek him. Of course, there are yet many other reasons.

II. What is it in Christ that leads men to seek him? 1. Foremost must be placed the fact that he seeks them. He came to seek and to save the lost. "We love him because he first loved us." 2. Then there are his invitations and promises. He has bidden men to seek his help and assured them that they shall not seek in vain. 3. Further inducement is his known power to respond to men's appeals and to satisfy their wants. His gracious and benevolent disposition renders it easy and congenial for people of all ages and conditions to seek him and the blessings he is so ready to bestow.

III. How shall men seek Christ? I. Sincerely. 2. In faith. 3. At once. In the timely present. "Now is the accepted time." We need him now, therefore we should seek him now. 4. Let us give up other seeking to seek and find Christ. Men are tired of their sectarian wranglings. They are wearied out with their ineffectual metaphysical analyses. They are sick of the poor results yielded by material research. They have lost confidence in their own self-will. They prize no longer their self-conceit. They long to be brothers in the embrace of one common Father. No one can bring them together but Christ. "All men seek for thee." May this unconscious prophecy soon be fulfilled!—J. R. T. (Adapted).

Suggested Texts and Themes

Entertaining God: "Behold, I stand at the door, and knock: if any man hear my voice, and open the door, I will come in to him, and will sup with him, and he with me." Rev. 3:20.

The Dangers of Life: "There is but a step between me and death." I Sam. 20:3.

Christ the One Satisfactory Solution of All Problems: "Lord, to whom shall we go? thou hast the words of eternal life." John 6:68.

The Church and Social Service: "Jesus therefore took the loaves; and having given thanks, he distributed to them that were set down; likewise also of the fishes as much as they would." John 6:11 (A.S.V.).

MIDWEEK FELLOWSHIP MEETING TOPIC

(Church Night or Suggestive Sermon Subject)

Theme: The Healing Touch.

TEXT: "And Jesus said, Who touched me?" Luke 8:45.

The whole scene is graphic. The afflicted woman hopelessly incurable. Now providentially near the all-sufficient Saviour. The crowd of pressing people. How the woman felt. What she said to herself. Now the question, "Who touched me?"

I. The question was not one of ignorance. Christ knew. It was to develop the woman's confession, strengthen her faith, and present her to his disciples and the people.

II. The answer to the question Who? It was this timid woman. 1. It was darkness coming into the realm of light. 2. It was disease coming into the region of health. 3. It was weakness recognizing Divine power. 4. It was extremity coming to the fountain of infinite resources. 5. It was self-abasement hiding itself behind the Redeemer. 6. It was faith recognizing Christ's graciousness and power. 7. It was humility and lowliness obtaining their reward. Immediately she was healed!

III. The purposed result of Christ's question. 1. It led to the woman's full confession, enlarged faith, and intensified experience of gratitude and joy. She explained all, v. 47. 2. It led to Christ's bestowal of commendation, comfort and peace, v. 48.

Learn the importance of individual contact with Christ. Behold Christ's great sympathy and power. Discover the simplicity of the way of salvation: trust in Christ and his healing, saving power and willingness.

CHRISTIAN ENDEAVOR SOCIETY TOPIC

Jan. 20. Indispensables for Life: What Provides *Real* Security? Matt. 6: 19-34.

SUNDAY SCHOOL LESSON

Jan. 20. Matthew Becomes a Follower. Matt. 9:9; Luke 5:27-39.

MEMORY SELECTION: "Those who are well have no need of a physician, but those who are sick; I have not come to call the righteous, but sinners to repentance." Luke 5:31, 32 (R.S.V.).

Matthew was a tax collector. Naturally he was unpopular. He was even despised. Yet Christ called him. In him we see a businessman who as a follower forsook his profitable employment to become a disciple of Jesus. Jesus plainly indicated that to follow him requires true repentance, not merely keeping the outward rules and religious observances. His reception of Matthew as a follower did provoke unfavorable discussion, but it also indicated that the socially outcast and unpopular can have in Christ a true friend.

SUNDAY: JANUARY TWENTY-SEVENTH

MORNING SERVICE

Theme: Doing Good Skillfully.

SUGGESTED SCRIPTURE READING: I Thess. 5:1-28. After-petition: May God bless to us this reading from his Word.

SELECTED HYMNS: "Lord, speak to me, that I may speak."—F. R. Havergal. "Take my life and let it be."—F. R. Havergal. "In the vineyard of our Father."—T. MacKellar. "Dear Lord and Master mine."—T. H. Gill. "O Jesus I have promised."—J. E. Bode.

CALL TO WORSHIP: "Thus saith the high and lofty One that inhabiteth eternity, whose name is Holy: I dwell in the high and holy place, with him also that is of a contrite and humble spirit, to revive the spirit of the humble, and to revive the heart of the contrite ones."

INVOCATION PRAYER: Almighty and eternal God, it has pleased thee to call us together into the communion of worship and service. Thou dost not invite thy children to the feast and then absent thyself. Before we begin to hunger the bread is ready, and before we thirst the water is at hand. Thou hast called us into a wondrous inheritance. May we have the lowly faith to claim it and to dwell among the unsearchable riches of Christ. We pray that we may enter more deeply into the glories of thy kingdom. Make us dissatisfied with our present attainments. May we press toward the mark of the prize of the high calling in Christ Jesus. Make us mindful of one another, and in tender sympathy may we bear one another's burdens. Unite us now in sacred reverence, and in the spirit of fuller consecration may we hide under the shadow of thy wings. Amen.—J. H. J.

Theme: Do Good Skillfully.

TEXT: "Let not then your good be evil spoken of." Rom. 14:16.

INTRODUCTORY: "Do good skillfully." That was the dictum of an ancient philosopher. It is in keeping with Paul's admonition here. The admonition is much needed now, and always has been needed. Goodness often has been discounted because it has been subject to so much blundering, so much folly, so much crudeness. It is one thing to do good and quite another thing to do it skillfully, in an unassuming, gracious manner, thus making it doubly attractive. It is remarkable that so much good is actually accomplished in spite of the careless, blundering way in which many people go about it. It shows the rare quality to goodness and how willing people are to accept it. And yet many a good deed is actually lost so far as its abiding value is concerned because it is not done skillfully. It is not enough to dispense charity, but the spirit of charity must be back of the deed. A person may be hardened by the ministry that is offered him. The unskilled manner in which it is dispensed turns sweetness into gall, so that he who receives actually is made to despise the one who gives. "Though I bestow all my goods to feed the poor," says the apostle, "and have not charity, it profiteth me nothing," and so its profit to the poor is quite limited and temporary. Sometimes persons who are committed to a good cause are hard to get along with. They may not know how to work with others or may be lacking in that grace and skill that are essential factors in the enterprise in which they are engaged. The manner in which a good deed is done may be even more important than the deed itself. Learn to do good, but above all learn to do it skillfully.

All the above is quoted from an editorial in *The Religious Telescope* and forms a long introduction to this brief sermon outline. The following points may well be amplified.

The Bible speaks much of the beauty of holiness. This implies wholeness, symmetry of character. Christians are witnesses for Christ; it is therefore their duty to make some fair representation before the world of what he is and what his religion is.

I. Their good may be unskillfully done and therefore evil spoken of when they so use their Christian liberty as to injure their brethren. That is what Paul was stressing in this chapter.

II. Christians may cause their good to be evil spoken of by undue sadness or moroseness. How likely we all are to turn sadness into sourness and thus make a really fine character repulsive Sadness, moroseness and sanctimoniousness all make a false representation of religion.

III. By narrowness. Good people often lay undue stress upon trifles. Paul says that religion does not consist in meat and drink, and to act as if it did is to slander the Gospel. Fanatics and bigots of all classes belie religion.

IV. By censoriousness. Christ's religion never justifies harsh judgments.

V. By hardness, or carrying right principles to excess. A businessman may be in all things severely conscientious, and yet no one likes him. Such hardness may be seen at times in family life. Christ's diamonds, like himself, ought to be full of beauty and grace. Let us not make indifferent things essential, which has a tendency to make essential things indifferent.

VI. By unseasonableness. Character is timeliness. True goodness has a fine perception of what is becoming to the persons, to the place, to the hour. We must have a care to judgment, sympathy, courtesy, or our good will be evil spoken of.

THEME PRAYER: O God of perfect truth and love, we seek after thy perfect life, but we fall so far short of it! Nevertheless, we beseech thee to give us the holy confidence of reaching forth toward perfection in thee. "Let patience have its perfect work" in us. We ask in Christ's name. Amen.

OFFERTORY SENTENCE: "Wherefore do ye spend money for that which is not bread and your labor for that which satisfieth not?"

OFFERTORY PRAYER: We would render unto thee, our Father, the glory due unto thy name, and would bring an offering and come into thy courts. Remember with thy gracious favor those who have brought these gifts and the causes for which they are brought. Let thy blessing so rest upon them that thy kingdom shall be advanced in the world. We ask in Jesus' name. Amen.

Illustrative Material

SEED THOUGHTS, HOMILETIC AND EXPOSITORY. Misrepresented Goodness: I. By sadness. II. By Narrowness. III. By hardness. IV. By unseasonableness. Work with judgment, sympathy, courtesy, or our good will be evil spoken of. —W. L. W.

We Have None Too Much: I. Let not your good be evil spoken of as we have none too much. II. We may cause it through ignorance. III. Through levity of temper. IV. Through moroseness. V. Through want of stability. VI. Through improvidence. VII. Through a number of little things which, like dust on a diamond, obscure its luster. —J. L.

Reputation: I. Easily destroyed. Guard it. II. It is very valuable. Wealth beside it is dross. 1. For our own sake guard it. 2. For society's sake guard it. 3. For the Church's sake guard it.—H. M.

Choice Illustrations on the Theme

DOING GOOD SKILLFULLY. A zealous if not overtactful street missionary once asked a city Arab, "Do you know Jesus?" "No, I don't know Jesus," was the reply, "but I know a friend of his, and I like her." Some good woman by doing good skillfully had done more than she knew for that boy.

CHEERLESS ADVERTISERS. The Rev. Dr. John Henry Jowett once said, "A little while ago I saw a half-dozen sandwichmen walking through the streets of London looking thoroughly pinched and starved and wretched, and their boards carried the advertisement as to where the onlookers could get 'The Best Dinner in London'! Famished wretches advertising the best dinners! Cheerless men and women advertising 'the joy of the Lord'! Heralds in whom there is no buoyancy advertising the Light of Life! No, it is the cheery spirit, the praiseful spirit, that offers the best commendation of the grace of God."

LOOK TO YOUR LIGHT

Has some one seen Christ in you to-day?
Christian, look to your heart, I pray,
The little things you have done or said,
Did they accord with the way you prayed?
Have your thoughts been pure and your words been kind?
Have you sought to have the Saviour's mind?
The world with a criticizing view
Has watched—but did it see Christ in you?

Has some one seen Christ in you to-day?
Christian, look to your life, I pray.
There are aching and blighted souls
Being lost on sin's destructive shoals,
And perhaps of Christ their only view
May be what of Him they see in you.
Will they see enough to bring hope or cheer?
Look to your light—Does it shine out clear?

—Source Unknown.

SKILLFUL TESTIMONY. We are told that it was Benjamin Franklin who discovered that plaster sown in a field would make things grow, that it was a good fertilizer. He told his neighbors; but they would not believe him. Early the next season he went into his field and sowed some grain. Close by the path where men would walk he traced with his fingers some letters and put plaster into them, then sowed the field broadcast. After a short time the seed sprang up. His neighbors as they passed that way were very much surprised to see in brighter green than all the rest of the field the writing in large letters, "This has been plastered." Franklin did not have to argue with his neighbors about the benefit of plaster for fields. This was doing good skillfully.

Some people profess to believe that there is no virtue in the teachings of Christ. But if they see that Christians are patient and gentle and unselfish, kind and thoughtful and pure, they will notice the difference in the human field and will read, "These people are truly Christians."—*5000 Best Modern Illustrations.*

EVENING SERVICE

Theme: The Life of Surrender and Trust.

TEXT: "He shall dwell on high," etc. Isa. 33:16, 17.

INTRODUCTORY: Here is the picture of the man who rests in God and is safe in the Rock. He is "dwelling on high."

I. First, the life of surrender and trust is a life of exaltation. "He shall dwell on high." Those who are kept secure are kept rejoicing. It is not an intermittent experience. "He shall dwell." It is a constant experience because it does not depend on circumstances, but depends on God.

II. Then, too, the life of surrender and trust is a life of safety. "His place of defence shall be the munitions of rocks." And because of safety there is perfect peace. "Thou wilt keep him in perfect peace, whose mind is stayed on thee; because he trusteth in thee."

III. Further, this life is one of continual satisfaction. "His bread shall be given him." There is no lack or leanness in the surrendered life. It is divinely fed with the Bread of Life. It is a life sustained and satisfied, a wholesome and happy life.

IV. Such a life is also one of beauty and refreshment. "His waters shall be sure." The Psalmist speaks of the happy situation of the good man: "He shall be like a tree planted by the rivers of water, that bringeth forth his fruit in his season; his leaf also shall not wither; and whatsoever he doeth shall prosper." The surrendered and trustful life has continual freshness and perennial beauty, with fruitfulness.

V. It is furthermore a life of vision and unlimited outlook. "He shall behold the land that is very far off." "The land of far distances." It is a mountain view. "He dwelleth on high." It is a high view. It is a far view. When one stands and looks down the vistas of eternity he learns a little of what this life means.—G. H. C. M.

Alternate Theme: God and Human Need.

TEXT: "The Lord stood by me, and strengthened me." II Tim. 4:17.

INTRODUCTORY: What do you and I need? It is easy enough to begin a list, starting with what we call "the bare necessities of life"—food, sleep, shelter, a job of work.

I. I am thinking of our need for friendship. That is not an acquired taste, nor something we can readily do without. The lonely life is unnatural. Indeed, solitary confinement is a form of punishment. Looking back quickly over our own life most of us have deep reason to be grateful to God for our friends, for those with whom we have traveled the miles and met the surprises and shocks of the way. Probably we are most grateful for one particular person, a wife, a husband, a parent, a special friend, who has shared life with us, been glad when we were glad, sympathetic and encouraging in our difficulties.

II. Here is another quite different need in all our lives. It is our need for forgiveness, for forgiving others, and being forgiven by them. You know the only way in which we succeed in living happily with one another is by forgiving and forgetting unhappy things which have happened between us which, if they remained unforgiven and unforgotten, would spoil and sour our relationships. Husbands and wives live together happily not because they behave perfectly toward each other—they don't—but because they forgive each other their imperfections. Parents and children get on well together not because the boy never does anything wrong and not because his father never makes a mistake, but because there is mutual forgiveness. Friends stay good friends not because they never hurt or offend each other, but because the hurts and offenses are forgiven and forgotten. We can and do live together by the grace of forgiveness.

III. But you and I have lived long enough to know that we cannot have these things in the way we need them, and when we need them most, on the purely human level; but aren't there some experiences of life which not even our best friend can share with us? Think of those moments just before a major operation, that time of fierce temptation, that day when an unexpected letter knocks the bottom out of things for us. Humanly speaking, you and I have to face these searching hours alone, but can we meet them alone? Well, what has happened for multitudes of men and women who have believed in Christ has been that at such times they have been upheld by a sense of the nearness of their Master. When St. Paul looked back to the hardest experiences of his hard life he wrote: "The Lord stood by me, and strengthened me."

Or think again about our need for forgiveness. Our friends forgive us and so make it possible for our friendship to continue, but can't we all remember times when something like this happened? In an angry or selfish moment, we deeply hurt one of our friends. Later we regretted it, honestly repented of what we had done, and out of the goodness of his heart our friend forgave us. We were happy with our friend again; but we were not happy inside ourselves. Why? Because by some deep instinct of the soul, we knew that the wrong we had done was not only an offense against our friend; it was an offense against the truth, against the right, against the good, in short, an offense against God himself. We have all sinned. We need that God should forgive us and God is ready to forgive, to forgive and to forget, putting our sins behind his back.

The friendship of Christ and the forgiveness of God—these reach down to you and me on the level of our deepest needs. "Our hearts are restless till they find their rest in him."—H. S. S.

Suggested Texts and Themes

Suicidal Sincerity: "And they cried aloud, and cut themselves after their manner with knives and lancets, till the blood gushed out upon them." I Kings 18:28.

A Retreat by the Brook: "And the word of the Lord came unto him, saying, Get thee hence, and turn thee eastward, and hide thyself by the brook Cherith, that is before Jordan." I Kings 17:2, 3.

Beside the Still Waters: "He leadeth me beside the still waters." Ps. 23:2.

The Shade of a Great Rock: "Behold, a king shall reign in righteousness, and princes shall rule in judgment. And a man shall be as a hiding-place from the wind, and a covert from the tempest; as rivers of water in a dry place, as the shadow of a great rock in a weary land." Isa. 32:1, 2.

MIDWEEK FELLOWSHIP MEETING TOPIC

(Church Night or Suggested Sermon Subject)

Theme: Strengthened with All Might.

TEXT: "Strengthened with all might." Col. 1:11.

Strength is required for the Christian's life. The source of all his ability is presented in this passage.

I. Let us think first of the Christian's need of strength. 1. He is to stand fast in the Christian profession. 2. He is to advance in the Christian life. 3. He is to work for his Lord. 4. He is to suffer for Christ—trials, temptations, afflictions. Surely he needs enduring power. He can do nothing worthy without strength.

II. Happily, strength is provided for the Christian. The might of God. The might of the Holy Spirit. The power of Christ. Such might is all-sufficient. "As thy days so shall thy strength be."

III. The process of strengthening the Christian. It is through God's almightiness. 1. This must be known. 2. It must be accepted. 3. It must be used.

IV. Some evidences that we are thus strengthened. 1. Abiding patience. 2. Activity. 3. Joyfulness.

CHRISTIAN ENDEAVOR SOCIETY TOPIC

Jan. 27. Committed to Christ. II Cor. 5:17; Eph. 4:20-32. (Denominational Day.)

SUNDAY SCHOOL LESSON

Jan. 27. Nicodemus a Hesitant Follower. John 3:1-10; 7:45-52.

MEMORY SELECTION: "Truly, truly, I say to you, unless one is born anew, he cannot see the kingdom of God." John 3:3 (R.S.V.).

Nicodemus was the man who came by night. He was a member of the Sanhedrin. He was strongly drawn to Christ, yet because of his scholarly caution and his official position found a public confession of Christ difficult. Later references to him indicate his continued interest and partial devotion to Christ, yet by his indecision and delay he lost much priceless fellowship with him. He is a type of those who must risk position and power if they are to be loyal to the Saviour. Let us be out-and-out Christians, loyal to Christ, enthusiastic in devotion to him.

SUNDAY: FEBRUARY THIRD

MORNING SERVICE

Theme: What Is Religion?

SUGGESTED SCRIPTURE READING: James 1:1-27.

SELECTED HYMNS: " 'Tis by faith of joys to come."—I. Watts. "O Everlasting Light."—H. Bonar. "Walk in the light, so shall thou know."—B. Barton. "My God, permit me not to be."—I. Watts. "Rise, my soul, and stretch thy wings."—R. Seagrave.

CALL TO WORSHIP: "Ask, and it shall be given you; seek, and ye shall find; knock, and it shall be opened unto you: for every one that asketh receiveth; and he that seeketh findeth; and to him that knocketh it shall be opened."

INVOCATION PRAYER: Our Father who art in heaven; hallowed be thy name; thy kingdom come; thy will be done on earth as it is in heaven. We thank thee that thou dost set before us a goal so high, an attainment so lofty. For in thee we find the realization of our highest ideal of goodness and of truth—and more! And to be like thee is our goal. Help us to find in thy searching precepts and requirements not discouragement, as demanding from us more than we are able to perform, but inspiration and courage. May they be to us a trumpet-call to high endeavor. Quicken, we pray thee, and multiply in us these impulses toward worthier things. May we be witnesses for Christ. May his life be our life, his deeds our deeds, his teaching our teaching. Through the indwelling power of his Spirit, may the high be not too high for us, the heroic not too hard. All of which we humbly ask in his name and for his sake. Amen.—H. C. Vedder.

Theme: What Is Religion?

TEXT: "Keep yourselves in the love of God." Jude 21.

INTRODUCTORY: It is not easy to frame a definition of religion. Religion is a full circle and we are in danger of being satisfied with a segment of it. So there are many errors made in seeking to define religion. They are due in every case to a partial or fragmentary view of truth. Let us notice some of the errors that have been made in seeking to define religion.

I. One mistake is to define religion as dogma. What do we mean by dogma? A truth becomes dogma to any mind the moment it is apprehended as proven beyond peradventure. A creed is a system of such truths. The malady of our age is credo-phobia. It is the fashion to say that creed is a matter of slight importance as long as we live well. But before we fall in with that assertion let us be sure that we mean it. The grocer whom you patronize must have a creed; he must believe that there are sixteen ounces to the pound, that sand is not sugar, that chicory is not coffee, and that honesty is the best policy. If he does not have a code of principles, that is to say, a creed made up of such simple truths, you will not patronize him. You will not cast your vote for a candidate who has not a creed; he must believe in an honest ballot, a sound currency, a just system of tariff, a wise adjustment of the rights of the individual states to those of the general government, etc. If you wish to cross the ocean, you will take ship with a captain who has a creed; who believes in sun and quadrant, in compass and chart. So in any department of life, a man is untrustworthy unless he have a creed; that is, unless he can say, I believe in something. So, indeed, should any man who is traveling on to eternity. He should satisfy himself at once and beyond misgiving of the truth or falsity of the great propositions that center in

God. But a creed is not the sum total of religion; it is a segment of the circle, but it is not the circle. We cannot be religious without a creed, but a creed alone will not make us religious.

II. A second mistake is to say that religion is a life. That is, it is a creed crystallized, vivified in good works. There is a measure of truth in this statement; for faith without works is dead. But good works are not all. They do not make a complete definition of religion; "for by the deeds of the law shall no flesh be justified." The hand like the head is a necessary part of the body, but not the whole of it; nor indeed the vital center of it.

III. A third mistake is to say or think that religion is a cult, or a particular form of worship. Rites and ceremonies are not to be belittled. The Church is of divine appointment. Its two sacraments, baptism and the Lord's Supper, were instituted by Christ himself. No man who loves the bridegroom will disparage or ignore the bride; our Lord himself honored the ritual of the house of God. But there is an immense difference between Churchianity and Christianity. Let us not, therefore, depend upon our church membership alone. A man may be a member of the church in good and regular standing and still have no place in the Lamb's book of life.

IV. A fourth mistake is to define religion as a sentiment. I would to God that we were all more tender of heart, more sensitive and quick to noble thought and purpose. The great truths are of such importance that our feelings should be profoundly stirred by them. "God!" "Calvary!" "The Judgment!" "Heaven!" "Hell!" There are worlds of meaning in these simple words; the very mention of each should thrill us instantly through and through. But while feeling is an important factor in religion, it must not be made to overshadow all. There is one thing better than feeling; that is duty. So let us attend to the affairs of our Christian life, praying God to keep our hearts warm and eager and full of the enthusiasm of truth and righteousness, but resolute, with or without feeling, to do what duty shall require.

V. Having canvassed some of the partial views of religion, let us approach its full definition in this injunction, "Keep yourselves in the love of God." But how? Can I force myself to love God? No. I enkindle my love toward God by contemplating him. But where shall I behold God? In the person of Jesus Christ. It is to this very end that he has made himself manifest in the flesh, that we might behold him and love him. Behold the beginning and the midst and the end of the whole matter: Love God. All else must follow. All noble purposes and all holy aspirations are under the dominion of love toward God. If we love him, our creed will follow; for we shall believe what he says. If we love him, we shall not fall short of the good works of a useful life; for we shall tread closely in the footsteps of him who went about doing good. If we love him, we shall honor his Church; because the Church is the bride of God. If we love him, our hearts will thrill in response to all the great verities which center in him.—D. J. B.

Theme Prayer: Vouchsafe unto us, O Lord, a steady devotion to the things that are true, honest, just, pure, lovely, and of good report, in the confidence that with these is the secret of life: through Jesus Christ our Lord. Amen.

Offertory Sentence: "To do good, and to distribute, forget not; for with such sacrifices God is well pleased."

Offertory Prayer: We recognize, our Father, that we are not our own, that we are bought with a price, we would therefore glorify thee in our bodies and our spirits, which are thine. Wilt thou therefore graciously accept and bless these offerings of thy people for the promotion of thy kingdom. We ask in Christ's name. Amen.

Illustrative Material

Seed Thoughts, Homiletic and Expository. Self-keeping: I. The work of self-keeping. 1. Keep an eye upon ourselves. An eye that is clear and true.

2. Keep a hand upon ourselves. A hand that is steady and strong. II. The means to be employed in self-keeping. 1. Be active. "Building up themselves." In order to conserve we must construct. "In our most holy faith." 2. Prayer is an occupation of upbuilding of Christian character. 3. Pray in the Holy Ghost. Encompassed by his power. Informed by his light. III. The Encouragement to be sought in self-keeping. 1. "Looking for mercy." "Building up yourselves." "Live soberly, righteously, and godly." "Cheering yourselves." Keeping yourselves." "Looking for the happy hope." "Looking for mercy." Still mercy, after our building, praying, keeping.—J. A. K. B.

Keeping in the Love of God: I. By building upon Christ. Go on building upon Christ. II. By praying in the Holy Ghost. What believer does not know his need of the Holy Spirit? III. By expecting mercy through Christ. "Looking also for the mercy," etc. IV. The effects of true spiritual religion. Happiness. Hope. Experience. Usefulness.—C. C.

Choice Illustrations on the Theme

THINGS TO BE AVOIDED. In order to keep ourselves in the love of God there are things to be avoided. We should shun carefully everything that would be likely to dampen the fervor of our affections or extinguish the holy fire. If we have taken Christ as our Master let us follow him. When a dog is following two men their parting shows which is master. Sin and holiness do not proceed along the same road. We must choose which way we will go. Avoid also the indulgence of a worldly spirit. We have read of a boy who tied his horse to his arm. The horse ran away and the boy was much injured. We must hold the world so loosely that it can never drag us with it.—H.

WISE STRATEGY. To keep ourselves in the love of God never parley with temptation. Temptation is an enemy outside the castle gate seeking by persuasive words to gain an entrance, but when once let in we will find it a Trojan horse full of armed men to overcome us. And never compromise with sin. Never say, "I will choose the least of two evils." Choose neither! Because it was cold the camel asked the Arab to let him put his head within the door of his tent. There being no hindrance, he got in with his forefeet. Then with his whole body. "Hold!" cried the Arab, "there is not room enough for two!" "Then," said the camel, "you had better get out!" That is the way it always ends. Compromises with sin are always dangerous.—*Preacher's Assistant.*

TO KEEP YOURSELF IN THE LOVE OF GOD. To keep yourself in the love of God there are things to be done. Religion is not a series of don'ts. We cannot pump darkness out of a room. It cannot be forced out. Open the windows and let in the light! So we cannot force evil out of the soul except by letting God in. What are some of the things that let light into the soul? What are some of the things that let God into the soul? They are such as these: prayer, study of the Bible, meditation, association with Christian companions, the preserving of a tender conscience, the engaging in every form of Christian service. If we would keep ourselves in the love of God we must cultivate the graces of the Christian life and imitate Christ in deeds of mercy and loving-kindness.—*Preacher's Assistant.*

IT REQUIRES SOME TIME. In these days many are so filled with bustle, and noise, and hurry, and excitement, and fret, and criticism, and everlasting talkativeness that they cannot discover the gentle tick of God's telegraphic messages or the soft cooing of the heavenly Dove, or the footsteps of the coming King. Neither can they know what is going on in their own hearts.—G. D. Watson.

IT REQUIRES ALONENESS WITH GOD. In these days of hurry and bustle we find ourselves face to face with a terrible danger, and it is this—no time to be alone with God. The world is running fast. We live in what is called the "age of progress," and we must keep pace with the times. So the world says. But the spirit of the world has not confined itself to the world. It is, alas, to be found among the professed people of God. And what is the result? The result is no time to be alone with God, and this is immediately followed by no inclination to be alone with God. This naturally greatly interferes with our "keeping ourselves in the love of God." —H.

EVENING SERVICE

Theme: Boasting in the Lord.

TEXT: "My soul shall make her boast in the Lord." Ps. 34:2.

INTRODUCTORY: It is high time that Christian folk followed the example of the Psalmist and gave themselves to the exhilarating practice of boasting in the Lord. We ought to do it more than we do, firstly because there is very good reason why we should boast, solidly, steadily, unashamedly. Then, too, we ought to do it because it would constitute a pleasant change from the tone of almost abject apology in which we find even convinced Christians speaking of the Faith and the Church which embodies that Faith. We have reason to do it, and examples manifold, if only we follow out the New Testament itself.

I. Let us then boast—though not of ourselves. God forbid! But let us, as we have cause, boast ourselves in the Lord. There are a multitude of matters about which we can boast, but just to show that we have cause to do so even in the most unlikely places let us consider now that which is held by many to be least worthy of any boast, that is, the Church. There are many ready to hurl destructive criticism at the Church. There is in fact so much in which our souls can boast of God as seen in his Church that it is hard to know where to begin. But come to the proof: let us now take some of the great New Testament assertions which from the beginning have been by many applied to the Church, and let us see whether or not these words of prayer and prophecy have come true. If they have, then we can boast indeed.

1. Take first the word of Jesus which is recorded for us at the beginning of the book of Acts. There, we are told, the Risen Lord said to his own: "Ye shall be witnesses unto me both in Jerusalem, and in all Judaea, and in Samaria, and unto the uttermost part of the earth." Now this has plainly and obviously happened. It has become progressively more plain and actual on the page of history from that day to this. Why then should we go around looking wistful, apologetic? This is the work of God and it is wonderful in our eyes. Let us then make our boast in the Lord.

2. Consider also the words of Jesus given to us in St. John's Gospel: "I say unto you, He that believeth on me, the works that I do shall he do also; and greater works than these shall he do; because I go unto my Father." Now, once again, it is plain, obvious, irrefutable truth that this has happened, in the mercy of God. Quantitatively, it is true that greater works than he did have since been done in his name. From obscure Galilee, from tiny Nazareth, from a little room in Jerusalem, power has gone forth from him to the ends of the earth. Why should we grovel? Why apologize? Rather let us make our boast in the Lord our God and all that he has done for us and is still doing toward us.

II. And further than this we can go. There may be those who would allow all that has gone before, and would yet feel that our claim to boast in God breaks down at one crucial point. A great deal of present talk about the unity of the Church is marred by unconsidered acceptance in the premises of the argument of the mathematical idea of unity as the only one that is valid. Yet this is not the case. We are all aware of that unity in diversity which characterizes, for example, a true family, or which is to be seen among the disciples of our Lord. I am not one of those who hanker greatly after anything approaching a lifeless, mathematically understood unity of the Body of Christ. I rather imagine that so long as men are men there must be diversities of calling, but the one Spirit.

III. But it may be that there are many who still feel critical; who are a little unconvinced. Certainly there are some who would wish to say: "This is all very well, but some plain and bitter facts still remain. The world is not yet Christian; individual Christians do not always love each other as they might; indeed, hypocrisy is still an all too prevalent sin."

Yet even so, and accepting the full burden of the incongruity between the ideal and the actual in many lives, still "My soul shall make her boast in the Lord." Is there any other political, social, ethical group of our day which takes men and women just as they are, rich and poor, ignorant and enlightened, vicious and cultured, black, yellow, red, and white, takes them all just as they come, young and old, hale and infirm, and receiving them all within the fold yet answers with the army of saints, making indeed its army of saints out of the very nondescript collection of humanity that gathers within its gates?

This is the Church to which we belong; this is the cause we are called to serve; this is the dimension of our discipleship of him who is the Head of the Church. We are a part of a huge, resolute army which is advancing resolutely, and will advance even more resolutely as all of us together imbibe the fighting spirit of the Psalmist and go to the conquest of other lands as our souls make their boast in the Lord our God.—S. M.

MIDWEEK FELLOWSHIP MEETING TOPIC

(Church Night or Suggested Sermon Subject)

Theme: Walking in the Truth.

TEXT: "I have no greater joy than to hear that my children walk in truth." III John 4.

Here is shown the anxiety the apostles displayed for the spiritual welfare of their flocks.

I. What is it to walk in truth? 1. It implies attachment to the doctrines of the Gospel. Error is dangerous. 2. It implies sincerity of conduct, not more profession. 3. It implies closeness of walk and conformity to the spirit of Christ. He is truth. Conform to his way.

II. The means by which such a walk may be promoted. 1. By a close acquaintance with the Word of Truth. "Let the word of Christ dwell in you richly." 2. By attendance upon the means of grace. "They that wait upon the Lord shall renew their strength." 3. By fervent prayer.

III. The motives by which we should be influenced. 1. For Christ's sake. 2. For the Church's sake. 3. For our own sake. Safety, comfort, usefulness, future glory.—B.

CHRISTIAN ENDEAVOR SOCIETY TOPIC

Feb. 3. United in Christ. Rom. 12:4, 5; Eph. 4:1-4. (Christian Endeavor Day.)

BULLETIN BOARD SLOGANS FOR THE MONTH

By Earl Riney

Knowledge is, in every country, the surest basis of public happiness.—Washington.

I cannot think of a man who is not wiser today than he was yesterday.—A. Lincoln.

It is possible to make a sound argument without a lot of noise.

A life of beauty and usefulness will never pass into nothingness.

The freedom of the individual is the core of American strength.

Freedom of religion does not mean freedom from religion.

Everything that you love is yours.

Practice courtesy at home if you wish it to become a habit.

There is no duty so much underestimated as the duty of being happy.—R. L. Stevenson.

A handful of common sense is worth a bushel of learning.

SUNDAY SCHOOL LESSON

Feb. 3. A Pharisee and a Repentant Woman. Luke 7:36-50.

MEMORY SELECTION: "If we confess our sins, he is faithful and just to forgive us our sins, and to cleanse us from all unrighteousness." I John 1:9.

This is a study of contrasting attitudes. The respectable Pharisee, interested in, yet not yielding to Christ. The sinful woman confesses, repents and is forgiven by Christ. She shows great love to him. To be self-righteous shuts Christ out of our lives. To desire to be different opens the way for him. This lesson reveals Christ's compassion for the sinful, and that unrighteousness prevents the understanding and following of Christ. Faith, love and confession are the doors to salvation.

SUNDAY: FEBRUARY TENTH

MORNING SERVICE

Theme: Divine Compensations.

SUGGESTED SCRIPTURE READING: II Chron. 25:5-9; Matt. 25:14-23.

SELECTED HYMNS: "How shall I follow him I serve?"—J. Conder. "Take my life and let it be."—F. R. Havergal. "Through good report and evil."—H. Bonar. "Jesus calls us o'er the tumult."—C. F. Alexander.

CALL TO WORSHIP: "The Lord is nigh unto all them that call upon him, to all that call upon him in truth. He will fulfil the desire of them that fear him: he also will hear their cry, and will save them."

INVOCATION PRAYER: Almighty and eternal God, creator of the universe and Father of our spirits, we worship thee. Far off from us thou never art, but by the unresponsiveness of our own hearts we keep thee distant. Grant unto us in this hour of opportunity the grace of receptiveness, that into hospitable souls we may receive thee, thou spirit of goodness and beauty and truth. Cross the inner thresholds of our hearts, lay hold upon our faith, steady our faltering spirits, and with such inner refreshment send us out to be soldiers of the common good, that we may be equal to all the demands that shall be made upon us. Graciously answer our prayer according to thy will, O God. Send down thy Spirit upon thy Church, that all nations may become disciples of Jesus Christ our Lord. In his name we pray. Amen and amen.

Theme: Divine Compensations.

TEXT: "The Lord is able to give thee much more than this." II Chron. 25:9.

INTRODUCTORY: Amaziah, King of Judah, hired for a hundred talents of silver an army out of the Northern Kingdom of Israel. A prophet warned him not to employ the army of Israel, "for the Lord is not with Israel." Amaziah, thinking of his big investment, possibly the modern equivalent of a quarter of a million dollars, asked the prophet, "But what shall we do for the hundred talents which I have given to the army of Israel?" The man of God answered, "The Lord is able to give thee much more than this."

When a man makes a sacrifice or suffers loss for the sake of conscience and in obedience to God, God has ways of compensating him and rewarding him.

Amaziah is not the only man who has been compelled to choose between obedience to God or self-denial. Soul or silver! Picture the matter again. Like some of our modern military aggressors Amaziah was devoured by ambition and vainglory. He coveted the domains of his neighbors, greedy of conquest. He had his eye on the land of the Edomites. There was probably no reason why he should, for the inhabitants of Seir apparently had done nothing to provoke an attack. But Amaziah desired more territory. He had raised an army, but desiring to be on the safe side, he had bargained for a hundred thousand men of Israel and paid the bounty. Just then the prophet confronts him with the announcement that if he takes the troops of Israel with him he shall be defeated. Now comes the struggle. What about that big bounty? The command of God had touched his pocket-nerve and it had sent a sensitive shock through his whole being.

I. Let us then consider first the duty faced. "Let not the armies of Israel go with thee." It was God's disapproval of union with the enemies of truth. And God's command will not bear delay. "Send the army of Israel away." But Amaziah hesitated because there was a self-made difficulty in the way. So today, duty and worldly profits or pleasures may stand in each other's way.

II. The difficulty stated. "And Amaziah said to the man of God, But what shall we do for the hundred talents which I have given to the army of Israel?" There was the divided mind, the difficulty faced. On the one side was the fear of God's displeasure, on the other, the hundred talents weighed down his purpose. How could he brook the loss of so large a sum?

III. The reward of obedience. It is suggested in the unanswerable reply, "And the man of God answered, The Lord is able to give thee much more than this." There was no promise of the restoration of the exact hundred talents of silver. But this, human obedience and Divine compensations. God is able to remunerate fidelity. Bring God into the matter. Bring God into your business, your pleasures, your social contacts, all your worldly interests. That may alter them altogether.

THEME PRAYER: We thank thee, our Father, that in our perplexities we have an ever-present guide, thy voice within. Help us to have good consciences. Illumine for us all the paths of duty and, having heard thy voice, may we obey it always and everywhere. In the name of Christ we ask. Amen.

OFFERTORY SENTENCE: "Every man according as he purposeth in his heart, so let him give; not grudgingly, or of necessity: for God loveth a cheerful giver."

OFFERTORY PRAYER: Thy kingdom come; thy will be done, on earth as it is in heaven. May we be helpers of the kingdom. To this end receive and bless the offerings which we bring. Use them for the advancement of thy cause and kingdom. Graciously use us also, and bless us as we lay our gifts upon the altar of service. In Jesus' name we ask. Amen.

Illustrative Material

SEED THOUGHTS, HOMILETIC AND EXPOSITORY. Consequences: I. It is the doing of a fool to disdain consequences. II. Amaziah's history makes plain when we should weigh consequences and be guided by them. III. Wherever we are sure duty leads there we should go. IV. To disdain consequences should never be done in a boasting or vainglorious spirit. V. There are Divine consequences for doing self-sacrificing duty. VI. Throw eternity into the scale of duty and interest.—K. H. B.

Compensations: I. Men's apparent interests are sometimes opposed to the commands of God. II. When this is the case apparent interests are to be sacrificed. III. For the alternative lies between total defeat and increased good. In either case the wisest thing is to give up the "silver" and obey.—K. H. B.

Choice Illustrations on the Theme

WHAT SHALL I DO? One man argues, "I can make more money selling dry goods than groceries, so I will deal in dry goods." But ultimately he adds, "There is more money in selling whiskey than either groceries or dry goods, so I think I will open a saloon." He looks at trade from his own standpoint. It seems that there are some men who really think that they are justified in such a course. They say that a man ought to look after his own interests. That is common sense; that is the first thing to be consulted, they say. There never was a greater mistake in this selfish world. The truth is that when a man deliberately marks out a course of conduct, and determines to pursue it without any consideration of God and fellow men he is in a very dangerous business. There are other things to be considered besides money. Soul-culture, helpfulness to others, influence for Christ, the increasing joys of a good life—these things are to be taken into account. If your business stands between you and God, let it go! There are Divine compensations.

BRING GOD IN. When the first English missionaries were sent to India Dr. Cope died on the voyage. Some letters of introduction to English gentlemen in India had been written. When others in the party arrived they went on shore and told how Dr. Cope had died and was buried at sea. As these knew nothing of the language of India the advice was given, "Take the first vessel that sails for England and go back home." One of the young men of the party said, "That is out of the question. I came here to preach the Gospel and, God helping me, I mean to do it." They said, "If you bring God into the matter, that alters it altogether." Bring God into your business, your pleasures, your social contacts, all your interests. That may alter things altogether.—Charles Garrett.

FIDELITY REMUNERATED. I know a widow whose husband died and left her with a little family to struggle for. She opened a little shop in the suburbs of the city, when one of the agents of a wine merchant waited upon her to ask her to be an agent for the sale of strong drink. She said, "Never a drop shall enter my house." He said, "It will help you very much." She said, "If it helps me some, it will harm me more. I have children around me, and whether I prosper or not, I decline to gain anything to the injury of my fellow beings."

She has done wonderfully. An intimate friend of mine went to see her and said, "I cannot understand how you get on, and why so many come to your shop, for they pass any number of good shops to come to yours." She said to her young son, "John, you are fond of ciphering; get your slate and put down how far off a man must live from my shop that God cannot bring him there." That settled it. God is able to remunerate fidelity.—Charles Garrett.

EVENING SERVICE

Theme: The Joy of the Lord Our Strength.

TEXT: "For the joy of the Lord is your strength." Neh. 8:10.

INTRODUCTORY: How different this is from what so many people think about religion. They consider religion to be a sadness, a weakness, far from being the "joy of the Lord," or any kind of joy. When Nehemiah called upon the people to joy in the Lord he at the same time told them what effect it would produce. It would not be sadness or weakness, nor would it produce either. It would be their strength.

I. First let us notice this fact that believers are called upon to rejoice. Christians do not rejoice as much as they ought. Paul said, "Rejoice in the Lord always, and again I say rejoice." We do not do it enough. All deep religion ought to be joyful. All strong religion assuredly will be.

II. But this "joy of the Lord," what is it? It is a joy which finds its source in the Lord. In its very nature it is pure. It is elevating. It is solid. It is durable. It is heavenly. It is divine.

III. How can we get it? It is the joy of which the Holy Spirit is the author. "The fruit of the Spirit is love, joy, peace." It is not something that we can get by seeking it for its own sake. It comes indirectly, by fulfilling its conditions.

IV. What are we assured that this joy will do for us? "The joy of the Lord is your strength." When Nehemiah called upon the people to rejoice in the Lord he told them at the same time, as we have said, what effect it would produce in them. It would be their strength. And it will be our strength. 1. It will support the Christian under all difficulties. 2. It will sustain us amid all temptations. 3. It will encourage the Christian in the performance of all duties. 4. It will make duties which without it would be burdensome and irksome to be pleasant. 5. It will encourage him in prayer. 6. It will incite him to persevere and to hold on to the end, for he who has the joy of the Lord for his strength will not rest in present attainments. It will do still other things for us. It will give value to our testimony, to the testimony of our life and influence, when others see us joyful in our religion. And it will enable us to accomplish more works for God, more service, for no one works well whose heart is not in it.

"The joy of the Lord is your strength." The joy of faith is strengthening. Christ came with glad tidings. Faith grows by fellowship with him. The joy of a free conscience is strengthening. The joy of Divine companionship is strengthening. The joy of love for Christ is strengthening, for what will not love for him constrain us to do? "The joy of the Lord is your strength."—H.

Additional Theme: Charging God Foolishly.

TEXT: "In all this Job sinned not, nor charged God foolishly." Job 1:22.

INTRODUCTORY: Here was a most commendable resignation to the will of God. Job was in deepest trouble. The two opposite states of prosperity and adversity equally require vigilance and caution. There is no crime more incident to those whose life is embittered with calamities and whom afflictions have reduced to gloominess and melancholy than that of repining at the determinations of Providence, or of "charging God foolishly."

I. Such are often tempted to unseemly inquiries into the reasons for God's dispensations. This is both foolish and wicked.

II. Such are liable to expostulations about the justice of that decision which condemned them to their present sufferings.

III. And such are likely also to look upon the lives of those whom they account happier than they are with an eye of malice and suspicion. Especially if they see those persons no better than they, they think themselves almost justified in murmuring at their own state.

IV. The unreasonableness of this attitude may be seen by reflecting upon the attributes of God. 1. He is creator. 2. He is wise. 3. He is just. 4. He is loving.

V. The unreasonableness of this attitude may be seen by reflecting upon the ignorance of man.—S. J.

Suggested Texts and Themes

The World's Only Hope: "There is none other name under heaven given among men, whereby we must be saved." Acts 4:12.

The Brotherhood of Men: "God hath made of one blood all nations of men," etc. Acts 17:26.

The Story Must Be Told: "How shall they believe in him of whom they have not heard?" Rom. 10:14.

Why Missions? "The love of Christ constraineth us." II Cor. 5:14.

Human Equality: "God will have all men to be saved, and to come unto the knowledge of the truth." I Tim. 2:4.

MIDWEEK FELLOWSHIP MEETING TOPIC

(Church Night or Suggested Sermon Subject)

Theme: The Momentous Question.

TEXT: "Is there any word from the Lord? And Jeremiah said, There is." Jer. 37:17.

The man who asked this momentous question was a solemn trifler. He was

King Zedekiah, threatened with a siege of Jerusalem. He sent for Jeremiah the prophet secretly to give him private audience as an ambassador from God. The king asked, "Is there any word from the Lord?"—any word of comfort? Can you give us any hope that the Chaldeans will again retire?

I. Note first that the king came with his question to the right quarter. To the prophet. To the man who had a living connection with God. Friend, carry your momentous questions to wise Christians, but especially to God.

II. Yet we know from the way the king treated the answer to the question that he came in the wrong spirit. Not that there was any gaiety or carelessness about his attitude. He was as solemn as could be when he asked the question. But he went away and by action showed he had been merely trifling with the question. The same is possible to us. It is too common among men.

III. The answer to the king's question was, "There is." "Is there any word from the Lord?" "There is." Failure to heed the answer brought great suffering to the king and to others. "Take heed how ye hear." Take heed how you treat what you hear.

CHRISTIAN ENDEAVOR SOCIETY TOPIC

Feb. 10. Christian Citizenship Overcomes Prejudices. Acts 10:19-28. (Race Relations Sunday.)

SUNDAY SCHOOL LESSON

Feb. 10. The Decision of Two Rich Men. Luke 18:18-23; 19:1-10.

MEMORY SELECTION: "Enter by the narrow gate; for the gate is wide and the way is easy, that leads to destruction, and those who enter by it are many. For the gate is narrow and the way is hard, that leads to life, and those who find it are few." Matt. 7:13, 14 (R.S.V.)

Each of these men finds himself confronted by Christ's challenge. One draws back. The other yields promptly. The rich young man was not willing to consecrate himself or his wealth to Christ. Zacchaeus, the taxgatherer, coming to know Christ yielded to him and began to pay fourfold all that he had wrongfully exacted from others. Jesus in both instances shows his concern equally for both rich and poor. Whosoever will may be saved.

SUNDAY: FEBRUARY SEVENTEENTH

MORNING SERVICE

Theme: The Earliest Name for Christianity.

SUGGESTED SCRIPTURE READING: Acts 9:1-22.

SELECTED HYMNS: "O gift of gifts, O grace of faith."—F. W. Faber. "Beneath the cross of Jesus."—E. C. Clephane. "My faith looks up to Thee."—R. Palmer. "Rejoice, the Lord is King."—C. Wesley.

CALL TO WORSHIP: "We have thought of thy lovingkindness, O God, in the midst of thy temple. As is thy name, O God, so is thy praise unto the ends of the earth."

INVOCATION PRAYER: Most gracious God, who art not far from any one of us, teach us how to call upon thee in truth. Stir up our hearts that we forget not all thy benefits. Day by day thou givest us our daily health and reason, our daily bread, and sunshine and work and rest. We bless thee most of all for thy daily patience, thy longsuffering mercy and restoring love. Thou knowest the secrets of our hearts, cleanse us from all pride and selfishness and graciously pardon all our sins. Strengthen our wills to do the right. Let thy countenance rest upon us as we wait together in thy house today. Let thy tender mercies rest upon us and upon all whom we love here and in all places of thy dominion. We ask through Jesus Christ our Saviour. Amen.

Theme: The Earliest Name for Christianity.

TEXT: "And desired of him letters to Damascus to the synagogues, that if he found any of this way, whether they were men or women, he might bring them bound unto Jerusalem." Acts 9:2.

INTRODUCTORY: This title, "The Way," seems to have been the earliest name for what we now call Christianity. It was the term by which the faith of Christ was spoken of chiefly perhaps among the Jews. The term means a peculiar doctrine or sect. Its application to Christians is most frequently used here in the book of Acts. Examples: 19:9, many "spake evil of that way"; 22:4, Paul said, "I persecuted this way unto the death"; again, 24:14, "after the way which they call heresy, so worship I the God of my fathers"; again, speaking of Felix he said, 24:22, "when Felix heard these things, having more perfect knowledge of that way." A fuller expression is used in II Pet. 2:2, "By reason of whom the way of truth shall be evil spoken of." Jesus himself had used the term in a very significant manner saying, "I am the Way," John 14:6. We may well compare with this the name "Christian," which was first applied to converts at Antioch, Acts 11:26. It began as a taunt and became accepted as an honorable title.

But of yet earlier use than the name Christian was this one of "The Way." Filling the title with the larger meaning of our later knowledge let us consider the title as a description of Christianity.

I. First, it is a way of thinking. It is a characteristic of Christianity that it has its own peculiar way of thinking about God, about man, about sin, about redemption or salvation. This way of thinking is claimed to be under the guidance of a special Divine revelation. The starting-point of this way of thinking is that God has "in these last days spoken unto us by his Son."

It may well be said that there is still a way of thinking characteristic of Christ's disciples. Within a large liberty, there are well-defined lines beyond which the thinking becomes disloyal to Christ and is unworthy of the Christian name. Yes, Christianity is a way of thinking.

II. Then, too, it is a way of feeling. Every true disciple of Christ is distinguished by his admiration for, his trust in, and love to the Lord Jesus Christ. In the Early Church the loyalty and the love were so strong that the disciples could endure shame and even death for his sake. "The love of Christ constraineth us."

And still this supreme motive, our "way of feeling" about Christ, should mark us off from all the world. Men should be able to "take knowledge of us that we have been with Jesus," that he has won our very hearts and that to us henceforth "to live is Christ." Everything in the way of power to serve and of Christian joy depends upon our maintaining fresh and strong this way of feeling. Yes, Christianity is a way of feeling.

III. As we have already intimated, it is also a way of working. Christianity is a thing to be promoted. Christ said, "Go ye into all the world, and preach the gospel to every creature." We call that his Great Commission. There are innumerable modes and methods characteristic of Christians in working for the glory of God and the good of men. They are so many we must not even begin to recount them. But truly Christianity is a way of working.

IV. Possibly equally important, if not more so, more fundamental, it is a way of living. Both by our lips and by our lives we are to express the holy gospel we profess. By their fruits of godliness and love the early Christians were known. The Christian way is a way of righteousness, of right conduct. It is a way of consecration, laying all our possessions and powers, all our attainments and opportunities upon God's altar, devoting them to his service.

V. It might well be added that the Christian way is a way of expectation. "All this here and heaven besides." Amplify.—R. T. (Adapted).

THEME PRAYER: Grant, our Heavenly Father, that the seed that has fallen into our lives this day may find fertile soil, and bring forth fruit. And wherein we ourselves have sown, do thou uproot the tares and give thy blessing to go with every act of good: for thy Name's sake. Amen.

OFFERTORY SENTENCE: "Charge them that are rich in this world, . . . that they do good, that they be rich in good works, ready to distribute, willing to communicate."

OFFERTORY PRAYER: O Thou who art the Lord and Master of us all, teach us to render day by day an account of our stewardship to thee. All that we have of time and talents and possessions are thine; and we are thine, bought with a price. We long to be good stewards of thy manifold mercies. Wilt thou graciously receive and bless and use these the gifts of thy people to the extension of thy kingdom of righteousness and peace in the world. We ask in Jesus' name. Amen.

Illustrative Material

SEED THOUGHTS, HOMILETIC AND EXPOSITORY. The Way: Familiar synonym for the disciples of Christ. See Acts 9:23; 22:4; 24:14, 22. It may have originated in Christ's claim to be himself the "Way."—P.

The Way: I. The Way is for lost wanderers. Man's need of a Way of salvation. This need arises out of man's ignorance, errors, sin, danger. Lost. II. The Way is Christ. "I am the Way." He is "the new and living Way." III. To what end? Way to God. To heaven. The Way is wisely planned. It is clear and plain. It is straight and narrow. IV. The Way is for all men. —T.

The Way: I. Discover it. It is not hard to find. II. Walk in it. Take no other. It is one of two. III. It is vain to praise it unless you make it yours. IV. Persevere in it. V. Point it out to others.—J. R. T.

Choice Illustrations on the Theme

WHAT IS TRUE RELIGION? Tennyson was walking one day in a beautiful flower garden where many flowers were blooming, and a friend said, "Mr. Tennyson, you speak so often of Jesus. Will you tell me what Christ really means to your life?" Tennyson stopped, and pointing down to a beautiful yellow flower said, "What the sun is to that flower, Jesus Christ is to my soul." That is true religion. Not a religion of opposition, not a religion of conquest, not a religion of destruction, but a religion that draws forth the good and beautiful in every system of human society.—Frederick B. Fisher.

GOOD WAY OF THINKING. A businessman who had wrecked his mind and body by the incessant and uncontrolled scramble for money went to see a great nerve specialist. He was considerably surprised when he was asked this question: "How much does your religion mean to you?"—so surprised, in fact, that he was unable to reply. The famous doctor then explained that there was one class of people he scarcely ever saw in his consulting room—the people who believe and practice the Christian religion.—F. A. Atkins.

RELIGION A WAY OF FEELING. It was Grace's first experience at a boarding school. A copy of the rules was handed to her as she entered. She read them with frowning brow and sinking heart. Keep those rules? She never could and she never would. It was intolerable! At supper Grace was introduced to the principal. What a lovely woman! How winning her smile! The next day Grace's admiration increased. Soon the girl became one of her most devoted adherents. Where were now the irksome rules? Her one desire was to please the principal. Love made easy the fulfilling of the commands.—*Christian Age*.

THE HONOR OF WORK. A noted physician gave this testimony. "When I was a medical student I attended an operation where a great surgeon did the work. His assistant failed to come, and he chose me to help him to save that life. How proud I was to be chosen to help this great man!"

Charles Spurgeon once said, "I realized that God could save the world without me, but when he told me that I might help him I praised him for the honor and the privilege."

EVENING SERVICE

Theme: Gifts and Service.

TEXT: "As every man hath received the gift, even so minister the same one to another, as good stewards of the manifold grace of God." I Pet. 4:10.

INTRODUCTORY: The gifts of grace whatever they may be are talents entrusted to us for the good of others. "Manifold" means many and diversified. Such is the variety of spiritual gifts and their manifestations. It is far too common for men to pride themselves upon their advantages, their strength of body, their gifts of intellect, the bestowments of fortune which they call their own. But the spirit of Christianity is altogether opposed to such a habit of mind. Peter, as well as other apostles, took occasion to remind Christians that their advantages should be estimated and employed in a very different manner. "As every man hath received the gift."

I. Consider the variety of gifts. Peter speaks here of "manifold" gifts, literally "variegated" or "many-colored," and so he exhorts to variety of service based upon dissimilarity of gifts. We say, "It takes all sorts to make a world." It takes all sorts to make a Christian world. With diversity comes room for mutual help and great varieties in service. "As every man hath received, so minister the same."

II. Consider our responsibility for our gifts. "As good stewards." All gifts are trusts. They are ours, but ours that we may use them. 1. The Christian's endowments, acquisitions and possessions are the free gifts of God's goodness. 2. The Christian's endowments, acquisitions and possessions are a trust which he holds from God and for which he must give account. 3. The Christian's endowments, acquisitions and possessions are designed for the service and benefit of his fellow men. This is an appointed service, a beneficial service, a mutual service. The principles embodied here, if honestly carried out, would revolutionize the Church and go far to regenerate the world. All powers are gifts. All gifts are trusts. What simplicity, what power, what unselfishness, what diligence, what regard for others' work, what humility as to one's own would fill the life fully moulded to these convictions!—A. M.

Suggested Texts and Themes

A Mistaken Policy: "But he helped him not." II Chron. 28:21.

When Wonder Wakes: "Stay yourselves, and wonder." Isa. 29:9.

The Treasures of Darkness: "I will give thee the treasure of darkness, . . . that thou mayest know that I . . . am the God of Israel." Isa. 45:3.

A Searching Question: "Offer it now unto thy governor; will he be pleased with thee . . . ?" Mal. 1:8.

The Peerless Blade: "And David said, There is none like that; give it me." I Sam. 21:9.

MIDWEEK FELLOWSHIP MEETING TOPIC

(Church Night or Suggested Sermon Subject)

Theme: The Great Name.

TEXT: "Holy and reverend is his name." Ps. 111:9.

Not all of the human race make this declaration, but all are going to make this declaration.

I. There have been and are great names to enrich the thinking of men, but they have been and are fading from age to age. Jesus is the great Contemporary. He does more for the world than all others combined. Whatever is done for the conservation of childhood, the upbuilding of manhood, is a glorification of his great name.

II. The name of Jesus shall bring in the new and better day for the human race. That new and better day is potential, not actual. It is a challenge to endeavor, not an example of achievement. The name of Jesus, all it has meant, does mean and can mean, is a challenge to us all to bring out the best that is in us, expended in behalf of our fellow men.

III. Only as the Church goes forth with Jesus' plan of sacrificial effort for redemption can it justify its existence. His name stands for universal love, sacrificial ministry, and heroic endeavor. In his name, we are saved from the perils of ecclesiastical hypocrisy, refined selfishness and the insidious perils of a smug complacency and the subtle suggestiveness of a luxurious ease, which in this hour threaten the life of the Church. —R. B.

CHRISTIAN ENDEAVOR SOCIETY TOPIC

Feb. 17. Christian Citizenship Promotes Brotherhood. Gal. 3:26-29; Prov. 22:2. (Brotherhood Sunday.)

SUNDAY SCHOOL LESSON

Feb. 17. The Family at Bethany. Luke 10:38-42; John 11:1-5, 24, 27.

MEMORY SELECTION: "She said to him, Yes, Lord; I believe that you are the Christ, the Son of God, he who is coming into the world." John 11:27 (R. S. V.)

Here is a home that welcomed Jesus, where he was loved and gladly served. It is the home of two sisters and a brother. They observed that friendly, personal relationship which marks the true followers of Jesus. The lesson shows how Christ may transform the everyday life in our homes. It pictures Jesus in the Bethany home as guest, teacher, friend and helper in the time of extreme need. It is very important that we dedicate our homes to him.

SUNDAY: FEBRUARY TWENTY-FOURTH

MORNING SERVICE

Theme: The Importance of Testimony to Religious Experience.

SUGGESTED SCRIPTURE READING: Ps. 66:1-20.

SELECTED HYMNS: "Come we that love the Lord."—I. Watts. "Stand up and bless the Lord."—J. Montgomery. "Thank and praise Jehovah's name."—J. Montgomery. "Praise, my soul, the King of heaven."—H. F. Lyte.

CALL TO WORSHIP: "Holy, holy, holy, Lord God Almighty, thou art worthy, O Lord, to receive glory, and honor, and power." "O magnify the Lord with me and let us exalt his name together."

INVOCATION PRAYER: We thank thee, our Father, for the things that happen in our inner lives as Sabbath after Sabbath we turn aside from our daily tasks to worship thee—for the consciousness of refreshment, the experience of cleansing, the reinforcement of power, the new light shining upon the pathway, the assurance that we are thy children, the sense of spiritual adventure, and the deep serenity of spirit. We pray, our Father, that such experience may not become our indulgence, but the motive for purer living, higher and better understandings, greater consecrations and eager sacrifice unto building thy kingdom. We pray that we may find ourselves not only in the world, but here for some great purpose. Help us to achieve that purpose. To this end bless our coming together this morning in thy house. Strengthen our faith. Enlist us anew in bringing about thy kingdom in our own hearts and in the whole world. We ask in the name of Christ. Amen.—M. K. W. H.

Theme: The Importance of Testimony to Religious Experience.

TEXT: "Come and hear, all ye that fear God, and I will declare what he hath done for my soul." Ps. 66:16.

INTRODUCTORY: True religion involves two things, an inward experience and an outward profession. The Psalmist had both. He was neither a cold formalist nor a timid believer. He had experimental enjoyment of God in his heart, and he was not ashamed to testify to it both by his lips and by his life.

I. Let us think first of the nature of religious experience. It is something God has done for the soul. The text we are studying limits attention to the Psalmist's personal experience of God's gracious dealings with him. Not what he had done for the world. Not what he had done for the Church in all ages. Not what he had done for historical individuals; but "what he hath done for my soul."

II. It is plainly evident that the Psalmist had made a point of keeping in mind the things which God had done for his soul. God had done great things for him in a temporal way, taking him from the shepherd's field to being a king. But he is speaking here of his soul, not his body nor position in the world. Unless David—and we assume that this is a psalm of David—had marked and treasured up God's dealings with him he could not have told them. The whole of his psalms show that this was his practice. And his example is worthy of imitation. "Forget not all his benefits." At least remember some of them. Such is the only course dictated by respect for God in his dealings with us.

III. The Psalmist felt the obligation also for declaring to others the things which God had done for his soul. "Come and hear." The general tendency and practice is to conceal God's dealings, though the relating of religious experience has great value. The Psalmist would have others learn what he had been taught. He would have others unite with him in praising the Lord for his mercies. He also yielded to strong feelings of gratitude for his blessings, out of the abundance of his heart testifying to God's goodness. Spiritual experience should be volunteered, not enforced. It should be told at suitable times. It may well be addressed only to congenial hearers—"all ye that fear God," that is, such as could understand and appreciate. It should be strictly personal: "what he hath done for my soul." It should be done in great modesty, in sincerity, in simplicity, and relating God's doings, not our own.

IV. Those who thus communicate their religious experience have much to tell. We all have. "I will declare." How much the true followers of the Lord have to tell, not merely of God's goodness in general, but of what he has done especially for them, in calling them, in pleading with them, in regenerating and accepting and sustaining and helping them in every way! Let us take this conduct of the Psalmist as a model. Let not shyness or timidity hinder, but with seriousness and sincerity and simplicity do this. It is not essential to salvation, but it is a great help both to ourselves and to others.

Why should we speak and not be silent? There is reason and value in connection with God, the duty and privilege of honoring him, of showing gratitude to him and to extol his goodness. There is reason and value in connection with those addressed. Our experience is likely to do them good in the way of instruction, encouragement and edification. And there is reason and value in connection with ourselves. It is good for our own souls. It will freshen our experience, enliven and quicken us and fill us with spiritual joy. Lastly, there is reason and value in connection with religion itself. It shows our religion, and true religion in general to be a thing not of gloom, but of gladness, joy and blessedness. Such testimony blesses us. It blesses others. It glorifies God.

THEME PRAYER: O God, our loving heavenly Father, forgive us for our lack of faith in thee and in thy Word. Clarify our eyes, that we may see; purify our minds, that we may understand; stir up our wills, that we may surely commit ourselves to thee and to thy purpose for us as messengers of the glorious Gospel. Through Jesus Christ our Lord. Amen.

OFFERTORY SENTENCE: "All power is given unto me in heaven and in earth. Go ye therefore, and teach all nations, baptizing them in the name of the Father, and of the Son, and of the Holy Ghost: . . . and lo, I am with you alway, even unto the end of the world."

OFFERTORY PRAYER: Thou hast said, our Saviour, that it is more blessed to give than to receive. It is both to advance thy kingdom and to promote our own souls' growth in grace that we have brought our offerings this day. Wilt thou graciously receive and bless them and by thy providence multiply their fruitfulness in thy service. We ask in the name of Christ. Amen.—H.

Illustrative Material

SEED THOUGHTS, HOMILETIC AND EXPOSITORY. Come and Hear: I. The subject of a good man's talk. What is it? The kindness of God to him. II. The desire of a good man to communicate. Why? That he may do others good. III. The audience that the good man seeks. "All ye that fear the Lord."

Communicating Christian Experience: I. Those that fear God take interest to his doings in the souls of men. II. Those to whose souls God has been gracious desire to tell what God has done for them. Not in pride, but in gratitude. III. Those who do thus communicate their religious experience have much to tell.—A. T.

Paul's Testimony. Throughout all his epistles it shines. Gems of personal allusion: "I obtained mercy." "Of whom I am chief." "By the grace of God I am what I am."

Choice Illustrations on the Theme

VALUE OF EXPERIENCE. The story is told of the artist Turner. Wishing to paint a storm at sea he went to the coast of Holland and engaged a fisherman to take him out in his boat in the next storm. He said, "Not only did I see the storm and feel it, but it blew itself into me till I became part of the storm. And then I came back and painted the picture."

VALUE OF TESTIMONY. Bishop Thoburn was once crossing the Indian Ocean on a boat on which were two Englishwomen who argued atheism for days in his presence. As the journey came near its end one of the women said: "Bishop Thoburn, we do not wish to be impertinent, but we wonder that you could listen respectfully to our arguments so long without being convinced." The bishop replied, "Madam, I have greatly enjoyed your conversation. I have never heard the case of atheism more brilliantly put. I am sorry that the journey is so nearly over. But I have enjoyed the conversation merely as an intellectual exercise. There was no more likelihood of convincing me of the nonexistence of God than of the nonexistence of myself. For I have known God for forty years."—*Christian Advocate.*

VALUES KEPT BY SHARING. Spiritual values are kept by sharing them. When men became followers of Jesus, he suggested that they go and tell others what had been done for them. Jesus knew the secret of spiritual growth. If you discovered the cure for cancer, would you keep it to yourself? If you have found the meaning of life eternal, can you afford to withhold it?

TESTIFY. Earnest Christians will never be like the rivers which flow into the Arctic Ocean—frozen at the mouth.

GRACIOUS WORDS. There is a blessed, healing power in words. They may comfort the sorrowing, hearten the discouraged, inspire the reluctant, put an end to loneliness, reconcile the estranged and, by the very music of them, build the cities of the soul. Our religion, says the Apostle, should find a voice in our words. Suppose we all tried, today, "words that are gracious and a means of grace."

EVENING SERVICE

Theme: Maxims for Living.

TEXT: "Whatsoever thy hand findeth to do, do it with thy might." Eccles. 9:10.

INTRODUCTORY: This injunction is as necessary today as when it was first uttered, but in all probability it is much more difficult to comply with than it was then. The trouble with our time is that it is so distressingly complicated, so that the more certain we are that something urgently needs to be done, the less certain are we what we ought to be doing. I cannot claim to have wisdom beyond the common measure, but I would offer for your consideration three simple maxims for the conduct of life.

I. The first is: Accept. The basic fact about our life is surely that it is not an affair of voluntary enlistment. And the beginning of wisdom is to accept this, not to regret it, not to wish it had been otherwise, but just to be willing to be what we in fact are here and now. This is our task.

Nor should we accept only where we are, but also what we are; I mean by that the kind of person one is, with one's specific powers and limitations. God has set each one of us at his post and given him his equipment; for those basic decisions he accepts responsibility himself, but he will call us to account for the use we make of them.

Furthermore, the task which is assigned to us is not so much to be perfect as it is that of redeeming, turning to good some situation which we did not bring about. You and I did not make this world as it is today. If we can leave some deeper impress of God upon the world where we have lived in it, if we can pluck good for others out of what threatened us with evil, then we have done what we were sent here to do.

II. In the second place, we must learn to select. To go through life saying regretfully: "So much to do, so little done!" may after all be but the expression of a pride which is not willing to accept the limitations of life on this earth. Some people, of course, are made careless and irresponsible by considerations of this kind: it means nothing to them that so many good causes are clamoring for their assistance. But there are others of a more serious turn of mind who feel helpless in face of so much need. We must learn to select, out of the hundred things we should like to do, the one, two or three that we know we must do.

But there is a difficulty here. To select, one must at the same time reject, and that is where the conscientious person is apt to hesitate. He asks, naturally enough: How am I to know that, if I neglect this, it will ever get done? The answer is that you must have faith, faith that when God tells you to do A and leave B, he will tell someone else to do B and leave A. We must not allow ourselves to imagine that we are the only persons who really care.

III. That brings me to my third point, for we have seen that something more than effort is needed, that faith is required as well. So the final maxim runs: Keep the Balance. That is to say, keep the balance between concentration of energy and freedom from anxiety. Two elements go to make up the true life; they are quiet confidence in God and valiant effort in his service, and we must find the right adjustment between the two.

The supreme illustration of this is Jesus. He is conscious that he is in the hands and under the protection of the Father, so that nothing can harm him till his hour arrives; at the same time he is eager to work while it is day, for the night cometh, in which no man can work. "Whatsoever thy hand findeth to do, do it with thy might"; find God's intention for your individual life and give yourself to the doing of it, while remaining free from care. For it is through the divine upholding and guidance that we become capable of decision and energy, as it is through valiant effort in his service that we win the assurance of his reality and power.

Theme: The Blind Spot: Bad Vision.

TEXT: "And there we saw the giants, the sons of Anak, which come of the giants: and we were in our own sight as grasshoppers, and so we were in their sight." Num. 13:33.

INTRODUCTORY: That was an inventory with the main fact omitted. It was an estimate which left out God. These explorers moved in the world of things which are seen. They never sallied forth on venturous quest into the realm of the unseen. Indeed, to them the unseen world did not exist. Spiritual presences and forces were disregarded in their count. They were not even named.

I. They saw nothing but physical giants, and they were dismayed. It has been charged against a certain officer that "he saw his enemy; he did not see his allies." It is a significant criticism and its application is very wide. The same defect of vision may be found among men and women who sincerely profess their concern for the kingdom of God. They see the enemy. They do not see their allies. They see the giants, but they do not see the Lord. Nor do they catch a glimpse of the mighty but secret forces which follow his command.

II. And this imperfect vision, this blindness to the friendly allies, breeds the mood of pessimism. We become possessed by an extensive and debilitating self-depreciation. "We were in our own sight as grasshoppers." We feel no more competent to capture the enemy's citadel than a grasshopper is able to subdue a fort.

And spiritual pessimism is the parent of moral paralysis. Nothing so saps our fighting power as the apprehension that we are sure to be beaten. The will eventually softens if it breathes the air of despair. When we estimate the combatants as "grasshoppers versus giant" we are undone.

III. Therefore it is of vital importance that we cultivate the spiritual sight which gives reality to the unseen world. There is a mystical food which is gathered from the harvests that grow on heavenly fields. Our spirits are fed on spiritual things, and they find their strength in the bread of life. Heavenly manna is the food of heroes. Courage is the product of grace. If we cut ourselves away from "the things which are not seen," we break communion with our spiritual supplies, and our powers will become anemic. We shall lack adequate resource, and when the giant appears we shall surely faint. And when the spirit faints the end has come!

IV. But, pre-eminently, when we see the giants, we must swiftly turn the eyes of the soul upon the Lord. If we are dismayed by an earthly king, let us fix our gaze upon the King of kings. The mighty Friend will give us confidence to meet the foe. "The Lord is my light and my salvation; whom shall I fear? the Lord is the strength of my life; of whom shall I be afraid?"—J.

Suggested Texts and Themes

Quenched Lamps: "Our lamps are gone out." Matt. 25:8.

The Church That Spends Itself Rich: "Give ye them to eat." Luke 9:11-17.

The Great Companion: "Now the God of peace be with you all. Amen." Rom. 15:33.

An Eternal Message: "I have a message from God unto thee." Judg. 3:20.

In the Diplomatic Service: "Now then we are ambassadors for Christ." II Cor. 5:20.

MIDWEEK FELLOWSHIP MEETING TOPIC

(Church Night or Suggested Sermon Subject)

Theme: God's Knowledge of Us.

TEXT: "These are the names of the men." Num. 1:5.

This is called the book of Numbers. It has been entitled, "The Muster-Roll of Israel." It treats of the hosts of God, the discipline of the army, and the special march from Sinai to Canaan.

I. God knows the number and the names of all who belong to him. "These are the names." He knows us individually and altogether. Comfort. Assurance.

II. The practical bearing of this great truth. 1. It should restrain us from sin. 2. It should promote sincerity of life. 3. It should promote humility of mind and life. 4. It should quicken reverence toward God. 5. It should comfort us in our troubles and sorrows. 6. It should assure us of salvation.

III. Seeing that God so intimately knows us it is our duty also to seek to know him in all love and obedience. 1. Confess him. 2. Trust and depend upon him. 3. Draw near to him. 4. Be grateful to him and joyful in him. 5. Seek to know his Word and will.

CHRISTIAN ENDEAVOR SOCIETY TOPIC

Feb. 24. Christian Citizenship Demands Responsibility. I John 3:16, 17; Rom. 15:1-3.

SUNDAY SCHOOL LESSON

Feb. 24. Peter, James and John. Mark 9:2; 10:35-40; Acts 4:13, 18-20.

Memory Selection: "We cannot but speak of what we have seen and heard." Acts 4:20 (R. S. V.).

These were special friends of Jesus. They became trained and tested and most useful followers. They belonged to the inner circle of friendship. Though with faults, they were especially devoted and loyal. In time, they proved their special ability to take responsibility. They were chosen by Christ to be with him on several special occasions. They were often chosen to help him. He had important work for them to do. He helped them and they helped him. It is a great privilege to be helpers of his cause and kingdom today.

SUNDAY: MARCH SECOND

MORNING SERVICE

Theme: Let Love Measure Your Giving (Financial Canvass).

Suggested Scripture Reading: John 21:1-25. After-petition: "Blessed are they that hear the Word of God and keep it."

Selected Hymns: "Saviour, thy dying love."—S. D. Phelps. "We give thee but thine own."—W. H. How. "O Lord of heaven and earth and sea."—C. Wordsworth. "O God of mercy, God of might."—G. Thring.

Call to Worship: "Holy, holy, holy, is the Lord of hosts: the whole earth is full of his glory." "Exalt in the Lord our God, and worship at his holy hill; for the Lord our God is holy."

Invocation Prayer: Almighty and most merciful God, again we take up the psalm of praise and magnify thy name; for thou art very good to us, beyond all thought and imagination, strengthening for toil, shielding from danger, cheering in sorrow. Pardon our ingratitude, our distrust, our disobedience. We would aspire to the greatness of soul that springs from communion with thy gentleness. Help us to be merciful that we may receive thy mercy, upright that we may go the way of thy righteousness, and pure in heart that we may see thee in thy holiness. Save us from narrow thoughts, contracted sympathies, mean actions. Enlarge our steps, and uphold us that our feet may not slip. Enlighten our darkness, and lead us through all our earthly pilgrimage, till the shadows lengthen and our little day draws near its sunset. Let thy mercy light upon those in trouble. Extend thy grace to all men, sending the gospel of thy Son abroad among the nations, and include our dear ones under the shelter of thy shield. We ask in Christ's name. Amen.

Theme: Let Love Measure Your Giving (Financial Canvass).

TEXT: "Lovest thou me? . . . Feed my sheep." John 21:17.

INTRODUCTORY: This text has been translated, "Do you love me? . . . Then feed my sheep." Paul says, "The greatest . . . is love." Henry Drummond's book on love is entitled *The Greatest Thing in the World.* Love is greatest because of what it is able to accomplish. Love motivated the first missionary. He said, "The love of Christ constraineth me." Love has kept missionaries going here and there across trackless seas and deserts and wastes, seeking out the most lowly and needy of God's children. Love builds homes and holds them steadfast and makes of them the bulwarks of nations. God so loved the world that he gave his only begotten Son. It is strange that the one thing that concerned Jesus as he was tenderly restoring fallen Peter, was: "Peter do you love me?—then feed my sheep."

The feeding of the sheep had much to do with Peter's love for Jesus. 1. The service in feeding the sheep was an unmistakable manifestation of his love. 2. The feeding of his sheep would serve to keep that love alive. 3. Only living things can grow.

I. Love manifests itself in service. "By this shall all men know that ye are my disciples, if ye have love one to another." Discipleship comes not through service, but service is the irrefutable evidence of discipleship. This is why Jesus' one concern about Peter was—do you love me? Demonstrate that love for me by feeding my sheep. Without sacrifice, nothing noble is achieved.

David was commanded to make an offering unto God, and the devastating pestilence would be stayed. (David do you love your people?) David came to Ornan, "Grant me the place of this threshingfloor, that I may build an altar therein unto the Lord: thou shalt grant it me for the full price: that the plague may be stayed from the people. And Ornan said unto David, Take it to thee . . . I give thee the oxen also for burnt offerings, and the threshing instruments for wood, and the wheat for the meat offering; I give it all. And king David said to Ornan, Nay; but I will verily buy it for the full price: for I will not take that which is thine for the Lord, nor offer burnt offerings without cost." No, indeed, I will not offer a burnt offering which cost me nothing. Your love for Christ will not be manifested through that which costs you nothing.

Do you love me? Then feed my sheep with that which costs you much. Is it the widow's two mites? Some of us would have to go pretty deep down in our pockets before it would cost as much.

II. Love is kept alive through sacrificial service. Disuse impairs machinery, paralyzes limbs, deteriorates organs. Love impounded makes for a dead sea. To live, love must flow; bear the burdens of others; meet the needs of the needy; give bread to the hungry; bind up the wounds of the mistreated; give hope to the hopeless. Do you love me? Is your love still alive? "Inasmuch as ye did it unto one of these . . . ye did it unto me." Feed my sheep. Continuing love calls for continuing sacrificial service. People have said, "We are not using the church so much now that the children are grown up and gone; so we are reducing our subscription." Your giving is not intended to buy service, but is an expression of the service you would offer because of your love.

III. Only living things grow. We cannot sing with Elizabeth Prentiss, "More love to Thee, O Christ, more love to Thee," except we keep feeding the sheep of the Good shepherd. Stewardship is a growing, and therefore, a living thing.—Paul Calhoun, D.D.

THEME PRAYER: O Thou, in whose

keeping what we seek or do is secure, we thank thee for all those through whose gifts of love we have been healed, for every treasured memory of kindnessess which have brightened our pilgrim way, for every generous deed which has enriched our souls we bless thy name. May we withhold no gift in which another may be blessed. In his name who gave himself. Amen.

OFFERTORY SENTENCE: "He which soweth sparingly shall reap also sparingly; and he which soweth bountifully shall reap also bountifully."

OFFERTORY PRAYER: We lay before thee here, Our Father, the gifts of our hands and the gifts of our hearts, both money and devotion. Wilt thou graciously accept and use both toward the building of a better world. In Jesus' name we ask. Amen.

Illustrative Material

SEED THOUGHTS, HOMILETIC AND EXPOSITORY. The Lord's Command: I. Its nature. Christ has a flock which he commends to all who love him. "Feed my lambs." "Feed my sheep." II. That love needs to be exercised as well as having an object. III. That love prepares us for service to Christ. IV. That love extends to his people. V. That love ought to show itself to the world.—A. G.

Lovest Thou Me? He puts the question to us thrice because there are three storeys in our nature. The uppermost is feeling. The middle one is intellect. And the basement is will. Jesus opens the door to each and asks, "Lovest thou me?"—C. H. S.

Love to Christ: It is not possible for that man to be a Christian who does not love Christ.—S.

Choice Every Member Canvass Illustrations

THE TOPCOAT. The topcoat is a most attractive garment for a Christian to wear. It is always in style, looks well, wears well. Why not wear it at Every Member Canvass time and all the time? It is comfortable even on a hot summer's day! "Above all these things put on charity."

THE GIVER'S BEST. Few of us are rich. Few of us have great and many talents. But all can be great givers, simply by giving our best to the Master, whatever it happens to be. Names do not matter. Position does not matter. Neither wealth nor fame matters. But our life does matter. Jesus, who saw so much in the widow's mite, can take the best we have, however small it may be, and accomplish wonders with it—provided we put it into his hands for his use.—H. W. Austin.

SACRIFICIAL GIVING. The closing verses of Samuel carry a strong lesson: "Neither will I offer burnt offerings unto the Lord my God of that which doth cost me nothing." Centuries before the coming of Christ, David knew that man's love for God was measured by self-sacrifice. He did not believe in cheap religion. Think of what vast sums are spent on worthless pleasures by its devotees; then consider how little our religion costs us. True religion deserves our best, not only in money but in time and devotion and sacrifice.—Archer Wallace.

TRY IT ON THE LANDLORD. You say you don't believe in tithing? Well, why not try eating—not in a systematic three-times-a-day manner, but spasmodically—the way nontithers give—every once in a while. Also try it on your landlord, pay the rent occasionally, when you feel touched by special emotion. Try it on your job—don't work regularly, every day, beginning at a certain hour, but come once in a while when you are peculiarly moved to do so. Funny, isn't it, how some of us treat the support of God's cause differently from everything else? Not even a fraternal order could exist if its followers supported it the way many want to support the church.

THE GIVER

The man who is a giver gains
A greater pleasure and attains
A surer progress than does he
Who lives his whole life selfishly.

This world is molded on the plan
That he who helps another man
Himself is helped in helping more
Than if he put himself before.

We must not, as a miser, hoard
The gifts into our coffers poured,
But freely, willingly must then
Share what we have with other men.
—Donald J. MacCargo.

A SHILLING HEART. "I'm sorry," said an Englishwoman who once was very generous in her poverty, but who had a large legacy left her. "I'm sorry but I cannot do as much as I used to do." "But how is that?" she was asked. "When I had a shilling purse I had a guinea heart, but now that I have a guinea purse I have only a shilling heart."

EVENING SERVICE

Theme: Thrifty Spending (Financial Canvass).

TEXT: "There is that scattereth," etc. Prov. 11:24-26.

INTRODUCTORY: We are accustomed to speak of the man who spends freely as a spendthrift and of the man who restrains his hand as on the way to wealth. But if that is our thought we are often and much mistaken.

I. There is such a thing as thrifty spending. "The liberal soul shall be made fat." Spending in works of benevolence is seldom known to impoverish a man, for it is seldom disjointed from calculation and economy in personal habits. In the highest point of view benevolence is a "lending to the Lord."

II. There is such a thing as unthrifty saving. Niggardliness tends to poverty. 1. Because it stints the energies. 2. It springs from a false or exaggerated view of the value of money. 3. It overlooks the happiness that wealth gives in its use.

III. Think therefore of the satisfaction of doing good. 1. Consider the reflex effect of actions. Indirect results are the wider and more important. 2. It is not sufficiently realized that whatever gives expansion to mind and heart, large views and broad sympathies, is so much gain in actual power.

IV. The question of selfishness or generosity in business. In time of dearth an avaricious proprietor keeping back his corn to secure a higher price brings down upon himself curses, while he who thinks of humanity more than personal profit earns the blessings of the poor. The maxim that "business is business" is true but may easily be pushed too far.

There are narrow and there are large hearts. Trust in riches leads to moral downfall. Ofttimes giving is getting.—P. C.

Alternate Theme: Too Close to the Borderline (Financial Canvass).

TEXT: "I will let you go, that ye may sacrifice to the Lord your God in the wilderness; only ye shall not go very far away." Ex. 8:28.

INTRODUCTORY: When Moses asked Pharaoh to permit the Hebrews to go out into the desert and worship their God, the latter consented on the condition that they would not go very far. They might serve God, but they must do it within reach of Egypt. He wanted them to remain near enough to Egypt that he could pull them back. Translated into modern terms it would read, Serve God, but do not go far enough from the world to break its grip. Serve God, but do it near the borderline. Accept Christ as a Saviour, unite with the Church, attend the church service Sabbath mornings (f you feel like it), but do not become so engrossed in religious matters that your religion will interfere with your social or business claims.

I. To the contrary Jesus said, "If any man will come after me, let him take up his cross and follow me." Too few grasp the full meaning of this required sacrifice. Too often our conception of obligation includes a large element of personal reserve. We feel too lightly the measure of obligation which flows out of our creation and redemption. Have we not had about enough of easy religion, a religion which crosses no great desire and calls for no unwelcome duty? When we come to realize deep in our souls that the Son of God clothed himself in human flesh and died on the cross for us, we will not remain near the borderline in our experience and practice of religion.

II. Leaving the children in Egypt. When Moses refused to shorten the distance to which the Hebrews could go in order to worship Jehovah, Pharaoh proposed a second compromise: "Go, but leave your children in Egypt." Modernized, this would read: Become Christians if you must but leave your children in the world. Go to church on the Sabbath (if you will), but leave your children at home. Let your children go to the Bible-school but do not take them to the public service. Two services are too long for them. They can stay in school all day; they can remain at the movies for four hours without weariness, but they cannot spend two hours in a religious service!

Some parents think they have fulfilled their obligation to their children when they have provided for their material and intellectual needs. Others are chiefly concerned to secure them social advantages. These are not to be neglected. But the responsibility of parents does not stop at this point. The child is spiritual as well as physical, intellectual and social. The spiritual is the governing element. It determines the way the others shall act. It gives moral direction to life. The greatest failure is not a financial or social one but a moral one. To neglect the spiritual training of children is to fail in the chief purpose of parenthood.

III. Worshiping God but leaving our money behind. Till the last, Pharaoh would let the parents go into the desert to worship. He would, though unwillingly, let the children accompany them; but they must leave their property behind. He knew that this would surely bring them back.

The young ruler, of the New Testament, wanted to follow Jesus, but refused to put his property into the surrender. When Prussia was converted to Christianity and the soldiers were immersed by the order of their king, they refused to let their right arms go under the water. They loved war and would not consent to having their sword-arms consecrated to the Prince of Peace. That reservation came to fruitage in the World Wars Numbers I and II.

The exception of property from consecration is not limited to ancient times. Many accept Christ and unite with the Church but refuse to put their pocketbooks into the surrender. They say that their uniting with the Church is a spiritual act, not a commercial one—as though self and possessions could be separated! Where the treasure is the heart will be also. A religion, made easy because it is cheap, is the very furthest possible from the type which Christ exemplified. When Peter urged Jesus to leave the cross out of his consecration, Jesus answered, "Get thee behind me, Satan: thou art an offence unto me."

Christianity has not lowered its conditions of discipleship. As we approach the end of life we will realize that the primal question is not, How much have you gotten? but How much have you given? It will not be, How much have you won? but How much have you done? It will not be, How much have you saved? but How much have you sacrificed? It will not be, How much have others done for you? but How much have you done for others? It will not be, How much were you loved? but How much did you love?—Rev. James Doig Rankin, D.D.

Suggested Texts and Themes

The Inquiring Heart: "Examine me, O Lord, and prove me; try my reins and my heart." Ps. 26:2.

The Contrite Heart: "I acknowledged my sin unto thee, and mine iniquity have I not hid. I said I will confess my transgressions," etc. Ps. 32:5.

The Cleansed Heart. "Wash me thoroughly from mine iniquity and cleanse me from my sin." Ps. 51:2.

The Consecrated Heart: "For thou, O God, hast heard my vows: thou hast given me the heritage of those that fear thy name." Ps. 61:5.

The Grateful Heart: "And he hath put a new song into my mouth, even praise unto our God," etc. Ps. 40:3.

MIDWEEK FELLOWSHIP MEETING TOPIC

(Church Night or Suggested Sermon Subject)

Theme: The People and the Church Treasury (Financial Canvass).

TEXT: "And Jesus sat over against the treasury, and beheld how the people cast money into the treasury." Mark 12:41.

In a court of the temple there was a chest with a hole in the cover. Near by Jesus was sitting. The people began flocking out of the temple. As they passed by—rich and poor—they dropped their offerings into the chest.

I. It was the people who dropped money into the chest. The impression we get is that everyone gave something. This is in accord with the teaching of Scripture, "Let none appear before me empty." Jesus wants all to give. This means rich and poor and those of moderate circumstances.

II. Jesus saw how much each giver was contributing. He noticed how some pompous men approached and with much display cast their rich gifts into the treasury. Then he observed a shabbily dressed working woman in the throng. Reaching the chest, she opened her hand and dropped two small coins into the treasury. And Jesus, reading her heart, knew that she had given all her living. Jesus sees how much we give today.

III. Jesus saw how the people cast in their gifts. This is most important. "Verily I say unto to you, That this poor widow hath cast more in, than all they which have cast into the treasury." With Jesus it was not so much a question of how much as how. The widow was actually giving more than the others. She gave of her heart, they of their purses; she of her love, they of their custom. He wants us to give according to our best abilities. We need not be ashamed if it is our sacrificial best. He wants us to give intelligently, cheerfully, graciously, lovingly.—Rev. Paul F. Boller.

CHRISTIAN ENDEAVOR SOCIETY TOPIC

March 2. Examples in Winning Others: Jesus Calls His Disciples. Mark 2:13-17; Mark 4:13-21.

BULLETIN BOARD SLOGANS FOR THE MONTH

By Earl Riney

The soul of all progress is the progress of the soul.

A loose tongue often gets its owner into a tight place.

Kindness is the golden chain by which society is bound together.—Goethe.

There is no road to success except a clear strong purpose.—T. T. Munger.

Thousands admire Christ who never become Christians.

God always has an angel of help for those who are willing to do their duty.

You can be lazy in your thinking as well as in your doing.

Never belittle the other person to make yourself seem important.

Life would be pretty dull if we always knew what was coming.

Happiness is a by-product of an effort to make someone else happy.

SUNDAY SCHOOL LESSON

March 2. "Our Beloved Barnabas." Acts 4:36, 37; 9:26, 27; 11:19-26; 13:1-3.

MEMORY SELECTION: "He was a good man, and full of the Holy Spirit and of faith." Acts 11:24.

Barnabas was a man who received very high praise. He was a good man, a trusted helper, and a hard worker. He was generous. He sold some land and gave the money to the church for the poor. He was sympathetic, a man known as "an encourager" or "son of consolation." His chief concern was not for recognition for himself but for Christ and the spreading of his gospel. He sponsored Paul when he needed it. He took a prominent part in the Jerusalem council. He went on long missionary journeys.

SUNDAY: MARCH NINTH

MORNING SERVICE

Theme: Jacob's Mistake and Ours.

Suggested Scripture Reading: Gen. 42:1-36.

Selected Hymns: "God moves in a mysterious way."—W. Cowper. "He leadeth me, O blessed thought."—J. H. Gilmore, "O let him whose sorrow."—H. S. Oswald. "How firm a foundation."—"K."

Call to Worship: "Trust ye in the Lord for ever: for in the Lord Jehovah is everlasting strength." "Thou wilt keep him in perfect peace, whose mind is stayed on thee: because he trusteth in thee."

Invocation Prayer: Almighty God, giver of all true thoughts and resolves and the rewarder of them that diligently seek thee; visit us, we beseech thee, in this place of sacred memories and aspirations that we may with a morning gladness of soul know and rejoice in that love in which all human griefs are transfigured and common things become divine. Make for us here a refuge from the stress and turmoil of earthly things. Dispel the clouds of our distrust and our coldness to the things which are spiritual and eternal. Unite us with our fellow worshipers here and everywhere who wait upon thee this day. Forgive our sins. Cleanse our hearts. Exalt our aims. Strengthen our purposes of good. And may thy Holy Spirit use us today and always in the service of thy kingdom. We ask in the name of Christ our Lord. Amen.

Theme: Jacob's Mistake and Ours.

Text: "And Jacob . . . said, . . . Joseph is not, and Simeon is not, and ye will take Benjamin away: all these things are against me." Gen. 42:36.

Introductory: In his long and tortuous career Jacob had had many sunless days, but the darkest and most tragic day of all was that at which he had now arrived. Joseph he took for dead. Simeon was a prisoner in Egypt. Mysterious hands were trying to clutch Benjamin and drag him from the sheltering of home. And all this happened simultaneously, and in a period of protracted famine, when sorrows would be more difficult to bear. It was the coming together of many evil things, the dark concurrence of them, that made the patriarch cry, almost in despair, "All these things are against me."

I. Now that dark hour which Jacob reached is an hour, I take it, which everybody reaches. There come days when that which tries the spirit is the simultaneous incidence of evils. Just as there are days when everything goes merrily, and every face we meet with wears a smile, and we are equal to every demand, and worries are lightly brushed away, so are there days when everything goes wrong. Every artist knows such days; he has mornings when his fingers lose their cunning. Every man of business knows such days, when all things seem to fall into a tangle. And how we all deal with the bad days of life, and react on them, and organize them, is one of the great abiding tests of character.

II. But the delightful comfort of our text is this, that Jacob was so utterly mistaken. Although he did not know it he was entirely misinterpreting his life. He took it for granted that Joseph had been slain, yet he was Prime Minister of Egypt. He pictured Simeon in an alien prison, yet the most powerful man in Egypt was his friend. He shrank with horror from the loss of Benjamin, yet a brother's heart was yearning over Benjamin, and longing to clasp him to its breast. Things never seemed darker to Jacob than just then. There was not one bright star upon his sky. In an agony that bordered on despair, he cried out "All these things are against me," and at that moment though he knew it not, everything was brightening toward sunrise.

III. That this is not an exceptional experience we may discover from the Apostle Paul. He too, like Jacob, had his period when everything seemed to be against him. Child of freedom, he found himself in bonds. With the wide world calling him, he was a prisoner. Eager to preach the gospel to the nations, he was fettered to a Roman soldier. And yet that hour, when all his heaven was dark, and everything seemed to be against him, lay right on heaven's highway to his dreams. Jacob cried "All these things are against me," and they were never brighter than just then. Paul cried, "All these things are against me," and just then the flowing tide was with him. I think when Paul and Jacob meet in glory, and talk over the vanished days of earth, they smile, and often say to one another, "Why, what stupid children we both were!"

IV. And perhaps we also, in overwhelming hours, are stupid children like that pair in glory. Just when we cry "All these things are against me," heaven's trumpets sound the distant triumph song. When tempted to cry "All these things are against me," be still a moment and meditate on Jacob. "There is a budding morrow in midnight." The day will dawn when you will wake to find that all things have been working together for your good. —M.

THEME PRAYER: We thank thee, our Father, for the hard things in life that may be transmuted into worthy character when we are led by thy Spirit. Help us to take what life brings to us of pain and adversity and use it as a means of spiritual growth. Through Jesus Christ our Lord. Amen.

OFFERTORY SENTENCE: "And he called his ten servants, and delivered them ten pounds, and said unto them, Occupy till I come."

OFFERTORY PRAYER: Our Heavenly Father, may we give of the best of our time, means, talent unto thee to be used in thy service that in our walk among men we may be a blessing, as we lay up treasure in heaven. We ask it in the name of Jesus Christ our Lord. Amen.—H. W. Austin.

Illustrative Material

SEED THOUGHTS, HOMILETIC AND EXPOSITORY. Mistaking God's Providences: I. Unbelief: "All these things are against me." "All." Indeed, what a little "all" compared with the benefits of God! Exaggerated. Bitter. II. Ungenerous. "Me ye have bereaved of my children." Untrue. III. Erroneous. "Joseph is not." Yet Joseph is, very much is. "Simeon is not." Wrong again. Simeon is alive.—C. H. S.

Wrong View of Life. "Joseph is not, and Simeon is not, and ye will take Benjamin away: all these things all against me." We undertake to pronounce judgment upon God's way in the world. Why don't we learn from our ignorance?—J. P.

Depression: In a fit of dejection Dean Hook once wrote: "My life has been a failure. I have done many things tolerably; but nothing well. As a parish priest, as a preacher, and now as a writer, I am quite aware that I have failed, and the more so because my friends contradict the assertion."

Choice Illustrations on the Theme

A DARK DAY MAY BE BEST. Smetham, the artist, in one of his charming letters, says something very suggestive about painting. He says that for painting certain parts of a picture a dark day is the best. And it may be that God, who made and loves the sunshine, knows that now and then dark days are best if our life is ever to be a thing of beauty. —M.

CROOKED PROVIDENCES. Suppose you were in the shop of a blacksmith and you were shown several sorts of tools, some crooked, some bowed, others hooked. Would you condemn the whole of them because they were not handsome? The smith makes use of them all for the doing of his work. And thus it is with the providences of God. They may seem to us very crooked and strange, yet they all help to carry on his work. We are too liable to misinterpret God's dealings and, like Jacob, say "all these things are against me."

VICTORY IN DEFEAT. A distinguished Japanese, who is now an American citizen, in a frank and careful study of Japanese philosophy says that in Japan the defeated man is always an object of scorn and contempt. Victory, no matter how obtained, is great but there is never any valid excuse for defeat. We know, however, that there can be defeat with honor; that sometimes in our own nation defeated men have been greatly respected by those who triumphed over them. Many of the saints of God have drunk the cup of humiliation to its dregs. Our Saviour died upon a cross. —Archer Wallace.

THE SPIRIT OF COMPLAINT. Momus, who according to Hesiod was the son of Night, was the god of criticism or the evil spirit of complaint. His carping spirit found fault with the perfect man Hephaestus made because there were no windows in the breast so that the thoughts might be read, and when he could not complain otherwise of the beautiful Aphrodite he grumbled because when she walked her sandals were heard. He is represented as the personification of a very unlovely and unjust disposition and the gods finally banished him from Olympus. But he still walks the earth and appears in our midst the same disturbing and depressing spirit. Jacob seemed to have some of that spirit. It was due to lack of faith, the fault in a good man.

EVENING SERVICE

Theme: The Boast of Babylon.

TEXT: "I shall be a lady for ever." Isa. 47:7.

INTRODUCTORY: The utterance of proud Babylon is identical with that of the vain and self-confident of all ages. The language in the individual puffed up with self-conceit is the same as that of the nation ruled by ignorance and pride. This expression, "I shall be a lady for ever," suggests that lengthened prosperity in the case of the ungodly leads to many evils.

I. First, it leads to false security. The Psalmist speaks of those who "trust in their wealth and boast themselves in the multitude of their riches." Job in the time of his health and gladness said, "I shall die in my nest." The tendency of riches and honors is to blind the heart to the future, and too often to steel it toward God.

II. It leads to presumption. "I shall be a lady for ever," that is in my own right. No contingency can arise to deprive me of my title and wealth. The prosperous man is likely to forget that he is as dependent upon God now as he was in his days of adversity.

III. It leads to boasting. "A lady" seems to imply something superior to others. Prosperity leads many to imagine that they are of a higher order of being. A woman assuming to be a lady gravely told an almshouse woman that in heaven itself the distinction would be observed. She virtually said, "I shall be a lady for ever."

IV. It leads to self-satisfaction. "A lady, I am that now." "I am rich and increased in goods, and have need of nothing." The Laodicean church spoke after this fashion. How dreadful a delusion! A lady! Self-styled, despised!

V. It leads to abandonment to luxury. "A lady for ever," that is, "I mean to be at ease, to enjoy life, to be in luxury." Let us beware, if our worldly position is prosperous, lest we live on the gifts rather than on the Giver.

VI. It leads to spiritual blindness. Prosperity dazzles the eye. The future is willfully disregarded. The boast of Babylon, "I shall be a lady for ever," is the boast of spiritual blindness, the boast of folly. Remember the desolation that came upon self-confident Babylon. Nor shall the future of those who disobey the Gospel be less severe.

Suggested Texts and Themes

A Promise for the New Year: "Behold I will do a new thing; now it shall spring forth; shall ye not know it?" Isa. 43:19.

Race Relations: "And whether one member suffer, all the members suffer with it." I Cor. 12:26.

Brotherhood Sunday: "Let no man seek his own, but every man another's wealth." I Cor. 10:24.

Giving and Getting: "There is that scattereth, and yet increaseth." Prov. 11:24.

Love at Home: "Be kindly affectioned one to another." Rom. 12:10.

MIDWEEK FELLOWSHIP MEETING TOPIC

(Church Night or Suggested Sermon Subject)

Theme: The Sins of Good People (Lent).

TEXT: "And Moses lifted up his hand, and with his rod he smote the rock twice." Num. 20:11.

Give the account, vv. 1-13. Moses sinned. There were several elements in his sin. It is an instance of the sins of good people.

I. In what did Moses' sin consist? 1. In departure from God's directions, and thus disobedience to the Divine command. 2. In immoderate heat and passion—anger. 3. In assumption of power, taking to himself the credit of supplying the people with water. 4. Lack of faith. 5. It was all publicly done, so the more dishonoring to God.

II. His sin was very painful to God. This is made plain by the story. "Ye believed me not!" It is not a light thing for a good man to sin. How sad when Christ "is wounded in the house of his friends"!

III. His sin was most disastrous in its results. Punishment came, v. 12. Even so, punishment for the sins of good people is gracious, intended to make God's own watchful against sin and to deter them from it.

1. Learn how candidly frank are the Biblical writers in recording their own sins. Moses records his own faults. In every case evidence of Biblical truthfulness. 2. We must not seek right ends by wrong means. 3. See the danger of departing in the least from any requirement of God. 4. Learn the importance attached to temperate speech, that "we sin not with our tongue." 5. Let us never think of ourselves as free from the danger of falling.—H.

CHRISTIAN ENDEAVOR SOCIETY TOPIC

March 9. Examples in Winning Others: Andrew Wins His Brother. John 1:40-42.

SUNDAY SCHOOL LESSON

March 9. Paul a Prisoner for Christ. Phil. 3:4-17.

MEMORY SELECTION: "One thing I do, forgetting what lies behind and straining forward to what lies ahead, I press on toward the goal for the prize of the upward call of God in Christ Jesus." Phil. 3:13, 14 (R. S. V.).

We can think of Paul as a brave follower of Christ, as a follower who gave all, and at last became a noble prisoner for him. He was willing to suffer, and, if need be, to die for him. This lesson portrays Paul's dramatic experiences, his radiant joy, his vital faith, his strength made perfect in weakness, and his utter dependence upon Christ. He is living still through his writings. This is a great lesson in Christian consecration.

SUNDAY: MARCH SIXTEENTH

MORNING SERVICE

Theme: The Secret Place (Lent).

SUGGESTED SCRIPTURE READING: Ps. 91:1-16.

SELECTED HYMNS: "Nearer, my God, to thee."—S. F. Adams. "My God, permit me not to be."—I. Watts. "Rise, my soul, and stretch thy wings."—R. Seagrave. "O for a closer walk with God." —W. Cowper.

CALL TO WORSHIP: "Give unto the Lord the glory due unto his name; worship the Lord in the beauty of holiness." "O magnify the Lord with me, and let us exalt his name together."

INVOCATION PRAYER: O God, who makest thyself known in the stillness, let us feel thy presence in this sacred place. Make us to be of the company of those who in times past have worshiped thee here in spirit and in truth. Through the voices of men and the instruments of praise give us uplift of heart and a sense of thy nearness. We would open our hearts freely to thy Spirit, our minds to thy law, and our wills to thy quickening energy. Keep us this day, we beseech thee, without fear, without sin, without distrust, and through meditation and prayer prepare us for another week of life and labor for thee and our fellow men. We ask in Christ's name. Amen.

Theme: The Secret Place (Lent).

TEXT: "He that dwelleth in the secret place of the Most High shall abide under the shadow of the Almighty." Ps. 91:1.

INTRODUCTORY: These words express a sense of entire security and untroubled peace. The secret place of the Most High, the shadow of the Almighty, how to enter into it—that may be a good way to express the Lenten ideal.

I. The central purpose of Lent is to bring us into the secret place of the Most High through close contact with the Lord Jesus Christ. We do this by going with him through that portion of his life which most perfectly reveals him. That is, of course, his last Passion and Death. Doubtless his whole earthly life was a passion; but in his last days that passion was concentrated and reached its height, just as the whole atonement is caught up and symbolized in the single figure of a cross.

That, then, is our Lenten employment, to draw near to Christ in these days of suffering, and to cultivate such sympathy as will help us to feel what he felt and will enable us to understand why it was necessary for him to do what he did. When we have done that we shall realize God's love and our own guilt and need as we should in no other way. If we use Lent in this way there is no doubt that we shall benefit immeasurably.

II. We do not question that we need to draw nearer to God. We desire a closer walk with him. Neither does anyone deny that this is not easy. It is not easy because it means the renunciation of many things and the concentration upon one thing. It means attention to matters that do not lie upon the surface of life. The sordid touch of the world is always upon us, the infection of its low ideals, its poor ambitions, its eating cares. It perplexes us and scatters our attention. How may we keep our eyes upon things above? The answer is that we need to withdraw ourselves. The posture of soul that inclines Godward, the relating of all things to the eternal so that life itself becomes worship—that is our quest.

III. But whoso would enter this secret place which is with Jesus Christ must take up a cross. We shall regulate our course by asking first what he would have us do. It was his will to make a sacrifice. We shall take our command from his example and make the sacrifice too. We shall give up what is hurtful. We shall give up even good things when they stand in the way of the best. But when we have really gone far in the way of Jesus Christ, that is, when our wills are really his, we shall not be able to speak of sacrifice any more, for that which is given up is not worth a thought in comparison with the perfect harmony, rightness of living, and peaceful security that are found in him.—P. H. R. (Adapted).

THEME PRAYER: To thee, O God, we lift our eyes, but it is thou who must lift our hearts. We are hindered in our devotion by many earthborn cares and circumstances. O help us that thy wisdom and strength shall overcome all hindrances in us! In this sacred season draw us near to thyself and restore unto us the joy of thy salvation. In Christ's name we ask. Amen.

OFFERTORY SENTENCE: "Ye know the grace of our Lord Jesus Christ, that, though he was rich, yet for our sakes he became poor; that ye through his poverty might be rich."

OFFERTORY PRAYER: O Thou Lord and Master of us all, we desire to render day by day an account of our stewardship to thee. All that we have of time and talents and possessions are thine; and we are thine, bought with a price. Give us opportunities for serving thee and our fellow men and grant us the courage and vision to use these opportunities aright. Wilt thou graciously accept and use these our morning offerings, blessing both the gifts and the givers. We ask in Jesus' name. Amen.—H.

Illustrative Material

SEED THOUGHTS, HOMILETIC AND EXPOSITORY. The Secret Place: I. The position indicated. We are to enter into and abide in the secret of God. 1. God's Word has its secret. 2. God's love has its secret. 3. God's purpose has its secret. II. The attitude. "He that dwelleth." To dwell means a fixed, settled, habitual mode of life. III. How attained? Christ supplies the answer, "I am the way." IV. The blessing enjoyed. 1. Dwelling. 2. Communion. 3. In the secret place of God's love. 4. In the secret place of his purpose. —B. P.

Secrets Enjoyed: I. Inwardness. II. Fellowship. III. Security. IV. Service. —J. T.

The Secret Place: I. In the secret place there is peace. II. In the secret place there is purity. III. In the secret place there is power. IV. How may I enter into this secret place? Jesus said, "I am the way." "I am the door."—J. W. C.

Choice Illustrations on the Theme

A PRESENT BLESSING. It was said of an old Puritan that "heaven was in him before he was in heaven." "Lay hold on eternal life." It is something for us to get hold of here and now. It is a thing of the future; but it is a thing of the present too, and even that part of it which is future can be so realized and grasped by faith as actually to be enjoyed while we are in the flesh. "The kingdom of God is within you."—H.

A PRESENT HEAVEN. A devout Scotchman, being asked if he ever expected to go to heaven, gave the quaint reply, "Why, mon, I live there." All the way to heaven is heaven begun to the Christian who walks near enough to God to hear the secrets he has to impart. There is such a thing as having an inner heaven in the heart. Pardon, peace, rest of soul, assurance of hope, abounding joy, and grace beyond measure, these and such as these are the experiences, even as we journey toward the gates of the celestial city, of all who walk so near to God that he can impart his secrets to them.—H.

THE SECRET PLACE

In the secret of His presence
How my soul delights to hide!
Oh, how precious are the lessons
Which I learn at Jesus' side!
Earthly cares can never vex me,
Neither trials lay me low;
For when Satan comes to tempt me,
To the secret place I go.

Would you like to know the sweetness
Of the secret of the Lord?
Go and hide beneath His shadow;
This then shall be your reward;
And whene'er you leave the silence
Of that happy meeting place,
You must mind and bear the image
Of the Master in your face.
—Unidentified.

DWELLING IN THE SECRET PLACE. I seriously doubt if Christians generally are as happy as they ought to be, as they have a right to be, and if they reveal to others the happiness they have as much as they should. Do we not, all of us, too generally put off "until we get to heaven," as we say, our expectation of a real, deep and happy experience of religion, or its joyous manifestation? I am convinced that this is true, and I want to make a plea for the experience and enjoyment of religion here and now, without waiting until we get to heaven, or for any future time whatsoever. "He that dwelleth in the secret place of the Most High shall abide under the shadow of the Almighty." It is to encourage and aid toward the accomplishment of this that we engage in our Lenten studies and devotion.—H.

EVENING SERVICE

Theme: Difficulties, or Rocks on Either Side.

TEXT: "And between the passages, by which Jonathan sought to go over unto the Philistines' garrison, there was a sharp rock on the one side, and a sharp rock on the other side," etc. I Sam. 14:4.

INTRODUCTORY: There are difficult periods in life where decision is of utmost importance. Life and honor or disgrace and death are dependent on the course to be taken at such times. This was a crisis in the history of Jonathan. Decision secured him life and honor. Ruin inevitably would have followed had he hesitated in indecision. The approach to the garrison would have been pronounced impassable by a less decisive and courageous mind. But nothing is too hard to be accomplished with the help of God on your side and a decisive perseverance.

I. Difficult extremes of the present are a skeptical spirit on one hand and a superstitious spirit on the other. Infidelity and superstition are like two rocks. The mind commencing an independent train of thinking and directing thought to the inquiry, "What is truth?" is met by the avowed infidel who begins with a subtle argumentation to burden and perplex the soul. On the other hand, superstition claims from the inquirer after truth implicit confidence in its priests and reliance on its ceremonies.

II. A second class of difficult extremes may be seen in the urgent claims of business and the temptations of leisure. The competition in business is fierce. The large portion of time and energy consumed in providing the bread that perisheth leaves but fragments of time and mental power for the interests of the soul. The less has first claim, the greater has second. But when the first has been answered there is little but exhaustion left. Yet the temptations of leisure have the same proportion as the demands of business. Mind and body endeavor to recruit expended energy. Then the allurement to pleasure becomes powerful.

III. A third class of difficult extremes may be seen in the danger of presumption on the one hand and the equal danger of despondency on the other. Presumption sometimes so infatuates the mind as to imbue it with an entire indifference to spiritual realities. But despondency discourages. The remedy must be prompt and decided faith, acquaintance with the Word of God, and a courageous decision of complying with its requirements.

IV. There are no rocks before the cross, though there may be one on either side.

Alternate Theme: Some Homespun Certainties.

TEXT: "The Lord recompense thy work, and a full reward be given thee of the Lord God of Israel, under whose wings thou art come to trust." Ruth 2:12.

INTRODUCTORY: The words we are to consider are part of the address of welcome Boaz gave to Ruth, the widowed Moabitess, who had left the country of her birth to begin life anew in the homeland of Naomi, her widowed mother-in-law. Simplicity and certitude were the marks of his speech to a lovely woman whose recent sorrows weighed so heavily upon her heart. I am attracted by the homespun certitudes of his teaching.

I. First, there is certitude concerning service. "The Lord recompense thy work," were the words that gushed up warmly from the heart of a man who had been deeply stirred by a story of family fidelity.

We are at a point in the story where the broken threads of life had been taken up again. What seemed to be best, they had done. Decisions had been taken on where to go, what to do and in what faith to live; especially the latter decision.

With reference to all this, Boaz used the word "recompense." Boaz was on sure ground when he encouraged a troubled soul with that of recompense. God will recompense the faithful.

II. In the second place, there is certitude concerning succor. "A full reward be given thee of the Lord God of Israel, under whose wings thou art come to trust," are words which have the stirring quality of a robust affirmation. That word "reward" repays study.

God's wings! Men who have made the prison house of cold exactitudes their dwelling place cannot understand this, but multitudes of simple-hearted people can testify that, taking cover under the wings of God, they have discovered the secret of undismayed confidence in all the changing scenes of life.

III. In the last place, there is certitude concerning sphere. In what circumstances are we likely to pass our days? Is there anything in this passage suited to the kind of life which may be ours? Assuring answers spring in plenty. What was the work on which with such confidence Boaz claimed God's blessing? Here is his own account of it: "It hath fully been showed me, all that thou hast done unto thy mother in law since the death of thine husband: and how thou hast left thy father and thy mother, and the land of thy nativity, and art come unto a people which thou knewest not heretofore."

So the "work" was the kindly, compassionate relationship of people in the common sorrow and losses of life. It was what they were to one another. Just their sticking to one another when things were difficult and lonely. Standing by one another when new things had to be faced. Being brave for another's sake when the future seemed empty.

What is more, the actors in this story, though unaware of it, were weaving strands in the divine pattern of life. What they were and what they did prepared the way for the coming of the Lord. From that scene of love and appreciative insight there runs a line at the end of which there stands Jesus Christ, the Saviour of the world.

All this is relevant to our tasks. If with love and devotion we do the common things; if we are faithful to one another in good or ill; if, trusting in Jesus Christ who is evermore calling us to the shelter of his wings, we do the hard things of our day and generation, we shall be blest.—H. J. F.

Suggested Texts and Themes

The Christian Accent: "And after a while came unto him they that stood by, and said to Peter, Surely thou also art one of them; for thy speech betrayeth thee." Matt. 26:73.

The Sin of Thoughtlessness: "And when he thought thereon, he wept." Mark 14:72.

The Christian Monopoly: "All [things] are yours." I Cor. 3:22.

Elective Affinity: "And being let go, they went to their own company." Acts 4:23.

Truth the Emancipator: "And ye shall

know the truth, and the truth shall make you free." John 8:32.

MIDWEEK FELLOWSHIP MEETING TOPIC

(Church Night or Suggested Sermon Subject)

Theme: Eternity in the Heart.

TEXT: "He hath set eternity in their hearts." Eccles. 3:11 (A.S.V.).

I. Then perhaps if we look carefully we may find it. Yes, an instinct for heaven. It does seem that God has put into the makeup of man eternal elements, spiritual aptitudes and longings, which seek to rise above the grossness of flesh and time.

II. The greatness of the human soul. Its capacity to receive, retain, develop, suffer, enjoy.

III. The necessity of soul culture. If we want a bright and lovely world, one we can enjoy as a paradise, we must endeavor to make our hearts right.

IV. Therefore the need of Divine influence. Who shall make these hearts of ours right? It is God's work. The Eternal within us seeks the Eternal, and nothing but the Eternal will feed it.

CHRISTIAN ENDEAVOR SOCIETY TOPIC

March 16. Examples in Winning Others: Paul Wins His Jailer. Acts 16: 25-34.

SUNDAY SCHOOL LESSON

March 16. Timothy a Dependable Follower. Acts 16:1-3; Phil. 2:19-24; II Tim. 2:1-5.

MEMORY SELECTION: "Let no one despise your youth, but set the believers an example in speech and conduct, in love, in faith, in purity." I Tim. 4:12 (R.S.V.).

Timothy was a man who could be counted on. The first Scripture passage tells of Paul's first acquaintance with him. The second, written late in Paul's ministry, tells of what a servant of Christ Timothy turned out to be. Paul's teaching in II Timothy concerning self-control and moral restraint may be used for temperance emphasis. There is an appeal here to young men brought up as was Timothy, in a godly home. There is appeal also for all Christian training. There is special appeal for Christian dependability.

SUNDAY: MARCH TWENTY-THIRD

Theme: Our Temptations (Lent).

SUGGESTED SCRIPTURE READING: James 1:1-27.

SELECTED HYMNS: "In the hour of trial."—J. Montgomery. "I need thee every hour."—A. S. Hawkes. "My soul, be on thy guard."—G. Heath. "O Jesus, I have promised."—J. E. Bode.

CALL TO WORSHIP: "They that wait upon the Lord shall renew their strength; they shall mount up with wings as eagles; they shall run, and not be weary; they shall walk, and not faint." "Wait on the Lord: be of good courage, and he shall strengthen thine heart."

INVOCATION PRAYER: It is a great privilege, O God, our Father, to have knowledge of the Gospel of Jesus Christ. It is in the name of Christ and by the power of the Gospel that we worship thee today and bind ourselves together in praise and aspiration and prayer. We are not worthy of the Gospel—that Christ should have humbled himself, lived a lowly life of service, endured the cross for us. This causes us to bow in humility. We can only thank thee for him, share our lives with him as he shared with us, let him be our ideal and example, accept him as our Saviour and follow him as our Lord. Hear our intercessions for all men. Bound in bundles of race and nationality, may they not be enslaved thereby, but in these find their nobler liberties. O Thou whose nearness is the answer to all our needs, help us in worshiping thee to lift our spirits above their weariness and littleness to thy eternal presence; and when our hour of worship is ended may the peace of it still possess us and its vision not grow dark. In Jesus' name we ask. Amen.

Theme: Our Temptations (Lent).

TEXT: "And lead us not into temptation, but deliver us from evil." Matt. 6:13.

INTRODUCTORY: The matter of our temptations is a most important and central Lenten theme.

I. The nature and uses of temptation. To live is to be tempted. Not to be conscious of life as a battle against temptation is already to have lost. Temptation is trial, testing, combat. To be kept from temptation would be to be kept from growth, from being men. What we pray is that we be not overcome by temptation, that strength may be equal to the demand. Arm us, O God, against temptation!

Temptation is a means of self-knowledge. Temptation brings the hidden truth to light. It is only when a man meets temptation that he knows the stuff that he is made of. Both the hidden weakness and the latent strength come to light. Peter, Judas, Paul, Thomas, Mark—there is no end to the list of those who reveal themselves to us by the light of temptation. Temptation is a great educator.

Many a man has thought himself in some peculiar sense hopeless because temptations have assailed him so fiercely. But it is no sin to be tempted. The sin lies in harboring temptation and temporizing with it.

II. The ways of dealing with temptation. 1. Avoidance. There is such a thing as willful walking into temptation. One has no right to expect help in a peril he needlessly invites. "Let him that thinketh he standeth take heed lest he fall." 2. Vigilance. "Watch and pray." Scripture has much warning against the dangers of sudden assault. Many a man is caught off his guard who could never be overcome when ready and alert. Sin is deceitful, has many masks, and appears in harmless, attractive guise. Sin is subtle, insidious, begins with little things, then habits are established that are hard to eradicate. "Watch, therefore." 3. "Watch and pray." Prayer, communion with God, brings the specific help and nourishes the sort of heart in which temptation does not readily take root. Prayer is a weapon no believer can be without. 4. And allied to this is a grasp of God's Word. The man whose mind is saturated with the Scriptures is armed. All great Christians have been mighty in the Scriptures. 5. And, finally, there is the presence of that pure and mighty Person through whom alone we may pray and who is the heart of the Word. In his might only can the battle be fought to victory. To look to him is to make every evil thing repulsive and impossible. United with him we hate what he hates and cannot but detest with all our hearts that fearful thing that nailed him to the cross. There is nothing that can so arm one against temptation as the sight of Gethsemane and the knowledge of what was in that bitter cup he had to drink. We cannot do despite to that love; and in the power of it which he imparts we are able to overcome.—P. H. R. (Adapted).

THEME PRAYER: O God, who knowest us to be set in the midst of so many and great dangers that by reason of the frailty of our nature we cannot always stand upright, grant to us such strength and protection as may support us in all dangers and carry us through all temptations. Through Jesus Christ our Lord. Amen.

OFFERTORY SENTENCE: "Every man according as he purposeth in his heart, so let him give; not grudgingly, or of necessity: for God loveth a cheerful giver."

OFFERTORY PRAYER: We would give unto thee, O Lord, the glory due unto thy name; we would bring an offering and come into thy courts. Remember in thy love those who have brought it and those for whom it is given. So follow it with thy blessing that thy kingdom may be advanced in the world. We ask through Christ our Lord. Amen. —H.

Illustrative Material

SEED THOUGHTS, HOMILETIC AND EXPOSITORY. God is better served in resisting a temptation to evil than in many formal prayers.—William Penn.

The realization of God's presence is the one sovereign remedy against temptation—Fénelon.

Every Christian is endued with a power whereby he is enabled to resist temptations.—Tillotson.

The time for reasoning is before we have approached near enough to the forbidden fruit to look at it and admire. —Margaret Percival.

Temptation: I. This prayer recognizes temptation as a part of the discipline of life. II. It traces to its source where it originates. III. It intimates that temptation generally results in sin. IV. It expresses on our part a shrinking from temptation through a sense of weakness. V. It is a joyful acknowledgment of God's power and strength to rescue us. —F. E.

Choice Illustrations on the Theme

TEMPTATION YIELDED TO OR RESISTED. If you apply a magnet to the end of a needle that moves freely on its pivot, the needle, affected by a strong attraction, approaches as if it loved it. Reverse the order, apply the magnet now to the other pole, and the needle shrinks away trembling as if it did not love but hated it. So it is with temptation. One man rushes into the arms of vice, another recoils from it with horror. According as the nature it addresses is holy or unholy temptation attracts or repels, is loved or hated.—*2500 Best Modern Illustrations.*

TEMPTATION RESISTED. I know a young, attractive fellow who is now up in Alaska doing a hard piece of work at small pay. Once he was a flyer and it seemed as though he might go a long way. His employers asked him to live in a way which he felt was very wrong. He gave up his place because he would not "fall down and worship" as they desired. It was hard for him to give up flying, but he is glad that he did not yield.

When temptation came to Jesus, his clean mind and common sense asserted themselves. He remembered again that which he had been taught at home and in the church. He said the thing which you and I must say hundreds of times if we are to live at our best: "Get thee behind me, Satan."—Clayton S. Rice.

THE SAFETY OF HIGHER LEVELS. Sportsmen complain that in Australia beautifully colored cockatoos perch on the highest branches of giant trees where rifle shots rattle on their brilliant feathers with no more force than a shower of hailstones. The birds evidently understand that there is a point where the bullets are ineffective. Having reached that lofty position, they are safe. It is equally true that there are people who live on such high levels of religious life and conduct that temptations are not nearly as strong as they are to those on lower levels.—Archer Wallace.

STAND UPON THY FEET! In the National Gallery in London there is (or was before the second Global War) a picture of Vittorio Pisano, an artist of the fifteenth century. In this picture a strong, manly youth is represented as standing beside an old man. The youth is St. George and the old man is St. Anthony. At the feet of St. George lies a dragon, dead, but hideous in aspect. At the feet of St. Anthony lies a tamed wild bear. These two men have won noble victories but in different ways. The dragon and the bear are symbols of those wild temptations which assail the flesh and which the old man has mastered and the young man has slain by one heroic effort. The circumstances and conditions that surround the human soul are never quite the same. The temptations that beset one man may not be the characteristic temptations of another. But whether it is St. George slaying his dragon or St. Anthony taming his bear, the victory is always won by manhood upon its feet. —W. A. Cameron.

PASSING UNSCATHED THROUGH TEMPTATION. It is said that the germs of the potato and vine disease are always floating in the air, but they can find no place of operation, no bed in healthy plants. But directly plants become degenerate, and unable to resist their attacks, then they sweep away the farmer's hopes in dreadful ruin. So it is with us. If only we were like our Lord, we should pass unscathed through a whirlwind of temptations. They would find nothing in us.—F. B. Meyer.

EVENING SERVICE

Theme: The God We Can Know.

TEXT: "For as I passed by, and beheld your devotions, I found an altar with this inscription, TO THE UNKNOWN GOD. Whom therefore ye ignorantly worship, him declare I unto you." Acts 17:23.

INTRODUCTORY: This is a day that demands the best in the presentation of the truth. People are critical. They are learning to detect and discard shams. Only that which proves its genuineness by meeting the exacting tests of life will endure, whether in religion or anything else. We must have a depth that comes from real experience if the religion of Christ is to mean what it ought to this age.

I. To many God is unknown. The altar in Athens inscribed TO THE UNKNOWN GOD is symbolic of the relation of many to God today. To multitudes God is still the Great Unknown. The actual objects of worship are those things in our lives to which we give the best of our time and devotion. In the midst of our absorption in the business of life, making a living and following our pet pursuits, some do pause to worship God, but too often he is unknown. Traditions that we have accepted without much thought and a feeling of fear for our own selves play a great part in our religion even yet. If that is all there is to our Christianity we are utterly selfish and God is to us the Unknown God.

II. But we can know God. All arguments to the contrary notwithstanding, here is a truth that we can experience as a foundation of our life. This is the message that we have for the world today, as Paul had it for his day. Paul had come to know God in a personal relationship that brought about the transforming of his life and brought satisfaction such as he had never known in the zealous days of his earlier life.

Christ is the supreme way to God. There is no other way to an acquaintance with his love and real character. Jesus came that we might come into a sacred intimacy with God whom men had known but imperfectly. Repentance and the exercise of faith are absolutely certain to result in a sense of forgiveness and the realization of the power to live a new life. There is no possible doubt about it. When conditions are met on the human side God does his part every time.

III. Consider also the power of the Gospel when God becomes real and near, living Truth. There is complete satisfaction in knowing God in Christ. We are so constituted that we never can be completely satisfied with anything less. Great is the day in our experience when this truth becomes real to us and we begin to act upon it. Our faith as Christians rests, even in this difficult day, upon a foundation that is surer than ever. Experience, as always, is still the test by which the truth must be demonstrated. The Gospel for this age is the same Gospel, a simple experience of faith, but verified by the hardest tests of which men are capable. Putting God to the test in the pressure of modern life, we find indeed that "he be not far from every one of us: for in him we live, and move, and have our being." The God we can know is the God Christ shows us.—J. R. C.

Suggested Texts and Themes

Religion for Two Worlds: "For bodily exercise profiteth little: but godliness is profitable unto all things, having promise of the life that now is, and of that which is to come." I Tim. 4:8.

Parental Responsibility: "And she went forth, and said unto her mother, What shall I ask?" (Salome to Herodias, who answered, "The head of John the Baptist.") Mark 6:24.

Self-denying Consecration: "He made the laver . . . and the foot of it of brass, of the lookingglasses of the women," etc. Ex. 38:8.

The Heavenly Vision: "Who art thou, Lord?" "What wilt thou have me to do?" Acts 9:5, 6.

MIDWEEK FELLOWSHIP MEETING TOPIC

(Church Night or Suggested Sermon Subject)

Theme: We Are Not Our Own (Lent).

TEXT: "Ye are not your own, ye are bought with a price." I Cor. 6:19, 20.

The youth first freed from home and parental restraints says, with masterful spirit: "Now my time, money, career, are my own. I have my own thought, my own way." Every man should in a sense be his own master; but this is but one turn of the affirmative. The other turn is self-abnegation. Only through both realizations do we get the Christian view of salvation. We are not our own.

I. A certain physical order owns us. My hand is my own; but if I put it in fire it burns, etc.

II. A certain social order owns us; capital and labor mutually dependent. We could not live but by conforming to the way of life, of city, state, etc. Government owns us.

III. The moral order owns us. It is penal; crime is punished; sin ruins.

IV. A divine redemptive order owns us. Its forces are inescapable. God, Christ, Holy Ghost, Church, creed, etc. "Bought with a price"—all the past, especially Calvary, is the price.

V. Self-possession is through Christ-possession. As in the other orders, a man wholly self-dependent becomes homeless, outcast, impossible. So in the case of his soul. Only by surrendering self do we find ourselves.

VI. This is the final and only way to power. It is in serving a higher that we ourselves get higher, stronger. The merely individual life is irresponsible. Without sense of responsibility no strength, no discipline.

Life is service. We are to ask Christ what he will have us do.—A. G.

CHRISTIAN ENDEAVOR SOCIETY TOPIC

March 23. Growing Up Spiritually. Phil. 3:7-15; James 1:19-27.

SUNDAY SCHOOL LESSON

March 23. Lydia Who Opened Her Heart and Home. Acts 16:6-15, 40.

MEMORY SELECTION: "A woman that feareth the Lord, she shall be praised." Prov. 31:30.

Lydia was Paul's first recorded convert in Europe. In opening her heart to the gospel and her home to the apostle her own life was completely changed. She was a business woman. She testified, told her story to others. She showed great hospitality. She was open-minded, gladly accepting Paul's teachings. Her industry and hospitality and zeal are all symbolic of the great service women have rendered to the Christian Church and to the cause of Christ ever since.

SUNDAY: MARCH THIRTIETH

MORNING SERVICE

Theme: Walking in the Spirit (Lent).

Suggested Scripture Reading: Gal. 5:1-26.

Selected Hymns: "More love to thee, O Christ."—E. P. Prentiss. "Lead us, O Father, in the paths of peace."—W. H. Burleigh. " 'Tis by faith of joys to come."—I. Watts. "Walk in the light, so shalt thou know."—B. Barton.

Call to Worship: "Blessing, and glory, and wisdom, and thanksgiving and honor, and power, and might, be unto our God for ever and ever." "O magnify the Lord with me, and let us exalt his name together."

Invocation Prayer: Almighty God, our heavenly Father, thou hast fashioned us for thyself. We cannot find rest till we find it in thee. Frail and mortal, as all things on earth are mortal, yet thou hast taught us to live as creatures capable of immortality and eternal life. We bless thee for these inner visions, these heavenly promptings, these spiritual instincts, these inextinguishable hopes. Teach us then, our Father, the importance, the gravity of life. Teach us to so number our days that we shall apply our hearts unto wisdom. Help those of us who are young and know now the seductions of the world that we may be kept from the great transgression. May we and they be so enamored of all things right and pure and lovely and of good report, that evil shall not be able to gain dominion over us. Vouchsafe, O Lord, to keep us this day without sin, in the name of Jesus Christ our Saviour we ask. Amen.

Theme: Walking in the Spirit (Lent).

Text: "Walk in the Spirit, and ye shall not fulfil the lust of the flesh," etc. Gal. 5:16-24.

Introductory: To strengthen us in this worthy walk is the very purpose of the Lenten observance. The Christian life is well conceived in this figure of walking. Text.

I. There are two ways, or roads, on either of which one may be walking, the broad or the narrow, the way of death or the way of life. Walking is living. It is our life's movement forward in this world. Is there a guide for the way? Where is the Guide? Here is Paul's answer, "This I say then, walk in the Spirit." There is one wise way to take, and by God's providing the safe Guide it is that of his Holy Spirit.

Two forces strive for the mastery in us, the flesh and the Spirit. It is easy and natural to follow the flesh; but to follow the Spirit goes against nature and requires self-sacrifice. Yet the easy way is the wrong way and the hard way is the right way. Bear in mind, the "flesh" does not mean our bodies. It means our fallen, sinful nature which lives for self-gratification.

The spirit of the world is that of the flesh. It walks by sight, not by faith. It takes the easy, luxurious way. It does as it wishes, always following its desires. It never sacrifices the low things for the high. It thinks always of the now, not of the future, of the material, not of the spiritual. The difference between the two ways is as broad as east is from the west. It is a radical difference.

II. The consequent results, or fruits. "These are contrary the one to the other."

1. For example, we shall not expect good, pure things from the fleshy heart. And we shall know that all good thoughts and deeds come from the Spirit-filled heart. For another thing, we shall see that there is no middle

position, that no one can walk east and west at the same time, not by the flesh and the Spirit at once.

Now the works of the flesh are such as these, lust, idolatry, strife, drunkenness, revelry, and many, many more. They are sins of abuse, of perverting God's good gifts to excess. They have wrought fearful harm in the world. They are plainly of the flesh. They often call for pity and forbearance. But of all the catalogue Paul plainly declares that they who do such things shall not inherit the kingdom of God.

2. The fruit of the Spirit. God be thanked, we need have no part or lot in such things or such results. We have a divine life to live and can have, by God's grace, power to live it. The fruit of the Spirit is love, joy, peace, longsuffering, gentleness, goodness, faith, meekness, self-control. Wonderful. Desirable. Cultivatable.

III. The method of conquering. "Walk in the Spirit." For one thing, live a positive life. There are two ways of dealing with every vice. One is to set to work directly to destroy it. The better way is the strategic way, to "overcome evil with good," to bring in as overwhelmingly as possible the opposite virtue. Walking in the Spirit means a steady movement forward. Let us accept this Lenten opportunity as a period for strengthening of purpose and the accepting of God's grace for a more steady and more progressive walk in a Spirit-led way.

THEME PRAYER: O God, who hast for Christ's sake given us the great gift of forgiveness of sins, we confess that we have indeed received less than our iniquity deserves. But lest we stop with this confession, grant us grace to follow on to share the fellowship of his sufferings, "who for us men and for our salvation came down from heaven." In this Lenten Season wilt thou enable us to draw near to thee. We ask in Jesus' name. Amen.

OFFERTORY SENTENCES "Lay up for yourselves treasures in heaven, where neither moth nor rust doth corrupt, and where thieves do not break through nor steal."

OFFERTORY PRAYER: It is with indeed grateful hearts we bring thee our offerings this day, our Father. Thou hast done great things for us whereof we are glad. Wilt thou graciously bless these gifts of thy people and use them toward the bringing in of thy kingdom. We ask in Christ's name. Amen.

Illustrative Material

SEED THOUGHTS, HOMILETIC AND EXPOSITORY. Walk in the Spirit: I. Here is first a duty enforced. The duty is to walk in the Spirit, which is the sum of all Christian character. Walking implies our course of action. II. There is, secondly, the consequent fruit of it. "Ye shall not fulfil the lust of the flesh." This is the motive.—T. M.

Flesh versus Spirit: I. The root of sin and evil. The flesh with its lusts. II. The opposite principle and root of life and righteousness. The Divine Spirit. III. The bounds of Christian conquest. "Shall not fulfil the lust of the flesh." IV. The method and way of conquering. "Walk in the Spirit."—J. B.

"Man's nature presents two sides. Walking in the Spirit is the preservative from the lust of the flesh."

Choice Illustrations on the Theme

WALK IN THE SPIRIT. Live a positive life. Use strategy against sin. To replace is to conquer. "Be not overcome of evil, but overcome evil with good." How cultivate the garden of the soul so as to preclude weeds? Ask the horticulturist. He says the way to preclude weeds is to cultivate flowers; at least, to grow grasses. There are said to be but four weeds which cannot be "run out" in this way—milkweed, live-forever, Canada thistle, and toad flax. To exterminate these requires a major operation. Napoleon's favorite aphorism was, "To replace is to conquer." Weeds can be run out of the soul by replacing them with their opposites. Selfishness, for instance, by a lively interest in others; by doing some good things for others; by putting oneself second in respect of others. The same in respect of miserliness, which can be crowded out by intentional generosity. The same in respect of jealousy and envy—really dogs in the manger, or dogs in the heart—which can be driven out by words of admiration for those of whom jealous, and words of praise for those envied. "To replace is to conquer."—Alfred H. C. Morse.

RUN HARD TO STAY. The *Christian Advocate* quotes from *Alice in Wonderland* the truthful paradox that "you have to run as hard as you can to stay where you are." It is certainly true in the Christian life that we will retrograde if we do not run. But we must run in the right direction and "so run that we may obtain."

LOSING GOD. The late Rev. F. S. Miller, missionary in Korea, illustrating how a man may lose his consciousness of God, tells of an old native man and his son who were on a train going to Seoul. When they looked for their railway ticket it could not be found. The conductor said he would come through again and for them to keep up their search. They hunted through their clothing and baggage and scolded each other. Finally the son opened up his underclothing and there in a secret pocket, wrapped in a paper, he found the ticket all safe and sound. "When you feel that you have lost God, do not search the heavens above or the earth beneath, just look in your heart," said Mr. Miller.

SPIRITUAL LIFE MAINTAINED. A fountain is not a fire, but it may illustrate how the Christian life may be maintained. In the London *Christian* we read that at St. Margaret's, on the South Coast of England, there is a well of water which is below the high-tide mark, so that when the tide comes in, the sea water covers the well. But the sea never gets in, although twice a day it passes over the top. How is it that the well remains fresh and pure? It is fed from the hills above. There is a constant source of sweet, pure water ever flowing in, keeping the salt, brackish water from entering and defiling the well. How can the Christian life be maintained? How is it possible, amid all the temptations and degradation of this world, for the Christian to be pure and sweet, always loving, tender and gracious? No man is equal to this task in his own strength. But there is a source of supply coming from the eternal hills of heaven that will be like a well of water within the Christian, keeping back from him the tides of evil, preserving him in the hour of trial, and filling him with the love of Christ.

EVENING SERVICE

Theme: Making Allowances.

TEXT: "The spirit indeed is willing, but the flesh is weak." Matt. 26:41.

INTRODUCTORY: There are times when it is hard to make allowances for other people. Even if we do forgive we are haunted by a lingering resentment. To make allowance when someone dear has failed us, to forget judgment in a great compassion, to go on trusting hopefully after the shock of discovered infidelity—that, which falls to the lot of many people though they very seldom speak about it, is one of the hardest tasks in human life.

I. Now it was such a task that met our Saviour in the Garden of Gethsemane. The hearts on whose fidelity he counted in one blinding flash were found to be unfaithful. The love that had been so terribly wronged wove the garment of mercy round the sinners. And so doing it saved their souls alive and led them onward to that brighter morrow when infidelities were all to be redeemed.

II. To understand that magnificence of attitude ponder a moment on the sleep of these disciples. It was not a venial fault of drowsiness; it was a heinous sin of infidelity. It is always a very grave offense if a sentry be found sleeping at his post. Often the penalty for that is death. And these men were not only there in comradeship; they were there to watch as well as to keep awake. Yet Jesus, toward his disloyal soldiers, who were also his disloyal lovers, maintained a pitying love that was redemptive. To condemn them would have been entirely natural. To keep them still within his heart was heavenly. So our Saviour points the better way for all who find their Garden of Gethsemane in the disloyalties of someone who is dear.

III. And then, mingling with disloyalty, think of the ingratitude involved. "What, could ye not watch with me?" For a moment put the accent upon me. Have not I been the best of friends to you? Have not I toiled for you and prayed for you? At the heart of it lies rank ingratitude. All the patient ministries of years are forgotten because the flesh is weak.

IV. He remembered it was long past midnight. He remembered the awful strain of the past days. He remembered the sorrow that consumed them, and their burden of unintelligible mystery. And all condemning wrath was swallowed up in an infinite compassion. "The spirit is willing, but the flesh is weak." Never was there kindlier allowance. It was the consummate handling of heaven. It issued not in tragedy, but in the richer loyalties of resurrection days.—M.

Additional Theme: The Christian in the World.

TEXT: "Not slothful in business; fervent in spirit; serving the Lord." Rom. 12:11.

INTRODUCTORY: The Christian religion is meant to be disseminated throughout the world, and this can only be done by its application to life in all its many departments and avocations.

We are therefore recreant to our trust if we refrain from taking Christianity with us into the world: if we refrain from bringing Christianity to bear on all the situations and occasions of life.

We rightly criticize those who, possessed of something good and worth while, refuse to take steps to share it with others.

It might be said that some callings positively do not lend themselves to the application of the Christian ethic. If anything, the contrary is the case. It is conceivable that the application of Christianity to certain undertakings might well be the extinction of that particular undertaking. That is the best thing that could happen to some businesses! But however menial or humble the work, Christianity ought to be the mainspring of all its activity.

I. The trouble with so many people is that they cannot regard Christianity as a leaven in the world. They regard religion as an "extra subject." Even if we accept this explanation as valid, it is astonishing what such people do make time for. But religion is not an extra subject. Religion is nothing if not a help in dealing with the myriad tasks and preoccupations of life.

II. There are still those about us who maintain their insularity as Christian theorists on the ground that the world and its affairs are "secular" in character. There are many people who, though not living in monasteries, live in cells. Their Christianity is hermetically sealed.

It is to be our imperative duty to take Christian principles with us into the world. How it would simplify the tasks of statesmen in hammering out policies if every consideration were made subordinate to a passion to establish God's kingdom on earth as it is in heaven! Happy is the man who can approach all the phenomena of life in this truly realistic manner and can impregnate all with a divine significance.

III. We often have strange material to work on. It is not always plastic and pliable, and it is hard to bring the mind of the Master to bear upon it. But it is amazing what can be done. We often find ourselves like Michelangelo taking rejected marble and working out in it a truly majestic conception of divine glory; or Copley Fielding, doing little masterpieces on tiny postcards. The truly good men of this world are they who, having the mind of the Master, emulate his methods in the world. We do meet men sometimes who are so actuated by Christian principles that their conduct is unconsciously Christian. No man can live on such a plane of soul if his Christianity be merely an adjunct to his life. It must be the mainspring of all his actions.

By witnessing for Christ by our lives we shall teach our contemporaries many things. We shall show them the incredible folly of conducting any business in this fleeting and transient world that is not in the Christian perspective. Let us so impress these values on people that they too will seek the pearl of great price.—C. W. P.

Suggested Texts and Themes

Our Brother's Burden: "Bear ye one another's burdens." Gal. 6:2.

Disclosures by the Way: "Did not our heart burn within us, while he talked with us by the way . . . ?" Luke 24:32.

Treating: "Woe unto him that giveth his neighbour drink." Hab. 2:15.

Be Vigilant: "Take ye heed, watch and pray: for ye know not when the time is." Mark 13:33.

The Immutable Christ: "But thou art the same and thy years shall not fail." Heb. 1:12.

MIDWEEK FELLOWSHIP MEETING TOPIC

(Church Night or Suggested Sermon Subject)

Theme: Pharaoh's Butler.

TEXT: "Then spake the chief butler unto Pharaoh, saying, I do remember my faults this day." Gen. 41:9.

There are said to be three words in the English language most difficult to pronounce. They are, "I am wrong." Circumstances taught Pharaoh's butler to say them.

I. From this story let us learn first the power of ingratitude. How easily the butler might have kept his promise! Are you ungrateful?

II. Secondly, let us learn the power of memory. The butler's memory went back two years. Then he saw Joseph in prison and his own broken promise. In memory God has given us a wonderful faculty. Use it well.

III. Thirdly, let us learn the power of a single event. What caused the butler to remember Joseph? The king's dream. How suggestive often are little things!

IV. Again, the power of conscience. The butler began to think about his faults. Sense of personal blameworthiness. Blessed monitor!

V. Lastly, the power of intercession. The butler interceded with the king for Joseph. This led to Joseph's freedom and exaltation. Think of the good we may do to others in this way.—H. R.

CHRISTIAN ENDEAVOR SOCIETY TOPIC

March 30. Techniques of Personal Worship. John 5:39; Matt. 6:5-8.

SUNDAY SCHOOL LESSON

March 30. Luke Physician and Historian. Luke 1:1-4; Acts 1:1, 2; 16:6-10; Col. 4:14.

MEMORY SELECTION: "You shall receive power when the Holy Spirit has come upon you; and you shall be my witnesses in Jerusalem and in all Judea and Samaria and to the end of the earth." Acts 1:8 (R.S.V.).

Luke's main contribution to the cause of Christ was in writing his Gospel and Acts. His work was that of an evangelical historian. Luke in his gospel gives not a few stories of Jesus not found elsewhere. It is to be remembered that he was a doctor, but willingly gave much time to his religious work. He was greatly gifted in literary style, and greatly advanced Christ's cause by writing for the Gentiles. He was a most helpful companion of Paul on different journeys. It is sure that this lesson teaches us the privilege and importance of being witnesses for Christ.

SUNDAY: APRIL SIXTH

MORNING SERVICE

Theme: All the City Was Moved (Palm Sunday).

Suggested Scripture Reading: Matt. 21:6-11.

Selected Hymns: "Ride on, ride on, in majesty."—H. H. Milman. "All glory, laud and honor."—John M. Neal, Jr. "When his salvation bringing."—John King. "O could I speak the matchless worth."—S. Medley. "All hail the power of Jesus name."—Edward Perronet.

Call to Worship: "And the multitudes that went before, and that followed, cried, saying, Hosanna to the son of David: Blessed is he that cometh in the name of the Lord; Hosanna in the highest."

Invocation Prayer (Palm Sunday): Thy mercy, O Lord, is new every morning, and every evening we have new cause to praise thee. We thank thee for this new day and its new hopes. We thank thee for thine own presence with us, our Strength and our Redeemer. Dwell in our hearts continually through thy Holy Spirit. We bless thee, O God, that thou hast given us thine own Son to be our King. Hosanna in the highest! Let his name endure for ever; let it be above every name. Subdue us once for all unto him. Come, Lord Jesus, and assert thy place in our hearts! Reign over all the children of men. Speak peace to those that follow thee and make them partakers of thy victory. Thine, O Lord, is the kingdom and the power and the glory and the victory and the majesty. All that is in the heaven and the earth is thine. Thou art exalted as Lord over all. May we this day enthrone thee as king of our lives. In thine own name we ask. Amen.

Theme: All the City Was Moved (Palm Sunday).

Text: "And when he was come into Jerusalem, all the city was moved, saying, Who is this?" Matt. 21:10.

Introductory: Preparation was being made for the Passover feast. Crowds had flocked to Jerusalem from many regions. There was much excitement, and into the midst of it all had crept the rumor that Jesus of Nazareth was coming and that the authorities had announced he must be arrested. Probably the majority sided with those in authority.

I. Note, first, that Jesus' entering into Jerusalem was in fulfillment of his own purpose. As he nears the city crowds come out to meet him. Those from Jerusalem turn back and escort him, while those from Bethany follow behind. They are singing, "Hosanna to the Son of David: Blessed is he that cometh in the name of the Lord; Hosanna in the highest!" "And when he was come near, he beheld the city, and wept over it."

Christ had "steadfastly set his face to go to Jerusalem," and even though he went with a broken heart, and even though it brought the agony of Gethsemane, he went steadily on believing it to be the will of his Father, and the fulfillment of a life purpose. He never for a moment let the praise and the acclaim of the crowd turn him from his true objective. He was entering Jerusalem for the last time. He had come for a purpose and that purpose must be fulfilled.

Israel had prepared for hundreds of years to receive the Christ, the Messiah. But he had come in such an unpretentious way, speaking directly to the hearts and lives of men and women, caring nothing for pomp and ceremony, a servant because he was their King, and a

King because he was their servant, revealing to them the love and character of God himself, and still Israel asks, "Who is this?"

II. This is the cry of the universal heart, "Who is this?" It is not now the impassioned cry of "Hosanna" to the King. The answer is in quieter tone, "This is Jesus, the prophet of Nazareth of Galilee." The enthusiasm is waning. He is no longer the great King, no longer will the hosannas rend the air, and before long the streets will be filled with a seething mob lusting for the blood of this Just Man.

1. Consider this, that though we may be elated for the time, though we may hear the hosannas of the crowd, the time comes when the shadow of a cross looms before us, as it did before him. There comes a time when we must look above and beyond the hosannas to the tragedy that awaits. Tragedy, yes, but more than tragedy, victory! The victory that Christ himself found, the victory of the cross.

2. Note also that this entry of Jesus into Jerusalem was the final offering of himself to the Jewish nation as their Messiah, as also to the entire world. And there came a time in your experience and mine when he offered himself to us, when our hearts were touched by his infinite love, and when we answered to our satisfaction the question. "Who is this?" If perchance he has thus come to you for the first time this Palm Sunday morning, are you ready and willing to respond to that call and say, "Thou art the Christ, the Son of the living God, my Saviour"?—After W. J. L.

THEME PRAYER: "Our Father, as we now remember our Redeemer's triumphant entry into the city, make us, we beseech thee, sharers in his devoted spirit. May he now and ever triumph in our hearts and let us lay ourselves in full and joyful homage before him, through the same Jesus Christ our Lord." Amen.

OFFERTORY SENTENCE: "If there be first a willing mind, it is accepted according to that a man hath, and not according to that he hath not."

OFFERTORY PRAYER: We come to thee with glad hearts bearing an offering not of palms to be strewn in thy pathway, O Christ, but of human hearts yearning for opportunity to serve thee in thy plan for the salvation of the world. Wilt thou graciously accept and bless and use these our gifts of gratitude for the forwarding of thy kingdom in all the earth. We ask in thine own name, O Christ. Amen.—H.

Illustrative Material

SEED THOUGHTS, HOMILETIC AND EXPOSITORY. An Exciting Inquiry: I. Who comes? "Who is this?" No temporal deliverer. A Divine King. The Son of God. World needing a Redeemer. To humanity needing a Ruler. To individual souls needing a King. II. In what manner does he come? Meek. Lowly. III. How ought we to prepare to receive him? Go forth to meet him. In holy desire. Putting away sin. Praying for his blessing. Ready to obey.—W. H. H.

The Triumphal Entry: I. By thus riding through the streets in state Christ claimed to be a King. II. What sort of a King he might have been had he so chosen. III. What kind of a King he is, or claimed to be. IV. The practical objects of this kingdom.—C. H. S.

Choice Palm Sunday Illustrations

HIS THRONE A CROSS. Palm Sunday heralded the King, but his throne was to be a cross. Christ deliberately put aside the promise of Palm Sunday. Not in the shouting multitudes but in the inquiring Gentiles before the Temple he saw the promise of victory. Not in the outward demonstrations but in the heart-hunger of humanity today he has his hope for a redeemed universe.—E. W. Caswell.

OTHER TRIUMPHAL PROCESSIONS. There are not lacking many historical events that will illustrate honors paid to heroes of days long gone by. Herodotus pictures Xerxes passing over the bridge of the Hellespont with the air filled with fragrance from the burning perfumes and his pathway strewed with branches of myrtle.

Only about thirty years after Christ's triumphal entry history records the magnificent honor paid to Pompey in Rome. For two days there was a great procession of captives, with many trophies, moving into the city along the *Via Sacra*. The brazen tablets bore the names of conquered nations, castles and cities taken.

As Alexander the Great entered Babylon flowers were scattered before him. Later the way of a Persian ruler was strewn with flowers for three miles and vessels filled with sugar were broken beneath his horses' feet, the sugar being the symbol of prosperity.—*5000 Best Modern Illustrations.*

PALM SUNDAY PROCESSION

Now near and nearer draws the throng,
Redoubling as it moves along.
It climbs the steep; the "Golden Gate"
It passes, pleased to celebrate
That meek prince riding to His throne—
While rings, in ever rising tone,
"Hosanna!"

Still the same motley groups appear.
Blind, lame and poor are ever near;
Still venal traders plot for greed;
Stalk priest and scribe of slippery creed.
Oh, for the Christ, and Christ-like men;
While sweet child-voices plead again—
"Hosanna!"

—Unidentified.

HE IS "REX." Jesus Christ is the mightiest moral personality in the universe. He is "Rex." And what men need more than anything else this very day is a sense of God in and ruling the world.—J. F. Cowan.

THE KINGLY CHRIST. Dear to the Christian world is the story of Christ's one day of triumph, Palm Sunday. The Church rejoices because even for one brief day he was hailed as King.

PALM SUNDAY ENTHUSIASM. Palm Sunday was the day of overflowing emotionalism. It was a wild, unbalanced crowd that surged over Olivet from Bethany and out to Olivet from Jerusalem. Emotionalism wins no battles, subdues no passions, checks no evils, rights no wrongs. The emotions that can be excited to wild cries of Hosanna, Hallelujah, can also be excited to cursings and maledictions. The figure that emotion sets upon the colt today, it will hand upon the cross tomorrow. The lips that will cry "Hosanna to our King" today, will cry tomorrow "We have no king but Caesar."

Suggested Palm Sunday Texts and Theme

A Wonderful Procession: "Thy kingdom come." Matt. 6:10.

The Royal Christ: "Yet have I set my king upon my holy hill of Zion." Ps. 2:6.

The Increasing Procession: "Behold, the world is gone after him." John 12:19.

The Desire of All Nations: "The desire of all nations shall come." Haggai 2:1-9.

Times of Visitation: "Because thou knewest not the time of thy visitation." Luke 19:44.

Christ as King. "The sceptre shall not depart from Judah." Gen. 49:10.

EVENING SERVICE

Theme: Caesar or Christ.

TEXT: "Thou art not Caesar's friend." John 19:12.

INTRODUCTORY: "Thou art not Caesar's friend." Well, what of that? What difference should that make?

I. It might make a world of difference in Pilate's worldly condition. Pilate was dependent on Caesar's favor. A frown from Caesar and in Pilate's life it is winter. A smile from Caesar and in Pilate's life it is glorious summer. If Caesar lifted a finger Pilate's place was empty. One word from Rome and Pilate was on the dust heap. And, therefore, when this boisterous crowd, shouting fiercely for the crucifixion of Jesus, reminded Pilate that imperial

Caesar was concerned in his judgments, they were bringing to bear upon him a mighty implement of fear. If they could not influence Pilate's reason they would seek to coerce his will. If everything else failed they would try the goad of fear. And so they cried out to him, as he wavered uncertainly in the seat of judgment: "if thou let this man go, thou art not Caesar's friend."

II. How did the uncertainty end? Pilate knew that Jesus was innocent, and yet he acted as though Jesus was guilty. Pilate was convinced of our Lord's integrity and yet he delivered him over to death. That is to say, the intimidation of the crowd was mightier than the constraint of his own conscience.

III. Now here we may seem to be a long way from Pilate, and from the critical choices which were presented to him, but the separating space is only apparent, and in reality we have traveled no distance at all. It is true that we do not wear Pilate's robes, and we do not share his power, but we stand precisely in the same place of judgment. Exactly the same choices are offered to you and me as were offered to him. We have to make our choice between principal and profit, between righteousness and expediency, between honor and safety, between integrity and ease, between Caesar and Christ; and we are exposed to essentially the same forms of menace and persuasion.—J.

MIDWEEK FELLOWSHIP MEETING TOPIC

(Church Night or Suggested Sermon Subject)

Theme: This Cup (Holy Week).

TEXT: "Can ye drink of the cup that I drink of?" Mark 10:38.

Here we get a glimpse into a dark old olive orchard, and we see our Master in an hour of agony that is beyond comprehension. He himself spoke of his suffering as a cup, Mark 14:26.

I. Once before he had spoken of this cup. 1. Men were asking to sit with him as companions in his glory. 2. "Are ye able to drink the cup?" 3. Now we begin to see the time when the cup was drained to its bitter dregs.

II. That was a hard cup. It held agony of soul, sweat of blood, loneliness. "What, could ye not watch with me one hour?" It held betrayal by a friend, suffering and death.

III. We who choose companionship with him today must face the same question, "Are ye able to drink the cup?" 1. We meet the cup of pain. 2. We taste the cup of sorrow. 3. We drain the cup of loneliness. 4. But do we drink the cup in a way that is to his glory, and do we walk with him?

Here is the call to companionship with Jesus. Life is barren and fruitless without him. We must drink the bitter cups with him or alone. Yet if we answer the call, we must share the cup. "Are ye able to drink the cup?"—with Him?

CHRISTIAN ENDEAVOR SOCIETY TOPIC

April 6. What Is Holy Week? Mark 11: 1-11; Mark 14-32-36.

BULLETIN BOARD SLOGANS FOR THE MONTH

By Earl Riney

Immortality like truth and justice lives within us.

Death is no more to be feared than birth.

Through their tears the sorrowful have first seen heaven's gate.

Heaven is only deaf when man's soul is dumb.

The best is the last of life for which the first was made.

Duty may be the mountain road to God.

Our opportunities often lie in the silences of God.

The good in us is God at work.

Sincerity and simplicity are two essentials in Christian character.

The law of living is the law of giving.

SUNDAY SCHOOL LESSON

April 6. A Fellowship of Many Followers. John 15:5-9; Phil. 2:14-16; Rom. 16:1-7.

MEMORY SELECTION: "By this my Father is glorified, that you bear much fruit, and so prove to be my disciples." John 15:8.

The early Christian fellowship was a society of real people, many of them obscure; but all played a real part. The Christian faith has been passed on ever since by ordinary people. They have been inspired of God and aided by the Holy Spirit. By the time of this lesson the group that began with a few fishermen had grown to a great company. In our day this movement is reaching all nations. Jesus taught us to pray "Thy kingdom come." It is coming. He never would have deceived us into offering this prayer were it not to have an answer.

SUNDAY: APRIL THIRTEENTH

MORNING SERVICE

Theme: Within the Doors (Easter).

SUGGESTED SCRIPTURE READING: Luke 24:1-32.

SELECTED HYMNS: "Welcome, happy morning."—V. H. C. Fortunatus. "The day of resurrection."—John of Damascus. "Christ the Lord is risen today."—C. Wesley. "Angels roll the rock away."—T. Scott.

CALL TO WORSHIP: "Now is Christ risen from the dead, and become the firstfruits of them that slept." "Thanks be unto God who giveth us the victory, through our Lord Jesus Christ."

INVOCATION PRAYER: Our blessed God and Father in Christ, we praise thee for this holy Easter morning. May we all be in the Spirit on the Lord's day. Lift our thoughts and affections and sympathies above earthly things. Enable us to enter into the heavenly tranquillity and holy Sabbath-keeping of thine own people. We thank thee for the empty grave. The Lord we love is risen indeed. May we be calm and trustful knowing that the reins of power are in his safe hands. Into thy holy keeping we commend one another, and all who are dear to us, the young and the old, those by our side and those far away. Make us each day by day more faithful and humble, more apt to catch thy whisper, more brave to carry thy cross. Purge our hearts from guile and envy and bitterness, and forgive all our sins, for, our Father, thou seest how much we need to be forgiven. We ask all through Christ our Saviour. Amen.

Theme: Within the Doors (Easter).

TEXT: "Then came Jesus, the doors being shut, and stood in the midst." John 20:26.

INTRODUCTORY: You remember the circumstances. Fear of arrest, defeat certain, hope gone, they were on the losing side. The world as they had planned and lived for it was quite impossible.

I. The miracle. It seemed certain to them that the cause of right, the great restoration of Israel and mankind, the very promises of God, were all doomed. Then the miracle—Jesus stood in the midst! And because he was in the midst, because he stood there, they thought of all the forces behind him. They were reminded of the power of God. Here was the Power greater than death. It was the incredible fact that, the doors being shut, hopes barred outside, Jesus the defeated Man, the lost Cause, was there, and the future assured! It must have been a great moment indeed. A desperate situation, a black outlook, an ominous future, a bleak and hopeless prospect—then, Jesus in the midst.

II. Then came the thought: "If God can do this, he can do anything!" Here was the Master whom they had seen arrested after betrayal, tried, sentenced, flogged, mocked, humiliated, spat upon, crowned with thorns, driven bleeding, crucified and buried—here was the Master alive, real, solid, in the midst, saying, "Peace be unto you." They were on the winning side; all was well!

III. Now there is one thing I have to stress, and it is this. The Christian religion, our hopes as well, are centered in the Person of Jesus Christ. They did not, nor do we, focus upon the words, the teaching of Jesus. They, and we, focus the attention upon Jesus, the Person of Jesus. The words, the teaching, do not redeem men. Jesus redeems men. The Living Jesus redeems men. It is this—when the doors are shut, when all hope is gone, when we are not sure about anything or anybody and ourselves least of all; when God and good seem defeated—Jesus comes, and stands in the midst—right inside. Jesus, the Living Christ, the Son of God—and he says, "Peace be unto you."

IV. That is the story of the redeemed libertines, drunkards, thieves, murderers, savages, cultured barbarians, men and women in the university, or unlearned who had forgotten God. That is the story: when people had been shut in, closed up, imprisoned, helpless, Jesus came in. Something happened. The sinner—whether a drug fiend, a drink fiend, a sex fiend, a blood fiend, or any sort of a devil—when he or she knew that there was nothing but failure, that nothing was certain but defeat, says that when Jesus came in—right inside of the heart and stood in the midst—there was peace, and victory. That is the story of Christianity. "If Christ be not risen, then our preaching is in vain." It is the fact that Jesus, the crucified Man, is greater than death, greater than time, greater than sin, and can redeem any man or woman, cast out any devil. That makes Christianity.

V. A last word. It is a mistake to think that Jesus enters only into the hearts and lives of very sinful people, or folk who are quite without hope. I am not preaching to bad people, although you and I are sinners. I want to stress this: there is no victory without Christ even in the lesser struggles. Nothing that is within your heart and mine can withstand his power if we let him in. The Easter message is not what Christ has done, but what Christ does. He has never stopped working miracles, and he never will—in any life, in any circumstances. He can be really there, risen, radiant, within the doors.—P. H.

Theme Prayer: We give thee thanks, O God, our Father, for the many voices that tell of thee, the many places where thy glory is revealed. But above all we thank thee for the revelation of thyself in Jesus Christ our Lord, whose Gospel, manifested in his word and cross and resurrection, reveals the deep secret of thy love for mankind. Help us to keep faith with him. Amen.—Harold E. Nicely, D.D.

Offertory Sentence: "If ye be risen with Christ, seek those things which are above."

Offertory Prayer: God and Father of us all, help us being risen with Christ to seek those things which are above, and to seek also the advancement of thy kingdom here upon the earth. Receive and bless the offerings which we consecrate this day to thy cause. In the name of Christ we ask. Amen.

Illustrative Material

SEED THOUGHTS, HOMILETIC AND EXPOSITORY. Peace from the Risen Christ: I. The blessing pronounced. "Peace." 1. Needed by minds perplexed with doubt. 2. By consciences oppressed with guilt. 3. By hearts burdened with sorrow. II. Who pronounced it? 1. He who had felt himself the need of it. 2. He whose death had purchased it.

3. He whose life secures it. III. When? 1. When the resurrection had ratified it. 2. When the disciples were seeking it.—N. H.

Immortality is the glorious discovery of Christianity.—Channing.

Our faith in God asks of him a risen Redeemer, and the faith is answered in a Saviour raised from the dead.—Bishop Fallows.

The resurrection of Jesus Christ is a certainty. If any fact, not merely of Christianity, but of history, stands on an impregnable foundation, this does. —E. P. Goodwin, D.D.

Choice Easter Illustrations

BEHIND THE DOOR. Dr. John Baillie tells how a man in his last illness asked his doctor what the future life would be like. Just then the physician heard his dog, which had followed him, scratching at the door. He told the patient that the dog knew nothing of what was happening behind the closed door but wanted to be with his master. He asked: "Is it not the same with you? You have no knowledge of what lies behind the door that opens into the future life, but you can rest assured that you will find your Master there.

THE EASTER MESSAGE. Moses and Elijah on the Mount of Transfiguration spake with Jesus "of his decease which he should accomplish." The correct rendering of this word "decease" is "exodus." Jesus talked with them about his exodus —his march out. Christ's death was not so much an event he was to suffer, as it was a victory he was to accomplish. As Moses by an exodus led his people to deliverance, so Jesus by his death emancipated his followers from the bondage of sin. This is the triumphant Easter message.—Archer Wallace.

THE PATH BEYOND. The Resurrection is a great hope to be cherished. "Now is Christ risen from the dead, and become the firstfruits of them that slept." Did you ever walk into a blind alley? You hurry along this narrow way till you come all at once squarely up against a brick wall. This was life before Jesus rose from the dead. It was a blind alley. The world had hoped and believed there must be some way out, but it had never found it. Jesus showed us the path to the beyond. He opened a door through the brick wall into the Garden of God. He brought life and immortality to light.—Stuart Nye Hutchison, D.D.

LIFE INDEED. Easter is the highest, holiest season of the Christian year, and of the Christian life, because on that first Easter morn Christ rose from the dead. The angel's words, "He is risen!" changed the sorrowing disciples into joyous witnesses. Since that day, millions have found life in him. Call the roll of all the Peters and Pauls, Polycarps and Tyndales, Luthers and Wesleys, Careys and Livingstones in the world—all are remembered today because they found life in the risen Lord.

Easter must become the most real and important fact in life to us just as it did to them. Without that, we do not really live here, and cannot hope for life hereafter.—Howard N. Reeves, Jr.

Quotable Easter Poetry

ROLL BACK, O CLOUDS!

Roll back, O clouds of darkness!
We greet the Easter morn!
This day within our troubled hearts
A gleam of hope was born,
For the spirit of the Risen Christ
Entered our hearts forlorn
And charged them with His radiancy
This glorious Easter morn!
—Velma Gray.

THE LAMPS OF FAITH

Turn on the lamps of faith,
Let there be light;
This is the day of wrath
And blackest night.

If you have things to say
To ease our pain,
I charge you say them now
And make them plain.

Turn from the oily word,
The slippery phrase:
Bring Christ and hope to men
These evil days.

Turn on the lamps of faith,
Let there be light;
When heaven and earth are dark,
Lamps should be bright.
—Charles Hannibal Voss.

An Easter Prayer

O Crucified Son of God, I pray
All hate and evil in me slay;
That I May live with spirit free
Not unto self, but unto Thee.

Risen, living, triumphant Lord,
Breathe in my soul thy living word,
That risen, I may walk with Thee,
Within appointed paths for me.

Ascended now upon Thy throne,
Thou wilt not leave us here alone.
Blest Spirit, walk Thou by our side
And bless us in this Eastertide.
—Chester M. Davis.

EVENING SERVICE

Theme: The Empty Grave (Easter).

Text: "Come, see the place where the Lord lay." Matt. 28:6.

Introductory: It is a garden. It is a garden with a grave in it. It is a new tomb where never man was laid. You can see by its size, position, adornments that it belongs to a family of wealth. The body of the crucified Christ had been placed therein and a great stone rolled before the entrance securely to seal it. All true. But the tomb is empty! To the early visitors the angel said, "Come, see the place where the Lord lay."

I. To prove the certainty of Christ's resurrection the angel first appeals to their senses. "Come!" "See!" There was much to see when the visitors came and looked. No body there! The grave-clothes aside and neatly wrapped! No signs of death! "Neither wilt thou suffer thine Holy One to see corruption."

II. In his ministering days Christ had distinctly and repeatedly predicted his crucifixion, his death, and his resurrection from the grave. He knew. He was truth incarnate. Now the grave is empty! "Come, see."

III. The enemies of Christ both believed and testified to his resurrection. Even the Roman soldiers reported his body gone. They believed that he had risen. The conduct of the scribes and Pharisees clearly indicates that in their own hearts and minds they feared that Christ would rise again. They sought to overthrow the true statement of their own guards by falsehood. The angel knew the truth and said, "Come, see the place where the Lord lay."

IV. The friends of Jesus bore witness to his resurrection. The angel announced positively to the women, "He is not here; he is risen from the dead." On their way to tell the disciples the good tidings Jesus met them. They knew his voice. They recognized him as their crucified and risen Lord. Soon after he appeared to the eleven when assembled behind closed doors, then to Thomas, then to five hundred brethren at once. There were other appearances and meetings until the day of ascension. He arose from the dead. "Come, see the place where the Lord lay."—H.

Suggested Easter Texts and Themes

The Call of Spring: "And he that sat upon the throne said, Behold, I make all things new." Rev. 21:5.

The Evidence of the Empty Tomb: "Come, see the place where the Lord lay." Matt. 28:6.

The Joy of Easter: "And they departed quickly from the sepulchre with fear and great joy." Matt. 28:8.

Christ's Resurrection the Promise and Prophecy of Our Own: "But now is Christ risen from the dead, and become the firstfruits of them that slept." I Cor. 15:20.

Science and the Resurrection: "But some man will say, How are the dead raised up?" I Cor. 15:35.

MIDWEEK FELLOWSHIP MEETING TOPIC

(Church Night or Suggested Sermon Subject)

Theme: The Touch of Faith.

TEXT: "Who touched me?" Mark 5:31.

Present the full account, vv. 25-34. The multitude thronged the Saviour but only one of the crowd "touched" him. It was the touch of faith.

I. The trembling suppliant. 1. Illness brought her to the Saviour. 2. Faith prepared her for a blessing.

II. The effectual touch. "The border of his garment." 1. There was a real cause at work. 2. There may be close contact with Christ without the effectual touch. 3. There cannot be a living touch between him and us without his knowledge.

III. The required confession. Avowal of hidden faith. 1. Our Lord called for acknowledgment in this case. 2. It led to fuller instruction of the woman and her deeper peace. 3. It developed her own faith and encouraged others. —A. R.

CHRISTIAN ENDEAVOR SOCIETY TOPIC

April 13. Easter—Day of Victory. (Easter.) John 20:1-18.

SUNDAY SCHOOL LESSON

April 13. Thomas and the Risen Lord. John 11:14-16; 14:1-6; 20:24-29.

MEMORY SELECTION: "Have you believed because you have seen me? Blessed are those who have not seen and yet believe." John 20:29 (R. S. V.).

This Easter lesson is based on Thomas' affirmation of belief in the living Christ. The story shows that he was a devoted but despairing follower of Christ. He was a disciple with honest doubt. But this doubt was changed to joyful certainty when Jesus personally talked with him. Comforted by the risen Christ his skepticism turned to faith. To considerable physical evidence brought conviction to Thomas. To what extent are we influenced by physical evidence?

SUNDAY: APRIL TWENTIETH

MORNING SERVICE

Theme: The Serpent behind the Hedge.

SUGGESTED SCRIPTURE READING: Eccles. 10:1-20.

SELECTED HYMNS: "My soul, be on thy guard."—G. Heath. "A charge to keep I have."—C. Wesley. "The world is very evil."—Richard of Cluny. "Jesus, my Strength, my Hope."—C. Wesley. "Christian, seek not yet repose."—C. Elliot.

CALL TO WORSHIP: "I will hear what God the Lord will speak; for he will speak peace unto his people, and to his saints." "Show us thy loving-kindness, O Lord, and grant us thy salvation."

INVOCATION PRAYER: Our Father, again we come to thee to offer our song of praise. The very thought of thee puts joy and peace in our hearts. We know no name that merits so much the songs which our voices can sing. Thou art the only hope of our contrite heart. Thou alone art the joy of all the meek. Thou art kind to even those who fall, and thou dost reward them that seek after thee. Be thou this day our only joy as thou our only prize shalt be. Be thou our glory now, so that some day we may see thy face and in thy presence rest, and find in thee our glory through all eternity. We pray in the name of thine own Son, our Lord and Saviour. Amen.—Rev. Garret Hondelink, B.D.

Theme: The Serpent behind the Hedge.

TEXT: "Whoso breaketh an hedge, a serpent shall bite him." Eccles. 10:8.

INTRODUCTORY: A common sight in Palestine today are the hedges and stone fences. Many of the hedges are of cactus. The stone fences are mostly of loosely laid up stones with the walls thick and somewhat shaky. As one journeys along the footpaths, caravan lines, or more modern roads, it is a common occurrence to see darting in and out here and there lizards of all sizes, shapes and colors, and sometimes even reptiles. In this verse by hedge is meant rather a wall or stone fence in the crevices of which lizards and reptiles have their abode. Not many are poisonous, but some belonging to the viper family are dangerous.

Hedges and walls are intended for protection, but of course one who breaks through is likely by the disturbance to contact a viper and may be bitten, or stung. The teaching is that any attempt to pull down or break through a wall, interpreted here as transgressing the laws of life which God has enjoined, is sure to bring out the hissing serpent with its sting.

Hedges are meant for protection, for homes and gardens and people. Let us think of some of the hedges or walls which God has erected for our safety.

I. One is the code of modesty or the sense of shame. Whatever tends to lessen the acuteness of the soul to things false, ugly or foul is sharply to be shunned. We may well beware of such literature as tends to reconcile us to odious things, of the company whose conversation and fellowship in some way, at first perhaps not very apparent, blights the bloom and dims the luster of pure feeling, of the amusements which filch away our time and the quick delicacy which has been evolved in our nature at an infinite expense. The sense of shame is a sacred thing. It is the nobility of nature. We ought wisely and sedulously to guard and heighten it in the fear of God.

II. Another gracious barrier which God has erected for our safety is the hedge of social requirements, or the code of courtesy. There are certain well-understood enactments of society which must be regarded by us. They may have no claim as moral laws or civil statutes, but nevertheless they are obligatory. And if we are so self-willed or self-sufficient, if we are so ignorant or so careless as to violate them, we must pay the appropriate penalty of general disregard.

The fact is that social conventions are the hallmarks of civilized living. They are the traffic rules which people have adopted for the better conduct of life. Their observance is the card proving one's right to membership in civilized society. There is no law against pushing one's neighbor aside on the street, but if one does so he proves himself a boor. There is no law against eating peas with a knife, but if one does so he marks himself ill-bred and unused to the amenities of civilized society. There is no law against discourtesy, but it just isn't practiced by the kind of people one wants to know.

III. We might mention a third sort of wall or hedge that ought not to be broken through, namely, the ordinary rules of business. The laws of business are the outcome of the experience of generations and are not lightly to be set aside. It is only a secular maxim that honesty is the best policy, but it is as true as gospel! One starting in business or anywhere along the way can hardly pay too much deference to the customs and traditions of the establishment in which his lot is cast, nor can he be too exactly conscientious about the prescribed obligations of time and usage and method and goods and cash.

IV. But I must not go on. There are many other hedges which God has placed about us. His commandments, not grievous but gracious walls of protection, parental restraints, maxims of health, maxims of truth, sentences of Scripture, lessons from teachers, and another very important restraint, the hedge of conscience. Conscience commands us with imperative voice, demanding that we keep well within the line of purity and sobriety and truthfulness and reverence. If we go beyond these lines we suffer. We suffer the condemnation of God, the disapproval of all wise and good men and women, the reproach of our own soul, and the loss of self-respect, which is one of the greatest evils that can befall us. "Whoso breaketh an hedge, a serpent shall bite him."—H.

THEME PRAYER: O God, in the knowledge of whom comes our eternal life, and in whose service is perfect freedom, defend us, thy humble servants, in all assaults of our enemies. By thy gracious forgiveness set us free from our sins so that we may live by the law of liberty. In the name of Christ we ask. Amen.

OFFERTORY SENTENCE: "Neither will I offer unto the Lord my God of that which cost me nothing."

OFFERTORY PRAYER: We would remember, our Father, that we are not our own, that we are bought with a price, we would therefore glorify thee in our bodies and in our spirits which are thine. It is for thy glory through the advancement of thy kingdom we bring these our offerings this morning. Wilt thou graciously accept and bless and use them to this end. In Christ's name we ask. Amen.

Illustrative Material

SEED THOUGHTS, HOMILETIC AND EXPOSITORY. Fences and Serpents: I. All life is given to us rigidly walled up. Obligations we owe. Relations in which we stand. Laws of nature. Laws of society. Laws of God. II. The laws are blessings. They are like the parapets on a mountain road that keep the traveler from toppling over the face of the cliff. III. Every attempt to break down the limitations brings poison into the life. We live in a great automatic system which by its own operation largely avenges every break of law. IV. Inflamed conscience or a palsied conscience is the result of all wrongdoing. V. The poison can be taken out. The sinless Son of God hath been made sin for us.—A. M.

Choice Illustrations on the Theme

NO DEFAULT. "Heaven never defaults. The wicked are sure of their wages, sooner or later."

THE TEN COMMANDMENTS A HEDGE. A good lady belonging to another communion once remonstrated with Dr. W. B. Robertson of Irvine. She said, "I hear that you have introduced some dreadful innovations into your church service." "Indeed!" he replied, "What innovations have we introduced?" "Oh," she said, "I hear you read the Commandments at the Communion." "Is that all you heard of?" was the reply. "We have introduced a far greater innovation than that." "What is it?" said the good lady, in some alarm. "We try to keep them," he replied.—*Life of W. B. Robertson.*

THE ECHO. Society is like the echoing hills. It gives back to the speaker his words, groan for groan, song for song. Wouldst thou have any social scenes to resound with music? Then speak ever in the melodious strains of truth and love. "With what measure ye mete it shall be measured to you again."

RETRIBUTION. Chaplain McCabe once talked with Admiral Schley in the harbor of Valparaiso. He asked him what he was thinking about during the battle of Santiago. Schley replied, "Well, you would hardly guess. In the midst of that thrilling engagement which resulted in the destruction of Cervera's fleet that Sunday morning, my mind was continually going back three hundred years when the Spaniards drove my ancestors out of Spain. I thought how strange it was that I was there to help pay that debt by the humiliation of that same nation."—*The Evangel.*

PUNISHMENT. The Belides were fifty maidens, daughters of Danaus. They all murdered their husbands on their wedding night. For this crime they are obliged to draw water from a deep well until they have filled up an immense sieve. Their punishment is therefore eternal.

EVENING SERVICE

Theme: Is Missionary Effort Justifiable?

TEXT: "Go ye therefore, and teach all nations," etc. Matt. 28:19, 20.

INTRODUCTORY: The biggest business in the world is the missionary enterprise carried on by the Church of Christ. Christianity is a missionary religion. After training his apostles Christ commanded them to go and make disciples of all nations. He took the whole world into his plan.

I. To those who are his loyal followers this is sufficient warrant for all missionary effort. Almost invariably those who obtain a true acquaintanceship with Christ and his teachings become enthusiastic propagandists. Finding it so satisfactory in their own life they recommend it to others and urge it upon them. After this fashion it has spread itself throughout the world. It was the intention of its Founder that it should propagate itself.

II. It is true also that the life of Christ's cause depends upon it. Without its missionary enthusiasm Christianity would deteriorate and vanish. Christians believe that they have a good thing in their religion and they are taught to impart good to others. There is no such thing as a selfish Christianity. If the history of missions should be written completely we would have a record of many of the world's most heroic deeds. And wherever Christ's religion goes it brings light and joy, a new life and a new hope. It has clearly demonstrated that it, and it alone, has the capacity of serving as the world religion, which is not true of any of the ethnic religions.

III. Christianity is responsible for many valuable by-products. Through its missions civilization is spread, markets are opened, and trade increased. It has been said that for every dollar England has invested in missions it gets ten dollars back in trade. Countries that are Christianized become greatly enriched.

IV. But the leading motive for missions is not and never should be a mercenary one. One outstanding motive is that in the Christian religion we have something too good to keep. The discoveries of curative medicines are never selfishly kept for the discoverers. The great question about the Christian religion is, Does it benefit the lands to which it is brought? It has benefited our Western lands. It has made them strong and multiplied happiness and comfort. In Eastern lands it acts in the same way to the extent to which it prevails. Where Christian influence has not come the world has made little progress. Where the religion of Christ has gone better sanitation, better education, better social conditions, better farming, better housing, and a better life have followed.

Christian people owe it to themselves and to the world at large to bring the Gospel of Christ to all men. Supremely they owe it to Christ himself who said, "Go ye therefore, and teach all nations, baptizing them in the name of the Father, and of the Son, and of the Holy Ghost: teaching them to observe all things whatsoever I have commanded you: and, lo, I am with you alway, even unto the end of the world."

Alternate Theme: The Voice of Spring (Springtime).

TEXT: "For, lo, the winter is past, the rain is over and gone; the flowers appear on the earth; the time of the singing of birds is come, and the voice of the turtle [dove] is heard in our land." Song of Sol. 2:11, 12.

INTRODUCTORY: The most obvious analogy which the spring suggests is that of life. I. Consider some of the natural characteristics of spring. 1. As intimated, life is the predominant feature. The sap is rising with its quickening energies through every plant and tree. The buds are opening with the elasticity and glow of life. The birds are nesting. Life everywhere is manifest. 2. And beauty shines forth in the spring. We see it in swelling buds and opening flowers. We see it in the early foliage, in the cloud-dappled sky and its moving shadows on the earth. We see it in the fresh clear landscape that looks as though the rain of winter and the sun of summer had combined to clothe it with rainbow radiance. 3. Joy and gladness also distinguish the springtime. Is your heart glad too? 4. We are impressed at this season with the riches and wealth that are manifested all about. 5. Youth and promise are also characteristic of the springtime.

II. We may well consider also the revelation concerning the Divine nature which spring affords. 1. Spring testifies to the faithfulness of God. Never do the seasons cease or fail of return. 2. Not less plainly revealed is the goodness of God. 3. And how many evidences of the Divine wisdom. Study a single leaf. Study growth, or the seasons. Design. 4. Consider the resources of God made known to us in the spring. The myriad world—life, fertilization, growth. God invites us by his love, encourages us by his wisdom and infinite power to trust in him.

III. Think also of the relation of spring to the doctrine of the resurrection. Life out of death. All the latent powers we possess of knowing, of loving, of having fellowship with God shall awake to life. The thrill of holy joy, the glow of Divine life shall be felt with new and spiritual meaning and we shall sing, "The winter is past," etc.—R. S. H.

Suggested Texts and Themes

My Responsibility: "Am I my brother's keeper?" Gen. 4:9.

The Call for Volunteers: "Who then is willing to consecrate his service this day unto the Lord?" I Chron. 29:5.

What of the Night? "Watchman, what of the night?" Isa. 21:11.

Where the Need is Greatest: "They that be whole need not a physician, but they that are sick." Matt. 9:12.

The Great Imperative: "Go ye into all the world, and preach the gospel to every creature." Mark 16:15.

MIDWEEK FELLOWSHIP MEETING TOPIC

(Church Night or Suggested Sermon Subject)

Theme: The Folly of Sordid Ambition.

TEXT: "And seekest thou great things for thyself? Seek them not." Jer. 45:5.

The point of this advice is "For thyself." This prohibition is directed at the folly of sordid ambition.

I. What is the nature of the great things prohibited? The verse evidently refers to things of the world, great riches, great honors, great positions, great power, great personal glory.

II. Why not seek such things for oneself? 1. For a first reason that great things for oneself ought never to be an ultimate objective. 2. Because such things are not essential to life and happiness. We are mistaken when we think they are. 3. And because they are associated with imminent perils: a. The danger of causing idolatry. b. The danger of causing us to subordinate duty to their acquisition and enjoyment. c. The danger that the seeking will involve us and others in much positive suffering. d. The danger that they exclude in their results the influence of better things. e. And because that manifestly such things are but transient and perishing. "The fashion of this world passeth away."

III. The supreme fact is that God has better things in store for his children. 1. Much greater treasures. 2. Much worthier titles. 3. Greater and much more worth-while privileges and blessings.

Seek best things first. Leave other things to God's disposal.

CHRISTIAN ENDEAVOR SOCIETY TOPIC

April 20. Enlarging Your Faith: Faith Is Power. Heb. 11:1; Phil. 4:8-13.

SUNDAY SCHOOL LESSON

April 20. Jesus and the Law. Matt. 5:17-20; Mark 10:17-22.

MEMORY SELECTION: "The law was given through Moses; grace and truth came through Jesus Christ." John 1:17 (R. S. V.).

We are now to have a series of lessons on the ten commandments and the teaching of Jesus concerning the law. This first lesson is an introduction. It is intended to show the attitude of Jesus toward Hebrew religious laws generally and the Decalogue in particular. He sought not to destroy the law, but to interpret it in vital terms of everyday living. Well might we study the contrast between law and grace. That is the suggestion of the memory selection. Law equals Judaism. Grace equals Christianity. Grace: 1. The divine message. 2. The heavenly gift. 3. The supernatural help.

SUNDAY: APRIL TWENTY-SEVENTH

MORNING SERVICE

Theme: The Secret of Security.

SUGGESTED SCRIPTURE READING: Ps. 112:1-10.

SELECTED HYMNS: "How firm a foundation."—Anon. "My God and Father, while I stray."—C. Elliott. "God is the refuge of his saints."—I. Watts. "He leadeth me, O blessed thought."—J. H. Gilmore. "Thy way, not mine, O Lord." —H. Bonar.

CALL TO WORSHIP: "Make a joyful noise unto the Lord; serve the Lord with gladness; come before his presence with singing." "Enter into his gates with thanksgiving, and into his courts with praise: be thankful unto him and bless his name; for the Lord is good; his mercy is everlasting and his truth endureth to all generations."

INVOCATION PRAYER: Eternal God, our heavenly Father, under the canopy of thy goodness we gather into thy house in faith and fellowship, lifting up our hearts in praise and thanksgiving and adoration. Each prays for all. Grant that all may escape from the loneliness in which we live into the freedom of a common aspiration and the joy of a common communion. To thy greatness we bring our littleness. To thy power we bring our weakness. To thy abundant grace we bring our hearts to be healed and cleansed and made pure by thy purity. Our Father, the days are thine. The work is thine. We are thine. Teach us how to adventure in thy name and trust in thy truth. Enlarge our hearts that we may add faith to faith and to faith add virtue, patience, brotherly love and joy. We ask all in the name of Christ. Amen.

Theme: The Secret of Security.

TEXT: "He shall not be afraid of evil tidings: his heart is fixed, trusting in the Lord." Ps. 112:7.

INTRODUCTORY: Most of us are affected by the fear of bad news. If we think we are immune we have only to recall the feeling that comes to us when a messenger boy hands in a telegram. We cannot avoid a shadow of anxiety. The fear of evil tidings is there, lurking behind the mind. It springs from the fact that this is an uncertain world, where there is always the risk that mischance or misfortune may befall us.

I. There is no assurance of immunity. Jesus drew a picture of a man who thought he had found security in a well-stocked barn. He settled down, saying to himself, "Soul, thou hast much good laid up for many years. Take thine ease; eat, drink and be merry." So far as he could see, he had provided against every emergency. But he had not reckoned with death. However we may try, none of us is immune or can make ourselves so. Those who try to build up security by increasing their possessions often find that they have only increased the burden of their anxieties. The Psalmist knew the one secret of security. Only faith can keep fear at bay and prevent it from invading the inward sanctuary where true peace has its dwelling.

II. The secret of security is a heart fixed on God and on the things which faith in God makes precious. If our hearts are fixed on God, he will take possession. If our hand grasps his, he will take hold of ours. If our anchor is cast among the things unseen—the great realities of God's love and care which Christ revealed—the anchor will hold in all the storms of life.

III. There are two things that spring from this experience. The first is the knowledge that whatever we may have to meet, God will see us through. We shall have the power in God to meet the situation. Peace has been defined as the "conscious possession of adequate resources." Whatever changes may come, God does not change and his grace has an infinite variety of resourcefulness. This is the secret of the peace which the world cannot give, and which it cannot take away. The roots of peace are in that simple faith. The more we rest on that conviction the stronger and deeper it becomes.

IV. But the heart fixed on God has a further secret of security. When our hearts are set on God and on his purpose we discover the real treasures of life and we know that these cannot be touched by its changes and chances. That is what Jesus bade us do. He warned us that we are living in an uncertain world. If our treasures are in money or power or the things on which many people set their hearts, we have no security from fear. Moth and rust corrupt; thieves break through and steal. The only way of security is to set our hearts on the things which cannot be affected by the most tragic events of time.

1. The real joys of life cannot be affected by time. Beauty and the power to enjoy it are indestructible. Beethoven had become deaf before he wrote his greatest work. He could not hear a note of it with the outward ear. But in his soul he was in touch with a world of beauty to which many people are strangers. The joy of love and friendship at its best does not pass with time or even with death. Our friends become more real to us after they have gone. Their true quality shines more clearly than ever in the radiance of eternity.

2. Above all, when our hearts are fixed on God's purpose we possess a satisfaction that cannot be threatened by accident or evil.

There is a familiar story of a Christian who was being threatened by a tyrant to force him to give up his faith. He threatened physical suffering, but was answered that "Suffering bringeth forth the peaceable fruits of righteousness." He threatened the loss of his goods, but was told, "My treasure is in heaven." At last he threatened the good man with the loss of his life. But quick as a flash came the reply, "My life is hid with Christ in God." —J. R.

Theme Prayer: O eternal Rest of the weary and of those who need poise and power for life's stern demands, give us the assured knowledge of thy truth. May we stand still and see thy salvation. So may we gain new hold upon thee. May we not be afraid of evil tidings, our hearts being fixed, trusting in thee. We ask in the name of Christ. Amen.

Offertory Sentence: "Bless the Lord, O my soul, and forget not all his benefits."

Offertory Prayer: Upon the first day of the week according as thou hast prospered us we would bring our offerings to thee, our Father. We would count it all joy to be used as helpers of thy kingdom. Bless us and the gifts of our hands, we pray in the name of Christ. Amen.

Illustrative Material

SEED THOUGHTS, HOMILETIC AND EXPOSITORY. Antidote against Fear: I. The truster in God shall not be afraid of evil tidings of persecution for the sake of Christ. II. He shall not be afraid of tidings of arduous duties. III. He shall not be afraid of tidings of worldly losses and afflictions. IV. He shall not be afraid of tidings of his own death. V. He shall not be afraid of tidings of judgment. His heart is fixed, trusting in the Lord.—A. S.

Our hearts fixed upon God, our feet upon the Rock of Ages, our house built firmly—we need fear no evil tidings.—S. B. J.

Established on God—here is a most remarkable type of man.—A. E. H.

"Greet the unseen with a cheer!"

The anxiety of the Christian partakes of the unreasoning terror of childhood. —S. B. J.

Choice Illustrations on the Theme

"MY HEART IS FIXED." An eminent Christian, eccentric but honest, said pleasantly and religiously that he was never afraid to open his letter bag. He was in full possession, we may conclude, of the *mens conscia recti*, the upright consciousness.—S. B. James.

ROUND OUR RESTLESSNESS HIS REST. A story is told by Dr. Rendel Harris of the time when he was staying with friends in Delaware. In the room where he slept the bed coverlet was made out of old brown linen and had been spun in old days by a godly grandmother. Over it she had worked with her needle Mrs. Browning's lines:

"God's greatness
Flows around our incompleteness
Round our restlessness His rest."

When asked in the morning how he had slept, he said, "How could I have slept other than well with such a text as that on top of me?"—Rev. F. R. Brunskill.

RELIGION NOT GLOOM. Oliver Wendell Holmes said that he might have entered the Christian ministry had he not met so many ministers who looked like undertakers. That is rather a libel on the undertakers for most of them we know are good-natured and cheerful. We think we know what Holmes meant. He was repelled by the gloom and sadness which some people regard as a mark of piety. There is no necessary connection between gloom and religion. True, we are told that Jesus wept but that is probably recorded because it was so unusual.—Archer Wallace.

ROOTED IN THE SHADOWS. Some months ago, in the late autumn, the writer was in the hothouse of one of our florists. We were in the cellar, and in the dimly lighted place one could see arranged in regular file long rows of flower pots. The florist explained that in these pots had been planted the bulbs for their winter flowers. It was the best for them, he said, that they be rooted in the dark. They would be ready for the open day a little later. Then their gay colors would cheer many hearts. Rooted in the shadows to bloom in the light.

Much of our Christianity is a sickly bloom because we have no quiet place in which the roots of faith may grow. We try to force the bloom before we have rooted ourselves in Jesus Christ. Return, O soul, to the secret place and linger there. A godly life, like the flowers, is rooted in the shadows to bloom in the light.—Costen J. Harrell.

"REST A WHILE." When President Coolidge was asked what he would do on retiring from the White House, his reply was, "Well, I am going back to Vermont and for a year or two I am going to whittle."

If you were born in the country, you know exactly what President Coolidge meant. You know the joy of "settin' around" and just whittling.

No angry, irritated, cross, vindictive person can whittle. It is the calm, contented, right-thinking individual who does this. It gives a man a chance to think and dream and compose his soul.

Why don't you do a little whittling? Do you ever relax? How often do you give body and soul a complete rest? An hour of placid, leisurely whittling every day would add years to your expectation of life.—Royal S. Copeland, M.D.

EVENING SERVICE

Theme: Riches You Cannot Lose.

TEXT: "Lay up for yourselves treasures," etc. Matt. 6:20.

INTRODUCTORY: In this country we have had recurring periods of financial depressions and serious losses. Sometimes banks have closed, hard-earned savings have disappeared, and businesses have failed. Over against such a situation we would name certain riches the value of which can never be lowered and the loss of which one need never sustain. To young people especially, yet to all people alike we commend investment in these riches one cannot lose.

I. Here is a treasure no person can steal from you, stock that will not go down in value, wealth always of supreme worth, the capacity to enjoy literature and art. For those who have cultivated this capacity there is genuine wealth in the vaults of their minds, vaults through which no stranger can break.

II. And closely associated with this goes the enjoyment of nature. Those who have eyes to see can still enjoy the sunset no matter if their income is affected by regrettable conditions. The same is true of all nature and of all art. This power of the soul is a possession we need to more fully appreciate. Wordsworth had become rich in the values which are eternal when he wrote:

"My heart leaps up when I behold
A rainbow in the sky:
So was it when life began;
So is it now I am a man;
So be it when I shall grow old,
Or let me die."

III. There is another treasure you cannot lose. It is the memory of rich experiences. Memory is a possession which makes one a personality. It is essential to personality and guarantees the future to each of us. Treasure which cannot be taken away, wealth no one can steal, is composed of happy recollections. You can carry with you down through the years happy memories of devotion to the best and finest you know. Is that not a treasure? It is wealth greater than any amount of bonds and stocks.

IV. Again, and emphatically, there is the treasure of abiding friendship. Charles Kingsley summed this up when he said: "A friend is one whom you can always trust, who knows the best and the worst of you, and who cares for you in spite of your faults." If you have such friends you are rich, possessing treasures that are real and abiding.

V. There is another and a higher relationship. It is a Divine friendship, friendship with the living God, whose very spirit lends a meaning and worth to all the human friendships we know. "I have called you friends."—After G. R. J.

Additional Theme: Secondhand Religion.

TEXT: "Jesus answered him, Sayest thou this thing of thyself, or did others tell it thee of me?" John 18:34.

INTRODUCTORY: Our Lord's challenge to Pilate enshrines an important religious principle. He might well ask us with reference to our own religious status, "Sayest thou this of thyself, or did others tell it thee of me?" Is your religious creed learned by rote? Is it a matter of mere verbal assent, or have you thought out your own religious position? Have you fought your way to faith in me? Out of the abundance of your heart does your mouth speak?

I. You may have been given religious teaching in childhood systematically and liberally, and have never made it your own. It is secondhand religion, and you have not made it first-hand. Others have told it to you, but you do not say it yourself. It has remained head-knowledge. The fuel is there, but it has never been set on fire. Perhaps the prevalence of religion of this nature may have prompted the policy which finds considerable vogue today: that of leaving the spiritual side of a child's education untended with the idea of letting him find his own way and choose for himself when he comes to years of discretion. This line is not followed in any other branch of knowledge. A pupil must build his own structure, but he builds upon the foundation of information acquired through centuries of research. The last word of science is taken into account.

II. On the other hand, a mere modicum of religious information may have been imparted to you in youth. Your theology may have been meager, but you have put it to the test of experience, and it has become part of your life, part of yourself. The reality of religious experience is no longer open to question, though there is a danger lest we may mistake a counterfeit experience for genuine spiritual experience. We are to "believe not every spirit, but to try the spirits whether they are of God." The religion of many people is defective because it does not pass from the realm of ideas into that of personal experience.

III. After all, a little faith goes a long way, and faith is not given to us to enable us to believe things which are difficult to believe, but to enable us to do things that are difficult to do. We are to use it, then, to develop our character, to show that degree of manliness and Godliness which ought to dignify the knowledge of our Lord Jesus Christ. "If these things be in you, and abound, they make you that ye shall neither be barren or unfruitful in the knowledge of our Lord Jesus Christ."

The call now comes to us to learn all we can of the spiritual love and so make it our own that we can declare to those who are less far on than ourselves, "that which we have heard, which we have seen with our eyes, of the Word of Life." That is firsthand religion.—J. T. I.

Suggested Texts and Themes

The Children's Friend: "And they brought young children to him." Mark 10:13.

The Christian and the State: "Let every soul be subject unto the higher powers." Rom. 13:1.

Dictators Always Fail: "He that sitteth in the heavens shall laugh." Ps. 2:4.

Worship is Worthwhile: "But as for me, I will come into thy house in the multitude of thy mercy." Ps. 5:7.

MIDWEEK FELLOWSHIP MEETING TOPIC

(Church Night or Suggested Sermon Subject)

Theme: A Man of Excellent Spirit.

TEXT: "This Daniel was preferred . . . because an excellent spirit was in him." Dan. 6:3.

It was not mere talent that raised Daniel to his high position. No doubt he was shrewd, able and clever. But a man's real strength or weakness is closely linked with his moral make-up. The heart, even more than the brain, determines the man. In Daniel we see a man whose conscience held a tight rein over his lower nature. We see that stern loyalty to principle is not inconsistent with the urbanity and courtesy of a perfect gentleman. We learn that the busiest man may be a man of prayer. Also that fervent piety can be sustained under circumstances most unfavorable to growth, together with the fact that a robust faith in God can carry one through the most trying circumstances.

I. Note first that this "excellent spirit" was a spirit of self-control.

II. Secondly, that it was a spirit of genuine piety.

III. Thirdly, that it was a spirit of unshaken faith in God. 1. Daniel was a man of purpose. 2. A man of prayer. 3. A man of perception. 4. A man of power.—J. T. D.

CHRISTIAN ENDEAVOR SOCIETY TOPIC

April 27. Enlarging Your Faith: Doubt Your Doubts. John 20:24-29.

BULLETIN BOARD SLOGANS FOR THE MONTH

A good investment is the time spent in God's house.

Conscience is the pulse of reason.

A sad saint is a poor saint.

The Christian life that is joyless is a discredit to God.

Human improvement is from within outward.

The Bible is common sense inspired.

If Christ is kept outside something must be wrong inside.

The reward of one duty done is power to fulfill another.

We do the greatest good by being good.

The Gospel is the balance wheel of character.

SUNDAY SCHOOL LESSON

April 27. Supreme Loyalty to God. Ex. 20:1-6; Luke 14:25-27; 16:13-15.

MEMORY SELECTION: "The law was given through Moses; grace and truth came through Jesus Christ." John 1:17 (R.S.V.).

Loyalty implies complete devotion to a person or cause. Duty to God is our first loyalty. He is our God and Father and bountiful Benefactor. Idolatry was the peculiar form of disloyalty common to many of the early Hebrews. Those forms of idolatry are not common in the same forms today. In our present time the issue of supreme loyalty is drawn at other points, but it is no less an issue.

SUNDAY: MAY FOURTH

MORNING SERVICE

Theme: Living in a Large Room.

SUGGESTED SCRIPTURE READING: Ps. 31:1-24. After-petition: May God reveal to our hearts and minds the truths of this great chapter.

SELECTED HYMNS: "How shall I follow Him I serve?"—J. Conder. "My dear Redeemer and my Lord."—I. Watts. "O where is He that trod the sea?"—T. T. Lynch. "Teach me, O Lord, thy holy way."—W. T. Matson. "How sweet the name of Jesus sounds."—J. Newton.

CALL TO WORSHIP: "The Lord is nigh unto all them that call upon him, to all that call upon him in truth. He will fulfil the desire of them that fear him: he also will hear their cry, and will save them."

INVOCATION PRAYER: O Lord, who hast brought us through the darkness of night to the light of this Sabbath morning, and who by thy Holy Spirit dost illumine the darkness of ignorance and sin; we beseech thee of thy loving-kindness, to pour out thy holy light into our souls, that we may ever be devoted to thee by whose wisdom we were created, by whose mercy we were redeemed, and by whose providence we are governed. And our gracious Father, ever ready to hear and answer the prayers of thy children, teach us the lesson of faith today by which our fears may be overcome; endow us with a glad and joyous spirit lifting us from any depression or despondency; and grant us the peace which passeth all our understanding, which is the forgiveness of our sins, the daily ministry of thy Spirit, and the friendship of the Christ. In his name. Amen.—M. K. W. H.

Theme: Living in a Large Room.

TEXT: "Thou hast set my feet in a large room." Ps. 31:8.

INTRODUCTORY: Many of us, I am sure, when we come to this verse in the Bible say to ourselves: "Well, that is not for me. I do not live in a large room. The place I occupy in the world is a very small one." The truth the Psalmist teaches here is that when we yield ourselves to Christ he so enlarges our vision and opportunity that we find ourselves in a different and larger world.

I. Circumstances can make of life a very small room. Here is a man who, in his youth, had thought of life as a great adventure out into a world of surprise and wonder. He finds himself instead tied down to his daily task, his whole world compressed within the narrow limits of his office or his workshop.

And his wife, how eagerly on her wedding day she had looked on to the future. Now her whole existence is a ceaseless round of cooking, sweeping, dusting and caring for the everyday needs of her household.

II. What are we to do when life closes in upon us? There are two ways in which we can enlarge a room. We can raise the ceiling or we can push back the walls. Jesus Christ does both when he enters a life. In our daily work Christ, if we take him into partnership, pushes back the walls and causes us to live in a larger world. A newspaper correspondent wrote: "I was on my way to fill a routine appointment. It was raining and I was tired and discouraged. Everything seemed so futile and meaningless. Then someone told me a parable: 'A certain man saw three men with their hammers and chisels cutting stones. "What are you doing?" he asked one of them. "I am chipping this 'ere bit of stone," he answered. When the next man was asked, he replied: "Earning my living for myself and my family." "And you?" he asked the third. "Building a cathedral," was the answer.' To him his daily task was a part of God's plan." Somehow that realization had pushed back the walls and admitted him into the larger room of God's universe.

III. What a small place the average woman in the home thinks she fills in a busy world. The largest Protestant group in America is the Methodist church. We think of John Wesley as the founder of Methodism, but it was not he, but his mother, Susannah Wesley. She was the wife of an Anglican minister. There were nineteen children in that tiny manse, and one woman's hands and heart to care for them all. Could you imagine a smaller place for her stupendous task than that poor cottage at Epworth? But God was there and he pushed out those walls till she could see the ends of the earth, and down to the farthest limits of time. As she held the baby Charles in her arms and sang him to sleep she saw by faith this son of hers the greatest hymn writer of modern times whose songs will be sung as long as the Christian Church endures. As she taught her little John of God and truth she could see by faith the untold millions who in his train would seek and find God.

IV. We see every day teachers on their way to school. What patience must be bound up with their work. Day after day, year after year, in the same place, with the same weary round of toil, ministering to a never-ending procession of children who pass on and seemingly forget them. How often that place where Providence has placed them seems so small, so unimportant. But let God push back the walls of the schoolroom till they see the men and women of the future trained by them who are shaping the destiny of the state and nation. The social, moral and spiritual battles of the future are to be won by men and women trained in the schoolrooms of today. Never in the world's history was there greater need for teachers as well as parents to realize the God-given opportunity which is theirs.

V. Trouble and adversity make life a small room. Christ and Christian faith can transform this into a large place. No place can be small to a soul in which Christ lives. It is not our outward circumstances that determine our world. It is the outreach and onreach of our sympathy and love.—S. N. H.

Theme Prayer: Make us, our heavenly Father, thine, entirely thine. Consecrate us to thy service. Consecrate us to thyself, that we may be given the more truly to thy work. Because we have so little in ourselves to assure us, may we look beyond every defeat and disappointment to the triumph of thy power in every righteous enterprise and find thy light on every road as yet untraveled. We ask in the name of Christ, who was wholly devoted to thy will. Amen.

OFFERTORY SENTENCE: "Honour the Lord with thy substance, and with the first fruits of all thine increase: so shall thy barns be filled with plenty, and thy presses shall burst out with new wine."

OFFERTORY PRAYER: We recognize, our Father, that we are not our own, that we are bought with a price; we would therefore glorify thee in our bodies and in our spirits, which are thine. Wilt thou therefore graciously accept and bless these offerings of thy people intended for the promotion of thy kingdom? We ask in Christ's name. Amen.

Illustrative Material

SEED THOUGHTS, HOMILETIC AND EXPOSITORY. Human Activities: They are not shut up within any narrow limits. I. These activities afford ample opportunities for the intellectual faculties. I. In nature. 2. In education. 3. In the Bible. Room for study. II. Their sphere affords ample play for the social sympathies. III. Their sphere affords ample play for the varied activities. Work to engage all our powers.

The Large Room: This room contains work adapted to draw out all our faculties. I. In this room there is work for our intellectual natures. There is a universe of study. II. In this room there is work for our social natures. We are members of a great and extended society. III. In this room there is work for our religious natures. We are made to worship. And there is an infinitely perfect God to worship. IV. This room contains work in which there is eternal freshness. Fresh work for every day. V. This room contains work to which there is perpetual promise. God has placed us in this large room.

Choice Illustrations on the Theme

CHRIST TRANSFIGURES LIFE. It is related of Murillo that, residing once in a convent as a lay brother, he used up all his canvas. As he was too poor to buy more, the cook jestingly threw him a napkin, saying, "Paint on this." Murillo took it and painted upon it the beautiful face of the Madonna which adorns the altar of the Capuchin Church and is known as the "Madonna of the Napkin."

One of the prizes of the Uffizi Gallery in Florence, again, is the "Madonna Della Sedia" of Raphael, one of the priceless pictures of the world, which the immortal artist painted upon the lid of a wine cask.

So Christ, the great Artist, can take the commonest lives and transfigure them, giving them immortal beauty by creating them in his likeness.—James Burns.

SMALL ROOM, LARGE SOUL. No place can be small in which Christ lives. A well-known minister has among his parishioners a woman who has been for years lying on a bed of weakness in a little room. To no one else perhaps does existence seem smaller than to a helpless invalid in a tiny room with nothing to do the livelong day but think, and count the figures on the wallpaper. In this room Christlike sympathy and love have pushed out the walls and made it as large as the world. The patient has for years made a practice of writing regularly to faraway missionaries. Her world is not bounded by four walls. It goes out far beyond them to India and China, to Africa and Iran, to Syria and Brazil. The love of Christ has set her in a large room.

A CONQUERING LIFE. A buoy is fastened securely to a rock at the bottom of the sea. The waves splash around it; it floats serenely in its appointed place. The tide rises and falls; it is still there. The Atlantic rollers come racing toward it; it mounts them one by one and rides upon them as they roll past. The tempest descends, the billows rush upon the little buoy, and for a moment it is submerged. But immediately it rises to the surface and is in its place again, unmoved and unharmed. What a picture of the conquering life! What a power and what a privilege for a soul to be able thus to rise lightly above every opponent, every vexation, never to sink into discontent, never to be overwhelmed with fear and doubt, always to be on top of the fretful sea of life!—*Sunday School Chronicle.*

LIFE SUBMERGED BY ACCESSORIES. There is an automobile story about a man who eagerly desired to purchase a number of accessories for his car. But the only way he could raise the money to do it was to sell his car itself and buy the accessories. So that is what he did. That is what the wild waves are telling us, that we are in danger of allowing the accessories of life to usurp the place of life itself.—H. E. Luccock.

HIS SOUL WAS FREE. Byron's "Prisoner of Chillon" tells of a man shut up in a dark dungeon on the shore of Lake Geneva. High up on the wall was a tiny window looking out across the lake to the mountains. The prisoner made footholds in the walls, and every day he climbed up so that he could for a moment or two look out from his prison toward the snow-clad Alps. The body was shut within his narrow cell but his soul was free to range the far distances.

EVENING SERVICE

Theme: Life with Wings.

TEXT: "They that wait upon the Lord shall renew their strength; they shall mount up with wings as eagles." Isa. 40:31.

INTRODUCTORY: The real zest of life is in its high experiences. We manage to endure much that is disagreeable and depressing if only now and then there come times of spiritual uplift, seasons of soul glow and sunrise. "They shall mount up with wings as eagles." This is our privilege. The soul has wings. It is free. It can mount up on wings in the joy of pure emotion. It can have upspringing by the might of faith, by the ardor of heavenly aspiration, on the swift wings of love, in the liberty of exultant hope.

With some these wings are often folded. They droop through sheer weariness. They trail frequently in the dust. "But they that wait upon the Lord shall renew their strength; they shall mount up with wings as eagles."

I. "They shall mount up with wings as eagles": with the vigor of eagles. In waiting upon God their faith becomes strong and lively. Love becomes pure and fervent. Hope becomes joyful and blessed. These graces, like the wings of an eagle, lift our souls upward and above.

II. "They shall mount up with wings as eagles": with the ease of the eagle. There is not alone strength and vigor for those who diligently wait upon God, but there is simplicity and ease. Religion is eminent and exalted in proportion as it is easy and unconstrained. Love makes duty a delight.

III. "They shall mount up with wings as eagles": with the elevation of eagles. With what majesty does the eagle soar through the heavens and pursue its lofty course! Here is fit emblem of the one who by waiting upon God mounts up with wings above the censures of the world and the hatreds that would retard his heavenward flight. His course is sublime. His eagle eye discerns the glories of the upper world.

MIDWEEK FELLOWSHIP MEETING TOPIC

(Church Night or Suggested Sermon Subject)

Theme: The Husbandman and His Garden.

TEXT: "Every plant, which my heavenly Father hath not planted, shall be rooted up." Matt. 15:13.

I. The presence of evil in the world constitutes a challenge to faith. In the face of firmly established wrongs, many have been led to doubt the goodness of God. If weeds are growing in a garden, one is inclined to think ill of the gardener, and sometimes the world seems to be a field without an efficient caretaker; briars and thorns grow unmolested and tares are found inextricably mingled with the wheat; the rain falls on all the plants, good and bad alike, and both prosper without respect of merit.

II. But we have the assurance of Jesus to this effect: "The Great Husbandman will finally vindicate himself of the charge of carelessness and neglect. Plants that are without divine origin will be uprooted and at length gathered into the fire and burned. The hour of reckoning and of final distinctions has not yet come. Nevertheless it is coming. Repent, for it is at hand; the ax is laid at the root of the tree, said John, and Jesus sounded the same warning in unforgettable words. The house with an unstable foundation is doomed to destruction; the fruitless tree will not be allowed to cumber the ground indefinitely; the plants that have shared the sunshine and rain of God's mercy will pass under the scrutiny of a just appraisal.

III. The final answer to all our questionings lies in the future with its unfolding judgments and sure processes of discrimination. Meanwhile, let us have faith in God, study to show ourselves approved unto him and watch and pray that we enter not into temptation!—W. L. G.

CHRISTIAN ENDEAVOR SOCIETY TOPIC

May 4. Making My Job a Christian Vocation. Eph. 4:11-16; Gal. 3:23-25. (Vocation Day.)

BULLETIN BOARD SLOGANS FOR THE MONTH

By Earl Riney

To be happy in one's own home is the ultimate of all ambition.

Christian marriage is costly in its demands but it is worth it.

Revere the mother, cherish the child, protect the family.—H. van Dyke.

Grace will last when gold is past.

Motherhood is the launching of an immortal soul on the sea of life.

Character is the will that has been educated.

Money is the servant of the wise and the master of fools.

Absent mothers are still with us in power.

The criticism of another may be open to criticism.

The workshop of character is everyday life.

SUNDAY SCHOOL LESSON

May 4. Warning against Profane Living. Ex. 20:17; Matt. 5:33-37; 23:16-22.

Memory Selection: "Thou shalt not take the name of the Lord thy God in vain." Ex. 20:7.

What is profanity? What is profane living? The commandment against taking the name of God in vain is concerned not only with profanity in speech, but also with all forms of insincere or careless profession of faith. The Scripture selections challenge us all to cultivate a spirit of reverence for God.

SUNDAY: MAY ELEVENTH

MORNING SERVICE

Theme: The Fine Art of Motherhood (Mother's Day).

SUGGESTED SCRIPTURE LESSON: Prov. 31: 1-31.

SELECTED HYMNS: "O happy home, where Thou art loved."—C. J. P. Spitta. "Thou gracious power, whose mercy lends."—O. W. Holmes. "Up to me sweet childhood looketh."—Anon. "Lord, I do not ask to stand."—Richardson-Bradley.

CALL TO WORSHIP: "One thing have I desired of the Lord, that will I seek after; that I may dwell in the house of the Lord all the days of my life, to behold the beauty of the Lord, and to inquire in his temple."

INVOCATION PRAYER: O thou, who broodest over our homes and art the unseen guest at every board, receive, we beseech thee, this our prayer for motherhood. Bring cheer to our own mothers. May they feel that the sacrifices of parenthood have been made worth while through the lives of their children. And help us that we may be worth the trust which has been reposed in us. In this little colony of heaven called home help us, O God, to be good citizens keeping all the traditions of the far country. To this colony may we be loyal. Toward all who dwell here may we be loving. And ever keep us true to him who is the center of its life. Amen.

Theme: The Fine Art of Motherhood (Mother's Day).

TEXT: "Thy mother is like a vine in thy blood." Ezek. 19:10.

INTRODUCTORY: There are three realms of spiritual value, truth, goodness and beauty. Out of the search for truth has come science; out of the search for goodness, philosophy and religion; out of the quest for beauty has come art. Perceiving all these and transcribing them into human life has given mankind the highest art ever discovered and practiced, the art of mothering.

I. In so far as a woman is able to embody the truth, the good and the beautiful in herself is she a success as a mother. Some mothers give their children a sense of beauty, but very little regard for truth. But first of all, before she can give them to her children a mother must have a desire for these things in her own life. Only so far as she makes them her own can she be successful.

II. But a second requirement after these qualities have been made her own, is that she be able to transcribe them, to make them live in the lives of her children. During the impressionable and plastic years the mother is the only one who has the privilege and responsibility of shaping life. And in so far as she can make truth, goodness and beauty her own can she reproduce them in the lives of her children and become a success in the great art of mothering. Many mothers seem to think they can teach their children what they want them to be. But there is a vast difference between knowing and being. Very few of us accomplish all the good we know. Very few people ever do wrong that they do not know better. Mothers must teach. They must impart information. But that is only a small part of their job.

III. Many mothers seem to think that their task is one of correction. Seeing all things that are wrong, they confine their task to pointing to mistakes and warning their children against them. Their stock in trade is "no" and "don't." They feel that if they can properly warn or frighten their children against the wrong way this will insure their doing right. Of all the ways of becoming a successful mother this is the poorest.

IV. Character is caught more than it is taught. The unusual mother is the one who can teach her children not only what is the good, the true and the beautiful, and warn her children against that which is false, evil and ugly, but who can set an example before them as well. But the way most successful mothers have succeeded in this fine art of mothering is by inspiration. To inspire one child is of greater importance than to impart information or to correct fifty. This is the lesson teachers and parents need to learn. It is not enough to instruct or to correct; the supreme task is to inspire.

This is true of the great mothers of history. The mother of Lincoln died when he was a boy. She had little opportunity to teach or correct; but somehow by her life and her love she inspired him with a challenge that lasted lifelong. Blessed is that mother who can leave an inspiration in the heart of her child!

V. No one knows whether civilization is going up or down. The answer to that question lies not in the hands of statesmen, politicians, businessmen, educators or preachers. The future lies in the hands and the hearts of mothers of the coming generation. If they fail we are doomed; for not science, discovery, industry nor big business, but the art of mothering is the key.

Is there love in your home? Paul was right when he said, "Love never faileth." It does not fail. A successful home is the home where love is the law of life. Is there religion in your home? You must have it if your home is to be what you want it to be.

Friends, the greatest art in the world is the art of mothering. It is the taking of truth, goodness and beauty on the part of woman and making it her own, and then transcribing these ideals, not on canvas, but on human life. It is the inspiring of her children to know and to be the best and the highest. It is this that our country needs above all else today.—C. F. B. (Adapted).

THEME PRAYER: Our Father, we pray for thy blessing upon our homes and all homes. We pray for children, that their lives may unfold in a haven of understanding. We pray for parents, that they may so live in patience, trust and joy, that their children may be led through the love of a father and a mother into the knowledge of the love of God. We bless thee for our own homes. May we make the houses of our habitation, though they be spacious or humble, beautiful with care and bright with love and, by thy grace, secure in peace. We ask in the name of Christ. Amen.

OFFERTORY SENTENCE: "Give unto the Lord the glory due unto his name: bring an offering, and come before him."

OFFERTORY PRAYER: We would make new investments today, our Father, in the cause of Christ. We bring in his name token gifts of wealth. We consecrate our talents. We pledge our lives to his service. May these investments bring profit to others and return unto us treasures laid up in heaven. In Jesus' name. Amen.—M. K. W. H.

Illustrative Material

SEED THOUGHTS, HOMILETIC AND EXPOSITORY. God Made Mothers That Way: A well-known preacher was remonstrating with his son for staying out late one night and thus causing his mother to lie awake worrying. Finally the boy said, "Well, I don't see why mother needs to keep awake on my account." The father answered, "Well, God made mothers that way; that's all I know." And there the argument ended.

House of God: Once I entered a home and found this sign hung up in the living room: "This is none other than the house of God, this is the gate of heaven." When this is a fact—of such is the kingdom of heaven.—P. F. B.

Choice Mother's Day Illustrations

MY ALTAR

I have worshipped in churches and chapels,
I've prayed in the busy street,
I have sought my God and found Him

Where the waves of His ocean beat;
I have knelt in the silent forest
In the shade of some ancient tree,
But the dearest of all my altars
Was raised at my Mother's knee.

I have listened to God in His temple,
I've caught His voice in the crowd,
I have heard Him speak where the breakers
Were booming long and loud;
When the winds played soft in the treetops
My Father has talked to me,
But I never heard Him clearer
Than I did at my Mother's knee.
—Unidentified.

THE WONDER OF A MOTHER'S LOVE. Here is a child. What is the power which can bring that child to the fullness of its possibilities? The strength of the mason and the carpenter can build a house for it to live in. The huge forces moving in a locomotive may bring to the city the food by which that child is fed. The club of a policeman may keep the house he lives in from violence without. But all these things together, though they may safeguard existence, cannot give that child his highest life. In order for the house he lives in to be a home, there must be the wonder of a woman's love. For the child's full growth in happiness, in confidence, and in serenity of soul, the gentle spirit of his mother is more powerful than all the world beside.—Walter Russell Bowie.

TRIBUTE TO MOTHERS. The literature of all ages has paid tribute to mother, and the chronicles of all nations acknowledge their debt to her. The sacred Word is full of the highest homage to mothers. "The Lord could not be everywhere, so he made mothers," said a Jewish rabbi. "Mother in Israel" has become a term of the highest regard. The Fifth Commandment, and the first with promise, says, "Honor thy . . . mother."

But it is in the New Testament that we find the culmination of the exaltation of motherhood in the life of Mary, the mother of Christ. From the time that the angel announced to her, "Blessed art thou among women," until the day that Jesus said from the cross to his beloved disciple, "Behold thy mother," she was ever the highest type of motherhood.—Author Unknown.

A TYPICAL MOTHER. When Sir Wilfred Grenfell, the famous Labrador doctor, was a youth attending Marlborough College in his native England, he had an experience which he never forgot, and which he related years later in his book, *Forty Years for Labrador*, as follows:

"My dear mother used to post me a little box of flowers each week. The picture of my mother, with the thousand demands and worries of a large school for small boys on her hands, finding time to gather, pack, address, and post each week with her own hands so fleeting and unessential a token of her love has a thousand times arisen in my memory and led me to consider some apparently quite unnecessary little token of my love as being well worth the time and trouble." This son affirmed that his mother had always been his idea of unselfish love.

Suggested Mother's Day Texts and Themes

Mother Valued: "Her children arise up, and call her blessed." Prov. 31:28.

Our Debt to Motherhood: "Render therefore to all their dues . . . honour to whom honour." Rom. 13:7.

God and Motherhood: "For God commanded, saying, Honour thy father and mother." Matt. 15:4.

A Holy Family: "Behold, I and the children whom the Lord hath given me." Isa. 8:18.

A Mother's Wages: "Take this child away, and nurse it for me, and I will give thee thy wages." Exod. 2:9.

The Wise Son: "My son, hear the instruction of thy father, and forsake not the law of thy mother." Prov. 1:8.

EVENING SERVICE

Theme: Christians Are God's Workmanship.

TEXT: "For we are his workmanship, created in Christ Jesus unto good works, which God hath before ordained that we should walk in them." Eph. 2:10.

INTRODUCTORY: Sometimes we hear a man boast that he is a self-made man. Paul boasted that he and all Christians are God-made men. But something happened to man. God's beautiful piece of handiwork was mared. So God had to make a "new man." It took love and power and wisdom to make man and it takes greater love and power and wisdom to remake man.

I. God has filled the world with his handiwork, beautiful evidence of his greatness and glory. The heavens and earth all proclaim this fact. Mountains and hills are beautiful things. A big river and a mountain stream are both lovely in their distinctive ways. The ocean is an overwhelming sight. The sky is marvelous in its beauty, whether we view it with all the color of a gorgeous sunset, or gaze up at its twinkling stars, or explore its riches through a great telescope. Truly the undevout astronomer is mad indeed!

II. But the most beautiful handiwork of God is beautiful people. The Bible is full of their portraits. These men and women walk across its pages, men and women of faith and love, of purity and purpose, of courage and conviction. Great giants they are, spiritual giants, the work of God's redeeming and sanctifying grace.

The old patriarchs were men of this sort. In Abraham and Isaac, Jacob and Joseph and Job we find these great men. Moses was a man of this type, and David and Samuel and Daniel, all the prophets, with such women as Ruth and Miriam, Esther and others; the little band of selected men who followed our Lord and became his disciples, and Paul who wrote the words of our text. These are but samples of God's handiwork.

When we see what some of these men were and what they became by the grace of God, we realize that nothing is too hard for God. The triumphs of his grace make a wonderful hymn of praise and we say, "Marvelous are thy works, O Lord God Almighty."

III. God wants to make such men and women out of us. It may be hard work and it may be long and tedious work. He may have to do a great deal of chastening and chiseling and testing and teaching and training.

It is in and through our Lord Jesus Christ that this re-creating work can and will be done. In Christ we have a new nature imparted to us. We are made alive, born again, born from above.

In Christ we are justified. Our standing before God becomes as though we had not sinned. His righteousness is imputed to us.

In Christ we are sanctified. This work of God's Spirit makes us over again, transforming us into the likeness of our Master.

In Christ we are adopted into the family of God. We are no longer strangers and foreigners, but fellow citizens with the saints, of the household of God.

In Christ we will be glorified; together with him we shall reign and rule and live at God's right hand.

IV. The purpose of this work of God is that good works may flow from our lives, and that he, our Creator and Recreator, may be glorified in these works. We are made good in order that we may do good, daily exhibiting this evidence of the work of grace in our hearts. He makes us new in order that we by our new walk, new obedience, new works, may show forth the praises of him who has called us out of darkness into marvelous light.

The flower by its fragrance and beauty shows forth the praise of God; the star by its shining proclaims the glory of him who created it; the mountains and hills and rivers and oceans by their majesty and greatness give honor to God. Is it too much to ask that each Christian should by his works, his life and words and acts, be to the praise of the glory of his grace? May we gladly and fully surrender to him that he may work his great work of grace in us and that we by our good works may be a "poem," for that is the meaning of the

Greek word "handiwork," be a real hymn of praise showing forth his glory. —Rev. J. Kenton Parker.

MIDWEEK FELLOWSHIP MEETING TOPIC

(Church Night or Suggested Sermon Subject)

Theme: The Duty and Privilege of Hospitality.

TEXT: "Rest yourselves under the tree." Gen. 18:4.

This invitation was introduction to hospitality. The full account in vv. 1-8. Hospitality is a common duty. It is a duty in which the best qualities of the soul are developed. It has rich rewards.

I. Let us think of this virtue in its source. It is a kind and generous heart. It is a grace of true religion.

II. Let us think of some of its attendant qualities. 1. Promptness. 2. Courtesy. 3. Admitting of no refusal. 4. Unsparingness.

III. The high esteem in which it is held. 1. It is pleasing to man. 2. Approved of God.

IV. Some of the rewards which it brings. 1. An angel may be entertained unawares. 2. Happy friendships may be made. 3. The gratitude of the person or persons entertained.

Abraham treated his visitors with true Eastern hospitality. May it not be that Christ comes often to us in the guise of a stranger? "Inasmuch . . . they did it unto him." Abraham entertained God in disguise. It might be well to give emphasis to the duty and grace of showing hospitality in church.

CHRISTIAN ENDEAVOR SOCIETY TOPIC

May 11. Is Your Home Fun? Col. 3:12-21. (Christian Home Sunday.)

SUNDAY SCHOOL LESSON

May 11. The Right Use of Sunday. Ex. 20:8-11; Mark 2:27, 28; Luke 4:16; 13:10-17.

MEMORY SELECTION: "Remember the sabbath day, to keep it holy." Ex. 20:8.

The Sabbath was ordained as a day of rest, of reverent meditation, and worship. In this lesson we may well consider the unholy practices of our modern weekends and the value and importance of observing the Sabbath for the purposes ordained. We may well consider also the physical and spiritual values of a weekly day of rest. Our mechanical age also raises many questions concerning Sabbath observance.

SUNDAY: MAY EIGHTEENTH

MORNING SERVICE

Theme: Apples of Gold.

SUGGESTED SCRIPTURE READING: Prov. 25:1-28.

SELECTED HYMNS: "Lord, speak to me that I may speak."—F. R. Havergal. "O Master, let me walk with thee."—W. Gladden. "Quiet, Lord, my forward heart."—J. Newton. "Lord, with glowing heart I'd praise thee."—F. S. Key. "O could I speak the wondrous worth." —S. Medley.

CALL TO WORSHIP: "Oh sing unto the Lord a new song: sing unto the Lord all the earth. Sing unto the Lord, bless his name; show forth his salvation from day to day."

INVOCATION PRAYER: O blessed Lord God, who art thyself the portion of thy people, make us joyful in thy house this morning. Save us from the gloom of evil and fear, so that we may walk in the light of thy countenance and rejoice and he glad all the day. Bring us and all our kinsfolk into this same blessed sunshine of thy love. Forgive us, our Father, for all our doubt, our sadness, and our dejection. Forgive us that we have lived like orphans, as though Christ had never died for us and risen again. Let thy mercy lighten upon us, according as we hope in thee. We ask in the name of Christ. Amen.

Theme: Apples of Gold.

TEXT: "A word fitly spoken is like apples of gold in pictures of silver." Prov. 25:11.

INTRODUCTORY: What a delightful picture! The imagination is captured by the beauty and elegance of the figure. The expression is so chaste, the picture conjured up in the mind by the words is so pleasing that we cannot but be impressed when we read or hear it. Apples of gold signify rich, ripe fruit, as sweet to the palate as they are attractive to the eye. And these apples are alluringly placed upon the table in a silver fruit bowl. The Authorized Version is "pictures of silver," but the better translation is "basket," or fruit bowl. The medium for displaying the apples is a silver basket. These rich, enticing apples are placed upon a shining silver dish which is embellished with delicate filigree work of silver.

Such, says the poet, is the fitly-spoken word. It does not jar upon you, it does not annoy and irritate you, it cannot offend you. On the contrary, it commends itself to you, for as apples of gold in a fruit basket of silver appeal to the natural senses so does the fitly-spoken word appeal to the moral sense.

I. The word in season. The fitly-spoken word is not only the right word, it is also a word spoken at the right moment, "a word in season." An ill-timed word is as unwholesome as an unripe apple. You and I need to exercise patience before we speak, for the fitting word is never spoken in haste or thoughtlessly. The fitting word must be spoken in a spirit of sympathy, understanding and love. As St. Paul has it, the truth must be spoken in love, and again, "let your speech be alway with grace, seasoned with salt."

II. The fact of counsel. The fitting word may be one of guidance, encouragement, warning, criticism, gratitude or praise. If it is one of guidance, then experience must bear the advice; if of encouragement, then sincerity must be the medium; if of warning, the word must be spoken in a spirit of understanding; if of criticism, in love; if of gratitude, without flattery and with genuine appreciation; if of praise, with restraint and yet with sincere approval. How futile it is to warn unless our warnings are shot through and through with understanding and love?

III. Words of encouragement. We are often reminded that for many people life is a difficult encounter and that there is always need for a message of good cheer. We might well faint and fail but for an occasional word of encouragement. Our Lord well knew how necessary it was to speak it, for often on his lips was that stimulating and cheering sentence, "Be of good courage." His followers too are to be ready to speak it.

IV. But it is not words of encouragement of guidance alone that are to be spoken. There is also the word of criticism. If this word of criticism is to be helpful it must arise not from prejudice, or envy, or jealousy, but from love. And have we any ground to criticize another unless we too have ourselves walked his way, tried to perform his work, and lived through a similar experience to his?

V. A word fitting all times and seasons is one of gratitude, yet how often is it withheld? It is always a gracious word, and, like mercy, it is twice-blessed, it blesses him who speaks the word as well as him who receives it. And how about the word of praise? After much labor, toil and trouble, after service well done, praise is always fitting. There is hardly a word so precious that falls upon the human ear when it is genuinely spoken.

We take our Lord as our example. He always spoke the fitting word. By an apt parable he warned, by timely admonition he criticized, with transparent sincerity he praised, with a kindly salutation he allayed fear and brought comfort. You and I can speak a message that will inspire, encourage, comfort and warn our fellows, and they will thank God for such an expression, for to them our word may be as an apple of gold in a basket of silver.—J. P. W.

THEME PRAYER: O God, who knowest our failures and our sins yet dost love us still, we cast ourselves upon thee. Pardon us, purge us, purify us! Make of us instruments fit for thy divine purposes. Lead us in the way in which thou wouldst have us to walk. Send us out to speak and live as messengers of thy great love. Though Christ. Amen.

OFFERTORY SENTENCE: "And whatsoever ye do, do it heartily, as to the Lord, and not unto men."

OFFERTORY PRAYER: May thy kingdom come and thy will be done on earth as it is in heaven. We bless thee that thou art willing to accept us as helpers of thy kingdom. To this end wilt thou accept and bless and use these offerings we bring thee this morning for the support and advancement of thy cause in the world. We ask in Christ's name. Amen.

Illustrative Material

SEED THOUGHTS, HOMILETIC AND EXPOSITORY. "Apples of gold" is a poetic name for the orange in more than one Eastern language. "Pictures of silver" may be a figure for the creamy-white blossoms of the orange tree.—Samuel Cox.

"Fitly spoken" is in the margin "a word in season"—a timely, opportune word.—Samuel Cox.

Excellency of Fitly-spoken Words: I. Words fitly spoken must be words fitted to exhibit the truth to the best advantage. II. They must be adapted to the mental mood of the hearer. III. They should be words spoken in the right spirit.—D. T.

Choice Illustrations on the Theme

POWER OF THE TONGUE. The tongue may be either a blessing or a curse. A taunt is one of the deadliest arrows in the quiver of our enemies. When arguments and persecution fail to move us, we fall before ridicule and mockery. Peter could draw a sword in the Garden and stroke for his master, but in the court he could not lose his tongue and speak for his Lord. Whispering and snickering campaigns are devastating. Many a Christian like Peter, and many a good cause has gone down under the withering fire of a vicious tongue—Walter R. Cremeans.

WOULDN'T IT?

Wouldn't this old world be better
  If the folks we meet would say,
"I know something good about you!"
  And then treat us just that way,

Wouldn't it be fine and dandy
  If each handclasp warm and true
Carried with it this assurance?
  "I know something good about you!"

Wouldn't life be lots more happy
  If the good that's in us all
Were the only thing about us
  That folks bothered to recall?

Wouldn't life be lots more happy
  If we praised the good we see?—
For there's such a lot of goodness
  In the worst of you and me.

Wouldn't it be nice to practice
  The fine way of thinking, too?—
You know something good about me!
  I know something good about you!
—Anonymous.

WORDS HAVE WINGS

How thoughtlessly we utter the little word that stings,
Forgetting every moment that little words have wings;
Like little birds, they travel, when once we let them start,
And long before we know it they lodge in someone's heart.

It pays to pause a moment before you speak a word,
For every word you utter has wings just like a bird;
Let none escape unheeded, send forth no poisoned stings,
Before you speak, remember that little words have wings.
—Alfred Barratt.

APPLES OF GOLD. A story was once related by Dr. J. H. Jowett concerning John Morel, mayor of Darlington. Passing through the town Mr. Morel met a fellow citizen who had just been released from jail, where he had served three years for embezzlement.

"Hello," said the mayor, in a cheery tone, "I'm glad to see you! How are you?" The man seemed ill at ease, and therefore very little else was said. Years afterward, according to the story related to Dr. Jowett by Mr. Morel, the mayor and the man met in another town and the latter said: "I want to thank you for what you did for me when I came out of prison." "What did I do?" "You spoke a kind word to me, and it changed my life."

KIND WORDS. Never lose a chance of saying a kind word. As Collingwood never saw a vacant place in his estate but he took an acorn out of his pocket and popped it in, so deal with your compliments through life. An acorn costs nothing, but it may sprout into a prodigious bit of timber.—W. M. Thackeray.

WOULD YOU?

If I knew that a word of mine,
A word not kind and true,
Might leave its trace
On a loved one's face,
I'd never speak harshly, Would you?

If I knew that the light of a smile
Might linger the whole day through
And brighten some heart
With a heavier part,
I wouldn't withhold it, would you?
—Unidentified.

EVENING SERVICE

Theme: The Vitality of Vision.

TEXT: "Where there is no vision, the people perish." Prov. 28:18.

INTRODUCTORY: The wise man never spoke truer words than when he said, "Where there is no vision, the people perish." We live by our visions.

I. Much of the joy of life is in our visions. Think, if you can, of what life would mean to you if all the bright anticipations of the coming days were suddenly blotted out. A prominent alienist said a few years ago that one of the most common causes of insanity is repression, the shutting up of lives in surroundings and circumstances where there is nothing to look forward to, where there are no anticipations.

II. Again, it is the vision that determines character. When Jesus met Simon first you remember he said: "Thou art Simon. Thou shalt be no more called Simon but Peter shall thy name be." Simon was inconstant and unstable, and because of this they had called him Simon. But Jesus told him that one day he would be Peter the Rock. Never for a day did that vision leave the apostle. Many times he sinned and fell, but always he arose, and followed the gleam that beckoned him on.

III. Again, it is the vision that makes us endure, that makes us strong in sorrow and loss. The agony of Jesus' passion, the mocking and scourging, the crown of thorns, the crucifixion, were all glorified by the vision he saw of what was to come after. He saw the welcome that awaited him in the Father's house and the throne that had been prepared. He saw the millions yet to come who would wash their robes and make them white in the blood that he shed that day, "who for the joy that was set before him, endured the Cross."

One cannot visit Quebec without thinking of the battle that was fought there a century and three-quarters ago between the French, under Montcalm, and the English, led by the gallant Wolfe. Early in the fight Wolfe was mortally wounded. As he lay dying on the field he heard a shout: "They fly! They fly!" Lifting himself half up, he cried, "Who flies?" "The French," was the reply. "Then I die happy," he said, as he fell back with a smile upon his face.

In that moment he saw the vision of the future. He saw Canada saved. He saw a whole continent under the dominion of the Anglo-Saxon race. He saw the glories of the centuries yet to come. What were wounds and death to that?

This it is that makes pain and loss and disappointment glow with the light of faith and hope. It is the joy that is set before us.

IV. It is the vision too that makes men achieve. A century ago men stood on the summit of the hills of Pittsburgh and saw the vision of the coming days. They saw those rivers, with their mighty possibilities. They saw the passes in the mountains through which the roads of the future were coming. They saw the iron and the coal that underlay those mountains awaiting the touch of the hand of industry. They saw the steady stream of Scotch-Irish settlers pouring through the Alleghenies. They saw it all and they had the vision of the city of the coming years. They saw the vision and they built a great industrial community.

God is giving us as a church another great vision. Every day thousands are passing by our churches, and behind them comes a vast and unnumbered multitude moving down the years. If we will listen, we will hear the tramp of their marching feet. Little children, men and women, old age—all are there. To the realization of the Church's vision we should solemnly consecrate ourselves.—S. N. H.

MIDWEEK FELLOWSHIP MEETING TOPIC

(Church Night or Suggested Sermon Subject)

Theme: Eventide Meditation.

TEXT: "And Isaac went out to meditate in the field at the eventide." Gen. 24:63.

Meditation was the same to Isaac that it is to us. Under all skies, in all times, thought has flowed in the same channel and observed the same laws. It is those who love to meditate who are the most open to impressions from nature and from grace. It is always the open eye before which the vision passes.

I. The Hebrew word here rendered "meditation" means also to pray. The meditation of any devout person will soon run into prayer.

II. We notice Isaac's time of meditation. It was in the evening. That is one of the choicest hours for meditation. The quiet gloaming, with its glamour and mystery, its long shadows and dying light, whispers into the heart of man. It has been well said, "Meditation is the twilight of thought." Its region lies between this world and the next, between definite ideas and dimest yearnings. No one ever loved Christ deeply, no one was ever strong or high or pure or deep in any way without meditation.

III. Let us therefore consider the moral advantages of meditation. 1. By it we acquire a competent knowledge of our own hearts. 2. By it we are enabled to form a just estimate of the world. 3. Meditation promotes rightness and purity of character, producing humbleness of mind and destroying its love for sin. 4. It places the soul under the influences of the Divine Spirit, who transforms and renews it in the image of Christ.—H.

Suggested Texts and Themes

Jesus Christ in Glory: "Received up into glory." I Tim. 3:16.

The Eternal World: "Father, I will that they also, whom thou hast given me, be with me where I am," etc. John 17:24.

Life Triumphant: "I came forth from the Father, and am come into the world: again, I leave the world, and go to the Father." John 16:28.

The Significance of Our Lord's Ascension: "He, because he abideth for ever, hath his priesthood unchangeable. Wherefore also he is able to save to the uttermost them that draw near unto

God through him, seeing he ever liveth to make intercession for them." Heb. 7:24, 25 (A.S.V.).

God's Drunken Men: "These men are full of new wine." Acts 2:13.

CHRISTIAN ENDEAVOR SOCIETY TOPIC

May 18. Churches for Our Country's Needs: Everybody Needs a Church. Matt. 9:36-38; Matt. 21:13, 14.

SUNDAY SCHOOL LESSON

May 18. Conserving the Family Heritage. Ex. 20:12; Mark 7:9-13; John 19:25-27.

MEMORY SELECTION: "Honour thy father and thy mother: that thy days may be long upon the land which the Lord thy God giveth thee." Ex. 20:12.

Let us love our homes. Let us love father and mother. Let us definitely aim at building the best possible family life. So much good has come to us through Christian family life that we should feel deeply the responsibility to preserve and pass on such good. The very purpose of this lesson is to confront all members of our classes with the facts of the present-day family situation. Also to challenge them to conserve the heritage that only wholesome family life can give.

SUNDAY: MAY TWENTY-FIFTH

MORNING SERVICE

Theme: An Unremembered Hero.

SUGGESTED SCRIPTURE READING: Rev. 21:1-7; 22:1-21.

SELECTED HYMNS: "Am I a soldier of the cross?"—I. Watts. "In the hour of trial."—J. Montgomery. "I need thee every hour."—A. S. Hawks. "Fight the good fight with all thy might."—J. B. S. Monsell. "Jesus still lead on."—N. L. von Zinzendorf.

CALL TO WORSHIP: "O Lord our Lord, how excellent is thy name in all the earth! who hast set thy glory above the heavens." "For thou, Lord, art good, and ready to forgive; and plenteous in mercy unto all them that call upon thee."

INVOCATION PRAYER: Our Father, whose hand is ever filled with bounty for thy children, whose mind is ever thoughtful for their good, whose heart is ever gracious toward their need, accept we pray thee, our gratitude. Be this our gratitude, O God, that we may seek to know thee more truly, to love thee more deeply, to serve thee more faithfully. Be this our consecration, that we ever seek thy kingdom, thy sovereign rule over us, the reign of Christ within us, and his abundant life all about us. May we be ever ready to greet a new day in the world when thy kingdom comes. May that kingdom be the light in our eyes, the passion of our hearts, the motive of our hands. Help us ever, O God, to prepare the way for the coming of the Christ into the lives of men. In his own name we pray. Amen.—M. K. W. H.

Theme: An Unremembered Hero.

TEXT: "There was a little city, and few men within it," etc. Eccles. 9:14, 15.

INTRODUCTORY: When Lord Byron looked upon the statue of himself created by Thorwaldsen, he said: "It is not like me; I look far unhappier than that." The great poet had allowed himself to fall into a spirit of sadness which, instead of opposing, he encouraged. This Byronic mood became popular all over Europe, this world-sickness, this pessimism regarding life and world politics.

Some two hundred years before Christ the people of Israel, though not falling into the same godless skepticism, were in a somewhat similar mood. The Jerusalem to which they had returned from exile was harassed by cruel enemies who were out the spirit of the inhabitants. Men wondered if life had any meaning. In the book of Ecclesiastes, an earnest man gave to the people of his day a message of hope based on his own experiences. This book is truly a tract for our times.

There was, says he, a city surrounded by powerful armies. The inhabitants were unable to resist their enemies by military force. That small city contained one man endowed with wisdom beyond the average and he delivered the city. What he did we can only surmise, but at any rate this wise man was of more value than the army to the beleagured city.

I. A little city may be delivered by one wise man. A large city requires a company of those in whose hearts the voice of God is heard. For a nation a solid company, scattered through the land of those who are convinced that in the way of obedience to the will of God lies the salvation of their country, is a necessity.

II. To do nothing because there is little that is obvious which presents itself is the attitude which too many adopt. This spirit of disillusionment must be eradicated. In the message of Jesus there is the power which can save the world. We are lost if we have no leader whose call we obey.

III. If we are to make something of our lives we must have something of the wisdom of the poor wise man. It will not be sufficient to adopt the way of the man who is just satisfied to live somehow or other without allowing any noble ideals to surge in his heart or any great ambitions to be all-powerful in his life. The Master is calling for men and women who will be loyal to him. They will soon discover that whatever he asks them to give, so he in his turn will give them something infinitely more valuable, for there will come to life a new joy and a new hope, the joy which comes to those who are wholeheartedly dedicated to a great and worthy service.

IV. But is is necessary to make the Christian witness as effective as possible. When Jesus saw the Jerusalem to whose temple he had first gone as a young lad falling under the power of leaders without vision, who were preparing the way for its final downfall, he wept over it. The same Master looks at the powerful cities of the world. He longs to gather the multitude of the dwellers therein under the banner of his love that they may deliver their city. Which of us does not see some step forward which we may take in order that we may more fully obey the will of Christ?—A. C.

APPLICATORY PRAYER: O thou who hast given thy Word as a lamp to our feet and a light to our path, dispose us meekly to receive it, and enable us carefully to obey it, that being upheld and guided in thy ways we may walk in holiness and righteousness before thee all the days of our life, and finally come into thine everlasting kingdom through Jesus Christ our Lord. Amen.

OFFERTORY SENTENCE: "Sell that ye have and give alms; provide yourselves bags which wax not old, a treasure in the heavens that faileth not, where no thief approacheth, neither moth corrupteth."

OFFERTORY PRAYER: Our heavenly Father, accept, we pray thee, this our contribution to thy service, which we now present. Help us to know that all we have and are belongs to thee—that we do not even own ourselves, that we are not our own, for we are bought with a price. Help us, then, to ever seek to glorify thee in our souls, our bodies, and our possessions, all of which belong to thee. For Christ's sake. Amen.

Illustrative Material

SEED THOUGHTS, HOMILETIC AND EXPOSITORY. The Poor Wise Man: Here is a very remarkable case. A little city in defenseless condition. A powerful army at the gates. It is rescued out of the hands of its enemies by one "poor wise man." I. The description suits well the Church. Its many enemies. Its comparative fewness. It is compassed about with those who would destroy. II. There comes a great king, Satan, the devil. The city seems ready to fall. III. There is found in the city a poor wise man. Who is he? He who saves the city must be he who saves us, our Lord Jesus Christ. The city is delivered. IV. What would be the behavior of the people in such a case? Overflowing gratitude, all possible honor? No, they did not so much as thank him. They even forgot him. "No man remembered that same poor man." V. Have we forgotten Christ?—W. J.

Choice Illustrations on the Theme

WHY THEY APPLAUDED: An audience of two thousand people had been requested not to applaud when Secretary of the Navy Frank Knox distributed diplomas to 547 new naval graduates of Annapolis, December 19, 1941. But when Secretary Knox came to one of the midshipmen he said:

"Remember your father did not lose his life, he gave it."

The "middie" thus addressed was Isaac Campbell Kidd of Long Beach, California, whose father, Rear Admiral Isaac C. Kidd, was killed at Pearl Harbor twelve days earlier by an attack of the Japanese.

Young Kidd, pale and composed, listened to this brief tribute to his father, smiled, shook the hand of Secretary Knox, returned to his seat, and requested that he be assigned to submarine duty.—W. J. Hart, D.D.

"BEFORE HONOR IS HUMILITY." An enduring friendship began when Dr. Will Mayo was in New York to receive an honorary degree from Columbia University. The other party to it tells the story:

"We were standing in line at Columbia University at Commencement in June, 1910, wearing borrowed academic gowns and about to receive degrees. Around us were a lot of notables whose faces we recognized. But we were put side by side and we looked at each other like a couple of dogs for a minute. Finally Dr. Mayo said to me, 'I don't know what I'm doing here,' and I said, 'You've got nothing on me, neither do I.' Then we both grinned and he said, 'Who are you?' and I said, 'To tell you the truth, I'm just a country editor from a little town in Kansas called Emporia and my name's White.' He grinned again and said, 'Well, all right, I'm just a country doctor from a little town in Minnesota called Rochester and my name's Mayo.' "
—Helen Clapesattle.

CHRIST AS GUIDE AND DELIVERER. In the sculptures and frescoes of the Catacombs, as well as in the symbolic art of early Christianity, the dolphin occupies a prominent place. The dolphins, called "the arrows of the sea," were in Greek mythology the great guides and deliverers of those in peril on the sea. Hence they are constantly found as a device on ancient coins. One of the famous stories connected with the dolphin is that Arion, the sweet singer, had so enchanted the dolphins with his music that when forced to leap into the sea to escape his enemies, he was borne by them in safety to Taenarum. He is seen riding on a dolphin's back, while he

"With harmonious strains
Requites his bearer for his friendly
pains."

In Christian symbolism the dolphin is taken to represent Christ as Guide and Deliverer.—*2500 Best Modern Illustrations.*

BRAVERY. When the battle of Coriole was being won through the stimulus given to the soldiers by the impassioned vigor of Caius Marcius, they mourned to see their leader covered with wounds and blood. They begged him to retire to the camp, but with characteristic bravery he exclaimed, "It is not for conquerers to be tired!" and he joined them in prosecuting the victory to its brilliant end. "The crown of life" is promised to those who are "faithful unto death." —*Austrian Teacher.*

EVENING SERVICE

Theme: The Vista of Memory (Memorial Day).

TEXT: "That they might set their hope in God, and not forget the works of God, but keep his commandments." Ps. 78:7.

INTRODUCTORY: Down the path of national life we have come through six great wars, Revolution, War of 1812, Civil, Spanish-American, World War I and World War II. Ties of kinship make the memory of those who served in these all most sacred. We do not glory in war, but in the unselfish sacrifice of all those who gave "the last full measure."

For the youth they gave and the blood
they gave,
For every marked or nameless grave,
We must pay with service true
Till the scales stand straight with even
weight,
And the world is a world made new.

The memory of the past serves the present if it lifts the present above the record of the past. If man recall and profit by what they recall forward steps are sure to be taken. Memory alone is sentimental. Linked with hope and effort it is vitalized. Memory has its place in war and in peace.

I. First, associate God with remembrance, with gratitude. There are few faculties of the human mind that we more seldom regulate and direct with Christlike principles than that of looking backward. But the past is noble and holy only as we see God's hand working in it. The past is "what God has done for us." Let us recognize him as the Giver of every good and perfect gift. It is the sure way of saving ourselves from falling into the habit of self-praise. If we see him we will not see what we think is our own cleverness and success, but his gracious Providence. We will not recall our sinful ways in such a manner as to become remorseful, but we will see him as a pardoning Father. We will recall the past, not to long for it and its departed blessings, but we will live in the present fully conscious of God's eternal presence.

II. Then memory of the past is related to the present. After all memory is but to fit us for the present. Past mistakes recalled will be helpful in avoiding them in the present. If memory weakens us for present duty it is not a blessing. If it strengthens it is a blessing. Memory of God's blessing in the past should make us conscious of his present power to aid. His answers to prayers in the past should send us on our knees today.

III. Memory is also related to the future. We are to live today with confidence, strengthened with memory of the past. We are to approach the future with hope that is born of that which memory recalls. The hope of the future draws memory for all that it may paint for us of beauty and happiness, sorrow and trial, in days yet to come. Hope of the future day without the memory of the past day is impossible.

Recall the years, with their blessings, national, family and personal. Recognize God's hand in the passing years. See his providences. Be instructed for the present by recalling the past. Be encouraged for the future by the blessings of the past.—J. W. R. (Adapted).

Suggested Memorial Day Texts and Themes

The New Memorial Day: "What mean ye by this service?" Ex. 12:26.

A Nation's Tribute to Its Heroic Dead: "This day shall be unto you for a memorial." Ex. 12:14.

Death for Others: "For none of us liveth to himself, and no man dieth to himself." Rom. 14:7.

Memorial Day and Its Lessons: "And he said unto me, Son of man, can these bones live?" Ezek. 37:3.

Heroes Are Immortal: "As dying, and, behold, we live." II Cor. 6:9.

Alternate Theme: From Sin to Service.

From the depths of sin to Christian service can be spanned in four steps.

I. The first step is Penitence. Luke writes of two men who went into the temple to pray. One was a Pharisee, the other a publican. The Pharisee faced himself in his prayer, telling of the good things he had done. There was no humility in him. He exalted himself.

The publican gave evidence of a penitent heart, as he cried, "God be merciful to me a sinner." Just as this publican approached God with a plea for mercy, so must every sinner come unto God with a penitent heart.

One day while Jesus sat at meat in the home of a Pharisee, a woman who was a sinner came into the room bearing an alabaster box of ointment. Standing at the feet of Christ, she washed his feet with her tears and wiped them with her hair, and anointed them with the ointment. More beautiful words cannot be found than those addressed to this penitent heart by Jesus. "Thy sins are forgiven. . . . Thy faith hath saved thee; go in peace."

The world is full of hearts bowed low with sin, grief and pain. They wish relief from the heavy load, anxious to exchange grief for joy, pain for peace. How can they do it? By coming to Jesus in true penitence.

II. The second step is Pardon. Jesus knows the human heart and the power of sin which crushes it. Relief is offered to those coming to him. His words never lose their beauty, "Come unto me, all ye that labour and are heavy laden, and I will give you rest. Take my yoke upon you, and learn of me; for I am meek and lowly in heart: and ye shall find rest unto your souls. For my yoke is easy, and my burden is light."

While Jesus lived upon earth, and since his death, resurrection and ascension, multitudes have come to the foot of the cross to find rest for their souls, and have heard the words of pardon, "Thy sins are forgiven."

III. The third step is Peace. The soul in sin has no peace, being out of touch with God. Out of harmony with God means discord in the life, and makes it impossible for us to fit into his plan and purpose. But when we come to God with penitent hearts and hear the words of pardon, peace floods the soul. "Therefore being justified by faith, we have peace with God through our Lord Jesus Christ." Christ is our peace, bringing us nigh to God by his shed blood. A great peace comes into the heart that ceases its warfare against God. Thus the transaction is effected from the place of alienation to that of favor.

IV. The fourth step is Power. A new factor comes into the life, for it becomes the abode of the Holy Spirit. No longer do we live in our strength to combat the powers of evil. The disciples were promised power for witnessing. "Ye shall receive power, after that the Holy Ghost is come upon you: and ye shall be witnesses unto me. . . ." The Holy Spirit is the source of power in the Christian.

We go forth to witness. It may be in Jerusalem, Judea, Samaria, or the uttermost parts of the world. We come to Jesus in sin and weakness, we go forth for him in forgiveness and power. Jesus said, "All power is given unto me in heaven and earth." His followers are to go forth to teach all nations. They will encounter difficulties beyond human strength to conquer, trials that will crush the human spirit, but their strength and power lies in the promise, "Lo, I am with you alway."—L. L. Wightman, D.D.

MIDWEEK FELLOWSHIP MEETING TOPIC

(Church Night or Suggestive Sermon Subject)

Theme: Three Looks on Memorial Day (Memorial Day).

TEXT: "What mean ye by this service?" Ex. 12:26.

To fathom "What mean ye by this

service?" let us take three Memorial Day looks.

I. First, the retrospective look. It is a day of memories. See again the battlefields and what they imply.

II. Secondly, the introspective look. Have we full appreciation of others' sacrifices? Are we guarding faithfully our heritage of freedom? Do we love the nation for which others died? Are we doing now what will bless the generations to come?

III. Thirdly, the prospective look. On Memorial Day we instinctively look into the future. The eternal campground; the great reunion.

CHRISTIAN ENDEAVOR SOCIETY TOPIC

May 25. Churches for Our Country's Needs: Mission to America. Matt. 26:16-20; Acts 26:19.

SUNDAY SCHOOL LESSON

May 25. God's Estimate of Human Life. Ex. 20:13; Matt. 5:21-26; 18:5, 6; Luke 9:51-56.

Memory Selection: "Thou shalt not kill." Ex. 20:13.

All human life is precious to God. It is so precious that nothing should be done to impair its well-being in any way. God who is the giver of life has placed about it every safeguard in commandment and teachings. Man was made in the image of God, so life should always be regarded as sacred and valuable. Jesus expanded this commandment to include not alone actual killing, but anger, hatred, injustice, and all mistreatment of others. If we use this as a temperance lesson, we may well show that the use of alcohol as a beverage is one source of suffering and loss of life.

SUNDAY: JUNE FIRST

MORNING SERVICE

Theme: Setting the Children in the Midst (Pre-Children's Day).

Suggested Scripture Reading: Deut. 6:1-12; Mark 9:33-37.

Selective Hymns: "Saviour, like a shepherd lead us."—Anon. "Shepherd of tender youth."—Anon. "How shall the young secure their hearts?"—I. Watts. "Once in royal David's city."—C. F. Alexander.

Call to Worship: "Oh, come, let us sing unto the Lord; let us make a joyful noise to the rock of our salvation." "Rejoice in the Lord, O ye righteous; praise is comely for the upright."

Invocation Prayer: We praise thee, our Father, that thou hast set the children in our midst. For their sakes do we raise four walls and a roof, and set the table. For their good do we carefully maintain schools and churches, libraries and gymnasiums, cities and streets, parks and playgrounds. For their happiness do we sacrifice and strain. For their prosperity do we plan and pray. But lo, they are leading us, and in their van is the Christ, now our Lord and Saviour, but once a child. Save us, and save the world's childhood, in His name we pray. Amen.—Bruce S. Wright.

Theme: Setting the Children in the Midst (Pre-Children's Day).

Text: "And he took a child, and set him in the midst of them." Mark 9:36.

Introductory: Next Sunday is Children's Day. Today we speak not to children but about them. We have a message for parents and teachers and all others especially interested in the well-being of children.

Steadily we have been learning that our one sure chance at tomorrow is with the child of today.

I. If we fail here, we have failed in everything worth while. It has been a long and hard fight to get laws that protect children from the crushing of labor in shops and factories. We have recognized the right of every child to be educated. In fact we compel everyone to attend school up to a certain age. We are now in the midst of that very important battle which seeks to establish the right of every child to be well born.

II. But there is a need for something even more vital than such considerations, important as they are. Every child has the inalienable right to a good example. No matter how many other things you may give, he will be poor without that. There is no more sobering question that a man may ask himself than this? "Am I furnishing an example that will steer my children right, or if they follow me will they end on the rocks?"

Juvenile courts and the unwritten records of youth's tragedies stagger us. The period through which we are passing will claim its ultimate cost out of the lives of the children. They pay. There is a yet most serious aspect, as we see homes being so rapidly broken. That tension creates an economic pressure upon boys and girls and young women, is breaking the morale upon which their future rests, and with their future ours is bound.

III. The challenge of childhood is put up squarely to this generation in a way in which it never has been put before. There is no more opportune challenge before us, and yet a great percentage of our people are not fully conscious of it. We may well be concerned over the neglect of the home. Fatherhood has been a neglected art. Men have thought that their greatest concern was for gaining of food and clothing and shelter and money for comforts and luxuries. The greatest gift a man can give his son is his own character consecrated to Christian living. Give us manhood and womanhood consecrated to Christ and the problem of childhood will fade.

IV. Every great social and religious problem ultimately returns to childhood for its solution. We can never save the world by the slow hard work of reclamation. We must save it by the spiritual cultivation which will root itself in childhood and youth. "Cure the children!" Is this not the most eloquent challenge ever hurled to those who are lovers of society and the world and are seeking to bring in a day of righteousness?

Do we realize it, that fully one-third of all the children of America know not Christ? The other two-thirds are poorly enough prepared. Jesus took a little child and set him in the midst of them. And the child stands there not alone to fathers and mothers, but to every man and every woman. Our responsibility is not for ours only, but all the children of all people. He who becomes a Christian finds himself linked in a crusade of unselfish sacrifice for world redemption. What an appeal for such a tangled hour when the most common word upon the lips of our generation is personal liberty. There is no room for such a phrase in the vocabulary of a Christian. The only right I have is the right so to live that others seeing me and knowing me and copying me may come to know Christ and live a Christlike life. The children are looking at you and me. God help us so to live that in their copying us they may never go wrong!—H. N. G. (Adapted).

Theme Prayer: We thank thee, our loving Father, for the simplicity of the gospel of Christ. The mind of a little child can grasp it, yet the wisest philosophers do not fully comprehend it. Help us to grow in a knowledge of him who himself was the gospel, even our Lord and Saviour, Jesus Christ. Amen.

Offertory Sentence: "Every man according as he purposeth in his heart, so let him give; not grudgingly, or of necessity: for God loveth a cheerful giver."

Offertory Prayer: We would remember, our Father, that we are not our own, that we are bought with a price, we would therefore glorify thee in our bodies and in our spirits which are thine. It is to this end we bring these our offerings this morning and set them apart to thy service. Wilt thou be pleased to accept and bless and use them, in Christ's name we ask. Amen. —H.

Illustrative Material

SEED THOUGHTS, HOMILETIC AND EXPOSITORY. A Child for a Text: Here Jesus commends to his disciples the childlike disposition. I. A child is remarkable for his considerateness of others. He loves everybody. II. A child is remarkable for his obedience to rightful authority. III. A child is remarkable for his contentment in the home circle. IV. A child is remarkable for his persistency of trust. V. Let the child teach us to modify our estimate of human greatness. VI. And our aims of attainment.—C. S. R.

Consider the danger and sin of standing in the way of children coming to Christ. The duty of bringing children to him. Our duty of ourselves becoming like little children.—J. V.

Choice Illustrations on the Theme

A DUTY TOWARD CHILDREN. The best thing a parent can do for a child is to take him to church, not send him—take him, not intermittently but regularly every Sunday and let him saturate his unconscious mind with the great ideals of religion. Let him hear from the pulpit, until they become part of his life, the noblest passages from the Bible. Let him learn to love the great hymns of the Church, which sing of faith and goodness and strength of character. Let him hear sermons; sometimes they may indeed be dull and musty and frequently they may be over his head, but they will give him the idea that honor, purity, righteousness and decency are virtues to be cultivated. He will get the conviction into his system so that it will never be eradicated, that a real man is one of character and honor.—Norman Vincent Peale.

COMMISSION THE CHILDREN. I saw a copy of Margaret Tarrant's painting, "Behold, I Send You Forth." In this picture Jesus was represented as standing in the midst of a group of children. For perhaps the first time in the history of religious art, most of the children are not facing Jesus, looking up into his face. The assumption is that they have already done that. Now their backs are toward him. His arms are outstretched, waving them from him, urging them to go forth and help him build his kingdom.—Charles D. Spotts.

THE HEART OF A CHILD

Whatever you write on the heart of a child,
No waters can wash it away.
The sands may be shifted when billows are wild
And the efforts of time may decay.
Some stories may perish, some songs be forgot;
But this engraven record, time changes it not.

Whatever you write on the heart of a child,
A story of gladness or care
That heaven has blessed, or that earth has defiled
Will linger unchangeably there.
Who writes it has sealed it forever and aye,
He must answer to God on the great Judgment Day.

—Clarence E. Flynn.

WORK FOR CHILDREN. A boy in India, seriously ill, was taken to the Baptist missionary hospital headed by Dr. and Mrs. John Carman. An emergency operation was successfully performed but the shock of the experience left the lad temporarily blind. When he began to regain his sight, the first object on which his gaze rested was Copping's picture of Jesus and the children.

Indistinctly he beheld the figure of the Master. "Who is that Man?" he asked. Dr. Carman explained that the person was Jesus and that because of him there were doctors and hospitals to heal the sick in India.

As his eyesight became more normal, the young patient saw not only Jesus but the children who were grouped about him. Then he heard from the doctor the story of the Saviour's love for all boys and girls.

Is not this a parable of what happens in the lives of Christians whose eyes are opened so that they see clearly? They behold not only Jesus but those around him. No one has an adequate vision of Christ if he sees the Master in lonely splendor. The Jesus of the Gospels is surrounded by people, and children are in the foreground of the portrait.

The disciples tried to blot the children out of the picture but Jesus rebuked them. "Suffer the little children to come unto me," he said. "Take heed that ye despise not one of these little ones."

The church needs to be reminded that it has only a partial view of its Lord unless it sees him seeking to bring boys and girls to himself. When a congregation of Christian people does not have a carefully planned and outreaching program of Christian nurture for childhood and youth something is wrong with its vision of Christ.

People today are talking about returning to Jesus. Let us be sure that we go back to the real Jesus and that we see him with children pressing around him and being welcomed into his arms.

EVENING SERVICE

Theme: A Great Day (Pentecost).

TEXT: "And when the day of Pentecost was fully come," etc. Acts 2:1-4.

INTRODUCTORY: It was a great day.

I. The preparations. It may seem strange to speak of God preparing for great occasions. But it is easy to see how many circumstances concurred to make ready for the gift of the Holy Spirit. 1. First, it was at the time of the Pentecostal Feast, the season of mild weather, of leisure, of easy traveling, of great concourses of people. 2. Secondly, the occasion gathered men from all parts of the world, the list of which can be seen in this passage. 3. Thirdly, there was the inner fitness, for Pentecost brought to the mind of every devout Jew the most tender and holy memories of his religion. 4. And, finally, there was the spiritual preparation. Quiet, reverent, expectancy. There was "one accord." Patient waiting. Prayers. Fellowship with the risen Christ. They were in that mood of receptivity which is always necessary to the receiving of a spiritual gift.

II. The coming of the Spirit. Great are God's promises. Great are their fulfillments. When we read how the Holy Spirit came we are satisfied that he descended as became him in power and great glory. It was with mighty winds of heaven, tongues as of fire, and a new power in man's highest gift of utterance. It converted cowering, dispirited, hiding fugitives into triumphant heroes filled with divine audacity.

III. The power. We have already suggested it. There is no one word, nor any number of words, that can depict the Spirit's influence. But we can speak of his power and the results of his power which are manifest. When we behold the marvelous transformations he wrought in the persons of the apostles, and behold with wonder how he has changed lives since; when we mark his great structure the Christian Church which he has called, gathered and enlightened through the centuries; when we have surveyed such effects of a more than human might, we often feel like asking whether we ourselves possess the Holy Spirit. But we should not be looking always for Pentecostal wonders; for there is "a still small voice" which works powerfully in the hearts and minds of men. Every holy and good impulse that moves within us is his work. The blessed Spirit has always come to those who in the place where God has placed them have obeyed his word, waited and prayed and sought to do his will.

IV. As we look back over the long past and the wonders of the Spirit's work, our minds turn to the future and the glories which we may expect. As all the marvels of our present mechanical civilization have been dormant for many centuries in this old earth, so with the word of God and his promises there are unimaginable latent riches awaiting the Spirit's hour.

Thanks be to God for the great day of Pentecost; for all it has given us in the past, for all it gives us every day, and for all the wonders of grace it is to give us in the future. And may we be enabled each one to receive a Pentecost, a pouring-out of the Holy Spirit into his own life!—P. H. R. (Adapted).

Alternate Theme: The Almost Incredible.

TEXT: "There shall be a handful of corn in the earth upon the top of the mountains; the fruit thereof shall shake like Lebanon." Ps. 72:16.

INTRODUCTORY: The idea of corn growing upon the top of the mountains of Lebanon is grotesque. But need we take these words quite so literally? This writer, as he looked away to the snow-capped mountains of Lebanon, let his imagination have full reign. He even saw corn on the tops of the mountains, and he uses this unique imagery to convey to his depressed countrymen something which he believed to be true. He says in effect to them, "If the Lebanites can grow corn almost up to the snow line, then who dare set a limit to what God can achieve, for he is the Lord of all life?" Yes, the Psalmist was aiming at bringing the people back to belief in the power of God. He was resolved to shake them out of their gloom and despondency into a state of wide-awake expectancy. I believe that this writer foresaw the time coming when God would make these words come true.

I. The first obvious lesson of our text is that nothing is impossible with God.

The Hebrew people looked with amazement at what the Lebanites had achieved. They were very conscious of their own failings and disappointments. But the Lebanites were only men. Nature still set limits on their achievements. The time would come, said the Psalmist, when all men should see that no limit could be set on the God of Nature who was the God of the Hebrew people.

And the day came when the greatest of all miracles happened. For men laid a crucified Jesus in a tomb, but death could not hold him. By the mighty power of God he rose triumphant. No longer need God's people be conscious of their failings and disappointments, for their God had shown himself to be Sovereign Lord of all the earth and of all the powers that be.

And this God is our God today. In many ways he has revealed his glory and power to us, and if we are truly his, then we do not doubt his power. For we know that with God nothing is impossible.

II. Let us notice, secondly, that men's expectations must never be limited by past achievements.

The Hebrew people would have been quite content if they could have emulated the Lebanites. Not so the Psalmist. He looked higher. He saw that greater things should yet be achieved than men had ever dreamed were possible.

How right he was. Men marveled at what Jesus did. Yet he declared to his disciples, "Greater things than these shall ye do." Truly, the Christian is called to sow in faith believing that miracles still happen. The mistake we all too often make is to measure the future by past achievement. Let us dare to disregard the scanty successes we have had in the past and learn to throw ourselves more wholeheartedly into the glorious work of the kingdom, firmly convinced of the all-conquering power and wisdom of God.

III. Note, thirdly, we are taught that the time shall come when the highest achievements of men will seem unimportant.

The Lebanites led the world in corn production. They had succeeded in overcoming natural difficulties. They were growing a rich harvest almost to the snow line. This was indeed a wonderful and commendable achievement. But the Psalmist sees a time coming which can only be compared with growing corn on the top of the mountains. And that day came when Jesus revealed the Truth to men's minds as he walked in the cornfields; as he changed water into wine and as he changed men's lives by faith in his power.

And this is the lesson our wonder-loving age still needs to learn: that the greatest achievements of men are really unimportant when compared with what the Master of life can do and is still doing in the lives of men. For he alone can redeem men's lives from futility, pettiness and sin. He alone can change men's lives and outlook. He alone can enable us to overcome our weaknesses, can comfort us in our sorrows, and enable us to triumph over our failures.

In the face of our needs how paltry are the best achievements of men. In the face of our needs only One can satisfy, even Jesus Christ, our Saviour and Friend. He indeed is the perfect fulfillment of the Psalmist's prayer and prophecy.—R. K. R.

Suggested Texts and Themes

The Meaning of Pentecost: "They were all filled with the Holy Ghost." Acts 2:4.

Power and Its Secret: "Strengthened with all might, according to his glorious power." Col. 1:11.

The Self-evidence of Pentecost: "Every man heard them speak in his own language." Acts 2:6.

Idle Money: "It is as when a man, going into another country, called his own servants, and delivered unto them his goods." Matt. 25:14 (A.S.V.).

MIDWEEK FELLOWSHIP MEETING TOPIC

(Church Night or Suggested Sermon Subject)

Theme: All This and Heaven Too.

TEXT: "Giving thanks unto the Father, which hath made us meet to be partakers of the inheritance of the saints in light." Col. 1:12.

In the spirit of joyfulness Paul stirs up his brethren to gratitude. The grounds of this thanksgiving are but various aspects of the great blessing of salvation.

I. Let us think first of the possession expected. "The inheritance." The word denotes that it is not a conquest, nor even a gift, but a legal right. Through Jesus Christ the saints become "heirs of God." "Saints in light." Light denotes knowledge, purity, safety, gladness, glory. The saints inherit all this and heaven too.

II. Secondly, the qualifications bestowed. "Made us meet." Made us sons to inherit. Adopted us, making us eligible for the privileges of sons.

III. The joy experienced in the present. "Giving thanks." Both for being "made meet" and for "the inheritance." The moment we read our title to this inheritance our souls are filled with boundless delight. And it is an increasing joy. "Always giving thanks." The joy of expectation never decreases. Yet it is a joy mingled with humility. We feel that "giving thanks" is all that we can do; for we merit not our rights to the kingdom here or hereafter.

CHRISTIAN ENDEAVOR SOCIETY TOPIC

June 1. Courtship and Marriage: Falling in Love Intelligently. Gen. 24: 61-67.

BULLETIN BOARD SLOGANS FOR THE MONTH

By Earl Riney

It is well known that a twisted childhood can mean a tragic life.

Parents must equip themselves to accept their responsibility.

A boy is apt to adopt his father's philosophy of life.

We live in the character house we build.

There is no better health preserver than a clear conscience.

A man is as big as the things that annoy him.

Beauty of character comes from fellowship with God.

The past cannot be changed; the future is still in your power.

The saints are sinners who kept on trying.

Every day can be the Lord's day.

SUNDAY SCHOOL LESSON

June 1. Christ's Standard of Moral Purity. Ex. 20:14; Matt. 5:27-32; Mark 10:2-9.

MEMORY SELECTION: "Thou shalt not commit adultry." Ex. 20:14.

God wants us as his children to be ever at our best. Unclean thinking, talking, and living degrades us. It also keeps us from having a Christian relationship with God and others. Clean thoughts and clean lives make us happy and greatly increase our influence for good upon others. Such also is one great contribution to the having of happy homes. Sex is one of the great factors for good or ill in the life of all people. Our commandment for today and the other Scripture references for this lesson give wise guidance for this area of life. Christ's standards are rigorous, but they must be so to preserve purity of life and the sanctity of the home.

SUNDAY: JUNE EIGHTH

MORNING SERVICE

Theme: Listening to the Flowers (Children's Day).

SUGGESTED SCRIPTURE READING: Song of Sol. 2:11-13; Rev. 22:1-7.

SELECTED HYMNS: "We plow the fields and scatter."—M. Claudins. "I love to tell the story."—K. Hankey. "Saviour teach me day by day."—J. E. Leeson. "I think when I read that sweet story of old."—J. Luke. "There's a Friend for little children."—A. Midlane.

CALL TO WORSHIP: "Suffer the little children to come unto me, and forbid them not, for of such is the kingdom of God."

INVOCATION PRAYER: Our Father, we are mindful this day how that Jesus called the little ones as lambs to his fold, placed his hands of blessing upon their heads, threw his arms of love round about them, and gave them the kindliest look. We know something of the cravings in the heart of a child. Its innocence is a cry for purity. Its weakness is a cry for strength. Its helplessness is a cry for protection. And its heart is a great plea for love. We bless thee for the little ones in our homes. May we deal with them as Jesus would deal with them were he in our place. We ask in his name. Amen—Rev. Garret Hondelink, B.D.

Topic: Listening to the Flowers (Children's Day [Object Sermon]).

TEXT: "The flowers appear on the earth; the time of the singing of birds is come, and the voice of the turtle [dove] is heard in our land." Song of Sol. 2:12.

Young folks, I ask you to look at this lovely bouquet of flowers. Admire it. Are they not very beautiful? Here in this book of the Bible Solomon spoke of flowers. "The flowers appear on the earth." Flowers tell us that the winter is past. Flowers are a very beautiful part of the spring. This Scripture verse speaks of the flowers as smiling, the birds as singing, picturing the great beauty of the springtime of the year and of the early summer.

Now let us think together for a little about these flowers I hold in my hand.

They have quite a few interesting things to say to us.

I. First, they tell us quite quickly and urgently that they are not weeds. They are valued and admired and loved, and they are the result of seed-sowing and much care. That is the way all admirable qualities even in our characters come, as the results of much thought and care and prayer and effort. "No excellence without labor" is a common proverb. Vices force themselves upon us, like weeds in a garden. To be good we must work at it. We must try and pray, and try and try and keep on trying.

II. Further, it is true to say that flowers are God's gifts. Spring is his gift. These beautiful days we are having are his gifts. So are the sunshine and the flowers. Listen! They whisper! This is what they say, "We are sent by God, who made us all." They are lovely types of many lovely gifts our heavenly Father sends us.

III. There is another interesting fact. Flowers often suggest to us the names of our friends, of human persons. We do not have them all here, but in many homes we have a Lily and Daisy and Violet and Ivy and Rose—all girls. There are boys too. There is at least one that I remember. Listen! Sweet William!

IV. Well that suggests another fact, that flowers are various. They are in great variety, simply countless. Boys and girls are not alike; but like flowers they all have names, and they all can live beautiful, fragrant and useful lives.

V. Then, too, flowers are planted. What can we learn from that? Well, planted things stay where they are put, don't they? Obedient children are a great comfort to their parents, and seeing them so is a great comfort and joy to everybody else!

VI. It might be added that flowers are companions. When we love people we are told to "say it with flowers." And flowers are a joy and blessing to sick folks. We decorate our rooms with flowers. They are like friends who come to visit us. We like them.

In closing let me remind you that Jesus is called the "Rose of Sharon." His was the most beautiful and most useful life. He is called "The chiefest among ten thousand and the One altogether lovely." I am sure we all love him, and this Children's Day we think especially of his gifts of the beautiful springtime when the "flowers appear on the earth."—H. (After T. B.)

THEME PRAYER: O Lord, who dost call thy servants in childhood, commanding them to remember their Creator in the days of their youth, we ask a blessing upon all children, that they may be led early to give their hearts to thee. Bless thou all parents and teachers and teach them thy law and grace, that all may be true children of thine. We ask in Jesus' name. Amen.

OFFERTORY SENTENCE: "Upon the first day of the week let everyone of you lay by him in store as God has prospered him." "Freely ye have received, freely give."

OFFERTORY PRAYER: Dear Father, from whose bounteous hand cometh every good and perfect gift, no offering that we can ever fully express our thanks for thy gift of children. Bless us as we bring our offering of money into thy treasury, and enable us to dedicate our precious children unto him who said: "Suffer little children, and forbid them not, to come unto me: for of such is the kingdom of heaven." We ask in Christ's name. Amen.

Illustrative Material

SEED THOUGHTS, HOMILETIC AND EXPOSITORY. Heaven lies about us in our infancy.—Wordsworth.

I love these little people: and it is not a slight thing when they, who are so fresh from God, love us.—Dickens.

Little works, little thoughts, little loves, little prayers for little Christians, and larger and larger as the years grow. —Rev. Chas. H. Parkhurst.

The first duty toward children is to make them happy. If you have not made them happy, you have wronged them; no other good they may get can make up for that.—Charles Buxton.

Children are the lambs of the flock. Christ said to the church, "Feed my Lambs." The lambs belong to the sheep and the sheep to the shepherd.—Rev. J. J. Barnhardt.

Children are the tomorrow of society. —Whately.

Choice Children's Day Illustrations

CHILDREN'S DAY. Some kind hearts have lived in every generation, but it is only within a few years that the older Christians have come into such perfect love and sympathy with children's needs as to set apart a Sunday for their especial benefit. Those who planned the grand day seem to enjoy it as much as the little ones, for the churches are full of grown-up people, many of them with silvery hair and wrinkled faces; but many of the wrinkles seem to be smoothed out by the happy, fresh looks that come over them when the children's voices are heard taking a prominent part in the worship. We older ones can testify that Children's Day has benefited us in many ways, and is the Sunday of the whole year which we enjoy the best.—Susan Teall Perry.

PERISHABLE PROPERTY. We once saw this sentence, "Perishable property; don't switch off," chalked on a car belonging to a freight train. Careless conductors sometimes leave freight cars on sidetracks for a day. But here was one that was not to be left even one day off the main track. It had fruit or something else on board which must be gotten to market at once. Those boys or girls in your class are "perishable property." Don't switch them off the track by any carelessness, or irregularity, or dullness, or severity of yours.—*5000 Best Modern Illustrations.*

WORK FOR CHILDREN. There is nothing in all the world as important as little children, nothing so interesting. If ever you wish to go in for philanthropy, if even you wish to be of any use in the world, do something for children.—David Starr Jordan.

CHILDHOOD MOLDED. When a thoughtful child was asked why a certain tree in the garden was crooked, he said he "s'posed somebody must have stepped on it when it was a little fellow."

BOTTLED SUNSHINE. We are all very glad and grateful during the cold weather that we have plenty of coal. Coal is sought for under the ground. The places where it is found and where workers dig it out are called mines, and sometimes they are a very long way below the surface. How does coal come into being? Many hundreds of years ago trees and leaves and branches fell on the ground and decomposed. Then in some earthquake or other upheaval of the earth this surface layer became buried, and there, far down in the earth chemical changes took place which altered it so that it became coal. Where did the quality of coal come from? The sun shone on the vegetation. The trees and shrubs and leaves drank in the sunshine and sealed it up within themselves; and when we put the coal on the fire that bottled sunshine is released and comes out in light and heat to help you and me and other people to live and work. Boys and girls, you can be bottled sunshine. Absorb and give out sunshine of joy and helpfulness.

Children's Day Quotable Poetry

CHILDREN'S DAY

Well may the church keep Children's
Day,
And thus draw near the Son,
Who gained His richest human realm,
When Children's hearts were won.

Well may the church keep Children's
Day,
And thus draw near the skies,
For in the children's sunny hearts
The light of heaven lies.

Well may the church keep Children's
Day,
She keeps her greatness then,
E'en now the Christ uplifts a child
Above all sinful men.

O, happy day! Oh, heavenly hour!
When thus the church shall stand,
Like Christ with smile and touch of grace
Amid the children's band. Amen.
—George Edward Martin.

ALL THINGS BRIGHT AND BEAUTIFUL

All things bright and beautiful,
All creatures great and small;
All things wise and wonderful,
The Lord God made them all.

Each flower that opens,
Each little bird that sings,
He made their glowing colors,
He made their tiny wings.

He gave us eyes to see them,
And lips that we might tell
How great is God our Father,
Who hath made all thinks well.
—Unidentified.

TRUST IN GOD, AND DO THE RIGHT

Courage, brother, do not stumble,
Though the path be dark as night;
There's a star to guide the humble—
"Trust in God, and do the right."

Let the road be rough and dreary,
And its end be far out of sight,
Foot it bravely! strong or weary,
"Trust in God, and do the right."
—Norman Macleod.

EVENING SERVICE

Theme: Some Homespun Certainties.

TEXT: "The Lord recompense thy work, and a full reward be given thee to the Lord God of Israel, under whose wings thou art come to trust." Ruth 2:12.

INTRODUCTORY: The words we are to consider are part of the address of welcome Boaz gave to Ruth, the widowed Moabitess, who had left the country of her birth to begin life anew in the homeland of Naomi, her widowed mother-in-law. Simplicity and certitude were the marks of his speech to a lonely woman whose recent sorrows weighed so heavily upon her heart. I am attracted by the homespun certitudes of his teaching.

I. First, there is certitude concerning service. "The Lord recompense thy work," were the words that gushed up warmly from the heart of a man who had been deeply stirred by a story of family fidelity.

We are at a point in the story where the broken threads of life had been taken up again. What seemed to be best, they had done. Decisions had been taken on where to go, what to do and in what faith to live; especially the latter decision.

With reference to all this, Boaz used the word "recompense." Boaz was on sure ground when he encouraged a troubled soul with that of recompense. God will recompense the faithful.

II. In the second place, there is certitude concerning succor. "A full reward be given thee of the Lord God of Israel, under whose wings thou art come to trust," are words which have the stirring quality of a robust affirmation. That word "reward" repays study. God's wings! Men who have made the prison house of cold exactitudes their dwelling place cannot understand this, but multitudes of simple-hearted people can testify that, taking cover under the wings of God, they have discovered the secret of undismayed confidence in all the changing scenes of life.

III. In the last place, there is certitude concerning sphere. In what circumstances are we likely to pass our days? Is there anything in this passage suited to the kind of life which may be ours? Assuring answers spring in plenty. What was the work on which with such confidence Boaz claimed God's blessing? Here is his own account of it: "It hath fully been showed me all that thou hast done unto thy mother in law since the death of thine husband: and how thou hast left thy father and thy mother, and the land of thy nativity, and art come unto a people which thou knewest not heretofore."

So the "work" was the kindly, compassionate relationship of people in the common sorrow and losses of life. It was what they were to one another. Just their sticking to one another when things were difficult and lonely. Standing by one another when new things had to be faced. Being brave for another's sake when the future seemed empty.

What is more, the actors in this story, though unaware of it, were weaving strands in the divine pattern of life. What they were and what they did prepared the way for the coming of the Lord. From that scene of love and appreciative insight there runs a line at the end of which there stands Jesus Christ, the Saviour of the world.

All this is relevant to our tasks. If with love and devotion we do the common things; if we are faithful to one another in good or ill; if, trusting in Jesus Christ who is evermore calling us to the shelter of his wings, we do the hard things of our day and generation, we shall be blest.—H. J. F.

Alternate Theme: Inside the Gates.

TEXT: "The inheritance of the saints in light." Col. 1:12.

INTRODUCTORY: Here is a glimpse of the heavenly world, a glance inside the gates. We get at least some very satisfying suggestion as to the beauty and blessedness and richness of the inheritance of the saints in light.

I. The place. "The inheritance." 1. It is a real world. 2. It is an inheritance. The privileges of religion are often represented as an heirship, or an inheritance. The pay of a soldier, the fees of a physician, the gains of trade, the wages of labor are not inheritance. Neither is this heavenly inheritance a reward of merit. All the riches of earth cannot buy it. The metaphor is drawn from Israel's "inheritance" of the land of Canaan.

II. The inhabitants, or inheritors. "The saints in light." Children inherit from the father. The inhabitants of heaven are the children of God, redeemed by Christ, made meet for heirship. That does not mean that we are made fit by our own merits. It does mean that the "saints" have a state of mind and feeling that is adapted to heaven, through God's Holy Spirit in their hearts. We may well think of: 1. Their number. 2. Their dignity. 3. Their employments.

III. Their condition. "In light." They are in a kingdom of light as contrasted with the kingdom of darkness and tears and anxiety and the transitory things of earth. We find this thought of light often used to describe the heavenly kingdom. God, who presides over it, "is light, and in him is no darkness at all." Christ is called "the light of men," "the true light," "the light of the world." The angels of that kingdom are "angels of light." All the descriptions of heaven represent it as filled with light and glory.—H.

Suggested Texts and Themes

Helps for Heart Gardens: "Awake, O north wind; and come, thou south; blow upon my garden, that the spices thereof may flow out. Let my beloved come into his garden, and eat his pleasant fruits," etc. Song of Sol. 4:16.

The Harvest of the Resting-time: "It is vain for you to rise up early, to sit up late, to eat the bread of sorrows: for so he giveth his beloved sleep." Ps. 127:2.

Heaven's Voices in Summer Echoes: "And they heard the voice of the Lord God walking in the garden in the cool of the day." Gen. 3:8.

At the Seaside with Jesus: "And it came to pass, that, as the people pressed upon him to hear the word of God, he stood by the lake of Gennesaret," etc. Luke 5:1-3.

MIDWEEK FELLOWSHIP MEETING TOPIC

(Church Night or Suggested Sermon Subject)

Theme: Sinning against Children.

TEXT: "Do not sin against the child." Gen. 42:22.

These are the words of Reuben. They

were to his brethren concerning Joseph. "Spake I not unto you, saying. Do not sin against the child?" What voices say this to us? Nature says it. The instinct of humanity says it. Experience adds its voice. Conscience repeats over and over again the same advice. The Church says it. God says it.

I. How may we sin against a child? 1. One way is by spoiling it. Honest training, wise training is needed. 2. Another way, the very reverse of the first, is by harshness. 3. A third way, far too common, is by bad example. 4. Joseph's brethren sold the child for silver. We surely never do that. 5. We may sin against the child by neglecting the means for its Christian culture and salvation.

II. What are some reasons why we should not sin against the child? 1. First reason, because he is a child. 2. Secondly, because by doing so you may blast his whole life. 3. Sin not against the child especially because children are Christ's favorites.—A. G. B.

CHRISTIAN ENDEAVOR SOCIETY TOPIC

June 8. Courtship and Marriage: Making a "Go" of Marriage. Eph. 5:22-33.

SUNDAY SCHOOL LESSON

June 8. Persons and Property. Ex. 20:15; Luke 16:1-12.

Memory Selection: "Thou shalt not steal." Ex. 20:15.

Chaos would result if the rights of ownership were not recognized. We all need to make a distinction between what is ours and what belongs to others. Any sort of theft breaks one of God's rules for living together. The teacher of this lesson may well raise the question as to whether the person who is tempted to gamble, steal or destroy can, in the light of the law of God and civilized society, afford to yield. This lesson permits also a strong emphasis upon stewardship. The right use of property is fundamental.

SUNDAY: JUNE FIFTEENTH

MORNING SERVICE

Theme: The Morning Road.

Suggested Scripture Reading: John 2:1-11.

Selected Hymns: "Come, we that love the Lord."—I. Watts. "O for a thousand tongues to sing."—C. Wesley "Jesus, thou joy of loving hearts."—Bernard of Clairvaux. "Children of the heavenly King."—J. Cennick. "Sometimes a light surprises."—W. Cowper.

Call to Worship: **"O come, let us** worship and bow down: let us kneel before the Lord our maker. For he is our God; and we are the people of his pasture, and the sheep of his hand."

Invocation Prayer: "By the knowledge that the Son of God loved us and gave himself for us may we rise to new life today. By the experience of forgiveness and the cleansing of our lives from all evil may we overflow with gratitude and praise. By the communion of our spirits with thee and with one another may we be filled with good temper. By the great high-calling of the kingdom of God may we rejoice in great tasks and do them with all our hearts. Bless us with thy presence and with the sense of thy nearness while we wait together in thy house upon thee this morning. We ask in the name of Christ. Amen.—M. K. W. H.

Theme: The Morning Road.

Text: "But the path of the just is as the shining light, that shineth more and more unto the perfect day." Prov. 4:18.

INTRODUCTORY: All life means progress. The path of the just, or righteous man, resembles the shining light in being small at the commencement. The path of the just resembles the shining light in its progressive character.

I. Let us not overlook the beauty of the figure of speech used. "The shining light." The reference is evidently to the light of day, the rising sun. It suggests morning beauty and gladness and increasing light.

II. We stop for a moment to make sure that we are on the right road. The Rev. Dr. M. K. W. Heicher expresses it thus: "One who knows the way directs us. He says that it is a morning road. It is a path of perpetual morning. That road that moves toward a gathering gloom and ends in darkness is not our road. This shines more and more unto the perfect day, a lovely noon when no shadow causes one to stumble or to fear."

We know a kindly aged gentleman who used to take a morning walk for exercise. He often passed the home of a little girl who liked his looks and called him "The Morning Man." He was a morning man walking a morning road.

III. The progressive aspect suggested. It is from dawn to full day. It has in it the light of goodness, of joy, and of glorious destiny. Again Dr. Heicher says: "One's eyes should be on the road but not cast downward at one's feet. That causes hesitating step. Looking ahead steadies the stride. Follow the gleam! When the gleam becomes a shining, follow the shining! When the shining becomes splendor, follow the splendor! When the splendor becomes the glory of God in the face of Jesus, follow the glory remembering that once he said, 'I am the Way.' "—H.

THEME PRAYER: O God, who hast made the heaven and the earth and all that is good therein, and hast shown us in Jesus that the secret of joy is a heart set free from selfish desires, and that finds its peace in thee, help us to find delight in all good and honest things and to rejoice always in thy truth and thy bounty. May the joy of the Lord be our strength, and we find that joy increasing as the days go by. We ask in Jesus' name. Amen.

OFFERTORY SENTENCE: "Thy kingdom come; thy will be done on earth as it is in heaven."

OFFERTORY PRAYER: In the name of Christ and unto the spread of his Gospel in the earth we dedicate this offering. May it receive, O Lord, thy blessing to carry unto men a finer appreciation of service, unto women a higher evaluation of their lives, unto children their rightful heritage of Christian nurture, and unto all a saving knowledge of thee. In Christ's name we ask. Amen.—Rev. M. K. W. Heicher, Ph.D.

Illustrative Material

SEED THOUGHTS, HOMILETIC AND EXPOSITORY. From Dawn to Noon: "The path of the just is as the shining light, that shineth more and more unto the perfect day." No nobler expression has ever been given to the great thought of Christian progress than these words contain. "Light of dawn" to the "perfect day." The depth of Christian joy should show the same increase.

The Path of the Just: I. The just. II. Their path. III. Our perfect day. IV. The crown of life.—H. B.

The Religious Life: I. Its beauty and excellence. II. Its pleasantness. III. Its instructiveness. IV. Its progressive nature and experience. V. Its issue in perfection of holiness and happiness.—H. G.

Choice Illustrations on the Theme

"WITH SONGS AND EVERLASTING JOY." We recently heard a man say that he was prejudiced against a certain clergyman because he was so cheerful. He thought a servant of God ought to regard cheerfulness as a sign of the superficial and the insincere. We disagre with him. That attitude is a leftover from the Dark Ages when men thought that God begrudged them happiness and they entered into monasteries and the women withdrew into convents so that they might remain unspotted from the world. Read Isa. 35.—Archer Wallace.

"OIL OF GLADNESS." Of Jesus it was said, "God, thy God, hath anointed thee with the oil of gladness above thy fellows." So, then, his followers owe it to the rest of the world to appear with cheerful faces, radiating the sunshine of hope and trust, of innocent fun and laughter that rises from the heart. "Joy," says Jean Ingelow, "is the grace we say to God." And we owe it to him every day for uncounted good things and happy experiences.

"REJOICE IN THE LORD ALWAYS." Some people think black is the color of heaven, and that the more they can make their faces look like midnight the more evidence they have of grace. But God, who made the sun and the flowers, never sent me to proclaim to you such a lie as that. We are told to "rejoice in the Lord always."—H. W. Beecher.

JOY OF CHRISTIANS. One of Haydn's friends asked how it happened that his church music was almost always an animating, cheerful, and even festive quality. The great composer replied: "I cannot make it otherwise. I write according to the thoughts I feel. When I think upon God my heart is so full of joy that notes dance and leap as it were, from my pen, and since God has given me to a cheerful heart it will be easily forgiven me that I serve him with a cheerful spirit."

EVENING SERVICE

Theme: An Appeal to Experiment.

TEXT: "O taste and see that the Lord is good: blessed is the man that trusteth in him." Ps. 34:8.

INTRODUCTORY: In introducing a sermon on this text the late Rev. John Henry Jowett said: "This confident and jubilant appeal comes at the end of a series of splendid testimonies such as might be heard at many a fervent experience meeting. One man confesses that he had once been enmeshed in multitudinous fears which had crippled his walk toward Zion: 'I sought the Lord, and he heard me, and delivered me from all my fears!' A group of cheery witnesses testified that in past days their faces had been clouded with sorrow because the sunshine had gone out of their souls: 'They looked unto him, and were lightened!' One man confessed that he had been in many a tight place, closely beset by powerful temptations: 'And this poor man cried, and the Lord heard him, and saved him out of all his troubles!' And then it seems as though the individual testimonies merge into one strain of triumphant assurance: 'The angel of the Lord encampeth round about them that fear him!' Now, out of these testimonies, and as their consequence, there issues a mighty appeal, 'O taste and see that the Lord is good; blessed is the man that trusteth in him!'"

I. Let us first think of this transcendent and gladdening truth, "The Lord is good." Goodness is an essential property of the Divine nature. He is originally, essentially, unchangeably, supremely good. We feel at a loss when we try to express how good he is. One way in which his goodness is manifested is in the provision he has made for conferring happiness upon his creatures. In Psalm 145:7, this attribute of goodness is extolled: "They shall utter abundantly the memory of thy great goodness." This attribute has different designations according to the different objects upon which it terminates. When it confers happiness without merit it is called grace. When it commiserates the wretched and makes them happy it is called mercy. When it defends the innocent it is called righteousness. When it delays to punish evildoers it is called patience and long-suffering. When it pardons the guilty it is called forgiveness. When it bestows blessings according to promise it is called truth. God's great goodness is especially manifest, supremely manifested, in his provision of Redemption through Christ.

II. Having been reminded of God's goodness let us hear the Psalmist's testimony as to the best way of knowing it. "O taste and see that the Lord is good." That means do not trust to hearsay. Do not be contented with the testimonies of others, or merely theoretical knowledge. Become experimental, and judge for yourself. Knowledge comes to us by way of three main channels. First, argument addressed to reason. Second, testimony addressed to faith. And third, experiment, which appeals to consciousness. Here the appeal is to experiment, a way open to all, a short, simple, safe way of testing.

III. A third and important inducement is added, the invariable blessing awaiting. "Blessed is the man that trusteth in him." Such a man has peace, inward satisfaction, calmness in the midst of trouble, resignation, hope, joy. This is not a promise of future blessedness only. It is a present blessing good for the whole life long.—H.

Alternate Theme: Forbidden Trees.

TEXT: "Thou shalt not plant thee a grove of any trees near unto the altar of the Lord thy God." Deut. 16:21.

INTRODUCTORY: The mere recital of Joyce Kilmer's "Trees" gives a sense of calm restfulness. There's music there.

Then there is our text: "Thou shalt not plant thee . . . any trees." Not any trees! Not even the trees that look at God all day! No, not any trees! Why this prohibition? Isn't God a lover of trees?

I. First, purity of worship is called for. The long story of heathen worship is strangely associated with trees. The darkened minds of heathendom devised all manner of weird outrages and thought of them as worship. Cruelties were a part of their worship. The gods they worshiped were not kind. Severe exactions were made upon natural affection and parental tenderness. There was nothing clean or sweet enacted around those grim altars hidden amongst the trees.

All these terrible things were practiced by the nations in whose lands the Children of Israel made their home at the end of their wilderness journey. Warnings against such terrible doings were made to them before they crossed the borders of those lands.

We begin to see why trees were prohibited. Nothing must be permitted that could suggest that there was anything in the worship of God like that. Worship was to be a clean thing, offered by a clean people. There is nothing that need be hidden.

Worship was to be a cleansing thing, not a defilement. It was to be sweet, pure, free and elevating. But all these warnings were unheeded. And strange it is, these evils, so gross and cruel, had a strange fascination for the hearts of the people when they lost touch with God. It is a terrible thought, that men who have seen God can go back to beastliness, to paganism. Only the pure in heart see God.

II. In the second place, an unhindered view of the altar is called for. The altar has primary importance. Not only wrong things, but things of secondary importance may obscure the altar. Things that in themselves are innocent become perilous when they hide the altar from view. All accessories to worship must be tested that way. Aesthetical things may become an intrusion.

What is it for which the altar stands? Sacrifice, and fellowship secured by sacrifice. I think this is a comprehensive answer. The altar is the meeting place between God and estranged children. Man cannot by searching find out God. Yet man, estranged, can be reconciled. Man, distanced, can be made nigh. Man, doomed, can be delivered. Man, lost, can be found. How? All the altars of the old order—indeed, all the altars of all the old religions of the world—hint at, point to the one great altar of man's redemption, the Cross of Christ.

Only dimly guessed, never clearly seen, but always there was a line that ran from the altars red with innocent blood to the Cross on which the Prince of Glory died. He was nailed to a tree, as the first preacher of the gospel put it. And as that same preacher elsewhere says, He bore our sins in His own body on the tree.

Through that Man on the tree repentance is given, forgiveness declared, reconciliation effected, and fellowship secured. That is the gospel. There is the altar that must not be obscured. No trees of ritual, ceremonies, ornaments or any human device must be allowed to hide the Cross of Christ. Trees must not hide the Man on the Tree.—H. J. F.

Suggested Texts and Themes

The True Spirituality: "But the mind of the spirit is life and peace." Rom. 8:6 (A.S.V.).

A Great Song: "Blessed be the Lord, the God of Israel; for he hath visited and wrought redemption for his people." Luke 1:68 (A.S.V.).

Human Blanks: "Every man hath his proper gift of God, one after this manner, and another after that." I Cor. 7:7.

The New Earth: "And I saw the holy city, new Jerusalem, coming down out of heaven from God." Rev. 21:2 (A.S.V.).

The Field of the Slothful: "I went by the field of the slothful," etc. Prov. 24:30-32.

MIDWEEK FELLOWSHIP MEETING TOPIC

(Church Night or Suggested Sermon Subject)

Theme: God's Rainbow Round His Throne.

TEXT: "And there was a rainbow round about the throne." Rev. 4:3.

The rainbow encircles the throne. The throne is the symbol of God's government. The rainbow is the symbol of covenant, looking back to Noah's bow, but with enlarged meaning.

I. The circle of promise. "Bow in the cloud." Old Testament covenant. Promise and prophecy.

II. The circle of truth. Promise assured by Eternal Truth.

III. The circle of providence. God's providence works out his promises. History.

IV. The circle of grace. New Testament covenant of grace. Pardon, Peace, Hope, Salvation.

V. The rainbow is round about the throne, indicating that all God's attributes and perfections are under its influence. God's promise surrounds his majesty. His grace surrounds his justice. His love surrounds his power. His glory surrounds his children. Think of the unspeakable delight this rainbow excites. Child of God, look up, and rest in God's promise, God's truth, God's grace, God's providence, God's love.—H.

CHRISTIAN ENDEAVOR SOCIETY TOPIC

June 15. Attitudes in Conduct: "Something for Nothing." Prov. 16:8; Lev. 19:11, 13.

SUNDAY SCHOOL LESSON

June 15. The Obligation to Be Truthful. Ex. 20:16; John 18:15-27.

MEMORY SELECTION: "Thou shalt not bear false witness against thy neighbour." Ex. 20:16.

Truthfulness is fundamental. It is fundamental to the best social, religious and economic life. Speaking the truth, acting the truth, being the truth are all-important. Truth both in speech and action must be learned and cultivated from our earliest childhood. We must be truthful in what we say about others. See the memory selection. The violation of this principle for the sake of expediency, thoughtlessness, or any other reason is unchristian. Jesus made plain that in his speech one should always be truthful even if personal suffering should be the result.

SUNDAY: JUNE TWENTY-SECOND

MORNING SERVICE

Theme: Which Is Life's Best Age?

SUGGESTED SCRIPTURE READING: Ps. 90:1-17.

SELECTED HYMNS: "Work, for the night is coming."—A. L. Coghill. "Today the Saviour calls."—S. F. Smith. "Brief life is here our portion."—Bernard of Cluny. "Tomorrow, Lord, is thine."—P. Doddridge.

CALL TO WORSHIP: "Thou art worthy, O Lord, to receive glory and honour and power: for thou hast created all things, and for thy pleasure they are and were created." "O Lord, how manifold are thy works! in wisdom hast thou made them all: the earth is full of thy riches."

INVOCATION PRAYER: O Thou who are the spirit of calm, alive in all living things, who art to be found by those whose hearts are pure, we wait silently in thy presence to hear thy voice and to worship thee together in thy house today. We bring to thee our confession of sins, for we are ashamed and sorry for all wherein we have displeased thee. We bring to thee our thanks for thine unnumbered gifts and benefits. We thank thee for the spirit of hope and expectancy in the hearts of men. We pray also for our brothers throughout the world, and for ourselves that we may be lifted out of the sordidness and confusion which engulf so much of mankind. Do thou so strengthen our faith and transform our vision that we may go forth into the light of day to work, and into the darkness of night to rest, all to the end of forwarding thy kingdom in the world. We ask in the name of Christ. Amen.

Theme: Which Is Life's Best Age?

TEXT: "My times are in thy hand." Ps. 31:15.

INTRODUCTORY: David places himself in God's hands and prepares himself to work to a divine timetable. He wants those "times" ordered and regulated by God.

That brings us to an interesting question. In one's life, which is the best time?

I. Our very wise grown-ups tell us that the age of seven is the ever-desirable age. Happiness and innocency are the joys of those at so tender an age. Their needs are all provided. No responsibility; no labor; a lovely age!

II. Along come others who say that fourteen is the ideal age. The mind is being trained; an appreciation of the beautiful things of life is now possible. Jesus, our Lord, before he was fourteen had pledged himself to give his time and talents to his "Father's business." David Livingstone was earning his living in a factory four years before he was fourteen, but he, too, already had dedicated himself to God's service, destined to mark him out as one of the world's heroes.

III. Others again favor the age of seventeen. For most, at this age, schooldays are ended. A new sense of responsibility begins. We are no longer treated as children. Even our parents begin to show that they regard us as growing up! Charlotte Brontë says: "At seventeen the joys of dreaming what we shall be make this age interesting." John Milton was a hymn writer at seventeen. The famous evangelist, D. L. Moody, had decided for Christ at that age.

IV. Against these earlier ages, many people choose the age of twenty-one as the ideal age. This, they say, is the perfect age. Now we "come of age." Now we have truly grown up. The threshold of manhood and womanhood has been crossed. Now, say so many, "we can do as we please." Can we? I remember One who, although He had passed the age of twenty-one, said, "I came not to please myself but to do the will of Him who sent me."

V. But there are people who tell us that we have set our ideal too low. Their view is that the ideal age is thirty-five. They reckon that if the average span of human life is, as the Psalmist says, seventy, then at thirty-five we have reached the halfway house. We live all over again life's golden moments. We count our successes: yet we are not too old to build new castles in the air. Halfway!

VI. I know some who put the ideal age as fifty. It is a wonderful age. Now instead of promising to do things, you boast of your achievements! Well, you "fifty's," what have you done? Is any life sweeter because of you? Frances Havergal did not reach the age of fifty by six years, yet her music and her faith have brightened all people everywhere, and Henry Lyte's last and greatest hymn entitled "Abide with me, fast falls the eventide," was written when he was fifty, and with it he ended his earthly ministry.

So let us of this age raise our "Ebenezer," and realize more than ever that "our times are in his hand."

What shall we say, then, of "Three score years and ten"? Hear one writer: "I feel in myself the future life. Winter is on my head, but eternal spring is in my heart. The nearer I approach the end the plainer I hear the immortal symphonies of that world which invites me." And yet, it may be a long time to the end of the journey.

Which is the best age, then? Indeed, who shall say? Each age as it comes to us is the best possible one for ourselves and for other people. Then, whether we finish our tasks at twenty-two or ninety, we shall be peacefully serene in the consciousness that our times are in His hands.—C. H. N.

THEME PRAYER: Grant us, O Lord, to know that which is worth knowing; to praise that which pleases thee best; to prize that which is precious to thee; and to hate all that is evil in thine eyes. So may we tolerantly search out and do what is well-pleasing unto thee. Through Jesus Christ, our Lord. Amen.

OFFERTORY SENTENCE: "Every man according as he purposeth in his heart, so let him give; not grudgingly, or of necessity: for God loveth a cheerful giver."

OFFERTORY PRAYER: What shall we render unto thee, Our Father, for all thy benefits toward us? We would call upon our souls and all that is within us to bless and magnify thy holy name. We would bring an offering and pay our vows unto thee in the presence of all thy people. Wilt thou graciously bless both the gifts and the givers, we ask in the name of Christ. Amen.—H.

Illustrative Material

SEED THOUGHTS, HOMILETIC AND EXPOSITORY. Short as life is, we make it still shorter by the careless waste of time.—Victor Hugo.

Still on it creeps, each little moment at another's heels, till hours, days, years, and ages are made up.—Joanna Baillie.

There is nothing of which we are apt to be so lavish as of time, and about which we ought to be more solicitous, since without it we can do nothing in this world. Time is what we want most, but what, alas! we use worst.—William Penn.

If time be of all things the most precious, wasting time must be the greatest prodigality, since lost time is never found again; and what we call time enough always proves little enough. Let us then be up and doing and doing to the purpose; so by diligence shall we do more with less perplexity.—Franklin.

Choice Illustrations on the Theme

WHICH AGE IS BEST? Just a few months before his thirty-fifth birthday Martin Luther nailed his famous Theses on the door of the Castle Church at Wittenberg which had blessed results all over the world. At the age of thirty-five Toplady reached the high water mark of his ministry in giving to the world that deathless composition, "Rock of ages, cleft for me." At sixty was the perfect age for John Bunyan for at that age the trumpets sounded for him on the other side. Frank Boreham used to write a new article on this theme each decade. At forty that was the best age, at fifty, at sixty, at seventy. Each of these ages in turn was declared the best! And there was truth in it too.—Rev. Charles H. Newland.

ETERNAL FRESHNESS. It was a great American, Julia Ward Howe, who said: "The longer I drain the cup of life, the sweeter it grows. All the sugar is at the bottom of the cup." That is the way we ought to grow old. Spiritually there need be no such thing as growing old. Many of the most eager, virile and forward-looking Christians have been far advanced in years. They knew that death itself was but a door.—Archer Wallace.

LIFE A BAG OF JEWELS. When a certain general was plundering a palace one of his soldiers found in a leather bag the crown jewels. The prize was worth millions, but the stupid soldier shook the glittering stones out among the rubbish, and went away boasting about the fine sack he had found for carrying his food. He did not know the value of the great treasure he had thrown away.

RESPONSIVENESS OF YOUTH. After asking ten different ministers the question, "What is the most discouraging things in your ministry?" the one who asked it was not surprised but interested to receive the same answer. What do you suppose it was?

"Spiritual apathy. Indifference to idealism."

But in reply to the question, "What is the most encouraging thing in your ministry?" the same men replied, "The young people in my parish."—C. M. Sheldon, D.D.

OPPORTUNITY. Each day is another opportunity to extend the lines of the forces of light and truth and happiness into the no man's land of ignorance, poverty and misery.

This is indeed a great day. All our life has been spent in preparation for it. Let us greet it with joy, treat it with reverence and expectation of blessings from it, and honor it, however humble our part in it, with our best endeavors for each of us has a great work to do this day.

EVENING SERVICE

Theme: The Menace of Overactivity.

TEXT: "Be still, and know that I am God." Ps. 46:10.

INTRODUCTORY: The sin of being too busy: Among all the numerous and grievous sins of life I am sure this one has a prominent place. It is a sin that provokes and permits many others. It allows the good things of life to crowd out the best. It permits the nonessential to take the place of the essential. The minor concerns push aside the great issues. If I permit my life to be too busy, the sins of omission mount like a black scourge to torture my peace of mind.

I. If my observations have been accurate, the sin of being too busy is one that attacks multitudes of good people in these furious days. One would naturally expect it to be otherwise. What advances have been made in the past years to add to the comforts and ease of life; and how the hours of leisure have increased! *The New York Times* recently computed one billion hours of leisure time in America every week. We have been able to lift many of the burdens of life. Electricity has given us the equivalent of thirty-five servants in the home. In her day my mother did most of her own work, but she never knew all the modern facilities of housekeeping, vacuum cleaners, and electric laundries, and the great host of time-saving, energy-sparing devices. She had six children, a large house, and a reputation for Dutch cleanliness, but how I have coveted the calm serenity, the quiet peace, and the unruffled poise of her life!

II. One would think that all the modern helps should give us more time for the simple virtues. On the contrary, life is an ever-increasing complexity. People have never been busier than they are today. If the proportion of achievement were equal to the proportion of energetic activity, what a world this would be! If men had improved as much in the past twenty-five years as automobiles have improved, we should be "a race of gods." Our forefathers were content to ride in oxcarts, while today some men chafe when they miss one section of a revolving door. In the midst of a growing inclination toward shorter working hours, better wages, faster communication, and more leisure, we are busier than we have ever been before.

III. Life in this kind of busy world keeps tearing us apart; we need those deeper forces that pull life together again. One of the great values of our Christian religion is the sense of the wholeness and unity that it gives to life. We lose our souls through the sin of being too busy. Religion unifies life. Worship compels a man to collect his widely scattered life.

IV. Humanity needs to seek and find the quiet places. In these hectic days we need to be alone with God and our own souls. Men who are too busy for the "quiet time" are "busier than God wants them to be." There ought to be a certain definite spot where we can keep our tryst with God. The world needs to hear: "Be still, and know that I am God."—F. H. O.

Alternate Theme: The Ministry of Silence.

TEXT: "Be still, and know that I am God." Ps. 46:10.

INTRODUCTORY: There are some things which have a message for us, but which we can only hear when the noises of other things are hushed, or when we can concentrate on listening to them to the exclusion of other distracting noises.

In the rush and hustle of our modern life how often do we face up to ourselves resolutely and firmly?

That section of the universal Church known as the Society of Friends may be mistaken in some of its opinions and customs, but its piety is very manifest—it has the spirit of true religion. One of its doctrines is that of the "Inner Light." That "Inner Light" often evinces itself in a vocal manner becoming the "Inner Voice." In view of this we may be led to ask ourselves whether or not we are robbing ourselves of a wonderful spiritual opportunity just by refusing to sit quiet sometimes and think about life and its final meanings. There certainly is need for the quiet mood of meditation. "Be still, and know that I am God."

And how difficult it is to create this spirit of absorption in the world of reality within; how hard to withdraw into the inner world from the superficial interests which take up so much of our daily interest!

Some time ago I read a letter from a man who had been at a service conducted by a young man who had adopted a very unusual method of preaching and praying. This young man would conclude a paragraph of his sermon or prayer, and then pause for a few seconds before proceeding. It was not due to a hesitancy on his part, but it was done, as he explained to the congregation, so that they might think about what he was saying. The writer of the letter said that at first it was very disconcerting for the hearer, but when he had overcome the first reaction to this unusual procedure and gave his mind to what was being said, that it made all the difference to its effect upon him. We get so accustomed in worship to being carried along by the words and worship of another that we ourselves give very little of our own intelligent participation to it.

Yes: it is this state of inner quietness, of directed attention, which helps us to crystallize the transitory thought engendered into the faith which holds and keeps us in the midst of untoward experience. Faith goes deeper than belief, its roots are in the subconscious life of a man, and it has the power of bringing all man's latent power to the aid of his desires. Stillness opens the way into the reservoir of spiritual power.

It brings us into contact with God through the resources of our own inner lives.

But this method is one that implies a humbling of oneself. To turn away, even for a short time, from such an attitude and face up to the questions of life within is a difficult matter, for it entails questioning our own accepted opinions and seeking to deliver ourselves from the mind-set which we have built up. Through such experiences as are thus possible to each one of us we discover our weaknesses, but also come to a knowledge of God.

We want this inner life to burst forth in all its glory; we want this desert of parched religious experience to blossom forth into the fragrant blooms of vitalizing faith, but how can we know and hear God within if all our attention is taken up with the activities of life to the exclusion of thought about life and seeking after God?

"Be still, and know that I am God."

Suggested Texts and Themes

Man's Search for God: "And ye shall seek me, and find me, when ye shall search for me with all your heart." Jer. 29:13.

God's Search for Man: "For the Son of man came to seek and to save that which was lost." Luke 19:10.

The Grace of Happy-heartedness: "I would have you to be free from cares." I Cor. 7:32 (A.S.V.). "Cast thy burden upon the Lord." Ps. 55:22.

The Perils of Unsettlement: "But I hold not my life of any account." Acts 20:24 (A.S.V.).

MIDWEEK FELLOWSHIP MEETING TOPIC

(Church Night or Suggested Sermon Subject)

Theme: Brought Out into a Wealthy Place.

TEXT: "Thou broughtest us out into a wealthy place." Ps. 66:12.

Often midnight is succeeded by noontide. The Psalmist found it so. He was in one moment in "the horrible pit," the next "his feet were set upon a rock."

I. Such an experience may come when least expected. Let us trust more, thus we may have the joys of anticipation.

II. Such experience may come when most needed. When we may have been wearied of the desert, thirsty, faint, then the oasis has suddenly appeared.

III. Such experience may come when not deserved. Israel was brought to Elim, "where were twelve wells of water, and threescore and ten palm trees," after they had murmured at Marah, Ex. 15:24, 27.

IV. The experience may come in a way we never anticipated. In ways as wonderful as Israel's through the Red Sea and the Jordan. The way to light has often been through "the valley of the shadow." Are you faint and weary? Be not overdistressed. You may be in the desert where are dangers and distresses; but has God no quails, no manna, no Elims left?

CHRISTIAN ENDEAVOR SOCIETY TOPIC

June 22. Attitudes in Conduct: "Keep Off the Grass!" I Sam. 12:4, 5; Matt. 9:12.

SUNDAY SCHOOL LESSON

June 22. The Sin of Greed. Ex. 20:17; Luke 12:13-21, 29-34.

MEMORY SELECTION: "Thou shalt not covet." Ex. 20:17.

This commandment deals with inward desire. Jesus' teaching on covetousness gives much emphasis on the same. We are to be unselfish. We are not even to wish for what belongs to another. The evils that result from greed are many and awful. Character is worth far more than possessions. Let us think of practical ways of overcoming greed. The story of the rich fool is very enlightening. The modern forms of greed are many. Selflessness is a fine virtue.

SUNDAY: JUNE TWENTY-NINTH

MORNING SERVICE

Theme: The Truth as It Is in Jesus.

SUGGESTED SCRIPTURE READING: Eph. 4: 1-32.

SELECTED HYMNS: "Thou art the Way." —G. W. Doane. "O God of truth, whose living Word."—T. Hughes. "Lead us, O Father, in the paths of peace."—W. H. Burleigh. "O Light, whose beams illumine all."—E. H. Plumptre.

CALL TO WORSHIP: "Honor and majesty are before him; strength and gladness are in his place." "Glory ye in his holy name: let the heart of them rejoice that seek the Lord."

INVOCATION PRAYER: O thou who didst create man and knoweth what is in him, suit a blessing to our individual needs this day. Work within us that spiritual and Divine renewal which we must have to receive thy blessings, or even to desire them. Increase our hunger and thirst for righteousness and enable us to use in a better way in the cause of truth and righteousness the powers which thou hast given us. Bless us each one and all together as we worship in thy sanctuary this day. In the name of Christ we ask. Amen.—S. P. O.

Theme: The Truth as It Is in Jesus.

TEXT: "As the truth is in Jesus." Eph. 4:21.

INTRODUCTORY: There is a school. In it Christ is taught. And Christ is learned. Where is this school? What is it? How is the instruction carried on? Who is the teacher? What is the name of its master? Christ, only Christ. He is known as "The Master." The truth taught? It is the truth "as the truth is in Jesus."

I. This truth comes to us attested by highest authority. The Teacher, the Messenger is the Son of God, "the brightness of his glory, and the express image of his person." He came to make known the eternal truth. From him we get the truth as it is in Jesus.

II. The truth as it is in Jesus is all truth and nothing but truth. It has no mixture of mistake, no element of error, no measure of disguise.

III. The truth as it is in Jesus is all interesting, of utmost importance. Men sometimes teach truth that does not materially concern us, is a matter of curiosity rather than of utility. Jesus did not come from heaven to earth to propagate matters of only trifling moment. The truth as it is in Jesus is of utmost interest and importance.

IV. The truth as it is in Jesus is complete. There is nothing that can contribute to our safety, peace or happiness, but what is fully contained in it. Nothing is overlooked. It is sufficient to "make the man of God perfect, thoroughly furnished."

V. The truth as it is in Jesus is most eminent and glorious in its nature. It makes revelations which the mind of man could never reach. It brings to light "the deep things of God."

VI. The truth as it is in Jesus shines by its own splendor. It needs no borrowed ornaments. Its own excellency is sufficient to commend it.

VII. Yet the truth as it is in Jesus is level to all capacities. It expresses itself in a way intelligible to peasant, prince, philosopher. "The wayfaring man, though a fool, shall not err therein."

VIII. The truth as it is in Jesus is most powerful in its effects. It sets the mind at liberty from the bondage of error and sin. It saves the soul. It sanctifies the heart. It transforms the life. It centers in Christ. It reveals

Christ. By his Spirit it accomplishes the saving work of Christ.

Let us love and reverence and cherish and practice the truth as it is in Jesus.

THEME PRAYER: O God, who hast given us minds that we may know thee, grant that our thinking may be honest and open in thy sight. Cast out from us whatsoever makes for false acts and thoughts, and bring us into the perfect freedom of thy truth. O Lord, we would believe. Help thou our unbelief. In Jesus' name. Amen.

OFFERTORY SENTENCE: Jesus said: "Give, and it shall be given unto you; good measure, pressed down, and shaken together, and running over, shall men give into your bosom. And with what measure ye mete, it shall be measured to you again."

OFFERTORY PRAYER: O God, the Father of lights, we praise thee for the light of this hour. We bless thee that we live to worship thee in the sanctuary and to bring offerings unto thine altars. Accept our unfeigned gratitude for the constant ministries of thy tender hand, for the undying love that will not let us go. As thou hast freely given us all things, even sparing not thine own Son, so would we make our gifts with free spirits and open hands. Through Jesus Christ our Lord. Amen.

Illustrative Material

SEED THOUGHTS, HOMILETIC AND EXPOSITORY. In the School of Christ: I. Then he is the Teacher. "Ye have heard Him." II. Then you receive continuous instruction. "Ye have been taught by Him." Gradual process. Not one act, but a long and patient discipline. III. The theme of the teaching is the Teacher. "Ye have not so learned Christ."—A. M.

Effects Produced on the Character by Reception of the Truth as It Is in Jesus: I. It produces humility of mind, but at the same time a new and elevated sense of dignity. II. It is a source of real happiness. III. It unites us with other Christians.—T. J. J.

Choice Illustrations on the Theme

DISTORTIONS OF TRUTH. There is a sight familiar on the hillsides of the Scottish highlands in the early hours of the day. While as yet the mist clouds cling to the lower reaches of the mountainside a sheep may be seen looming high in the haze of a cloud curtain. The sight is startling. The sheep takes on an exaggerated and grotesque dimension. When the sun is up the false proportion passes with the mist of the morning. The uncanny thing gives place to nothing more formidable than a patient sheep at its morning pasture.

So it is with all distortions of truth. Whatever reality lies in the psychical and the occult may be cheerfully left to the light of day. The occult can never be a substitute for the religion of life. The cults and mystery religions do not possess the power to recreate and maintain character. Distortions disappear when the mist atmosphere passes into the warm light of day.—J. H. C. Macaulay.

CHRIST THE TRUTH. Christ is the Truth because he came to reveal truth. He is in himself the substance of all revealed truth. He came to teach about God. What could we have known about God, of his mercy, his faithfulness, his truth, his justice but for the revelation of them that is made in Christ? "He that hath seen me hath seen the Father." He came to confirm the truth. He came to set up a kingdom of truth, to establish truth, to set up a kingdom in which truth reigns. And Christ came to use the truth. He remakes men by means of the truth. He brings truth to bear on their understandings. By his Holy Spirit he leads men to desire the salvation of Him who is the Truth.—J. W. Reese.

TRUTH VITALIZED BY CHRIST. A beautiful story is told of Sir Hubert Herkomer, the great painter. His father was a poor man, and the professor brought him from his native Germany to live with him in his beautiful house near London. The old man used to model in clay in his early life, and now that he had leisure he took to it again in his old age. But his hands trembled, and the work showed signs of imperfections. It was his one sorrow. At night he went to bed early and when he had gone his son would go into his studio and take his father's poor work and make it as beautiful as possible. When the old man came down in the morning he would look at the work and rub his hands and say, "Ah, I do it as well as ever I did!" So Christ took the best teaching uttered before him and refined it into beauty. The words of the old law became beautiful words of truth and life when vitalized by the touch of Jesus.—*Good Words.*

JESUS THE TRUTH. Christ is the Truth in the highest sense of that word. Some by that word mean literal accuracy of speech. But Christ is the saving Truth. He is incomparably the most important of all truth. Other truth may affect our intelligence, our conscience, our personal freedom, but this truth affects our soul, our character, our eternity. And he and his truth contradict and refute the world's falsehoods. It has the power ultimately to subdue the world. "Great is truth and it shall prevail." Great is Christ the Truth incarnate, and he shall prevail.—R. W.

EVENING SERVICE

Theme: Playing the Fool.

TEXT: "Then said Saul, I have sinned . . . behold, I have played the fool." I Sam. 26:21.

INTRODUCTORY: There are different ways of playing the fool, some harmless, others intrinsically noble. It is a charming thing to play the fool with children, and none but the humble and the wise can do it. You never find starchy people on their hands and knees, transmuted into elephants or horses. On the other hand, there was something very noble in the conduct of the great apostle Paul when he became a fool for Christ's sake. But if there be one thing written clearly in the Scripture it is that he who sins is playing the fool.

I. One mark of a fool is that he pays too dearly for what he gets. That is where every sinner plays the fool—he pays a thousandfold too dear for what he gets. With a dulled intellect, or a corrupted body, or a shrunken heaven, or a blighted home, he pays for the satisfaction of an hour. The sinner gets "Verily I say unto you they have their reward." But the sinner pays such a terrific price for it that at the end of the day he has to cry with Saul, "I have played the fool."

II. Another mark of folly is a credulous and easy confidence. It is because the world contains so many fools of that kind that knaves and tricksters flourish. Some flashy company is floated, which from first to last is nothing but a swindle, and the amazing thing is that multitudes of people go and put their money in that company, "playing the fool." But I say that every man does that who invests his capital in sin. Sin is the greatest imposture, the flashiest concern that ever lured an unsuspicious public. And yet what multitudes take sin's prospectus as if it were a gilt-edged security. Sin promises liberty, and it gives slavery. Sooner or later every man who sins, and who thinks cunningly to reach his ends by sinning, has to admit with Saul, "I have played the fool."

III. Another characteristic of the fool is that he forgets the things that really matter. One sees that in the cleverest of criminals. A man commits a crime, and with infinite pains he hides the traces of it. But one thing he forgets, and that one thing leads to his detection. And then he says to himself in bitterness of soul, "I've played the fool." That is what every sinner does. He forgets the very things that matter. It is a fatal thing to forget conscience. The fool hath said in his heart there is no God. Be sure your sin will find you out, often in the hour when you seem safest. That is why every man who sins with a high hand, and thinks to get the better of high heaven, sooner or later has to say with Saul, "I have played the fool."—M.

Theme: Courage for Every Day (Additional).

TEXT: "Be strong and of a good courage." Josh. 1:6.

INTRODUCTORY: Joshua had been right-hand man to Moses and now he is given the responsibility of leading the people. His task was not easy and it would demand all his time and thought and strength. So he is urged to take courage for his task. No one can fulfill his purpose in life without this virtue.

Yet courage is not confined to the exceptional circumstance. There are brave lives in every realm. The average person is called to spend much time in unheroic surroundings. Courage is needed to do the task which produces no thrill of publicity.

I. There is no point in seeking to discriminate between physical and moral courage, for all heroism is at bottom moral, but there is a great difference between that display of courage which brings us the praise of those who look on and the quiet heroism of being and doing where no medals are given and no fine words are said. There was once a group of people discussing heroism and exchanging among themselves stirring and inspiring experiences. One of their number, a woman, had been silent throughout until she was asked: "And what form of courage do you practice?" In the sudden, tense silence which fell upon those who had been talking so glibly of their heroic ways this woman quietly answered: "I practice the heroism of going on." Just so! Where, indeed, would be the great stories of heroic deeds if it were not for the thousands who face life with indomitable courage and practice the grand heroism of going on?

II. We need courage to keep straight. Joshua was advised to keep in the way of God. Verse seven urges him to "turn not to the right hand nor to the left," but to remain in that way which God had given through Moses. No matter who we are or where we are none of us can keep to the Christian path without courage. We are promised that if in all our ways we acknowledge God then he will direct our paths. And Jesus bluntly said that no man having put his hand to the plough and looking back is fit for the kingdom of God. How easily we repeat these words! How difficult it is to follow them!

Yet without the courage of keeping to our course we cannot fulfill the task given to us as Christian people.

III. We need courage to trust in God. Yes! If religion means anything it means the heroism of trust in God! In verse nine Joshua is reminded of this: "For the Lord thy God is with thee whithersoever thou goest." But Joshua would not always find it easy to believe that God was with him. Such a promise did not mean that he would escape trouble.

Christians are not hothouse plants that droop and die when the first chill wind touches them. And chill winds there are in plenty. To trust through all demands the utmost courage.

Christ did not come into the world to make life easy, but to make men great. Only trust can do that, trust which takes Christ at his word and acts upon it. And such a trust demands courage, the heroism of a faith that falters not at the world's question, "Where now is thy God?" but answers with quiet assurance, "Though he slay me yet will I trust him."—A. E. W.

Suggested Texts and Themes

Life's Oases: "They came to Elim, where were twelve wells of water, and threescore and ten palm trees: and they encamped there by the waters." Ex. 15:27.

Christ's Manifold Dominion: "On his head were many crowns." Rev. 19:12.

The Grave in the Garden: "And in the garden a new tomb." John 19:41 (A.S.V.).

The Message of the River: "And everything shall live whither the river cometh." Ezek. 47:9.

Christians Getting Tired: "Let us not be weary in well doing." Gal. 6:9.

MIDWEEK FELLOWSHIP MEETING TOPIC

(Church Night or Suggested Sermon Subject)

Theme: The Hidden Wells of Life.

TEXT: "And God opened her eyes, and she saw a well of water." Gen. 21:19.

In this hidden well, which Ishmael's prayer uncovered, lies many a true lesson if only we have the right sort of a pitcher to dip and draw.

I. How came the well to be there just where and when it was wanted? The Arab shepherds who dug it never meant it for wandering travelers, but for their own flocks. God guided the steps of Hagar to it in her time of extreme need.

II. Life is full of hidden wells, stored-up blessings ready at the right moment to supply the answer to prayer. "And God opened her eyes, and she saw a well of water; and she went, and filled the bottle with water, and gave the lad drink."

III. God foresees our prayers as well as our necessities. God is so great and so wise that nothing escapes his thought and care.

IV. Prayer itself is a hidden well, a secret source of strength and joy and wisdom not only in times of trouble but always.

CHRISTIAN ENDEAVOR SOCIETY TOPIC

June 29. Attitudes in Conduct: "It's Smart *Not* To———" Dan. 1:3-18; I John 3:7, 8.

SUNDAY SCHOOL LESSON

June 29. Christ's New Commandment. Mark 12:28-34; John 13:34, 35; 15:10-14.

MEMORY SELECTION: "A new commandment I give to you, that you love one another; even as I have loved you, that you also love one another." John 13:34 (R.S.V.).

Here we have commended the law of love, the rule of love, the practice of love. It is a wonderful thing to live in love to God and to others. How can we learn this? How can we practice it? A life of love is a life of happiness. There is no surer way to be happy. Let us try to measure the greatness of God's love to us, of Jesus' love for us. This lesson gives fine opportunity to note the relationship between Old Testament love-teachings and those of Jesus, especially in this his "New Commandment."

SUNDAY: JULY SIXTH

MORNING SERVICE

Theme: The Man Who Nearly Let Go.

SUGGESTED SCRIPTURE READING: Ps. 73: 1-28.

SELECTED HYMNS: "God is the Refuge of his saints."—I. Watts. "Almighty fortress is our God."—M. Luther. "Wait my soul, upon the Lord."—W. F. Lloyd. "Who trusts in God a strong abode."—J. Magdeburg. "Call Jehovah thy salvation."—J. Montgomery.

CALL TO WORSHIP: "The secret of the Lord is with them that fear him; and he will shew them his covenant." "My soul shall be joyful in the Lord: it shall rejoice in his salvation."

INVOCATION PRAYER: We worship thee, our Father, the Giver of every good and perfect gift. Unceasingly thou sendest thy blessings down upon us. Thou gavest us thy supreme Gift, even thine own Son to save us. He is our one and only Hope. We would touch the hem of his garment and be made whole. May we see thy royal Son and his royal glory this day. May we feel deeply thy love. May we look forward with great expectation to the end of all thy designs for us all. In Christ's name we ask. Amen.—Rev. Garret Hondelink, B.D.

Theme: The Man Who Nearly Let Go.

TEXT: "But as for me, my feet were almost gone; my steps had well nigh slipped." Ps. 73:2.

INTRODUCTORY: It is not sure who wrote this psalm. It may have been Asaph, as author; or it may have been for Asaph, as in the margin. It records the reflections that troubled the writer concerning the Divine administration in view of what he saw of the prosperity of the wicked. His were thoughts that might occur to any mind, do often occur, arising from the fact wicked men seem often so successful and happy, living in prosperity and dying apparently without pain or alarm, while so many of the good are poor and sorrowful in their lives.

But the general teaching of the psalm is in the first verse, that "God is good to Israel, even to such as are of a clean heart." This is not the world of retribution or final settlements. There is a future state where the inequalities of the present system will be adjusted. The character of God will be vindicated, with justice for all.

I. This is the story of a man who nearly let go. He was in a perilous crisis. "But as for me, my feet were almost gone; my steps had well nigh slipped." Caught in a world that seemed unfriendly, he was about as low as possible without complete collapse. He nearly gave up the friendship of God who had been the bright spot in his experience. He was about to go out like Judas in the night, without God and without hope. It was a perilous crisis in a good man's life.

II. Some causes of the crisis. We have intimated some of them. They were many. 1. First, he had cherished a wrong spirit. "I was envious at the foolish," v. 3. It was when he saw the prosperity of the wicked. They were even proud and blasphemous, yet God seemed to show no disapprobation, while, on the other hand, he was chastened and afflicted. 2. So he had come to doubt the Divine Sovereignty, saying, "Doth God know? and is there knowledge in the Most High?" v. 11. If God were Sovereign how could such wickedness succeed? 3. He forgot the future, where inequalities could be adjusted and justice brought to prevail. 4. He forgot the Divine Fatherhood. 5. And he endeavored to extricate himself by the aid of human reason alone. "When I thought to know this," v. 16. In fact, this crisis was not an innocent one. He was at fault both in his attitude and his reasoning.

III. But note the deliverance from the crisis. "It was too painful to me; until I went into the sanctuary," vv. 16, 17. The deliverance was a flash of light when he went into the secret place of communion with God. The difficulty was not to be solved by any human reasoning, nor by man away from God. The only solution was to be obtained by a near approach to God himself. There the mystery could be solved and there it was solved. "Then understood I their end," literally the "after things." That solves the difficulty. God reigns. There will be a judgment; which means that there will be exact and equal justice done to all.

IV. In closing, the way of prevention of such crises is recorded. 1. A confession of folly, v. 22. 2. An expression of confidence, v. 23. 3. An affirmation of trust, v. 24. 4. A testimony of gratitude, vv. 25, 28.

Learn (a) That a querulous spirit is a source of spiritual danger. (b) That a record of past experience is the safeguard of today. (c) That there is development through worship. It was through worship the Psalmist came to understand. (d) That God is our refuge and strength and a very present help in trouble.—H.

THEME PRAYER: Teach us, our Father, the secret of faith in thee. We would believe; help thou our unbelief. Forgive us that in our vain restlessness we have sought so much other then peace, and pity us in that we have so sadly failed as we have sought it. Grant us wisdom, faith and courage to seek thee anew and to walk in the way of thy will. We ask in the name of Christ. Amen.

OFFERTORY SENTENCE: "For ye know the grace of our Lord Jesus Christ, that, though he was rich, yet for your sakes he became poor, that ye through his poverty might be rich."

OFFERTORY PRAYER: Gracious God, we thank thee for thy bounteous provision for our needs. We adore and praise thee for thy Son Jesus, who, though rich, became poor that we through his poverty might inherit eternal riches. In his name we dedicate these offerings to thee. Amen.

Illustrative Material

SEED THOUGHTS, HOMILETIC AND EXPOSITORY. Men always grow vicious before they become unbelievers.—Swift.

Difficulties of Unbelief: Intellectually the difficulties of unbelief are as great as those of belief, while morally the argument is wholly on the side of belief.—T. Arnold.

Faith's Peril and Rescue: I. Its peril! When the Psalmist saw "the prosperity of the wicked." 2. When he observed the apparent desertion of the righteous. II. Why was the Psalmist's faith in peril? Because he harbored a wrong spirit. "I was envious." 2. Because he had narrow views. III. The rescue of faith. 1. Through holy influence. "I went into the sanctuary"—into the presence of God. 2. Through clearer views. "Then understood I their end." 3. Faith becomes more vigorous than before. He becomes not only satisfied, but jubilant. "Whom have I in heaven but thee!"—J. L.

Choice Illustrations on the Theme

THE PAIN OF INFIDELITY. An English scientist who lost his faith wrote, "I am not ashamed to confess that with this negation of God the universe to me has lost the soul of loveliness which, at times I think, as think at times I must, of the appalling contrast between the hallowed glory of that creed that once was mine and the lonely mystery of existence as I now find it. It is impossible for me to escape the sharpest pains of which my nature is susceptible." It was to this sharpest pain that the lonely man of the Seventy-third Psalm was about to consign himself. He nearly let go. He nearly gave up his faith. In that there is both peril and pain.—H.

"WHEN GOD DIED." Dr. Edward A. Steiner once wrote an article with the strange title: "When God Died!" We hurriedly turned the pages to learn of the date of his demise and we found the answer. God had died in the life of a brilliant young man not by reason of unbelief, but because of an inner sin that had eaten out the vitals of his religious experience, and for that young man God was dead.—Frank S. Lankard.

THE PAIN OF INDECISION. The writer of an internationally famous newspaper column says that fully fifty percent of all letters that come to his desk begin: "My problem is. . . ." We believe him. Most people have difficulties which harass them and they are looking for advice and help. We once lived in a fishing village on the Atlantic coast where the fishermen agreed that the most anxious time was when the boat was "tacking," with sails wildly fluttering before being set in a decided course. Spiritual indecision is an anxious time and wise, kindly people, who can help others to become spiritually adjusted, are badly needed.—Archer Wallace.

TRAGEDY OF UNBELIEF. In a large manufacturing town a man lay on his deathbed. While well and strong he and his son both professed to be infidels. But under the test of his latest days his confidence in his unbelieving principles broke down; there was nothing in them to sustain him. His son, desirous that his father should die as he had lived, went to fortify him, and said, "Father, be a man and stick to it." "Ah!" he replied, "but there is nothing to stick to."—*King's Business.*

THIEVES OF FAITH. An Illinois thief stole $500 worth of shoes, the entire stock of a store, and in addition played a trick on the dealer by leaving all the empty boxes, putting them back just where they belonged. One after another the customers arrived the next day, and the dealer pulled out box after box only to find that each was empty.

That was a unique theft, but something much like it takes place all the time in the spiritual world. For there are many thieves of faith, writers and speakers who make it their business to destroy belief in God, in Christ, in the Church, in religion. But they always leave the boxes. They always leave the shell of what they have taken, in order to fool people into thinking that they have taken nothing at all. But pull out the boxes, try to get any comfort and strength out what they have left, and you will see that the theft has been complete.—Amos R. Wells.

EVENING SERVICE

Theme: Divine Compensations.

TEXT: "The Lord is able to give thee much more than this." II Chron. 25:9.

INTRODUCTORY: Amaziah, King of Judah, hired for a hundred talents of silver an army out of the Northern Kingdom of Israel. A prophet warned him not to employ the army of Israel, "for the Lord is not with Israel." Amaziah, thinking of his big investment, possibly the modern equivalent of a quarter of a million dollars, asked the prophet, "But what shall we do for the hundred talents which I have given to the army of Israel?" The man of God answered, "The Lord is able to give thee much more than this."

When a man makes a sacrifice or suffers loss for the sake of conscience and in obedience to God, God has ways of compensating him and rewarding him.

Amaziah is not the only man that has been compelled to choose between obedience and self-denial, soul or silver. Consider the facts and implications in this case.

I. First, the duty faced. "Let not the armies of Israel go with thee." It was God's disapproval of union with the enemies of truth. And God's command will not bear delay. "Send the army of Israel away." But Amaziah hesitated because there was a self-made difficulty in the way. So today, duty and worldly profits or pleasures may stand in each other's way.

II. The difficulty stated. "And Amaziah said to the man of God, "But what shall we do for the hundred talents which I have given to the army of Israel?" There was the divided mind, the difficulty faced. On the one side was the fear of God's displeasure, on the other the hundred talents weighed down his purpose. How could he brook the loss of so large a sum?

III. The reward of obedience. It is contained in the unanswerable reply, "And the man of God answered, The Lord is able to give thee much more than this." There was no promise of the restoration of the exact hundred talents of silver. But this, human obedience and Divine compensations. God is able to remunerate fidelity. Bring God into the matter. Bring God into your business, your pleasures, your social contacts, all your worldly interests. That may alter them altogether. —H.

Suggested Texts and Themes

The Religious Use of Holidays: "Return unto thy rest, O my soul." Ps. 116:7.

Elective Affinity: "And being let go, they went to their own company." Acts 4:23.

The Mercy of Oblivion: "God . . . hath made me forget." Gen. 41:51.

The Wonder of that Night: "In the night in which he was betrayed." I Cor. 11:23 (A.S.V.).

The Problem of Poverty: "Ye have the poor always with you." Matt. 26:11.

MIDWEEK FELLOWSHIP MEETING TOPIC

(Church Night or Suggested Sermon Subject)

Theme: Spiritual Sowing.

TEXT: "And he taught them many things by parables, and said unto them in his doctrine, Hearken; Behold, there went out a sower to sow," etc. Mark 4:2-20.

By the seaside. Taught in parables, a new system of teaching, excellent vehicle for spiritual truth. "Hearken"! Important. Parable of the sower. Its language is figurative, drawn from the processes of nature. It exhibits the kingdom of God in its beginning, its processes, and its results.

I. The sower. Every man a sower, especially teachers, preachers, etc.

II. The seed. The Word of God. The Gospel.

III. The soil. Human hearts.

IV. The sowing. It should be liberal, diligent, indiscriminate. "How beside all waters."

V. The growth. Not always alike. Varies with the nature of the seed, the soil, the showers, the sunshine.

VI. The harvest. The end of the sowing, tilling, culture, toil, is fruit, results, harvest. There is harvest in time. There is harvest in eternity.

1. All gospel sowers are doing the Master's work. 2. Take heed how and what you hear. 3. What are the thorns that overgrow the ground? 4. How do they choke the seed? 5. The seed is heavenly. Is the soil kindly, prepared, grateful, fruitful?—J. R. T.

CHRISTIAN ENDEAVOR SOCIETY TOPIC

July 6. "Thou Shalt Have No Other Gods." Ex. 20:1-6.

BULLETIN BOARD SLOGANS FOR THE MONTH

By Earl Riney

Democracy at work is the articulate voice of the people.

The first security for civilization is a family in its own home.

The success or failure of a nation depends in part on adjustments to present complexities.

How can I know my neighbor if I don't know myself?

Christ and his cross is better than the world and its crowns.

Good example is one of the loudest bells to call people to church.

Faith is trusting God in the dark.

Pardoned sin makes peace within.

Christian growth comes not by wishing it but by willing it.

Measure men around the heart.

SUNDAY SCHOOL LESSON

July 6. In the Time of the Judges. Judg. 2:8-17; 21:25.

MEMORY SELECTION: "Blessed is the nation whose God is the Lord." Ps. 33:12.

We are now to study the period in Jewish history from the Judges to Solomon. The period points out the struggle of the Hebrew people between true and false religions. It puts emphasis on the love of God for the people at all times, as also his justice and his constant effort to lead them back to him. The people were responsibile to God and fidelity to him held the only promise for the future. We may well study the influence of occasional individuals whom God raised up to champion his cause.

SUNDAY: JULY THIRTEENTH

MORNING SERVICE

Theme: Wanted, a Prophet.

SUGGESTED SCRIPTURE READING: I Sam. 3:1.

SELECTED HYMNS: "God, in the Gospel of his Son."—B. Beddome. "The Spirit breathes upon the Word."—W. Cowper. "Lamp of our feet."—B. Barton. "O Word of God incarnate."—W. W. How.

CALL TO WORSHIP: "The hour cometh, and now is, when the true worshippers shall worship the Father in spirit and in truth: for the Father seeketh such to worship him."

INVOCATION PRAYER: Almighty God, our heavenly Father, thou hast revealed thyself as a God who openeth thy hand and giveth abundance to the children of men. Wherein any of us lack, it is not because thou dost not place gold and silver in the mountains, nor cover the plains with plenty; it is by human selfishness and greed that some are made to suffer lack. Grant us wisdom to correct our mistakes, and this hour deliver our hearts from all selfishness, make them thankful for every material and spiritual blessing and make them great with mercy and sympathy, and inspire our wills to do loving service. May this be the experience of all of us as we worship together this morning. We ask in the name of Christ. Amen. —M. K. W. H.

Theme: Wanted, a Prophet.

TEXT: "The word of the Lord was precious in those days; there was no open vision." I Sam. 3:1.

INTRODUCTORY: From Moses to Samuel, a period of several hundred years, there was no acknowledged prophet in Israel. The natural consequence was that such intimations of the Divine will as were now being given made a deeper impression and were highly valued.

I. There are times without open vision. The time had been one of religious stagnation and stupor. Men had sunk into a dead level of dullness and formality and routine. Men lived their lives in a humdrum, languishing sort of a way, without intensity of feeling or earnestness. There are times when heaven seems far away, when men have faith only in what they can see and handle.

1. "There was no open vision." Why? There was no prophet. Wanted, a prophet! There was no man to act as a go-between, to communicate God's message to his people, no chosen witness with prophetic gift.

2. Again, there was no open vision because the people were not in the proper mood to receive the vision. The soil was not congenial to the growth of prophets. It was a time of deep spiritual dearth.

3. With the loss of vision truth is lost. This is especially true of the stern truths, as accountability to God, the guilt and doom of sin, the final judgment, little fear of God before men's eyes.

4. But it is a glad fact that such times are not permanent. God never wholly deserts his people.

II. There are times when open vision is lacking, but there are times also of open vision. Heaven then is near to men. They are sensitive to spiritual impressions. The things that are unseen and eternal appear. There is religious activity and progress.

III. But there is no time without the word of God. Though the vision is at times withholden God is always with us in his word. It is sufficient and sure that he still speaks. Samuel represented a renewed and more extensive dispensation of the word. The spoken word, like the written, has never been lost.

Visions may be interrupted, prophets may be lacking, but not the continuity of revelation. That has never ceased.

1. But the word of God requires a human ear to hear. The sons of Eli lacked the ear that hears God's voice. Samuel had a sensitive ear.

2. And the word of God requires human lips to speak it. Wanted, a prophet! Wanted, messengers of truth! Wanted, witnesses for Christ.—H.

THEME PRAYER: We praise Thee, our Father, for the sacrament of life, for its great adventures, its glorious opportunities, for love which though it constrains, so blesses us, for the duties in which we may forget ourselves, and the loyalties in which losing ourselves we find thy presence and benediction. Teach us thus the Master's secret in whose Name we pray. Amen.

OFFERTORY SENTENCE: "Vow, and pay unto the Lord your God: let all that be round about him bring presents unto him that ought to be feared."

OFFERTORY PRAYER: O God, as we worship with our offering, may we see thine image and thy superscription indelibly minted on all the money in the world. Out of thine abounding goodness thou hast entrusted us with greater or lesser stores of wealth. May we acknowledge our trust by rendering regularly unto thee the firstfruits of the things which are thine. Amen.

Illustrative Material

SEED THOUGHTS, HOMILETIC AND EXPOSITORY. Open Vision: This phrase has been a difficulty to interpreters. It has been explained as referring to the times in earlier Jewish history when God appeared in pillars of fire and cloud by angelic ministry. It has also been explained as referring to the open and authoritative promulgation of Divine truth. It has been noticed as a feature of human history that it divides into alternate periods marked by the possession or the lack of spiritual insight. There are times of open vision. Heaven then is near to men. They are sensitive to spiritual impressions. The gift of vision is diffused. The things that are unseen and eternal appear. There are periods of religious activity and progress.—M. C. S.

Choice Illustrations on the Theme

VISION AND THE INDIVIDUAL. A few summers ago, up on Mt. Tom in Massachusetts, I saw this incident. Quite a company of people were on the lookout tower on the summit of the mountain on a clear day. It seemed as though the whole state of Massachusetts and a large part of Connecticut and Vermont were spread at our feet. The crowd of people were looking at the scene, quietly and deeply impressed, when a woman with a high-pitched voice pointed to a little speck of a house in Holyoke far beneath us, and cried out to the whole company, "Look! That's where I live." My first thought was: How strange that a person with such a majestic landscape to look at should be interested in finding only the familiar spot where she lived. But I soon came to see that such a feeling is perfectly natural and that the preacher had better remember the little streets where people live, even when he is up on a hilltop. It is the preacher's task not only to take people up into a high mountain of vision, but also to enable them from that outlook to see clear down the valley to the little house in a side street where they live day by day.—Halford E. Luccock.

WITNESSES NEEDED

Christ has no hands but our hands
To do His work today;
He has no feet but our feet
To lead men in His way.
He has no tongue but our tongues
To tell men how He died;
He has no help but our help
To bring them to His side.
—Annie J. Flint

NEEDED, MEN OF VISION. Robert Louis Stevenson cherished the ideal of perfection in literary style, and he toiled like a galley slave to reach it. Sir Joshua was continually touching up every picture that remained in his studio. Burne

Jones often saw what his admirers failed to see—the difference between what he had painted and what he wanted to paint; and he continually strove to make his work perfect. The names of Livingstone, Grenfell and Schweitzer remind us of notable accomplishments in other fields of human endeavor. What can you and I do? It depends on the nobility of our spirit and on the sensitive quality of that spirit in becoming sure of God and of God's plan for our lives. —G. Ray Jordan.

VISION OR LACK OF VISION. Three stonemasons working on a cathedral were asked in turn what they were doing. The first answered, "I am waiting until it is 5 o'clock"; the second said, "I am making seven dollars a day"; and the third answered, "I am building a cathedral." The first man was a drudge, the second was a money-maker, and the third was an idealist. The three men outwardly seemed to be doing the same thing, but inwardly they were far apart and were living in different worlds. These three men are ever with us and are at work on every job; and probably all three of them are in each one of us, one or another of them coming to the top on different days as we are in different moods.—*The Continent.*

EVENING SERVICE

Theme: The Conditions of a Happy Life.

TEXT: "Whoso trusteth in the Lord, happy is he." Prov. 16:20.

INTRODUCTORY: This proverb builds on the ground that all of us desire to be happy. Philosophers in all ages of the world have been trying to find out what is man's greatest good. Varying answers have been given. There are even those who question whether life is worth living at all. But they are extreme pessimists. The Westminster divines gave answer that "the chief end of man is to glorify God and enjoy him forever." That is a fair approach to the words of this proverb, "Whoso trusteth in the Lord, happy is he." It is a fact that the results of thousands of years of experiment and experience, both before and after Solomon's day, are well set forth in the words of our text, "Whoso trusteth in the Lord, happy is he."

I. Let us think first of the principle here set forth to be exercised. "Trust." Trust signifies dependence, reliance, confidence. Trust in the Old Testament and faith in the New are practically synonymous. Trust is the ground on which people find freedom from the bondage of sin, as also from the painful sense of condemnation due for their sins. And everyone knows and sometimes feels that he is a sinner.

But the knowledge of God's gracious character brings trust in him. The infinite love of God, the rich provisions of his grace, the pleasure he takes in the welfare of his people all warrant the soul to trust in him.

Of course trust in God is opposed to self-confidence. It is opposed to trust in the law, or in moral duties. This would be like a man treading on soft yielding ground incapable of supporting his weight. The man who trusts in God through Christ places himself, his soul, upon a rock firm and immovable.

II. Let us think now of the delightful influence of such trust. "Whoso trusteth in the Lord, happy is he."

1. Such trust ennobles, elevates and dignifies a man. These bring a sense of happiness. "Happy is he."

2. The trusting man is happy in having the sense of God's love and favor. It calms his mind. "Thou wilt keep him in perfect peace, whose mind is stayed on thee." The stayed mind is a great source of happiness.

3. It cheers and supports him in darkest seasons. All God's people in all ages have found it so.

4. It gives strength to conquer sin and temptation.

5. It produces positive joy.

6. It conquers the fear of death and produces the hope of heaven.

There are a great many other blessings that accompany the trusting life, more than can be numbered, "Whoso trusteth in the Lord, happy is he."—H.

Suggested Texts and Themes

The Base Line: "Begin at my sanctuary." Ezek. 9:6.

The Cry of the City: "Men groan from out of the city." Job 24:12.

Looking Backward: "And thou shalt remember all the way which the Lord thy God hath led thee." Deut. 8:2.

The Aftermath of Sin: "They shall loathe themselves for the evils which they have committed." Ezek. 6:9.

A Noble Record: "He clave to the Lord, and departed not from following him, but kept his commandments." II Kings 18:6.

MIDWEEK FELLOWSHIP MEETING TOPIC

(Church Night or Suggested Sermon Subject)

Theme: Over-the-Wall Fruitfulness.

TEXT: "Joseph is a fruitful bough . . . whose branches run over the wall." Gen. 49:22.

This was his father's blessing and prediction for Joseph. The words remind us of Jesus' saying, "I am the vine, ye are the branches: He that abideth in me, and I in him, the same bringeth forth much fruit." They take our thoughts to an eastern vineyard. A thrifty vine. Clusters overhanging the wall. Extras available to passers-by.

I. Think of the branch that bears fruit over the wall. Fruit beyond. Ministry to those outside our particular vineyard. Contrary to the spirit of selfishness. Exclusiveness is not Christianity.

II. This over-the-wall fruitfulness is a mark of the branch of the True Vine. 1. Christianity enlarges sympathies. 2. It offers deliberate consideration of others' wants. 3. It results in unconscious, unchecked fruitfulness. Every branch of the Vine which is Jesus runs over the wall somewhere, enriching others.

III. How may this over-the-wall fruitfulness be secured? 1. It depends on the measure in which we receive Christ. 2. It depends on our submission to Divine culture. 3. "The branch that bears much fruit is proud to stoop with it."—C. N.

CHRISTIAN ENDEAVOR SOCIETY TOPIC

July 13. "Thou Shalt Not Bear False Witness." Ex. 20:16; Ps. 15:1-5.

SUNDAY SCHOOL LESSON

July 13. Deborah a Woman of Courage. Judg. 4:4-8; 5:1-7.

MEMORY SELECTION: "Be strong and of a good courage; be not afraid, neither be thou dismayed: for the Lord thy God is with thee whithersoever thou goest." Josh. 1:9.

The dangers from which Deborah saved the people were both physical and moral. But the greater emphasis should be placed on the call upon the people for return to God. The best blessings come to those individuals and nations who honor God and do his will. This lesson is laid at a time of a great national emergency. Deborah as a woman of unusual courage and ability as a leader arose, rallied the tribes, and saved the day. We should interpret her achievements in the light of the standards of the age in which she lived.

SUNDAY: JULY TWENTIETH

MORNING SERVICE

Theme: The Power to See.

SUGGESTED SCRIPTURE READING: II Kings 6:1-17. After-petition: May God reveal to our minds and hearts the truths of this great passage.

SELECTED HYMNS: "'Tis by faith of joys to come."—I. Watts. "O for a faith that will not shrink."—W. H. Bathurst. "Lord, I believe; Thy power I own."—J. R. Wreford. "Give me the wings of faith to rise."—I. Watts.

CALL TO WORSHIP: "I will lift up mine eyes unto the hills, from whence cometh my help. My help cometh from the Lord, which made heaven and earth." "I was glad when they said unto me, Let us go into the house of the Lord."

INVOCATION PRAYER: Help us, O God, to come into thy house in the childlike spirit which was commended by Jesus. In simplicity and sincerity we desire to worship thee. We open our hearts and release our deepest prayers through the words of our hymns and strains of music. May thy word to us reach expectant hearts and may we stand ready to put it into practice in daily life. Release us from all bonds that hinder us from reaching heights of worship. Deliver us from error, and open our minds to truth; remove prejudices and hatreds from our hearts and cause them to glow with love; re-engage our energies in great causes and set our eyes upon the vision splendid, when the kingdom of Christ shall prevail in the hearts of men. Grant unto us ministry of thy presence now while we wait together before thee in this morning's worship. We ask in Christ's name. Amen.—M. K. W. H.

Theme: The Power to See.

TEXT: "And Elisha prayed, and said, Lord, I pray thee, open his eyes, that he may see." II Kings 6:17.

INTRODUCTORY: Once when a comet appeared in the heavens an astronomer made a tour of some country villages to tell the people the facts about the beautiful object which night by night attracted so much attention. Among other things he told of calculations as to the enormous length of the comet's tail. A villager treated this part of the lecture with contempt, saying, "I saw the comet myself, and its tail is just four feet long. How are we to believe a man who comes here to tell us that it is ever so many millions of miles?"

Now that was the common sense of ordinary sight pitted against the common sense of the higher insight into nature which is won by scientific investigation. Sight against sight. Sight against the power to see. Human sight against seeing the invisible. Sight beyond the reach of your sight and mine. Sight from the power to see.

The servant of Elisha, when the eyes of his spirit were opened, saw. It was by the aid of a new telescopic faculty, a new spiritual faculty. "And Elisha prayed, and said, Lord, I pray thee, open his eyes, that he may see. And the Lord opened the eyes of the young man; and he saw: and, behold, the mountain was full of horses and chariots of fire round about Elisha."

I. In looking at the account one cannot but be impressed with Elisha's strong and unshaken confidence. Imagination deals with fiction; faith with fact. "Faith is the faculty which reaches to that which is beyond the senses. It apprehends invisible things to be as certain as the things which we see."

II. No prospect could be more unpromising and gloomy than that which confronted Elisha and his servant. It looked as if they might as well dash themselves against the mountain itself as to contend against a force so numerous and well-equipped. But just then it was that the prophet's faith and confidence shone forth. With clear eyes fixed on the unseen, Elisha answered cheerfully, "Fear not: for they that be with us are more than they which be with them." Then, looking at his servant, he prayed, "Lord, I pray thee, open his eyes, that he may see." Prophets are seers. The greatest and wisest and purest men are in a true sense prophets. They see further, see deeper, see more than other men.

III. Some hold that a man's life is rich in proportion to his material possessions. No fallacy was ever more misleading. A man is rich only in proportion as he has power to see. One man will find more pleasure in a flower which he is too poor to buy than another will find in some earthly paradise all his own. Your poet is a seer. Your artist is a seer. Your Christian is a seer.

IV. From all this it follows that our daily prayer for ourselves and others should be for the power to see. Faith is to sight and reason what the telescope is to the naked eye. 1. God is the unseen but constant factor in the lives of men and women. 2. The army of God camps between the trusting soul and his enemies. 3. The spirit world is near to us, not distant. 4. Through prayer we may may pass from the life of sight into the life of faith. 5. The prophet Elisha in the midst of the Syrian host is a type of every defender of the truth. He was alert. He was calm. He found refuge in prayer. 6. Think, too, of our angelic allies! "Behold, the mountain was full of horses and chariots of fire round about Elisha."

THEME PRAYER: Give us the wings of faith to see thee and something of thy working in the world. Open thou our eyes, O God, that we may behold thee in all thy splendor. Remove the scales from our spiritual vision, that we may see that thou hast come to us in so many ways, but especially in the person of thy Son, Jesus Christ. Amen.

OFFERTORY SENTENCE: "Vow, and pay unto the Lord your God: let all that be round about him bring presents unto him that ought to be feared."

OFFERTORY PRAYER: O Lord, who didst count no suffering and anguish too great to bear for us, we pray that we may respond with deep spiritual appreciation of thy sacrifice. As we come now with the offering of our hands, help us to bring it in the spirit of such a response. Receive it and multiply it to the glory of Thy name. For Thy love's sake. Amen.

Illustrative Material

SEED THOUGHTS, HOMILETIC AND EXPOSITORY. The Power to See: Here is a scene worthy of the pencil of the finest artist, but a scene of such simplicity and beauty that no artist could improve it. It represents the triumphal struggle of simple unarmed truth against the massed and mailed battalions of error. Lord, open our eyes that we may see!—W. J.

Faith and Sight: Faith is to sight and reason what the telescope is to the naked eye.—R. V.

Invisible Realities: The scope of human penetration is limited. Even with our wonderful organs of vision there are many material things which we cannot perceive. Besides material objects there are immaterial things which the age cannot perceive. Beyond all this there is the spiritual world.—T. H.

Ignorance of the unseen is due to the limitations of the senses.—J. H. T.

Choice Illustrations on the Theme

STAGES OF FAITH. The late Rev. Dr. J. S. Jones, of England, wrote: "There are three stages in men's views of the world. The first stage is that of glowing optimism when everything seems rosy—that is the stage of ignorance. The second is that of a deep and brooding pessimism as one views the world's misery and sin—that is the stage of realism. The third is that of a calm faith, which does not ignore the hard and cruel facts but fully believes that good is the end of all—that is the stage of triumphant faith."—Archer Wallace.

FAITH AND SIGHT. A minister was preaching on Glasgow Green a few years ago when someone asked permission to speak, and made his way to the platform.

"Friends," he exclaimed, "I do not believe what this man has been talking about. I do not believe in a hell, in a judgment, or in a God, for I never saw any of them."

He continued talking in this way for a while, when another voice was heard from the crowd. "May I speak?" The infidel sat down; the next man began.

"Friends, you say there is a river running not far from this place, the River Clyde. There is no such grass and trees growing around me where I now stand; there is no such thing; that also is untrue. You tell me that there are a great many people standing here. Again, I say that is not true; there is no person standing here save myself. I suppose you wonder what I am talking about; but, friends, I was born blind. I never have seen one of you, and while I talk it only shows that I am blind or I would not say such things. And you," he said, turning to the infidel, "the more you talk the more it exposes your ignorance, because you are spiritually blind, and cannot see."—*Life of Faith.*

HOW FAITH SEES

With reason's eye we seek out God
And catch sweet glimpses of His face,
But when we cannot see, Faith comes
And trusts Him where we cannot trace.
—Unidentified.

THE INVISIBLE BROUGHT NEAR. The radio has seemingly brought the invisible world near. It has made it much more real and apprehensible by our human mind. No thoughtful man can hear the clear and natural tones of a human voice speaking to him out of absolute silence and void from two thousand miles away and not have a solemn realization of the actuality of the viewless spiritual world. We find in this experience a wonderfully appealing illustration and analogy by which to make real the things which lie beyond our mortal ken, but which by faith may be brought into most intimate communion with our souls.
—Robert C. Hallock, D.D.

EVENING SERVICE

Theme: Strained Piety or Being Righteous Overmuch.

TEXT: "Be not righteous over much." Eccles. 7:16.

INTRODUCTORY: In this wicked world, at first sight one might conclude this a very unnecessary warning. Who ever heard of any man saying, "I have been ruined because I went to church too often, read the Bible too much, or prayed too frequently?" Yet here is a Scripture caution, "Be not righteous over much."

It is plainly a warning against strained or overdone religion. It is indeed quite a possible thing for religion to run wild, for goodness to be pushed on wrong lines, for it to be strained, arbitrary, exaggerated.

I. This strained piety or overdone religion sometimes manifests itself in a doctrinal way. This is somewhat common in these days, though we think not so much so as in former times. It seems evident that there is far less doctrinal "You can and you can't; you will and you won't; you shall and you shan't, and you'll be damned if you don't." Yet there is danger with some people lest they become doctrinal overmuch, create articles of faith, make vague creeds, or interpretations of creeds that few if any can accept. There are people of a certain temper that make this mistake.

II. Such strained or overdone piety sometimes is revealed in morbid religious introspectiveness. There is, of course, such a thing as righteous self-examination. It is a duty to look closely into one's own heart and life. And yet this duty is often misconceived and pressed to false issues. Men sometimes get morbid about the state of their health, constantly weighing themselves, feeling their pulse, reading about medicines. We all feel that such solicitude is a mistake. It is a sign of a morbid and miserable condition of mind. Yet such a thing can happen in religion. It is not very common we think. But there are Christians who become oversolicitous about their religious state, curious about obscure symptoms. Such a habit may prove very mistaken and hurtful. It is spiritual morbidity. It is morally weakening, takes away peace of mind, and is very likely to rob life of joy and brightness.

III. And, again, such strained and overdone piety reveals itself sometimes also as an overexacting conscientiousness. There is such a thing as "suffering from an overpampered conscience." Some really good people do so suffer. They have an overfastidious moral sense. It is a legal maxim that "the law concerneth not itself with trifles." Courts are always impatient of "frivolous and vexatious charges." But some Christians are forever arraigning themselves at the bar of conscience about arbitrary, frivolous and vexatious things. It is a great mistake. A true and noble conscience is tender, quick, imperative; but it is also large and generous and intelligent as is the eternal law of which it is the organ.

IV. Yet again, such strained piety sometimes reveals itself in a person's inordinate culture of some special virtue. For some reason or other a man conceives a special affection for a particular excellence. It engrosses his attention. He harps upon it. Every conversation gets around to one subject. This extreme love for any one virtue may easily become a snare.

V. We remark, lastly, that such strained piety or overdone religion sometimes reveals itself in striving after impracticable standards of character. It is a fine characteristic of Christianity that it is so sane and reasonable and practical. It never demands or expects impossibilities. Fanciful ideals discourage and exhaust and distort us. "Learn of me," says Christ. Yes, let us go back to him. He was without excess. Nothing is more wonderful about our Lord than his perfect naturalness, his absolute balance, his reasonableness, his reality.—After W. L. W.

Suggested Texts and Themes

The Transmission of Truth: "Who received living oracles to give unto us." Acts 7:38 (A. S. V.).

Flee, Follow, and Fight: "Flee these things . . . follow after righteousness . . . fight the good fight of faith." I. Tim. 6:11, 12.

The Christian Art of Anger: "Be ye angry, and sin not: let not the sun go down upon your wrath: neither give place to the devil." Eph. 4:26-27.

The Royal Man in Public Life: "But Daniel purposed in his heart that he would not defile himself with the portion of the king's meat, nor with the wine which he drank," etc. Dan. 1:8.

The Attestation of Sonship: "Jesus said unto them, If God were your Father, ye would love me." John 8:42.

MIDWEEK FELLOWSHIP MEETING TOPIC

(Church Night or Suggested Sermon Subject)

Theme: Walking with God.

TEXT: "And Enoch walked with God: and he was not; for God took him." Gen. 5:24.

The patriarch Enoch did not see death. In some mysterious way he was taken up from this temporal life and translated into the life of glory.

I. The distinguished character of Enoch. 1. Walking with God. His faith gave him knowledge of God, confidence in God, enjoyment of God. 2. Witnessing for God to his generation.

II. The excellence of his piety. 1. It began in early childhood. 2. It was manifest in the face of evil times. 3. It grew in spite of scanty privileges. 4. It continued to the close of life.

III. The reward of his good life. He was translated that he should not see death. God took him because he loved him. 1. Here is a striking proof of immortality. This anticipation of the resurrection was itself a prophecy of the heavenly life. 2. Here a striking proof of the Gospel. 3. The peaceful quiet of a good man's end is little short of translation. 4. Walking with God is walking to God.—P. C.

CHRISTIAN ENDEAVOR SOCIETY TOPIC

July 20. "Remember the Sabbath Day." Ex. 20:8; 31:12-17; Mark 2:23-28.

SUNDAY SCHOOL LESSON

July 20. Gideon a Man of Faith and Humility. Judg. 6:11-17, 25-27; 8:22, 23.

MEMORY SELECTION: "Teach me thy way, O Lord, and lead me in a plain path." Ps. 27:11.

Here is a story of a brave leader, as we would say today, of a man to match the hour. The lesson includes four incidents in the story of Gideon. These include his call, the confirmation of the call, the tearing down of the heathen altars, and his military victory. His self-effacement when confronted by the divine call and his courage when once assured of divine help are notable. Once assured he answered the call in great faith. Yet he was so humble that he refused to be king.

SUNDAY: JULY TWENTY-SEVENTH

MORNING SERVICE

Theme: Salt and Sacrifice.

SUGGESTED SCRIPTURE READING: Ps. 96:1-13, 100:1-5. After-petition: May God bless to us this reading from his Word.

SELECTED HYMNS: "Come, let us join our cheerful songs."—I. Watts. "Glory to God on high! Let praises fill the sky."—J. Allen. "O worship the King all glorious above."—R. Grant. "Angel voices ever singing."—F. Pott. "Come, thou Almighty King."—Anon.

CALL TO WORSHIP: "Let the words of my mouth, and the meditation of my heart, be acceptable in thy sight, O Lord, my strength, and my redeemer."

INVOCATION PRAYER: Almighty God, revealed to us in thy Son, we know that thou alone art God. Thou didst create us, and all things by thy sovereign power. By thy grace and might sustain us this day. We come bowing before thee with sacred joy. We raise high our thankful songs, and would fill thy sacred courts with resounding praise. Wide as the wideness of the sea is thy mercy. Vast as eternity is thy love. Firm as the mountains doth thy truth ever stand. Unending as thyself is thy grace. Bind us then unto thyself that thy life may flow into us, and through us into the life of all mankind. Through Christ we ask. Amen.—Rev. Garret Hondelink, B.D.

Theme: Salt and Sacrifice.

TEXT: "And every oblation of thy meat offering shalt thou season with salt," etc. Lev. 2:13.

INTRODUCTORY: The historical value of the book of Leviticus is very great. That its elaborate rituals looked beyond itself there can be no doubt. They contain prophecy of things to come. They shadow forth the Gospel. They are replete with "the gospel of the grace of God." The whole book has much to do with the laws of sacrifices and the sanctification of feasts.

I have read of a reporter who visited a Chinese "Joss-house" in San Francisco. An intelligent Chinese man who could speak a little English was in charge. The reporter asked him why the Chinese put tea cups of wine and tea and rice before their god; did they believe that their god would eat and drink? "Oh, no," said the Chinese attendant, "that's not what for. What you like self, you give god. He see. He like see."

Too many Christians in making sacrifices to God offer only what they would about as lief spare as not, instead of giving what they like themselves.

The Levitical directions about seasoning of sacrifices are very interesting and suggestive. The text emphasizes their seasoning with salt. In this same chapter we discover that other things besides salt were necessary. They were to bring frankincense, a sweet scent. Their meat offerings were to be seasoned thus. They were to bring oil. And they were to bring salt. Salt had its own symbolism.

I. For one thing, salt was the symbol of the covenant. The Scriptures frequently mention "the covenant of salt." It is written that when God gave the kingdom to David he did so by "a covenant of salt." Eating salt together in the East is a pledge of amity and friendship. The "covenant of salt" meant an indissoluble pact. Salt was used in the sacrifices and offerings of the Israelites doubtless with the same idea of honor and fidelity.

II. Salt also was a token of communion. In the East especially it is the token of fellowship. When an Oriental has once eaten of a man's salt, he will do him no harm. It is a token of friendship, of communion. Our sacrifices for God should have always this element of the spirit of fellowship with him.

III. Further, salt is the emblem of sincerity. "With all thine offerings thou shalt offer salt." Intense sincerity should always mark all that we do for God.

IV. But especially is salt the type or emblem of purifying power. With all our sacrifices, and in all our relations to our heavenly Father, we have need to bring a great deal of this salt. If we come before God with holy things we must seek to be holy as he is holy. It is written, "Without holiness no man shall see the Lord." Certainly without holiness no man can serve the Lord.

We are told that in Buddhist temples a tall and broad-leaved lily stands directly in front of the altar. The idea is as beautiful as is its workmanship. This pure white emblem suggests that all offerings on sacred shrines should be simple and sincere. This truth applies with tenfold force to the worship of God and all service for the Christian sanctuary. God who is a Spirit would have us worship him in sincerity and in truth, in the beauty of holiness.

"With all thine offerings thou shalt offer salt."

THEME PRAYER: O God of surpassing greatness, we acknowledge and confess thee to be the Lord of all the earth, far beyond all human knowledge; yet hast thou drawn near to us and redeemed us in Christ. For this we adore and bless thee. O God, seen of no human eye, heard to no human ear, whom yet our souls confess and our hearts crave, we praise thee for thine always upholding power and love. May we fear no fall with thy power beneath us and in our weaknesses help us to surrender to thy strength. Through Jesus Christ, our Lord. Amen.

OFFERTORY SENTENCE: "In the morning sow thy seed, and in the evening withhold not thine hand: for thou knowest not whether shall prosper, either this or that, or whether they both shall be alike good."

OFFERTORY PRAYER: God of all being, we would worship thee in the bringing of our offerings this day. The heavens are thine and the earth with all that therein is. We thank thee, O Lord, that thou hast ordained a wondrous partnership whereby we, thy human stewards, may administer thine earthly riches and give thee back a portion, that thy kingdom may come and thy will be done on earth as it is in heaven. Bless these gifts and the givers to that high purpose; in Jesus' name. Amen.—Jesse H. Baird, D.D.

Illustrative Material

SEED THOUGHTS, HOMILETIC AND EXPOSITORY. True Worship: I. Its nature. Devout exercises of the soul. 1. It is a necessity of man's nature. 2. It is an evidence of man's greatness. Kinship with God. II. Its object God. III. Man becomes assimilated to the object of his worship. How important, then, that our knowledge of God should be intelligent, correct, Scripture, true. IV. Its spirit. "In the beauty of holiness." 1. In reality. 2. In simplicity. 3. In beauty of soul.—J. O. K.

Worship: Lay hold of the Divine ideal, the beauty of Christ. Worship God through him and in his likeness, laying our noblest and best, our best thoughts and our best feelings and our noblest actions on the high altar of dedication to him.—A. B.

Choice Illustrations on the Theme

THEY THAT WORSHIP HIM. In the Tate Art Gallery in London there is a famous picture by Alphonse Legros, entitled "Women at Prayer." It shows a number of women praying in a church. Some bow in deep contrition, other faces show intense ecstasy, reverent awe, or the anguish of doubt. There are faces which reveal weariness of spirit while others appear indifferent or even flippant. Thus the artist seeks to show that worship may be a very different thing because of the totally different spirit in which people approach God.—Archer Wallace.

WHAT WORSHIP DOES. Worship was the impelling motive that sent the wise men on the long, long journey to the cradle of the Christ. When they came to Jerusalem they asked: "Where is he that is born king of the Jews? for we have seen his star in the east, and are come to worship him. . . . And when they were come into the house, they saw the young child with Mary his mother, and fell down, and worshipped him: and when they had opened their treasures, they presented unto him gifts; gold, and frankincense, and myrrh." They came not to get but to give. Their gifts followed worship.

Worship is the key that opens the treasure first of the heart then of the hand.

WORSHIP A THRILLING EXPERIENCE. Worship ought to be a thrilling experience, like going back to the old home for Thanksgiving, or voting for president, or meeting old friends in a foreign land, or witnessing a historical pageant about some great event in which one's ancestors took part, or sitting across from some really great man and talking to him for half an hour, or watching a sunrise over the Grand Canyon or a sunset through the Golden Gate.

We need worship, just as we need to have experiences like those noted above, in order to give life deeper overtones and richer colors. In worship we are really going home for Thanksgiving, going back to a well-loved ritual to express our gratitude to God for all the good things that have enriched our lives. In worship we do a greater thing than cast a vote for president, we reaffirm our loyalty to the eternal order of the universe, and our allegiance to the God whom we seek to serve. Just as it is a great joy in a foreign land to meet old friends who speak our language and understand our ways, so in the worship service we share a common experience with others whose citizenship is in heaven and who have kindred loyalties to Jesus Christ and aspirations for his prevailing kingdom on the earth.—Albert W. Palmer.

EVENING SERVICE

Theme: Caught in One's Own Snare.

TEXT: "Whoso diggeth a pit shall fall therein: and he that rolleth a stone, it will return upon him." Prov. 26:27.

INTRODUCTORY: The supposed pit was such as are made to catch wild animals. They are concealed with a covering of boughs and earth. The maker is assumed to approach one incautiously and falls into his own trap. The picture of the rolling stone is of a man pushing it to a height to hurl it down upon an enemy. Its weight causes it to fall back and crush the author. The principle is that sin brings its own retribution. Let us consider some cases in which such things might happen.

I. One instance is that of the deceiver. The pit is a snare. It is meant to deceive. But those who deceive are likely to be deceived. They have blinded the faculty of truth. They have acclimatized themselves in a zone of falsehood. In the very belief that they think this well for them they prove themselves deluded.

II. Another instance is that of the swindler. This man may entrap unwary folk who trust his offers. At first he may thrive and fatten on his ill-gotten gains. But his success is almost sure to be short-lived. Swindlers rarely prosper long.

III. Another instance is the tempter. A person who imitates the work of the evil one may have a wicked triumph over weakness and ignorance. He may succeed in luring his victim to shame and ruin. But he is a short-sighted self-destroyer. Every tempter prepares his own pit of destruction. There is a pit prepared for the devil and his angels.

IV. The most foolish one of all is the opponent of Christ. The Jews rejected him, laid snares for catching him. He turned the shame upon their own heads. In the end they accomplished his death. But they were punished in the frightful overthrow of their city. 1. The world's overthrow of Christ would mean the world's ruin. 2. Everyone who plots against the kingdom of heaven unwarily plots for his own undoing.—P. C.

Suggested Texts and Themes

Triumphant Thanksgiving: "And he took the cup, and gave thanks." Matt. 26:27.

The Secret of Joy: "Happy is that people . . . whose God is the Lord." Ps. 144:15.

Nameless Saints: "Salute Philologus, and Julia . . . and all the saints which are with them." Rom. 16:15.

Residual Religion: "And the residue thereof he maketh a god." Isa. 44:17.

The Statue of Liberty: "I will establish my justice for a light of the peoples." Isa. 51:4 (A. S. V.).

MIDWEEK FELLOWSHIP MEETING TOPIC

(Church Night or Suggested Sermon Subject)

Theme: Love Returned, or God Loves Those Who Love Him.

Text: "I love them that love me." Prov. 8:17.

These words do not set forth that God's love is produced by ours. Its source is in himself. Nor that it is since ours. It is eternal. Nor that his love is dependent on ours. It is unchangeable. Nor that his love is only for those who love him. For he gave the greatest proof of his love while we were enemies.

I. Those who return God's love in Christ have the evidence of his love to them. Love in us proves God's love for us. No one can ever say that his love to God is rejected. He values our hearts too much to discard them.

II. Those who return God's love in Christ receive special manifestations of acceptance from him. Inner experience. Answered prayers. The Spirit's comfort. The joys of communion. Success in labor.

III. Those who return God's love in Christ have the position and titles of his loved ones. Called Brethren, Friends, Sons of God. Given many endearing titles and relationships.

IV. Those who return God's love in Christ give him special gladness. "There is joy in the presence of the angels of God over one sinner that repenteth."

Make God glad! Love him because he first loved you. Love him deeply. Serve him devotedly.—R. A. G.

CHRISTIAN ENDEAVOR SOCIETY TOPIC

July 27. Money Is Spiritual Power. Mal. 3:8-10; Mark 12:41-44.

SUNDAY SCHOOL LESSON

July 27. God Prepares a Leader. I Sam. 1:20, 24-28; 3:1, 16–4:1.

Memory Selection: "The child Samuel grew on, and increased in favour both with the Lord, and also with men." I Sam. 2:26.

As he grew up Samuel was faithful to his duties in the Lord's house and obedient to God's will. Thus he became a man to whom God could entrust a great task. He became a great prophet trusted by the people. He was a child of prayer, dedicated by his mother to God. He was well prepared for leadership and responsibility. Let us learn the lesson of good home background and the responsibility of parenthood.

SUNDAY: AUGUST THIRD

MORNING SERVICE

Theme: I Had Fainted Unless—.

SUGGESTED SCRIPTURE READING: Ps. 27:1-14. After-petition: May God reveal to our minds and hearts the great truths of this lesson from his Word.

SELECTED HYMNS: "Wait, my soul, upon the Lord."—W. F. Lloyd. "If thou suffer God to guide thee."—G. Neumark. "God is my strong salvation."—J. Montgomery. "Cast thy burden on the Lord."—Anon. "Who trusts in God a strong abode."—J. Magdeburg.

CALL TO WORSHIP: "O come, let us sing unto the Lord: let us make a joyful noise to the rock of our salvation. Let us come before his presence with thanksgiving, and make a joyful noise unto him with psalms. For the Lord is a great God, and a great King above all gods."

INVOCATION PRAYER: O God, once more the call to worship is heard across the busy tideway of our lives. May it sound like a silver bell in our hearts, luring, impelling and commanding. And when the evening shadows gather, may we still rejoice in the sweetness of thy presence. Quicken our faith, O thou Spirit of God, that our experiences may be deepened. We believe, yet help our unbelief. By faith may we see more deeply into the heart of things. By faith may we incline our ears unto the still small voice. By faith may our minds discover higher truth, our hearts respond to the love of Christ, and our wills be found in harmony with thy purposes.—M. K. W. H.

Theme: I Had Fainted Unless—.

TEXT: "I had fainted, unless I had believed to see the goodness of the Lord in the land of the living." Ps. 27:13.

INTRODUCTORY: How very expressive the word "faint" is in biblical phraseology. It indicates not only that physical strength is gone, but that courage, hope and spirit have departed also. One who faints is one whose heart becomes water, and who is helpless in the face of terrible foes when he should be strong.

I am sure that we all have oftentimes been weary and faint in our minds. If there is a real antidote for fainting to be found in the Bible, surely men ought to make use of it.

I. I had fainted unless I had believed. It is faith, first of all, which preserves a man from fainting when the odds are great, when the future is dark, and when human resources seem futile and unavailing.

Darkness descends at times upon every life. It may be short or it may be long-continued. It may come in the form of sorrow, disappointments or suffering. We acknowledge that men must then walk by faith rather than by sight. It is a fine and rewarding act of faith to slip our hands into the hands of the Lord, and to let him lead us one step at the time.

But notice that the Psalmist in the

text said: "The goodness of the Lord in the land of the living." He not only had faith to believe that what God did was best; he had faith to believe that he would see God's goodness while he was yet alive.

What can religion offer a man today? Have faith that you shall see the goodness of God which has ever been around about you but has been hidden perhaps by your own spiritual blindness.

II. There must also be prayer. "Men ought always to pray, and not to faint." Thank God, we can always pray and prayer will keep Christians from fainting and from despair. (Amplify.)

III. The third antidote for fainting is waiting on the Lord. Isaiah says: "Even the youths shall faint and be weary. . . . But they that wait upon the Lord shall renew their strength. . . ."

1. Waiting on the Lord is, first of all, having patience with God and his great purposes. Our human vision is very limited. It is also imperfect and defective. Let us give God time in the many things that trouble us, and be very patient lest we wear ourselves out. For there is nothing like fretting to wear out the life and the soul of a man.

2. There is this additional idea in the word "wait" which the old Hebrew prophet used. It is the idea of entwining ourselves round about the Lord as the vine entwines itself round about the giant oak. As the strength of the oak becomes the strength of the clinging vine, so the strength of the Lord becomes the strength of the clinging Christian.

3. But there is a positive promise also in the prophet's words. His strength shall be renewed. He shall be equal to any task, any duty, any mission, any emergency. God has provided us with an antidote for any fainting.—Rev. Stuart R. Oglesby, D.D.

THEME PRAYER: Grant us, O Lord, in all our duties thy help, in all our perplexities thy counsel, in all our dangers thy protection, and in all our sorrows thy peace; for the sake of Jesus Christ our Saviour. Amen.

OFFERTORY SENTENCE: In token of our joy, and of our giving of our lives in service to God we now make our offering, reverently, with prayer, and in the spirit of sacrifice. It is the privilege of all God's people thus to share in carrying our triumphant joy of today to all the world.

OFFERTORY PRAYER: We offer here, O Lord, our token gifts. Some will come out of plenty. Some will come out of poverty. Some will come from those who know joy. Some will come from those who know sorrow. All will be coins of sacrifice. Thou knowest, O Lord, how to suit a blessing unto each giver. We pray thee graciously so to do. In Christ's name we ask. Amen.—M. K. W. H.

Illustrative Material

SEED THOUGHTS, HOMILETIC AND EXPOSITORY. Unless I Had Believed: I. God's goodness is often a matter of faith rather than of sight. II. We faint because we do not see it. III. But we must hold fast to what we know of God's goodness and trust where we cannot know.—M. R. V.

Faith Expects: I. Faith expects to see the goodness of the Lord. II. Faith expects to see that the forces of God are adequate to overcome the forces of evil, that the eternal right must prosper. III. Faith awakens fortitude. It gives strength of heart and hope. It inspires courage. It nerves the arm. IV. Faith leads to fidelity. To be full of faith leads to faithfulness.—J. M. C.

Choice Illustrations on the Theme

I HAD FAINTED UNLESS—FAITH. A father was nursing his little daughter on his knee. Just then a friend came in, and, picking her up, walked off with her down the garden. The little one experienced neither surprise nor fear, so her father said, "Aren't you afraid, darling?" "No," she said. "But you don't know who has you?" "No," was the prompt answer, "but you do, father." That was enough. She was "in sight of" her father, and faith in her father's loving care banished fear.—W. Hetherington.

GOD'S GOODNESS. A lady visited a cemetery in New England and read the epitaphs and the thing that impressed her most was the fact that all the brief obituaries were words of tenderness and praise. With a twinkle in her eye she said to the sexton: "Evidently there are no bad people buried here." Probably the truth is that in our calmer and more reflective moments we know that love is nearer the truth than any other mood.—Archer Wallace.

UNLESS I HAD BELIEVED TO SEE—GOODNESS. One writer uses this beautiful illustration: "A king is sitting with his council deliberating upon high affairs of state involving the destiny of nations, when suddenly he hears the sorrowful cry of his little child, who has fallen down, or been frightened by a wasp; he rises and runs to his relief, comforts his sorrows and relieves his fears. Is there anything unkingly here? Is it not most natural? Does it not even elevate the monarch in your esteem? Why then do we think it dishonorable to the King of kings, our heavenly Father, to consider the small matters of his children? It is infinitely condescending, but is it not superlatively natural that being a Father he should act as such?"

HAVING A SENSE OF GOD. John Ruskin, much interested in art, maintained that no artist or sculptor could do good work if he confined himself to a representation of human achievements. He must represent the work of God: the flowers of the fields and the grass; the leaves of the trees and the fruit of the garden; tiny woodland streams or the vast expanse of the ocean. If that be true is it unreasonable to say that in our lives we must imitate the divine? We cannot lift ourselves up by our own bootstraps. We must have a deep sense of God and be sustained by the inspiration of his life within.—Archer Wallace.

EVENING SERVICE

Theme: A Popular Delusion.

TEXT: "Say not thou, What is the cause that the former days were better than these? for thou dost not inquire wisely concerning this." Eccles. 7:10.

INTRODUCTORY: Impatience leads some to disparage the present and see the past through rose-tinted atmosphere. It is not founded on any adequate information.

I. The delusion stated. "That the former days were better than these." "The good old times." The proposition may be understood as applying to: 1. Individual experience. 2. To human history.

II. The delusion exemplified. Greeks looking back to the age of those who fought at Marathon. The Romans recalling the greatness of the republic. Englishmen mourning over the passing of the good old days of the Tudors. Old men regretting the vanished days of their childhood. Men once rich lamenting the disappearance of their wealth.

III. The delusion explained. Two things account for it, the instinctive idealization of the past, and the equally instinctive depreciation of the present. Past ills forgotten. "Distance lends enchantment to the view." Present evil things appear worse. Present pleasure is seldom as happy as its pursuit.

IV. The delusion disproved. It is founded upon false judgment. 1. The standard is mistaken. 2. The comparison is incomplete. It will not do to contrast the dark side of the present with the bright side of the past. Cease complaining. Make the best of the present instead of dreaming about the past. This foolish comparison and complaint is based upon ignorance, marked by forgetfulness, indicative of a spirit of discontent, is wanting in manly resoluteness, and is lacking in religious trustfulness and hopefulness. —P. C.

MIDWEEK FELLOWSHIP MEETING TOPIC

(Church Night or Suggested Sermon Subject)

Theme: How to Get Rich.

TEXT: "And God said, Ask what I shall give thee." I Kings 3:5.

These are God's words to Solomon. Relate the account. "Thou art coming to a King; large petitions with thee bring." We look for prosperity from the same source. It is obtained in the same way. "Ask what I shall give thee" is a God-signatured check in hand.

I. Asking is the simplest method.

II. Asking is the Divinely appointed method. Matt. 7:7.

III. Asking is the only method. Purchase? Impossible. Deserts? We have not any.

IV. Asking is the certain method. Never yet has failed. Never will fail.

V. Asking is the abundantly-enforced method. The whole Bible "Ask." The promises and exhortations say "Ask." God says, "Ask and ye shall receive."

VI. Asking ever has been the supremely successful method. The history of the Church evidences it. Individual Christian experience proves it. All traceable to prayer. How get rich? Ask.

Suggested Texts and Themes

Active Compassion: "Jesus went about all the cities and villages, teaching . . . healing. . . . But when he saw the multitudes, he was moved with compassion," etc. Matt. 9:35, 36.

Compassion Commended: "Go, and do thou likewise." Luke 10:37.

Compassion Denied: "The same servant . . . found one of his fellowservants . . . took him by the throat," etc. Matt. 18:28-30.

Need Poverty Be Permanent? "For ye have the poor always with you; but me ye have not always." Matt. 26:11.

The Test of the Street: "The same servant went out, and found one of his fellowservants, which owed him an hundred pence: and he laid hands on him, and took him by the throat, saying, Pay me that thou owest." Matt. 18:28.

CHRISTIAN ENDEAVOR SOCIETY TOPIC

Aug. 3. Eternal Influences: What Do You See? John 1:35-39; Ps. 66:5; II Cor. 4:18.

BULLETIN BOARD SLOGANS FOR THE MONTH

By Earl Riney

A vacation should be a rest, a joy, an experience and a preparation.

God made the country and man made the town.

A telephone pole never hits an automobile except in self-defense.

It is no sport if the fish jump into your boat.

Take a vacation and relax; it allows your soul to catch up with your body.

Nothing is really work unless you would rather be doing something else.

Religion is much more a matter of feeling and attitudes than it is of knowledge.

Every experience becomes a part of your personality.

Our souls are dyed the color of our thoughts.

The beautiful is not always good, but the good is always beautiful.

SUNDAY SCHOOL LESSON

Aug. 3. Samuel Judge and Prophet. I Sam. 7:5-17.

MEMORY SELECTION: "Direct your hearts unto the Lord, and serve him only." I Sam. 7:3.

This lesson shows Samuel at work as a prophet, a priest, and a judge. His mission was to keep the people alive to the authority and requirements of God. By his influence he promoted unity among the various Hebrew tribes. He set a precedent for the great prophets of later generations. The class may well discuss the necessary requirements for Christian ministers of today.

SUNDAY: AUGUST TENTH

MORNING SERVICE

Theme: Sins of Ignorance.

Suggested Scripture Reading: Lev. 5:1-19.

Selected Hymns: "Not all the blood of beasts."—I. Watts. "A voice by Jordan's Shore."—S. Longfellow. "How gentle God's Commands."—P. Doddridge. "Father of mercies, in thy Word."—A. Steele. "God in the gospel of his Son." —B. Beddome.

Call to Worship: "Great is the Lord, and greatly to be praised in the city of our God, in the mountain of his holiness. . . . Walk about Zion, and go round about her: tell the towers thereof. Mark ye well her bulwarks, consider her palaces; that ye may tell it to the generation following. For this God is our God for ever and ever: he will be our guide even unto death."

Invocation Prayer: Our Father, God, our hearts are restless till they rest in thee. Something deep and haunting in our hearts draws us to the altar of prayer. Make us responsive to the inner voice. Lift us out of any dullness or coldness. Drive fear from our hearts. Fill them with love. May we come unto thee, our Father, with a child's unspoiled spontaneity and a child's heart of expectancy. Deal with us this hour, O God, that we may become more truly thy sons, and that we may be truer brothers of our fellow men. May thy love dominate us. May our every word and deed manifest the love of Christ. Help us to release an overwhelming tide of love in the world. In Jesus' name. Amen.—M. K. W. H.

Theme: Sins of Ignorance.

Text: "Though he wist it not, yet is he guilty." Lev. 5:17.

Introductory: In the Levitical law sins of ignorance were taken for granted and provided for. One of its sections begins with these words, "If a man sin through ignorance." Our text says, "Though he wist it not, yet is he guilty."

There is a story concerning an English railway signalman. There was an accident through his mistake by which a number of persons lost their lives. An inquiry was held. It was found that the signalman had in his possession a book of instructions which if they had been attended to the accident could not have occurred. But this book, the man confessed, he had never read. Result, the accident. How many of the sins of professing Christians could be traced to a similar culpable ignorance!

The word rendered "ignorance," in this Levitical law, will bear also the translation of "inadvertence." Inadvertence is a kind of acted ignorance. A man frequently does wrong from lack of thought. He carelessly and hastily blunders into a course, erring because he did not study to be right. There are sins of this kind committed every day. There is a saying, "Evil is wrought by want of thought as well as want of heart." Sins of ignorance, sins of inadvertence, is there any actual guilt in them? The Levitical law says there is. Our civil law says there is. It says "Ignorance of the law is no excuse."

I. Yes, ignorance may be culpable. The law is supreme, not our ignorance. If we break the law our deed is recorded against us. We must bear the blame. Also the law is supreme aside from any man's opinion about it.

II. Another fact. By the teaching of this text concerning the culpability of ignorance, men's consciences will be aroused. By this teaching men will be impelled to study the law. All right-minded people will begin to say, "Let me know what God would have me to do. We do not wish to be breaking the law, or leaving God's commands undone." The Psalmist exclaims, "Who can understand his errors? cleanse thou me from secret faults." Conscience can be informed and educated. It should be. The right-hearted man will seek its enlightenment, through good counsel, through the study of good examples, and especially through God's Word.

III. Consider also this: It is not possible that ignorance should be a justification of sin, because if it were so then it would follow that the more ignorant a man was the more innocent he would be. That is an absurdity. Then, too, if the guilt of an action depended entirely upon a man's knowledge we would have no fixed standard at all by which to judge right and wrong. Many do not seek to know. There is a saying, "There are none so blind as those who will not see." The laws of nature are invariable. They do not provide for ignorance. They demand that we shall learn or suffer. The fact is that the ignorance of many people is to a large degree willful. To those who really wish to do right there is a Divine Word which can be to us all a lamp unto our feet and a light unto our path.—H.

THEME PRAYER: Almighty and most merciful Father, before thee and one another we confess our sins in thought and word and deed. We are ashamed and sorry for all wherein we have displeased thee. In spirit and in truth we do repent, and of any whom we may have wronged we seek forgiveness. Purify our affections in the love with which thou hast first loved us, and lead us in the way of thy will, which is our peace, through Jesus Christ our Lord. Amen.

OFFERTORY SENTENCE: "What shall I render unto the Lord for all his benefits toward me? I will take the cup of salvation, and call upon the name of the Lord. . . . I will pay my vows unto the Lord now in the presence of all his people, in the courts of the Lord's house, in the midst of thee, O Jerusalem. Praise ye the Lord."

OFFERTORY PRAYER: O Lord, our God, who art ever bountiful in thy dealings with man, who openest thy hand and satisfiest the desire of every living thing, make us as gracious in our giving as the Master, who taught that it is more blessed to give than to receive. Amen. —Arthur H. Limouze.

Illustrative Material

SEED THOUGHTS, HOMILETIC AND EXPOSITORY. Sins of Silence: I. Sins may lay in silence as in speech. II. The force of influence. Good influence grows. Evil multiplies. III. From influence and example there results responsibility. One can as easily evade the law of gravitation as the law of human responsibility, to God and to man.—W. J. D.

The Sin of Conniving at Wrongdoing: I. The sins of men cannot evade witnesses to give evidence when justice demands it. 1. The law of God commands it. 2. The welfare of society demands it. II. In concealing evidence against sin we involve ourselves in serious guilt. We so dishonor God, disobey his law, decrease our own antipathy to sin, and encourage trespassers in their wrongdoing.—F. W. B.

Choice Illustrations on the Theme

PRETENTIOUS IGNORANCE. Paintings were not her specialty, but as she gazed at a beautiful copy of Millet's "Gleaners," her admiration of the work called forth enthusiastic comment. "What a wonderful picture!" she exclaimed. "And how natural it looks!"

"But what are those people doing?" she inquired, as she bent nearer to read the title. "Oh, yes, I see, gleaning millet! How perfectly fascinating!"

QUOTATIONS CONCERNING IGNORANCE. "Nothing is more terrible than active ignorance."—Goethe. "Ignorance is a prolonged infancy only deprived of its charm."—De Boufflers. "Ignorance is a dangerous and spiritual poison, which all men ought warily to shun."—Gregory. "Ignorance is the dominion of absurdity."—Froude. "A man may live long, and die at last in ignorance of many truths, which his mind was capable of knowing, and that with certainty."—Locke. "Ignorance, when voluntary, is criminal, and a man may be properly charged with that evil which he neglected or refused to learn how to prevent."—Johnson. "Ignorance is not innocence, but sin."—Robert Browning. "The receipt for perpetual ignorance is: be satisfied with your opinions and content with your knowledge."—Elbert Hubbard. "To be ignorant of one's ignorance is the malady of the ignorant."—A. B. Alcott.

IGNORANT OF IGNORANCE

With ignorance wage eternal war,
To know thyself forever strain,
Thine ignorance of thine ignorance is
Thy fiercest foe, thy deadliest bane:
That blunts thy sense, and dulls thy taste;
That deafs thine ears, and blinds thine eyes:
Creates the thing that never was,
The Thing that ever is defies.
—Richard Burton.

THE SIN OF COMPLACENT IGNORANCE. Transgression may ensue from lack of knowledge that such conduct is forbidden; or it may be that knowing the prohibition disobedience is speciously excused on some vague plea that circumstances warrant it or expediency condones it. In such cases ignorance, if it be really ignorance at all, is self-induced and therefore the more culpable. Amid such reprehensible forms of ignorance may be placed carelessness, the mind too placid to rouse itself to inquiry; indiscrimination, the habit of ignoring vital principles; self-excusing, finding exceptional circumstances which extenuate faults and condone misconduct. A religious fault is neglect of Scripture, not "coming to the light lest our deeds should be reproved," (John 3:20). Another is satisfaction with a state of conscious darkness. Another is plausible sophistry, entertaining the delusion that because there is not determined willfulness in wrong we are less responsible and less to be condemned. A complacent ignorance is the softly gliding stream which flows onward to the rapids.—W. H. Jellie.

EVENING SERVICE

Theme: Profitless Mirth.

TEXT: "For as the crackling of thorns under a pot, so is the laughter of a fool." Eccles. 7:6.

INTRODUCTORY: In Eastern countries where fuel is scarce every combustible shrub, brush and bramble is seized upon for necessary cooking fires. I have seen grass twisted in knots and stalks cut in bits so used. Of course the blaze is bright, hot, but soon extinct. In cooking a meal the fire must be fed constantly. So is worldly mirth "as the crackling of thorns under a pot."

I. It is noisy. It is nosier than if there were more in it—more reality, more substance. It is crackling, noisy, showy, even boisterous, with the sound and appearance of great hilarity and enjoyment.

II. Yes, noisy, but short-lived. The point of comparison in the text is the loud crackling and short duration of the fire, with small results. Flimsy materials are quickly kindled. They blaze up for a time with much noise and show, but soon die away. That is the picture of the pleasures of a fool. Even if there were enjoyment in it physical limits are put on all gay pleasures. There comes a time of life when such frolic becomes as difficult as it is disgraceful. There is not in society a more ridiculous object, even in its own circle, than a tottering, antiquated, bedizened devotee of fashion.

III. And such mirth is unintelligent. "The old fool!" We have already intimated that this is so. Besides it is sure that grief will come and shorten the amusement. Losses and reverses will shorten it. Health is sure to fail. The pursuit of worldly frolic is unintelligent.

IV. And this implies the final fact that it is unprofitable. It does not pay. If there were nothing else such pleasure must be foolish, short-lived, and unprofitable because at best it cannot be extended to judgment and eternity. We are making no criticism of mirth. Christianity has higher joys. "Godliness is profitable in all things, having promise of the life that now is and of that which is to come."—H.

Suggested Texts and Themes

Temperance and Triumph: "Every man that striveth for the mastery is temperate in all things." I Cor. 9:25.

The Challenge of Discontent: "I count not myself to have apprehended: but. . . . I press on." Phil. 3:13, 14.

The Test of the Trivial: "He that is faithful in a very little is faithful also in much." Luke 16:10 (A.S.V.).

The Testimony of the Face: "The shew of their countenance doth witness against them." Isa. 3:9.

Harvest Begun: "Now is Christ risen from the dead . . . the first fruits of them that slept." I Cor. 15:20.

MIDWEEK FELLOWSHIP MEETING TOPIC

(Church Night or Suggested Sermon Subject)

Theme: A Study of Silence.

TEXT: "A time to keep silence." Eccles. 3:7.

The writer of Ecclesiastes is declaring that to everything there is a season. In this verse he says that there is a time to keep silence. Many writers have extolled silence. Says Carlyle, "Silence is more eloquent than words." Kossuth says, "The unspoken word never does harm." Lord Beaconsfield stated, "There is no diplomacy like silence." Said George Herbert, "Speak fitly, or be silent wisely." Let us note several kinds of silences.

I. There is the silence of emotional fullness. Great emotions choke utterance. This is true of painful emotions. Those of sorrow, surprise, remorse, despair may so rush upon one as to prevent speech. And great joyful emotions often act in the same way. The returning prodigal son was so full of joyous feelings with his father's welcome that he could not speak.

II. There is the silence also of Christian resignation. It indicates a loving and joyful acquiescence in the will of our all-wise and all-loving heavenly Father. The Psalmist said, "I was dumb, I opened not my mouth; because thou didst it." Such silence reveals highest wisdom and highest faith in God.

III. Again there is the silence of deep self-respect. This was the silence Christ displayed before his judges. It was the silence of moral majesty. The same at times may wisely be shown by his followers.—B. I.

CHRISTIAN ENDEAVOR SOCIETY TOPIC

Aug. 10. Eternal Influences: You Can Read, Can't You? Acts 8:26-35; Prov. 4:5-13.

SUNDAY SCHOOL LESSON

Aug. 10. The Beginning of the Kingdom. I Sam. 9:1, 2; 10:24-27; 13:5-7, 19-21.

MEMORY SELECTION: "The Lord will not forsake his people for his great name's sake: because it hath pleased the Lord to make you his people." I Sam. 12:22.

Saul was chosen for a great work. He began well, strong in body and in spirit. Later he forgot to depend upon God for guidance. He had some great problems, attacks by surrounding nations, lack of weapons for warfare, and lack of a unified and centralized government. But he was a great leader and gifted with military prowess. Let us think about and ask what may be the required qualities of a good leader today.

SUNDAY: AUGUST SEVENTEENTH

MORNING SERVICE

Theme: Authority.

SUGGESTED SCRIPTURE READING: Matt. 7:1-29.

SELECTED HYMNS: "O Christ, who didst our tasks fulfill."—L. F. Benson. "Thou art the Way: to thee alone."—G. W. Doane. "O Light, whose beams illumine all."—E. H. Plumptre. "Father of all, to thee."—J. Julian. "Lord, speak to me, that I may speak."—F. R. Havergal.

CALL TO WORSHIP: "They that wait upon the Lord shall renew their strength; they shall mount up with wings as eagles; they shall run, and not be weary; and they shall walk, and not faint."

INVOCATION PRAYER: It is a great privilege, O God, our Father, to have knowledge of the Gospel of Jesus Christ. It is in the name of Christ and by the power of the Gospel that we worship thee today, and bind ourselves together in praise and aspiration and prayer. We are not worthy of the Gospel—that Christ should have humbled himself, lived a lowly life of service, endured the cross for us. This causes us to bow in humility. We can only thank thee for him, share our lives with him as he shared with us, let him be our ideal and example, accept him as our Saviour and follow him as our Lord. Our Father thou has shown us thy greatness, and we humble ourselves before thy power. Thou hast shown us thy love, and we rise with joy in response to the revelation of thy goodness. Thou hast taught us thy holy law; forgive us that we have broken thy commandments. Lord, have mercy upon us, and incline our hearts to keep thy law. Amen.

Theme: Authority.

TEXT: "He taught them as one having authority." Matt. 7:29.

INTRODUCTORY: The verdict of history on any event is usually more correct than the contemporary view. Time is also needed fully to assess the importance of the life of a man. It is always interesting to ascertain what people thought of men during their lifetime. Of Christ it was said, "He taught them as one having authority."

I. By all means let us accept the verdict of authorities (we shall be unwise not to), and in so doing we pay them the compliment of acknowledging their hard work and hard thinking, but remember that we accept what they say on faith because most of us lack the means and the ability to verify their statements. We believe, for example, that the sun is about 93,000,000 miles away from the earth, not because we have proved it but because we were taught it at school. I want to make a plea for honesty in the matter of religion and to urge you to be as ready to accept an authoritative statement about it as you are about other things.

II. When I wanted to learn to play the piano I went to a music teacher, to someone who knew something about it, and I accepted what he told me. The fact that I cannot now play the piano doesn't mean there is nothing in music and that my teacher didn't know what he was talking about. It is due to the fact that I didn't put into practice what he told me. In religion, however, so many feel that they know all about it and therefore do not need the guidance and advice of experts. Moreover, some will accept the statement of anybody who has made a name for himself in another sphere but who is unqualified to speak about religion. Someone has said, "When I want to know about the age of the earth I go to a geologist; when I want information about the motion of the planets I go to an astronomer. When I want to know about God I go to the pure in heart."

III. As we accept by faith the findings of science, let us also accept by faith the findings of religion. In this age of specialists let us go to the authorities in religion as in other things. First and foremost let us go to the Bible, especially to the New Testament, and in particular to the words of Christ, who spoke as one having authority because he was authority, coming from God as a supreme revelation of God.

Let us, then, observe what faith means and what faith does to those around us who are Christians and then let us test our findings by our own experience. Until we have done this let us at least reserve our judgment for only as we accept Christ and his teaching and test them by experience have we a right to speak about God, Redemption, forgiveness of sins; only then have we a right to judge of the reality of spiritual things. Science, using the methods of a science, cannot help us here, but when a man says from the depth of his own personal experience, "I know in whom I have believed," the evidence of his life is worthy of consideration.

IV. If a man doesn't believe there is beauty in a sunset sky or music in a rippling brook, you cannot prove it to him. If he says he is experiencing the emotion of love, sympathy, benevolence, hatred, anger or fear, you cannot take him into a laboratory and prove it. Do not try to use the scientific method in realms which are outside its scope. As St. Bernard said, "To reason about things which are beyond reason is unreasonable." In religion, experience is the only test and the only man whose testimony counts is the religious man's. "He taught them as one having authority." If men were as ready to accept the utterances of the saints as they are to accept the statements of the scientist, this would be a better place and mankind happier.—W. E. B.

Theme Prayer: O God, we thank thee that so much of thy will has been revealed for and to us in Jesus Christ. We would know more of him and his commands. Help us, we pray, to repledge our obedience to him. Give us courage and unselfishness to keep his commandments. In his own name we ask it. Amen.

Offertory Sentence: "God so loved the world, that he gave his only begotten Son, that whosoever believeth in him should not perish, but have everlasting life."

Offertory Prayer: With heartfelt thanksgiving, our Father, do we make our offering in Christ's name. Unto all the holy uses of thy Church may it be applied, and grant that it may abound unto all comfort, all peace, all strength, and all salvation unto those for whom it is given and those who give it, for thy Son's sake. Amen.

Illustrative Material

SEED THOUGHTS, HOMILETIC AND EXPOSITORY. Christ knows. He is the authority for the soul.—W. P. Philpot.

Christ's Authority as Teacher: I. The nature of this authority. It was the authority of truth. II. It arose from the purity of his character. It was the authority of a good life. III. It was the authority of heaven. God confirmed what he said.—F. W. P. G.

Christ As Preacher: I. He was a model as to the matter of his preaching. 1. He taught himself. He had nothing higher to present than himself. 2. He had nothing that the world required more than himself. II. He was a model as to the manner of his teaching and preaching, which was unconventional. 1. His positiveness. 2. His self-assurance. 3. His naturalness. 4. His freshness. 5. His suggestiveness. 6. His definiteness. 7. His tenderness. 8. His faithfulness. 9. His consistency. 10. His devoutness.—D. T.

Choice Illustrations on the Theme

CHRIST'S MAGIC POWER. In the earliest Christian art, that of the Catacombs, Christ is represented as the Greek Orpheus, with the lyre in his hand, drawing everything to him by his magic spell. These early Christians, standing near to the Greek civilization, chose this out of all the figures of Greek mythology to express their ideas of the Lord whom they loved and worshiped. Orpheus was the greatest of all musicians. So wonderfully did he play that when his fingers touched the instrument the beasts of the field drew near and the birds were arrested in their flight, and even the things of nature gathered spellbound around him.

It was thus that the early Christians thought of Christ. They felt his drawing power, the strange spell which he had over everything. Possessed in their hearts, he transfigured nature, but most of all he transfigured them. He banished by his music the low and bestial instincts which raged within them, and made the most coarse and intractable gentle and obedient.—J. Burns.

THE AUTHORITY OF CHRIST. Let us ask how Christ's authority was asserted and claimed? By the tone of his teaching; by his ministerial acts as, for example, the cleansing of the temple; by his miracles as, for example, when he commanded the unclean spirits and they obeyed him. Upon what was his authority based? It was not based upon force, or craft, or popular regard, but upon right and upon conscience. His words are authoritative because they are true, his commands because they are righteous. He wields the personal authority of love. In all his authority is Divine, as he is. His authority—nature knew it, Satan confessed it, angels recognized it, men felt it. The message of heaven is, "In the name of Jesus every knee shall bow."—J. R. Thompson.

CHRIST AUTHORITY IN RELIGION. Jesus is our authority in religion. About all the things of which he spoke he spoke truly. The world has taken him at his word, in all that he said about goodness, greatness, character, religious service, the Fatherhood of God and the brotherhood of man. We are only striving to grow up to his levels. Not one word he said is antiquated; not one truth is outgrown; not one promise has failed. Trusting him and proving him right in all beside, shall I not trust him in this question of eternal life?

CHRIST THE EXALTED ONE. Jesus had no earthly possessions. At his birth he borrowed a manger from the beasts of the field; he preached a sermon in a borrowed boat; he rode into Jerusalem on a borrowed beast; he ate his last supper with his disciples in a borrowed room; and he was buried in a borrowed grave. Yet he stands the living, risen Son of God, stripped of all earthly possessions, saying, "All authority has been given unto me in heaven and on earth."

EVENING SERVICE

Theme: "Listeners Hear No Good of Themselves."

TEXT: "Take no heed unto all words that are spoken; lest thou hear thy servant curse thee." Eccles. 7:21.

INTRODUCTORY: It is an old saying, "Listeners hear no good of themselves." The writer of Ecclesiastes intimates that the wise man who remembers his own mistakes and offenses will judge leniently of others. Indifference to idle praise or idle blame well becomes the possessor of wisdom. It certainly is true that idle curiosity to know what others think or say of us is likely to be a source of much mortification. The servant who waits on us and from whom we expect special reverence would probably, if we could hear him without his knowledge, say much about us that would surprise and mortify us. Of course then the conclusion is that we ought not to be too eager to hear our character analyzed and discussed. There may be a good deal in the old saying, "Where ignorance is bliss 'tis folly to be wise." "Listeners are likely to hear no good of themselves."

I. This does not imply that we should pay no attention to what others think and say about us. "A good name is rather to be chosen than great riches, and loving favor rather than silver and gold." What a force public opinion is! We cannot see it, nor touch it; and yet it is a great factor is shaping the character and actions alike of men and nations. Public opinion may be utterly wrong. Then it is our duty to oppose it at any cost. But some of us might well pay a little more heed than we do to the tone of thought and feeling around us. If one sees that his acts and life are giving pain to others, that he is a stumbling block to his neighbors, even though it only be to those whom he would consider weaker brethren, if he go on his way recklessly regardless of what men may say or think, surely he will not be able to free himself of guilt. By such thoughtlessness we are likely to harden, irritate or mislead our fellows. This verse does not say that we are to pay no attention to what others think or say of us.

II. But it does say that we should not be too curious to know what other people think of us. We are all one family closely united, and at every point we are hurting or helping one another. There are many whose lives are darkened for a whole day because someone has said a severe word about them and the report of it has reached their ears. It is foolish to make too much of the world's opinion; for think how much idle gossip is floating about everywhere. He is a wise man who is not anxious to hear too much.

III. While this is true, there is one thing sure, that we should always be anxious to know God's opinion of us and to have his approval. One may say, "I do not mind so much what men say about me; but, oh, that I knew God's opinion of me!" It is easy to know. Hear what Jesus said to his disciples the night before his crucifixion; "For the Father himself loveth you, because ye have loved me." Do you love Christ? Then you are loved of God.—W. P.

Suggested Texts and Themes

The Master Musician: "Glory to God in the highest, and on earth peace." Luke 2:14.

The Competent Guide: "Lord, to whom shall we go? thou hast the words of eternal life." John 6:68.

The Path-maker: "No man cometh unto the Father, but by me." John 14:6.

The Cultivation of Meditative Piety: "Isaac went out to meditate in the field." Gen. 24:63 (see also Ps. 1:2 and 143:5).

An Immediate Decision: "Now if ye will deal kindly and truly with my master, tell me," etc. Gen. 24:49, 50.

MIDWEEK FELLOWSHIP MEETING TOPIC

(Church Night or Suggested Sermon Subject)

Theme: The Insatiableness of Desire.

TEXT: "All the labour of man is for his mouth, and yet the appetite is not filled." Eccles. 6:7.

"All the labour of man is for his mouth," that is, for self-preservation and enjoyment, eating and drinking being taken as a type of the proper use of earthly blessings. The sentiment here is general and does not refer to any particular person. Such appetite is never satisfied with what it has but is always crying for more.

I. The appetite is indeed an imperious master. "All the labour of man is for his mouth." However varied a man's works may be they all have this end in common, to appease the hunger of his ambition. This appetite grows by what it feeds on and so never cries "Enough!"

II. This insatiable desire affects the characters of us all. Intellectual gifts do not argue the absence of it. Material poverty does not guarantee its absence.

III. Insatiable desire disappoints the hopes of all "Yet the appetite is not filled." Such desire often misses enjoyments that are within its reach through grasping after those that are beyond its power. There is danger in self-indulgence. There is difficulty in keeping the lower nature in subjection.—P. C.

CHRISTIAN ENDEAVOR SOCIETY TOPIC

Aug. 17. Christian Virtues: "Thy Neighbor As Thyself." Luke 10:25-37.

SUNDAY SCHOOL LESSON

Aug. 17. The Tragedy of Saul. I Sam. 15:17-22; 18:6-9; 31:3, 4.

MEMORY SELECTION: "To obey is better than sacrifice, and to hearken than the fat of rams." I Sam. 15:22.

Here was a king who failed. Why did he fail? Note his anger and jealousy toward David. Note his loss of trust in Samuel as God's spokesman and in God himself. See also his growing fear of his own position. He was moved by pride, love of applause, impatience. Leaders of today will fail also if they allow the weaknesses which marred the life of Saul.

SUNDAY: AUGUST TWENTY-FOURTH

MORNING SERVICE

Theme: The Writer's Inkhorn.

SUGGESTED SCRIPTURE READING: Rev. 1:10-20, 21; 1-7.

SELECTED HYMNS: "Lamp of our feet, whereby we trace."—B. Barton. "The Spirit breathes upon the Word."—W. Cowper. "Father of mercies, in thy Word."—A. Steele. "How precious is the book Divine."—J. Faucett. "God in the gospel of his Son."—B. Beddome.

CALL TO WORSHIP: "As the hart panteth after the water brooks, so panteth my soul after thee, O God. My soul thirsteth for God, for the living God."

INVOCATION PRAYER: O Lord! Our gracious Father, we pray for thy blessing to rest upon us in our worship this morning. Guide us, we pray thee, when we try to meditate together upon thy holy will. And let the word of thy grace run and be glorified among us, and all our hearts and minds be affected and hallowed by the truth as it is in Jesus. Thou who hast promised to be present with thy people, and to grant their requests in the name of thy well-beloved Son, regard us, we humbly beseech thee, with thy favor; and for the sake of him who is our only Saviour and Mediator with thee fulfill thy promise on our behalf, that our thoughts being lifted up, and our desires drawn forth unto thee, we may render unto thee acceptable worship; through Jesus Christ our Lord. Amen.

Theme: The Writer's Inkhorn.

TEXT: "One man among them was clothed with linen, with a writer's inkhorn by his side." Ezek. 9:2.

INTRODUCTORY: No one ever had such divine dreams as Ezekiel. In a vision he had seen wrathful angels, destroying angels each with a sword, but in this text he sees a merciful angel with an inkhorn. The receptacle for the ink in olden time was made out of the horn of a cow, or a ram, or a roebuck, as now it is made out of metal or glass, and was therefore called the inkhorn, as now we say inkstand. Men speak of the power of the sword, of wealth, of office, of social influence. Today let us think of the power for good or evil in the inkstand.

You mistake, says someone, it is the pen that has the power. No, my friend, what is the influence of a dry pen? It is the liquid which the pen dips out of the inkstand that does the work.

I. First we mention that which is purely domestic. The inkstand is in every household. It awaits the opportunity to express affection or condolence or advice. Father uses it; mother uses it; the sons and daughters use it. It tells the home news; it announces the marriage, the birth, the departure, the accident, the last sickness, the death.

That home inkstand, what a mission it has already executed, and what other missions it will yet fulfill!

II. Furthermore, the inkstand of the businessman has its mission. Between now and the hour of your demise, O commercial man, O professional man, there will not be a day when you cannot dip from the inkhorn a message that will influence temporal and eternal destiny. There is a rash young man running into wild speculation, and with as much ink as you can put on the pen at one time you may save him from the Niagara rapids of a ruined life. On the next street there is a young man started in business, who through lack of patronage, or mistake in purchase of goods, or want of adaptation, is on the brink of collapse. One line of ink from your pen will save him from being an underling all his life and start him on a career of success.

III. But especially great are the responsibilities of the author's inkhorn. When a bad book is printed you do well to blame the publisher, but most of all blame the author. The malaria rose from his inkstand. The poison that caused the moral or spiritual death dropped in the fluid from the point of his pen. But blessed be God for the author's inkhorn in ten thousand studies which are dedicated to pure intelligence, highest inspiration, the grandest purpose. They are the inkstands out of which will be dipped the redemption of the world. The destroying angels with their swords seen in Ezekiel's vision will be finally overcome by the merciful angel with the writer's inkhorn.—T. D. T.

THEME PRAYER: Our Father in heaven, we thank thee for thy holy Word which is contained in the Scriptures. We bless thee that there the Word became flesh and dwelt among men. So may thy Light, thy Truth, thy Power dwell in us as we find thee and our own highest self in the sacred page. Bless all worthy writings and all true and noble writers. May truth abound everywhere. We ask in the name of Christ. Amen.

OFFERTORY SENTENCE: "Honour the Lord with thy substance, and with the firstfruits of all thine increase: so shall thy barns be filled with plenty, and thy presses shall burst out with new wine."

OFFERTORY PRAYER: For the wonder of the world and the beauty of the earth, for the discoveries of science and the treasures of art, for the power of music and the wealth of literature, for all work as a means of grace and of growth we would give thee hearty thanks this morning as we bring these offerings for thy cause. Amen.

Illustrative Material

SEED THOUGHTS, HOMILETIC AND EXPOSITORY. "Look, then, into thine heart and write!"—Longfellow.

"And choose an author as you choose a friend."—Wentworth Dillon.

"There are authors in whose hand the pen becomes a magic wand: but they are few."—Lady Montagu.

"The pen is the tongue of the hand; a silent utterer of words for the eye."—Henry Ward Beecher.

"To write well is to think well, to feel well, and to render well; it is to possess at once intellect, soul, and taste."—Buffon.

Choice Illustrations on the Theme

GOLDEN RULE IN LITERATURE. A resident of Utica, New York, realizes that a newsdealer has his own responsibilities. He declines to handle anything that is not up to his standard. Sometimes, he said, some magazines come through from his wholesale dealer that he cannot approve. These unrequested periodicals he at once wraps up and returns. Said he to a Utica editor: "I will not sell to anyone else's daughter something that I will not let my own daughter read." That's the Golden Rule in action. "Love worketh no ill to his neighbor."—W. J. Hart, D. D.

EMBALMED IN BOOKS. The great and good do not die even in this world. Embalmed in books, their spirits walk abroad. The book is a living voice. It is an intellect to which one still listens. —Samuel Smiles.

HONEST WRITING. As for my labors, if they can but wear one impertinence out of human life, destroy a single vice or give a morning's cheerfulness to an honest mind—in short, if the world can be but one virtue the better, or in any degree less vicious, or receive from them the smallest addition to their innocent diversions—I shall not think my pains, or indeed my life, to have been spent in vain.—Steele.

ARTIFICIAL LEARNING. The picture of some of those wise fools, spoken of in Matthew 11:25, has perhaps never been sketched with more telling irony than by James M. Barrie in his play, *The Admirable Crichton*. The characters are a family of society people and their butler wrecked on a desert island. They are possessed of an impressive variety of sophisticated learning and skill. They know Burke's *Peerage* by heart. They have complete mastery of the technique of auction bridge. In the knowledge of good form for all occasions, a court reception to a hunt, they are letter perfect. Yet they would have speedily starved to death had it not been for the butler. He alone had the knowledge of the common, elementary processes of sustaining life. Their crazy jumble of artificial learning had about as much connection with elementary human needs as if they had lived in the moon.—H. E. Luccock.

LEARNING BY DOING. A Korean Christian repeated the Sermon on the Mount without a mistake, and the missionary who heard it said it would do little good unless he practiced it. Whereupon a smile broke over his face as he said, "Why, pastor, that's just how I learned it. I am only a stupid farmer and could not remember it, so I learned one verse at a time and then went out and practiced it on my neighbors until I had the whole sermon bit by bit.—*Daily Bible*.

EVENING SERVICE

Theme: The Unsatisfied Eye.

TEXT: "The eye is not satisfied with seeing." Eccles. 1:8.

INTRODUCTORY: This was a common proverb. Thomas à Kempis applies it thus, "Endeavor, therefore, to withdraw thy heart from the love of visible things and to transfer thyself to the invisible." This is about the same as Paul's statement, "The things which are seen are temporal; but the things which are not seen are eternal," II Cor. 4:18.

I. Consider first the wonder of the eye itself. In its chambers of imagery are flung the pictures of the universe, the aspects of nature, the shapes of art, the symbols of knowledge, the faces of love. It is a magic glass both telescope and microscope, viewing an insect's wing or taking in the expanse of heaven, sentinel of the passions, signal of the conscious soul. It is kindled by a light within more glorious than light without, and never satisfied with seeing.

II. This suggests the mysterious power behind the eye. The eye that is not satisfied with seeing is the spirit within. The mind of man is the eye of man. Atoms do not see; it is the man that sees. Man has a body but is a soul. If man were only mortal he would be satisfied with seeing.

III. Let the eye of the soul be educated if one would detect the true significance of life. Then will he discern the real blessedness of every joy, the right look of every affliction, and realize the presence of God and the value of spiritual things. What we really need is not more things, but better sight. It is the eye of the soul we must constantly rely upon.—E. H. C.

Theme: The Pool and the Conduit (Additional).

TEXT: "He made a pool, and a conduit, and brought water into the city." II Kings 20:20.

INTRODUCTORY: No one who has visited Palestine and knows anything of its climate and geography will fail to realize the vital importance of its water supply. In a land of very few rivers, where drought lasts for several months of the year, no boon is greater than the discovery of a deep unfailing well or a reservoir built to conserve water.

Thus, I think it can stand as a symbol, a parable of what the Church of Christ is in the world and our relation to the Church.

I. I like to think of the Church as a reservoir, fed continuously from the springs of God; a reservoir into which has flowed all the best of the ages in faith and knowledge, in righteousness and truth, in holy endeavor and aspiration.

No wonder men in all ages have turned their eyes with longing to the Church, believing that they could find in that reservoir water to quench their thirst. The Psalmist expressed this longing in language of unforgettable beauty: "As the hart panteth after the water brooks, so panteth my soul after thee, O God. My soul thirsteth for God, for the living God: when shall I come and appear before God?" And there is no doubt this thirsty traveler, when he entered the sanctuary, found the refreshment and experienced the renewal he sought, as men have done ever since in all parts of the world.

II. But this water of life must be brought into the city, into our homes, into our business relationships, into the council chamber, into every interest and activity of human life. Hezekiah not only built a "reservoir" on the Judean Hills outside Jerusalem. He made a conduit to bring water into the city.

And that is a picture—a parable—of what God is calling us to do today.

What does it mean? It means that each one of us must be a channel through which God's grace is ever flowing, bringing the refreshing water of life into the dry and thirsty places of human habitation; it means that each one of us in his own way and in his own sphere must be a channel of purity to cleanse all that we know to be foul and unclean: it means that through us is ever coursing the energizing, redeeming power of God's Spirit—bringing Christ's values to bear upon every aspect and problem of life until "the wilderness and the solitary place shall be glad for them; and the desert shall rejoice, and blossom as the rose." We cannot remind ourselves too often and too seriously that the Christian life must function in this way. It must be open at both ends, filled in order to flow, purified in order to purify, quickened in order to quicken, enriched in order to make rich.

III. Whatever goodness there is in the world, whatever improvement we have seen in outlook and practice—whatever reform, whatever progress has been made in social life and economic conditions, it can all be traced back to the influence and activity of certain individuals whose lives were channels of God's truth—mediums through which the "water of life" flowed to bring refreshment, joy and peace into the city.

No, without us, we who are God's appointed channel, the pure water of life will not reach the city.—R. G. A.

Suggested Texts and Themes

The Secret of Happiness: "It is more blessed to give than to receive." Acts 20:35.

Daily Diligence: "Exhort one another daily." Heb. 3:13.

Lovers and teachers: "A lover of good. Teachers of that which is good." Titus 1:8; 2:3 (A.S.V.).

Culture and Crop: "It was planted in a good soil by great waters, that it might bring forth branches, and that it might bear fruit, that it might be a goodly vine. Ezek. 17:8.

MIDWEEK FELLOWSHIP MEETING TOPIC

(Church Night or Suggested Sermon Subject)

Theme: The Changing and the Abiding.

TEXT: "All the rivers run into the sea; yet the sea is not full; unto the place from whence the rivers come, thither they return again." Eccles. 1:7.

No particular sea is intended, though some have fancied that the peculiarities of the Dead Sea gave occasion for the thought. But as a statement of fact the text is correct. There is suggested by this figure both change and permanence.

I. The changing. The face of nature changes. The handiwork of man changes. See prostrate palaces, fallen temples, buried cities. And great historical characters and people have passed. Science too is working miracles of change and invention.

II. The abiding. Yes, there is change; but many things remain. Such features of human life as birth, labor, sorrow, care, struggle, death; love, pleasure, success, honor, these remain. We still have with us also the false, the cruel, the licentious, and many other evils. How long are they to remain? But we still have the spiritual element, the supernatural, the Divine. And we have, blessed be God, the truth of Jesus Christ. Heaven and earth may pass away, but his words "will not pass away." They are with us still. And they will remain, and grow to enlighten our ignorance, cheer our sorrow, conquer our sin, light up our eternity, and enrich us with the blessings that are beyond all compute.—P. C.

CHRISTIAN ENDEAVOR SOCIETY TOPIC

Aug. 24: Christian Virtues: "Humbly with Thy God." Micah 6:8; Mark 9:33-37.

SUNDAY SCHOOL LESSON

Aug. 24. David Becomes King. I Sam. 8:1-5, 14-16; 22:1, 2; II Sam. 5:1-5.

MEMORY SELECTION: "Man looketh on the outward appearance, but the Lord looketh on the heart." I Sam. 16:7.

Here is the story of a shepherd boy who grew up in Bethlehem and became a dependable and greathearted king and leader of the people of Israel. He grew up on a farm, was kind, courageous, and joyful in spirit. He was industrious, resourceful, free from the spirit of revenge, understanding of others and spiritually-minded. It may well be noted that he used every opportunity to prepare himself for the work to which he was called.

SUNDAY: AUGUST THIRTY-FIRST

MORNING SERVICE

Theme: Life's Three Dimensions (Labor Day).

SUGGESTED SCRIPTURE READING: Rom. 12:1.

Selected Hymns: "O brother man, fold to thy heart."—J. G. Whittier. "When thy heart with joy o'erflowing." —T. C. Williams. "I thank thee, Lord, for strength of arm."—Robert Davis. "Jesus, thou divine companion."—Henry van Dyke. "We thank thee, Lord, thy paths of service."—C. W. Laufer.

CALL TO WORSHIP: "Who shall ascend into the hill of the Lord, and who shall stand in his holy place? He that hath clean hands, and a pure heart, he that walketh uprightly and doeth righteousness. He shall receive the blessing from the Lord, and righteousness from the God of his salvation."

INVOCATION PRAYER: As this anniversary of honor to labor begins we would lift up our eyes unto the hills and remember that thou, our Father, workest even until now. Thou art not a God of idleness, but the Great Comrade of all men and women who toil for honest ends and noble causes. Help us to do our work day by day. Help us to preserve our ideals, and keep our human contacts Christlike and unembittered. Reveal to us day by day some new fragment of thy truth. Take what we have tried to do and build it into thy kingdom in mystic fellowship with all other eager-hearted men and women who seek to be partners in creative toil and sharers in the joy and labor of our Lord. Bless us each and all together as we worship in thy house this day. We ask all in the name of Christ, our Saviour. Amen.

Theme: Life's Three Dimensions (Labor Day).

TEXT: "Not slothful in business; fervent in spirit; serving the Lord." Rom. 12:11.

INTRODUCTORY: In this message Paul charges us to be diligent in business. If you were to ask a wise man to tell you what are the main objectives in a good man's existence, he might reply: "The overcoming of evil; the attainment of happiness; and the knowledge of God." None of these are possible without work.

I. It is a false interpretation of the Genesis story that makes labor the penalty for sin. Labor is the antidote for sin. God gave man work as a blessed means of overcoming temptation. Labor is God's safeguard against corruption everywhere in his creation. The angels have their appointed tasks, and every tiniest insect must work or starve. It is the running water that is fresh and pure. It is the man who works whose lips are clean and whose heart is pure.

II. The attainment of happiness is only possible through work. One of Watt's paintings is entitled, "When poverty comes in at the door, love flies out at the window." There is a shabby and neglected room with signs in it of former wealth and plenty. The secret of the change in the circumstances of the household is the laziness and slovenliness of the woman there. Instead of busying herself with her pressing household cares, she is caressing a pet dove. Her workbasket lies overturned on the floor, its contents scattered around. Through the open window one can see the untended roses returning to their wild condition through neglect. The woman is beautiful, but the home is a wreck because she is slothful. The artist pictures the wolf of poverty and hunger coming in at the door on one side while peace and happiness are going out at the other. There is no real happiness or contentment anywhere in this world apart from work. Those who seek it in idleness are doomed to certain disappointment.

III. Still further God reveals himself to us through work. That is a false conception of God that represents him as sitting in idle majesty above a world he once created, but which he has long since abandoned to its fate. His work is always going on. And Jesus worked. At the outset he said: "Wist ye not that I must be about my Father's business," and, "My Father worketh hitherto, and I work." To understand and know God, we must work also.

IV. In this work, which is an indispensable factor of our existence, we are bidden to be diligent. What is diligence? It is industry. It is earnestness, the habit of concentration. And diligence is haste. It is the realization that the opportunity is passing. But Paul's words mean more than this. He addresses himself to the man as he is a citizen of this world, and also to the man as he will be, a citizen of a world to come. He must maintain an equipoise between the two. How may this be accomplished? By blending worship with our work, whatever that work may be. Of what value is diligence if it is not used in the purpose for which it was intended? Serving God has four parts. It is a belief. It is a profession. It is worship, and it is obedience to his will, and each one of these may be a part of every conscious act we perform. Would you make the most of life that has been given you? Be diligent in business and use your diligence in serving the Lord. —S. N. H.

THEME PRAYER: Give thy blessing, we pray thee, our Father, to our daily work, that we may do it in faith heartily as to the Lord, and not as unto men. All our powers of body and mind are thine, and we would fain devote them to thy service. Sanctify them and all the work in which we engage. In Jesus' name. Amen.

OFFERTORY SENTENCE: "Now ye have consecrated yourselves unto the Lord, come near and bring sacrifices and thank offerings into the house of the Lord."

OFFERTORY PRAYER: Eternal God, who hast committed to us the swift and solemn trust of life, giving us all things that pertain unto godliness, keep us ever awake to the instant claims of thy holy will, so that nothing that is ours may be withheld from thee. Take now, we beseech thee, these gifts of our devotion, using them to the purposes of thy kingdom. In Christ's name we ask. Amen.

Illustrative Material

SEED THOUGHTS, HOMILETIC AND EXPOSITORY. Business and Religion: I. A life of active usefulness is obligatory upon all of us. II. There is nothing in the busiest life as such which is incompatible with the claims of personal religion. III. So far from the active duties of life presenting any barrier to our proficiency in personal religion, they are the very field in which its highest graces are to be exercised and its noblest triumphs are to be achieved.—D. M.

Business Life: I. It is a school of Christian Energy. II. It is a school of patience. III. It is a school for the attaining of knowledge. IV. It is a school of Christian integrity.—T. D. T.

Worship at Work: I. Here is the diligent hand. II. The fervent heart. III. The single eye.—J. L.

Choice Labor Day Illustrations

SAVED BY LABOR. We have known foolish parents who have permitted their children to grow up in little Edens, free from all care or any need of labor. The time comes by and by when they, too, are compelled to drive them out of their easy Paradise, and bar the gates behind them, that they may save their souls by the sweat of their brows.—S. N. Hutchison, D.D.

NOT HANDS BUT SOULS. A Great Christian leader protested against the use of the word "hands" as it is generally applied to those working in factories and elsewhere. He said it suggested a mean estimate of these people, as though they had neither heads nor hearts. He contrasted the estimate placed upon human beings in Scripture: "And the same day there were added unto them three thousand souls." We may be sure that there will be less soulless labor in the world when we learn to think of men and women in Christ's higher and worthier way. "How much better is a man than a sheep."—Archer Wallace.

THE DIGNITY OF SERVICE. "How prone man is," says a writer, "to want to be first! At the altar of Neptune every officer who had fought in the battle of Plataea wrote the names of those who had done the best service, and each one wrote his own name first and that of Themistocles second."

In his third epistle John describes Diotrephes as one "who loveth to have the pre-eminence." Once when Jesus's disciples asked, "Who is greatest in the kingdom of heaven?" Jesus called a little child and set him in the midst of them, and said, "Whosoever therefore shall humble himself as this little child, the same is greatest in the kingdom of heaven."

This humility which is exemplified in John's answer to the Jerusalem priests and Levites sent to him is also illustrated by the story of Professor Stuart of Andover. One of the students asked him one day where he could find someone to saw a load of wood he had bought.

"I am out for that kind of a job myself," said the professor. "I will saw it if I may."—Rev. John F. Cowan, D.D.

THE BLESSING OF TOIL

The toil of brain, or heart, or hand,
  Is man's appointed lot;
He who God's call can understand,
  Will work and murmur not.
Toil is no thorny crown of pain,
  Bound round man's brow for sin;
True souls, from it, all strength may
    gain,
  High manliness may win.
—Thomas W. Freckelton.

WORK

Work, work; well, what of it?
Do you wonder now why I love it?
Why I wouldn't want heaven on couches
    of ease,

Or be blown there by winds from the
tops of the trees,
But had rather reach port over tempest-
tossed seas,
And stand like a man if I do it.
—A. C. D. Noe.

PERSEVERANCE IN WORK

Diamonds are only chunks of coal
That stuck to their jobs, you see.
If they'd petered out, as most of us do,
Where would the diamond be?

It isn't the fact of making a start,
It's the sticking that counts, I'll say;
It's the fellow that knows not the mean-
ing of fail,
But hammers and hammers away.

Whenever you think you've come to the
end,
And you're beaten as bad as can be,
Remember the diamonds are chunks of
coal,
That stuck to their jobs, you see.
—Unidentified.

EVENING SERVICE

Theme: Words to a Worker (Labor Day).

TEXT: "Whatsoever thy hand findeth to do, do it with thy might," etc. Eccles. 9:10.

INTRODUCTORY: Man is the worker here described. This is a call to work as a prelude and accompaniment both of duty and enjoyment.

I. He is furnished with capacity to work. He has bodily organs, mental endowments, with speech and reason.

II. He is located in a place of work. The world is a vast workshop in which every creature is busily employed.

III. He is appointed to the destiny of work. Even in Eden man was set to dress the garden and keep it. After the fall beyond the garden's precincts he was commanded to till the ground and earn his bread by the sweat of his brow. He is still charged to be a worker, a Christian apostle even saying that "if any would not work, neither should he eat," II Thess. 3:10.

IV. And man is impelled by a desire to work. Under the compulsion of his own nature and of the constitution of the world man is constrained to work. He desires labor for his hands and exercise for his mind. The normal man is impelled by a desire for work.

V. Then this verse goes on to give advice to the worker. First, to earnestness. "Whatsoever thy hand findeth to do, do it with thy might." Do it with earnest energy. Half-hearted work wastes time, spoils the work, and demoralizes the worker. Be impelled by the great fact that the present is the day of opportunity. Do all your work under the sense of the great value of time. This life's work must be done in this life.—P.C.

Alternate Theme: What Do You Expect from Your Religion?

TEXT: "I will pray the Father, and he shall give you another Comforter, that he may abide with you for ever; even the Spirit of truth." John 14:16, 17.

INTRODUCTORY: What do you expect from your religion? What do you expect the church to do for you? What do you think religion has to offer you? What do you expect when you come to worship? How many people ever stop to ask themselves those questions? Yet we ask them about other things. If we go to the theater we expect to be amused. When we buy a book we expect to be informed. If we send our children to school we expect them to get equipped. But what exactly do you expect to derive either from your religion or from your worship?

I. Now we have a psychological law to the effect that we can only attend to something if we have something to attend with. If you had no curiosity nothing new or novel could attract your attention. If you had no pride you could be insulted or humiliated without resentment or any impulse to defend yourself. If you had no ambition others could pass you in the race of life without stirring any impulse to emulate them. And if you had no expectation regarding your worship, your religion or church, then nothing happens. You have cultivated nothing to attend with and consequently find nothing to attend to. On the other hand, you may receive nothing from your religion or worship because you are expecting the wrong thing. It is just as fatal to expect the wrong thing from your worship as to expect nothing. So I am back again at the question with which we started: What do you expect from your religion?

II. Now, the answer to that question can only be given by asking another: What did Christ promise? Let us know what Christ actually promised and we have the answer to our question.

Here in our text you will find all that he promised, all that we have a right to expect from our worship or our religion or from the church; and indeed all that we need for life. No less than four times in this address our Lord lays emphasis upon the Comforter, the Strengthener, the Spirit of Truth. These disciples wanted to know many things, but Christ refuses to reveal more. He will send the Comforter, the Spirit of Truth; he alone will enable them to meet all things. That is what you and I can expect from our worship and from our religion. Here is what we should expect from our church. Here is what we ought to expect and what we ought to be able to find in the atmosphere and life of the church. This is what we should expect religious education to do for our children, to give them the Spirit of Truth, to give them that strength that is needed for life. "I will pray the Father, and he shall give you another Comforter, that he may abide with you for ever; even the Spirit of truth."

III. Now if you think hastily you may feel that if this is all religion, worship and the church can offer, then it is far too little. I want to know, you tell me, what religion and worship can offer in a day such as the one through which we are passing with its moral, social and political contradictions. I want to know what meaning the tragedy of the last few years can have in the purposes of God. I want to know what religion can give youth that they may be able to avoid the sorrow, suffering and frustration of our generation.

Would it not have been better, you ask, had Christ given us a system of truth rather than the vague Spirit of Truth? Would it not have been more in keeping with an ordered universe had he laid down forms of worship in which all could have participated? Or had he laid down rules for a form of government that all could have obeyed? Why did he not give us a catalogue of moral and spiritual duties that we could have taught authoritatively to our children and in which they could not have been mistaken?

That is how our minds naturally tend to think when we stop to consider what Christ promises, or what our religion has to offer. It offers so little and we need so much. There is a strain of that in every one of us: we tend to be afraid of our freedom; we crave an infallible system.

IV. That God refuses to give. Not in some hard dry system of religious forms or ethical creed, but in the spirit of truth, the spirit of love, are religious gifts to be found.

That is what your religion and worship offer you: not a body of readymade rules that helps you to act automatically; not a system that will meet the contradictions and tragedies of life without remainder, but the spirit of truth in which every duty will be perceived and obeyed, every contradiction met and every tragedy overcome.

Have you received the spirit of truth? Where the Spirit of the Lord is, there is liberty—liberty from the debilitating conflicts, peace-breaking doubts, liberty to walk in the way, the truth and the life of him who promised that he would pray the Father and he could send another Comforter, even the Spirit of Truth.—J. G. M.

Suggested Labor Day Texts and Themes

The Dignity of Service: "I am among you as he that serveth." Luke 22:27.

No Work, No Food: "This we commanded you, that if any would not work, neither should he eat." II Thess. 3:10.

Divine Workers: "My Father worketh hitherto, and I work." John 5:17.

The Happy Laborer: "The sleep of a labouring man is sweet, whether he eat little or much," etc. Eccles. 5:12.

MIDWEEK FELLOWSHIP MEETING TOPIC

(Church Night or Suggested Sermon Subject)

Theme: God Planted a Garden.

TEXT: "And the Lord God planted a garden eastward in Eden." Gen. 2:8.

Here is a beginning of the description of the Garden of Eden.

I. "The Lord God planted a garden." In this garden provision was made for the happiness of man. 1. The garden was beautiful. 2. The garden was fruitful. 3. The garden was well watered.

II. "The Lord God planted a garden." In this garden provision was made for the daily occupation of man. 1. Work is the law of man's being. His work should be accepted as from God. This will dignify and inspire the worker. 2. The man who lets God put him to his trade is likely to be successful. 3. Work is the benediction of man's being. It makes him happy. Indolence is misery. Work is one of the truest blessings we have. It occupies our time. It keeps us from mischief. It supplies our temporal wants. In enriches society. It wins the approval of God.

III. "The Lord God planted a garden." And in this garden provision was made for the spiritual obedience of man. He was in best surroundings, under best spiritual influence and association. God gave command to obey. A penalty was annexed in case of disobedience. Sin entered the garden. The remedy for sin was graciously provided in a Garden. Since then we have another chance.—J. S. E.

CHRISTIAN ENDEAVOR SOCIETY TOPIC

Aug. 31. Giving Honest Measure. Luke 6:38; Luke 19:1-10.

SUNDAY SCHOOL LESSON

Aug. 31. The Reign of David. II Sam. 5:6-10; 8:13-18.

MEMORY SELECTION: "As for God, his way is perfect; the word of the Lord is tried: he is a buckler to all them that trust in him." II Sam. 22:31.

David was strong. He was kind. He was just. He showed these traits as a king. The passages chosen for this lesson show the great ability of David as a statesman in the establishment and ruling of his kingdom. An important thought for today is the need of wise and God-fearing statesmanship in all nations. David did earnestly desire to do God's will.

SUNDAY: SEPTEMBER SEVENTH

MORNING SERVICE

Theme: Lend a Hand.

SUGGESTED SCRIPTURE READING: II Cor. 6:1-18.

SELECTED HYMNS: "Ye servants of the Lord, each in his office wait." P. Doddridge. "Take my life and let it be."—F. R. Havergal. "Lead on, O King Eternal."—E. W. Shurtleff. "The Son of God goes forth to war."—R. Heber. "O Jesus I have promised."—J. E. Bode.

CALL TO WORSHIP: "Hear, O Lord, when I cry with my voice: have mercy also upon me, and answer me. When thou saidst, Seek ye my face; my heart said unto thee, Thy face, Lord, will I seek."

INVOCATION PRAYER: We assemble ourselves together this holy Sabbath morning, our Father, to seek thy face and favor. Prepare us in heart and mind for thy promised blessings. Lighten our spirits with the shining of the Sun of Righteousness, and help us this day to rest in thee and to serve thee in sincerity and in truth. Grant us, O Lord, our God, the vision of thyself that belongs to the pure in heart. Fill our hearts with so much of love and grace that evil thoughts and purposes shall find no room within us. May the love of Christ constrain us to purity and useful living day by day. May the temple of our hearts be holy. Keep us from falling into sin, our Father, and when we are in danger either through the device of men or the temptations that rise out of the evil desires of our own hearts, be thou near to protect and save us. We ask all in the name of Christ our Saviour. Amen.

Theme: Lend a Hand.

TEXT: "We then, as workers together with him, beseech you also that ye receive not the grace of God in vain." II Cor. 6:1.

INTRODUCTORY: We are living in an age when many appeals are being made. No one can escape hearing them, for seldom a day passes without an appeal being made for some good cause or other. What effect does the appeal have upon you? That will depend upon the way in which the appeal is put over. The Apostle Paul certainly knew the art of appealing. Think of his appeal to the Corinthians. I appeal to you as a worker together with God, do not receive the grace of God in vain.

I. What a high and holy privilege is conferred upon man. What dignity—that he should be called a worker together with God. And yet we do not seem to give much thought to this. Many do not count it a privilege. Sometimes we think the work we do is not of any great importance, that we or our work do not count for much in the great scheme of things, and so it is done halfheartedly, or perhaps it is not done at all. That is wrong. We do count far more than we think. We are workers together with God.

II. Our duty and privilege to lend a hand. This phrase was once used by a beautiful woman in prayer: "All that thou dost ask of us, Lord, is just that we lend thee a hand." Just to lend a hand in lowly yet beautiful ways is a very wonderful thing. And Christ today makes his appeal for workers, and yet more workers. "The harvest truly is great and the laborers are few." Will you lend a hand? Christ says: "I need help, your help. I need your time, talent and money. I need your love—the love that is ready to spend and be spent, in order to carry on my ministry in the world." Remember:

He has no hands but our hands
  To do His work to-day.
He has no feet but our feet
  To lead men in His way.
He has no voice but our voice
  To tell men how He died.
He has no help but our help
  To lead men to His side.

III. We are not sent into this world just for our own selfish ends. We are meant to lend a hand to a good deal that needs to be done. There are wrongs that cry to heaven to be righted. When Jesus was arrested in the Garden the soldiers bound his hands, and every time we refuse to respond to the promptings of the Holy Spirit of God to lend a helping hand, we, too, bind his hands.

We do not pretend to understand in all its fullness the mystery of the love of God in Christ on Calvary, but the wonder of that love never fails to make its appeal. Can I, can you, in the face of such love, refuse to lend a hand?—J. W. P.

THEME PRAYER: Take our hands, our Father, and let them move at the impulse of thy love. Be in our hearts that we may love thee and thy cause in the world. Be in our eyes that we may see the need. Be in our minds that we may comprehend the urgency of the needs; be in our feet that we may run upon thine errands, and in our hands that we may do thy work. In Jesus' name. Amen.

OFFERTORY SENTENCE: "I will offer to thee the sacrifice of thanksgiving, and will call upon the name of the lord."

OFFERTORY PRAYER: We would bring to thee, our Father, these our token gifts of gratitude for all thy mercies. Thou dost open thine hand and satisfy the wants of every living thing. Out of thy fullness have we all received. Wilt thou graciously accept these expressions of our thanks and use them for the good of others. We ask in Christ's name. Amen.

Illustrative Material

SEED THOUGHTS, HOMILETIC AND EXPOSITORY. The Dignity of Life: I. We are chosen to be fellow workers with God. A great honor. Partners. To share in forwarding the great work of God in the world. II. In what sense are we fellow workers with God? 1. As a farmer in the fields works with the elements. 2. As the mariner works with the wind. 3. As an ambassador not the king, but acting for him and reporting to him. III. The admonishment: "That ye receive not the graces of God in vain." "Grace" means favor. It also means the Gospel for the world. How may we receive it in vain? 1. By not believing it or in our mission. 2. By despising it. Failure to value it. 3. By neglecting it. By laziness, doing nothing about or with it. Or by being too busy, utterly failing to co-operate with God in his work. In either case we miss the dignity of life.—H.

Choice Illustrations on the Theme

WORKING TOGETHER WITH GOD. God calls us into the fellowship of his activities. Let us not underestimate the work he has given us to do. Stradivarius, the famous old maker of violins, did not. Whilst plying his calling he used to say:

When any master holds twixt hand and chin
A violin of mine, he will be glad
That Stradivari lived, made violins
And made them of the best. . . .
For while God gives them skill,
I give them instruments to play upon.
God using me to help Him. . . .
If my hand slacked I should rob God.
Leaving a blank behind instead of violins
He could not make Antonio Stradivari's violins without Antonio.

We are workers with God.

YOUR HANDS. In that delightful book *My Lady of the Chimney Corner,* in which A. Irvine tells the story of the most beautiful life he ever knew, the story of his own dear mother, in one passage he makes her say in her quaint way, "God takes a hand wherever he can find it, and just does whatever he likes with it. Sometimes he takes a bishop's and lays it on a child's head in benediction; then he takes the hand of a doctor to relieve pain, and the hand of a mother to guide her child, and sometimes he takes the hand of an old creature like me to give a bit of comfort to a neighbor. But they are all hands touched by his Spirit, and his Spirit is everywhere looking for hands to use."

Take my hands and let them move
At the impulse of thy love.

Dorcas' Needle

The Acts of the Apostles tells the story of a very homely person named Dorcas. It expressly says, "She was full of good works." She was not by any means a brilliant person. She had no outstanding gifts, but there was one thing she could do. She could use her hands. She knew how to knit and sew and cut out garments, and so she consecrated her gift to the Master. "A needle and thread were little enough, but to each were added four fingers and a thumb, and lovely things of far-reaching importance were done by her." She was clever at cutting out and making things. She wanted to help, and so all her spare moments were spent in planning and making garments for needy folk. One day the King shall say of Dorcas and all her followers: "I was ill-clad and you clothed me. Inasmuch as ye did it unto the least of these, my brethren, ye did it unto me."—Rev. J. W. Price.

CALL TO MISSIONS. The older of two men was once urging upon the younger the claim of Christian work in mission countries, and the latter answered with an excuse that had a familiar ring: "But I have never felt any compelling call to give my life in that way." "Are you sure that you are within calling distance?" was the disquieting reply. Some of us keep out of calling distance—intentionally so.

EVENING SERVICE

Theme: The Song of the Pilgrimage.

TEXT: "The Lord spake unto Moses, Gather the people together, and I will give them water! Then Israel sang this song, Spring up, O well; sing ye unto it." Num. 21:16, 17.

INTRODUCTORY: The people of Israel were on a pilgrimage, travelers in a wilderness journey. They came to need water. How many things we need on our human pilgrimage! "The Lord spake unto Moses, Gather the people together, and I will give them water." When they got it they sang a grateful song. It has been called, "The Song of the Pilgrimage."

I. Notice first that the water of this well was a promised supply. "The Lord spake unto Moses, Gather," etc. His promises to us, how great, how many, how meaningful!

II. The supply promised here was a Divine supply. "I will give thee water." How many the people, how numerous the flocks and herds! God alone could give supply, and he did. The supply of grace we need is a Divine supply, and suitable to our case. So was the water of the pilgrim well.

III. Observe, too, that it was not alone a suitable supply, but an abundant supply. "I will give them water," plenty for the need. Abundance of water! Abundance of grace for us all!

IV. But do not forget the song. These people had not been singing for years. They came together for the digging of this well, and now they sang this song: "Spring up, O well; sing ye unto it! 1. It was a faith song, a song of expectation. As they dug awhile the water did begin to spring. 2. It was a cheerful song, a grateful song, a unanimous song. 3. It was a prayer song. "Spring up, O well," was virtually a prayer to God that he would make the well spring up, only it was Faith's way of saying her prayer.

They began with a promise, but turned the promise into a song, and the song into a prayer. A good example for us. Also let us keep in mind that we are only pilgrims. The well was not the goal—a place to halt, but not to settle.—S.

Theme: The Ministry of Silence (Additional).

TEXT: "Be still, and know that I am God." Ps. 46:10.

INTRODUCTORY: There are some things which have a message for us, but which we can only hear when the noises of other things are hushed, or when we can concentrate on listening to them to the exclusion of other distracting noises.

In the rush and hustle of our modern life how often do we face up to ourselves resolutely and firmly?

That section of the universal Church known as the Society of Friends may be mistaken in some of its opinions and customs, but its piety is very manifest—it has the spirit of true religion. One of its doctrines is that of the "Inner Light." That "Inner Light" often evinces itself in a vocal manner becoming the "Inner Voice." In view of this we may be led to ask ourselves whether or not we are robbing ourselves of a wonderful spiritual opportunity just by refusing to sit quiet sometimes and think about life and its final meanings. There certainly is need for the quiet mood of meditation. "Be still, and know that I am God."

And how difficult it is to create this spirit of absorption in the world of reality within; how hard to withdraw into the inner world from the superficial interests which take up so much of our daily interest!

Some time ago I read a letter from a man who had been at a service conducted by a young man who had adopted a very unusual method of preaching and praying. This young man would conclude a paragraph of his sermon or prayer, and then pause for a few seconds before proceeding. It was not due to a hesitancy on his part, but it was done, as he explained to the congregation, so that they might think about what he was saying. The writer of the letter said that at first it was very disconcerting for the hearer, but when he had overcome the first reaction to this unusual procedure and gave his mind to what was being said, that it made all the difference to its effect upon him. We get so accustomed in worship to being carried along by the words and worship of another that we ourselves give very little of our own intelligent participation to it.

Yes: it is this state of inner quietness, of directed attention, which helps us to crystallize the transitory thought engendered into the faith which holds and keeps us in the midst of untoward experience. Faith goes deeper than belief, its roots are in the subconscious life of a man, and it has the power of bringing all man's latent power to the aid of his desires. Stillness opens the way into the reservoir of spiritual power. It brings us into contact with God through the resources of our own inner lives.

But this method is one that implies a humbling of oneself. To turn away, even for a short time, from such an attitude and face up to the questions of life within is a difficult matter, for it entails questioning our own accepted opinions and seeking to deliver ourselves from the mind-set which we have built up. Through such experiences as are thus possible to each one of us we discover our weaknesses, but also come to a knowledge of God.

We want this inner life to burst forth in all its glory; we want this desert of parched religious experience to blossom forth into the fragrant blooms of vitalizing faith, but how can we know and hear God within if all our attention is taken up with the activities of life to the exclusion of thought about life and seeking after God?

"Be still, and know that I am God."

MIDWEEK FELLOWSHIP MEETING TOPIC

(Church Night or Suggested Sermon Subject)

Theme: The Christian's Race.

TEXT: "So run, that you may obtain." I. Cor. 9:24.

This is a word addressed to Christians.

I. The Christian life is a race to be run. "So run." There is but one Divine course, the "way of life." We enter the course by faith and are kept in it by faith.

II. For this race preparation is necessary. 1. Enrollment. 2. Putting off unsuitable costume. 3. Laying aside every weight.

III. This race also implies certain self-denials and training. 1. Suitable diet. 2. Avoiding luxuries. 3. Rigid sobriety, temperance. 4. The bracing up of mind and resolution.

IV. For this race must be run with spirit and devoted resolve. 1. Looking to the goal. 2. In exercise of lively hope and joy. 3. With invincible faith and expectation carried on to the very end. "So run, that ye may obtain."—B.

Suggested Texts and Themes

Pray Ye: "Pray ye: Our Father which art in heaven, Hallowed be thy name." Matt. 6:9.

Love Ye: "Love ye your enemies, and do good, and lend, hoping for nothing again." Luke 6:35.

Do Ye: "Therefore all things whatsoever ye would that men should do to you, do ye even so to them." Matt. 7:12.

Fearless Service: "Might serve him without fear." Luke 1:74.

Ethics and Etiquette: "Why do thy

disciples transgress the tradition of the elders?" Matt. 15:2.

Only Weatherwise: "When it is evening, ye say, it will be fair weather." Matt. 16:2.

CHRISTIAN ENDEAVOR SOCIETY TOPIC

Sept. 7. I Go On Learning. II Tim. 2:15; Deut. 6:4-9.

BULLETIN BOARD SLOGANS FOR THE MONTH

By Earl Riney

We enjoy ourselves most in the work we do best.

A job is an intimate relationship between employee and his boss.

A teacher of any vital subject should be an authority.

Remember a child is at the mercy of those who teach him.

Here's hoping that the nation's labor pains will give birth to full production.

Economists believe the average family can be self-supporting.

The best things in your home are what money can never buy.

It often shows a fine command of language to say nothing.

For a man to live at his best he must live creatively.

The deadly enemy of a man's happiness is routine monotony.

SUNDAY SCHOOL LESSON

Sept. 7. A Humble and Greathearted Leader. II Sam. 12:1-7, 13-15; 18:32, 33; 24:24.

Memory Selection: "Create in me a clean heart, O God; and renew a right spirit within me." Ps. 51:10.

Through this lesson we may well seek to come to an appreciation of the great capacity of David for patient understanding, thoughtful sympathy, and for a generous forgiveness of those who had wronged him. His people were devoted to him. The lesson covers David's sin and repentance, his magnanimity toward Absolom, his greatheartedness, and his desire to offer no cheap sacrifice to God. The God who brought such great good out of David's life, with all its mistakes and sins, can do the same for us.

SUNDAY: SEPTEMBER FOURTEENTH

MORNING SERVICE

Theme: Forward—To What?

Suggested Scripture Reading: Ps. 122:1-9; Isa. 62:1-12.

Selected Hymns: "I love thy kingdom, Lord."—T. Dwight. "Glorious things of thee are spoken."—J. Newton. "Triumphant Zion, lift thy head."—P. Doddridge. "Soldiers of Christ, arise." —C. Wesley. "How beauteous are their feet."—I. Watts.

Call to Worship: "He that dwelleth in the secret place of the most High shall abide under the shadow of the Almighty. I will say of the Lord, He is my refuge and my fortress: my God; in him will I trust."

Invocation Prayer: Almighty and Eternal God, draw nigh unto us as we gather again with joy into thy sanctuary. For all the divers memories we bring with us from the past days and weeks, for sunshine and storm, for lake and forest, for sea and mountain, and for the benedictions of this glad season, we thank thee. Be graciously in our midst as we rejoice together. Let our joy be thy joy, and thy ways our ways. And so fulfill upon and within us the true and the good of all our yesterdays. So fill our hearts with thy grace that we shall have no hatred or bitterness toward anyone. Let our will be good will, our ways the ways of peace. Keep us diligent in friendliness, eager in creative work. And in the leavening of life by love grant us that victory which the world can neither give nor take away. To that end be with us as we share together the triumphant joy of him who said long ago: "Be of good cheer; I have overcome the world." In his name we pray. Amen.

Theme: Forward—To What?

TEXT: "Speak unto the children of Israel, that they go forward." Ex. 14:15.

INTRODUCTORY: The children of Israel had just left Egypt, their long years of bondage being ended. (Give circumstances, their fears, etc.) All God asks is that we give him a chance. To go forward bravely, relying on God, is to invite the miracle. Never were people more surprised.

In religion there can be no going back. The cry is always "Forward."

I. To what are we to go forward? To more knowledge. The first essential to any other progress is progress in knowledge, pressing into clearer and fuller knowledge of God and his revelations of himself. But let us not forget that Christianity is a life as well as a creed, and there are certain practical directions in which a forward movement seems to be called for. One is in relation to Christian character and the Christian standard of living. Forward, then, to higher life. No worthy character can be formed without a basis of belief. But, on the other hand, what is the good of a foundation if it is never built upon?

If we are to go forward to higher life we must practice the presence of God in worship, prayer and the study of his Word. The best way to convince the world of the truth and the worth of our religion is to live it.

II. Forward, too, to fuller service. We shall be known by what we have done more than by what we have said. I hope that, like the Apostles, our memorials will be our acts.

III. What are the hindrances to progress? The history of the children of Israel suggests three:

First, we shall not go forward if we look back. Jeremiah describes the people asking their way to Zion with their faces thitherward. "I will go anywhere," said Livingstone, "provided it is forward."

Secondly, another hindrance to progress is to go round instead of going forward. The Sunday service, hymn, prayer, sermon, the round of observances, no new victories, no new visions, no new hopes, no added strength, no fuller service. Day after day, week after week, year after year, the same fixed round.

A third hindrance is fear. Our desperate difficulties will either dampen our courage or set fire to it. No army can march on a retreating mind. No ship can keep afloat if the hold is filled with water. No church can hope to conquer if its outposts are manned by waterlogged souls. "I can do little," said St. Teresa, "but I with God can do much." The future lies with those who will go forward.—J. B.

THEME PRAYER: O thou, Lord of the harvest, the field is vast, the harvest is abundant, but the workers are too few. Enlist us all anew, we pray thee, in thy cause. Thou hast warned us through thy Son that we should do thy works while it is day, keep us from the misuse of those talents which thou hast committed to our trust. Enable us to perform our several duties with such care and diligence that our work may never be reproved in thy sight and that we may receive thy approbation at the time of accounting. Amen.

OFFERTORY SENTENCE: "Not every one that saith unto me, Lord, Lord, shall enter into the kingdom of heaven; but he that doeth the will of my Father which is in heaven."

OFFERTORY PRAYER: Our Lord and Master, we are grateful to thee for the privilege of being stewards in Thy Kingdom. Forgive us when we fail to make a faithful acounting of that stewardship. Accept these gifts and multiply them in the service of the brotherhood of men, and the building of thy Church. Through Jesus Christ our Lord. Amen. —William Samuel Hess.

Illustrative Material

SEED THOUGHTS, HOMILETIC AND EXPOSITORY. Excelsior: I. Going forward supposes difficulty. II. To go forward implies decision and energy. III. To go forward implies patient endurance. IV. This going forward implies an object.—J. H.

Progress: I. The necessity for progress is a condition for healthy life. II. The directions in which progress should be sought. 1. Forward to clearer conceptions of truth. 2. Forward to fuller development of the church's social life. 3. Forward in works of Christian beneficence. 4. Forward individually in the cultivation of spiritual life.—J. L.

Forward: I. Advancement demanded. Forward, upward, heavenward, Godward. II. Recognition of obstacles. III. Obstacles can be surmounted. IV. Obstacles may contribute to our advancement. V. Forward, encouragements are many.—W. J.

Choice Illustrations on the Theme

SAFETY IN PROGRESS. Flying birds are never taken in a fowler's snare.—Archbishop Seeker.

FORWARD THE TRUE DIRECTION. David Livingstone having broken fresh ground among the Bakjatlas, wrote to the Directors of the London Missionary Society explaining what he had done, and expressing the hope that it would meet with their approval. At the same time he said he was at their disposal "to go anywhere—provided it be forward"!

PROGRESS HINDERED. A gentleman was walking on the Parade at Llandudno and was watching a pretty little vessel with its white sails shining in the sunlight. "How is it that this ship does not seem to be moving?" he said to a seaman standing by. "Her sails are spread and there is plenty of breeze, but she seems to make no progress." "She's anchored, sir," replied the sailor. "That's just how it is with many of us," said the gentleman in answer. "There is everything to help us on our heavenward journey, but we can make no progress at all because we are anchored to something here on earth—some sin indulged in, or some worldliness we cannot give up."

It is also true that sometimes a church gets anchored.—*Best Modern Illustrations.*

CALLED TO HOE. I found in a small country church away up among the hills of Vermont a certain deacon of great wealth, who was one of the most zealous and self-denying members in that little church, and known throughout the whole community for his good works. I ventured to ask him one day why he was pursuing a course so unusual for rich men. His reply was, "When I became a Christian and began to read my Bible with appreciation of its meaning, I read that I was called into the vineyard of the Lord, and I made up my mind at once that I wasn't called to eat grapes, but to hoe: and I've been trying to hoe ever since."—*Christian Endeavor World.*

EVENING SERVICE

Theme: The Reward of Serving Christ.

TEXT: "If any man serve me, him will my Father honour." John 12:26.

INTRODUCTORY: The followers of Christ should ever be distinguished by love to him and active exertion to promote his glory. The text and the preceding verses describe the service of Christ and its reward.

I. Consider the nature of this service. It is not a condition of serfdom—far from it—but one of perfect freedom. It is not something menial, but of great distinction, emphatically royal. It is through infinite grace that we are accepted as laborers together with God, that there is a union of Divine and human agency in the kingdom of Christ. Well may we think: 1. Of the Master who is served. 2. Of the men who serve. 3. Of the object contemplated, the evangelization of the world. 4. And of the constraining motive, the love of Christ. Such service comprehends both love for our Divine Master and rejoicing in his triumphs. "We love him because he first loved us." "The love of Christ constraineth us."

There can be no cheerful, effective and acceptable service without this love. And the proof of our love is that we consecrate all that we have and are to his service, and that we rejoice when our own work or that of others is crowned with success. This service implies diligence, cheerfulness, a willing mind and fidelity. It implies love to God, love to men, active zeal and prayerful faith.

II. But notice that no such service is without reward. "If any man serve me, him will my Father honour." God honors those who serve his Son. 1. Sometimes, often, by crowning their labors with success. Even often in this world. In the midst of the Church. Whatever a man's rank may be, the most useful after all are the most honored. Let a man deserve position and his fellow Christians will not be backward in bestowing it. 2. God honors such by bestowing upon them his friendship and presence. "I have called you friends." 3. By making them the recipients of his grace. All right-minded men esteem it an honor to be able to confer blessings upon others. 4. There is a final honor we will not here dwell upon—that of raising them to the blessedness and glory of heaven. "Come ye blessed," etc. "In his presence there is fulness of joy," etc. "They shall be mine," etc. "That where I am, there shall my servant be."—H.

Additional Theme: God Glorified by Mystery.

TEXT: "It is the glory of God to conceal a thing." Prov. 25:2.

INTRODUCTORY: Among the many ministries of God to arrest and stimulate his children one of the kindliest and commonest is the attractive power of the secret. There is something fascinating in a secret. It makes us eager, curious and alert. And God, who knows our frame, often arrests and stimulates our hearts by a kindly ministry like that. It is the glory of God to conceal a thing, and he, who is a very loving Father, does it in the interest of his own.

I. Think how interesting this world becomes through that attractive power of the secret. The world would be a dull, dead place without it. God does not scatter coal upon the fields: he hides it in the bowels of the earth. He conceals the iron and the diamonds, and buries the pearls under the ocean floor. He does it because he loves us and longs to have us quickened to activity. It is the secret of the stars that has led to all the triumphs of astronomy. It is the secret of the strata that has urged men to the study of geology. All science, all discovery, all search for the uninhabitable Poles, is the response of man to the challenge of the secret. How the secret of an uncharted land played like a magnet on Columbus! How the secret of the sources of the Nile haunted and captivated Livingstone! The world ceases to be a dull, dead place, and grows fascinating and alluring, in that divine ministry of secrecy. Every astronomer outwatching the lone night, every chemist in his laboratory, every explorer in the heart of Africa, every philosopher brooding on the infinite is the child accepting the summons of the Father to come and play a game of hide-and-seek, and it is in playing that we are so happy.

II. Again one remembers how the secret adds to the attractiveness of life. It would be very difficult to live without it. The boys used to tell us in the war how they came to loathe the long, straight road. Walking is always a somewhat dreary business when the road stretches out for miles ahead. What gives it charm, so that we walk alert, and sometimes quite forget that we are fagged, is the surprise and unexpectedness of things. It is that unexpectedness, that secret hidden in the future, that upholds us, and keeps the heart young, and gives not a little of the charm to life. When Abraham fared forth, he knew not whither he was going. Had he known everything that lay before him, would he have started with that gallant heart? Doubtless there are some of us who have experienced the very bitterest of suffering. You have had dead sorrows or living sorrows—and living sorrows sometimes are the sorer. And I ask, could you have traveled radiantly, and wakened singing but for the divine ministry of secrecy? It is the glory of God to conceal a thing, and he does it because his children are so dear to him. He does not want the heartbreak of tomorrow to blind us to the sunshine of today. He keeps us interested, alert, alive, free to enjoy and grapple with the day, through the beautiful method of the secret. To wrest the secret from tomorrow is to wrest the radiance from today.

III. That unfailing attraction of the secret, too, is one of the charming things in personality. We are always interesting to one another because we never fully understand one another. There are books which I have read once, and I never want to read these books again. I have mastered them, exhausted them, moved through and passed beyond their little message. But there are other books, like Shakespeare, like the Bible, that I come back to for the hundredth time, and they are alluring and attractive still. They inspire me, yet they escape me. And it is that mysterious element, that inscrutable and secret element, which God has lodged in every human breast. You say, "I know him perfectly." But you never do. In the most commonplace and ordinary breast there is something beyond the reaching of your hand; something inscrutable, mysterious, secret, too deep for the sounding of any earthly plummet or any analysis of human brain.

That is why sometimes we are all a little lonely, though we be honored with a troop of friends. And that is why, to the end, we are always interesting to one another—it is the haunting attraction of the secret. The beautiful thing is that God put it there. It is the glory of God to conceal a thing. He wants us to take an interest in one another, and to comprehend things "with all the saints." The world of nature, the journey we all take, the men and women we meet with as we journey—perhaps we have never thought how much they owe to the divine ministry of secrecy.—M.

Suggested Texts and Themes

God Requires Our Best: "But whatsoever hath a blemish, that shall ye not offer: for it shall not be acceptable for you," etc. Lev. 22:20-25.

Peter in the Firelight: "And the servants and officers stood there, who had made a fire of coals; for it was cold . . . and Peter stood with them, and warmed himself." John 18:18.

The Many-sided Christ: "He appeared in another form." Mark 16:12.

The Great King: "Art thou a king then? Jesus answered, Thou sayest that I am a king." John 18:37.

Justifiable Retribution: "Behold also, the gallows fifty cubits high . . . made for Mordecai," etc. Esther 7:9.

An Assassin's Deception: "I have a secret errand unto thee. . . . And Ehud put forth his left hand, and took the dagger," etc. Judg. 3:19-21.

MIDWEEK FELLOWSHIP MEETING TOPIC

(Church Night or Suggested Sermon Subject)

Theme: The Gospel's Conquering Power.

TEXT: Thanks be unto God, which always causeth us to triumph in Christ." II Cor. 2:14.

I. Religion today has to hold her own amid governments, and armies, and navies, and universities, and huge industries where capital and labor are organized on a world-wide scale. Mere sentiment, tradition, respectability, music, eloquence, are not enough for a situation so exacting; and if churches—indeed, if Parliaments and Congress—are to survive, they must display what Ruskin has called the lamp of power.

II. The most hostile witnesses agree that among the early Christians such power was manifest. "We cannot deny it," said the priests, when an impotent cripple was healed. "These men," complained the Philippians, "do exceedingly trouble our city." "They turn the world upside down," protested the Thessalonians.

III. It was revolution, not by blows, but by ideas; and Danton himself was not more audacious than Peter and John, when—unlearned though they were—they faced the Sanhedrin. About Stephen's preaching there was that which could not be resisted. And as for Paul, when he was a prisoner at Rome, chained and penniless, he faced the Emperor with an air of quiet mastery which Napoleon would have envied. "Conquests!" wrote he to Corinth—"we are more than conquerors."—P. W. W.

CHRISTIAN ENDEAVOR SOCIETY TOPIC

Sept. 14. The Art of Making Decisions. Josh. 24:14, 15; Ps. 37:5, 6.

SUNDAY SCHOOL LESSON

Sept. 14. David's Religious Contribution. II Sam. 7:18, 19, 25-29; 23:1-4.

Memory Selection: "Serve the Lord with gladness: come before his presence with singing." Ps. 100:2.

The passages chosen for our lesson emphasize the religious contribution David made to Israel and to succeeding generations of God's people. Among notable elements were his bringing up the ark to Jerusalem, his establishing the order of singers and fostering worship, preparing materials for the Temple, writing many of the Psalms, and the passing on a strengthened faith in God's messianic promises. Think how much we owe to David today. Think of the importance that a national official should be a worshiper of God.

SUNDAY: SEPTEMBER TWENTY-FIRST

MORNING SERVICE

Theme: On Walking with God.

Suggested Scripture Reading: Ps. 23:1-6; Ex. 33:12-23.

Selected Hymns: "Guide me, O thou great Jehovah."—W. Williams. "Gently, Lord, O gently lead us."—T. Hastings. "Lead us, heavenly Father, lead us."—J. Edmeston. "Father of love, our Guide, our Friend."—W. J. Irons. "He leadeth me, O blessed thought."—J. H. Gilmore.

Call to Worship: "The Lord is nigh unto all them that call upon him, to all that call upon him in truth. He will fulfil the desire of them that fear him: he also will hear their cry, and will save them."

Invocation Prayer: We thank thee, our Father, for the builders of this house. Let us honor them before thee by appreciating the beauty unto the inspiration of our souls. We thank thee for the servants of the temple, the ushers at the doors. We would honor them before thee by catching their spirit of good will to the warming of our hearts. We thank thee for the singers of the sanctuary. We would honor them before thee by lifting our own voices in hymns of praise. We thank thee for the Divine Presence in this dedicated place of prayer, and would honor thee by the deep devotion of our very lives. Bless us all while we here worship thee together, we ask in the name of Christ. Amen.—M. K. W. H.

Theme: On Walking with God.

TEXT: "And Enoch walked with God." Gen. 5:24.

INTRODUCTORY: The poets and saints of religion have for generations interpreted life as a walk, human existence as a journey, and man as a pilgrim. If in the spiritual realm we could rediscover the art of walking, we should build up our spiritual health. In this chapter there is the record of one man who mastered well the art of walking. His name was Enoch. Nearly his whole biography is given us in four words. "Enoch walked with God." It would be interesting to know how many other things about him. But we do know the most important matter. We know how he managed his inner life. He had a steady companionship with an invisible Friend. "Enoch walked with God." That is as simple and as true a description of religion as you can find.

I. Almost any experience that makes you aware of your own limitations and of your need for more than human help can start you on the adventure of walking with God. The book of Genesis says, "Enoch walked with God after he begat Methuselah." That was the experience that started him—the birth of his first child. And that was the experience that has started countless other men and women. Recall how vivid God was to you when first you looked into the cradle and saw your own baby.

But plenty of other experience can start men in this adventure. Many fellows started walking with God when they went away into the armed services. Many girls have thought more seriously about God when they began college or nurses' training away from home. A tragic failure, a sudden illness, a tight business situation—all these are events that can start men walking with God. Only remember that while Enoch started with the birth of his first child, he kept on walking with God through all his days. The kind of friendship with the Eternal which he thus cultivated must have built beauty and worth, steadiness and permanence into his character.

II. The art of walking with God is to be learned by the simple process of taking one step at a time. That is the way we all learned how to walk with our feet. And we learn how to walk in the spiritual realm in exactly the same manner.

To be a Christian you do not have to leap from the place where you are to the kind of character and life that you see in Christ. All you have to do is to say sincerely, "O Master, let me walk with thee," and then take the first step that his influence indicates for you and then the next. That is the most valuable kind of religion for the period in which we are living. For we cannot see very far ahead. We are living in what aviators or mountain climbers or sailors would call a time of low visibility. In such a time we shall wear ourselves out with worry and anxiety and dread if we spend our time trying to peer into a future which it is impossible to pierce. But we can keep steady and go forward strongly if we will go one step at a time.

III. In following this method of "one step at a time" we must constantly guard against shortsightedness. Dr. Willard Sperry warns us that "the single step must always be taken in the direction determined by the very long views of life." "One step at a time" must be a religious method. We are not urging ourselves merely to take the next step, but to take the next step with God. And he is never shortsighted. He sees far horizons that we cannot perceive in our time of low visibility. We are safe only when we take the next step that his Christlike influence inspires us to take.—Rev. Guthrie Spears, D.D.

THEME PRAYER: O thou great Companion of our souls in times of sorrow and also of joy, give us the steadfastness that trusts in thee even when we feel the bitterness of evil. "Shall we not receive evil?" And shall we not much more than conquer it through him who "hath borne our griefs, and carried our sorrows"? Permit us to walk with thee and fellowship with thee here and inherit with thee the home eternal. In Christ's name we ask. Amen.

OFFERTORY SENTENCE: "Thou shalt remember the Lord thy God: for it is he that giveth thee power to get wealth."

OFFERTORY PRAYER: Almighty God, bountiful Giver of all good, from the first creation, as we bring our offering unto thee, give us the realization that thou art working today—still creating and molding and fashioning, out of our gifts and our lives, to establish thy kingdom, even a new heaven and a new earth in the hearts of men. Consecrate thou the gifts we bring, and grant that with all our offerings our surrendered spirits may sing forth the honor and majesty of thy name: through Jesus Christ our Lord. Amen.—Albert B. McCoy.

Illustrative Material

SEED THOUGHTS, HOMILETIC AND EXPOSITORY. Walking with God: I. A safe walk. II. A useful walk. III. A pleasant walk. IV. A profitable walk.—R. N.

Enoch: I. The history of Enoch. II. The character of Enoch. III. The conduct of Enoch. IV. The reward of Enoch.—J. A. J.

Enoch's Walk: I. Walk confidently with God. II. Walk obediently with God. III. Walk humbly with your God. IV. Walk patiently with God.—H. M.

Enoch: I. His piety. Walking with God includes: 1. A true knowledge of God. 2. Cheerful obedience to God. 3. Devotional intercourse with God. Meditation, Prayer, Praise. II. His association with God gave: 1. Assimilation. 2. Dignity. 3. Pleasure. 4. Security. III. His peculiar reward: 1. Translation. 2. Immortality.—J. B.

Choice Illustrations on the Theme

WALKING STEP BY STEP

One step thou seest then go forward boldly,
One step is far enough for faith to see;
Take that, and thy next duty shall be told thee,
For step by step the Lord is leading thee.
—Unidentified.

ACQUAINTANCE WITH GOD. When Mark Twain was in Berlin he received an invitation asking him to call upon the Kaiser. "Why, papa," exclaimed his little daughter, after contemplating the missive for a moment in speechless awe, "if it keeps on this way there won't be anybody left for you to get acquainted with but God." An amusing remark; but in saddest seriousness how many there are who have a wide circle of acquaintance and yet have never come to know Him whom to know aright is life eternal.—*Autobiography of Mark Twain.*

WALKING WITH GOD. Fellowship with God is a blessed experience. "It is good for me to draw near to God," is a common sentiment of Christians; but the drawing near and living near are not nearly so common as attainments. How different is the failure of many to realize the presence of God from the experience of nearness realized by some! Brother Lawrence, the simple-minded cook, tells us that for more than sixty years he never lost the sense of the presence of God, but was as conscious of it while performing the duties of his humble office as when partaking of the Holy Supper.

Say to yourself over and over again every day and many times in the day: "God is here." "God is with me." "God is within me." "God is my Father." "I am God's child." "I am in my Father's presence." "God is love, and God loves me." Abide in him. Let his words and will abide in you. Cultivate this habit of mind, this grace of intercourse with God, and by and by you will arrive at the state of an unbroken and delightful consciousness of his nearness.—*Upward Steps.*

EVENING SERVICE

Theme: Difficulties of Disbelief.

TEXT: "Lord, to whom shall we go?" John 6:68.

INTRODUCTORY: Many had apostatized and it was natural now for Jesus to submit the question of continuing with him to the twelve, "Will ye whom I have chosen, on whom I have bestowed apostleship, who have seen the evidence of my Messiahship, will ye also leave me?" This was the time to try them. And this is the time to try all Christians, when many professed disciples grow cold and turn back. Then we can suppose Jesus addressing us and saying, "Will ye also go away?"

With characteristic ardor and promptness Simon Peter answered him, "Lord, to whom shall we go?" This implied their firm conviction that Jesus was the Messiah and that he alone was able to teach and save them.

It was one of Peter's noble confessions, the instinctive promptings of a genuine heart and ardent love. The whole occurrence suggests a line of inquiry toward unbelievers concerning the difficulties of unbelief.

I. Suppose we give up the Christian faith, what shall we have instead? Wise men are bound to look at consequences. If you were asked to leave your house, would you not inquire where you were to go? And are we to concern ourselves more about shelter for the body than a home for the soul?

It is easier to pull down than to build up, to spoil a picture than to paint one, to tempt a man than to save one, to ruin life than to train it for heaven. Disbelievers and all opposers of the Christian faith are doing this easy work, and to them we must put the practical question, Give up religion, and what then?

II. Give up the idea of God? And what then? You would refuse to throw away the poorest covering until you knew what you were to have in return. Will you, then, recklessly give up the idea of the living, loving personal God at the bidding of any man? Remember that you can put away the mystery of God, and you get in return the greater mystery of godlessness. The wax flower on your table was made, but the roses in your garden grew by chance, forsooth!

III. Give up the idea of the future? And what then? If a man should ask you to throw away a telescope, would you not inquire what you were to have in return? Will you, then, throw away the faith-glass through which you read the solemn and wondrous future? Christian revelation tells us that death is abolished, and heaven the goal of human spirits. Renounce this and what does the skeptic give?

IV. Shut your Bible? And what then? The Bible says "The Lord is my shepherd," etc. The tempter says, "You have no thirst that you cannot slake at the muddy pool at your feet." The Bible says that "God is a present help in time of trouble." The tempter says, "Dry your tears and snap your fingers in the face of the universe." The Bible proclaims the forgiveness of sins. The disbeliever says, "You have never sinned." The Bible says, "In my Father's house are many mansions." The disbeliever says, "Your mansion is the grave; get into it, and rot away."

Some kindly advice. 1. Keep this question straight before you. 2. Inquire of the tempter his power to provide an alternative. 3. Be sure the alternative is worth having. 4. And you will find that if you leave the Divine life and aspect of things there is nothing but outer darkness.—J. P.

Additional Theme: Christlike Compassion.

TEXT: "A certain Samaritan, as he journeyed, came where he was." Luke 10:33.

INTRODUCTORY: Our Lord, true poet that he was, had a great liking for pictorial teaching, and in all the pictures of his gallery none is more remarkable than this one. It is a beautiful etching of benevolence, and as such it is immortal. But men have loved, right down the ages, to find in it something more than that. They have loved to find in this Samaritan a delineation of the Lord himself in his infinite compassion for mankind.

I. That feature is that the Samaritan came just "where the man was"—came right up to him, and handled him where he lay. When he saw, as he came down the hill, that in the hollow yonder there had been a struggle—when he saw that battered figure by the road, with the robbers probably in concealment—how naturally he might have halted till some Roman convoy had come up; but, says Jesus, he came just where he was. The Priest saw him; the Levite looked at him; the Samaritan came right up "where he was." How perfectly that exquisite touch applies to the Lord, who was the teller of the story, in his infinite compassion for mankind!

II. Think for a moment of the Incarnation. Tell me, what was the Incarnation? It was the Son of God, seeing the need of man, and coming in infinite mercy where he was. Not speaking as by a trumpet from high heaven; not casting down a scroll out of eternity; not sending Gabriel or any of the angels to proclaim the loving fatherhood of God. No, this is the glory of the Incarnation, that when man was bruised and battered by his sin, Christ, the Son of God, the good Samaritan, came just where he was. He came to the inn, where the travelers were drinking; to the cottage, where the mother prayed; to the village, where the children romped; to the fields, where happy lovers wandered. He came to the marriage feast and to the funeral; to the crowded city and to the sea; to the agony and to the Cross. Show me where folk are lying ill at home, and I can show you Jesus there. Show me where men are tempted of the devil, and I can show you Jesus there. Show me where hearts are crying out in darkness, "My God, why hast thou forsaken me?" and the beautiful and amazing thing is this: that I can show you Jesus there. Where man has suffered, Jesus Christ has suffered. Where man has toiled, Jesus Christ has toiled. Where man has wept, Jesus Christ has wept. Where man has died, Jesus Christ has died. He has borne our griefs, and carried our sorrows, and made his grave with the wicked in his death. The good Samaritan has come just "where he was."

III. And when we follow the footsteps of the Lord, does not the same thing at once arrest us? Why, that is just what the people marked in Christ, when they contrasted him with John the Baptist. If you wanted John, you had to search for John. You had to leave the city and go into the wilderness. And there, "far frae the haunts of men," was John the Baptist, a solitary figure. But Christ was genial, kindly and accessible, a lover of the haunts of men, the friend of publicans and sinners. Simon Peter was busy with his nets, and Christ came where he was. Matthew was seated at the receipt of custom, and Christ came to him. The poor demoniac was in the graveyard, there to be exiled till he died, and the glorious thing about our good Samaritan is that he came exactly where he was. Where is that bright girl from Jairus' home? We have been missing her happy smile these days. Where is Lazarus? We used to see him daily. Is he ill? We never see him now. I only know of each of them that Christ came where he was. Go to the penitent thief upon the cross, and tell him there is someone who can save him. Only he must come down, and leave the city, and fly to the wilderness and he will find him. There are many who offer paradise on these terms when men are powerless and cannot move a finger; but Christ came "where he was." That is exactly what he is doing still. Behold, I stand at the door and knock. No one needs to fly away to find him. The Word is nigh thee, even in thy mouth. "Just as I am," is a very gracious hymn: but I want someone to write me another hymn: "Just where I am, O Lamb of God, you come."—M.

Suggested Texts and Themes

An Outlet to Life: "I perceive that virtue is gone out of me." Luke 8:46.

Asking Jesus to Depart: "And, behold, the whole city came out to meet Jesus: and when they saw him, they besought him that he would depart out of their coasts." Matt. 8:34.

Dominant Interests: "For to me to live is Christ." Phil. 1:21.

Building on the Good in Men: "Behold an Israelite indeed, in whom is no guile!" John 1:47.

Jesus Singing: "And when they had sung an hymn, they went out." Mark 14:26.

Jesus in the Pew: "Then cometh Jesus from Galilee to Jordan unto John, to be baptized of him." Matt. 3:13.

MIDWEEK FELLOWSHIP MEETING TOPIC

(Church Night or Suggested Sermon Subject)

Theme: When the Master Calls.

TEXT: "And they call the blind man, saying unto him, Be of good cheer: rise, he calleth thee." Mark 10:49 (A.S.V.).

I. It is always good cheer—or "comfort" as the old King James Version has it—when the Master calls. Yet you and I dread to hear his voice. Like the disciples to whom the Master came walking on the seas, we are troubled and cry out for fear. To them our Lord himself spoke words similar to those spoken to the beggar by his followers, "Be of good cheer; it is I; be not afraid!"

II. To Bartimaeus the call meant joy unspeakable, the opening of his eyes, his weakness done away, his dearest desire granted—the thing he would have above all else was sight.

III. Why do we fear when he calls? Rather let us be of good cheer: let us run to him and follow him.—J. A. M.

CHRISTIAN ENDEAVOR SOCIETY TOPIC

Sept. 21. Resources for Times of Crisis. Eph. 6:10-18; Phil. 4:13.

SUNDAY SCHOOL LESSON

Sept. 21. Solomon Begins His Reign. I Kings 1:38-40; 3:5-9; 8:27-30.

MEMORY SELECTION: "Trust in the Lord with all thine heart; and lean not unto thine own understanding. In all thy ways acknowledge him, and he shall direct thy paths." Prov. 3:5, 6.

This lesson presents the promising beginning of Solomon's reign. It goes on to tell how he built the Temple in fulfillment of his father's wishes. There is shown his sense of worship in his remarkable prayer at the dedication of the Temple. The whole account manifests the need of divine wisdom in national life. It was needed then. It is needed now.

SUNDAY: SEPTEMBER TWENTY-EIGHTH

MORNING SERVICE

Theme: Short Bed and Narrow Covering.

SUGGESTED SCRIPTURE READING: Luke 14:1-35.

SELECTED HYMNS: "My God, permit me not to be."—I. Watts. "My soul, be on thy guard."—G. Heath. "Am I a soldier of the cross."—I. Watts. "In the hour of trial."—J. Montgomery. "Jesus, I my cross have taken."—H. F. Lyte.

CALL TO WORSHIP: "The Lord is my light and my salvation; whom shall I fear? the Lord is the strength of my life; of whom shall I be afraid? . . . One thing have I desired of the Lord, that will I seek after: that I may dwell in the house of the Lord . . . and to inquire in his temple."

INVOCATION PRAYER: We thank thee, O God, that thy fatherhood, so righteous, so loving, so sacrificial, was made manifest unto us through the life and character of Christ and his death and resurrection. We rest our faith on him. His loving deeds while on earth tell us that thou art a God of love. His words are expressive of thy mind. His plan for the kingdom is that which thou dost entrust us to bring to pass. We thank thee that we find him the light of our lives, the shepherd of our souls, the door into nobler living, the bread which nourisheth our spirits, the vine in which to abide. Grant us ability to draw close to him and receive from his abundance of life. While we worship in thy house this morning grant us each and all together thy richest blessing. We ask in the name of Christ. Amen. —M. K. W. H.

Theme: Short Bed and Narrow Covering.

TEXT: "For the bed is shorter than that a man can stretch himself on it: and the covering narrower than that he can wrap himself in it." Isa. 28:20.

INTRODUCTORY: One can hardly imagine a more unpleasant position for a man to find himself in than that here pictured. He arrives from a long journey tired and footsore, or comes in from a hard day's work, and longs for "nature's sweet restorer, balmy sleep." On reaching his bed, however, he finds it altogether inadequate for comfortable rest. The bed is too short and the covering too narrow. That is the picture which the prophet Isaiah here presents. So should it be to Israel in their calamities and in their efforts for comfort, which would utterly fail them.

So the picture has a meaning. God has so made man that there are two things necessary to his comfort. One is sleep. The other is clothing. But man's body, after all, is only a picture of his inner being. Just what the body needs materially that the soul needs spiritually.

I. Let us then notice, as a first fact, that men do make for themselves beds for their minds and souls to rest upon. They must have beds and they must have covering. The Jewish beds were only mattresses laid on the floor; and the cover was a quilt or sheet laid over it in which the person wrapped himself. In this adage there is an illusion to the condition of one who being weary and inclined to rest goes to bed that he may have refreshing repose, only to find the bed too short for him, the covering too narrow to wrap himself in, so that instead of getting agreeable warmth and refreshment he becomes cold, restless and uneasy. This painful state represents the distressed and disappointed condition of those who hide themselves under falsehood and refuges of lies in order to obtain either temporal or spiritual deliverance. Beds too short and coverings too narrow!

II. What are some of the beds men make for themselves and upon which they vainly seek to rest? 1. One man makes for himself a bed of gold. He becomes a merchant prince, a millionaire, and he says to himself, "Soul, thou hast much goods laid up for many years; take thine ease, eat, drink, and be merry." He makes riches his God, seeks in them his happiness. But his lands are still too narrow and his estate too small. He does not find rest. 2. Other men have been ambitious. One says, "I want to be famous. I want to be a man of note." The man succeeds, but, like that said of kings, "Uneasy lies the head that wears a crown." The bed is too short, the covering too narrow. 3. Another may seek sensual pleasure; but the result is no better.

But still more significant, let us turn to think of some spiritual bed-makers and their mistaken dependence. 1. Here is one who rests his mind and heart on what is known as natural religion, the religion of nature, the light of reason. But his longings are not satisfied. The bed is too short, the covering too narrow. 2. Another seeks to satisfy himself with what is known as ceremonial religion. He rests in forms and ceremonies, but finds the bed shorter than he can stretch himself upon. 3. Another makes the mistake of finding a false confidence in a comparison with others. "I am as good as they are." Nothing practical about that! 4. Another rests upon self-excuses. "I have had no chance." "I have no time for religion." "I have no power for self-renewal." All too short!

III. The real need. It is of a larger and truer conception of God. Of his grace. Of his pardon. Of his hope. Of the rest of soul he gives, and of the peace and happiness and usefulness of life he offers. The religion of Christ contains all that we need. "Plenteous grace with thee is found, grace to cover all my sin." It is plain that some religions are false and inefficient, the bed too short and the cover too narrow. But the salvation of Christ is an abundant salvation. The all-important question is, Do we possess it? In our heart's experience have we got it?—With acknowledgments to J. B.

THEME PRAYER: O God, be Thou our guide along the highway of today! If fog and darkness beset us, let the white life of thy Son be the light that shall bring us to our desired haven, with hearts courageous and banners unstained. And help us to be good reflectors of his Light to our fellow travelers. Amen.

OFFERTORY SENTENCE: "Many, O God, are thy wonderful works which thou hast done, and thy thoughts which are to us-ward."

OFFERTORY PRAYER: O Master, who didst sit over against the treasury not to count the gifts but to read the hearts of the givers, search our hearts as we give today and inspire with the example of thy love the offering which we now dedicate to thy service. Amen.

Illustrative Material

SEED THOUGHTS, HOMILETIC AND EXPOSITORY. Delusive Expectations: This proverb contains a soul of truth for every age and people. I. The words apply to the world's offers of satisfaction to man's nature. II. They apply to false confidences. 1. Self-help. Moral improvement. 2. Mere formal religion. Religious observances. 3. Comparison with others. "Common sins I shudder at. I love culture. I am a good husband, wife, sister, brother." No, God looks at the heart. III. Self-excuses. 1. "The temptation was so subtle and my nature weak." 2. "I was surrounded with bad examples and influences." 3. "I have had no time for religion." 4. "I have no power for self-renewal." Vain excuses. IV. Vain hopes. 1. "After all it may be otherwise than the preachers say." 2. "I may repent at the last." That is you will sin no more when you have no more power to sin!—G. M.

Choice Illustrations on the Theme

AMBITION A DISAPPOINTING COVER. In an old fable there was a magic skin the wearing of which would get a person everything he wished. But each wish that was granted shrank the skin; and by and by when the wearer got what he wished the skin squeezed his breath out. The fable is true. The magic skin is false ambition. Every time the false ambition is attained the person shrinks.

A man in one of our large cities was worth several hundred thousand dollars, but he was so miserly that he denied himself the comforts of life, not even allowing himself sufficient food and a comfortable bed. He had lived wholly for self. Before he died he said, "I have made a great mistake, putting the wrong things first in life." His false ambition proved a short bed and narrow covering. Ambition is nothing for a soul to rest upon.

EXCUSES TOO NARROW. Considering excuses, we are reminded of a colored man who was visited in prison by a social worker. When asked why he was there he replied, "Dey say I took a watch. I made a good fight. I had a dandy lawyer, an' he done prove an alibi wif ten witnesses. Den my lawyer he shore made a strong speech to de jury. But it wasn't no use, suh; dey gives me ten monfs."

"I don't see why you were not acquitted," said the visitor.

"Well, suh," explained the prisoned, "dere was shore one weak spot 'bout the defense—dey found de watch in ma pocket!"—*Religious Telescope.*

WEALTH SHORT BED, NARROW COVERING. One who had traveled far talked of the saddening sight of the "exhausted" diamond mines of South Africa—mines completely worked out. There are exhausted gold mines in Western Australia while on this continent the apparent fabulous wealth of the Klondike is only a memory. Paul wrote of the riches of Christ and Dr. Weymouth translates the text, "The exhaustless wealth of Christ." Here is wealth that will not diminish, mines that will never be exhausted. On the other hand it is true that "the pleasures of sin are soon explored."—Archer Wallace.

UNAWARE OF LACK. A story which has extra significance is the one that the late Rev. Dr. William L. Stidger related under the title "Lost Harmony." He told the traditional incident of Ole Bull visiting John Ericsson after the latter had refused again and again to attend one of his concerts. He insisted that he had no time for music. Ole Bull carried his violin with him to see Ericsson, took it apart, asked for help, put it back together, and began playing a few bars of "marvelously sweet music." As Ericsson listened, his soul was stirred. "Tears glistened in his eyes, and when Ole Bull paused he said softly, 'Play on! Don't stop. Play on! I never knew before what it was that was lacking in my life.'" How many people are unaware of their lack in spiritual possessions. The bed is short, the covering narrow; they are distressed in the cold and know it not.

EVENING SERVICE

Theme: The Common Fault of Self-Deception.

TEXT: "There is a generation that are pure in their own eyes, and yet is not washed from their filthiness." Prov. 30:12.

INTRODUCTORY: A common fault of hypocrisy and Pharisaical self-righteousness is self-deception. Yet such are not "washed of their filthiness." They have not cleansed their hearts either because they have not examined themselves and so know nothing about their real state, or else because they care nothing about it and refuse to regard it in its true light. Result, pride, "lofty eyes," v. 13. Self-deception in regard to the guilt of sin is a most common delusion, especially of minds not spiritually enlightened.

I. Consider, first, the temptation to this evil. 1. People have strong motives to think well of themselves. For the sake of peace of mind people desire to stand well with their own conscience. So they lie to it. They hoodwink it. They cajole it. If these measures fail they smother it. 2. Pride also makes us desire our own approval. 3. And fear is another cause of self-deception. The feeling of danger passes when we persuade ourselves that we are innocent.

II. It is important to know what are some of the causes of self-deception. 1. One is purely from an inclination to flatter oneself. It helps to produce the delusion, "wish father of the thought." 2. It is aided by any prevailingly low standard of morals. 3. It is encouraged by the example of others. "Comparing ourselves among ourselves."

III. What are some of the bad results of this evil of self-deception? 1. A whole generation may mistakenly count itself pure in its own eyes. 2. Our self-deception does not cleanse us. It only asserts what is false. 3. And it does not hide sin, as we seem to hope. It is not even a successful cloak. 4. And, surely, it does not save from punishment. Sinful in itself, it only adds to sin.

IV. Pray "Cleanse thou me from secret faults." 2. Pray, "God be merciful to me a sinner."—C.

Additional Theme: The All-Sufficient Christ.

TEXT: "Who is sufficient for these things?" II Cor. 2:16.

I. This question was asked by the Apostle Paul in writing his second letter to the church at Corinth, and it is a question that finds an echo in our hearts; for how many times have we asked it or felt like asking it. In our own homes, with our family and loved ones, there are often problems that arise that are too much for us. As Paul said, in view of what he was facing in his ministry to the church, "Who is sufficient for these things?"

In the business world also there are

conditions over which we have no control. There are problems that come up that are too much for us—problems of the relation of employer to employee, problems of government regulation, problems of supply and demand, problems of competition. We want to meet these problems, and we want to meet them in the right way, but how can we? "Who is sufficient for these things?"

Or, it may be in our association with others in the community problems and difficulties arise. And it may be even in the church, and if so, that is harder to bear than it is on the outside, because we expect a Christian spirit in the church, and if we do not find it, we are not only disappointed, but we feel nonplused and say to ourselves, "Who is sufficient for these things?"

In our individual lives also, we run into so many problems of so many different kinds that we find ourselves asking this same question over and over again.

II. As we face these problems we are glad to know that the Apostle Paul, who asked this question, also had the answer to it, for he said, "Our sufficiency is of God." Suppose then instead of looking to our own insufficiency, we look to the sufficiency of God in Christ.

1. In his nature and character he is sufficient, as is said in Hebrews: "He is the first begotten of the Father." It was he who made the world itself, he who upholds all things by the word of his power.

2. His sacrifice is sufficient—sufficient to purify heavenly things as well as earthly things, so that once for all he has prepared to take away sin by the sacrifice of himself and to perfect forever them that are sanctified.

3. In his position and power he is sufficient, for when he had purged our sins, he sat down on the right hand of the Majesty on High. He is all-sufficient—and he is ours—our great High Priest in the heavens on the right hand of God himself, our Lord and our Saviour.

III. And because he is sufficient, he is able to meet every need of man. Suppose we begin on the plane of national and international problems. Can he solve them? Yes, he can and will by taking his power and reigning. In the meantime, can he meet our needs? He certainly can. When we look to the mission fields we see a demonstration of the fact that he can, in that he preserved the churches of China, Korea and Japan so that they came through the terrible experiences of the past years with a vigor and vitality that is an evidence of the sufficiency of Christ.

He is sufficient for the needs of the individual. Though that individual be a lost sinner, steeped in sin, he is able to save unto the uttermost all those who come unto God by him. And what about our own individual problems? Is he able to meet them? He is. "If any of you lack wisdom, let him ask of God, that giveth to all men liberally, and upbraideth not; and it shall be given him." "He is able to keep you from falling, and to present you faultless before the presence of his glory with exceeding joy."

Whether in the home, in business, in society, in the church, no matter where, he is sufficient.

We may feel like asking why God allows us to be tempted and tried and have so many problems and difficulties, why it is so hard for us to act like children of God in our own homes, in our business, and in the world at large? Is it not just because he wants to prove us? That we may realize our own insufficiency, that we may not try to live in our own strength, but that we may rely upon him who is all-sufficient, and that more and more our sufficiency may be of him?

May we learn in our own experience the all-sufficiency of Christ, that he is not only sufficient for our salvation, but that he is sufficient for life, with all of its trials and problems, and is sufficient for death, and the great hereafter. Because we put our trust in him, and commit our way unto him, may we be able to say, as many others have been able to say before us, "Our sufficiency is of God, who also made us sufficient."—Rev. W. C. Cumming.

Suggested Education Week Texts and Themes

Education for Today and Tomorrow: "Say not thou, What is the cause that the former days were better," etc. Eccles. 7:10.

Jesus the Matchless Teacher: "The people resort unto him again; and as he was wont, he taught them again." Mark 10:1.

Christ and Culture: Acts 19:9.

Let Us Grow Up: I Cor. 13:11.

Thank God for Leaders and Followers: Judg. 5:2.

Christian Illiteracy: "My people are destroyed for lack of knowledge." Hos. 4:6.

MIDWEEK FELLOWSHIP MEETING TOPIC

(Church Night or Suggested Sermon Subject)

Theme: Religious Education (Education Week).

TEXT: "Train up a child in the way he should go: and when he is old, he will not depart from it." Prov. 22:6.

The matter of religious education is of supreme importance. The Bible tells us so. Modern psychology tells us so. Experience tells us so.

I. The duty. 1. Train them early. 2. Train them intellectually. 3. Train them morally. 4. Train them religiously.

II. Ways this duty is to be performed. 1. By precept. 2. By example. 3. By discipline, wise and kindly. 4. By education, the best possible.

III. Some encouragements toward the discharge of this duty. 1. Regard to the happiness of the child. 2. Regard to the happiness of the parents. 3. Regard to the happiness of society. 4. Supremely, with regard to the will and kingdom of God.

CHRISTIAN ENDEAVOR SOCIETY TOPIC

Sept. 28. Making the Best of Second Choices. Col. 3:17; Eccles. 9:10.

SUNDAY SCHOOL LESSON

Sept. 28. The Glory of Solomon's Empire. I Kings 4:20-26; 11:4-8.

MEMORY SELECTION: "A man's life does not consist in the abundance of his possessions." Luke 12:15 (R. S. V.).

The Scriptures chosen for this lesson describe the superb glory of Solomon's kingdom. The material wealth, the personal riches, the political alliances, the public buildings, and the administrative organization all are glimpsed. Yet there were always present evil tendencies that ultimately undermined this glory. How successful was Solomon? Note the peril of earthly glory. Note the folly of trusting in such things.

SUNDAY: OCTOBER FIFTH

MORNING SERVICE

Theme: How Having Faith Helps Others.

SUGGESTED SCRIPTURE READING: Acts 27:1-44.

SELECTED HYMNS: "Jesus, Saviour pilot me."—Edward Hopper. "Rock of Ages, cleft for me."—A. M. Toplady. "God is the Refuge of his saints."—I. Watts. "O God, the Rock of Ages."—E. H. Bickerseth. "Who trusts in God, a strong abode."—Various.

CALL TO WORSHIP: "Seek ye the Lord while he may be found, call ye upon him while he is near: let the wicked forsake his way, and the unrighteous man his thoughts: and let him return unto the Lord, and he will have mercy upon him; and to our God, for he will abundantly pardon."

INVOCATION PRAYER: We praise thee, O God, our Father, maker of heaven and earth, who hast set our world among the planets and the stars, who hast also set our feet upon it, and who by the laws of nature provideth us with food and shelter and raiment.

We praise thee, O Christ, of sterling character, of unique purpose, of ultimate worth, for the salvation which thou hast wrought out for us, wisdom for ignorance, righteousness for sin, eternal life for mortality.

We praise thee, O Holy Spirit, "nearer to us than breathing," for thy inspiration and direction. Help us in our efforts to know thee and to that end direct this service. Amen.—M. K. W. H.

Theme: How Having Faith Helps Others.

TEXT: "Wherefore, sirs, be of good cheer: for I believe God." Acts 27:25.

INTRODUCTORY: It might seem as if what a man believed were no concern to anybody but himself, that that is his own affair and his alone. But as a matter of fact what a man believes has profound and pervasive social consequence. It affects the lives of all he comes in contact with. It inspires or depresses them. And all this is more beautifully illustrated in the story of the shipwreck of St. Paul than perhaps in any other piece of Scripture.

I. Note, for instance, how the faith of Paul made him intensely and practically useful. We could well imagine somebody dilating on the compelling preaching of St. Paul, but quite certain that in storm and shipwreck he would be altogether useless. And yet in such an hour, when things were darkest, Paul was the most useful man on board, and he was so because he believed God. The same thing is profoundly true of Jesus, who lived in a perfect and unwavering faith. That did not make him an ineffectual dreamer; it made him intensely and socially useful. It filled the nets, and fed the hungry folk, and restored the withered arm to service, and brought joy and singing to the home at Bethany. We help people by what we do. Perhaps we help them more by what we are. We prove ourselves useful when we give our money. We are still more useful when we give ourselves. And no man has his whole self to give in all the expansion of his possibilities until he as aligned himself with God.

II. Note again how the faith of the apostle brought new hope to everyone on board. These despairing souls were saved by hope. One moment there was not a star in all their sky. They were driving on to certain death. The best of them would be crying to their gods; the worst would fall to cursing and blaspheming. And then, like the first faint flushings of the dawn, hope came stealing into every heart because there was one on board who believed God. Things were just as dark as they had been before. There was no cessation of the raging storm. They were still driving on to an iron shore, their ship the sport and plaything of the elements. But one man believed God, and because of that was radiant and serene, and it brought hope into the heart of everybody. What, does it not matter what you believe? It mattered supremely for these despairing sailors. It matters every time. Have faith in God, have it for yourself; be strong and quiet and confident because of it, and everybody on shipboard is affected.

III. For that is always one of the fruits of faith. Faith radiates the atmosphere of hope. The presence of a strong and living faith calls out the music of a thousand hearts. A son may be a prodigal, and everybody may think him past redemption. But his mother never thinks him past redemption, because of the faith in her big mother-heart. And because of the faith in the heart of the Lord Jesus hope has downed on millions of people, who, like these shipwrecked sailors, were despairing. It is a great thing to give weary people hope. And in all our weakness one sure way to do it is the old true way of Jesus and of Paul. Have faith in God. Live it out in storms. Be strong and quiet when others cry in terror. And in mysterious ways we cannot trace hope will dawn upon the hearts of men.

IV. Not only did the faith of Paul give hope; it also gave the blessing of good cheer. It brought the comfort of a happy confidence to every desponding heart on board. I have read somewhere of an ocean liner caught in the fury of a terrific storm. Men were panic-stricken, women screamed; and then the captain smiled. And the faith that lay behind that smile, that the ship he knew so well would weather through, brought good cheer to every soul on board. So was it with St. Paul. He believed God and he could smile. When others were terror-stricken and beside themselves he could give thanks and quietly take his breakfast. And men, seeing it, forgot their fears, and plucked up heart again, and all because one person believed God. It is a fine thing to do kindly helpful deeds. It is one of the very finest in the world. But there is something finer than the helpful hand; it is the helpful heart. To be brave and radiant when things are darkest has an impact upon everybody, and for that one must believe God. My dear friend, longing to cheer others, begin by having faith in God. A strong faith is the secret of all helpfulness. Nothing can ever take the place of that. This is the victory that overcomes the world—even your faith.—M.

THEME PRAYER: Almighty God, who by thy Spirit helpest our infirmities and out of thy fullness hast given to each one of us some peculiar grace and faculty, help us to hold in trust for thee and thine our own diversities of gifts and so administer them in good will and humbleness that thereby others may be blessed and we ourselves grow in grace and knowledge. In Jesus' name. Amen.

OFFERTORY SENTENCE: "Not every one that saith unto me, Lord, Lord, shall enter into the kingdom of heaven; but he that doeth the will of my Father which is in heaven."

OFFERTORY PRAYER: Help us, our Father, to see that we abound in this grace also, the grace of giving. Wilt thou bless these contributions of thy people to the increase of thy gospel of peace and good will in the world. We ask in Christ's name. Amen.

Illustrative Material

SEED THOUGHTS, HOMILETIC AND EXPOSITORY. Be of Good Cheer: I. Paul was strong because he believed. Faith makes men strong. Remember Christian that wherever you are placed you are to be the one person to comfort those around you who may have weaker faith. 1. Paul's faith was in God. "I believe God." 2. Believing God he believed his message. 3. And he did that when there was nothing else to believe in. 4. And he was not ashamed to say so. II. Paul being strong spake words of cheer to others. So must we. There are Little-Faiths and we need strong-faith people to encourage by telling that you "believe God as he told you."—C. H. S.

Faith: I. Faith is the acceptance of what God says as sure and final. II. Christian faith must be exercised in the face of difficulties. III. Those who have such faith are sustained by God as their actual needs require. IV. Faith vigorously uses all the means of self-help. It is no supine influence in life.—S. J. M.

Choice Illustrations on the Theme

HAVING FAITH HELPS OTHERS. There was a storm at sea. The passengers were all afraid and thought themselves in great danger. One woman saw the face of the captain and he smiled. Faith is creative of faith. It created faith in this woman. Her faith created faith in others. All the passengers became full of faith and full of courage. Having faith helps others.—H.

ANOTHER CASE OF FAITH WORKING. Two little Japanese girls of Tokyo were comparing experiences after the earthquake. One had gone with her parents to the Buddhist temple where immense throngs, silent and hopeless, had passed before the idols. "Our parents just looked at the gods and scowled," said the child. The other little girl had attended a service held by the Christian missionary. "Our people looked up to God and sang!" she replied. Then with good courage the people turned to the task of rebuilding their homes, and thereby put new hope into the hearts of all with whom they came in contact. —*Youth's Companion.*

FAITH KEPT BRIGHT. A woman who was showing a beautiful, massive piece of family silver, apologized as she took it from the cupboard where it was kept. "Dreadfully tarnished!" she said. "I can't keep it bright unless I use it!" That is just as true of faith as it is of silver. Tucked away in the Sunday closet of the soul, and brought out only for show, it needs apology. It is bound to be tarnished. You can't keep faith bright unless you use it.—*Sunday School Times.*

FAITH CREATING COURAGE. The war has had curious effects on many people. The story is told of a woman who left her fortune to the town that shall give its name to the successful combat. She at least had no doubt of the victory of her country. The story calls to mind the old incident during Hannibal's siege of Rome. Some man in the city gave courage to the defense by purchasing for a large sum the plot of ground outside the walls on which the tent of the invading general stood.

THE INFLUENCE OF SHOWING FAITH. A gentleman was crossing on the ferry from New York to Brooklyn. The tide was running very high and the boat crashed into the dock. In a moment all was confusion. The gentleman noticed a little girl sitting on the knee of one of the hackmen, who evidently was her father. The little chin began to quiver, the tears started to her eyes, and a cry of fear sprang from her lips. But turning and looking into her father's face, she saw him laughing. Instantly, without having anything explained, the tears dried, the little mouth straightened out, and the cry of fear gave place to a merry laugh.

EVENING SERVICE

Theme: Self-mastery.

TEXT: "And every man that striveth for the mastery is temperate in all things," etc. I Cor. 9:25.

INTRODUCTORY: The picture is that of preparation for the Greek games, the exercises of wrestling, boxing or pitching the bar of quoit, in which every entrant strove to excel. The entrants practiced abstinence from all things that would excite, stimulate or enfeeble. It means they did all they could to make the body vigorous, active and supple. A much-esteemed garland was publicly bestowed upon the victor.

I. In studying this passage notice first that the Christian life is a striving after an end. "We press toward the mark." "We strive to enter in." "We work out our salvation." It is an active life of effort toward a goal.

II. The manner of the strife. It must be "lawfully," in harmony with the Divine rule and will, not according to our own whims or impulses. Men guided by Christ are not in doubt as to what they ought to do or as to the result.

III. The object of Christian striving. To develop self-mastery. To keep the body under. To keep the soul on top. To lead a temperate and Divinely approved life.

IV. The motives Paul mentions. 1. Lest he be a castaway. Paul seems to have made more of that motive than we do. "Lest by any means, when I have preached to others, I myself should be a castaway." In the Greek games a castaway meant one who had been pronounced by the judges to be disqualified. To Paul it meant loss of favor with God and its fruition. "In thy favour is life." 2. The other was to gain a crown, the victor's garland, precious, imperishable, the eternal award.—H.

MIDWEEK FELLOWSHIP MEETING TOPIC

(Church Night or Suggested Sermon Subject)

Theme: Traveling Toward Home.

TEXT: "The righteous also shall hold on his way." Job 17:9.

That master allegorist, John Bunyan, has not pictured Christian as carried to heaven on "flowery beds of ease." He loses his burden at the Cross, but is nowhere delivered from the necessities incident to the way—climbing, watching, fighting, footing it all the way.

No man knew better the difficulties of the way than did Job. This text is his confession of faith, most commendable, most valuable.

I. Let us think first of the traveler. "The righteous." Honest, upright, the truly Christian. In the Bible the Christian is frequently compared to a traveler. But no traveler reaches his journey's end by merely starting on the road. We must journey all the length, every mile of the road if we would reach the desired end.

II. The road. The Christian travelers are represented as "on their way." They shall "hold on," shall persist. The way may be unknown, perilous, narrow, circuitous. Discouragements the travelers may have, shall have; trials of patience and hope; through want of watchfulness they may slumber; through want of diligence they may stumble; but "the righteous also shall hold on his way."

III. That means persistence. The road may be long, rough, uphill, downdale, across rivers, over mountains, and lifelong; but the traveler has the strong staff of God's promises, the sword of the Spirit, his feet are shod with the preparation of the gospel of peace, and by God's grace he "holds on his way."

IV. That means arrival. Home!

On any morning—
Think of stepping on shore
And finding it Heaven!
Of taking hold of a hand
And finding it God's hand;
Of breathing a new air
And finding it celestial air;
Of feeling invigorated
And finding it immortality;
Of passing from storm and tempest
To an unknown calm;
Of waking up, and finding it—Home!

—Unidentified

CHRISTIAN ENDEAVOR SOCIETY TOPIC

Oct. 5. What Is the Church? Matt. 16:13-19; Acts 2:41-47.

BULLETIN BOARD SLOGANS FOR THE MONTH

By Earl Riney

The fall season reminds us of beauty, patience and fruitfulness.

What others say cannot hurt you unless you let it.

Inferiority is not a fact; it is a condition of mind.

Do you think that folks that disagree with you are stupid?

Your character is better credit than your pocketbook.

Successful finance is spending less than you earn.

Seek wisdom and guidance from God that you may avoid life's pitfalls.

The cake you don't eat today may supply you with years of future happiness.

It is better to light a candle than to curse the darkness.

The place of need is the place of opportunity.

SUNDAY SCHOOL LESSON

Oct. 5. Jesus Dedicates His Life. Matt. 3:16–4:11, 17.

MEMORY SELECTION: "Lo, I come . . . to do thy will, O God." Heb. 10:7.

We now begin the study of the Gospel of Matthew. In this lesson we see Jesus choosing God's way. This is shown in his temptation, his baptism, and in the beginning of his lifework. We note his consecration, his self-discipline, and the divine approval of the task before him. "I have come to do thy will, O God." This is his theme and his purpose. A dedicated life then and now grows in the desire and ability to do God's will day by day.

SUNDAY: OCTOBER TWELFTH

MORNING SERVICE

Theme: Though the Vision Tarry.

SUGGESTED SCRIPTURE READING: Ps. 27:1-14.

SELECTED HYMNS: "Wait, my soul, upon the Lord."—W. P. Lloyd. "If thou but suffer God to guide thee."—G. Neumark. "Cast thy burden on the Lord."—Anon. "As pants the hart for cooling streams."—Anon. "Rise, my soul, and stretch thy wings."—R. Seagrave.

CALL TO WORSHIP: "They that wait upon the Lord shall renew their strength; they shall mount up with wings as eagles; they shall run, and not be weary; and they shall walk, and not faint."

INVOCATION PRAYER: Our God and Father, we gather to wait upon thee this day. We would tarry for the heavenly vision, and when it is given help us to be obedient to it. O thou whom the hosts of heaven obey, and whose commandments to us are not grievous, incline our hearts to serve thee as we ought. Help us to perform duty not in dread, but as constrained by the power of thy love. Help us today to live in the joy of thy strength, to keep thy law, and to be honored with some service to our fellow men. In thy great compassion forgive our shortcomings, and make us heirs of thine everlasting kingdom through the gift of thy grace in Christ Jesus. We ask all in his name. Amen.

Theme: Though the Vision Tarry.

TEXT: "Though the vision tarry, wait for it; because it will surely come, it will not tarry." Hab. 2:3.

INTRODUCTORY: No one can fail to have visions unless he is devoid of imagination.

I. What is a vision? It is an inward view, an image or series of images larger, grander, deeper than one's bodily eye can see. Life without vision would be drab indeed. There are false visions and true. Those that are false usually have this world for their boundary and the things of the world for their substance. They generally relate to self, to one's own aggrandizement, to one's own enjoyment or gratification of some desire of the natural mind and heart. But there are visions true, that come from God and bring men near to God. That sort of vision is supernatural, spiritual. It is seen by faith, and by faith alone.

That vision in your eyes, whence comes it? You have been seeing justice, righteousness, peace, good will, love prevailing in the world, in society, in self. Whence comes it? Whence your dream? We have been having dealings with God and perhaps are not aware of it. It is only the unusual one who realizes that he is thinking God's thoughts after him. That vision of your eyes of the better day, of the coming of the kingdom, know you not that you are seeing the purposes of God?

Though that vision tarry, wait for it, keep it in your eyes, because it will surely come, it will not tarry.

II. What is implied in such waiting? 1. Sometimes it implies pain or a degree of impatience. M. K. W. Heicher has said, "What pain is to the body that waiting is to the soul of man. Children can scarcely wait for Christmas to come. Some men have grown old waiting for the seed which they have sown to bring forth a harvest or the bread which they have cast upon the waters to return." 2. Always such waiting implies a firm persuasion of the being and reality of what God has promised. Faith makes unseen things visible and future things present. It is "the substance of things hoped for." 3. Such waiting, "though it tarry," implies a deep humility joined with reverence and love. Rightly waiting upon God implies high apprehensions of him and low apprehensions of ourselves. Humility waits. Reverence waits. Love waits. 4. But true waiting does not give up. Fervent desire fails not, but continues. 5. And it is patient. "Though the vision tarry" the waiting soul is not discouraged by the longest delays. The prophet Habakkuk calls it "standing upon a watch-tower." That implies the opposite of sloth and weariness. Waiting upon God does not imply indolence, but activity, not neglect of means, but diligent use of them.

III. Note also the reasonableness of such waiting on our part. 1. We are but servants. 2. What God has promised must be worth waiting for. 3. God has long waited upon us. He has had great patience with us; shall we not patiently wait for his time and grace? 4. Forget not also that the very sweetness of our blessings are usually proportioned to the time we have waited for them.

Therefore wait. Wait in patience. Wait in faith. Wait in confidence. Wait in hope. Wait in cheerfulness. Wait in action. Let your waiting be humble, patient, prayerful, persistent, brave, active. "Though the vision tarry, wait for it; because it will surely come, it will not tarry." Wait for it! Don't give it up!—Acknowledgments to R. B.

THEME PRAYER: Help us, our Father, to hear thee saying, "Wait on the Lord, be of good courage, and I will strengthen thine heart." Help us to wait as a servant waiting for his master, as a child waiting for his parents, as a traveler waiting for the directions of his guide, as a mariner waiting for his pilot. Though the vision tarry, help us to wait for it because the fulfillment will surely come. In Jesus' name we ask. Amen.

OFFERTORY SENTENCE: "God so loved the world that he gave his only begotten Son, that whosoever believeth in him should not perish, but have everlasting life."

OFFERTORY PRAYER: With heartfelt thanksgiving, our Father, do we make our offering in Christ's name. Unto all the holy uses of thy Church may it be applied, and grant that it may abound unto all comfort, all peace, all strength, and all salvation unto those for whom it is given and those who give it, for thy Son's sake. Amen.

Illustrative Material

SEED THOUGHTS, HOMILETIC AND EXPOSITORY. Waiting on the Lord: I. A humble waiting. II. A patient waiting. III. A persistent waiting. IV. An active waiting. Faith without works is dead. Prayer without works is just as dead. The sick man must use the remedy if he would get well. The businessman must be fervent in his business. The soldier must keep his powder dry. V. Be brave in waiting. "Wait" is a large word. We must take it at its full meaning.—H. J.

The Duty of Waiting: I. Wait in prayer. II. Wait in simplicity of soul, as a humble child willing to be guided by God's will. III. Wait in faith. IV. Wait in quiet patience.—C. H. S.

Choice Illustrations on the Theme

CAMP PATIENCE. One of the great Arctic explorers named his camp in the snowy waste, Camp Patience. There he waited for the opportunity to make his dash for the Pole. To be ready and to wait was essential to the success of the venture.—M. K. W. H.

VISION. How does it come about that we have a vision of a better day? Whence comes that vision? Do men just naturally dream splendid things like that? You have been seeing justice, righteousness, peace, good will, love prevailing in the world, in society, in the self. Whence your dream? What is the ultimate source of good? This is a problem —where does good come from? It overwhelms the other problem—where does evil come from? In spite of evil, why is it that high vision persists in the eyes?—M. K. W. H.

VISION CHERISHED. Our air castles are the children of our youth. They should be no less, however, the heritage of manhood, middle and old age. No life can keep alive that does not have newborn visions. When the fires of enthusiasm cease to burn, the mind ceases to dream and the hands to create. I have seen many who begin life and its pursuits with zest and promise. But because such people are not able to keep alive their dreams and sustain their ideals, life is impoverished and becomes a drudgery.

WE LIVE BY VISIONS. The wise man never spoke truer words than when he said, "Where there is no vision the people perish." We live by our visions. A man without vision is a man without hope, and a man without hope is a man without life. He whose thoughts and aspirations are bounded by the narrow horizon of today, who has no vision and plan for what lies beyond it, is to be pitied. On the other hand, where there is vision there is life. It is the vision that quickens the pulse and rouses the spirit and sends men forth to victory.—Rev. S. N. Hutchison.

VISION RETAINED. One of Frank Dicksee's, the English artist's, most inspiring pictures is one to which he has given the title, "The Ideal." It represents a youth climbing up a steep ascent, and having reached with infinite difficulty a high and shining peak. His uplifted eyes are full of the fire of aspiration; his arms are eagerly outstretched. In the wreathen mist in front of him there is a Figure which he strains to reach, but which has left the earth and is rising towards the heavens. Still the Figure beckons the youth to follow, to struggle, to attain. This is the young Christian, not dolorous, but triumphant, seeking as his prize the high calling of God in Christ Jesus.—James Burns.

Suggested Texts and Themes

A Good Man's Opinion of Himself: "Christ Jesus came into the world to save sinners; of whom I am chief." I Tim. 1:15.

The Opinion of a Rich Fool: "Soul, thou hast much goods laid up for many years; take thine ease, eat, drink, and be merry." Luke 12:19.

A Man of Set Opinions: "One thing I do, forgetting the things which are behind, and stretching forward to the things which are before." Phil. 3:13 (A. S. V.).

An Apostles's Opinion of Future Bliss: "For I reckon that the sufferings of this present time are not worthy to be compared with the glory which shall be revealed to us-ward." Rom. 8:18 (A. S. V.).

The Ideal Community: "Thou shalt be called, The city of righteousness, the faithful city." Isa. 1:26.

EVENING SERVICE

Theme: The Sounding of Silver Trumpets.

TEXT: "And the Lord spake unto Moses, saying, Make thee two trumpets of silver," etc. Num. 10:1-3.

INTRODUCTORY: In this passage and its connections the law of the silver trumpets is recorded. The commission was given to Moses as leader of the people. There were to be two trumpets, yet both formed out from one piece of silver. The law of their various uses was also given.

I. Let us notice first that they were to be of silver. They were not to be cast, but of hand-beaten work, and of a shape no doubt suitable for their purpose. But that they should be of choice silver speaks of their worth, white, brilliant, precious, also that they were for important uses.

II. They were to be blown to call the people to the sanctuary worship. "Blow ye the trumpet in Zion." "Blessed are the people that hear the joyful sound."

III. They were to be blown for the journeying of the camps. The Gospel trumpet calls us, "Move on; advance; go forward!"

IV. They were to be blown for the animating and encouraging of their armies when they went out to battle. For alarm. For call. For inspiration. "If ye go to war blow with the trumpets," v. 9. It signified an appeal to heaven for the decision of the controversy.

V. They were to be blown for the commencing of seasons. "At the beginning of your months ye shall blow," etc. v. 10. Anniversaries have religious meaning and importance.

VI. For the solemnizing of their sacred feasts they were to blow the trumpets. One of the feasts was called the Feast of Trumpets, Lev. 23:23, 24. Trumpets were blown in connections with their sacrifices also. II Chron. 29:27, to intimate with what joy and delight they performed their duty to God. It has been well said, "Holy work should be done with holy joy."

Let us remember to blow with the silver trumpets in our days of gladness in our families and in our own hearts; also for our country's sake in days of victory and triumph.—H.

MIDWEEK FELLOWSHIP MEETING TOPIC

(Church Night of Suggested Sermon Subject)

Theme: Seeking for Christ.

TEXT: "Go your way, tell his disciples and Peter that he goeth before you into Galilee." Mark 16:7.

I. Oftentimes we look for Jesus in the wrong place. He is risen: he goeth before you in the activities of life. The place where he lay in the sepulchre is but a memory. You must come where he is bringing dead souls to life.

II. We should go where there is sorrow, toil, trial and human need; you will find him there; on battlefields, among the wounded; he and his angels are there.

III. Do not seek him so much in past experiences, but in present duties. Do not linger about the tomb of your losses and failures. He is among the crowds of struggling people. You may commune with him, but still better, you can accompany him personally, all the way.

IV. The resurrection is the receipt of the soul as an evidence that the debt was paid on Calvary. We may believe that Jesus paid it all when he cried, "It is finished!" but the receipt is necessary to show mankind. The risen Christ is the evidence that the debt of sin is paid.—E. W. C.

CHRISTIAN ENDEAVOR SOCIETY TOPIC

Oct. 12. What Happens When We Worship? Matt. 18:19-22; Ps. 100.

SUNDAY SCHOOL LESSON

Oct. 12. Jesus Describes the Christian Life. Matt. 5:1-12.

MEMORY SELECTION: "Let your light so shine before men, that they may see your good works, and glorify your Father which is in heaven." Matt. 5:16.

This lesson features the qualities which Jesus expected his followers to develop. The Beatitudes are in contrast with the ideas of the secular world. They afford opportunity for careful interpretation of the principles which should enter into Christian living and make it different. They throw light also on the search for happiness. The Christian life is a happy way of living. Blessed are those who hear the word of God and keep it.

SUNDAY: OCTOBER NINETEENTH

MORNING SERVICE

Theme: Secret Reserves.

SUGGESTED SCRIPTURE READING: II Pet. 1:1-21.

SELECTED HYMNS: "Rise, my soul, and stretch thy wings."—R. Seagrave. "O for a faith that will not shrink."—W. H. Bathurst. "Forward! be our watchword."—H. Alford. "O then to whose all-searching sight."—N. L. von Zinzendorf. " 'Tis by faith of joys to come." —I. Watts.

CALL TO WORSHIP: "Praise ye the Lord. Sing unto the Lord a new song, and his praise in the congregation of saints. Let Israel rejoice in him that made him: let the children of Zion be joyful in their King."

INVOCATION PRAYER: In deep reverence, O God, we bow before thee in worship. In the presence of thy holiness we feel unworthy and without any right to stand before thee; but in the presence of thy love we come with hearts that are full of joy. Accept our worship, O thou holy, loving Father; may it please thee and may it minister unto us peace of heart and calmness of spirit, strength to labor, joy in living, and the forgiveness of our sins.—M. K. W. H.

Theme: Secret Reserves.

TEXT: "Strengthened with might by his Spirit in the inner man." Eph. 3:16.

INTRODUCTORY: Since the war we are all so far familiar with military technique that we can understand that the fate of a battle can depend upon the disposition and availability of reserves. Though all may seem lost, if one is able to summon a sufficient number of reserves, the situation may be saved, and retreat sometimes turned into advance. So also in the financial battle it is all-important that there be reserves adequate to meet the situation.

Do you know anything of this kind of thinking in your own life? Is there any fund of reserve power or energy, of which you know? If so they lie deep in that "inner man" of which St. Paul speaks. There are few of us who have not known what it is to be jaded, worn out nervously, and sometimes spiritually exhausted. St. Paul would pray for us as he did for the Ephesian Christians in days of testing, "that God would grant you, according to the riches of his glory, to be strengthened with might by his Spirit in the inner man."

I. Consider first this fact that reserves have to be built up. We know how in warfare an offensive has to be delayed until the reserves are ready. The "secret reserves" on a bank's balance sheet are built up through years of public service. They consist of property, buildings, land, investments, etc. Make sure that you are giving God's Spirit a chance to strengthen you with might in the inner man. Similarly, it is the man who has been steady in his Christian habits; who has thought much about these things, lived with his Lord, kept to public worship and fellowship; it is he who possesses reserves in the day of stress.

II. Another point to be stressed is that the best part of your reserves and mine are secret, in the sense that they are unseen, God-given. As you build them up and develop them, you cannot see them, any more than you can see what you are doing when you charge a battery with electricity. When it comes to using them, they will often be as complete a surprise to you as to others. How many people, sorely tested by some unexpected blow, have said to me, "I don't know how it is that I've been able to get through."

III. The way to divine resources. It has been said that 75 per cent of the people in our churches never pray, and as large a percentage never read their Bibles devotionally. We will not stop to examine these figures. They are not mine. But even supposing they are only faintly correct, may we not find here, and in other things like them, the reason why the Christian army, in this country at any rate, is not strikingly effective today? There are no reserves behind it.

Prayer happens to be the way to power. It is the way to develop faith in Divine Resources and to get to know that they are there. Through the intimacy with God that prayer gives we come to know, too, just the way in which God wants us to meet the situation and let his power through.

A prayerless Christian should be something of a contradiction in terms. If we have been failing in this matter, let us start again. Start intelligently, making Jesus the starting point, discovering what he says about it, and finding out what he did, and beginning our own experiments from there. Let us build up a Christianity with reserves, a church with reserve power behind it. Then we shall be an army whose accent will be victory instead of defeat.—C. H. P.

THEME PRAYER: Almighty God, grant to us thy children such a consciousness of thy indwelling presence as may give us utter confidence in thee. In all pain and weariness and anxiety may we throw ourselves upon thy besetting care, that knowing ourselves fenced about by thy loving omnipotence, we may permit thee to give us health and strength and peace; through Jesus Christ our Lord. Amen.

OFFERTORY SENTENCE: "I beseech you therefore, brethren, by the mercies of God, that ye present your bodies a living sacrifice, holy, acceptable unto God, which is your reasonable service."

OFFERTORY PRAYER: Not by measure would we give, O gracious Giver of all; for we can never give as thou hast given. Nevertheless, we would ask thee to help us to increase our offerings with the increase of our blessings, temporal and spiritual. May our material offerings ever be enhanced by richness of personality, and may our acknowledgments of thy bounteous love ever flow forth to bless. We ask it in the name of thy Son, our Saviour. Amen.—Hurd Allyn Drake.

Illustrative Material

SEED THOUGHTS, HOMILETIC AND EXPOSITORY. The Inner Man: I. Everyone has an inner man, a better self. He feels in his soul the touch of God. II. What does the outer man put on? 1. Dress. This is the first thing we see in another. 2. Manners. The manners are beneath the dress, make the dress more impressive and beautiful. 3. Mind. Deeper still. 4. Morals. Deeper yet. III. The inner man. 1. It is soul consciousness. 2. It is conscious relation to God. "My Father." 3. But along with this consciousness of sin—omission, commission, a falling short. 4. Consciousness of goodness as well as sin. Repentance, gratitude, aspiration.—A. R.

Strength within: I. In the "inner man." The central and highest life. Too often our effort is alone to change the outer man. We must go much deeper. In that "inner man" the "strength" has to do with conscience, motives, thoughts, affections, spiritual converse with God. II. And how? By the Spirit—supernatural power. III. The result. "Might," true might, ever increasing might. Begin inside.—J. V.

Choice Illustrations on the Theme

RESERVES. Some autos and airplanes have what is known as reserve tanks. When the gasoline gets too low you can switch over and count on the reserve. Maybe you have always been able to manage on the ordinary supply, and have never had consciously to switch over to the reserve. You have been very fortunate if this is so; but sooner or later in a life such as this our reserves will be tested.—C. H. Powell.

CHRISTIAN STRENGTH. The Christian needs to be strengthened with might in the inner man. The might which the Christian needs is conveyed through the agency of the Holy Spirit. This might is in answer to prayer. This might should be sought as from an inexhaustible source.—G. Brooks.

THE SPIRIT'S GIFT OF STRENGTH. The Christian has great need of strength. The region where strength is required is in "the inner man." It is in the moral and spiritual nature that reinforcement is required to do duty, withstand temptation, and stand steadfast in right. What is the source from which this strength is derived? It is the gift of God through the influence of the Holy Spirit. The law of its bestowment is "Through faith," that is, through the exercise of faith.—A. F. Muir.

STRENGTH OUT OF WEAKNESS. The most striking symbol in Venice is the winged lion with the Gospel in its paw. It meets you everywhere in that queen of cities which rears itself out of the waters of the Adriatic. And it is a fitting emblem. For this is the emblem of St. Mark, the patron saint of Venice, in whose honor the matchless Byzantine cathedral was built.

But one might say of all emblems surely the lion, the bravest of the beasts of the field, is the least fitting for St. Mark. Was it not he through cowardice turned aside and fainted by the way, forsaking the great apostle in his first missionary journey, and in the hour of his deepest need? Was it not St. Mark whom Chrysostom held up to high scorn calling him "maimed finger," the scornful epithet applied to those who maimed themselves in order to escape military service? All of which is true. But it is to be remembered that at the last St. Mark "witnessed a good confession." He conquered his hereditary weakness, and is a noble illustration of those who "out of weakness were made strong." And this is the highest form of valor.—J. B. Burns.

EVENING SERVICE

Theme: A King Who Gives in a Kingly Way.

TEXT: "My God shall supply all your need according to his riches in glory by Christ Jesus." Phil. 4:19.

INTRODUCTORY: Paul and his colleagues were poor. Here Paul acknowledges the kindness and generosity of the Christians at Philippi, and declares his confidence that God will reward and enrich them from the glorious treasures of his providence and grace. "My God," etc.

I. Let us think first of the need of Christians. "All your need." The Christians at Philippi were just as much in need as were the apostles. It was a time of persecution, of great tribulation. Under fierce persecution these early Christians could not well succeed in their secular affairs. But the text also presupposes that we too are needy creatures, full of temporal and spiritual wants. We are in want as sinners and need salvation. We are in want as believers and need grace to overcome foes that are not alone strong, but often artful and cunning and sometimes fascinating to appetites within our own hearts and minds. "All our needs." They are very many and our needs are very great.

II. But here comes in the assurance that God will supply all our needs "according to his riches in glory." The phrase "riches in glory" is a glorious phrase. It implies the fullness of God, grace sufficient. It has been expressed as "according to the greatness of his goodness," also as "according to the inexhaustible riches of his grace." This "according to" suggests the rule of supply. It suggests that whatever God does is done in a way worthy of himself. The King gives in a kingly way, according to his office, according to his infinite ability. This is not commonly the case among men, for the most wealthy are not always the most liberal. But God is a glorious Giver. Nothing short of infinite good is at his disposal, and he gives accordingly. "He giveth liberally and upbraideth not," "according to his riches in glory." The Agent is God. "My God will give" expresses the confidence of Paul arising from his knowledge of God's ability and the love he bears to his servants. He also implies that the gifts will be appropriate, skillfully adapted to the necessities of his people.

III. The apostle then tells us the Medium of this supply. "By Christ Jesus." "My God shall supply all your need, according to his riches in glory, by Christ Jesus." Christ is the Medium of supply. He is the way to the Father and the channel of communication between God and us. God in the supplies he grants has a special regard to Christ. Our Great High Priest is infinitely precious in the sight of God, and therefore there is nothing too good or too great to give for his sake. All the riches of his grace and infinite blessings for his people are to be given through Christ.

How wonderful the love of God in providing such a Fountain, such a Channel of Supply! "My God shall supply all your need according to his riches in glory by Christ Jesus." He is the King who gives in a Kingly way. He is our Father!

Suggested Texts and Themes

A Square Issue Squarely Met: "But when Peter was come to Antioch, I withstood him to the face, because he was to be blamed." Gal. 2:11.

The Triple Tyrant: "The sting of death is sin; and the strength of sin is the law." I Cor. 15:56.

Christian Socialism: "All that believed were together," etc. Acts 2:44, 45.

The Atoning Sorrow: "And about the ninth hour Jesus cried with a loud voice," etc. Matt. 27:46.

The Rising Road: "The way of life is above to the wise." Prov. 15:24.

MIDWEEK FELLOWSHIP MEETING TOPIC

(Church Night or Suggested Sermon Subject)

Theme: Food for Soul and Body.

TEXT: "Give us this day our daily bread." Matt. 6:11.

I. The prayer suggests more than a crumb and crust doctrine. It means all that nourishes life, all the wants of man beyond the primary need of food for the body, clothes for the outside, shelter from the elements.

II. The soul needs nourishment. A starved soul in a well-fed body is not the logic of life that is life indeed. The world has been greatly benefited by those who wrought nobly, by well-nourished souls when their bodies were lacking; but the ideal is to nourish the whole being, body and soul.

III. God intends that we obtain such balance that souls and bodies share in his good gifts. The balanced life is the contented life. The normal life is the happy life. The sane life is the efficient life. Some people want too much. Some are satisfied with too little. Let us ask God in his wisdom to give us just enough.—R. B.

CHRISTIAN ENDEAVOR SOCIETY TOPIC

Oct. 19. How Can the Church Affect World Order? Acts 17:24-28; Isa. 2:2-4. (World Order Sunday.)

SUNDAY SCHOOL LESSON

Oct. 19. Jesus Demands Sincerity. Matt. 6:1-8, 16-18, 22-24.

MEMORY SELECTION: "Where your treasure is, there will your heart be also." Matt. 6:21.

After condemning insincere practices of his day, Jesus demanded sincerity from his followers. Well may we examine ourselves in the light of Christ's standards. In the matter of worship this is especially important. How do we pray? How sincere are we? There is a great difference between those who pray to be heard of men and those who talk to God and mean what they say. Even service is of little value without sincerity of purpose. Let us examine ourselves.

SUNDAY: OCTOBER TWENTY-SIXTH

MORNING SERVICE

Theme: The Ministry of Music.

SUGGESTED SCRIPTURE READING: Pss. 149 and 150.

SELECTED HYMNS: "Angel voices ever singing."—F. Pott. "Holy, Holy, Holy, Lord God Almighty."—R. Heber. "Come, thou Almighty King."—Anon. "Sweet is the work, my God, my King."—I. Watts. "Now thank we all our God." —M. Rinkart.

CALL TO WORSHIP: "Seeing then that we have a great high priest, that is passed into the heavens, Jesus the Son of God. . . . Let us therefore come boldly unto the throne of grace, that we may obtain mercy, and find grace to help in time of need."

INVOCATION PRAYER: Our Father, whose hand is ever filled with bounty for thy children, whose mind is ever thoughtful for their good, whose heart is ever gracious toward their need, accept we pray thee our gratitude. Be this our gratitude, O God, that we may seek to know thee more truly, to love thee more deeply, to serve thee more faithfully. Be this our consecration, that we ever seek thy kingdom, thy sovereign rule over us, the reign of Christ within us, and his abundant life all about us. May we be ever ready to greet a new day in the world when thy kingdom comes. May that kingdom be the light in our eyes, the passion of our hearts, the motive of our hands. Help us ever, O God, to prepare the way for the coming of the Christ into the lives of men. Bless us that we may have skill in attracting little children to him, in showing youth his excellence, in bringing men and women his wisdom, in blessing age with his comfort, in offering to all his grace of forgiveness and of peace. And that which we would bring to others may we accept for ourselves ever knowing that each of us has no other Saviour than him who is the Saviour of the world. In his own name we pray. Amen.—M. K. W. H.

Theme: The Ministry of Music.

TEXT: "I will open my dark saying upon the harp." Ps. 49:4.

INTRODUCTORY: One hesitates to speak of music because words fail to express its meaning, beauty or power. It has its spring in the senses. Its appeal is to the heart. It is difficult to analyze its spell.

I. It is a refuge from materialism. When the mind is bewildered by contradiction it seeks release in an overworld of harmony. It has always been so. Music not alone expresses the moods of the mind, but gives a glimpse of a world which lies beyond. The musician uses tones as the poet uses words.

No other art stirs men so deeply, so entirely in body, mind and soul; no other sways him with such magic spell. Music is at once the most sensuous and the most spiritual of the fine arts, and therein lies its power and its peril. For not all music is noble. But at its best this art makes the soul jubilant with praise and tender with prayer, and lifts us to the gates of heaven.

II. What is music? Ask the poets what it is that sends the plowboy whistling to his task, and they will tell you a song. Beethoven said that it is more than a concord of sweet sounds; it is something from a higher world that we cannot describe. Music, they tell us, is an echo of heaven; a hieroglyphical and shadowed lesson of the world; a voice from the irrevocable past; the great mysticism; the beautifier of time: a silver key to the fountain of tears; love in search of a word; a rose-lipped shell that murmurs of the eternal sea that brought us hither, and upon which we set sail when we go hence. But when we have gleaned all these images of speech we do not know what music is.

III. Let us think of the priestly ministry of music. A priest is one who speaks of God for man, as a prophet is one who speaks for God to man. But music does both of these. There is an ever-struggling impulse in man to send his soul heavenward. Music does this where words fail. But just so truly is it a message which comes to us from God.

The Bible is a great book of music. It begins with a creation hymn, when the morning stars sang together and all the Sons of God shouted for joy; and its music though sometimes faint is never hushed. The Psalter is a hymnbook. Indeed it is a great organ with keys of black and white on which is played all the high, tender, plaintive, aspiring, triumphant music of the soul in its quest for God amid the shadows of time. The Magnificat was the cradle lullaby of Jesus, and there must have been many wayside songs in the house of his pilgrimage. On the last night when he had eaten the parting supper they sang a hymn and wended their way to the Garden of Sorrow; and from the upper room the hymn has echoed, like a refrain, to the ends of the earth, giving the Christian ages their motive and their melody. —J. F. N.

THEME PRAYER: We would bless thee at all times; may thy praise be ever upon our lips. Amen.

OFFERTORY SENTENCE: "Give, and it shall be given unto you; good measure, pressed down, and shaken together, and running over, shall men give into your bosom."

OFFERTORY PRAYER: O God, who art the source of all generosity and the spirit behind all sacrifice, help us always to find our stronghold in thee, and not in any abundance of earthly riches. We thank thee for all thy mercies; may we trust thy loving-kindness, and be strengthened by it. With the fruits of our hands, O Father, may we also bring thee the homage of our hearts, through Jesus Christ our Lord. Amen.—William H. Hudnut, Jr.

Illustrative Material

SEED THOUGHTS, HOMILETIC AND EXPOSITORY. On Wings of Song: "And when they had sung an hymn, they went out." Matt. 26:30. I. Music can fill our minds with beauty and drive away depressing moods. It can be a comfort in time of trouble and can take us out of ourselves and lift us into an emotional state that is wider than our immediate experience. It can bring us into the Divine Presence. Great music, great art, and great poetry are aids to true worship. II. The hymns of the Christian Church constitute a spiritual treasure for all humanity. We need to put more emphasis on singing; as Christians we need to learn to sing our great hymns instead of complaining that we do not know them when they are used in our churches. We live at our best when we meet life with a song in our hearts and on our lips.

Choice Illustrations on the Theme

THE MINISTRY OF MUSIC. Music is a divine art, a universal language, a vehicle of worship, and a soothing, inspiring and saving force. Old and young, rich and poor, learned and unlearned, all alike acknowledge the strangely weird and fascinating power of music. It is grateful and refreshing as the breezes of the mountains. It is stimulating as the breath of spring. It comes to the mind like an enchantment from the world of infinite harmonies where God himself is found. It blesses us. It blesses others. It pleases God.—*5000 Best Modern Illustrations.*

HEATHENISM LACKS MUSIC. Heathenism has no hymnbooks. Buddhism, Brahmanism, Confucianism, Mohammedanism and paganism do not break forth into songs of joy. How could this be expected of religions whose gods inspire only fear and dread? Charles E. Scott, of China, describes the Buddhist chants as "weird," with "A vein of sadness in them as of joy unattained, of hope unrealizable," and goes on to say. "They give many people a sense of unutterable homesickness."—*Sunday School Times.*

MUSIC WINS TO CHRIST. We have read of a Grecian mother who saw her child on the brink of a precipice. To shout to it might only quicken its vagrant feet to wander closer to the edge, or so startle it with fear as to cause it to tottle over. She lifted her voice in a familiar hymn and lured the little one back to her side. So many a sinner has been led to Christ, won by the singer of some sweet song.—H.

GOSPEL SONGS IN THE CHURCH. Some religious leaders advocate the dismissal of Gospel Songs from the music of the church. Their reasons for this is in the statement that Gospel Songs are not worshipful. Dr. John Greenfield, the Moravian hymn authority, in discussing the difference between a hymn and a Gospel Song gives this definition: "The hymn is addressed to God in praise, adoration, worship and prayer. The Gospel Song is addressed to the people, bringing to them God's message and plan of salvation with the promises and warnings, personal testimony and experience, or an appeal to the people to yield themselves to Christ."

The purpose of every church is not alone worshipful, but also evangelistic. Both Gospel Songs and hymns should be in every church hymnbook.

VERY SIGNIFICANT. When the body of a well-known infidel rested in his home on the banks of the Hudson river, some years ago, the telegraph carried this intimation regarding the funeral service: "There will be no singing." That was very significant. The undertone of all Christian teaching is that every experience can be turned to good account and thus made an occasion for rejoicing.—Archer Wallace.

EVENING SERVICE

Theme: Wine the Mocker (Temperance).

TEXT: "Wine is a mocker, strong drink is raging: and whosoever is deceived thereby is not wise." Prov. 20:1.

INTRODUCTORY: "Wine is a mocker," translated also "a scorner." "Strong drink is raging," translated also "a brawler." Liquor is thus personified and represented as doing what men do under its influence. They scoff at what is holy, ridicule all that is serious, and under strong drink become noisy, insolent, and no longer masters of themselves or restrained by the laws of morality or decency.

I. Wine is a mocker because it allures the weak. It makes great promises. Strong drink is to some pleasant and to all stimulating. It goes with genial companionship. It appears to favor good fellowship. It pretends to heighten joy, cure illness, and strengthen the weak.

II. Wine is a mocker because it deceives the unwary. The danger that lurks in the cup is not seen at first. The evil it produces comes on by slow and insidious stages. Every victim of its terrible results was once an inoncent child. It is a daring piece of presumption to think one can escape its snare.

III. But, thirdly, wine is a mocker because it brings ruin on its victims. It has no pity. It hounds its dupes to destruction. Too late they discover that they are slaves. The victims are disgraced and degraded. We should allow no quarter to such a vile deceiver.—P. C.

Suggested Texts and Themes

Strong Drink a Snare: "Keep me from the snares which they have laid for me." Ps. 141:9.

How to Get Poor: "The drunkard and the glutton shall come to poverty." Prov. 23:21.

See for Yourself: "By their fruits ye shall know them." Matt. 7:20.

The Way It Ends: "The wages of sin is death." Rom. 6:23.

The Delusion of Personal Liberty: "For none of us liveth to himself." Rom. 14:7.

MIDWEEK FELLOWSHIP MEETING TOPIC

(Church Night or Suggested Sermon Subject)

Theme: Social Worship.

TEXT: "If two of you shall agree," etc. Matt. 18:19, 20.

There are always facilities for social worship. Opportunities everywhere. There are no difficulties in the matter of numbers. "Two or three" are enough, rich or poor, young or old. Distance does not prevent, for a few neighbors can come together. Time is not a limit, for any hour may be chosen.

I. Some inducements to social worship. 1. One is the promise of Christ's presence. "There am I in the midst." 2. Another, the promise of answers to prayer. "It shall be done."

II. The character of social worship. 1. Concord. If there be one thing all desire in common ask for it. 2. Prayer in itself is a privilege. 3. Joyful expectancy. Count on the promises of these verses.

III. Some requisites for social worship. 1. "In my name." 2. The spirit of obedience. 3. The recognition of Christ's presence.

IV. The advantages of social worship. They are many. Some of them. 1. It promotes spirituality of heart and mind. 2. It promotes spiritual acquaintance with other Christians. 3. It leads to more freedom with our friends in conversing upon the things of the kingdom. 4. It adds greatly to our comfort, strength and Christian joy. 5. It brings blessings upon others through prayers answered. 6. It is a stimulus to secret worship.

CHRISTIAN ENDEAVOR SOCIETY TOPIC

Oct. 26. This Is Our Protestant Faith. Rom. 1:16, 17; II Tim. 3:15-17. (Reformation Sunday.)

SUNDAY SCHOOL LESSON

Oct. 26. Jesus' Test of Faith. Matt. 7:12, 15-27.

MEMORY SELECTION: "Not every one that saith unto me, Lord, Lord, shall enter into the kingdom of heaven; but he that doeth the will of my Father which is in heaven." Matt. 7:21.

Jesus states plainly that the test of discipleship is doing the will of God. Christian influence lies in what we actually will and do, through the help of God. Saying is not enough. The test of faith is conduct. Genuine religious faith bears fruit in life. In this demand for doing the will of God and for doing his words rather than merely hearing them, he challenges the easygoing profession of religion so prevalent in this day.

SUNDAY: NOVEMBER SECOND

MORNING SERVICE

Theme: Shibboleth, or Bigotry's Password.

SUGGESTED SCRIPTURE READING: Matt. 12:1-30. After-petition: May God bless to our hearts this reading of his Word.

SELECTED HYMNS: "Who is on the Lord's Side?"—F. R. Havergal. "How shall I follow Him I serve?"—J. Conder. "Through good report and evil, Lord."—H. Bonar. "Thou art the Way, to thee alone."—G. W. Doane.

CALL TO WORSHIP: Holy, holy, holy, Lord God Almighty. Thou art worthy, O Lord, to receive glory and honor and power." "O magnify the Lord with me, and let us exalt his name together."

INVOCATION PRAYER: Our Father, be gracious to us with all the graciousness of thine own Person. Keep thou our hearts to the rhythms of heavenly truth, to the melodies of the skies, and to all that is angelic and Godlike. Speak again, O Christ, such words as thou didst speak even when wearied by the wellside, and when hungry hearts turned to thee for the bread of life, and when the outcast sought restoration. May we lose no word of thine which thou shalt speak to us this day. May thy Word come winging home to our memories, and build itself a precious place in all our hearts. We ask through Jesus Christ our Saviour. Amen.—Rev. Garret Hondelink, B.D.

Theme: Shibboleth, or Bigotry's Password.

TEXT: "Then said they unto him, Say now Shibboleth: and he said Sibboleth: for he could not frame to pronounce it right." Judg. 12:6.

INTRODUCTORY: It seems a singular thing that in a country as small as Palestine there were in the past, and still are, different dialects or ways of pronunciation by the people. You will recall that at the time of Christ, at his trial, the apostle Peter was recognized by the high priest's servant as a Galilean. He said, "Thy speech betrayeth thee." We know that even today people in some parts of England cannot say ham or house. Here among us in meeting people you are likely to say, "He is from New England." "She is from the South." "That person is a westerner." Well, really, what is a shibboleth? It is a test word, or it is a pet word of some party. It has come to be counted as a sort of password in society or politics or religion.

I. Now, how did the word originate? It came about through this incident related in the book of Judges, in the story of the Ephraimites, of the time of Jephthah. To save their lives these Ephraimites could not sound the letter "h," but said Sibboleth instead of Shibboleth. Ever since the word has been used as a sort of proverbial expression. It means any word, or doctrine, or form, or fashion which, whether we will or not, whether rightly or wrongly, justly or unjustly, we are required to pronounce or agree to as a test. It is intended to reveal what side we are on. As we have said, it has come to be a sort of password in society, in politics, or in religion. Communities have their shibboleths. Society has its shibboleths. Social life has them many, and some of them terribly cruel. Politics has them.

II. Sad to relate, so does religion have them. In religion shibboleth is often bigotry's password. There are not a few vain and man-made shibboleths in religion. 1. Many of them are in connection with things absolutely nonessential, most often identified with some form of sectarianism. There are peculiar notions on various points of belief. Some are just human whimsies on the precise character and importance of certain church ordinances. Some have to do with church polity and methods of government. Many of them are trivial. Very few of them have any great importance. 2. They do harm. How? They dishonor Christ, often working interference with his authority. They divide Christians, leading to sectarianism and lack of Christian unity. They trample on the rights of conscience, of which God alone is the judge. They sometimes lead to bad spirit which dishonors God and our common Christianity.

III. To be sure, there are some true shibboleths in religion. There are two great truths in religion: man a sinner and Christ a Saviour. Another true shibboleth of God is repentence for sin. Another is faith in Christ. But these and such as these are not sectarian. They have no elements in them of bigotry, nor do they divide Christians. Christianity as taught by its Divine Author is a spirit of kindness, tenderness, forbearance. It commends and enjoins the charity that beareth all things, believeth all things, hopeth all things. In the Gospel we are to make allowance for one another's differences, and bear with one another's infirmities, and bid Godspeed to one another's efforts. There are shibboleths which are legitimate and essential to the maintenance of vital truth and goodness among men. There are principles which constitute the very foundation stones of God's temple. These are to be defended and guarded without compromise. It is not our own measuring line which is thus applied. It is not our standard that is set up. It is not our speech to which conformity is required. It is the pronunciation which God demands. And yet it becomes us to be extremely cautious in the pressing of passwords lest we should substitute our own pronunciation for God's and shut out any of the children of the kingdom.—H.

THEME PRAYER: We are so prone to be self-centered and forgetful of others and to think of ourselves more highly than we ought to think. Lord, forgive us. Help us to be more brotherly. We want to begin today. Amen.

OFFERTORY SENTENCE: "I beseech you therefore, brethren, by the mercies of God, that ye present your bodies a living sacrifice, holy, acceptable unto God, which is your reasonable service."

OFFERTORY PRAYER: O God, with our gifts we would present ourselves. Bless the offerings we bring. Use them for the furtherance of thy cause and kingdom, and bless us as we bring them. We ask through Christ our Lord. Amen.

Illustrative Material

SEED THOUGHTS, HOMILETIC AND EXPOSITORY. Shibboleth: These Ephraimites could not for the nonce become Gileadites, nor for their life could they make that little change in their speech. The language of Palestine was diversely spoken in the different provinces. The English of Northumbria cannot pronounce the "r." In China there are dialects that differ in one valley from the next.

Bigotry. Bigotry and sectarianism do great damage in the fact that they hinder the triumph of the Gospel.

In the memory of common hardships and common trials, and common prayers, and common tears, let us be brothers forever.—T. D. T.

Bigotry is often the child of ignorance. You seldom find a man of large intellect who is a bigot.—T. D. T.

Choice Illustrations on the Theme

SOCIAL SHIBBOLETHS. Goodness of heart and purity of life and language are not always the tests of admission to what is termed good society. With some it is education. With others it is elegance of manners and accomplishments. And some estimate the worth of their neighbors by the length of their purses. With multitudes dress is the countersign. The idol of fashion is set up and we are expected to bow down daily and offer devout homage. In many assemblies the garment decides the position. One of our great generals, it is said, went modestly to one of our fashionable churches on a great funeral occasion. Upon his applying for a place it transpired that the plain cloak which wrapped his person was barely sufficient to gain him a seat inside the door. It was almost literally, "Stand thou there." During the service the cloak fell back far enough to reveal the mark upon the shoulders. Then came most profuse apologies with the pressing invitation, "Come up higher, and sit thou in a good place."—Goyn Talmage.

RACE RELATIONS. On Morningside Heights in New York City is a structure called the "International House." There one may dine with men and women of more than forty nationalities. He may sit in the lobby and discuss Omar Khayyám with a Persian, or Lao-tse with a Chinese, or Gandhi with a Hindu. It is, as it were, an "asylum of refuge" from the furious racial prejudices of the everyday world. It is a deliberate effort to face the conflict by understanding the other party and, through such understanding, working out a new relationship.—H. A. Overstreet.

RACE

A yellow man and a black man
Walked in the white man's street;
Both knew the feel of friendless soil,
Both knew the taste of defeat.
They paused outside a great stone church
To hear the white folks sing;
The voices praised in sweet accord
Jesus Christ, their King.

The yellow man and the black man,
The brown, the white, the red,
Go into the church together,
And each man bows his head.

They pray their Lord to help them
To live as brothers should;
God looks down on His children
And smiles, and says, " 'Tis good."
—Elizabeth H. Moore.

WHAT'S THE USE? One of the great indignations of my life was to find certain women in Christian churches in America who would give money and time to a foreign misionary society for work among peoples ten thousand miles away but who would not open the doors of their homes to students and persons of other races in their own cities, strangers and foreigners in America. What is the use of preaching Christ abroad when we deny him by such acts as these at home? —Pearl S. Buck.

EVENING SERVICE

Theme: Does It Pay to Be Good?

TEXT: "For thou, Lord, wilt bless the righteous; with favour wilt thou compass him as with a shield." Ps. 5:12.

INTRODUCTORY: It would seem quite unworthy to be good only from the motive of profit, because it pays. That would appear to be extreme selfishness and of doubtful acceptance with God. Yet this is at least one motive presented and even commended in the Scriptures. In I Timothy 6:6 we read, "Godliness with contentment is great gain." In the fourth chapter, v. 8, it is stated still more definitely, "Godliness is profitable unto all things, having promise of the life that now is, and of that which is to come." "All this and heaven besides!"

It cannot be doubted that this motive is appealed to not once or twice, but many times. So it seems a proper, though uncommon theme for a minister to preach upon. Here in our text the same motive is presented when it is said, "For thou, Lord, wilt bless the righteous; with favour wilt thou compass him as with a shield."

I. The first question that arises is, "Who are the righteous?" Surely not the self-righteous, nor the presumptuous, nor the conceited, nor those who call themselves righteous. This happens to be a term by which the people of God are known. It is a term by which they are distinguished from ungodly men. In Isaiah we read, "Say ye to the righteous that it shall be well with him." Such character is derived, not self-created. Its source is the grace of God. No sane man says, "O God, I thank thee that I made myself a Christian!" It is God who enlightens the mind, renews the will, changes the heart. It is the justifying righteousness of Christ that brings pardon for our sins and acceptance as the sons of God.

II. As a result we witness the blessedness of the righteous. "For thou, Lord, wilt bless the righteous." 1. He has blessed them. Their preservation is a proof of it, and their interest in Christ and their connection with his people show them to be those whom the Lord has blessed. 2. He will bless them. With temporal good. With spiritual influences. With communion with himself. With the conduct of his providence.

III. There is, thirdly, a special sort of blessedness suggested. "With favour wilt thou compass him as with a shield." The suggestion is that of a shield composed of the Divine favor. That is, as a shield is thrown round or before one in the day of battle to protect him, so will God throw his protection around the righteous. Of course, this implies that we have enemies. "Sure I must fight if I would reign." It implies also weakness and frailty, that we are in danger of being overcome if without the Divine protection. But it distinctly implies also the Divine favor as a shield that will protect, defend and save. God's love and providence will keep us safe on every side. How important to be encompassed with the shield of Omnipotence, of love, of immutable grace! Such protection would be effectual. "Compass him." "Hast not thou made an hedge about him . . . ?" Job 1:10. "I, saith the Lord, will be . . . a wall of fire round about." Zech. 2:5.—H.

Suggested Texts and Themes

The Schoolmaster: "Wherefore the law was our schoolmaster to bring us unto Christ, that we might be justified by faith. But after that faith is come, we are no longer under a schoolmaster." Gal. 3:24, 25.

Concord and Glory: "It came even to pass, as the trumpeters and singers were as one, to make one sound to be heard in praising and thanking the Lord," etc. II Chron. 5:13, 14.

Spiritual Perspective: "Our light affliction, which is but for a moment, worketh for us a far more exceeding and external weight of glory; while we look," etc. II Cor. 4:17, 18.

The Immediate Call and Response: "Straightway he called them: and they left their father . . . and went after him." Mark 1:20.

The Immediate Duty: "Straightway on the sabbath day he entered into the synagogue." Mark 1:21.

MIDWEEK FELLOWSHIP MEETING TOPIC

(Church Night or Suggested Sermon Subject)

Theme: The Unsearchable Riches of Christ.

TEXT: "Unto me, who am less than the least of all saints, is this grace given, that I should preach among the Gentiles the unsearchable riches of Christ." Eph. 3:8.

I. Think first of Paul the man. We are struck by his humility. He considered himself "less than the least of all saints." This was no mock humility, no mere affectation of humility. It is the way he felt especially in view of God's call.

II. For notice, secondly, the ministry he had received. It was to preach Christ, and especially among the Gentiles. He counted this call a call of grace, of God's great and loving favor shown to him. All work for God should be so regarded, accepted as a privilege. It was so Paul regarded this call into Christ's service.

III. This becomes all the more apparent when we think of the message he was to proclaim. It was "the unsearchable riches of Christ." What a contrast with his own conscious unworthiness! And what a message! "The unsearchable riches of Christ." 1. The riches of heavenly knowledge. 2. The riches of redeeming love. 3. The riches of pardoning mercy. 4. The riches of sanctifying and satisfying grace. 5. The riches of consolation and hope. 6. The riches of immortality and glory. 7. All of them riches in Christ and all of them "unsearchable," higher, more valuable than any possible computation.

Here are riches for all nations, wealth for all the world. Here is suggested the duty and privilege of proclaiming the good news.—B.

CHRISTIAN ENDEAVOR SOCIETY TOPIC

Nov. 2. What's One Vote Worth? Rom. 13:1-8; I Kings 19:9-12.

BULLETIN BOARD SLOGANS FOR THE MONTH

By Earl Riney

Thanksgiving Day is our national time for saying grace.

Cease minimizing your blessings and exaggerating your misfortunes.

We should give expressions of thanksgiving every day.

Enjoy the going and stop thinking so much about getting there.

A man without a purpose is like a ship without a rudder.

He that brings sunshine into the lives of others cannot keep it from himself.

Only a life lived for others is a life worth while.

We win by tenderness; we conquer by forgiveness.

If you want to put the world right start with yourself.

God's mercy is the only match for the world's misery.

SUNDAY SCHOOL LESSON

Nov. 2. Jesus' Power and Human Need. Matt. 8:5-17.

MEMORY SELECTION: "He took our infirmities and bore our diseases." Matt. 8:17 (R. S. V.).

In this selfish and secular age we need to realize that Jesus used his marvelous power to help people. He gives clear indication that power should be directed toward human good, not to oppression or destruction. The recent development of power in the hands of men (atomic energy, for instance), compels attention to the necessity of spiritual purpose in the appropriation and use of all power. There is great human need in the world today. There is great power in the hands of Christians to help meet it.

SUNDAY: NOVEMBER NINTH

MORNING SERVICE

Theme: Like a Tree (Autumn).

Suggested Scripture Reading: Ps. 1:1-6; Isa. 61:1-4.

Selected Hymns: "Songs of praise the angels sang."—J. Montgomery. "Now thank we all our God."—M. Rinkart. "With songs and honors sounding."—I. Watts. "To Thee, O Lord, our hearts we raise."—W. C. Dix. "We plough the fields and scatter."—M. Claudius.

Call to Worship: "Lift up your heads, O ye gates; and be ye lift up, ye everlasting doors; and the King of glory shall come in. . . . Who is this King of glory? The Lord of hosts, he is the King of glory."

Invocation Prayer: We thank thee, O Eternal Father, for the brightness of this autumn Sabbath. We pray thee to touch our eyes that they may be open to the beauty of the earth. Make sensitive our minds that they may be filled with wonder and responsive to all that is beautiful and good and true. Open our hearts by the warm pressure of thy love that they may respond to thy grace, to the sympathy of Christ and the guidance of thy Holy Spirit. May our souls find in thee the satisfaction of all their needs! Amen.—M. K. W. H.

Theme: Like a Tree (Autumn).

Text: "That they might be called trees of righteousness, the planting of the Lord." Isa. 61:3.

Introductory: Feeding our souls upon the beauty of trees resplendent in their autumnal glory, here and there we see one that combines with splendor of color a beautiful symmetry of form. Its branches spread gracefully in every direction and in perfect balance. We may be sure that such a tree has not attained its symmetrical proportions overnight. It is a beautifully formed tree because it has grown that way, uncrowded and unhampered.

It is just so with God's people, whom the prophet calls "trees of righteousness, the planting of the Lord." If we would be well-rounded men and women, not one-sided or cramped or peculiar, we may be sure that we cannot attain this well-balanced poise of personality by any trick of magic or sudden transformation. We must grow that way. We can achieve well-balanced character only by living well-balanced lives.

Some years ago Dr. Richard C. Cabot, of Boston, Massachusetts, wrote an interesting book entitled, *What Men Live By*. The four elements of life that Dr. Cabot presented as the things by which men live are Work, Play, Love and Worship. The distinguished author argued that each of these four phases of living is indispensable to our health and happiness, and to the development of a well-poised personality. Upon the cover of this book as a symbol of its message was a quatrefoil cross, a cross with its four beams, or arms, of equal length. The obvious suggestion was that symmetry of life could only be attained by giving due place to each of these four vital experiences.

It is reported that Dr. Cabot's formula and the cross that symbolizes it are used in the diagnosis of patients in one of the great medical clinics of the United States. To discover the cause of certain maladies the diagnostician investigates the patient's habits with respect to these normal expressions of life. The resulting report is graphically summarized by the use of the Greek or Maltese cross, each of its four beams representing one of the four "things that men live by," and being made abnormally long or abnormally short to represent the place it has held in the patient's life.

There are other ways than that employed by Dr. Cabot to designate the essential attitudes and activities of a well-ordered life. But the vital truth is plain enough. Each of us will one day be what he is day by day becoming. By the grace of God we have certain advantages over trees, but there are laws of growth for the soul as well as for the grove. And we can attain a fine symmetry of character and the beauty and health of a well-poised personality only by living well-balanced lives every day. That involves serious self-examination and strict self-discipline. It involves careful attention to habits of thought and word and behaviour. It involves a humble and gracious attention to the duties we owe to God and to our fellow men. At the same time it involves a happy and generous response to all that is good and true and beautiful in the world about us. It involves toil and laughter, smiles and tears, prayer and praise. Most of all it involves yielding our hearts to the perfect Lord of Life.—Rev. Henry Wade DuBose, D.D.

THEME PRAYER: Almighty God, gracious Father of men and angels, who openest thine hand and fillest all things with plenty; teach us to use the gifts of thy providence soberly and temperately, that our temptations may not be too strong for us, or our affections sensual and unholy. Grant, O Lord, that the blessings which thou givest us may minister neither to sin nor to sickness, but to health, holiness and thanksgiving; that in the strength of thy provision we may faithfully and diligently serve thee, may worthily feast at thy table here, and be accounted worthy to sit down at thy table hereafter, through Jesus Christ our Lord. Amen.

OFFERTORY SENTENCE: "And if thou draw out thy soul to the hungry, and satisfy the afflicted soul; then shall thy light rise in obscurity, and thy darkness be as the noonday."

OFFERTORY PRAYER: O Lord our God, who art ever bountiful in thy dealings with man, who openest thy hand and satisfiest the desire of every living thing, make us gracious in our giving as the Master who taught that it is more blessed to give than to receive. Amen.

Illustrative Material

SEED THOUGHTS, HOMILETIC AND EXPOSITORY. Trees of Righteousness: I. They are trees. 1. That is they have life. 2. Have dependent life. 3. Life of growth. II. They are goodly trees. "Trees of righteousness." 1. Afford shelter. 2. Adorn the world. 3. Give fruit. —H.

Trees of Righteousness: I. In what respect do they represent Christians? 1. Supply needs. 2. Objects of beauty. II. The planting of the trees. "Planting of the Lord." Our spiritual welfare. —G. W. H.

Trees of Righteousness: I. Description of God's people. "Trees." II. The planting. "Of the Lord." 1. He chooses their position. 2. He visits them with renewing power. III. Their purpose. "That he might be glorified." 1. Shelter. 2. Beauty. 3. Fruit.—W. H. J.

Choice Illustrations on the Theme

AUTUMN BEAUTY. No one can walk forth through the countryside, in these fall days, without a thought of Carruth's words describing the beauty of the day: "Some of us call it autumn, and others call it God." That is indeed suggestive. With bountiful hand God supplies our common needs. Yet he also adds the fair scenes of earth, the love of dear ones, and all these he crowns with Christ, our Saviour.—*Christian Herald.*

THE PLANT WIZARD. Luther Burbank is well called the plant wizard, and by his fifty years of notable service is worthily celebrated. He has produced the Burbank potato; the high gluten wheat; from the dewberry and raspberry a new and superior berry; changed the hard-shelled walnut into a soft-shelled, and improved the quality of the wood; improved several varieties of apples and other fruit, and produced new kinds; evolved wonderful roses and other flowers; taken the spines from the cactus and made it food for stock. In like manner our Divine Lord takes the bitter, thorny, unlovely lives of men and transforms them by his grace into beauty, fruitfulness and glorious usefulness. In his hands even the most unpromising are made into his own likeness.—*Homiletic Review.*

TREES AND POSTS. Every community is divided into saved people and unsaved. I call them trees and posts. When you put in a tree it begins to grow. When you stick in a post it begins to rot. We pastors have a delightful time watching trees grow. But it is a sad business watching posts decay.—A. C. Dixon.

EVENING SERVICE

Theme: The Christian's Wardrobe.

TEXT: "Put on therefore, as the elect of God, holy and beloved, bowels of mercies, kindness, humbleness of mind," etc. Col. 3:12-14.

INTRODUCTORY: Clothing is to a considerable extent the badge of character. Paul is telling these newly enlisted Colossian Christians to clothe themselves with the essential spiritual graces, and recounts some of the parts of such a wardrobe. He enumerates some of the fair garments or excellent graces of the renewed man.

I. Put on, he says, "a heart of compassion." This is the true meaning of the term "bowels of mercies." Is it not beautiful that the series should begin with pity? We all so often need it. We all should make definite effort to "put it on."

II. Put on "kindness." That is to all, perhaps especially to those who are our equals and need no special compassion. Kindness is a wider term and a wider grace. It should be quite universal. It always takes pleasure in obliging and avoids injury.

III. Put on "humility." Humility needs to go along with compassion and kindness. It is fostered by a true view both of our sinfulness and of the blessings bestowed upon us.

IV. Put on "meekness." That is a quiet, gentle spirit which will calmly endure disappointments and slights, not constantly seeking to vindicate itself.

V. Put on "long-suffering." Patience. It is difficult to exercise toward our fellow men, our fellow sinners. But it is a beautiful grace.

VI. Put on "forbearance and forgiveness." Forbearance is often the first step toward frank forgiveness. A Christian spirit will hail the first signs of repentance and will exact no unreasonable humiliation. Be "ready to forgive."

VII. "And above all these things put on love." That is the "bond of perfectness," the finishing, the binding, the completing Christian garment. 1. No Christian character is complete without love. 2. Love is the crowning Christian grace. 3. Love binds together all other Christian graces. 4. Love should make a harmonious whole of one's character. 5. It should perfect the strength of Christian character and give unity of spirit and purpose to the whole life. —E. S. P.

Additional Theme: The Ministry of Titus.

TEXT: "For this cause left I thee in Crete, that thou shouldest set in order the things that are wanting." Titus 1:5.

INTRODUCTORY: Here we are told why Paul left Titus in Crete. The situation and the spiritual condition of the people there is summed up in one blistering verse: "They profess that they know God; but in works they deny him." Because of this, said Paul, "Left I thee in Crete, that thou shouldest set in order the things that are wanting."

Crete was a hard place. The Cretans were persuaded they were sufficient of themselves. Titus was disappointed with the position as he found it. Then he received a stimulating message from Paul—a message which gave him eyes to see that his little world was so much raw material out of which something good could be created. A world in which there was so much evil was not a reason for despair, it was an opportunity for exercising his Christian-creative power.

I. The men that matter. Titus was to be the man through whom the Cretans were to discover the power that could give redirection to their aims and desires. The possibilities for good inherent in a difficult situation are determined by the Christian mind brought to bear on it. Ships are all right, it is the men in them that matters most. Slavery is doomed when Lincoln throws the force of his personality against it. Africa, so dark, is flooded with light when Livingstone goes in with heart and mind aglow with Christian truth and Christ-inspired love. Cannibals become Christians when transforming grace is revealed and accepted through the life of Mary Slessor. General Booth saw in the slums of London not only the scum of humanity, but souls for whom Christ died.

Titus had to stand alone. Paul did not remain with him. He was left in Crete to battle with the awkward situation. Yet he was not alone, for the Lord whom he served was with him. When one life sincerely co-operates with God, great things are possible. All the problems of life must be tackled as Titus tackled Crete. What life hands to us is the raw material out of which something worth while must be created.

II. To face the hard facts of life with all the strength we have is the only way to achieve results, but none of us are sufficient of ourselves. We need the conviction that Christ will fulfill for us his great promise: "Lo, I am with you alway." Then, whether we walk in the light or in the dark, we know it is not a lonely way. Jesus faced his "Crete" as he found it, knowing his Father was with him. His faith never faltered. Faith in God gives us an enlarged conception. We come to see that our corner of the world is a bit of God's world, and so, when we do our best, we are helping to increase the music of heaven in this world of discord. A new gladness comes into life when we learn that God has a place for us in this world; a place that only we can fill. Life for so many people is so ordinary, because it is purposeless. Life is only delivered from ordinariness when we see our task, our God-given work, and try to do it with all our heart, mind and soul.

III. Real progress depends on discovery, and the ability to use the discovery wisely. Titus discovered that Crete was a dark place, but later he made another discovery. It was this: Crete was not entirely soulless, therefore not entirely hopeless. No position is completely hopeless, no person beyond redemption when seen in the light of God's power as Jesus revealed it. That truth has yet to grip the heart of mankind. Anything less than a belief in the redeemability of the worst through the grace of God is only a partial recognition of the Christian message. Unless we believe that this spark of goodness can be fanned into a flame we have no gospel to preach and no inspiration for supporting the work of the kingdom of God.

IV. Crete still exists. We are a long way from the day when this epistle was written, but there are still Crete-like places—people at home and abroad who are imprisoned in Crete-like experiences. To be a modern Titus is not less difficult than in the days of this early disciple. How challenging are the facts of our modern world which call for a power which can transform and renew!

How urgent is the need for the dauntless spirit of Titus finding expression through our daily life! Do we feel the challenge of this modern Crete in which we live? And when we see it do we realize that by Christ's help it can be transformed, made new? If so, let us pray that God may help us to be a modern Titus, bringing our experience of Christ and his power to bear on this mass of evil material—evil material in which there are possibilities for good. Only a flame of sacred love burning in our hearts can make us a modern Titus. —J. C. M.

Suggested Texts and Themes

The Danger of Looking Back: "Remember Lot's wife." Luke 17:32.

The Snare of the South Wind: "And when the south wind blew softly, supposing that they had obtained their purpose, they weighed anchor and sailed along Crete, close inshore." Acts 27:13 (R. S. V.).

The Insensibility of Selfishness: "They considered not the miracle of the loaves: for their heart was hardened." Mark 6:52.

The Policy of Compromise: Acts 19:35-41.

The Master Workman: "Is not this the carpenter?" Mark 6:3.

MIDWEEK FELLOWSHIP MEETING TOPIC

(Church Night or Suggested Sermon Subject)

Theme: The Happy People.

TEXT: "Happy is that people . . . whose God is the Lord." Ps. 144:15.

This is quite contrary to what many people mistakenly think. Yet happiness is universally desired and sought after.

I. In this Scripture we are called upon to think as to who are the happy people. The text says, "Happy is that people . . . whose God is the Lord." This means that they are blessed in having God for their Lord; but it means also that they themselves are happy.

II. What are some of the features of the happiness God's people possess? 1. They are happy in the sense of having God's favor. 2. They are happy in the peace that faith gives them. 3. And they are happy too in a happiness that is permanent. The world can neither give it nor take it away. God is their sun and shield, their refuge, the strength of their hearts, their exceeding great reward and their portion forever.—B.

CHRISTIAN ENDEAVOR SOCIETY TOPIC

Nov. 9. This Is Africa! Acts 16:6-10; John 3:18-21.

SUNDAY SCHOOL LESSON

Nov. 9. The Compassion of Jesus. Matt. 9:1-9, 35-38.

MEMORY SELECTION: "When he saw the crowds, he had compassion for them, because they were harassed and helpless, like sheep without a shepherd." Matt. 9:36 (R. S. V.).

Jesus was the great Helper. He always felt concern for others. When he saw the crowds he had compassion on them. Appeal may well be made to all of us to develop more of Jesus' sensitive spirit. This may well prove a missionary motive. We are responsible for taking an active part in the extension of the Christian message throughout the world. Compassion is a great grace. It should be an active one in the lives of us all.

SUNDAY: NOVEMBER SIXTEENTH

MORNING SERVICE

Theme: The Christian Walk.

SELECTED SCRIPTURE READING: Eph. 5:1-33.

SUGGESTED HYMNS: "Walk in the light, so shalt thou know."—B. Barton. "'Tis by the faith of joy, to come."—I. Watts. "My soul, be on thy guard."—G. Heath. "A charge to keep I have."—C. Wesley.

CALL TO WORSHIP: "The Lord reigneth; let the earth rejoice; let the multitude of isles be glad thereof. Clouds and darkness are round about him: righteousness and judgment are the habitation of his throne."

INVOCATION PRAYER: Almighty and eternal God, Creator of the universe and Father of our spirits, we worship thee. Far off from us thou never art, but by the insensitiveness of our own hearts we keep thee distant. Grant unto us in this hour of opportunity the grace of receptiveness, that into hospitable souls we may receive thee, thou Spirit of goodness and beauty and truth. Cross the inner thresholds of our hearts, lay hold upon our faith, steady our faltering spirits, and with such inner refreshment send us out to be soldiers of the common good, that we may be equal to all the demands that shall be made upon us. We pray in the spirit of Jesus Christ. Amen.—Harry Emerson Fosdick.

Theme: The Christian Walk.

TEXT: "See then that ye walk circumspectly, not as fools, but as wise." Eph. 5:15.

INTRODUCTORY: Of all the figures of speech which men have devised to describe the Christian life there is none so apt as that which depicts it as a walk. We are bidden time and again by the Biblical writers to walk in the ways of the Lord, to walk by faith and not by sight, to walk not after the flesh but after the spirit, to walk worthy of the Lord.

The metaphor is a good one. The life of the man of God is more like a walk than anything else; not an aimless meandering, but a walk with a direction. The Christian believer is a pilgrim walking through life with Christ as his goal, wth God as his guide and with the Spirit as the supplier of his endurance.

Nobody was more attracted by this conception than the Apostle Paul, and in this chapter he uses the metaphor three times.

I. His first call to men is to walk in love, and in so doing he draws attention to the supreme quality of the true Christian life.

The trouble is that many of us have a complete misconception of what it means to be a Christian. We have thought of the Christian life as a grim obedience to a list of rules, as a striving with clenched teeth to fulfill a catalogue of stiff duties, as a faithful endeavor to practice a lofty morality. But the criterion by which we are approved or condemned of God is the criterion of love. Are we loving or are we loveless? We can be just and yet unloving. We can be upright and yet radiate no spirit of holy affection. We can be moral and yet spread no Christlike fragrance around us. Do we love as Christ loved? This is the standard and, in the end, is the only true morality.

II. The Apostle also bids men walk in wisdom. But the wisdom of which the Apostle speaks is not even wisdom as the world regards it. For him wisdom is doing the will of God. To walk in wisdom is to subdue our wills, to submit our desires, to subordinate our ambitions to the will and purpose of him in whom all the treasures of wisdom are found. And in all this we must never forget that what is wisdom in the eyes of God may seem foolishness in the sight of men. So in countless ways what appears to be foolishness to the world is in reality the true wisdom of God. To discover our place in the great, divine purpose, to find and fulfill our part in the kingdom of Christ and to carry out that which the will of God has ordained for us, in spite of the world's parrot-cries of "Waste!" or "Folly!" is to walk in wisdom, the wisdom of God.

III. The other call which the Apostle addresses to us is to walk in the light. "Walk," he says, "as children of the light." What is this light but the light of the revelation of God, the light of Truth? It is the light of the knowledge of the glory of God in the face of Jesus Christ. The treasure-store of that Truth and the torch of that light God has placed before us in the Bible. In our hands as we step forward upon our pilgrim's progress, it will be for us what the cloud of day and the pillar of fire by night were to the children of Israel long ago, and what it has always been for men of God in all the ages since.

The world is often dark and stormy, and the path we have to take is sometimes rough and hard. The Word of the Lord is a lamp of divine truth for every one of us. It is a lantern that may appear old and rather battered. But be assured of this above all—it will light us home.—G. W. H.

THEME PRAYER: We come to thee, O Master, asking thy forgiveness. Many times we might have spoken a good word for thee, but we did not; we might have witnessed to thee, but we let slip our opportunity. Put in us a spirit of courage and help us to seize every chance to speak out clearly and effectively for thee. Amen.

OFFERTORY SENTENCE: "Now ye have consecrated yourselves unto the Lord, come near and bring sacrifices and thank offerings into the house of the Lord."

OFFERTORY PRAYER: O God most high, in whose hand our breath is, and whose are all our ways, we thank thee for another anniversary of our national independence. We praise thee that thou hast called us unto liberty. O God, grant that we may use this rich gift, not as an occasion to the flesh, but as an opportunity to serve one another by love. May the offering now presented in worship be a sacred part of our service. For Jesus' sake. Amen.

Illustrative Material

SEED THOUGHTS, HOMILETIC AND EXPOSITORY. Wise Walking: I. A course warned against. "Not as fools." II. The course recommended. "Walk circumspectly, as wise." 1. Walk by wise rule. 2. In the spirit of wisdom. 3. After good examples. 4. In good company.—J. B.

Wary Walking: I. We must walk humbly. There is no peace for pride. II. We must not overload ourselves with this world's gear.—H. J. W.

Walk Circumspectly: I. Walk circumspectly, that is diligently, carefully, that you may keep within the line of duty. II. Walk circumspectly that you may escape the snares in the way. III. Walk circumspectly that you may do every duty in its time and place. IV. Walk circumspectly that your good may not be evil spoken of.—J. L.

Choice Illustrations on the Theme

A GOOD MAN'S WALK. A Boston daily once said that whenever Phillips Brooks went down town the whole neighborhood brightened. Men felt their hearts warm as if the sun had broken through the murk and the dim alleys of the city.

WALKING WITNESSES. Francis of Assisi once said to a young monk, "Brother, let us go into the town and preach Christ." They walked through the crowded streets. Francis paused to speak to some folk he met or to lay his hand on some children's heads. And so on until evening. "Father, when shall we preach?" inquired the young men. "My son," came the reply, "what have we been doing all day but preaching?" —Archer Wallace.

UNCONSCIOUS INFLUENCE

When I met him I was looking down,
When I left him I was looking up.
—Unidentified.

A WORD OF WARNING. An elderly man I once knew told me of an experience that befell him in his young days. Having attached himself to a group of foolish young men whose morals were not above reproach he seemed to be destined to go the slippery way, but a word of warning changed his whole career. "One day when walking alone I met an old man who knew me. He was obviously aware of my foolish and indiscreet ways. Surveying me with admiration he said, 'My word, you are developing into a fine-looking fellow; what a credit you must be to your parents.' Then patting me on the shoulder he added, 'If the devil ever gets hold of the likes of you he could make a capital sinner out of you.' Then he was gone. He had said enough. It was a word fitly spoken, for it became the very turning point in my career."—J. Price Williams.

WARNINGS ARE IMPORTANT. An electric bell tinkled sharply beside the florist's desk. "Frost!" he said, and ran hatless to the greenhouses. "The fires had sunk," the florist explained on his return. "The watchman had fallen asleep. But for my frost bell I'd have lost hundreds of dollars. Frost bells are now pretty generally used by florists and fruit growers," he went on. "An electrical contrivance is connected with the thermometer, and when the mercury falls to a certain point—you regulate this danger point to suit yourself—a bell rings a warning in your house or office. Many a crop of winter fruit and flowers has been saved in the past year or two by the clever little frost bell." If Christians could only have a frost bell attached to them in some way, so that they might be plainly warned of the fact that they are getting cold, it might save many a Christian from being spiritually frostbitten and also save the Church from great losses.—*5000 Best Modern Illustrations.*

WALKING AND FINDING THE WAY. Following the crowd is not to find the way. Not to have a clear purpose for life is to wander around without any definite sense of direction. We cannot hope to get anywhere if we do not know where we are going. That is what the world is slowly discovering. It is lost because it has lost the way. But the Christian has Christ as his sure and competent guide. Without him the race can never reach its goal; with him, the soul cannot miss it.

Suggested Texts and Themes

The Immediate Blessing: "And straightway coming up out of the water, he saw the heavens opened, and the Spirit like a dove descending upon him." Mark 1:10.

The Immediate Testing: "Immediately the Spirit driveth him into the wilderness." Mark 1:12.

A Week's Work: "There are six days in which men ought to work." Luke 13:14.

The Midnight of the Soul: "Who is among you that . . . walketh in darkness, and hath no light?" etc. Isa. 50:10.

The Grafter: "Every one loveth bribes and followeth after rewards." Isa. 1:23 (A. S. V.).

EVENING SERVICE

Theme: Infatuated Hearers.

TEXT: "Speak unto us smooth things." Isa. 30:10.

INTRODUCTORY: We have heard of two jugglers who gave exhibitions of skill. One stood with back to a large board. The other threw deadly knives that struck and stuck close to his body, between his legs, under his arms, past his ears, over his head, each side of his neck. The art was not to hit him. I wonder, do any of us preachers ever juggle thus with truth? It seems that even in Isaiah's time there were people who preferred that kind of preaching. They said to the prophets, "Speak unto us smooth things." It does seem unaccountable that any intelligent human beings should ever become so foolishly infatuated that they should prefer deceit to sincerity and falsehood to truth. Strange as it may seem, there are such people still, preferring to be willingly deceived in the highest of all concerns, the concerns of the soul.

I. First let us ask just what is it to speak smooth things? It is not to be confounded with kind and affectionate things. God, our heavenly Father, is in himself both loving and kind beyond all expression. Nor is it to be confounded with a prudent presentation of truth, so as to avoid as far as possible the preconceived prejudices of people.

II. Why, then, do any persons ever desire to have spoken to them only smooth things? Well, in the first place it is common to the natural heart of man to like to hear only agreeable things. It is true also that the refinements of modern society and taste lead many to prefer and ask for only smooth things. But there is a more important reason. As a rule we do not like to be told of our sins. It wounds our pride, disturbs our self-complacency, lowers us in our own self-esteem.

What did those people in ancient Israel want? They wanted what is desired by every age, namely, to be entertained. "Speak unto us smooth things." In the church today possibly a certain amount of instruction may be tolerated in the so-called preliminaries of the service for the sake of the entertainment that follows. But people ask to be entertained with light music, with stories, with something that will give pleasant excitement, or even a degree of intellectual delight; but do not prophesy; do not become rigorously moral. "Speak unto us smooth things."

III. What is the final result of thus hearing only smooth things? It lowers the general standard of religion and morality. It starves people, for it is only upon the nourishment of truth that they can grow spiritually. It is against the true interests of the hearers themselves. It grieves the Holy Spirit. It lulls souls to sleep. It is also a great sin and violation of trust on the part of the messenger. God says always to his prophets, "Speak my words unto them."—H.

MIDWEEK FELLOWSHIP MEETING TOPIC

(Church Night or Suggested Sermon Subject)

Theme: Things for Which Jesus Gave Thanks (Thanksgiving).

TEXT: "Father, I thank thee." Matt. 11:25.

I. First: He gave thanks for bread. "And he took the seven loaves . . . and gave thanks" (Matt. 15:36). He took the simple loaves of a boy's lunch and thanked God for them. The practice of gratitude made Jesus thank God for the scantiest fare.

II. Second: He gave thanks for a gospel that is within the grasp of everyone. "I thank thee . . . because thou . . . hast revealed them unto babes" (Luke 10:21). Here is gratitude for a God who is within the reach of everyone, even the least. You and I will examine this gospel anew and our hearts will be grateful that we have this gospel.

III. Third: He gave thanks for the sacrificial service which he could render to others. He took bread and gave thanks saying, "This is my body which is given for you" (Luke 22:19). My Master gave thanks for a body broken in the service of others.

IV. Fourth: Jesus gave thanks for a prayer that was answered. "Father, I thank thee that thou hast heard me" (John 11:41). It was a request for life—immortal life if you will. He thanked God that, through faith, death is conquered.

If Jesus could practice thanksgiving in spite of all the difficulties of his day, you and I will find reason for thankfulness in the commonplace routine of our private lives.

Today my step will be a little lighter because I have said in my heart, "Father, I thank thee."—Rev. Hugh I. Evans.

CHRISTIAN ENDEAVOR SOCIETY TOPIC

Nov. 16. Religious Liberty in America. John 8:31, 32; Gal. 5:1-6.

SUNDAY SCHOOL LESSON

Nov. 16. Jesus Commissions the Twelve. Matt. 10:1, 5-7, 24-27, 34-39.

MEMORY SELECTION: "He that findeth his life shall lose it: and he that loseth his life for my sake will find it." Matt. 10:39.

Jesus lets his friends help him in doing his work in the world. Great honor is thus won. We may well think of ways in which we can do this, also of the joys that come in so doing. The mission to which Jesus called the Twelve and the instructions which he gave them in preparation for it provide guidance in discovering the mission he has for us. There is guidance for our own preparation also.

SUNDAY: NOVEMBER TWENTY-THIRD

MORNING SERVICE

Theme: A National Hymn of Thanksgiving (Thanksgiving).

SUGGESTED SCRIPTURE READING: Ps. 33: 1-22.

SELECTED HYMNS: "We plough the fields and scatter."—M. Claudius. "Come ye thankful people, come."—Henry Alford. "Praise to God and thanks we bring."—W. C. Gannett. "Now thank we all our God."—Martin Rinkart. "Now sing we a song for the harvest."—John W. Chadwick.

CALL TO WORSHIP: "The mighty God, even the Lord, hath spoken, and called the earth from the rising of the sun unto the going down thereof. Out of Zion, the perfection of beauty, God hath shined."

INVOCATION PRAYER: Heavenly Father, who art the Giver of every good and perfect gift, we thank thee for our creation in thine own image, for thy preserving mercy through all the days of our life, for the protection and comfort of our homes, for all who love us and whom we love, for healing in sickness, deliverance in danger and comfort in sorrow, for the work given us to do and the strength wherewith to do it, and for the innumerable mercies of thy mindful providence; and above all for the coming of thy beloved Son into the world, for the gracious words he spake, for the merciful work he did, for his bitter passion and atoning sacrifice on the cross, and for his mighty resurrection from the dead; for the pardon of sins, the means of grace, the indwelling of thy spirit, and the life everlasting. Amen.—J. W.

Theme: A National Hymn of Thanksgiving (Thanksgiving).

TEXT: "Rejoice in the Lord, O ye righteous," etc. Ps. 33:1-22.

INTRODUCTORY: This is not so much a national as it is an international hymn of thanksgiving. It has in it universal elements; therefore, on the principle that the greater includes the less, it is just as applicable to America, to Britain, or to any other nation, as it was to Israel. Its three leading thoughts are as follows:

I. That the source of national prosperity is in God. Hence, there is a constant need to heed the ancient admonition, "Beware lest thou forget Jehovah thy God . . . and lest thou say in thy heart, My power and the might of my hand hath gotten me this wealth." To leave God out, and to boast of our self-sufficiency, is to present a pitiable spectacle. What have we that we have not received from him? His loving providence is over all, and is over us all the time.

II. Thankfulness for the past and the present. The Jew, whose religion was largely a thing of temporal rewards, looked upon super abundant prosperity as a sign of God's favor. With us, in this Christian age, there is a clearer recognition of spiritual values.

A national hymn of thanksgiving, suitable to the present, ought to take account of the revolution of things, and include the following particulars: 1. Thankfulness for the awakening of a new national conscience, a stronger national heartbeat, and a heightened sence of corporate national existence—with all its implied responsibilities. 2. Thankfulness for the awakening of a new spirit of patriotism. The profiteer is tabooed. 3. Thankfulness for the awakening of a new spirit of idealism. We have begun to rise above national consideration; to exalt manhood above money; to seek enlargement of life, more than enlargement of wealth; and this will go on. 4. Thankfulness for the awakening of a new sense of national destiny. We have come out of our semi-isolation to take our place in the sisterhood of free nations, in the struggle for a higher civilization—and the end is not yet.

III. Hope for the future. This is a strong note in Israel's hymn of thanksgiving. Hope is based upon what God is, and upon what he has already done. Praise is given for his uninterrupted goodness. There is no broken link in the chain of his mercies.

Rowland Hill tells the story of a rich man who sent a poor friend a sum of money, with a note which said: "More to follow"; and this he kept up as long as the need lasted. So it is with the gifts of God; there is no end to them. "The goodness of God endureth continually."

THEME PRAYER: Almighty Father, we give thee thanks for all thou hast given us richly to enjoy, for our health and our vigor, for the love and comfort of our homes, for the joys of friendship, and for every good gift of happiness and strength. We thank thee, too, for the gifts of freedom and peace that we enjoy in this land under thy divine guidance. We beseech thee to give us the vision to appreciate thy bounty, and to use thy precious gifts for the aid of our fellow men; thereby praising thy name, and speeding the day when thy kingdom shall be established on earth. Amen.—Rev. Henry Fisher.

OFFERTORY SENTENCE: "Every man according as he purposeth in his heart, so let him give; not grudgingly, or of necessity: for God loveth a cheerful giver."

OFFERTORY PRAYER: Lord of the harvest, we come with thanksgiving to present in worship an offering unto thee. For all the bounties thou bestowest, for all the wealth thy mercy lendeth, for all the blessings thy love sendeth, we praise thee, Lord of all. Help us now to come with real and deep devotion to this act of worship. Bless the givers and the recipients, and glorify thy name through both. For Jesus' sake. Amen.

Illustrative Material

SEED THOUGHTS, HOMILETIC AND EXPOSITORY. The Brimming Cup (Ps. 23:5): This shepherd psalm is a carol of the heart. It is a song at a banquet. Its centerpiece is this brimming cup. I. It is our national cup. In it are: 1. Our fair possessions. 2. Our free institutions. 3. Our fruitful resources. 4. Our religious heritage. II. It is our domestic cup. 1. It is brimming with comforts. 2. Ruddy with affection. 3. Rich in opportunities of helpfulness. III. It is our personal cup. 1. This is a good time to be alive. 2. Ours is a good land to live in. 3. We have a good Lord to love and serve.

Choice Illustrations on the Theme

A MARK OF MANHOOD. Yes, thankfulness must be cultivated. And somehow the mark of greatness in men is their spontaneity in giving thanks. Thankfulness is a real test of growth. No baby is grateful. Take your darling out of his crib when he is suffering the pangs of colic, walk the floor with him, lose precious hours of sleep, and when you put him down he will never say: "Thank you so much, Daddy!" We do not blame him because he is a baby. But, do you know, to continue to be unthankful is to be always but a baby. Only moral dwarfs and pygmies are ungrateful. Learn therefore to grow up in this grace of being thankful "in everything," and not only in being and feeling thankful, but "in everything" giving thanks as the blessed Word has commanded us.—O. L. Ice.

THANKSGIVING TOO LATE. A sick man who was sensing his unmindfulness of God's mercies when in health, said to Billy Bray, his visitor:

"Billy, I'm so happy now that if I had the power I'd shout from the housetop my praise and thanksgiving to God!"

"Ah lad," replied Billy, "what a pity

thou didst not shout when thou hadst the power!"

"Do not," said Alexander Maclaren, "let the empty cup be your first teacher of the blessings you had when it was full!"

WHAT DO WE SEE? A certain man was asked to talk to a company of businessmen about the depression. He tacked up a big sheet of white paper. Then he made a black spot on the paper with his lead pencil and asked a man in the front row what he saw. The man replied promptly, "A black spot."

The speaker asked every man the same question and each replied, "A black spot." That was what he had expected. Then with calm and deliberate emphasis the speaker said: "Yes, there is a little black spot, but none of you saw the big sheet of white paper. That's my speech."

What do we see? Of course, there is a "black spot." But do we see the big sheet of white paper, which represents our opportunities, our advantages, our blessings, and the challenge of today and tomorrow? Matthew Arnold wrote of Wordsworth that he "saw life steadily and saw it whole." That inspiring phrase expresses wisely and well the comprehensive conception of life which we all need. We see the spots. We see the obstacles, the clouds, and the depressions. But do we see enough? Do we see the heights and the lights of God's firmaments?—*The Standard*.

STOP AND THINK. We need to stop taking things for granted—especially things that have been bequeathed to us through "blood, sweat, and tears." Our modern conveniences—electricity, radio, automobile, and many others—have become such second nature that we do not stop to think they were perfected for us at a cost of time, effort, energy on the part of our fellow men. Even our democracy —won by fire and sword and bloodshed— is now simply taken for granted. Our faith and our church we also take for granted—our church, which has as its sign the cross, symbol of the supreme sacrifice, and which has been bequeathed to us by the undying devotion of millions of Christians.—M. R. Burroughs.

EVENING SERVICE

Theme: Jacob's Remembrance of Past Blessings (Thanksgiving).

TEXT: "I am not worthy of the least of all the mercies, and of all the truth, which thou hast shewed unto thy servant." Gen. 32:10.

INTRODUCTORY: Jacob's character was far from faultless, yet he had fine and noble traits. He was a man full of energy, active, enduring, resolute. Therefore his infirmities became more conspicuous than they would have been in a man of a quieter and more restful nature. Say what one will of him, he was a master in the art of prayer, and he that can pray well is a princely man. For another thing, he did not fail in remembering God's goodness to him, and in humble gratitude. Humility is a great grace, and far too rare. Humility is not telling falsehoods against oneself. It is forming a right estimate of oneself. Jacob was perfectly honest and sincere before God when he said, "I am not worthy of the least of all the mercies, and of all the truth, which thou hast shewed unto thy servant."

I. Consider first the estimate which Jacob made of his own character. "I am not worthy of the least of all thy mercies." 1. This acknowledgment implies that he was a true believer in God. 2. And it implies that he was a devout worshiper of God. 3. It implies that he sought to be a sincere follower of God.

II. Notice, further, his grateful acknowledgment of the Divine goodness. "All the mercies." 1. They were abundant mercies. 2. They were unceasing mercies.

III. Lastly, we see his conscious unworthiness of such peculiar blessings. "I am not worthy of the least." 1. It is the language of dependence. 2. It is the language of grateful recollection.

In view of all that God has done for

us can we be content to go through life without humility, gratitude, and trying to serve him?

Alternate Theme: All That Is within Me (Thanksgiving).

TEXT: "Bless the Lord, O my soul: and all that is within me, bless his holy name." Ps. 103:1.

I. What is there within one to bless the name of the Lord? Answer: There's a poet in your soul. You may recall that in reading Chaucer John Masefield discovered, "I too am a poet." Or the stationmaster in Mrs. Miniver on the occasion when he looked up at her and said, "There'll always be roses." By no science, or logic, did the stationmaster say that. I say he was a poet if in his life he never spoke any other words. There's imagination, emotion, intuition in every one of us. Too often we have let them die from disuse. The poet in our souls needs to be recognized or resurrected or awakened.

What is the preacher talking about? Does he mean to make writers of poems out of us all? No. That, to say the least, would not be desirable. The derivative meaning of the word "poet" is that he is one who makes. We have limited the word to making verses, but sometimes we escape from that limitation. We have seen gardens that men have planted and tended until they become expressions of imagination, emotion and intuition—something made by the poetic faculty, poems. Even a business can be made a poem, but this can be done and only can be done where men have time. In the Orient the rug dealer, the brass merchant, the jeweler, often handles his merchandise with a tenderness born of the poetic qualities. If the click of the cash register must be forced there is no time for poetry.

A poem is a thing made with imagination, emotion and intuition; thus homes have been made, thus some men have followed their handicrafts making things, thus some have sung their songs and played out their music.

Now all that I have said is for the purpose of broadening our idea of the poet, so that the most prosaic of us, or the one who has let the poet die in him, or the one in whom it has never wakened may look up and say, "I too am a poet."

There's a poet in your soul! Then apprehend God, grasp God, with all the poetry that is within you. Let imagination, emotion and intuition apprehend God and bless him! There is a poet within us and with the poet we must bless the Lord.

II. What is there within me with which to bless the name of the Lord? There's a patriot in my soul! Perhaps it is a little easier to convince ourselves that we have the patriot temperament than to bring ourselves to acknowledgment that we are poets. How seldom does our patriotism rise above vainglory and narrow nationalism and making the eagle scream! But there is a patriotism that glories in national good and sorrows for national evil. There is a patriotism which sees the alabaster cities gleam in the future and works and endures and waits and prays that they may become reality. There is a true patriot in our souls. A small boy was walking by my side when all unexpectedly he placed his hand in mine and said, "I'm going to be like Abraham Lincoln." It was the birth of the patriot in his soul.

What is the meaning of this restless striving in us, this mortal fight, these dissatisfactions with Congress or government or party or common custom? These are the soul's call for a better day and a better country. These are the strivings of the patriot. There is a patriot in us. And the point is that with the patriot in us we must bless the Lord. With all that is within me bless his holy name!

III. With what that is in us shall we bless the Lord? Let all that is within me bless his holy name! There's a poet in your soul; there's a patriot in your soul. You scarcely recognize the poet; you'll admit the patriot. I have another word I now want to use, and it is the right word to use, and yet you will not like it as applied to you. "I too am a ——." The word is saint. Said the African chieftain who found the Christ, "I'm condemned to be a saint."

Why do I have these twinges of conscience? Because there is good in me. Because it demands the evil to be gone. Because I'm condemned to be a saint.

A publican is praying, "God be merciful to me a sinner." How does he know he's a sinner? Why should he pray? How can he have any expectation that God will have mercy? Because deep down within him there is a saint —a saint crying for expression, for liberation, for his own sainthood. Yes, there's a saint in you. The saint may not be easily recognized, not enough of a saint to talk about, but the good man won't die in you. It is that in a man more fundamental than either the poet or the patriot in him. It was placed there when God created the world including man and said, "Behold it is very good." There's a good man, a saint, in your soul. And therewith a man should praise God. Let me read how a saint praised God, a saint who had committed grievous sins, lies and adultry and murder. Here is the saint praising God. (Read selections from Psalm 103 —having read for patriotism from Psalms 104 and 105.)

Can we not catch this man's mood and temper and let experience of iniquity and transgression and sin be transmuted into the ecstasy of forgiveness with which the good man within us praises the name of the Lord?

Yes, "all that is within me bless his holy name." What is within me? There's a poet in my soul. There's a patriot in my soul. There's a saint within my soul. These three were within the soul of David. By the poet in him he wrote the 104th Psalm. By the patriot in him he wrote the 105th Psalm. By the saint in him he wrote the 103rd Psalm. Poet, Patriot, Saint— these were the three-in-one of the soul of David.

"Bless the Lord, O my soul, and all that is within me, bless his holy name." —M. K. W. H.

Suggested Thanksgiving Texts and Themes

The Crowned Year: "Thou crownest the year with thy goodness; and all thy paths drop fatness." Ps. 65:11.

God Governing the Nations: "O let the nations be glad and sing for joy: for thou shalt judge the people righteously." Ps. 67:4.

The Full Table of the Year: "Oh that men would praise the Lord for his goodness, and for his wonderful works to the children of men!" Ps. 107:8.

The Thankful Attitude of Mind: "Enter into his gates with thanksgiving." Ps. 100:4.

Forgotten Mercies Remembered: "Then spake the chief butler to Pharaoh, saying, I do remember my faults this day," etc. Gen. 41:9-12.

Benefits of Thanksgiving: "It is a good thing to give thanks unto the Lord." Ps. 92:1.

MIDWEEK FELLOWSHIP MEETING TOPIC

(Church Night or Suggested Sermon Subject)

Theme: The Safe Deposit.

TEXT: "An inheritance incorruptible, and undefiled, and that fadeth not away, reserved in heaven for you." I Pet. 1:4.

Include vv. 3-5. Peter begins with a doxology, an outburst of praise. "Blessed be God," etc. Present praise. Reverent praise. Loving praise. Intelligent praise. Grateful praise. Praise especially for a great hope. An expectant hope. A living hope. A future hope. A heavenly hope. It is called an inheritance, a sure inheritance, heirship that is certain, a safe deposit.

I. What is the substance of this inheritance? No doubt there is a glance toward Canaan, which was the promised possession of the wandering Israelites. But there is more direct reference to the inheritance of grace here and hereafter, "reserved in heaven."

II. What are the characteristics of this inheritance? 1. It is incorruptible. All things earthly have in them the seeds of decay. Some heirships are far from secure, but fade away like a flower cut from its stem. 2. It is undefiled. The inheritance of Israel in Canaan was defiled. In heaven there "entereth not anything that defileth." 3. It fadeth not away. The fairest things of earth fade. Not so heavenly things.

III. What is implied by the reservation of the inheritance? 1. It is reserved, laid up, deposited for the heirs. 2. And the heirs are guarded for the inheritance. 3. The emphasis is upon the fact that the inheritance in trust is sure. It is incorruptible, undefiled and fadeth not away as do so many earthly hopes and inheritances. It is an inheritance reserved, held, kept securely for the heirs like a trust-fund inheritance in a bank. It is an inheritance that is sure.—A. M.

CHRISTIAN ENDEAVOR SOCIETY TOPIC

Nov. 23. Examples from Jesus: How Jesus Expressed Thanksgiving. Matt. 11:25-27; Matt. 26:26-28; John 19:25-27.

SUNDAY SCHOOL LESSON

Nov. 23. Jesus' Thanksgiving and Ours. Matt. 11:2-6, 25-30.

Memory Selection: "The Lord hath done great things for us; whereof we are glad." Ps. 126:3.

It has been asked, Do we thank God for God? Do we thank God for Jesus? We all more often thank God for material things than we do for spiritual things. A study of Jesus' prayer of thanksgiving may help us in our giving of thanks. The Lord hath done great things for us. Our gratitude should be founded upon the great blessings which Jesus' life and ministry have brought to us and to all mankind. They are such as healing for life's ills, hope for all classes of people, help in bearing life's burdens—all the word "salvation" means.

SUNDAY: NOVEMBER THIRTIETH

MORNING SERVICE

Theme: Experimental Religion.

Suggested Scripture Reading: Col. 1: 1-19.

Selected Hymns: "Jesus, I my cross have taken."—H. F. Lyte. "Children of the heavenly King."—J. Cennick. "Happy the souls to Jesus joined."—C. Wesley. "Give me the wings of faith to rise."—I. Watts. "Blest be the tie that binds."—J. Fawcett.

Call to Worship: "What shall I render unto the Lord for all his benefits toward me? I will take the cup of salvation, and call upon the name of the Lord. . . . I will pay my vows unto the Lord now in the presence of all his people, in the courts of the Lord's house, in the midst of thee, O Jerusalem. Praise ye the Lord."

Invocation Prayer: Almighty God, our heavenly Father, we have heard thy gracious summons calling us to the house of prayer. We would come like children going home, eager and expectant and glad. May there be no reluctance in our spirits when we turn to the holy privilege of fellowship with thee. To this end wilt thou graciously forgive our sins, and remove the hindrance of our guilt, so that there may be no barrier between our hearts and thine. Draw us from our far wanderings to the cross of Christ. May we find our joy through his sorrows and our life in his death. May we be eagerly willing to give him homage and to crown him Lord of all. We ask in his name. Amen.

Theme: Experimental Religion.

TEXT: "And knew the grace of God in truth." Col. 1:6.

INTRODUCTORY: A man took his friend to visit a great scholar. On leaving the home the visitor said to his host who had introduced him, "Dr. C. has splendid talents. What a pity he has not been educated." What the visitor meant was that no school or college could, in his mind, equal the life experiences of the everyday world. Experience is education. At least, no education is complete without experience. There are different kinds of knowing. There can be knowledge without experience, knowledge lacking the experimental.

I. Paul in writing to the Colossian Christians spoke of their "knowing the grace of God in truth." What did he mean? He did not mean mere knowledge. He meant more than that. He meant that the religion of the Colossians was experimental. They knew the grace of God "in truth." They had found it. Yes, but they had also felt it. They had experienced it. They had been moved by it. They had been changed, transformed by it. Paul entitles them "saints and faithful brethren." They had what is designated by the old-fashioned words, "experimental religion."

II. How did they come to this experience? The answer of the apostle is "by the grace of God." What does that imply? Grace means the free love and favor of God. The whole plan of salvation is perfectly free and gratuitous. "The grace of God that bringeth salvation hath appeared." 1. The contrivance of salvation is of grace. 2. The accomplishment of salvation is of grace. 3. The application of salvation is of grace, for no human merit can secure the renewing influences of the Spirit. The religion of the Colossians was not mere knowledge. It was experimental. They "knew the grace of God in truth."

III. The importance of such knowledge. It is all-important. It is supremely important. Religion is not religion at all without it, without this experimental element. It is important for pardon. It is important for peace. It is important for hope and for joy. True experimental religion gives all of these. Nothing short of this does it give them. The Colossians had borne such fruits "since the day that they heard and received the gospel." "They knew the grace of God in truth." They knew it sincerely, really, feelingly, experimentally.—H.

THEME PRAYER: O God, teach us that thy kingdom is not a kingdom of this world but an invisible kingdom of the heart and experience. May it come in our home and church and town and nation, through Jesus Christ our Lord. Amen.

OFFERTORY SENTENCE: "Thou shalt remember the Lord thy God: for it is he that giveth thee power to get wealth."

OFFERTORY PRAYER: O Lord of infinite power and wisdom, we acknowledge our debt to thee for all that we possess and are. We thank thee for Christ, in whom all the treasures of grace are ours. In his name and for his sake we bring our offerings. Wilt thou graciously accept them at our hands and use them for the upbuilding of thy kingdom? We ask in Christ's name. Amen.

Illustrative Material

SEED THOUGHTS, HOMILETIC AND EXPOSITORY. The Gospel of Grace: I. It is only by hearing and believing the Gospel that, like the Colossians, we can "know the grace of God in truth." II. The method of its propagation. It is by preaching. This is the Divinely instituted means of disseminating the Gospel. III. It is propagated by men thoroughly qualified for the work. IV. To whomsoever the Gospel comes it is imperative duty to believe and receive it.—G. B.

Experience: The only faith that wears well and holds its color in all weathers is that which is woven of conviction and set with the sharp mordant of experience.—J. R. Lowell.

Choice Illustrations on the Theme

THE VALUE OF EXPERIENCE. In his autobiography S. S. McClure says he asked Robert Louis Stevenson how he knew so well the feelings of extreme fatigue which he describes in his hero in *Kidnapped*. Stevenson laughed and said he had been through all that himself. Experience—that is what makes books, great books. It is the life of men in relation to God that makes the Psalms and many other parts of the Bible so vital today. Jesus said, "We speak that we do know, and testify that we have seen." I know a minister of very ordinary scholarly attainments whose experience of the things of God is so real and vital that it carries many a sermon to a successful issue.

EXPERIENCE THE "TUG UP." A gentleman passing along a city common one day saw a blind boy flying a kite. Laying his hand upon his shoulder as the boy turned his sightless eyes up, the gentleman said: "My son, why do you fly the kite when you cannot see?" "Oh," said the little fellow, with his sightless eyes flashing, "I like to feel the tug up, sir." And it is this "tug up" that Christians of all ages of the Church have felt and that has caused them to rejoice when others have done nothing but sigh and moan. Experience is the "tug up."

THE EVIDENCE OF EXPERIENCE. A doctor was discussing religion with a minister. "I cannot understand that a man like you still believes such fables," said he. The minister replied: "Supposing that you had learned of a remedy that consistently cures a certain sickness. Supposing that this remedy had not only cured hundreds of your patients, but you as well. Would you not have confidence in this remedy?" The doctor said, "Certainly!" Then the minister continued, "It is just so with my faith. It rests upon experience. Others may speak of fables, but I know what faith has done for me and thousands of others. Formerly my heart was full of unrest. I did not know why I was in the world. I had no answer to the most important of questions. Then Christ came into my life and since then I have been a new creature. Now I have peace, comfort and all else that I need." Such an experience is the most conclusive answer to all doubts.—*500 Best Modern Illustrations.*

LIFE ENRICHED BY EXPERIENCE. A story is told of the artist Turner, that one day he invited Charles Kingsley into his study to see a picture of a storm at sea. Kingsley was wrapt in admiration: "How did you do it, Turner?" he exclaimed. Turner answered: "I wished to paint a storm at sea, so I went to the coast of Holland and engaged a fisherman to take me out in his boat in the next storm. I was bound to the mast. Not only did I see that storm and feel it, but it blew itself into me until I became part of the storm. And then I came back and painted that picture."

Turner's experience is a parable of life and religion.—Bishop Slattery.

EVENING SERVICE

Theme: The Secret of a Happy Life.

TEXT: "For who knoweth what is good for man in this life, all the days of his vain life which he spendeth as a shadow?" Eccles. 6:12.

INTRODUCTORY: The writer of Ecclesiates seems to take a sad view of life. Life is short, he says. It is uncertain, he says. It is unsubstantial, like a vapor, he says. Who knoweth what is good for a man in this life, wealth or poverty, health or disease, or is it better as one has said, "Give me neither poverty nor riches," the golden medium he thought?

The question of the text has been repeated many times since the writing of Ecclesiastes. The stoic has said, "The chief good for man in this life is to take everything just as it comes, maintain stolid indifference, like a cold, unmoved statue amid either storms or sunshine."

The Epicurean said, "Eat, drink and be merry. Indulge your senses, and banish all thought and care about the future." The miser says, "Get all you can; give as little as you can; heap up riches and treasure." The ascetic says, "Treat the world with disdain and scorn, retreat from it, and trample upon all its associations and joys."

But there are far better answers in the light of the New Testament.

I. It tells us that it is good for a man to be in right relations with God. The prodigal could not be happy while away from his father, at variance with him. And no man can be really happy while away from God and at variance with him. It is good for a man to surrender himself and be on God's side. There will be harmony in his heart and peace in his mind.

II. It is good for a man to accept God's plans and providences for him. A man cannot be happy who doubts God's goodness and wisdom and power, or whose will runs counter to God's will. The mind of Christ was a surrender of his will to his Father.

III. It is good for a man to trust the love of God and his final awards. —F. W. B.

Suggested Texts and Themes

The Lift of Love: "Thou hast in love to my soul delivered it from the pit." Isa. 38:17.

Divine Dimensions: "What is the breadth, and length, and depth, and height," etc. Eph. 3:18.

The Cry of the City: "Men groan from out of the city." Job 24:12.

The Journey of a Day: "I must walk today." Luke 13:33.

The Mislaid Faith: "And he said unto them, Where is your faith?" Luke 8:25.

MIDWEEK FELLOWSHIP MEETING TOPIC

(Church Night or Suggested Sermon Subject)

Theme: Have Faith in God's Goodness.

TEXT: "Man shall not live by bread alone." Luke 4:4.

Have we not heard the expression, "I had to do it; my bread and butter depended upon it"? It was an excuse for not living up to the ideal. It implied that temporal wants should be supreme over the spiritual and eternal.

I. It brings up the question: "How much shall it profit a man if he gain the whole world and lose his own soul?"

II. But what does the Book say? "Be not anxious, saying what shall we eat?" "Seek ye first his righteousness, and these things shall be added unto you." "Will in no wise fail thee." "In nothing be anxious, but in everything let your requests be made known unto God. And the peace of God shall guard your hearts." "God shall supply every need of yours."

III. We should have the faith that is shown by loyalty to our Captain. If we will do our part, God will not fail us. Put him to the test, and see if he will not keep his word. "All authority hath been given me in heaven and on earth." It is not given to us. It will be safe for us to obey and trust him who has it.

IV. Were these sayings for others, and not for us? They were written for our admonition, that we, with the teachings and the examples before us, might show fullness of faith in the answering goodness of God.—J. H. M.

CHRISTIAN ENDEAVOR SOCIETY TOPIC

Nov. 30. Examples from Jesus: How Jesus Dealt with Individuals. John 4:1-26; Mark 10:17-22.

SUNDAY SCHOOL LESSON

Nov. 30. Jesus' Law of Doing Good. Matt. 12:1-14.

MEMORY SELECTION: "Do not imitate evil but imitate good. He who does good is of God; he who does evil has not seen God." III John 11. (R. S. V.)

Jesus placed the welfare of human beings above the traditions of men.

He showed that laws, institutions, business dealings, and things in general are to be tested by what they do to people. Some things are conducive to spiritual development, others to weaken and destroy personality. This is supposed to be a temperance lesson. In such case we may well record and teach that beverage alcohol is one of the most destructive forces in the world today.

SUNDAY: DECEMBER SEVENTH

MORNING SERVICE

Theme: The Promised Shiloh (Advent).

SUGGESTED SCRIPTURE READING: Matt. 21:1-17.

SELECTED HYMNS: "O Jesus, King most wonderful."—Bernard of Clairvaux. "O Christ, our King, Creator."—Gregory the Great. "All hail the power of Jesus' name."—E. Perronet. "Rejoice, the Lord is King."—C. Wesley. "Crown him with many crowns."—M. Bridges.

CALL TO WORSHIP: "Let Israel hope in the Lord: for with the Lord there is mercy, and with him is plenteous redemption." "I wait for the Lord, my soul doth wait, and in his word do I hope. My soul waiteth for the Lord more than they that watch for the morning: I say, more than they that watch for the morning."

INVOCATION PRAYER: Eternal Father, as we gather in thy house, we come with hearts prepared by the many intimations around us of the approach of another holy Christmas season. As humble shepherds rejoiced at the sound of the angels' song, may we be filled with joy as we hear again the story of thy love. As wise men brought their gifts to the Infant King, so too we would bring the richest treasures of our devotion and lay them before thy majesty. As seekers in the past followed the star that led them to the shrine of thy birth, so may we find some source of guidance to the fulfillment of our need, and in this hour of worship may we find thee, whom to know is life eternal. Through Jesus Christ, our Lord. Amen.

Theme: The Promised Shiloh (Advent).

TEXT: "The sceptre shall not depart from Judah, nor a lawgiver from between his feet, until Shiloh come: and unto him shall the gathering of the people be." Gen. 49:10.

INTRODUCTORY: The word "Shiloh" means "peace." This is a prophecy of the coming of Christ, "the Peaceful One." He has been called "The World's Tranquilizer," his grand design being to give peace to men's souls and peace to the world.

I. The prophecy contains a revelation as to the appearing of Christ. "Until Shiloh come." He was to come and the world was to be the scene of his wondrous works. Two things are specified. 1. He was to be of the tribe of Judah. That such was his human descent is carefully specified in the genealogy of Christ in both Matthew and Luke. 2. He was to come before the rule and authority of the tribe of Judah should cease.

II. And the prophecy has connected with it a statement in what way his people would come to him. "Unto him shall the gathering of the people be." More literally in the Hebrew it reads, "Unto him shall the gatherings of the peoples be." It includes all the peoples of the Gentiles as well as of the Jews. 1. They are to be gathered to his cross as the source of salvation. 2. They are to be gathered to his cause as his devoted followers. 3. They are to be gathered to his Church as the visible friends of his kingdom. 4. They are to be gathered to his royal standard as his loyal and obedient subjects. 5. Finally, they are to be gathered into his eternal dominion to share in its blessings for ever and ever.

Are we ready to welcome him and his reign? Are we ready actively to aid in bringing in his full reign in the world? —B.

THEME PRAYER: Almighty God, we beseech thee, grant unto thy people grace that they may wait with vigilance for the advent of thy Son, our Lord, that when he shall arise from thy right hand to visit the earth in righteousness and thy people with salvation, he may not find us sleeping in sin, but diligent in thy service and rejoicing in thy praises, that so we may enter in with him unto the marriage of the Lamb; through his merits who liveth and reigneth with thee and the Holy Ghost, ever one God, world without end. Amen.

OFFERTORY SENTENCE: "Thy kingdom come."

OFFERTORY PRAYER: Our Father, put thy blessing upon the gifts we bring this morning in Christ's name for thy great work in the world. Send them forth with our sympathy and love, and make real to us that it is "more blessed to give than to receive." And this we ask for Jesus' sake. Amen.

Illustrative Material

SEED THOUGHTS, HOMILETIC AND EXPOSITORY. Shiloh: I. The coming One predicted. II. The character of the King and his kingdom. The name "Shiloh" means "Peaceable," or "Peace-bringer." The name intimates that the King who is to come will bring tranquility to his people. III. The completeness of his rule. "Unto him shall the gathering of the people be." The Christian religion is the fulfillment of the hope of Israel. Do we rejoice in our knowledge of Jesus as King?—W. S. S.

Revelation of the Advent of Christ: I. This is the language of prophecy. II. The prophecy contains a revelation of the coming of Christ. III. It is a revelation connected with the time in which he should appear. IV. It is an announcement showing in what way his people shall come to him. V. It suggests Christ's purpose in gathering his people to himself. It is to give them rest, peace, here and hereafter.—C. S.

Choice Advent Illustrations

THE KINGLY CHRIST. The words "sceptre" and "lawgiver" applied to the coming One suggests kingship. That is why we connect his Advent with thought of the Triumphal Entry. Dear to the Christian world is the story of Christ's one day of triumph, Palm Sunday. The Church rejoices because even for one brief day he was hailed as King.

SHILOH AS KING. Because of the distance of time and the difference of customs it is not easy for us to grasp how perfectly Jesus made plain his claims to be the appointed Messiah and King of the Jews. "This thing was not done in a corner." It was perfectly plain to every intelligent Jew, and so plain to the men in positions of authority that they were compelled to "do something about it." He claimed to be nothing less than Almighty God's chosen person to effect the salvation of the individual soul and the salvation of the Hebrew people, and the transformation and salvation of human society. Jesus Christ claims to be the only Saviour of us all, and the triumphal entry is absolutely typical of the response that we each must make to that claim. Will he look round about and find us treating him as King, or frigidly looking upon him as a pretender to be quickly disposed of? Will we crown him or crucify him?—*S. S. Times.*

A LOVE KING. The prediction of his advent pictures Christ not as a force-king but a love-king, peace-bringer. He was to be God's sort of a king. That is, he would reign only by the consent of the reigned-over. He would not force himself upon the people by dint of the power he could exercise. He wanted their glad, gracious acceptance.

THE PEACE BRINGER. In the Doré Gallery in London there is a picture the foreground of which consists of a group of people of every condition, all turning beseeching looks upon a faraway figure. It is the Christ, wearing robes of dazzling whiteness, bearing a cross, with a hand uplifted beckoning these weary, brokenhearted ones to come to him. That is the Christ who draws all men unto himself. "Unto him shall the gathering of the people be." A Christ who is only a heavenly teacher, a faultless pattern, a strong friend, is not what this sorrowing, sinning world needs most of all. It needs one who is pitiful toward the penitent, who has power to forgive, who can restore ruined lives. —*Westminster Teacher.*

Suggested Advent Texts and Themes

Messiah's Rightful Dominion: "And the government shall be upon his shoulder." Isa. 9:6.

The Complete Manifestation: "God, who at sundry times and in divers manners spake in time past unto the fathers by the prophets, hath in these last days spoken unto us by his Son." Heb. 1:1, 2.

The Healing Sun: "But unto you that fear my name shall the Sun of righteousness arise with healing in his wings." Mal. 4:2.

The Desire of All Nations: "The desire of all nations shall come: and I will fill this house with glory, saith the Lord of hosts." Hag. 2:7.

EVENING SERVICE

Theme: Finding the Lost Star (Advent).

TEXT: "When they saw the star, they rejoiced with exceeding great joy." Matt. 2:10.

INTRODUCTORY: There is a legend which tells of the Wise Men losing the star as they journeyed from the East. Finally they found it again, reflected from the surface of the water in a wayside well.

I. Some people have lost the star of Guidance. They have lost direction. They have lost a sense of destination. Which means that life has become meaningless and purposeless. They may have water in the water bags. They may own a caravan of stuff. They live but have not life.

II. This does not mean that from their point of view they are necessarily pathetic. Having lost the star, having no direction, they still have directions. Every man who has lost his direction still has many directions to follow. Having lost North by the clouding of the star, all the directions are still there to follow, if he can possibly correct for that human tendency to move in a circle. But the fact remains that for life, creative living, happiness, directions are not enough, just to go here and there—there must be some direction that has meaning, purpose, destination and destiny in it. For that, man needs a guiding star.

III. Many have lost the star of Peace. We have lost this star in many places in the world. If there is no peace in many places, is it not possible to have peace in one place? If there is no peace in wide spaces, can there not be peace in one narrow spot? Peace may be found in one man's heart. In another's. Peace in the units may eventually become peace in the mass.

IV. The star of Love must not be lost. It is by that star that men come alive. It is by the warmth of human relations that they lose their coldness. It is by love that they rise to the heights of manhood and become Christlike. Guidance: He said, "I am the Way." Peace: He said, "My peace I give unto you." Love: He laid down his life: "Greater love hath no man than this, that a man lay down his life for his friends."

V. There are many people who have lost the Christ. Where, how shall they find him? As we pour our heart's devotion into some dry well that others may drink, it may be that they will look over our shoulders into the well below and see his star shining again in the sky. —M. K. W. H.

Additional Theme: The Difference Christ's Coming Makes (Advent Time).

TEXT: "In every thing ye are enriched by him." I Cor. 1:5.

INTRODUCTORY: The gift of Christ to the world is unique because in him alone have we a true revelation of God and an unconquerable power to live aright.

The difference that Jesus Christ has made cannot be adequately measured and dated. Like leaven in the meal, Christ's influence is essentially in the new spirit which has entered life through him.

I. In the first place, his is the spirit of Wholeness. Jesus is always challenging us along with the disabled man, "Wilt thou be made whole?" God's will for us is that no part of our personality shall be unexercised, misused, discordant or withered, but that everything about us shall be unified like separate sounds to produce glorious harmony.

Only when a man finds something greater than himself to which he can give himself, can his life be pulled together and unified. Life organized around low obsessions like drink, success or self, will in the end split up and go all to pieces. So there comes One with healing hands to master and enthral us. All our interests are harnessed to his plan. The old futility and inward conflicts go for evermore. We are made whole.

II. Christ's is also the spirit of Truth. The answer to the materialist's argument that Christianity is dope, a soporific, a chloroform mask that is fantasy and make-believe, could never have produced One who lived out his claim: "I am the Truth." No book has played so great a part in the world as the Bible has done in Christianity. Again and again the Bible has initiated education, literature and culture. Far back in the fourth century it was this spirit in the Church that gave rise to the first traces of elementary schools. The medieval universities and public schools were originally Christian foundations. The greatest work of the great classical painters, Fra Angelico, Leonardo da Vinci, Michelangelo and Raphael was in sacred subjects, in the birth, death and rising again of Christ. Music became ever richer in chant, anthem and mighty oratorio.

Consequently one thing Christians need supremely is a truthful mind. Not necessarily a profound intellect, but rather the mental attitude that does not plunge down the first path which opens out or follows blindly every popular slogan but rather that follows fearlessly where the Truth leads and that thinks a little harder about Christ than any other subject.

III. Then again, Christ's is the spirit of life. "I am come that they might have it more abundantly." Life does not depend on how long we live but on how much we live. Are we living or passing the time? Life we may have, but without Christ we have not life abundant.

Henry Drummond, at one of his famous student meetings in Edinburgh, read a letter from a man who had made a shipwreck of his life and who signed himself with the Greek word for death, "Thanatos." He seemed a hopeless case. About a year later Drummond reminded his students of that letter and said: "I have in my pocket tonight another letter from 'Thanatos,' in which he says he is a changed man—a new creature in Christ Jesus." Jesus has released a new power reinforcing life—"the power of an endless life." Christ takes a world full of unpromising material—shady individuals like the woman at the well, hotheads like the sons of Zebedee, misguided fanatics like Saul of Tarsus, young men about town like Francis of Assisi—none of them really getting anywhere with their lives, but you would not have recognized them after Christ had transformed them.

We can never assess the influence of Jesus Christ. He has touched our life at so many points that the more we contemplate the difference he has made, the more we must say: "In everything we are enriched by him."—J. L. C.

MIDWEEK FELLOWSHIP MEETING TOPIC

(Church Night or Suggested Sermon Subject)

Theme: Christ Cannot Be Hid.

TEXT: "And from thence he arose, and went into the borders of Tyre and Sidon, and entered into an house, and would have no man know it: but he could not be hid," etc. Mark 7:24-30.

Christ goes outside of Palestine, into a country of the Gentiles. Tyre and Sidon were renowned for their commerce and wealth. He entered into a house and "would have no man know it." Why? Partly for quiet. Partly lest he should arouse the Jews more bitterly against him. But "he could not be hid."

I. Christ cannot be hid because great need will seek him out.

II. Christ cannot be hid because true love will surely find him.

III. Christ cannot be hid because earnest faith will ever lead to him.

IV. Christ cannot be hid because his own heart will betray him.

V. Christ cannot be hid because his disciples will make him known.

1. Witness-bearing is to continue until the whole earth is filled with his glory. 2. The true disciple cannot be hid any more than his Master.—A. R.

CHRISTIAN ENDEAVOR SOCIETY TOPIC

Dec. 7. Examples from Jesus: How Jesus Utilized Prayer. Mark 6:46; 14:32; Luke 23:34.

BULLETIN BOARD SLOGANS FOR THE MONTH

By Earl Riney

Christmas sets our days to music.

Christmas is not myth nor mockery but both a fact and a faith.

The Christmas spirit never asks how much must I do, but how much can I do?

Next to the help of God is the good will of unselfish friends.

You will not find any success rules that work during the coming year unless you work.

Believe that the task ahead of you is never so great as the Power behind you.

The stars still point the way for wise men.

We all need the Christmas song in our souls: why not tune in?

A miser is a rich pauper.

He has bad food who feeds on others' faults.

SUNDAY SCHOOL LESSON

Dec. 7. Jesus the Great Teacher. Matt. 13:24-35, 53, 54.

MEMORY SELECTION: "Whence hath this man this wisdom, and these mighty works?" Matt. 13:54.

Jesus was a teacher come from God. He himself said, "Learn of me." This lesson should lead us to wish to learn more about the things that Jesus taught and to try to obey them. He taught from a boat. He taught in the fields. He taught in the synagogues. The content, the method, and the effect of his teachings contain things we need to learn and know. One of his great themes was the growth of his kingdom. His kingdom is and should be important to us.

SUNDAY: DECEMBER FOURTEENTH

MORNING SERVICE

Theme: The Daystar in the Heart (Advent).

SUGGESTED SCRIPTURE READING: II Pet. 1:1-21.

SELECTED HYMNS: "O Come, O Come, Immanuel."—Latin. "Lift up your heads, rejoice."—T. T. Lynch. "Watchman, tell us of the night."—J. Bowring. "Hark, the glad sound, the Saviour comes."—P. Doddridge. "Draw nigh, draw nigh, Emmanuel."—Latin.

CALL TO WORSHIP: There shall arise a star out of Jacob. The people that walked in darkness have seen a great light; they that dwell in the land of the shadow of death, upon them hath the light shined."

INVOCATION PRAYER: By the day's dawning, O God, our meditations have been turned toward him who is the Light of the World. As the day advances toward its noontide our hearts have high hope of his high noon when all the world shall be flooded with his light. And may there be no afternoon, no declining of his shining, no night of darkness. The vision of the Celestial City is one wherein there is no night. It is his glad day we greet, which shall know no ending. We thank thee for the return of the Advent season wherein we greet the coming of our Lord, our Saviour. As ancient prophets saw his coming and kindled their hopes for a better day, so may we in the foregleams of this Christmastide catch visions of his kingdom. Prepare us, O God, to celebrate with joy this blessed season of the year. Grant us victory over sin. Cast out all low motives, unholy passions, all dark and malignant thoughts and prejudices from our minds, and fill our lives with truth and grace and joy and peace. In the name of Jesus and for his sake. Amen.—M. K. W. H.

Theme: The Daystar in the Heart (Advent).

TEXT: "We have also a more sure word of prophecy," etc. II Pet. 1:19.

INTRODUCTORY: Christmas is no longer confined to one day—the 25th of December. It begins weeks before and extends weeks beyond. The period before Christmas Day may be a strenuous time of shopping and many other activities. There is always the danger that its real significance may be crowded out of our thinking and living. It is well for us to pause and consider the real meaning of this holy day. This is nowhere better expressed than in the carols we sing at this time of the year.

I. First, the carols tell us that Christmas is a celebration of the birthday of Jesus.

> God rest ye, all good people
> Let nothing you dismay;
> The God of all good Christians
> Was born on Christmas Day.

It was on Christmas Day over four hundred years ago. The monks at Erfurt monastery were assembled to sing Advent hymns. One of their number, Martin Luther, was missing. He sat alone in his cell, reading the story of the Bethlehem shepherds. Later he wrote a cradle hymn about the Christ child who was born:

> Away in a manger, no crib for his bed,
> The little Lord Jesus laid down his sweet head;
> The stars in the heaven looked down where he lay,
> The little Lord Jesus asleep on the hay.

Yes, we seem to need to be reminded of that fact—Christmas is the birthday of Jesus. Let us observe it primarily as such.

II. Again, Christmas is a time of Christlike generosity, directed especially toward the needy. This means more than an exchange of gifts between friends.

If we substitute the word "Christmas" for "Holy Supper" in one of our American poems, we get this result:

The Christmas is kept indeed
In whatso we share with another's need,
Not what we give but what we share,
For the gift without the giver is bare.
Who gives of himself with his alms feeds three,
Himself, his hungering neighbor and me.

III. Moreover, the birthday of Jesus is truly observed when Christ is born in our hearts and we know him from a personal experience. How well is this said in the hymn, "O Little Town of Bethlehem":

O holy child of Bethlehem,
Descend to us, we pray;
Cast out our sin, and enter in,
Be born in us today.
We hear the Christmas angels,
The great, glad tidings tell;
O come to us, abide with us,
Our Lord Emmanuel.

IV. One more thing, Christmas involves a world-wide fellowship of all Christians. It reminds us of the supranational character of our Christian faith. We know that on Christmas Day the carols will be sung in every land the world over.

The God of Jesus is not the God of any one land or group of nations. He is the God of all who love and serve him regardless of nationality. We have a fellowship with Christians of every land, including even enemy nations.

In Christ there is no east or west
In Him no south or north;
But one great fellowship of love
Throughout the whole wide earth.

V. On that first Christmas night, the angels sang to the shepherds: "Peace on earth to men of good will." And we sing with hope in our hearts:

It came upon the mid-night clear,
That glorious song of old,
From angels bending near the earth
To touch their harps of gold:
"Peace on the earth, goodwill to men,"
From heaven's all gracious king;
The world in solemn stillness lay,
To hear the angels sing.

—Rev. Paul F. Boller.

THEME PRAYER: Almighty and Everlasting God, who art the Brightness of faithful souls and the desire of all nations; so fill the world with thy glory and show thyself by the radiance of thy light that all the peoples of the earth may be subject unto thee; through Jesus Christ our Lord. Amen.

OFFERTORY SENTENCE: "Vow, and pay unto the Lord your God: let all that be round about him bring presents unto him that ought to be feared."

OFFERTORY PRAYER: Receive the offerings which we bring to the holy altar and use them if it pleases thee for the coming of thy kingdom. Open our hearts that we may give to the needy so that none may go hungry, and create in us the desire to share our happiness with others. Amen.

Illustrative Material

SEED THOUGHTS, HOMILETIC AND EXPOSITORY. The Advent Call: "Ye shall be unto me a holy people." Deut. 7:6. This call expresses what the Lord would have us be—what he would have in us. I. First, a people who know the time of the kingdom of God. A people who know that with the coming of Christ the night is gone. A people who know that the time to awake is at hand. II. Secondly, a people whose walk is in the light, laying aside the works of darkness, putting on the armor of light. III. Thirdly, a people who seek light and power in communion with God.—C. B.

Choice Illustrations (Advent)

CHRIST IS THE DAWN. A band of fugitives was crossing an eastern desert. The night was dark, but they determined to push on. Soon they lost their way and had to spend the night in anxiety and fear. It seemed as if the night would never pass. But almost all at once the sun arose, bringing daylight and showing the way of safety. Not one of them ever forgot that sun-rising. So to the people of this world in their wanderings. They were lost—lost in the darkness of sin. But the Dayspring from on high hath visited us, has arisen upon us, making plain the way of eternal safety. Christ is the Dawn. Christ is our Dayspring, and the purpose of his coming was to give us the light that will lead us to eternal bliss. This is the Advent message.—H.

THE DIVINE IN THE HUMAN. He sent his comfort to me, relieved my anxiety, answered my prayers by the coming of Titus (II Cor. 7:6)—just a dear personal friends of Paul's own! That brings the Eternal down from the infinite heavens into such a thing as the timely advent of a friend. . . . Therefore and on that word the whole message of Advent seems to turn. The very Love of God himself came among us as a Man. Therefore the infinite and Eternal Father, that he may win the love and trust of his heedless, willful children, goes all the length that even Love can go and gives himself to them in the Man Christ Jesus of Nazareth and Calvary. . . . He sent Paul his comfort by the coming of Titus. He sends you and me and all men his salvation, his Love, his very self in Jesus of Nazareth, the Son of Man, for Whose coming among us as a little helpless Child the Church is keeping again, in memory, her Advent-watch.—Archibald Alexander. D.D.

ADVENT AND PEACE. Toward the close of the War of 1812, the country was shrouded in deep gloom; the harbors were blockaded, commerce destroyed, products moldering in the warehouses, the currency depreciated.

In February a ship drew near to New York, bringing the commissioners from Ghent, and the news that the treaty of peace was signed. Men rushed breathless to the city, shouting, "Peace, peace!" From house to house, from street to street, amid waving torches, all went shouting, "Peace, peace!"

More joyful is the news of peace brought from God by the angels. We, too, should not keep silence, but repeat the news of peace till all the world shall hear.—P.

ADVENT AND THE NEED. The world's supreme need at this Christmastide is that room should be made for the Child. The world has come nigh to perishing because it has made room for everything except the one thing needful—that love which came on Christmas Day. The need of the world is God, and nowhere can that need be satisfied save by the coming of the Child. Long years ago St. Chrysostom, speaking of the Holy of Holies between the cherubim, said, "The true Shekinah is man." And that saying is ever true. For there is no way by which love can manifest itself save through human hearts and hands and lips. Personality is the means by which God could manifest the highest in him, and in the fullness of time the Child was born who was destined to reveal in a life of love that God is Love. Christmas is not the commemoration of an isolated fact. It is the day of all days on which we are to realize that the coming of God to man in his Holy Spirit is a continuous process, and that we each of us on this day can become tabernacles for the indwelling of the most High.—Norman MacLean, D.D.

EVENING SERVICE

Theme: Following the Star (Advent).

TEXT: "We have seen his star in the east, and are come to worship him." Matt. 2:2.

INTRODUCTORY: The Saviour still offers the star-guidance to the solution of the many duties and difficulties which perplex and distress our minds.

I. And if we are really determined to find the Christ, and worship him, we shall be ready and eager to follow his star. But there are crowds of people who are very keen to reason about Christ who are not equally disposed to become his disciples. They are "all there" if life be regarded as a debate, but they are not to be found if life is regarded as a crusade! They will argue a case but they will not follow the star. They are willing to be astronomers discussing stars—they are not willing to be navigators, trusting the stars to guide them across the pathless deep. They are great in "making points," they are poor in making journeys. They may go so far as to say, "We have seen his star"; they will not add, "We are come to worship him."

II. Now, there is no life so dark and rayless as to be without a single star. In every soul there is some little gleam which is the star of God, and the price of finding the Sun is to follow the star! For instance—here is a radiant beam of starlight shining upon the pilgrimway: "He that loseth his life shall find it." That star is shining—who is willing to follow it and see where it will lead? And if we refuse to follow the star, how can we expect to find the Christ?

III. And what is the good of turning our back upon the star and then sitting down to discuss some theme in high theology? How can any man expect to come into the blazing blessedness of the atonement who will not follow the star of sacrifice? How can a man, who immures himself in the prison of selfish interests, expect to touch the glowing mystery of Calvary? We ought surely to understand—for it is one of the noble laws of life—that there are many questions which can only be answered by following the star.

IV. We can only understand some things by going to see them. Many of our grimmest difficulties are settled by just striding out after the star-gleam which has already been given. Theological knots are untied as we go along our dutiful journey. Some things are revealed to us as we just step out. We follow the star and we find the Sun. We "live ourselves" into light and sight.

V. The wise man takes the road and follows the star. We are going to learn precious little about Jesus if we remain rebellious to his will. Here is the secret of the only promising quest. "We have seen his star in the east, and are come to worship him."—J.

Alternate Theme: Tidings of Good Things (Advent).

Text: "How beautiful are the feet of them that . . . bring glad tidings of good things." Rom. 10:15.

Introductory: The Bible is the messenger of glad tidings. It is not a book of cheap romanticism. It is realistic, unsparing in its judgments, serious as life itself at its deepest levels is serious. Nonetheles it is supremely the book of glad tidings. It pulsates with good news. It is the most joyful book in the world. At the beginning "the morning stars sang together and all the sons of God shouted for joy." At the end a great multitude which no man can number are singing hallelujah choruses.

I. In the good news of this Book let us think first of the glad tidings of God's sovereignty. St. Paul, in our text, is quoting from the book of the prophet Isaiah: "How beautiful upon the mountains are the feet of him that bringeth good tidings, . . . that saith unto Zion, Thy God reigneth!"

The sovereignty of God is one of the great truths by which men live, and its message is needed today as much as, perhaps more than, ever. In days of national calamity the prophets of Israel bade the people remember that whatever happens God is God. Nothing can dethrone him. They might be hard put to it to explain the untoward things which had come to them, but God was not at the mercy of even the most untoward events. The last book in the Bible, written in the teeth of bitter persecution, contains the same victorious assurance as this word from Isaiah, "Hallelujah, for the Lord God omnipotent reigneth." This surely is glad tidings indeed. To tell men that all is vanity, that there is no purpose in their lives or in the world—there is nothing inspiring about that. But to be assured that all is not vanity, that there is a purpose in our lives and in the world, that the things which happen are not outside but within the orbit of an omnipotent will, that goodness and truth will be finally victorious, there is something joyous and inspiring about that. "How beautiful upon the mountains are the feet of him that bringest good tidings, . . . that saith unto Zion, Thy God reigneth!"

II. Glad tidings of the kingdom. St. Luke tells us that Jesus "went throughout every city and village, preaching and showing the glad tidings of the kingdom of God," and St. Paul relates how he had labored night and day to establish the kingdom of God at Thessalonica, and had "exhorted them—that they should walk worthy of him who had called them unto his kingdom and glory." This is the second piece of good news borne by the feet of them that bring glad tidings of good things—the establishment and progress of the kingdom of God on earth, the kingdom in which faith and charity, hope and love, joy and peace hold sway.

Good news is always exhilarating and inspiring. Here is good news in very deed and truth. The kingdom of God is here in the world. God reigns supreme in heaven, but he reigns also, and more and more, on earth. "Therefore, my beloved brethren, be ye stedfast, unmoveable, always abounding in the work of the Lord, forasmuch as ye know that your labour is not in vain in the Lord."

III. The third and last message of glad tidings is the message to which our ears are specially attuned at this Christmastide. "Behold," said the angelic messenger in Luke's lovely Nativity story, "behold, I bring you good tidings of great joy. . . . For unto you is born this day in the city of David a Saviour." That is the need which the Christmas gospel supplies. To sinful men it brings deliverance from their sins, setting their feet on a new and upward road. To guilty consciences it brings pardon and peace. To a lost world it brings recovery and hope. "Immanuel, God with us." There is good news for a sinful world, for a guilty world, for a lost world. How beautiful are the feet of them that bring glad tidings of such good things.—A. S. H.

AN APPROPRIATE ILLUSTRATION. When Tennyson was a young man he wrote from Marblethorpe: "I am housed at Mr. Wildman's, an old friend of mine in these parts. He and his wife are two perfectly honest Methodists. When I came I asked her after news, and she replied, 'Why, Mr. Tennyson, there's only one piece of news that I know—that Christ died for all men.' And I said to her, 'That is old news and good news and new news,' wherewith the good woman seemed satisfied."

Suggested Advent Texts and Themes

The Rising Star: "There shall come a Star out of Jacob, and a Sceptre shall rise out of Israel," etc. Num. 24:17.

Necessary Preparation for the Coming of Christ: "And he shall go before him in the spirit and power of Elias, to turn the hearts," etc. Luke 1:17.

The Greatest Guest: "Where is he?" Matt. 2:2.

The Fullness of the Times: "That in the dispensation of the fullness of times," etc. Eph. 1:10.

God's Prehistoric Choice: "According as he hath chosen us in him before the foundation of the world," etc. Eph. 1:4.

MIDWEEK FELLOWSHIP MEETING TOPIC

(Church Night or Suggested Sermon Subject)

Theme: Gospel Adornment.

TEXT: "Adorn the doctrine of God our Saviour in all things." Titus 2:10.

The word "doctrine" here used means "instruction." It means any and all the great truths set forth in the Gospel, in God's Word. The word "adorn" means "decorate" or "beautify."

I. The wonderful possibility. To adorn or beautify the truth of God. The best illustrated Bible is the conduct of the people who profess to take it for their guide and law.

II. The grandeur of Christian doctrine. It is the "Gospel in shoes," the living, walking, attractive Christian. 1. The Gospel consists not in speculation. It is something to be displayed in conduct. 2. It is something to be lived from within. Its adornment is from within. It is what the Christian really is. "Truth in the inward parts." 3. It is something to be lived with Christ. 4. Consider how Christ adorned the doctrine, by his life of friendliness, sincerity, purity, serviceableness. Adorn the doctrine after his pattern.—H.

CHRISTIAN ENDEAVOR SOCIETY TOPIC

Dec. 14. Examples from Jesus: How Jesus Used the Scriptures. Matt. 4:1-11; Luke 4:16-22; Luke 24:27. (Universal Bible Sunday.)

SUNDAY SCHOOL LESSON

Dec. 14. Jesus Dispels Fear. Matt. 14:22-33.

MEMORY SELECTION: "Take heart, it is I: have no fear." Matt. 14:27 (R.S.V.).

Fear is a great weakness. Jesus would have us face life unafraid. Jesus calmed the fear of others. This lesson should bring to us an unwavering trust in Christ. His disciples should be unafraid. We should have a growing feeling of security in God's world. Yet we should also take care of ourselves and not expect or demand miraculous deliverances. "Fear not." This was the angel's Christmas message. It is a needed message still.

SUNDAY: DECEMBER TWENTY-FIRST

MORNING SERVICE

Theme: A Perfect Christmas (Christmas).

SUGGESTED SCRIPTURE READING: Luke 2:1-20.

SELECTED HYMNS: "Good Christian men, rejoice."—Holst. "Angels o'er the fields."—Old French Carol. "I hear along our street."—Old English Carol of the Hearth, by MacKinnon. "O come, all ye faithful."—Latin. "Joy to the world, the Lord is come."—I. Watts. "O Little Town of Bethlehem."—Phillips Brooks. "The first Noel."—Traditional. "It came upon the midnight clear."—E. H. Sears.

CALL TO WORSHIP: "Arise, shine; for thy light is come, and the glory of the Lord is risen upon thee. . . . And the Gentiles shall come to thy light, and kings to the brightness of thy rising."

INVOCATION PRAYER: Eternal God, who hast revealed thy purpose in the Holy Child of Bethlehem born under the shadow of the cross, open our hearts to the joy of his coming. Deliver us from doubts and fears through faith in him who is our ultimate victory. Where there is hate renew in us the spirit of good will. May we welcome the Great Guest, who maketh all things new. Pour out thy Spirit upon all mankind, and grant that this Christmas may bring us nearer to a world ordered in thy will which will be our peace. Regard all thy children, O Heart of Love, in their need, and lead us in the way everlasting. Amen.

Theme: A Perfect Christmas (Christmas).

TEXT: "When they saw the star," etc. Matt. 2:10-12.

INTRODUCTORY: What makes a perfect Christmas? Surely this text tells. It tells the story of a perfect Christmas.

I. Perfect because it was a day of joy. When they saw the star, they rejoiced with exceeding great joy. They saw a star and said, "It is his star. It stands for the newborn King of the Jews, the Messiah, the Saviour." Signs and tokens and symbols are sources of joy. The other day I opened a book and there dropped into my hands a pressed flower, "the wonderful Edelweiss which alone blooms amidst the eternal snow." As I looked at the flower I was again in Switzerland, I could see the mountains, I could hear the calls of the goat-herds and the tinkling of the bells, I could live over again the happy days of years ago—there was joy in my heart. The wise men had joy because a new star was a new sign, a thing of great portent. Therein lie the possibilities of much joy, using the less to suggest the greater. One flower becomes a garden. The line of a song stands for all the anticipated joy of heaven. The touch of a hand stands for an eternal friendship. A single word contains a volume. What presence can be summoned by a sign! When one grows old with what signs of retrospection and anticipation one may drive away the cares that infest the day. The wise men—I always think of them as old men—had a joyous Christmas Day.

II. A perfect Christmas Day, a day of joy—but joy alone does not make a perfect day. Some might rejoice in the star until in their intense gladness they lose the significance of the star. Some have a happy Christmas with the Christ left out. Some let the star lead them to the door of the house and then never enter to see the Christ Child. The Magi entered the house, saw the Child and worshiped. To make the day perfect add worship to joy.

What happens when a truly reverent soul worships the Christ? I think there is the "silence of beholding,"—just looking. Once a group of us stood upon Sunrise Mountain, Silver Bay, in the early morning. We watched the East change from crimson to orange, to yellow, to gold, to radiance—we looked until our souls appropriated the glory. So I suppose those men of old looked upon the wonderful Christ Child until their souls appropriated his glory—and then they prayed. No rush of words, no exclamation of praise—the prayer of intense longing to exchange ugliness for beauty, sinfulness for righteousness, dullness for radiance. For a perfect Christmas day add to joy, worship, reverent and humble and silent gazing upon his glory, and then petition to become like him. But not yet is Christmas altogether perfect, some things need to be added to joy and worship.

III. And when these wise men had worshiped they opened their treasures and presented gifts, gold, frankincense, myrrh. Not patronage—patronage precedes not follows worship, their gifts were tokens of loving service. A perfect Christmas, to joy add worship and to worship service.

Open the treasures, the caskets where the precious things are kept. Did we do this what rich gifts we would give the King!

I once saw a woman radiantly happy because like the widow whom Jesus watched at the temple treasury she gave all she had. Young men who have opened their caskets have found lives of achievements inside to dedicate to him.

IV. "They returned into their country by a different road"—joy, worship, service, obedience. Who can go back to Herod after he has had a perfect Christmas with the Christ? I cannot bow at the feet of evil after I have opened my casket at the feet of Jesus. Herod says, "Come back to me, I would worship, too"; the tempter is always willing to promise to worship. Herod says, "Come back to me," but the voice of God says, "Travel a different road."

So many of us are always going back to Herod. So many of us enter the room and bow before the Christ and then go back to the old evil things—we are enticed by the glitter of the king's palace after we have walked in the litter of the stable where the Christ Child lies.

Go back a different road and every good thing of the old road will be transplanted and bloom by your doorstep. Should you have two flowers in your hand, lay both at the feet of Jesus and surely there will come into your hands many more to give.

A perfect Christmas—Joy, Worship, Service, Obedience. I see the star, I worship the Child, I open my casket, I go back by a new road.—M. K. W. H.

THEME PRAYER: Most mighty and merciful Father, God of us all alike, let the consciousness of thy presence be in our hearts this Christmas Day. Help us to carry into our daily lives the knowledge that all men, whatever be their speech, their color or their creed, are thy sons and our brothers. Make us to understand that only as we have love for our fellow men can we properly keep the day which no man can keep alone. Give to us the gifts of patience, kindness and forbearance toward our fellow men. Open our hearts to understanding and our spirit to justice for all. In the unity of common faith in thy universal Fatherhood and in thy holy law of love, we ask this, in the name of Him in whose honor we keep Christmas. Amen.—R. Taylor.

OFFERTORY SENTENCE: "And when they had opened their treasures, they presented unto him gifts; gold, and frankincense, and myrrh."

OFFERTORY PRAYER: O God, our heavenly Father, we thank thee for the gift of thy dear Son. Grant that we who have received him in our hearts may joyfully go forth with him on many errands. Bless those who toil for thee in far-off places; comfort them in their loneliness; and unite our work to theirs. Accept the gifts we now make; receive our prayers; and use us for the sake of thy Son, Jesus Christ our Lord. Amen.

Illustrative Material

SEED THOUGHTS, HOMILETIC AND EXPOSITORY. The Visit of the Wise Men: "And when they were come into the house, they saw the young child with Mary his mother," etc. Matt. 2:11. Wonderful events were connected with Christ's birth. Appearance of the celestial choir. The astonished shepherds. A little later the visit of the wise men. I. The persons. Styled "wise men." Probably of those skilled in astronomy. Whence they came, "From the East." Some think Arabia. Most likely Persia. II. The journey. 1. The cause of it, "the star." 2. The journey itself. Probably about two weeks. 3. Its termination. "Where the young Child lay." III. The worship they presented. 1. Bowed in great humility. "Fell down at his feet." 2. In great reverence, "And they worshiped him." 3. In great generosity. They opened their treasures and "presented unto him gifts, gold, and frankincense, and myrrh." IV. Some suggested lessons. 1. A tacit reproof to the Jews. They paid no attention to the event. 2. An interesting illustration of Divine providences. 3. The homage due to Jesus.—B.

Choice Christmas Illustrations

CHRISTMAS BRINGS A NEW SPIRIT. A few years ago one of our illustrated papers contained a picture showing how Christmas appeared to two classes of people. It was Christmas Eve. The snow was falling thick and fast, and the ground was covered with a white mantle. The curtains of a house were so arranged that those upon the street could look in and see the blazing fire, the tree burdened with gifts, the happy faces of the parents, the radiant faces of the children.

Outside were two figures; one, a woman thinly clad, with an old shawl drawn tightly around her head, and the other, a little child in rags and tatters. Both were looking into the brightness which they could not enter.

Gradually, as the result of the teachings of the Master, all are coming to understand that those outside in the snow belong to him quite as much as those in the light and warmth; and few in our modern life can be happy with their own joys unless they have done something to add to the joy and comfort of others.—A. H. Bradford, D.D.

CHRISTMAS OPEN-HEARTEDNESS. The true "open-heartedness" of Christmas is well expressed in these verses:

My door is open wide to-night,
The hearth fire is aglow;
I seem to hear swift passing feet,
The Christ-Child in the snow.

My door is open wide to-night,
For stranger, kith or kin;
I would not bar a single door
Where love might enter in.

The new year will be better than the old if we can preserve the mood of Christmas so completely that it shall fashion our lives for the next twelve months.

CHRISTMAS ALL THE YEAR. There is a little poem, only a scrap of verse that found its way into the columns of a country newspaper. It told of a man riding on horseback through a bit of timberland in one of our southern states. It was a bright day in October, and he was jogging along enjoying the air and the scenery, when all at once he came upon a little clearing in which was a tiny cabin, almost falling to pieces. In the doorway of the cabin an aged Negro woman was standing. Her back was bent with the hard toil of the years and her hair was snow white, but her eyes were as bright as the stars. The man called out: "Good morning, Aunty! Are you living there all alone?" Looking at him with a smile on her withered old face, she answered: "Yes, Massa, jes' me and Jesus." The traveler said that as she spoke a hush fell over it all. He seemed to see a halo about the ramshackle old hut, and he thought he could see some-one standing there beside her, and his form was as the form of the Son of God.

Christ is everywhere in our thoughts and plans at Christmas time. But every day could be transfigured if we carry him with us down through all the days of the year.—S. N. Hutchison, D.D.

KEEPING THE GLOW OF CHRISTMAS. During pre-Christmas days the spirit of generosity and kindness fills the earth. Hearts are softened, as we think of the Christ Child in the lowly manger, and selfishness hides its face. Love and pity occupy the throne, and a spiritual glow warms the hearts of men.

There is but one way to explain this. The Spirit of the Christ, which is the spirit of love, takes hold upon us, as we listen to the angel's song and meditate upon God's wonderful gift to men. His birthday gives us the opportunity to express this spirit, and the spiritual glow is created within us. To almost everyone Christmas is the happiest time of the whole year, because our hearts are warmed with love which the infant Jesus brought with him when he came to earth "on that solemn midnight, centuries ago."

Oh, if we could maintain that spiritual glow all through the year, and be as "fervent in spirit" after Christmas as on that blessed day.—Robert Tate.

Quotable Christmas Poetry

LIGHT A CANDLE

Light a candle in the window,
Bright and bonny may it glow,
So its gleam may guide the Christ-Child
In his journey here below.

Gifts of love and Merry Christmas,
'Neath our tree are loaded high,
Light a candle in the window,
For the Christ-Child may be nigh.

Light a candle in the window,
Also light one in your heart.
Let it ever shine for Jesus,
Light the Christ-Child in the dark.

—Evelyn Dewhirst.

GIFTS OF THE WISE MEN

A surgeon brings a laughing lad
With twisted limbs made strong—
A teacher brings brave visions,
A singer a silver song.

An engineer brings bridges,
A mason a temple wall—
A mother brings a trembling prayer,
And love illumines all.

I wonder what the Christ-Child did
With myrrh the magi bore,
And gold and frankincense! These gifts
He uses evermore!
—Earl Bigelow Brown.

EVENING SERVICE

Theme: The Compassion of Jesus (Christmas).

TEXT: "And Jesus went forth, and saw a great multitude, and was moved with compassion toward them, and he healed their sick." Matt. 14:14.

INTRODUCTORY: We see the long lines of people mailing Christmas presents, showing the spirit of kindness all over Christendom in an effort to make others happy. For one week all jealousy, hatred, selfishness are hidden and forgotten through the spirit of love and sympathy.

I. The curtain is lifted on human life for a short time and shows that the real heart of humanity is wonderfully kind. Whence comes this Christmas spirit of love and sympathy? There was no Christmas at the time of Jesus. Jesus gave to meet men's greatest needs and make them happy as though every day were a Christmas day. He met a man blind from birth. He didn't simply say: "I am sorry for you," and walk on. He might have said: "I am in a hurry and it is the Sabbath." He might have said: "I will heal you for $300." He saw a man's present suffering and need and treated his eyes and he saw. What did he give the blind man? A new world. What did he do to the blind man? He lifted him from a despised beggar to a self-respecting man, able to earn a living and to care for others. How big and valuable was this present? The biggest it was possible to give him to be enjoyed the rest of his life.

II. Take as an example the despised woman at the well. His gentle spiritual talk opened her vision to a new spiritual world. She became so happy that she forgot her water bag and ran to tell others that she had found the Christ. Are not others affected in the same way? He gave her the greatest blessing possible. It lasted with her life. It blessed others. Compare this gift with our small temporary gifts.

III. Peter and John healed the lame man at the gate—a blessing for life. He was so happy, went walking and leaping and praising God.

IV. So Jesus and his disciples after him showed the Christmas spirit, giving largest possible gifts for present need. They endured. They were given to friend or foe, to high or low. All men were sacred to them because they were human.

V. Succeeding generations, filled with the Christ-spirit and stirred by reading of his sympathy and helpfulness, felt inspired to follow in his footsteps and chose a day which they called Christmas in his honor.

VI. Suppose every nation should observe every day as a Christmas day and forget hate and selfishness and just learn to be kind? The day would arrive when the dream of the poet would come true—of a "parliament of nations and a federation of the world." The cold exacting world longs for sympathy and a helpful loving spirit.—E. H. C.

Alternate Theme: The Road to Bethlehem (Christmas).

TEXT: Matt. 2:7-12.

INTRODUCTORY: There is an old carol in which the shepherds ask: "How far is it to Bethlehem?" The angels reply: "Not very far, not very far." At any rate the Bethlehem we treasure—that of the spirit—is not very far. At Christmas time we are all sure of that. So we make one more pilgrimage to Bethlehem.

I. Along this road we shall discover that the Bethlehem road is not a thing apart by itself. Thus the Via Dolorosa is not very far removed; neither is the road that leads to Samaria where he declares that "God is a Spirit and they that worship him must worship him in spirit and in truth." The glad worship of Christmas time should center there.

II. This highway of the mind leads to where the ideal and the real blend. When this happens there may be some confusion; especially if we walk only by sight. Surely the faith factor was not absent when those searchers after truth, missing the guidance of the star for a while, still journeyed on. It is this perspective we need for days like these. Herod and his crowd are near, but the star shines and the angels sing.

III. The star and the song are symbols of that realm of life that by inference we are apt to label unreal. Hence, while we are bound to the poetry of dream and vision it is imperative that we should remember the spiritual reality of which these things are the medium of expression. Someone has said that "the true realism—that is, the track toward that ultimate goal—is in the inner life rather than the physical environment. It is by way of the wings and not the hands."

IV. The folk of the East depended on the stars. They knew next to nothing about "light years," and the stars seemed near and friendly. Long and lofty thoughts often came to them as they contemplated the heavens.

We, too, taking the shepherds' way, must surely be led to the more specific aspects of our faith. What Herod bade them do for his evil design they do adoringly—they "search out exactly concerning Him." And, in the last analysis it is in turning to the specific tasks that the vision is saved.

This special pilgrimage cannot long endure, and this is probably all to the good. We return to the world of "hard facts." Christmas is followed by the New Year, and the season of Lent soon comes with its different emphases. We are warned not to betray the object of our search back there. In a world like this it is so easy to betray one's own cause. It is easy to fall a prey to hate, and the spirit of man, destined for fellowship with the highest, becomes seared thereby.

V. Another warning came to these ancient pilgrims, and for the same reason: that the holy child might not be, even unwittingly, betrayed. They were warned to go home "another way." There is a sense in which all who journey to Bethlehem and bow there in adoration do return another way.

"Another way!" Out of the way maybe. For many the way of sacrifice. It is only natural that the weary pilgrim should ask why another way at times. But when he realizes that supreme values are at stake—goodness, beauty, truth and love—then, by God's grace, obedience is added to adoration.

How far is it to Bethlehem? Sing the traditional songs, and maybe catch the overtones of angels' voices; follow the star by way of imagination, and bow in adoring wonder with the great devout souls of the centuries and you, too, will be there.—T. C. O.

Suggested Christmas Texts and Themes

The Two Census Books: "There went out a decree from Caesar Augustus, that all the world should be taxed." Luke 2:1. "They which are written in the Lamb's book of life." Rev. 21:27.

Five Points of the Christmas Star: "And his name shall be called Wonderful, Counsellor, The Mighty God, The Everlasting Father, The Prince of Peace." Isa. 9:6.

Christmas Good Will: "If God so loved us, we ought also to love one another." I John 4:11.

The Peerless Christ: "Christ is all, and in all." Col. 3:11.

Where Is He? "Where is he that is born King of the Jews?" Matt. 2:2.

The Greatest Name: "Thou shalt call his name Jesus, for he shall save his people from their sins." Matt. 1:21.

MIDWEEK FELLOWSHIP MEETING TOPIC

(Church Night or Suggested Sermon Subject)

Theme: Jesus Excluded (Christmas).

TEXT: "There was no room for them in the inn." Luke 2:7.

Joseph and Mary resided at Nazareth. The enrollment or poll tax required their journey to Bethlehem. Here Christ was born.

I. First let us look at the illustrious travelers. Both Joseph and Mary were in the royal line of Judah. The account given of Joseph is short but significant—"a just man." A man of religious integrity. Mary was a woman of most exalted character. Her condition is stated in Matthew 1:18.

II. Notice the journey they took. It was from Nazareth to Bethlehem. It was a distance of near a hundred miles, and in that period slow and of considerable risk and difficulty. At length they reach the end of their journey.

III. Probably great numbers were arriving at the same time and for the same purpose. This may account for there being no place for suitable reception. "There was no room in the inn." The place was preoccupied. They, therefore, had to retire to the outer buildings intended for pack animals and cattle. Here Jesus was born. Wonderful condescension of God! Wonderful meaning for us!

IV. It seems Christ's exclusion from the inn was purely accidental and not designed, though it contains important lessons for us. "No room!" Today the world makes room for its own. Why is Christ excluded? Why not more room for him? Why? Why is there so little room for him: In our thoughts. In our conversation. In our reading. In our social pleasures. In our business. In our civic, national and international affairs. In his own Christmas! Christ crowded out!

CHRISTIAN ENDEAVOR SOCIETY TOPIC

Dec. 21. "In the Fullness of Time." Gal. 4:1-7; Isa. 9:6, 7.

SUNDAY SCHOOL LESSON

Dec. 21. Emmanuel—God with Us. Matt. 1:18-25.

MEMORY SELECTION: "Thou shalt call his name Jesus: for he shall save his people from their sins." Matt. 1:21.

This lesson is the heart of Christmas. Through Matthew's narrative and interpretation of the meaning of Jesus' birth we are led to know that God has come among men in the person of Jesus his Son, and for the express purpose of providing a Saviour for the world. This study may also help us to a growing awareness of God's presence always.

SUNDAY: DECEMBER TWENTY-EIGHTH

MORNING SERVICE

Theme: Inquiry of the Past (End of Year).

SUGGESTED SCRIPTURE READING: Rev. 10:1-11.

SELECTED HYMNS: "While with ceaseless course the sun."—J. Newton. "Days and moments quickly flying."—E. Caswell. "O God, our help in ages past."—I. Watts. "Rise, my soul, and stretch thy wings."—Robert Seagrave. "Ring out wild bells."—Alfred Tennyson.

CALL TO WORSHIP: "Then Samuel took a stone, and set it between Mizpeh and Shen, and called the name of it Ebenezer, saying, Hitherto hath the Lord helped us."

INVOCATION PRAYER: Almighty and most merciful Father, who hast given us grace in times past, and hast mercifully brought us to see the end of another year, grant us that we may continue to grow in grace and in the knowledge of thy dear Son. Lead us forward by thy Spirit from strength to strength, that we may more perfectly serve thee. Stir up the gift that is in us. Increase our faith as thou dost increase our years, and the longer we are suffered to abide on earth the better may our service be, the more willing our obedience, the more consistent our daily lives, the more complete our devotion to thee. Grant this our prayer, which we offer in the name of Jesus Christ thy Son, our Lord. Amen.

Theme: Inquiry of the Past (End of Year).

TEXT: "Ask now of the days that are past." Deut. 4:32.

INTRODUCTORY: Some are so thoughtless as to pay no attention to the past. They ignore it. They ask nothing of it. Yet the past can be a great teacher. Asking of the past may spur us on by bringing to us a humbling consciousness of the poor use we have made of our time. Or it may bring a suitable sense of the Divine goodness and forbearance. Or it may bring earnest resolve to correct in the future those things which were evil in the past. It is especially true that to ask of the past may bring to us a sensible appreciation of the value of time.

I. It is our wisdom to "ask of the days that are past." 1. Because the past is in existence now. 2. Because for the past we are responsible. 3. Because the past is full of useful lessons.

II. Ask of past blessings, as to how they have been received. Blessings material, blessings spiritual, how have they been received? 1. As from God? 2. As undeserved mercies? 3. In a thankful spirit? "Ask now of the days that are past." Consider them. Learn from them.

III. Ask of past opportunities, as to how they have been used. 1. Opportunities for improvement, for getting good, mental good, moral good; have these opportunities been turned to profit or are they lost forever? 2. Opportunities for doing good, to the bodies of men, to the souls of men, to the ignorant, the sorrowful, the erring, have we improved these?

IV. Ask of past sins. Have they been repented of? Have they been forsaken? Have they been pardoned? How about our sins of omission? How about such sins as irreverence, unsubmissiveness, ingratitude against God? Of injustice, untruthfulness, uncharitableness against men?

He is wise who obeys this injunction and "asks of the days that are past."

THEME PRAYER: Almighty God, our heavenly Father, with whom a thousand years are as one day and one day as a thousand years, we the children of a brief time would draw near to thee as we stand at the end of another year and seek pardon for past failures and guidance for the future. Teach us to so number our days that we shall apply our hearts unto wisdom. Help us to realize the infinite significance of life's opportunities. Forgive the sins of the past. Above all teach us to walk during this coming year in trustful fellowship with thee, through our Lord Jesus Christ. Amen.

OFFERTORY SENTENCE: "If there be first a willing mind, it is accepted according to that a man hath, and not according to that he hath not."

OFFERTORY PRAYER: Great Giver of the rolling years, we thank thee that when we are but marred clay in thy hands, thou dost not cast us away from thy presence, but dost begin to shape us again, other vessels to thy glory. At the end of this year, we are especially conscious of our failure to yield ourselves wholly to thee. As we come bearing gifts, may we bring the acceptable offering of yielded lives, to let thee have thine own way with us in the days to come. We ask in the name of Him who gave all to us. Amen.

Illustrative Material

SEED THOUGHTS, HOMILETIC AND EXPOSITORY. Inquiry of the Past: We can never consent to give the past to oblivion. God requires that which is past, and he requires us to remember it. And it is wisdom to do so. I. There is something very solemn in thought of the days that are past. For one thing, they never return, while their moral results remain forever as subjects of future responsibility. II. Ask of the days that are past what they have to say concerning the world. III. Ask of the days that are past what they have to say concerning ourselves. IV. Ask of the days that are past what they have to say concerning our Lord and Saviour.—W. J.

The Voice of the Past: I. The past speaks of the value of time. Who can say of the past year or years that time has gone as he wished? II. The voice of the past calls us to a grateful sense of God's goodness and mercies. III. The voice of the past calls us to correct in the future the things which have been evil.—J. F.

Choice Year's End Illustrations

THE PROPHET AT YEAR'S END. When weighed down by a consciousness of our own and others' failings during the year now dying it is small comfort to be reminded that "a historian is a prophet looking backward." But what if the reverse of that celebrated definition is true? "A prophet is a historian facing forward." Though even he dare not foretell any change in man's past deeds, he can, if he is truly God's prophet, with complete confidence forecast many a change in the souls of men. And such a transformation can in actual fact change God's eternal record of the past. If the historian interprets the future in the light of the past, the prophet interprets the past in the light of the future. When a man's trend, however feeble or wavering, is Godward, he is on his way toward that better man he is to be. His future interprets both his present and his past. God's prophet, then, sees each Old Year darkness transfigured by the possibilities of the New. —*Monday Morning.*

FORGET TO REMEMBER. In Newport there stands what was once a magnificent mansion, now in ruins. Its story would have delighted an author like Dickens. Years ago a wealthy family, intending to "crash" Newport society, bought the house. A great dinner was arranged and many invitations sent out. But no one came. Humiliated beyond tears, the family walked out never to return, leaving the house just as it was. Through the years it has stood, a monument to wounded pride, and no one is allowed to forget. How much more sensible and Christlike was the attitude of the philosopher Kant, who, when hurt by a man named Lampe, wrote on his memorandum pad: "Remember to forget Lampe." A good motto, but a better one is, "Forget to remember."

Today, as we stand at the threshold of a new year, let us forget "those things which are behind," the old hurts, disappointments, failures, mistakes, and remember to "press toward the mark for the prize of the high calling of God in Christ Jesus."—B. D. Stevens.

YEAR'S END

"This year may be my last"
Ah, let us bow reluctant heads
At this the threshold now,
And as the chime of warning fades,
In solemn silence go.
Before us lies a trackless space,
Unseen, unknown, untried;
But let us not forget the grace
Of God, the Unseen Guide.
As one more space of Time hath dawned
To spread her silent wings,
Then let us all the more abound
With greater, nobler things.
A wise Creator framed the world,
And for a season man
May here enjoy, as was of old,
The bounties of his hand.
So let us look to him who holds
The future in his power;
Whose hand man's destinies enfolds—
Controls forever more.

—W. D. Smith.

ETERNAL YOUTH. "Memory is given to us," said a great man, "so that we might have roses in December." In a European art gallery there is a picture of an old man and a young girl sitting before an open fireplace and watching the flames tossing in fantastic shapes. Under the picture are the words: "She is thinking of the future; he is dreaming of the past." Yet the distinctive thing about the Christian life is that the best is ever on before; the best is yet to be. It was in the closing stages of his life that Paul wrote, "I press on toward the mark." There is no such thing as growing old for the Christian.—Archer Wallace.

EVENING SERVICE

Theme: The Finality of the Gospel (Watch Night).

TEXT: "The word was made flesh, and dwelt among us." John 1:14. "When he had opened the book." Luke 4:17. "He closed the book." Luke 4:20.

INTRODUCTORY: Christ was the Word, God's Word, like an opened book. He opened the book and he closed the book. There in a sentence is the purpose of the life of Christ.

I. First, he opened the book. We believe that God has never left himself without witness. He has spoken to man through nature, through instinct, through conscience, through personal contact with other men, through the history of the human race. In every age men may hear his voice speaking in life's many and varied situations, a voice from within and a voice from without. The Bible is the supreme witness to this speaking of God to man. Through its pages God has again and again spoken to men's needs and passed judgment on men's error.

"He opened the book." He opened the book because he alone had the right to open the book. I have never forgotten an experience told me by my first music teacher, a converted Jewess. She was greatly puzzled by certain passages in Isaiah. No one could explain them to her satisfaction. Suddenly she saw that the life of Jesus gave them new meaning. He had opened the book. That was the discovery of the Early Church. "And beginning at Moses and all the prophets, he expounded unto them in all the scriptures the things concerning himself." Anyone who wants to understand the Bible should begin with the life of Christ. Once that life becomes real the rest of the Bible discloses its meaning. Begin with Christ. He opens the book.

II. He also closes the book. This does not mean that we can now dispense with God's witness through the Bible and nature and conscience and the rest. Christ handed the book to the attendant to be used again. But he closed the book because he himself had more to give to men than could be found in any book, even the Bible. St. Paul said he was the end of the law. He was more than a spoken or written word could be. He was the Word made flesh. A distinguished scholar has said that the Incarnation was God's way of writing theology. The witness of God in Christ is final.

III. Here is the heart of our religion. He opened the book because he closed the book. "God who at sundry times and in divers manners spake in time past unto the fathers by the prophets, hath in these last days spoken unto us by his Son."

Another year ends tonight. We express our hopes for the year that is to come. We wish each other well. We cannot of ourselves do more. God can do more. He does not only speak to us. He comes to us. He gives us something we can see and handle—a human life lived completely in his power. By this we judge the past. By this we interpret the present. By this we are led into the future unafraid. "Lo, I am with you alway." This is no word from the heavens only nor only in our hearts. It is the promise of One who "himself hath suffered being tempted, he is able to succour them that are tempted." Therefore, as we go forward, I do not offer you my good wishes. I do not even offer you the church and its worship and fellowship. I do not even offer you this book. I offer you Jesus, the same yesterday, today, and forever, because if you have him you will have all else beside.—R. L. A.

Year's End Texts and Themes

Be Ready in the Morning: "Be ready in the morning, and come up in the morning unto mount Sinai," etc. Ex. 34:2,3.

The Christian's Taking Account of Time: "A wise man's heart discerneth both time and judgment." Eccles. 8:5.

The End of the Year: "Then shall the end come." Matt. 24:14.

New Year Optimism: "Tomorrow the Lord will do wonders among you." Josh. 3:5.

God Alone is Unchanging: "Thou art the same, and thy years shall have no end." Ps. 102:27.

Watch and Pray: "Take ye heed, watch and pray," etc. Mark 13:33-37.

MIDWEEK FELLOWSHIP MEETING TOPIC

(Church Night or Suggested Sermon Subject)

Theme: Holding Fast.

TEXT: "Take fast hold of instruction; let her not go: keep her; for she is thy life." Prov. 4:13.

A short but urgent admonition. The tenacious grasp of the shipwrecked sinking sailor on floating spar or plank illustrates the kind of grasp with which wisdom is to be held.

I. The necessity of holding fast. 1. Divine wisdom is an attainment. 2. Divine truth is spiritual. It belongs to a different region from that of everyday experiences in the world. 3. It is morally exacting. It concerns our conduct. It urges us with lofty mandates.

II. How we may hold fast. 1. Attention must be directed to it. Let us turn our minds to Divine truth by voluntary resolve. 2. Truth must be realized in practice. There is no better way of holding fast to instruction than by obeying it.

III. The advantage of holding fast. 1. It fulfills duty to God. 2. It is to our own souls' profit. 3. Truth shows us the way to salvation. 4. It is an immediate source of life. To lose it is to starve. To hold it fast is to secure eternal life. —P. C.

CHRISTIAN ENDEAVOR SOCIETY TOPIC

Dec. 28. "What's This Year Been Worth to Me?" II Cor. 13:5; Phil. 4:8.

SUNDAY SCHOOL LESSON

Dec. 28. Wise Men Seek Jesus. Matt. 2:1-12.

MEMORY SELECTION: "Ye shall seek me, and find me, when ye shall search for me with all your heart." Jer. 29:13.

It is an honor to bring gifts for Jesus and to worship him. The story of the Wise Men is especially appropriate for our study right after Christmas. It suggests that the wisdom, wealth and glory of the world be brought to Jesus' feet. There are also missionary implications in it—the representatives of the Gentile world coming in quest of the world's Saviour. The story may also serve as an inspiration to us to consecrate ourselves to Christ at the beginning of the New Year. It is always the part of wisdom to see Jesus as Saviour and to follow his leadings day by day.

SECTION VIII. The Junior Pulpit. A Church-School Year of Suggestive Sermons for Children and Youths

JANUARY 6. Topic: The Door of the Year (New Year).

The old Romans called the first month of the year January after the name of their god Janus. His name comes from a word meaning a door. Janus was the great janitor who opened the door of the year, and the door of every human life. The people and pagan priests prayed to Janus at the begining of every day and when they began any work. They also had a great festival for him on the first day of January, and finally they reckoned the beginning of the year from his festival.

Janus had a temple in Rome. The gates of this temple were closed when there was peace in the land and they were open during war.

A strange thing about this god who opened the door of the new year was that he had two faces. There was an old face looking backward, and a young, bright, eager face looking forward into the future.

Those Romans were right in thinking that someone did open for them the door to let in the new year. They were right, too, in seeking his blessing when they began any new work or entered upon the duties of a new day. They did not know as we do that the real name of him who opens the door of the year is Jesus. It is he "that openeth and no man shutteth, and shutteth and no man openeth." Jesus it is who stands guarding the doors and gates of life. And you young folks are looking forward wondering what Jesus has put into the new year for you.

One thing it will bring us is opportunity—opportunities to do good and to get good. The Greeks thought that that big word, Opportunity, was a goddess. If you have not seen it, someday you will see their picture of Opportunity. You will notice that the person is bald behind, but with a little tuft of hair in front. They said that once Opportunity went past anyone not even Jupiter himself could catch her.

So you see to use opportunity we must take hold of her as she comes to us.

I hope that every one of you young friends will look out every morning to see the bright, shining face of opportunity, and that as she comes you will use her—use her in school, use her at home helping mother, use her when you play with your companions. Remember also that it is Jesus who sends opportunity to us, making a door for each day through which we can go out to do good and get good.—Rev. Lloyd Morris.

JANUARY 13. Topic: The Bread (Talk on Communion Sunday).

It seems that whenever I talk to you boys and girls that I am always remembering things of my boyhood. And the thing I am remembering today is that sometimes I got hungry. Now that is not unusual for a boy, is it?

And when I got hungry my grandmother would say, "I'll spread a piece of bread with butter for you." "No, I want some cake." And very often she would say, "No, if you're hungry you will be willing to eat bread." And she was right—and we had a word for real hunger in our house—we called it "bread-hunger." That is, hungry enough to be willing to eat bread.

Once when he was a boy my son had bread-hunger. It was Thanksgiving time and we had a big family party with turkey, and dressing, and sweet potatoes, and everything that goes with such a dinner. We had come almost to the end of the dinner before we noticed that this small boy had eaten nothing but bread. He had been so very hungry, and bread tasted so good that he wanted nothing but bread. He had bread-hunger.

This incident suggests the thought of the bread we use in observing the sacrament of the Lord's Supper. When we have Communion each Christian eats a little portion of bread. Now as I told you last Communion Sunday, that is just a token, a symbol. The bread is the symbol of Jesus, the symbol of his power to satisfy one's spiritual hunger, and people may come to Communion with a kind of bread-hunger.

Jesus said, "I am the bread of life." It is as if he had said, By me you will get strength of spirit. By me you will become strong in character. I will feed the deep part of your nature. I will help you grow toward Christian manhood and womanhood.

And so when we partake of the bread it is a symbol that we accept him for the deepest needs of our lives.

I hope that everybody here this morning has bread-hunger, hunger for the Living Bread of Life.

One day a friend of mine was in a great and wonderful bakery. He saw the machinery for preparing the dough for the bread. He looked into the ovens. And he came out of the bakery and ate no bread.

That's just what one might do here. Come into the church, and see all its loveliness, listen to the music, even hear in a sort of way the Scripture reading, but go through and not eat any of the bread. Everything we do here is that we may know Jesus better. He said, "I am the bread of life." And we must be bread-hungry.—M. K. W. H.

JANUARY 20. Topic: The Legend of the Outstretched Hand.

In one of the great churches in Spain there is a curious and unusual crucifix. It is of gold and is studded with jewels. But the unusual thing is that only one hand of the almost life-size figure of Jesus is nailed to the cross. The other hand is lifted from the cross and seems to be pointing to something.

There is an appropriate legend told by way of explanation of this unusual figure of Christ. It is said that long ago two young people pledged themselves to each other with a vow of lifelong love and faithfulness. They were engaged to be married. But the man broke his vow. The broken hearted girl in her anguish came to the foot of that cross, seeking there some comfort from the Crucified Christ, who knew so well what suffering was. There as she knelt, the legend says, Jesus raised one hand from the cross and stretching it over the girl said, "Be comforted! I am the witness." Through the centuries the hand has thus remained, states the legend, outstretched in tenderness to all sufferers and in silent witness to wrong doers that he sees and cares.

The legend has doubtless had far-reaching influence in the neighborhood of that church. The outstretched hand of the figure on the cross and the story have helped to make real to many simple-minded people the sympathy and compassion of Jesus.

I need not tell you that legends have grown numerous about the cross. In crude and superstitious ways people have set forth their devotion and their hope. We need not be superstitious, but we do well to seek the spiritual facts behind the legends, and then learn to appreciate the great truths thus symbolized.

One of the greatest of ancient writers once cried out, "Oh, that someone would stretch out a hand!" He had come to the end of his resources. His life principles, noble though in many ways they were, when tried out were found wanting. The man needed more than his philosophy could give. The Christian faith is that in Jesus the cry of the human heart is always answered. And that, young friends, is the truth behind the legend of that curious crucifix in that church in Spain.—Adapted from Rev. F. C. Hoggarth.

JANUARY 27. Topic: How a Great Treasure Was Discovered.

Recently I read a most interesting story by an English minister named W. D. Lewis. He was telling how Jesus saw the goodness in the heart of the little man, Zaccheus of Jericho, who had climbed a tree to see Jesus as he passed by. You remember the story and how Jesus went home with Zaccheus to dinner. This story reminded Mr. Lewis of the story I am going to tell you now. The story is concerning a certain South African ostrich hunter named O'Reilly who some years ago sought shelter one winter's night at a solitary farmhouse near the banks of the Orange River.

As Mr. O'Reilly entered the farmer's home he overheard a dispute between the children which was being settled by the mother. While playing on the banks of the river near by the children had picked up some pretty pebbles, and it was the possession of one of these which gave rise the the quarrel. The pebble shone and sparkled by candlelight, and was so unlike any other stone that they had ever seen that the mother made arrangement with Mr. O'Reilly that he should try to sell it at Graham's Town, and then share the profits with her. The stone proved to be a magnificent diamond of twenty-one and a quarter carats, which the man sold for five hundred pounds, equal to two thousand five hundred dollars. On the site of this farm now stands the prosperous little city named Hopetown.

A few months later a native Hottentot came wandering toward the same place with a brilliant stone, which he offered for sale to a certain man who gave him what he asked for it, two hundred pounds' worth of goods. Next day the man parted with his bargain for twelve thousand pounds in gold, about sixty thousand dollars, bought a large tract of land, and bothered himself about diamonds no more. This diamond was the famous eighty-three carat called the "Star of Africa," but afterwards known as the "Dudley Diamond," because it became the property of the Countess of Dudley.

We are told that today the diamond is worth about two hundred and fifty thousand dollars.

Now here is something to think about. The men and women and boys and girls who lived in the vicinity of Zaccheus' home appreciated him not much more than did that Hottentot the diamond he had. But Jesus saw Zaccheus for what he was, a child of God. Jesus was not mistaken. And the lesson for us is plain. We don't know men and women, boys and girls, when we know them only on the surface. Let us try to get underneath, and we shall discover many hidden treasures. Let us get into the hearts of the people we meet.

FEBRUARY 3. Topic: Homes of Other Countries—Switzerland.

From time to time I mean to give you young folk brief descriptions of homes of other countries. There is no place like home. The people in distant lands love their homes the same as we do ours. And it is good for us to know something about how other people live. Like travel, it has educational value. It increases our knowledge, enlivens our imagination, enlarges our world, and widens our sympathy. This morning let us look at some typical homes in Switzerland. Of course there are quite a few small cities and large villages there where the houses are similar to those in other parts of the world. But the typical Swiss homes are in the Alpine regions. These are in the country spaces among the mountains. They are called chalets. These are the typical homes and much alike, though differing somewhat in size. They all have steep roofs and wide summer time flower-filled balconies on the gable end second story front. They are very picturesque and well suited to the wonderful scenery.

They are all made of wood and in the pure mountain air look remarkably spick-and-span. At first sight these dainty cottages seem little suited to the storms and frosts of a Swiss winter. But in reality they are very strongly built. The snow slips easily from the high-pitched roofs. The roofs all have widely overhanging eves. These help to make the house snug, but they also make very useful shelters for great piles of firewood. The homes are heated mostly with large wood-burning stoves that keep the rooms inside warm and cosy.

Often in winter time the snow is so deep that the ground floor level is completely buried, and then the family live chiefly in the upper story. This can be reached by an outside staircase which runs up to the wooden balcony.

Large stones are always seen on the roof of a chalet. These are put there to make it heavy, so that it may not be blown away when a strong wind sweeps down from the mountains.

You know that dairying is one of the active employments of the Swiss farmers. You all know about Swiss cheese, and how good it is. In still higher parts of the mountains in the summertime there are fine pastures. Then some members of the family leave their homes, take the cattle higher up into the hills and herd them there. Here they live for several months in rough wooden huts and spend their time in looking after their herd and making the milk into cheese.

Of course you know that cheese making, though one of the great crafts of the Swiss people, is not their only employment. The cultivation of grapevines, fruit trees and garden products flourishes. Cattle-breeding is largely carried on. There is also manufacturing of silks, cotton goods, leather, woodenware, jewelry, and especially of watches. I would not be surprised if some of you boys and girls have Swiss watches on you now. If not, you may get one when you are a little older. But I am sure you are interested in the Swiss people, and will be still more so. And I think you will be more interested than ever in their homes, all kept so neat, well-tended and much loved. All the world around people are alike in love for home. I close with the words of a writer of both beautiful and meaningful poetry, Henry van Dyke:

. . . Home, sweet home;
For there the heart can rest.

FEBRUARY 10. Topic: The Serpent behind the Hedge.

TEXT: "Whoso breaketh an hedge, a serpent shall bite him." Eccles. 10:8.

The vineyards in Palestine are generally surrounded with hedges. These are not of bushes growing out of the soil, but of stones or lumps of hardened clay thrown loosely together and covered at the top with thorns. In the sides of these hedges or walls serpents find a favorable place to lodge. The robber breaking through the hedge to steal the fruit would be likely to disturb the serpents, and they would spring up and bite him.

In Solomon's reference to this too common occurrence he wishes to teach us some important truths about our lives; that God has placed hedges around us; that we often have the disposition to break through them; and that if we do pain and sorrow will surely follow.

Let us think of some of the hedges God has placed around us. We have to break a hedge to do wrong.

I. First we mention God's commandments. Every one of us, even the youngest, should know them. They are Divine hedges for our safety.

II. Then there are also parental restraints. God has placed our parents in their position. Their restraints are as a rule wise and good. Young children do not understand their parents' care. They often feel it irksome; but it saves from much evil and sorrow. Hedges with respect to our associates, to books, and habits, and amusements are usually good and kind and wise.

III. Then there are principles we are taught by teachers and friends. Teachers are always anxious to fix truths and good maxims in our minds, in the minds of all the young that they may be in them as moral hedges against the time of temptation.

Now, young people are often tempted to break through these hedges. God's restraints are not always welcome, neither are those of their older friends. Hedge-breaking has its fascination. We are tempted by our own hearts, by evil companions, and by Satan, the evil one. There are surely many tempters, and very many temptations.

But, young friends, there is a serpent behind the hedge. If we do wrong we certainly will suffer. The way of transgressors is hard. Punishment is not always visible, but surely follows the deed. It follows in the sense of shame, in the stings of conscience, in the displeasure of God. The serpent's bite is sure. "Whoso breaketh an hedge, a serpent shall bite him." Beware of the deceitfulness of sin. Pray for grace to be kept from it. Christ can keep us from sin. He also can heal our serpent-bites. Look to him for help and safety from sin.—Rev. W. Osborne Lilley.

FEBRUARY 17. Topic: The Single Eye (Hindu Legend).

TEXT: "If therefore thine eye be single, thy whole body shall be full of light." Matt. 6:22.

This morning I am to bring you a legend that comes from far away India. It is called a Hindu legend. But first I want to tell you about our text and what those words mean that speak of the single eye. That is a peculiar expression. "If thine eye be single"; what does that mean? It means seeing steadily, unwaveringly, not confused. It means not seeing double, but fixedly, focused on one subject. For an illustration, ropedancers, in order to steady themselves, fix the eye on some object on the wall and look steadily at that—not at the rope, not at the people. Or if one is crossing a stream on a log or a footboard, if he will look steadily at some object across on the other side, he will be in little danger of dizziness or falling. The single eye is one therefore fixed on a single object, steadily, not confused, without wavering.

But now for our Hindu legend. It has to do with this same thought.

A Brahmin teacher appointed a day on which to test the skill of his pupils with bow and arrow. He placed an artificial bird in the top of a high tree, then calling together his pupils he told them to make ready to shoot off its head.

To the first one called he said, "Do you see the bird on the top of that tree?" "I do," replied the pupil. "What else do you see?" asked the teacher. "I see yourself, my brothers, the tree, and the bird," said the pupil. "Stand aside," said the teacher.

Then he called the others, one by one, and they replied in almost the same words until he came to young Arjuna. That was his name, Arjuna. When Arjuna had drawn his bow and taken aim the teacher said to him, "What do you see?" "I see only the bird," he replied. "Describe the bird to me," said the teacher. "I see only its head," answered the pupil. "Then shoot!" shouted the teacher. The arrow sped straight to the mark and cleft the head of the bird from its body.

Now, young friends, let me tell you this, that the secret of good marksmanship is the secret of the Christian life. We need the single eye, the single aim, the single purpose. This is what we learn from the legend. Like Paul we should say, "This one thing I do."—H

FEBRUARY 24. Topic: The Happiness of Being Trusted.

This morning I am bringing you a brief account from a magazine called *King's Treasuries.* Its stories are vouched for as true. They indicate the fact that young people enjoy the experience of being trusted.

A little white sign with modest black letters close to the grass beside a path caught a certain boy's attention as he passed. The sign read only, "Please," in the quietest way, and so the boy stuck to the footpath and did not cross the grassplot to reach the gate by a short-cut. That boy was a visitor for the day at Princeton. He saw also a great many fellows older than he swarming over the campus, but all heeding the quiet little sign by keeping quite carefully to the many good walks laid out for them.

None of the signs read "Don't," or "Keep off," and there were no wire barriers to guard the lawn. Just a few small signs which simply read "Please."

On a country road near Philadelphia there is a border of wonderful rose bushes running nearly a quarter of a mile in length. The flowers hang over the light fence behind which the bushes are growing. Anyone passing could gather great bunches of roses without being seen by the caretaker on the owners grounds. But these roses bloom in all their glory unmolested. There are no signs forbidding touch. There are perhaps two or three small notices which simply read, "These roses are under the protection of the public." The owner says that he never has lost any of the roses since the signs were put there. The public does protect them gladly.

Young friends, there are more persons than perhaps you think who like to trust you in just these cheery, expectant ways. They know they can count on you to do the square thing under cheerful "Please" or "Kindly" or "Thank you." Boys, girls, show that you do not need the Don'ts" and the "Musts," and the iron fence and penalties. It's great to be trusted. Let's be worthy of it.—H.

MARCH 2. Topic: Bird Gospel Carriers.

You have all heard about carrier pigeons. Explorers of the Artic regions sometimes let them loose with messages for home. Armies often use them too in strategy or to carry news. You have heard also of branding birds, putting a little circle of light metal on a bird's leg to indicate its high breed, or to discover its migrations.

But it is not pigeons or canaries I am to tell you about just now, but a man in Canada who brands wild ducks and geese. His name is Jack Miner. Some years ago he scratched his name and address and a short Bible verse on a light metal band, clasped it on the leg of a duck, and then released the duck again. He owns a farm near Kingsville, Ontario, Canada. On the farm is a small lake which he uses as a bird sanctuary. The ducks and geese can come, be protected and fed, and no harm befall them. In the past few years he has caught and branded thousands of ducks and geese with his name and a short Scripture verse. Mr. Miner and his wife prepare the bands to be placed on the legs of the ducks. Every day they choose a different Bible verse and keep a record, so they can tell at what date the bird left their lake.

When people in far away regions catch or kill a duck or goose with one of these bands on it they write to Mr. Miner, returning the band and telling where they found it. In this way he can put a mark on a map of the bird's trip. From that he has learned more about the migratory routes of ducks and geese than any other man. He is counted an authority.

But it is especially about these birds as Gospel-carriers, or winged missionaries, I am asking you young folks just now more especially to think. Let us notice just how this missionary work comes about.

In one case a duck was shot down by a hunter in Columbia, South America, three thousand miles away from where it started its journey. Around its leg was found the band with its verse: "Let us consider one another," (Heb. 10:24). What better verse could be sent to the people of South America!

When the first Eskimo shot one of the geese and found the band, he brought it to a missionary. The missionary read him the verse and explained its meaning. The same thing happened in different cases, so the Bible verses became the themes of the minister's sermons to the Eskimos and Indians. So you see the verses on the birds' legs helped to spread the words of the Gospel among the people of the north country.

So Mr. Miner has been doing a double service to mankind, both conserving the game supply and spreading the Gospel of Christ in many parts of the world. Truly, God makes use of the birds of the air to become his winged missionaries of love and truth.—H. (With acknowledgments to J. E. Pearson.)

MARCH 9. Topic: Know Your Church: The Ground Plan (1).

(Note: As pastor in a parish with a well-planned and beautiful church I wished that all the children and youths might understand and appreciate its architecture, windows, symbols, furnishings, etc. It would help them to know and admire not alone the building itself, but to feel increased reverence and loyalty toward it, all of which would help to promote a lifelong attachment to Him in whose honor it was built. Not all churches may have exactly the same features, but the following outlines may prove suggestive for such talks by other pastors calling attention to various phases and furnishings for the same purpose.)

This morning I am asking you young friends to think only of the floor of this church. Just imagine that there is no building here above the floor. See only this broad expanse of tiles.

Now as you see the floor without the building I should like to ask you, What is the shape of the floor? Suppose you were to draw the floor plan on a piece of paper, what shape would it be? Begin at the door of the church—better at that inner door. Notice that you would draw a straight line across and then two straight lines up the sides until you came to this wider section of the church. Here you would draw another straight line outward on each side, then lines at right angles again; then two lines out again until you came to the floor section of the chancel. Now add the shape of the floor of the chancel. Do you see what you would have? On paper you would see that it is the shape of a cross.

And above the cross is a window with a wonderful picture of Jesus. And the prints in his hands which you can see remind us that he was nailed to the cross and gave his life for the world. He gave his life for you and me that we might have abundant life.

And because he is the world's Saviour we build churches in his name. And don't you think it fine that we sometimes build churches in the shape of a cross so that each time we see the church or enter we think of his sacrifice for us?

It is because he sacrificed for us, and gave us a ground plan at great cost, that we try to build churches like this one strong and beautiful. With such a ground plan we must build a great church.

Now, when you go home, take a pencil and paper and draw a ground plan of this church and see whether you can remember what I said.—M. K. W. H.

MARCH 16. Topic: Know Your Church: The Buttresses (2).

The other day two strange boys, one about eleven and the other about twelve, came to the church-house and asked permission to see the church. And so I brought them to this room and we looked over the church together. They knew a lot about a church building. They saw immediately that which I pointed out to you a week ago, that the floor plan of the church is in the shape of a cross. They made many comments and asked many questions.

One of the boys said, "Does the church have any buttresses?" I was surprised, for I didn't think that he knew about buttresses. I wonder if you know what a buttress is?

I said to the boy, "This church does not have flying buttresses like those of certain great churches in Europe, but it has a few small close buttresses."

Now, it is no use looking around here to see whether you can locate the buttresses. They are on the outside of the church. They are something like pillars built against the outside walls so that they do not topple over. They support the vault of the church which you can see from the inside.

After this service look on the north and south sides of this building to see whether you can find the buttresses. You will discover that they strengthen the church against falling down. They are very important.

But I have been thinking of the buttresses all of us have. For example, none of us could do without food, could we? There is a story that there was once a man who trained his horse to do without food, but just as he got it trained it up and died! Well, you and I cannot get along without food. But I do not raise any food. I don't have a garden, nor raise cattle for milk and meat. Neither do you. You see the farmer is a kind of buttress to our lives, but we don't think much about him.

Also the man who goes down into the mine and digs out iron, or copper, or gold, or silver. Many things that we use are made of metal. But we don't dig any metal. The miners are buttresses.

Think, too, of what the government does for us—the policeman who keeps us safe, the people who give us clear fresh water. Your teachers at school are buttresses, holding you up so that sometime you can support a weight.

And that is what we try to do here at the church—buttress you up so that you will not break down, topple over as a man or woman.

Once there was a man who said, "I can do all things through Christ which strengtheneth me." That meant if Christ was holding him up, if Christ strengthened him, if Christ was his buttress, he could be marvelously strong. And so can you.

Let us thank God for the buttresses of our lives. Let us thank him especially for Christ, the buttress of our souls.—M. K. W. H.

MARCH 23. Topic: Know Your Church: Tokens (Communion Sunday) (3).

This morning, boys and girls, I shall talk to you about tokens. First let me give you some examples of tokens. One of the commonest I know is a little piece of paper just about an inch long and less than an inch wide, on one side of which is a little paste and on the other side a picture of George Washington. And down in the corner is the number 3. You all know that I am speaking of a postage stamp. And the number 3 means that it costs three cents.

But of course you also know that a little piece of paper that big is not worth three cents. A little piece of paper that big is worth practically nothing at all. What is a stamp then? It is a token. You place a stamp on the letter and that means that the U. S. promises to carry your letter anywhere in the United States that you want it to go. I write a letter to my father three thousand miles away in Pennsylvania and for three cents the Government carries my letter three thousand miles. That's pretty good, isn't it?

And that stamp on the letter means that I have paid the three cents. So by that stamp I say, "I have paid three cents." And by that stamp the Government says, "I'll carry your letter." You see it is not the value of the paper in the stamp that counts; it is what the stamp means. The stamp is a token.

There are so many tokens. Let me give you one that I used as a boy. I think you many not understand it, but some people in the church will. It is just two fingers up like this. It meant to us boys, "We're going in swimming." You see we could signal quite a distance to each other and by that token meet at the old swimming hole.

Well, then, what is a token? Another word for it is sign or symbol. It is one thing that means another thing.

Today in this service those who openly follow Christ are going to use a little bit of bread as a token, and a small portion of the juice or wine of the grape. Now just a fragment, a crumb of bread is in itself almost nothing. But Jesus said the broken bread—that means my broken body; and the red wine of the grape—that means my life, my blood, given up for you. And so the bread and the wine are the tokens that Christ's body was broken and his life was given up for you and me.

And so the cross before you becomes a token. Bread, wine, the cross—these mean more than they are. It is one thing meaning another thing.

Now I want you to notice something. We do not treat things by what they are, but by what they mean. Here is a little piece of paper and I say it is only paper, I'll throw it away. And you say, "No, it is a postage stamp; it has meaning; don't throw it away."

So we treat things with respect, with reverence, because of their meaning. We Christians have great reverence for the bread, the wine, the cross on this day because they mean that Christ died for us. He loved us so greatly that he was willing to give up his life for us. We have great reverence for the tokens of Christ's love.—M. K. W. H.

MARCH 30. Topic: The Search for the Sea.

In a Sunday-school magazine I recently read an account of a man who has a summer cottage on the coast of Maine. At vacation time he decided to start a Sunday-school class for some little children living on an island not far from the shore. He went over in his motorboat and met the boys and girls who had come together. "How many of you have seen the Atlantic Ocean?" he asked. His little friends stared at him with blank faces. No one answered or raised his hand. Of course they were quite young, but all their lives those little folks had been within sight and sound of the Atlantic Ocean. It was a major fact of their existence. But none of them had ever heard it called by any name.

Is not this an illustration of what happens in the experience of a good many young children today? God is all about them, but he is not recognized.

Did you ever hear the story of the fishes that were in search of the sea? I am going to tell it to you this morning for the comfort and cheer of any of you who might be mystified concerning God and how to find him. I know you often think of this matter. God is very near. And he is our heavenly Father and delights to have his children near him and speak to him and love and trust him. And he is near us all the while, not far from any one of us. So the story I am bringing has an important meaning, which I am sure you will discover as we go along.

Once upon a time there was a young fish that had heard other fishes talking about the sea. One day this young fish thought to himself, "I will go and find the sea." But it searched for a long while, and could not find it.

By and by it met another fish and asked, "Can you tell me where I may find the sea?" But the fish said, "No; I have often wished to see it, for I have heard so much about it, but I do not know where to look."

Pretty soon the young fish met another fish, an old and wise fish, and asked, "Can you tell me where I may find the sea?" And the old fish said, "Why this is the sea; you are swimming in the sea; you have been in it all the time."

So, dear young friends, do some of you sometimes look for God, wondering where he is, thinking he is far away and difficult to find, when all the while he is near, "in him we live and move and have our being"? "God is round about us, nor need we be afraid." That is what we sing in one of our hymns. God is with us, near us, all about us, so near that he knows our tiniest thought. He is thinking of us, protecting and caring for us, giving us all good things. Let us never think of him as far away, but as our very present Friend and Helper.—H.

APRIL 6. Topic: Children Who Helped Jesus (Palm Sunday).

TEXT: "The children crying in the temple, and saying, Hosanna to the son of David." Matt. 21:15.

When this account of the first Palm Sunday says that the children were crying in the temple it does not mean that they are sad. Far from it. They were shouting because they were glad. The children admired Jesus very much, and he loved them too. He loved to have them near him, and even when he was busy he would not allow his disciples to send them away. He once told the grown people that they should all of them have the spirit of teachable children before they could enter the kingdom of heaven.

So the children, of course, loved Jesus. And because they loved him they were a great help to him. One little boy helped him one day by supplying his lunch that he might feed five thousand people. At another time a crowd of children did something for him that helped very much, though they perhaps did not know how much. It was on a day that we now call Palm Sunday. It is given that name because on that day when Jesus rode into Jerusalem the people put palm branches all along the road where Jesus was to ride. They sang and shouted for him. There was a big crowd, and many children were there. We don't read anything about what they then said or did; but in the afternoon Jesus was in the temple and the children were there too. In the temple were people who sold things. Here was a table where some men changed money for some of the people who came to worship, and they charged too much for it. They cheated. And over yonder was a table where some other men sold doves for the sacrifice, and charged the poor people far too much for them. Jesus was much displeased about it. He drove these traffickers out of the temple calling the men thieves and robbers, for it was very wrong for them to be there. The little children helped him in this way, by cheering him. They shouted over and over again, "Hosanna to the son of David! Hosanna to the son of David!"

Thus they gave Jesus encouragement. Now, "encouragement" is a long word, but its meaning is very plain, and it is one thing that children can easily do. Encouragement means putting heart into someone. It means helping someone to be brave and cheerful and to do the thing that may be hard.

I think that Jesus liked to have children near him, not alone for their sakes, but for his sake too, because they helped him by their enthusiasm. No doubt the children on Palm Sunday gave Jesus courage of heart that helped him all through that last week of his life. I am sure that when Judas betrayed him in the garden it must have helped Jesus when he thought of the children who loved him, and when he hung on the cross that he was better able to bear the pain because he could still hear ringing in his ears the shouting of the children so dear to him, "Hosanna to the son of David!"

Young friends, remember this that Jesus still needs the songs and the enthusiasm and the encouragement of children. When he needed them then they did not fail him. And the children must not fail him today. He is counting on you to help him in every good work, in the home, in the Bible-school, and in the church, and in all the world. Are you going to help the work of Jesus as the children in the temple did? —After Rev. Peter H. Pleune, D.D.

APRIL 13. Topic: A Wonderful Surprise (Easter).

The fact of Easter is a wonderful surprise—the great surprise of life out of death. It means resurrection. It means that Christ has risen. It means that because he lives we shall live also.

Let me give you an illustration of the Easter thought, for the mysterious meaning of Easter can be best grasped by comparison, by illustration. One of the most beautiful insects we ever see is the dragonfly. With its iridescent wings, its graceful flight, who has not been charmed by it in summer days? Yet it was once a grub lying in a pond. Then came the change. It emerged from its lower form of life. It found itself endowed with powers which were entirely new, and with a beauty which before it could not boast. So shall it be with the Christian. "There is no death, what seems so is transition," sings our poet Longfellow, with the assured hope of immortality.

I know a minister who each winter grows daffodil bulbs in his study. He says: "I have watched them growing, shooting up their spikelike leaves and flower stalks. And yet, until the flower naturally expanded have I ever caught any hint of scent. Then, in a flash, it arrives like a benediction and sprays my room with fragrance. This is the hope that I hold out for all of us who are steadily, patiently growing here. One day as the flower opens the scent will come." It is the day of our triumph. But its blessing lies in the long, slow growth of the here and now passing days. This is true for us all, the youngest of us all, and the oldest of us all.—H.

APRIL 20. Topic: The Nests and Eggs of Birds.

The last time we talked about birds we considered their food and how they get it. This time let us think about their nests and eggs. In the first place, let us know this, that only birds have feathers, and all birds come from eggs. Also that different kinds of birds build different kinds of nests. It is a fact too that all bird younglings need a great deal of food and care.

Most birds build nests, but the nests are not by any means all alike. Different kinds of birds use different materials, and the shapes and forms and places of the nests are very different. Many of the birds that live in fields and pastures use grass and horsehair for their nests. Birds that live in the woods are likely to use leaves and fibers and small rootlets. Birds that live in marshes use cattails and rushes. Most swallows build their nests of mud, usually lined with feathers or soft materials.

Let us think of the nests of some of them. For example, mourning doves build a shabby nest, almost flat and made of twigs. The Baltimore Oriole is one of the best nest-builders. When finished it looks like a gray bag hanging from some slender limb of a tree. It is sometimes lined with grass and bark and bits of rags and paper. Our little ruby-throated hummingbird builds a very small but beautiful nest. It is like a tiny cup about the size of half a walnut, made of bits of moss and other plants and lined with plant down. It is found on a rather low limb of some bush or tree. On the other hand, the barn swallow, the eve swallow and the chimney swallow build their nests of mud. The cliff swallows build their nests in a deep hole in the side of some sandy vertical bluff. The meadowlark builds its nest on the ground in some pasture lot where the grass is tall. As a rule the nest is very much hidden. It is made of grass and roofed over with the same material. The chimney swift, which is also a swallow, plasters its nest of mud on the inside of a chimney or a silo. The flycatcher makes its nest in some hole in a tree trunk.

Now we have time for just a word about the eggs. The eggs of birds are all pretty much alike, only they differ greatly in size and color. Inside every egg there is food for a baby bird that is to be hatched. As the little bird grows inside the egg it uses up the food, and by the time it is ready to come out it fills the whole egg. Of course you know that the eggs will not hatch unless they are kept warm. So the mother bird or father bird sits on the eggs all the while to keep them always warm.

Some birdlings are strong enough to run about as soon as they are hatched, like the little chickens or young partridges. But most newly hatched birds have to be carefully looked after by the father and mother birds for a good many days or weeks.

Now, young friends, what happy suggestions we here find concerning such Bible expressions as "Abide under the shadow of the Almighty" (Ps. 91:1), or putting our trust "under the shadow of thy wings" (Ps. 36:7), or this, "Because thou hast been my help, therefore in the shadow of thy wings will I rejoice" (Ps. 63:7).—H.

APRIL 27. Topic: Where Birds Live.

In our past studies together as young folks, concerning various kinds of birds, we have considered mostly single individuals, as to their size, color, habits, etc. But this morning let us think a little more closely concerning birds in general, and especially about where they live. Some birds live in the same part of the world the whole year through. Of course many birds do not. Very many of them have summer homes in one part of the world and winter homes in another part of the world. These we call migratory birds. We watch for their coming in the spring, and we see them in large numbers preparing to leave us in the fall. Some of these so-called migratory birds make long journeys between their summer homes and their winter homes. Their distant flights take them to places where they are most fitted to live. It is said that the hot forests near the Equator have hundreds of kinds of birds. But a great many never go so far south.

Some of the birds that do not fly south, or migrate, are such as the cardinals, the nuthatches, the woodpeckers, the chickadees, the crows, the blue jays, and the owls. But many others do fly south to find warmer climates in our winter. To mention only a few of the great many of such are the robins, the warblers, the kingfishers, the herons, the wrens, the cowbirds and the tiny hummingbirds.

You no doubt wonder how any birds that stay in the cold northern weather can find anything to eat. Sometimes they do have a very hard time when there are long spells of snow covering the ground, or storms of sleet that encrust with thin ice the limbs of trees and branches and plants. To be sure, in the winter it is not easy for the birds to find insects for food, for there are no insects flying about. But there are many hidden under the bark of the trees. The nuthatches and a great many other winter birds eat these insects and especially insect eggs hidden under the bark of trees and plants. Others of them, such as the cardinals and blue jays eat quantities of weed seeds and the berries that are found on mushes and trees, such as bitter sweet, barberries, dogwood, mountain ash, huckleberries, bayberries and holly.

It is a beautiful custom that many people have, boys and girls and older people also, of putting out feed for the birds in winter, especially when there has been a long stormy time. Some hang apples and pieces of suet on trees, or put seeds under the trees. Some have feeding-boards and shelves and cover them with various kinds of food. Some suspend on strings pieces of hard fat, which the birds peck at and greatly enjoy.

Now, I think I have said enough for this time. But the subject is so interesting that we might go on for a good while. Maybe we will go into the subject more fully some other time. But enough has been said to show how important it is for us to cultivate acquaintance with the birds, with their needs, and how we can serve them. Besides, in doing so we will serve ourselves, cultivating the graces of thoughtful kindness and appreciation of these beautiful examples of God's creation. —H.

MAY 4. Topic: The Homes of Other People—Cave-dwellers.

In a former talk about the homes of other people our topic was the homes of Switzerland. Those of the mountain regions are called chalets, and are very cosy and comfortable. But this time we have a far different theme, the homes of cave-dwellers.

Thousands of years ago men and women instead of building themselves houses lived in caves and hollows in the rocks. These are the oldest known of dwelling-places, and caverns are now often discovered which show traces of former inhabitants, such evidence as charred bones, flint weapons or implements, pieces of earthen pots, also sometimes pictures of deer or other animals roughly cut in the rock walls by artists of the Stone Age.

Many hundreds of years ago when the Canary Islands were discovered stories were told of savages who lived in caves and burrows in the rocks. These caves vary greatly, some of them being merely rough holes in the rocky mountainside while others have had walls built in front, porches added, and open spaces covered with roofs.

In the mainland of Africa there are not a few cave-dwellings, in Algeria and others in the South. One of these South African caves is very large and at one time sheltered a whole tribe. On its rocky walls are to be seen some of the quaintest, uncouth portraits of animals which were drawn long ago by prehistoric artists.

In China and other parts of Asia there are also caves which were used as homes. But perhaps the most interesting of all these primitive dwellings are to be found in Mexico. They are in the range of the Sierra Madre mountains. In this district remains of ancient cave homes are still to be found and many evidences of having been occupied. Some of these Mexican caves are very large and are divided into a number of rooms. A low wall at the entrance serves as a protection against bad weather, and often a terrace of adobe, or sun-baked mud, is built in front. Three stones in the center of the floor served as a fireplace, and the smoke found its way either out at the entrance or through cracks in the rock above.

When the cave-dwellings are situated high up on the steep mountainside wooden ladders lead up to them, or sometimes rough steps are cut in the cliff. Sometimes a notched tree trunk was used as a stairway.

There are some such dwellings now in use in the western part of our own country. Flowers and curious cactus plants grow in front of the caves. The dress of the women is brightened by the gay handkerchiefs they wear twisted around their heads. Long lines of clothes hang out to dry in the wind or are spread upon the rocky ground.

These all, and many others, are examples of primitive homes. They show the home instinct of all human beings. The best homes on earth are just a fulfilling of that instinct. Young friends, let us all make much of our homes, and seek to improve and make them the very happiest of dwelling places.—H.

MAY 11. Topic: Are You a Wasp? (Nature Study).

What do you know about wasps? Most people if asked that question would answer right away, "They sting." Certainly they do sting. I found that out several times to my sorrow! But is that all we know about wasps? It seems quite unfortunate that a wasp should be known almost exclusively on account of its sting, when it has so many other interesting qualities.

A wasp is a most ingenious papermaker. It is said that the first maker of paper learned the art from the wasp. He discovered the process and practice the wasp uses in building his nest, which is of a kind of homemade paper. Our manufacturers of paper in these days use almost the same method as the wasp.

Then, too, if you examine a wasp's nest, which is far from safe to do, you will find that it is built most cleverly. In fact, the wasp is an exceedingly clever architect, not alone in the way the rooms are arranged, but in the way the various pillars are placed to support the galleries which contain the cells for the eggs, for the newborn wasps, and for the honey.

Another remarkable thing about a

wasp is the way his wings are arranged. He has two pairs of wings, a front pair and a back pair, but they are close together. The pairs are so arranged that they can hook into each other when the wasp wants to make an especially strong flight. That is a little like an airplane with four motors. The wasp can use part of the motors or all of them, just as he wishes.

Now, don't you think it a little strange that an insect so highly endowed as this should be known not on account of his clever way of folding his wings, or his unique power of making paper and building his nest, but only because of his sting? It hardly seems fair, does it? Yet it is true that most people think only of his sting. I suppose it is because he can use it so very effectively and seems to do so on such little provocation.

Now I wonder if that does not explain the whole matter? Why we do the same thing. I have heard people say of someone who is ill-natured and cross, "He is a wasp!" That term "wasp" is used to denote one who is irritable, or ill-natured, or has a sarcastic tongue. So you see that this stinging quality of the wasp has not only given him a bad name, but has given a descriptive name for bad qualities in other things and even in people.

Look out, young friends. For one bad quality in character and life can overshadow and almost obscure a great many good ones. In the Old Testament it is said, "Naaman was a mighty man, but he was a leper." It is very important that we should look out for that little word "but." A boy or girl may be very nice looking, but proud. A person may be very clever, but selfish; very pleasant, but disobedient; very good-mannered, but careless. One bad quality may overshadow a number of good ones. It is very important that we not alone cultivate good characters, but also well-balanced characters that grow in beauty and usefulness and in good report.—H. With acknowledgments to W. S. H. Wylie.

MAY 18. Topic: Automatic Goodness.

The very highest form of goodness is spontaneous, natural, automatic goodness. You have all seen, and I suppose used, the automatic machines in our railway stations and other public places. You know that for one cent you can get weighed or measured, you can try the strength of your hand's grip, the blowing capacity of your lungs, or be supplied with a somewhat limited assortment of candy. Each machine is made to work one way and do one thing. They are automatic, self-acting. They cannot do anything else but what they were made to do. Of course they are machines, not people—not boys and girls!

But our goodness ought to be like that. Anyway, it ought to become so—automatic. We must practice doing good and being good, being kind and helpful constantly until that becomes the habit of our life, until our goodness crowds out all the badness. If you do that gradually you will find your love becoming self-acting and automatic. If you have anything to do, do it as love would do it. The loving way to do anything will then be your first thought. You will become naturally, spontaneously good. You see, goodness requires practice and study just as much as baseball or mathematics or grammar, before you can become expert in it.

Of course we must have the help of God or we will fail; but he is always ready to help if we ask him.

I have heard of a man in a legendary story who was offered by the angels that God would fulfill any wish he might express. He was a good man, and this was his wish: "My wish is that I may do a great deal of good unconsciously." I think that was a prayer that he might be automatically, spontaneously good.

Most of us do not practice enough goodness, kindness, helpfulness. Sometimes we are automatically good and sometimes automatically bad. Others are influenced by our example, both bad and good. We cannot live alone, like Robinson Crusoe. Therefore, let us practice goodness. Let us cultivate goodness, more and more goodness, and nothing but goodness. That is the way to have our goodness grow toward being automatic goodness.—Adapted from Rev. James Learmount.

MAY 25. Topic: The Puff Adder That Plays Possum (Nature Study).

Most boys and girls don't like snakes. Some girl's don't even like to hear about them. But the kind I am going to tell you about this morning is perfectly harmless. Sometimes it is called an adder, and that doesn't sound so bad. The fact is that most all snakes are harmless. The only harm they do is to scare you. Of course I know that city folks do not have much chance to see or know about snakes, unless it is when they go on vacation or visit the country.

The snake I am going to tell you about is named the *Heterodon Contortrix*. That is its scientific name; but it is too hard to say or remember, so we call it by its common name, the Puff Adder. When I tell you about its doings you will say it ought to be called the Bluff Adder, for that is what it does, bluffs its way in the world. It is a great "bluffer." But is commonly called the Puff Adder because it blows itself up to look big.

The Puffer Fish is found down in the Florida region. It puffs itself up so that it looks too large for the bigger fish to swallow it. A brother of mine sent me a peculiar Puffer Fish that he found on a shore down in Mexico. It is called the Porcupine Puffer Fish because it not only blows itself up, but it has sharp quills like a porcupine all over it. That makes it both big and harder for the larger fish to swallow.

But I am telling you about this Puffer Adder. Although harmless he is short, thick, and has markings not unlike some rattlers. He looks poisonous, but is not. He has some queer tricks. We might call them adder antics. If you corner him he puts up a terrific bluff. He pulls himself up and hisses and coils and strikes with a fury that is calculated to scare the daylights out of you. But if you don't scare, then he promptly puts on another performance. He writhes in agony, sometimes drawing parts of his body throught his open jaws. Then he flops on his back and apparently dies. You can pick him up, hang him on a fence or a limb of a bush and he is as lifeless as a piece of rope. But it is all a bluff, playing possum. If you hide and watch, pretty soon he will roll over, and, seeing no enemy, will wiggle off just as fast as he can.

These adder antics are just ingenious devices he uses to protect himself from harm, first by making himself look bigger than he is, and then by playing possum as though he were dead. But I was not thinking so much of the adder puffing himself up to look big. I was thinking of puffer people. I heard one boy say to another the other day, "Don't you think yourself big!" The boy was a puffer, a bluffer. He inflated himself. He was proud. He boasted. I suppose girls sometimes boast themselves, but I am too polite to say so!

Anyway, young folks, it is bad to be a puffer. Don't do it. My text for this little talk is Proverbs 16:18, "Pride goeth before desctruction, and a haughty spirit before a fall."—H.

JUNE 1. Topic: Foresight and Hindsight (Temperance).

TEXT: "A prudent man foreseeth the evil, and hideth himself." Prov. 22:3.

Young friends, did you ever see an animal with his eyes almost in the back of his head, nearly behind? The hare in England and Scotland, which is a large rabbit, has its eyes so far back that it will often come quite near to a person in front before it sees him. The hare is a very fast runner, but not so good a fighter. Its safety is in running away from danger while its enemies are behind. When I was a boy in Scotland the rich people used to gather near a high hill, called Dechmont, and hunt the hare with fast-running greyhounds. Two of the hounds would be fastened on a leash, and when the hare was found the men would slip the leash and the hounds would run after the hare side by side, just like a team of horses. The hare would watch with its eyes partly behind, and when the hounds got too near would dodge and try to escape.

So, you see, the hare needs hindsight, for its enemies are behind.

Now, what I wonder is this, if you boys and girls have eyes behind?

But because you are young your enemies and dangers are practically all ahead, and as the text says, you need prudence and foresight rather than hindsight. If you had eyes behind that would not help you very much, for the life upon which you are entering has its dangers ahead.

One of the dangers I am thinking about this morning is that of strong drink. Did you ever see a drunkard staggering along and in danger of falling into the ditch? I hope not. But I fear you have in these days of so much intoxication. Well, if that man had had foresight, he never would have gotten into that sad condition. And remember this, that he did not get that way all at once. It took him a good while, just as it takes you a good while to learn things at school. If he had used foresight, and seen himself in the gutter, he never would have tasted the drink. He often uses hindsight now, and looks back at the time when he was a promising boy; but that does not help him. My dear young friends, look ahead to see what strong drink will do. Never touch it, for it is dangerous. And do all you can to keep others of your young companions from touching it. God has put your eyes in your forehead that you may look ahead. "A prudent man foreseeth the evil, and hideth himself." That is, he stops before he begins. That is the one good and safe rule.—Rev. William Armstrong.

JUNE 8. Topic: A Boy to Whom God Could Speak (Children's Day).

TEXT: "I have lent him to the Lord." I Sam. 1:28.

There is a beautiful picture I think you all have seen. It is of a fine-faced boy kneeling in prayer. Many a mother has taught her child to pray by looking at that picture. Sir Joshua Reynolds painted it. He thinks this is how Samuel looked when saying his prayers.

Samuel was a child of many prayers. Hannah, his mother, had prayed to God to give her a baby boy. She had promised that if God would anwser she would give the boy back to serve God in his tabernacle, or church.

God did give her a son, and she kept her promise. She taught him to know God. And when he was old enough she brought him up to God's house and left him there in training for God's service.

Year by year, regularly, she came to see him, bringing with her on each visit new clothing made with her own hands.

Samuel became a little doorkeeper in God's house. He opened the doors, lighted the lamps, ran on errands. He slept in one of the courts of the house and was faithful in all that was given him to do.

I am thinking of other boys and the teaching they received. King Alexander the Great gathered boys into his camp, and trained them to become warriors and fight for him. Which kind of education do you think is best for a boy? I would rather see a lad trained to serve God than just taught to fight. Would not you?

This story tells us how God can save a country by using a boy. It is wonderful what God can do with a child. He can speak through the mouths of babes. He has often used a child to give a message. Out of a child God can make a prophet.

Why did God use Samuel? Why did he not go to some wise man to carry his message? Why was not some old man trusted with it? I believe there are some good things God can do better through a boy or girl than he can do through an older person.

When will God first speak to a child? I don't know. Many of the best people in the world have been led to Christ in their early childhood.

A girl of eleven once applied for church membership. Her home was good but not definitely Christian. There was a little hesitation about it, until, after careful examination, the church received her. Within three months the entire family was led to Christ and came into church fellowship. "A little child shall lead them."

Did God really speak to Samuel? And did Samuel speak to God? The radio is wonderful. You can hear people speak from halfway round the world. It is a greater miracle to hear God speaking, and equally great when God speaks to a little child. Happy is that boy or girl who can hear God's voice, who can know God's secret, and who can speak to and for God.

When reading about Jesus there is nothing said about him from the time when he was twelve years of age until we find him a man of thirty just beginning his gracious ministry. It is something like that with Samuel. We know of him as a child, and then we lose sight of him until we see him a good man serving God. I wonder what will become of you from the time you are fourteen until the day when you are twenty-five! You love God now, and you love to go to church; will you still love him when you are a man or a woman?

Samuel's life grew to be a greatly honored one. He opened the first school for prophets, or ministers. It was he who called Saul to be the first king of Israel. It was he who found David, the shepherd lad, and anointed him to be king. When Samuel came to be an old man, the people all showed deep respect for him saying that he had lived well. They will say the same of us if we live as Samuel did in such a way that God can speak to us.—Rev. Charles W. Watch.

SEPTEMBER 7. Topic: An Animal Story.

You all know what a giraffe is, that very tall animal with a very long neck. And you know what a lion is, that powerful fellow that roars so loudly and is called the king of beasts. Now I am going to tell you a story I read not long ago in an English paper about a mother giraffe, a baby giraffe and a lion. Doesn't that sound interesting?

The lion had been out all night hunting for his dinner, but without success. He was returning hungry to his den when he discovered a group of giraffes quietly browsing under a clump of trees. Standing a short distance from the other giraffes was a mother giraffe with her baby at her side. The lion knew that he could not catch one of the big giraffes, as they had long legs and could run much faster than he could. But with the baby giraffe it was different. He could catch it easy enough he thought.

Quietly and stealthily he began to creep through the high grass, edging closer and closer to his prey. But just then the mother giraffe caught a glimpse of the lion's big green eyes gleaming in the grass. Immediately she stamped her feet on the ground and in a flash the whole group of giraffes was gone.

The mother giraffe also ran and made her baby run as fast as his legs could carry him; but he was too young to run very fast. The lion was overtaking them. What then do you think the mother giraffe did? She turned and faced the lion. She had no claws or fangs as he had, but she had one weapon—her long and powerful legs. She gently pushed her baby right under her tall body. The lion went round and round her body, waiting for a chance to pounce upon the little giraffe.

This was kept up for quite a while, until once the baby giraffe got out from under its mother. The lion made a pounce, when something came between him and the baby giraffe. It was the powerful foreleg of the mother giraffe. The attempt of the lion was kept up until he got tired and slipped away into the tall grass and was gone.

Now, young friends, our lives have dangers. But of one thing we can be sure; it is of God's care and watchfulness over us. He is our heavenly Father and we are safe in his keeping. You know in the 46th Psalm it is said, "God is our refuge and strength, a very present help in trouble" (Ps. 46:1). Keep near to God. Stay under his gracious shadow, and there no power on earth can harm you.—H.

SEPTEMBER 14. Topic: About Growing.

Do you know that there is something that every one of you young people can do that I cannot do, that your father and mother cannot do, nor the Governor of this State, nor the President of the United States, nor the King of England? You can all grow, and we cannot. Some of us grown-ups can grow this way—sidewise. But we cannot grow any taller, and our arms and legs cannot grow any longer, no matter how hard we try.

This time of year we are surrounded with flowers and fruits and vegetation. Let us see if we cannot learn something about growing from plants and flowers and trees.

Now the first thing we do if we want a plant to grow is to put a seed into the earth and let it have moisture and heat. Where does moisture come from? From the rain. Where does the rain come from. From the clouds. Where do the clouds come from? From the rivers and lakes and the ocean. Where does heat come from? From the sun. All helping the little plant to grow. How God must like to see things grow, when he makes all these great things help even a tiny plant to grow!

It is an interesting fact too, that when a little plant or tree begins to grow it grows in two directions—down and up. The root grows down and the stalk grows up. The roots always grow down to get food out of the soil. The stalk always grows up toward the light.

And every boy and girl that is good for anything also grows in two ways. The body, with its muscles and bones, grows. It doesn't grow down into the earth the way roots do. If the only way we grew was in muscles and bones we would be of no more importance than a horse or an elephant, because they have much stronger bodies than we do. It isn't bigness that makes us. But you young folks grow in another way. Your mind grows as well as your body. And your soul grows. You have bodies, but you are souls. And it is because your mind and soul grow that you learn about God, about right and truth and love—about God's love and your great value in his sight.

Now there is another thing about plants and trees. They have enemies. There are bugs and worms and ants that eat their leaves and suck their juices. There are grubs and slugs and centipedes that eat their roots.

Just so we have enemies that injure the body and enemies that injure the soul. We have to fight measles and whooping cough and scarlet fever and other diseases, and we have to fight also against evil desires and temptations and bad tempers and appetites. And just as the little plant often would die unless the gardener came to its help, killing the bugs and the worms, so we would yield to our enemies, temptation and passion and evil thoughts, were it not for the help our heavenly Father gives us in Christ our Saviour. He is the Gardener of our souls.

But why does the gardener help the little plant? Because he knows what it will become if it is only helped to grow. The gardener sees what that little plant may become, so he helps it to fight the bugs and worms. And so it is because Christ, our Saviour, saw what we may become that he came to help us, and does help us to fight and conquer our temptations. It is because he knows that we have immortal souls that he comes to help us grow more and more beautiful, more and more wise, more and more useful, now and through all time to come. Let us yield ourselves to our Divine Gardener and Friend, that he may help us to grow in grace and beauty and helpfulness and bear the fruits of usefulness in the world.—E. J. W.

SEPTEMBER 21. Topic: The Sermon the Sunflower Preaches.

This morning I want to tell you young people about a great sermon that is preached to me every morning of late. The preacher is a flower that grows in my garden and the sermon is its life. It is not a fine flower, either, not the kind you will find growing in beautiful gardens and parks in company with tulips and dahlias and roses, but it is a humble plant that is content to grow in out of the way places and in forgotten corners.

A little while ago I planted some of the seeds of this flower and they are blooming now. When I go out in the early morning every one of the blossoms is facing the sun which is just peeping through the trees. At noon they have lifted up their heads and are looking straight up into the face of the sun. At evening I find them turned to the West, as though eager to catch the last rays of the setting sun. During all the days of their youth they follow the sun in his course across the sky. At last, grown large and heavy with seed, they can no longer turn as of old. Then for the last time they turn from giving their farewell kiss, back to the East, to stand and greet the sun each day on his return. They seem to say, "If we cannot longer follow him, and can gain but one greeting in the day, let it be a greeting of the morning, a greeting of joy, when the sun comes forth in all his strength to run his course."

How many boys and girls know the name of my preacher, and how many have ever heard the sermon? The preacher is the familiar sunflower, the sun-seeker, and we call it that on account of its habit of keeping its face toward the face of the sun.

The lessons I learn from this roadside flower is this: If we seek the face of God as earnestly as this flower seeks the face of the sun, God will bless us and help us to grow strong and beautiful. In II Chron. 7:14, we read: "If my people . . . shall humble themselves, and pray, and seek my face, and turn from their wicked ways; then will I hear them from heaven, and will forgive their sin." So, young friends, keep your faces toward God, in the morning, and at noon, and at evening. Seek him as earnestly as the sunflower seeks the sun and God will bless you greatly all your days.—Rev. A. J. Cohee.

SEPTEMBER 28. Topic: The Pedometer.

TEXT: "Keep thy heart with all diligence; for out of it are the issues of life." Prov. 4:23.

This past summer in the mountains a man showed me a little instrument which to me was very interesting. It was called a pedometer, and it told a man about how far he had gone. The instrument was about the size of a watch and looked very much like a watch. Every time you took a step the instrument registered one. You may not realize how much of a jar you give your body each time you take a step, but it is considerable. By a delicate arrangement the hand of the pedometer will move by the jar of each step. A man can easily measure about how far he steps, and in that way he can tell about how far he has gone.

When my friend would start out on a tramp up to one of the lakes or peaks or some beautiful point, he would set his pedometer and hang it from a pin in his pocket. Then when he got home he could look at it and tell how far he had gone, and then, you see, he could tell how tired to be.

It was indeed a very interesting thing to me, for while I had often heard of a pedometer I had never before seen one. After I looked at it I said to my friend:

I. "Will it tell you where you have been?" And he had to answer "No," that the only thing it would tell was how far he had gone. He might have been to a very beautiful place, or to a very ugly one; but the pedometer would not show which it was.

Now, young friends, there is something more delicate than the pedometer which will tell us where he have been.

Our hearts will tell us whether we have been to a good place or a bad one, and it is the only thing that will. I am sure that that is one of the reasons we are told to keep our hearts with all diligence.

II. "Will this little instrument tell you what you have been doing and who your companions were?" Again he would say "No," and that it would only show about how far he had gone. He might have been on a mountain trail with evil companions who would have delighted to push him off a steep place for all the pedometer could tell. He might have been doing great good with those steps that the instrument numbered or he might have been on an evil errand. It could not tell.

III. Now that more delicate instrument, which we call the heart, alone can tell us whether our errand was good or bad. It can tell us at the end of the day whether our feet have carried us on good errands or bad ones, whether our steps have done good or evil.

The pedometer is a wonderful little instrument. If I had one I surely would take mighty good care of it. But while I do not have one of them God has given me something far more wonderful; a heart which will not alone tell me how far I have gone, but also the thing that took me on the errand. Surely I must take good care of such an instrument as that.

"Keep thy heart with all diligence, for out of it are the issues of life."—Rev. John A. McAfee.

OCTOBER 5. Topic: The Migratory Birds (Fall Season).

There is a very interesting verse in the prophecy of Jeremiah which tells of the instinct of the birds that migrate in the fall and return in the spring. I call your attention to this prophecy just now because this is the time when the many birds are gathering and going, or getting ready to go to the South lands. The reference I am thinking about is in the eighth chapter of Jeremiah, seventh verse. It tells that the stork in the heavens, the crane and the swallows, and many other so-called migratory birds, know their appointed times. This is the way the verse reads, "Yea, the stork in the heaven knoweth her appointed times; and the turtle and the crane and the swallow observe the time of their coming; but my people know not the judgment of the Lord."

It is a very remarkable thing that in the whole world there seems to be no place suitable all the year round for birds of the migratory nature. It seems all the more wonderful that these untaught and unthinking creatures should shift their habitations and make long voyages through the air with the changes of the seasons. God has imprinted upon their nature that wonderful instinct which enables them to determine when to go and which direction to take.

But, young friends, we too have an instinct. At the "appointed time" the birds feel an impulse within that they must be going. They congregate together, like swallows in the fall, and are soon off on their long journey. As I said a moment ago, we also have an instinct. It is an instinct for God. We have movements within. We often feel them, are aware of them, especially when we are young, resulting from conscience, from hearing God's Word, from the movement of God's Spirit in our hearts. And when we hear, it is our duty and privilege to obey the voice of God, to yield to the instinct which makes us want to know him and love him and serve him.

There is another fact about the birds, that they do not delay to make their start, or they might get caught in the winter and perish with the cold. Young friends, when you hear God's call do not delay to start. "Now in the accepted time." "Today is the day of salvation."—H.

OCTOBER 12. Topic: The Spider Crab (Nature Study).

In summertime a good many boys and girls are able to go to the seashore for a vacation. When exploring the rock pools left after the tide has gone out you may find some very remarkable little animals which are worth watching in order to learn something of their habits. Among these you are quite likely to find some that are known as spider crabs. These crabs look quite a little like spiders, and I suppose that is the reason for their name. They have very long legs and will try to run away when you disturb them.

But the most peculiar thing about these crabs is their ingenious way of disguising themselves in order to escape from their enemies. They camouflage themselves. They dress themselves with sponge or seaweed, or any other sea-growth in their vicinity. They attach these growths to their backs with their claws. It is very interesting indeed to watch one of them scratching his back until he has made a rough place in his shell in which he "plants" pieces of sea-growth. He pressed them into these scratches in his shell, pressing them down with his claws, so they can take root, just as a gardener does when he transplants flowers from their pots into his garden.

This makes the crab feel secure. When lying on the ground covered with these growing things on his back his enemies are fooled. They see only the growing things and not the hidden crab himself.

There is another trait possessed by the spider crab. When he fights with another crab, or is attacked by an enemy and in the battle some of his camouflage covering gets torn off, he goes to some quiet nook and carefully examines himself. He feels all over his back with his claws, and when he finds a bald place he plants fresh pieces of seaweed, or whatever he wishes to grow, on the vacant spot.

I think that possibly the best lesson we can learn from our spider crab is one concerning his custom of self-examination. I wonder if it would not be a good thing for us as young folks, and older folks too, now and again to examine ourselves and see if we have suffered any harm in life's experiences! Are any of us less diligent in our work, or more careless than we used to be? Have we become more thoughtless, or selfish, or disobedient during the past few months? Do we find that we have developed any tendency to become untruthful, or unkind, or impolite? Have we sometimes forgotten to read our Bibles, or neglected our prayers? Well, these may not be the very pleasantest things to think about, but they are good things to think about, and point the way to amendment and growth in character. Let us all test ourselves sometimes and see if we are really growing in grace and in the knowledge of Christ, and in likeness to him. This is one of the very best means to mending our ways and becoming more beautiful in character and more useful in life.—H. With acknowledgments to W. S. H. Wylie.

OCTOBER 19. Topic: The Jumping Spider (Nature Study).

Not long ago we had a study together about spiders. We noticed that there are hundreds of varieties of spiders and that they are found in many parts of the world. The name "spider" comes from the word "spinner." The spider is a spinner. Out of fine gossamer threads he spins his silken web to make his home and his trap to catch insects upon which he feeds. There are so many different kinds that we cannot name them all. A few names are the Garden-spider, the House-spider, the Grass-spider, the Wolff-spider, the Round-web-spider. There is a Water-spider that binds bits of leaves together to make a raft and floats about seeking his prey. There is another spider called the flying-spider. He doesn't really fly, but he spins a little cloud of film and lets the wind pick him up and carry him any distance. All spiders have eight legs, but different varieties have two, four, six, or eight eyes. It was the Trapdoor-spider we considered before. But this time we will think together about another interesting one known as the Jumping-spider.

As we have said, like the Trapdoor-spider, this variety is found in many parts of the world. The Trapdoor-spider is not often seen because when he sees us he hides in his hole and shuts tight the lid. And the Jumping-spider is hardly seen because his jumping movement is so very quick and he is so small.

A number of naturalists have been interested in the behavior of these Jumping-spiders, or spiders that jump. Various methods have been employed to determine just how they jump; but the action is too quick to be observed accurately by the unaided human eye. Photography with a high-speed flash brings out every detail not only of the act of jumping, but of the use of the safety line as well.

Now it is this fact of having a so-called safety line that makes the Jumping-spider so interesting. Such a provision, that of the safety line, is most astonishing. When the Jumping-spider gets ready to jump from any height he carefully leaves a safety line attached to something solid behind him. The safety line is made up of a number of filaments like exceedingly fine silk threads, emerging from his spinnerets, and if the spider misses in his jump the safety line enables him to haul himself back up to the perch.

That is a strange provision; don't you think so? But, young friends, when you make a wrong jump, you have no provision by which you can get back where you started! I thought that might be a good thing for us to think about in connection with our study of the Jumping-spider.—H.

OCTOBER 26. Topic: The Power of Perseverance (Nature Study).

I don't know whether you boys and girls like oysters or not. If you live near the seashore you probably do, and most older people in this community like them very much. Not only do many people like oysters, but there are many creatures in the sea that like them too. And that is what we are to talk about this morning. One of the chief oyster eaters in the sea is the starfish. As you probably know, the starfish has that name because of its being shaped like a star. It is a soft, flabby creature which looks as if it were made of jelly. In the center there is a body and a big mouth. From this center long limbs reach outward. These long limbs are covered with suckers which enable the animal to grip any object, like a limpet clings to a rock.

Now the oyster lives in a two-sided shell. Whenever it is attacked or frightened it closes its shell very tightly. But the starfish likes oysters very much. How do you suppose he gets that oyster held so tightly inside his strong double shell? How is it possible for that soft, flabby, jellylike starfish ever to get that oyster? Well, he does get it, and this is how.

The starfish puts his arms around the oyster and grips him tightly. Then fastening his suckers on each half of the shell, he begins to pull in such a way as to draw the shell apart. The oyster can hold tight against a sudden pull, but is not able to hold out against a long-continued and steady pull that never lets up for a moment. The starfish does not get tired nor give up. He just keeps on pulling until at last the oyster has to yield. He just has to give up.

Now, boys and girls, what an example that is of the power of persistence, which is one of the great secrets of success in every department of life and work! It is well for you young folks to learn very early in life what an important thing persistence is in study, in play, in work, in attaining success in anything you undertake. Learn from the starfish never to give up nor give in, but stick to your purpose until what you are doing is crowned with success.

Now, all this holds true in religion, as well as for success in study or business or in learning a trade or profession. No doubt, like sermons for big people, you think this little sermon for you should have a text. I think so too, and have chosen this one, "Be ye stedfast, unmoveable, always abounding in the work of the Lord" (I Cor. 15:58).—H. With acknowledgments to W. S. H. Wylie.

NOVEMBER 2. Topic: Making Faces.

Every day as we walk along the street we meet many people and look into many faces. Some of these faces are hard and unpleasant, others are pleasant and beautiful. At one time, not many years ago, each of these faces had the privilege of expressing kindness and beauty. We know that in ten years from now, as today, we shall see hard, cruel faces as well as noble and kind ones. These faces are going to be made by the boys and girls of today. That is sure.

Now, as the artist makes his picture line by line, so are we just as surely making faces. We can see the artist at work because he works on the outside of his picture. We cannot see our friends or ourselves at work because it is all done on the inside. The artist works with a brush, but we work with thoughts, words and deeds. Whenever we are tempted to say an unkind word or do an unkind deed to hurt others, then we ourselves receive the greater harm. In time they may forget our cruelty, but it is built into our lives and finds its way to our faces, where it is seen by the world.

In the theater men paint their faces to fit the parts they play. If they are to represent a wicked man they make their faces look wicked. In life, whatever part we play our faces grow to look the part.

We should all desire to have beautiful faces, which stand for character. When the artist paints a picture he has a model to follow. If the model is ugly he paints an ugly picture, and if the model is beautiful he paints a beautiful picture. When we say that boys and girls may be Christian we mean that they may take for their lives the most beautiful model. We always think of Jesus having a beautiful face because his life was beautiful. If we follow his life and teaching we cannot have hard, cruel faces for the world to see. God meant all faces to be kind and noble, and therefore he has given us his Son as our life model.

We must always remember that what the poet says is true for us:

Beautiful thoughts make a beautiful life,
And a beautiful life makes a beautiful face.

—Rev. Chester J. Armstrong.

NOVEMBER 9. Topic: A Slave Boy Who Became a Bishop (Missions).

If you had looked down upon the shore of Africa in the Yoruba country long ago, you might have seen a black boy playing about. If you had watched, you might have seen him suddenly seized by strangers who landed from a ship, and carried off to be pushed cruelly into the hold of a Portuguese slaver. You have heard, perhaps, that long ago such wicked deeds were done, and money was made by seizing and selling as slaves the poor, helpless Africans.

Following this boy you might have seen that he was wretched enough, till, by a kind Providence, he was rescued and set free. He was taken to Sierra Leona, and one of the very first things he did was to beg a halfpenny to buy an alphabet card for himself, so anxious was he to learn to read. He was such a bright boy that in six months he learned to read, and in five years entered college, where, not long after, he was made a tutor. Could an American white boy do much better?

The most important event of the boy's life was his becoming a Christian and giving himself to Christian service. Time went on, and from being a tutor, Samuel Crowther became a minister, and then, in 1864, was made a bishop. He was the first black bishop of modern times in Africa. He planted mission stations all along the banks of the Niger River. He had wonderful wisdom and tact in dealing with different people, and won their confidence in a remarkable way.

This man also was quite a discoverer,

and was given a gold watch by the Royal Geographical Society of England as a reward for his travels and researches. He assisted in translating a part of the Bible and a part of the prayer book into the language of the natives. Although he had learning and honor, he was one of the humblest of men. His humility increased as others appreciated him more.

One of the most intense longings of the good man's heart was to find his mother from whom he was torn as a boy, and tell her about Jesus. He could not hear anything about her, nor find her in any way.

But one day a most wonderful thing happened. A woman came to be baptized, and the Bishop examined her to see if she understood and was ready for baptism. He found that she was indeed a Christian; but he also found that she was his own mother. It was hard to tell which of the two was more joyful, as the Bishop baptized his mother and received her into the church. He called her "Hannah, the mother of Samuel."

In 1891 this first black bishop entered into rest. His life and labors were wonderful, and his memory still blooms, like a white flower in the dark soil of Africa, the land he loved.

NOVEMBER 16. Topic: Watching the Ships.

TEXT: "There go the ships." Ps. 104:26.

God made the sea. Man made the ships. And it must have taken a long time for man to learn to make them, the swift and beautiful creatures they are. As we imagine ourselves watching them we may learn some useful lessons, for we too are like ships on God's great sea. Everything depends on how the ships go.

I. "There go the ships." Every ship has a captain. You know that they cannot go of their own accord. Someone must manage the helm, regulate the sails, control the engine. And all these must be obedient to the captain's orders. Who is your captain? Is it Jesus Christ? If so, the ship will sail prosperously and arrive safely. If you think of him as first in every plan, at school, at home, Sundays and weekdays, then he is your Captain. If you consider before you speak whether your words will please him, and before you act whether your deeds will honor him, then he is the Captain of your ship.

II. "There go the ships." Every ship has a chart. The captain studies the chart and directs his course accordingly. If you could see and understand the chart which the captain is studying you would understand the ship's course. And we have a chart for life's voyage. It is God's Word. When we are in doubt as to the Captain's orders, or the perils of the sea, let us consult the chart. It has the instructions for our guidance.

III. "There go the ships." What do they carry? They are not empty or idle. A few of them are pleasure yachts; but you may feel sure that a ship on the sea as a rule carries freight of more or less value. You eat and drink, you play and sing, you work and think; but that is not all, nor indeed the most important part of life. What is the freight you carry? Is it poor or valuable? In other words, what is your character? It will be a grand thing if when you come ashore you have brought what will be a treasure in the sight of God.

Yes, "There go the ships!" God prosper them, one and all! But much more may God prosper you, dear young friends. You have only one voyage to make. One life is given to each of us. That is why we are so anxious that you may not be wrecked. With Jesus for your Captain, the Bible for your chart, and a good character for your treasure, may you have a happy arrival some sweet day!—Rev. H. Elvet Lewis.

NOVEMBER 23. Topic: He Sings in Winter (Thanksgiving Nature Sermon).

On a winter day when the breeze blew cold our children insisted on going sliding. Most of our neighbors were hugging their stoves, and no sounds came from the lee of the woods. But suddenly a cheerful song whistled from the top of the spruce across the road, "Chickadeedeedee, chickadeedeedee." we just gazed and smiled, but felt with Emerson,

> Happy to meet you in these places
> Where January brings few faces!

This black-capped titmouse with his white mask bobbed along the twigs and pecked vigorously into one cranny after another. He was enjoying life:

> This scrap of valor just for play
> Fronts the north wind in waistcoat grey.

At night he would hide in the hollow of a tree or shelter himself from the cold in a nest. But now he was feasting on the eggs and larvae of bark beetles, gipsy moths, tent caterpillars, or plant lice, and saying grace as he ate.

That was the best part of it. He was saying "Thank you" to God while he dined. What fun to listen, "Chickadeedeedee, chickadeedeedee." He made me think of that line in Psalm 147:7, "Sing unto the Lord with thanksgiving."

St. Paul once wrote to the people in a church that he started (I Thess. 5:16-18, R. S. V.), "Rejoice always, . . . give thanks in all circumstances." Later he repeated the advice (Eph. 5:18-20, R. S. V.), "Be filled with the Spirit, . . . always and for everything giving thanks in the name of our Lord Jesus Christ to God the Father."

It was too cold for us to stand there watching our friend in the tree, and we did not remain to slide very long. But on returning home the children did tell Mother of the song which the chickadee had sung, "Thank God whatever happens" (I Thess. 5:18, Godspeed). Then, while we warmed our fingers, I went on to explain that our friend would soon be adding his "feebee" call to the "chickadee" song. In balmy weather he will be saying, "Feebee—Spring's here—Love me." His mate will line a home in a hollow birch and lay six to ten eggs in it. Our summer visitors will have returned. Soon he will be too busy filling eight empty mouths to take time off to whistle. But while Mrs. Chickadee hatches their second big family you may hear him stop to "give thanks."

And why not we?—Rev. Donald B. Howard.

NOVEMBER 30. Topic: How They Stopped the Engine.

In the early days of railroading the engines were given names. Now they are usually given numbers. I have a story for you boys and girls this morning about an engine that had a name. I will tell you the name a little later. The story is one concerning the early days of railroading, and though I cannot really vouch for it I got it from a good source and think it reliable. But it is an interesting story anyway, and I think you will agree with me that it has some valuable suggestions.

One dark night when a railway conductor was taking three passenger coaches through to the division point of his run he noticed the headlight of a locomotive back of his train. He immediately informed the engineer of the fact, and both began wondering what it might mean. The train was running at high speed, but the headlight in the rear kept steadily gaining on them.

As there were no lights back of the headlight they concluded that it must be an empty engine that seemed to be chasing them. The road twisted along the banks of a stream in such a way as to permit anyone looking back to see what was going on in the rear for a considerable distance.

The conductor ordered the engineer to put on more steam, and the engineer pulled the throttle wide open. Then followed a wild chase. Pursuer and pursuing engine grew dim in the distance. Everyone in the cars believed that the engineer on the pursuing engine must be crazy.

At last an idea struck the engineer. He recalled the fact that a locomotive can make little progress on greasy rails.

The contents of two large cans of oil were poured on the track from the rear of the last passenger coach. The scheme worked. Soon the headlight of the pursuing engine grew dim in the distance. What it was safe to do so the train stopped and backed up to solve the mystery. A peculiar sight met the eyes of the crew.

One of the finest engines on the road, called the "Davy Crockett," had broken away from the hostler up the line and started down the track on a voyage of destruction. The oil poured on the track had baffled all the destructive abilities that the locomotive possessed. There stood the "Davy Crockett" puffing and snorting and pawing like a wild Texas steer, the driving wheels buzzing around on the greased rails like a fly-wheel in a machine shop, but hardly moving at all.

Not a sign of an engineer was found and the fireman of the train that was being chased mounted the engine and shut it off. They towed it into town, and there found a dispatch ordering them to sidetrack out of the way of the runaway; but the oil had saved them.

Well, boys and girls, a little oil at the right time will save other things besides engineers. It can save boys and girls and men and women. The oil of kindly speech is one saving sort, the oil of civility, the oil of politeness, the oil of the "soft answer" that "turneth away wrath." I have heard of a man who always carried with him a little can of oil. He hated unpleasant sounds. So he would put a drop of oil on a rusty hinge, a creaking door, or a piece of machinery. Things were so much better where he had been that people liked him and spoke of him as "that kindly man with the oil can."

A little oil in the right place is a good thing—don't you think so?—H.

DECEMBER 7. Topic: The Tongues of Frogs and Toads (Nature Study).

I recognize that talking about any sorts of tongues is a rather delicate matter. But that is hardly true concerning frogs' tongues and toads' tongues. You may be interested in hearing some not very well known facts about the tongues of these little animals.

Probably the most remarkable thing about the ordinary type of frog and toad is the way the tongue is placed in the mouth. Instead of being fastened low at the back of the mouth, with the point toward the lips, as is the case with people, frogs and toads have the tongue fastened in front with the point toward the throat. That is exactly the opposite to the way our tongues are set.

Now in some ways this is a very convenient arrangement. When the frog or toad sees a nice little insect or worm, he quickly darts out his tongue, catches his dinner with the point, and curling it backward, quick as wink pushes it down his throat. That is easy! Don't you think so?

But when it comes to speaking, that would be quite another thing if our tongues were made that way. If our tongues were fastened in front, with the point down our throats, I do not see how we could speak at all. I don't think we could.

Of course sometimes that might be quite an advantage, for then we might not be able to say some things that would be better left unsaid! If anyone were about to say something unkind or untrue, it would really be a good thing, don't you think, if his or her tongue were pointed down the throat?

Now, while it is true that we cannot reverse our tongues, there is another thing we can do. We can reverse our intention when we are about to say things we ought not to say. Another thing we can do. We can always think before we speak, asking ourselves whether it is a kind thing, a true thing, and a necessary thing we are about to say, or whether it would not really be better not to say it.

There is quite a little in the Bible about this matter of our use of the tongue. It may be that you think this little sermon ought to have a text, like other big sermons do; but I am not going to repeat a text just now on such a personal matter. Instead I will give you a good one to look up when you get home. I will tell you just where to find it. Look it up. It is the third chapter of the Epistle of James. It is real interesting reading!—H. With acknowledgments to W. S. H. Wylie.

DECEMBER 14. Topic: If Christ Had Not Come (Advent or Christmas. Alternate).

There is an interesting story which appeared some years ago telling of a little boy who had a dream on the night before Christmas. What he dreamed was that he saw himself up and dressed very early the next morning and running down to the school ground to meet his playmates. To his astonishment their was a vacant lot at the corner where he would usually see his beautiful school building, with a sign at the vacancy. On the sign were these words, "If Christ had not come." Then in his dream he hurried over to the town hospital where he and some of his friends were to gather early Christmas morning with gifts for some sick children. There again he saw only an empty space and the same sign, "If Christ had not come." Though he was much bewildered, he thought of the early Christmas morning service at his church and ran quickly in that direction expecting to meet his parents there to worship. Astonished, he was only greeted once more by a vacant lot and that same strange sign, "If Christ had not come." At that point he was shocked awake from his dream. Then he saw its meaning. What a loss to the world and what a difference it would make if Christ had not come. Yes, how many great blessings the world would have missed, and we each would have missed, if Christ had not come! On this Christmas Day, let us thank God anew for his great and loving gift of Christ our Saviour and Friend and Giver of life eternal.

There are people who do not know about Christmas. And, sad to relate, there are said to be some wicked people who would abolish Christmas and do away with all the customs and observances that have entwined themselves around this day of days, if that were possible. Of course it is not possible. Christmas is here to stay and be more and more widely and more gladly observed. But if there were no Christmas would we love little children and one another as much? We think of Christmas always as a good time, a kind and happy time, every hour of it brimming with cheer and gladness. In the long calendar of the year it is the one day when, as if by common consent, men and women open their shut-up hearts freely and strive to share with one another the blessings they have received. The spirit of Christmas is essentially the spirit of good fellowship, benevolence and unselfish service. The joyous thing about Christmas is that we realize for all too brief a season that life is more than making a living. We take time to stop and smile and be friendly with everybody. We look into one another's souls and see kindness, gentleness, sympathy and understanding. So long as this is true we may rest assured that no one will ever be able to cut Christmas out of the calendar, nor out of the heart of humanity.

Christmas is a lovely thing;
Angels' chorus, carols ring,
Yule logs blazing, children sing.

Christmas is a heavenly thing;
Skies a-glowing, winds a-blowing,
Cherub music, love bestowing.

Christmas is a spacious thing:
Heaven's embracing proclamation,
Every nation, whole creation.

—H.

DECEMBER 21. One Boy's Christmas Treasure Hunt (Christmas).

Once there was a boy who got his Christmas presents in an unusual way. Instead of having them all piled up under the Christmas tree or tied to its branches he had to hunt for them. All he found on the tree when he came downstairs on Christmas morning was a piece of paper folded up and tied to a branch. He wondered where his presents were, but he saw his name on the little paper. He untied it, and when he had unfolded it he read: "Look up in the attic behind the trunk in the southwest corner." He ran up and to the corner, and sure enough there was a big trunk, and behind it he found a newly-wrapped package. He undid the package as fast as he could, and inside he found a new football, and a pump to pump it up. And there too was another folded paper. It said, "Fourth from the floor; third from the left; look behind me."

He wondered what that could mean—fourth what? and third what? He went back downstairs and looked around. Suddenly he noticed the bookshelves. He counted up from the bottom—one, two, three, four. Then he found the third book from the left, a big thick one, and he pulled it out. Reaching in, sure enough, there was a little package. He pulled it out and there was a new fountain pen, just what he wanted! Around the pen was wrapped another little paper.

He was pretty excited by this time, and could hardly unwrap the paper which told him to go to the last house on the street and say to whoever came to the door:

"I can float on the water, I can fly over snow;
I'll carry you through the air, So let's go!"

A lady came to the door, someone he knew pretty well. There was a twinkle in her eyes as she said, "Merry Christmas!" The boy answered:

"I can float on the water, I can fly over snow;
I'll carry you through the air, So let's go!"

"Okay," she answered, "that's the password. You look inside that closet over there under the stairs." There, standing against the wall, was a pair of new skis, and then he understood what the words of the queer rhyme meant.

I cannot tell you all the places he had to look that day and the presents he found. All I know is that he had the best time he ever had on a Christmas Day, and he never forgot what fun he had hunting all his presents.

Now, I want to tell you a secret. I have found that being a Christian is something like that. God has lots of wonderful things he wants to give us, but he does not give them all at once, and he does not put them out in plain sight for us to just pick up. He wants us to go on a treasure hunt. He tells us where to look for things and what to do to find them.—Rev. L. P. Van Slyke.

DECEMBER 28. Topic: The Legend of Ho Sien-ju (Chinese Folklore).

As I have told you before, young friends, I have a brother who for many years has been a missionary in China. He has sent me many stories recounted to him by the Chinese. One of these stories I am to give you this morning. It gives the account of one of the goddesses they honor and that not a few ignorantly worship. The story states that once upon a time there lived in China a very beautiful maiden named Ho Sien-ju. Her father was a storekeeper in a little town in Hunan. When she was born only six hairs grew on top of her head and never any more came. But her parents must have gotten her a wig, for her pictures show plenty of hair.

She is said to have been a fox originally, but was changed into a beautiful woman. She lived on a "ling," or notch, in the top of a mountain. She had a dream in which she was told to grind up and eat mother-of-pearl, by which she was promised the ability to fly and also to be immortal.

She obeyed. She decided never to marry. She spent her time flying from mountain to mountain or riding on the clouds. Her fame spread far and wide. The Empress invited her to visit her court; but just before arriving she suddenly disappeared and became an Immortal, as a reward for her goodness and for her religious zeal. She has been seen several times since—they say.

She is pictured with a lotus flower in her hand. Once in a while she is shown playing a reed organ. You will find her picture in books, on pieces of china, on fans, or beautifully embroidered on silk.

If you wish to hear more about this fox-lady-immortal come with me to Chinese fairs and markets and hear the story-tellers as they paint in glowing language all her doings. We will find it a little difficult to get near enough, for there are many other listeners greatly interested—though they have all heard the stories many, many times before.

It is surely an interesting story, but it shows how people in ignorance of the true God are prone to create gods in their own minds and imagination. A story once begun grows, and is told over and over again until it comes to be believed.

"For all the gods of the nations are idols: but the Lord made the heavens. Honour and majesty are before him: strength and beauty are in his sanctuary. Give unto the Lord, O ye kindreds of the people, give unto the Lord glory and strength. Give unto the Lord the glory due unto his name" (Ps. 96: 5-8).—H.